PROJECT APPRAISAL IN PRACTICE

Project Appraisal in Practice

The Little-Mirrlees method applied in Kenya

by

M. FG. Scott
J. D. MacArthur
D. M. G. Newbery

HEINEMANN EDUCATIONAL BOOKS
LONDON

Heinemann Educational Books Ltd
LONDON EDINBURGH MELBOURNE AUCKLAND TORONTO
HONG KONG SINGAPORE KUALA LUMPUR IBADAN NAIROBI
JOHANNESBURG LUSAKA NEW DELHI

ISBN 0 435 84786 4

First published 1976

Published by Heinemann Educational Books
48 Charles Street, London W1X 8AH
Printed in Great Britain by
Richard Clay (The Chaucer Press) Ltd,
Bungay, Suffolk

PREFACE

This book is an attempt to show how a method of project appraisal can be applied in practice. The method is described in Little and Mirrlees, *Project Appraisal and Planning for Developing Countries* (Heinemann, 1974), which is a successor to their well-known OECD Manual[1]. Although several case-studies based on the latter have been published[2], this is the first to bring in some important new developments. It is also the most comprehensive and sustained attempt to estimate a set of shadow prices in this way for a particular country that has yet been published.

Part I opens with a summary chapter which outlines the method and summarizes the results. The authors' experience shows that many potential users of the method are reluctant to apply it because they feel it is too complicated and time-consuming. To meet this criticism, the summary chapter not only gives the essentials of the method in a relatively short space, but also suggests numerous short-cuts which can be employed. One of the aims of the study has been to devise such short-cuts, but this was only possible on the basis of a set of more carefully worked-out estimates. Otherwise, how can one know where a short-cut is leading? Part I is therefore written at several different levels, particular problems being studied in more detail in subsequent chapters.

These problems are, we believe, the main ones that have to be faced if shadow prices are to be used. Although they are considered here in the Kenyan context, they are mostly not peculiar to Kenya but are to be found, in developing and even developed countries, all over the world. The discussions of, for example, the unit of account, rates of interest, inflation, weighting benefits, shadow wages, private profits, skilled labour, economies of scale, and the problem of making what are essentially interdependent estimates, are all of very general applicability and interest. The great advantage of discussing them in a particular context is that the expositor of the method is forced to derive an estimate at each point, and cannot escape by the easy route of enumerating the considerations which (ideally) should be taken into account. The result is that the reader can see more clearly where the weaknesses lie and what is practicable.

It is true that time and effort are needed to produce good estimates, but this is an investment which, once made, greatly cheapens the cost of subsequently providing good project appraisals. Once the foundation is laid, it is relatively quick and simple to build more on top of it. In fact, there have already been several case-studies which have used preliminary versions of the shadow prices given here, and in Parts II and III there are two more. These are of interest both as examples of the way in which the method can be applied and in their own right, since they refer to matters which are of current importance in many countries besides Kenya.

Part II is an economic appraisal of some of the land settlements forming part of the famous Million Acre Settlement Programme, probably the largest programme of its kind anywhere in Africa. Large-scale farms which had been operated by white settlers were divided up into much smaller plots for African farmers. The whole operation was carefully planned, and individual budgets were drawn up for different types of farm. Subsequently, a large-scale sample survey of the settlement farms was undertaken over four years from 1964/5 to 1967/8. From the data thus made available it has been possible to compare the profitability of the different systems of farming (large-scale, High Density settlements and Low Density settlements) and also to compare the plans with the results so far achieved. The comparisons are made both at market prices and at shadow prices, so that private and social profitability can be compared.

Since many comparisons were made, it is not easy to give a brief summary of the results, but we may mention four here. First, while High Density settlements on average were socially more profitable than the large farms they replaced, the average Low Density settlement was only about equally profitable.

Second, this comparison looks very different at market prices: the average High Density settlement then appears little better than the large farms, while the average Low Density one looks appreciably better. This contrast is due, in the main, to the relatively low weight we have given to gains accruing to the relatively well-off Low Density farmers. Third, the valuation of land at market prices turns out to be a poor guide to its social value. Finally, the overseas finance linked to the settlement programme made an important difference to its social profitability. Without that finance, the average settlement of each type (but especially the Low Density) would have been less socially profitable than the large farms they replaced. Many countries have considered or are engaged in land reform or in other types of rural development programmes, and the lessons about the social evaluation of such projects which can be learned from this analysis are highly relevant.

Part III is concerned with a very different type of agricultural project, though one which is also of topical interest to many other developing countries. Such countries typically produce low quality meat for the domestic market and for low-value exports. The Green Revolution creates a real opportunity for fattening cattle on feed-grains to produce high value beef for export to sophisticated markets. If this opportunity is taken, it should be possible to avoid the rather gloomy prospect of surplus grain production forcing down prices for developing countries' grain exports, and to create instead a new income-elastic export market for the grain processed into beef. The project studied in Part III is an experiment to determine whether this is true for Kenya, and the results show that it is, and that it is privately and socially very profitable there. The findings appear to be transferable to similarly placed countries provided certain conditions are met, and the methodology developed in the appraisal should be widely applicable. Although local research is needed to adapt the project to local conditions, the cost of this research can be very much reduced if the procedures described in Part III are followed.

It is sometimes argued that the most important task facing a government is not to *select* individual projects, but to frame *policies* which will lead to the efficient working of projects already in existence, thus creating a climate in which sensible proposals for new projects are generated. This may be so, but it is sometimes forgotten that a good method of project appraisal is by implication a method for devising and evaluating policies more generally. These wider implications are emphasized throughout the study, and examined in some detail in Part III.

This book is addressed, in the first place, to economists who are concerned with the problems of economic development. It should be of particular interest to those working in consultancy firms, in aid agencies, or in government service, and to academics whose subject this is. Development depends on productive investment, and governments have played an increasingly important role in the selection and design of projects in developing countries. What can the economist contribute to the improvement of this process? The authors are under no illusion that their contribution is the only, or the most important, aspect of project selection and design. They do believe, however, that it is *an* important aspect, and one which a professional economist is particularly suited to study. Nor do they think that this book is the last word on the subject. On the contrary, project appraisal is an art which can only be learned by practising it, and which must evolve as more skilled practitioners take it up. There are many problems which others must solve. It is a fascinating subject, which the authors strongly recommend to their fellow-economists. Decisions have to be taken about projects, and must inevitably be based on imperfect knowledge. The question is whether and how an economic analysis can help. The authors believe that it can, and hope that this book will provide enough of the 'how' to convince others that this is so.

Our work is an outcome of the Nuffield College Project, supported by the Leverhulme Foundation, and organized by Ian Little and Maurice Scott, to promote case studies of investments in developing countries and discussion of the principles involved. The research got under way in the summer of 1969, when John MacArthur and Maurice Scott visited Kenya and toured some of the settlement areas. They were ably assisted by Teresa Gregory (then Hayter), and accompanied by Nicholas Stern, whose study of small-holder tea in Kenya has already been published. These visits were financed by the Ministry of Overseas Development. Further visits were made by

MacArthur and Scott in 1970 and 1973, and Matthew Oakeshott collected some very useful data in 1971. David Newbery's main visit to the Beef Research Station at Lanet was made in 1970, and he revisited it in 1972 and 1973.

We are indebted to a great many people for inspiration, encouragement, advice and help of all kinds. Our main intellectual debt is to Ian Little and James Mirrlees. We have also benefited from others who have been associated with the Nuffield College Project, and in particular John Flemming, Ian Heggie, Gordon Hughes, Vijay Joshi, Deepak Lal, Francis Seton and Nicholas Stern. Sudhir Mulji was not only a persistent and constructive critic, but also provided invaluable technical help in processing computerized data. Adrian Spencer-Smith arranged the transcription and processing of the basic farm survey records. Martyn Dowell, Jean Nicholls and Clive Payne gave computing assistance and advice. Research assistance came from Monica Dowley, Teresa Gregory and Roger Kojan, and secretarial assistance from Anna Baidoun, Teresa Blaber, Paula Greenwood, Margaret Macdonald, and Mabs Simmonds.

Our studies were undertaken with the agreement of the Kenya Government and (for Part III) of the Food and Agricultural Organization of the United Nations, which also financed one of David Newbery's visits to Kenya. We received help and encouragement from many Kenya Government officials, especially in the Ministry of Agriculture, Ministry of Finance and Economic Planning, the Department of Settlement and the Central Bureau of Statistics. We would like to mention in particular Mr H.Mule, who suggested the choice of project for Part III, and who arranged a seminar in the Ministry of Finance and Economic Planning to discuss all our work; also the Director of Settlement for arranging our tour in 1969, during which our endless questions were patiently answered by many Settlement Officers, Agricultural Advisers, farmers and other workers. We were supplied with statistics on various matters by Mr J. Ferguson, Mr L. P. Mbuthia and Mr B. D. Mucai of the Department of Settlement, and data and other help, especially on the economic surveys of the settlements, by Messrs A. Barnett, R. Clough and J. Exeter of the Ministry of Finance and Economic Planning.

Mr J. Peberdy of the Ministry of Agriculture, and Dr M.

Creek and Messrs Redfern and Miles of the Beef Research Station gave hospitality and assistance for the study in Part III. That study is especially indebted to Mr H. A. Squire, the Project Economist at the Beef Research Station, and also relies on the work of Mr G. Beddoes, the Cost Analyst of the Beef Industry Development Project. Valuable comments on earlier drafts were provided by Messrs T. Aldington, B. Cracknell, J. Peberdy, L. Smith, H. A. Squire, R. von Kaufmann and Mrs M. Simpson.

On all our visits we received advice and help from the staff of the Institute of Development Studies, University of Nairobi. On our first visit in 1969 we were provided with office accommodation by the Acting Deputy Director, Professor E. Rado, and on our last, in 1973, the Director, Professor D. P. Ghai, arranged a series of seminars at the Institute for us.

To all those mentioned, and to others we have been unable to mention but who gave us the benefit of their time and knowledge, we offer our thanks. The list may look long for a book of this length but what is presented here is only the tip of the iceberg. Some of the rest is in our files and work-sheets, but most of it is data that others have collected and analysed and we have used. They are not responsible for our use of it, but we could have done nothing without them.

Reader's Guide

As readers have different interests, we offer the following suggestions.

For readers in a hurry, summaries of each part are in Chapters 1, 11 and 18.

Readers whose main interest is in the methodology of shadow pricing should read, in addition, those other chapters of Part I which concern items they want to consider more fully than does the summary Chapter 1. They will also find particular shadow-pricing problems discussed in Chapter 15 of Part II, and Chapters 19, 20 and 21 of Part III.

Readers mainly interested in land settlement (or land reform) should read the whole of Part II, together with Chapters 1 and 5 from Part I.

Readers mainly interested in livestock projects should read the whole of Part III, together with Chapter 1 from Part I.

CONTENTS

PART I

PART III

A Feasibility Study of Intensive Cattle Feeding

LIST OF TABLES

PART I

PART III

LIST OF FIGURES

NOTES

1. *Technical Data*

The currency used is the Kenyan shilling (Sh) divided into 100 cents and the Kenyan £ = 20 shillings. Cents and £ are *always* Kenyan cents and £.

The exchange rate used is £1 = US $280 or US $1 = 7.14 sh. Until the sterling devaluation of 1967 the Kenyan pound was at parity with the British pound, since then it has been linked to and has floated with the US dollar.

All measurements in Part III are metric, the ton is a metric ton of 1000 kg. Conversions are:

1 kg	=	2.2 lb
1 hectare (ha)	=	2.47 acres
1 Mcal	=	1 Megacalorie or 1 million calories
1 bag of maize	=	90 kg.

2. *Tables*

Details may not add to totals because of rounding.

—	means 'zero'
..	means 'not applicable'
n.a.	means 'not available' or 'not known'

3. *Abbreviations*

AFC	Agriculture Finance Corporation
AI	Artificial insemination
AP	Accounting prices
AR	Accounting ratios
ARC	Agricultural Research Council of Great Britain
ARI	Accounting rate of interest
BRS	Beef research station
CCB	Canned corned beef
CDC	Commonwealth Development Corporation
CDW	Cold dressed weight
CF	Covered freight rail wagon
CLB	Central Land Board
CSC	Cotton seed cake – provides protein in rations fed to cattle
DFA	Disease free area
DM	Dry matter
D of S	Department of Settlement
EIU	Economist Intelligence Unit
FAQ	Fair average quality (beef grade)
FAO	Food and Agriculture Organization of the United Nations
FES	Farm Economic Survey
F/Q	Forequarters (of beef)
GAQ	Good average quality (beef grade)
GDP	Gross domestic product
GPT	Graduated personal tax
GFAQ	Good *or* fair average quality (beef grade)
HA	High Altitude
HD	High Density
HMG	Her Majesty's Government
H/Q	Hind quarters (of beef)
IBRD	International Bank for Reconstruction and Development (World Bank)
IDA	International Development Association
ILO	International Labour Office
IRR	Internal rate of return
KCC	Kenya Co-operative Creameries
KMC	Kenya Meat Commission

KSU	Kenya Stock Unit – a modified LSU
KTDA	Kenya Tea Development Authority
LA	Low Altitude
LD	Low Density
LDC	Less developed country
LDSB	Land Development and Settlement Board
LMD	Livestock Marketing Division of the Ministry of Agriculture
LRMC	Long-run marginal cost
LSU or LU	Livestock Unit – is the reference animal that eats a standard amount of feed (6 kg of 90 per cent airdry feed per day in this case). Animals of different size, age or sex can be expressed as proportions of LSU. Land area can be measured by the number of LSU which it can support. See Appendix A.20.
ME	Metabolizable energy – a measure of the energy concentration of a ration
MP	Market prices
MPB	Maize and Produce Board
MUM	Minerals, Urea and Molasses – a supplement for the rations fed to cattle
NEP	North Eastern Province, formerly the
NFD	Northern Frontier District
NPV	Net present value
OIE	Office International des Epizooties
P	Passed (meat free of measles)
PDV	Present discounted value
PV	Present value (usually of a single item or category of items)
R	Retained (because of the presence of measles)
ROR	Rate of return
SCF	Standard conversion factor
SD	Standard deviation
SFT	Settlement Fund Trustees
WHO	World Health Organization

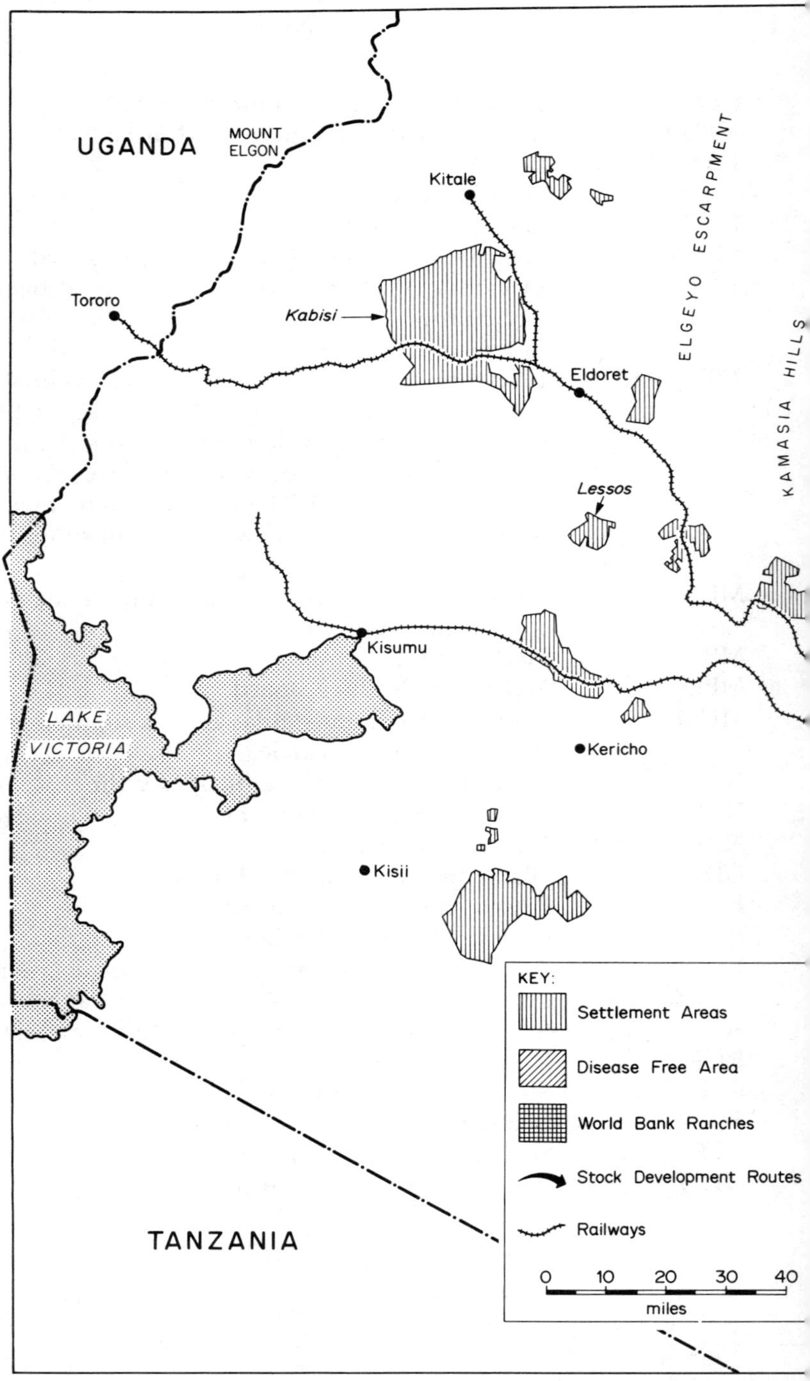
UGANDA
MOUNT ELGON
Kitale
ELGEYO ESCARPMENT
KAMASIA HILLS
Tororo
Kabisi
Eldoret
Lessos
Kisumu
LAKE VICTORIA
Kericho
Kisii
KEY:
Settlement Areas
Disease Free Area
World Bank Ranches
Stock Development Routes
Railways
0 10 20 30 40
miles
TANZANIA

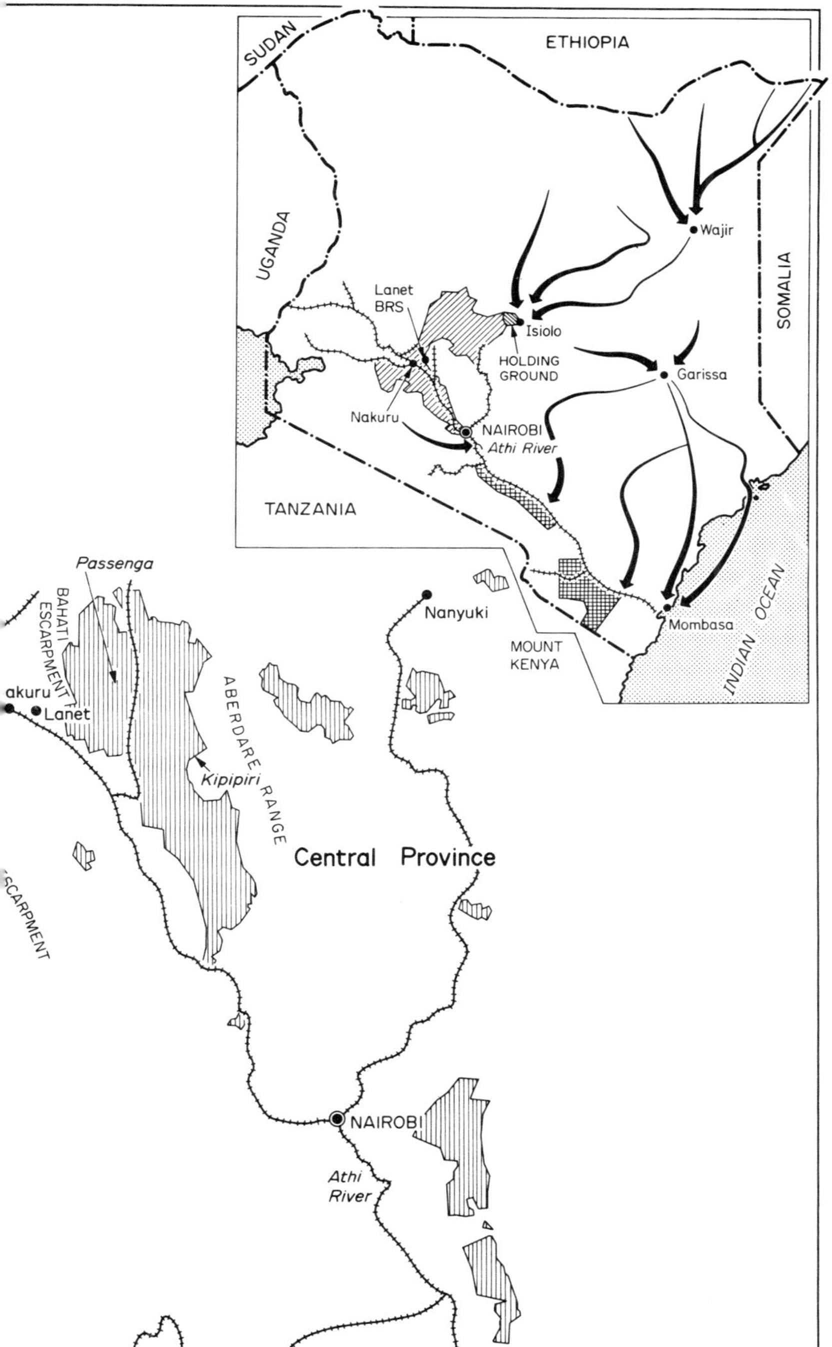

SUDAN
ETHIOPIA
UGANDA
SOMALIA
Wajir
Lanet
BRS
Isiolo
HOLDING
GROUND
Garissa
Nakuru
NAIROBI
Athi River
TANZANIA
Mombasa
INDIAN OCEAN
MOUNT
KENYA
Passenga
BAHATI
ESCARPMENT
akuru
Lanet
ABERDARE RANGE
Kipipiri
Nanyuki
Central Province
SCARPMENT
NAIROBI
Athi
River

PART I

A SET OF ACCOUNTING PRICES FOR KENYA

by

M. FG. Scott

CHAPTER 1

Introduction and Summary

INTRODUCTION

1.1 INTRODUCTION

This part shows how we have estimated a set of shadow prices (or accounting prices as we shall call them) for Kenya. The goods and services covered are those which are inputs or outputs of the Settlements considered in Part II or the beef research station considered in Part III (although beef itself is dealt with in that part). They are likely to be inputs or outputs of many other projects as well. We have not, however, attempted to estimate accounting prices for everything, and in particular we have not estimated them for non-traded outputs nor for non-commercial outputs like health, education, defence, etc.

Our estimates refer, in the main, to accounting prices in the years 1967 to 1969. 1967 is the last year of the economic survey of the Settlement Schemes studied in Part II, and 1969 was the year in which we made our principal visit to Kenya and also the year to which a great deal of the data given in the ILO Report, 1972, refers. For imported goods, the accounting ratios (i.e. the accounting price divided by the market price) depend in the main on rates of import and excise duty. Provided these do not change, the accounting ratios will not change very much. For exports, the situation is less clear, and fairly large changes did occur in the past for two we examined: pyrethrum and (to a much lesser extent) butter. For bulky goods which switch from one category to the other, the swings can be very large indeed—maize being the prime example. It seems likely, therefore, that a careful updating of the figures is needed for the principal export items, but may be less important for the imports. Non-traded goods and services, being a weighted average of a great many other items, are almost certainly much less variable, and we hazard the guess that the same is probably true of the accounting ratios for labour of different kinds.

Ideally, estimates of accounting prices similar to those presented here should be prepared in the planning offices of developing countries themselves. This would have many advantages over our estimates. More, better, and more up-to-date information would be available. A wider range of expertise could be called upon. For some items, it is necessary to know or interpret government policy before one can make a suitable estimate (e.g. for shadow wages of unskilled urban labour), and, if the estimates are to be taken seriously, and their full implications for government economic policy realized, it is desirable that they should carry the authority of the Government itself, and be properly understood by it. This can best be achieved if the estimates originate with the Government. If such estimates were available, the task of someone called upon to evaluate the social costs and benefits of a *particular* project would be considerably eased. The 'overhead cost'[1] of preparing these estimates could be spread over the very large number of projects which come up for government approval, and a greater consistency in making the estimates would be secured.

The estimates would not only be of value for project selection, however. A systematic attempt to estimate accounting prices for a wide variety of goods and services leads on to a critical review of the whole price structure of the economy. Ideally, actual prices and costs should reflect social values and social costs, so that private efforts are directed to socially beneficial ends in the most efficient ways. While it is probably impossible to make very precise estimates of social costs or benefits, wide and varying differences between one's estimates of accounting prices and the corresponding market prices at least suggest that there is something which is worth further examination and needs to be explained. There may be good reasons for some of the differences, but, equally, there may not. Accounting prices also have far-reaching implications for the way in which national income is conventionally measured.

[1] This cost can easily be exaggerated. It should probably be measured in man-months, not man-years, see Chapter 10.

It is hoped, therefore, that the estimates presented here will serve as an example of the kind of work which government planning offices could well do for themselves. How far they can be imitated, or improved upon, in countries other than Kenya depends partly on the data available. So far as Kenya is concerned, there is little doubt that the estimates could be much improved, especially by the further analysis of certain items, but also by making greater use of the local expertise. The author does not want to claim much for these estimates. If they act as a stimulus to work elsewhere, they will have achieved one of their main objects.

In project appraisal we have to predict the future. The prices used to value inputs and outputs should be prices expected to rule in the future, when the project is implemented. This means that we should allow for the effects of technical change, changes in government policies, and other factors which change relative costs and prices. It is important to bear this in mind in what follows, since it helps to put some of the problems which arise in estimating shadow prices into their proper perspective. There are undoubtedly severe problems to be solved, but they are not of a different order from those involved in estimating future market prices. One has to be content with approximate solutions, and theoretical perfection has to be abandoned. It is easy to point out the flaws in any practical set of rules one cares to invent, but that does not mean that they are useless. So long as they help to improve decisions on projects, they are useful. If one wants to criticize constructively (or even destructively!) the rules presented here, one should show that some alternative set of rules would be likely to improve project choice—unless one takes the view that prices are altogether irrelevant to project choice, which would be difficult to defend.

The rest of this chapter gives an outline and summary of the whole of Part I, and we warn the reader that no further summaries are provided in the following chapters. In this chapter we refer to the more detailed discussion in later chapters, so that the reader interested in some particular problem can pursue it there. We also suggest short-cut methods which can be adopted if data and time permit nothing better. We review the accounting ratios which are the result of the whole exercise, and comment on their implications for project selection and for some other economic policies. Finally, we list the main factors which account for divergences between market and accounting prices and which we have tried to bring in to our analysis.

1.2 OUTLINE OF THE METHOD–PUBLIC SECTOR PROJECTS

The following outline briefly explains the method of estimating accounting prices used throughout this book. That method is explained and discussed much more fully in Little and Mirrlees, 1974. To avoid repetition, we do not refer the reader to them at every point for further elucidation: this paragraph must be taken as a comprehensive reference which makes that unnecessary. Much of what follows is also concerned with particular points not dealt with in their more general analysis.

1.2.1. *The unit of account or numeraire*

If the benefits and costs of projects are to be consistently and efficiently weighed up, so that decisions about project selection and design are improved, they must be expressed in commensurable terms. They consist, in reality, of bags of maize, gallons of milk, lorries, petrol, man-hours of different kinds of labour, etc. What we seek to do, in Part I of this book, is to show how all these and many other outputs and inputs can be expressed in terms of a single unit of account, or numeraire, which is uncommitted foreign exchange in the hands of the Government.

For a private individual, the obvious unit of account to use is money. If one shilling more is spent on this, then there is one shilling less to be spent on that. Shillings, for the individual, are homogeneous. By analogy, we could say that foreign exchange is a Government's money. Its liquid reserves consist of foreign exchange, which can be used to purchase any goods and services on world markets. By expressing it in terms of a single currency convertible into any others at known exchange rates we can make it homogeneous. For convenience, we choose Kenya's own currency for this purpose, but we are still referring to foreign exchange (for further discussion see Chapter 2).

Although foreign exchange is the unit of account, and

projects are to be selected and designed so as to maximize their value in terms of foreign exchange, this does not mean that we assume that the Kenya Government pursues the mercantilist objective of maximizing its foreign exchange reserves, or that improving the balance of payments is all that matters. We assume that the objectives pursued are the improvement of the standard of living of the citizens of Kenya, having regard to the distribution of income and to constraints imposed by the scarcity of resources, the balance of payments, fiscal problems and the like. We do *not* assume that all benefits and costs of a project take the form of actual increases or decreases in the Government's foreign exchange reserves. We merely seek to express the actual benefits and costs in terms of *equivalent value* to such increases or decreases.

Our results could in principle be expressed either as absolute accounting prices, or as accounting ratios. The former give the values of physical units of commodities in terms of the unit of account. The latter are the ratios of accounting prices to market prices. Although we give a few absolute accounting prices (e.g. for certain kinds of labour) all our results are expressed as accounting ratios, as these are generally more useful.

1.2.2 *The essentials of the method*

The simplest way to explain how we estimate the accounting ratios is to imagine that we already know them for a great many goods and services[1], and now require to estimate some more. We then ask, if a project were to require a particular input, where would it come from? Suppose that we think that the main source would be from extra imports, reduced exports, or extra home production, and that other home consumption would not be much affected. In that case we can analyse the cost of supplying the good into components for each of which we know the accounting ratio, and in this way we get the accounting cost of the good itself. It is a weighted average of the accounting ratios of its cost components. This is the method which we use for most goods and services. In some cases, however, it seems probable that home consumption would be affected as well as home production and trade. The extra demand made by the project would bid up prices and

[1] But what if we don't? This is discussed in 1.2.7.

consumers would switch to other goods. In so far as that happens we need to work out the accounting cost of those other goods, and they must be included in the weighted average of accounting ratios we need.

Thus far we have only mentioned what we call the '*resource costs*'. Besides these, we bring into the reckoning shifts in income distribution caused by our project, and we take account of net benefits received (or net costs incurred) by those outside the public sector. These occur in various ways described below, and to evaluate them requires a system of weights to convert them into our unit of account, which is foreign exchange in the hands of the Government. In many cases, the purchase of an input will not result in significant benefits accruing outside the public sector. There will then only be the resource cost of the input to consider. Where, however, significant private benefits do occur as a result of the purchase, we subtract their social value from the resource cost in order to get the accounting cost of the input. This procedure is to some extent novel and certainly controversial. We shall not attempt an extended defence of it here[1]. We must, however, make the following points very briefly:

1. Considerations of income distribution and what we may call 'the fiscal problem' are involved in many projects in practice (e.g. what charges should be made for water in an irrigation scheme? On what terms should loans be made to settlers?). It is an illusion to believe that projects can be designed and selected ignoring them. Our system of weights is one way of bringing them in.
2. In principle, one could work out the income effects of a project and show them separately, leaving it to the ultimate decision-makers to weight as they see fit. In practice, this would be much more complicated than our method, would be unlikely to lead to consistent decisions, and would probably not be done explicitly at all. Furthermore, it would be unpractical to present decision-makers with more than a very few alternatives to choose between. Consequently, it would be difficult to influence the design of projects in the required way,

[1] See Little and Mirrlees, 1974, Chapter 4.

since the designers must have some quick way of choosing between a great many alternatives. Unless one is to rely on *their* judgements on weighting, they must be given prices which reflect a centrally determined system of weights.

3. The probable result of having no system of weights is that equal weights will be given to benefits accruing to rich and poor, and that fiscal considerations will be neglected. In so far as these mistakes are corrected, the corrections will tend to be haphazard and inefficient. The realization that project appraisals neglect these factors will mean that less weight will be given to their conclusions, and more to subjective judgements or 'hunches'. This will tend to worsen project selection and design.

Having said this, it must be recognized that the set of weights put forward here is not the only one which could be considered reasonable. We have tried to make it consistent with the Kenya Government's statements and actions (see Chapter 3), but our interpretation of them is open to question. It would be valuable to conduct a sensitivity analysis to determine which accounting ratios would be appreciably changed by a change in the weights. Unfortunately, we have not been able to do this, but such experiments as we have performed suggest that a great many would not be much affected. The most sensitive items are probably the wages of urban unskilled workers and the social cost of family labour on the settlement farms. The former is a small component of most other prices, and the latter, though crucial for an evaluation of the settlements themselves, is not otherwise important. We do not believe, therefore, that the set of accounting prices presented here stands or falls depending on whether the weights used are judged to be about right.

So much for the essence of our method. We now consider the main kinds of goods and services in more detail. Wherever possible, we suggest short-cuts as well as describing what we have actually done. References to later chapters are also given, so that each question can be considered at different levels of simplification.

1.2.3 *Traded goods*

Consider a project which has, as an input, X shillings of, say, bottles which are imported. The customs duty on these is $33\frac{1}{3}$ per cent, assuming that no special rebate is allowed, and we estimate the port handling, rail freight and wholesale margins as in Table 1.1, col. (1) (see further in Chapter 9). To estimate the accounting ratio for bottles we then look up the accounting ratios for each of these inputs in Table 10.1. The code numbers in col. (2) of Table 1.1 may be helpful here. The ratios are shown in col. (3), and the result of multiplying them by each input in col. (4). Adding up col. (4) then gives the accounting cost of imported bottles, and, since we set the market price at one, this is also their accounting ratio. The total cost of bottles for our project is then 0.75 X shillings at accounting prices.

Table 1.1

Estimating the accounting ratio for bottles, T 3

Input	Proportion of wholesale price (1)	Code number (2)	Accounting ratio (3)	Accounting cost, (1) x (3) (4)
Imports, c.i.f.	–0.592	P 1	1.00	–0.592
Duty	–0.198	P 10	0.00	0.000
Port handling	–0.040	N 13	0.77	–0.031
Rail marginal cost	–0.020	N 18	0.90	–0.018
Rail price–marg. cost	–0.020	N 19	0.67	–0.013
Wholesaling	–0.129	N 27	0.78	–0.101
Total	1.000	T 3		0.755

Sources: Col. (1), Table 10.2. Cols. (2) and (3), Table 10.1.

Notes: The estimates of rail freight assume that the project using the bottles is located at Nairobi. If the project were located elsewhere, and transport costs were important, an adjustment would be necessary.

Several points may be noted. The accounting ratio for imports c.i.f. is simply 1.00, since this is foreign exchange paid out by a public sector project. The accounting ratio for the import duty is zero, since this is a transfer within the public sector–what the project pays out the Customs and Excise receive. The weighted average accounting ratio for all the other inputs (port, rail, wholesaling) works out at 0.78. This suggests the following short cut: divide the wholesale cost of any imported input into three parts, the c.i.f. cost, the duty and the rest, and work out the accounting cost by multiplying by accounting ratios of 1, 0 and 0.8. As a further short cut, and if one had no information about the magnitude of the 'rest', one could take it at 20 per cent of the wholesale price, which seems fairly typical[1].

The signs in Table 1.1 may need explanation. A negative sign denotes an input into bottles, and the 'output' of bottles is shown as positive. The net sum of inputs and output is zero, whether at market prices or at accounting prices. With an import like bottles all this is straightforward, but exports can be more complicated, and it is important to take care over the signs. Suppose, for example, that maize is an input into our project, and that, had we not used it, the maize would have been exported. Then we lose the foreign exchange value of the exports (which therefore enters with a negative sign in just the same way as the import cost of bottles) but we *save* the port handling costs and probably some rail freight as well. These savings are, in a sense, complementary outputs of our project, and enter with a positive sign, and this explains why such items relating to exportable products are positive in Table 10.2 (maize is further discussed in 7.1).

The case of maize shows that our procedure can be applied even if the input with which we are concerned is not *actually* exported or imported. It is enough if the effect of our using it is to reduce exports or increase imports elsewhere in the economy. This is very important, because it means that our relatively simple procedure can be applied, for example, to bottles even if they are produced in Kenya as well as being imported. We have, in fact, regarded as many products as we reasonably could as tradeable in this sense (all those given a code number starting with T and many others as well), the main criterion being whether a substantial value of trade was taking place or not. Can we justify this? For many of the products, imports do account for the bulk of supplies. Where domestic

[1] The arithmetic average for all imports in the T category, excluding fuel oil which is atypical, is 21 per cent, and half the observations lie between 15 and 25 per cent.

production is important, and the product is also imported, the effect of increased demand by a project may well be *both* to increase imports *and* to increase domestic production, and not *just* to increase imports as we have implicitly assumed. Nevertheless, our procedure should still give a good approximation to the accounting cost, since the marginal cost of home production may (and in a well-regulated economy *should*) roughly equal that of imports when both are reckoned at accounting prices.

This argument applies even when there is a quota, which should be adjusted by the Government to maintain the above equality. We have not, in fact, made any special allowances for quotas. They were not important for many products in 1969, but have become increasingly so recently, especially after the worsening in the balance of payments in 1971. With the subsequent improvement, it is to be hoped that the additional restrictions imposed will be relaxed. In a quota-ridden economy the estimating procedure adopted here, which relies on the use of published information on tariff and excise tax rates, would be inappropriate, as would our concentration on accounting *ratios*. These ratios would vary widely, both from commodity to commodity and from time to time, as the experience of India and Pakistan suggests[1]. Instead, and following the argument in the preceding paragraph[2], one should probably use *absolute* import prices and *absolute* accounting prices. The data are then more difficult to collect[3] and to use, although still a considerable improvement on the use of market prices. This is just one more example of how the widespread use of controls makes it difficult to exercise rational economic choice.

Although the short-cut procedure described above can be applied to many traded goods, and particularly to imported goods, it is advisable that any major agricultural traded goods should be looked at more carefully. Maize is the leading example in Kenya (see 7.1). Its accounting ratio has fluctuated

[1] See Bhagwati and Desai, 1970, p. 353 *et seq.* and Lewis, 1970, Chapter 4.

[2] See also Little and Mirrlees, 1974, Chapter 9, for further discussion of how to deal with the case of a fixed quota.

[3] This may not always be true, at least for the direct inputs into a project, for which it may be easier to get information on absolute border prices than on domestic market prices.

widely in the past, fundamentally because of good and bad harvests and the price stabilization efforts of the Marketing Board. Care is needed in choosing an appropriate ratio to project into the future. Maize is a large component of consumption, and its accounting ratio is also an important determinant of that of non-traded agricultural products and of rural wages. Its ratio should therefore be estimated fairly accurately. For agricultural exports it can also be the case that marginal export revenue is much lower than average export revenue. Examples for Kenya are coffee and butter and probably to some extent pyrethrum (see Chapter 7).

1.2.4 *Non-traded goods and services*

Where no substantial volume of trade takes place, we call the good non-traded (all items whose code number starts with N). In most cases we assume that increased demand by a project leads to increased output of the good, and does not appreciably affect consumption of it. This simplifies matters because we need only consider the cost of production of the good, and not the items for which it substitutes in consumption. But is it a reasonable assumption? We make three points by way of justification.

First, we concentrate on long-run marginal costs (including capital costs, for instance), rather than short-run ones. The latter may be higher or lower than the former at a particular point in time, but on average one would expect them to be roughly the same, and it is clearly unpractical to attempt to forecast or allow for widely fluctuating short-run marginal costs in a general study of this kind. In the particular circumstances of a particular project, it might be worth making a special estimate for the short-run marginal cost of an important non-traded input, but we cannot do that here.

Second, and considering the average long-run position, it seems reasonable to assume as we do that output of non-tradeables keeps pace with demand, and that the extra demand of the project is foreseen.

Third, it seems reasonable to assume as we do that for most of non-traded manufacturing, transport, distribution, building and construction, long-run marginal costs are either independent of output or else fall gently as output expands. In either event, prices may change very little as a result of the extra demand of the project, and hence consumption elsewhere may be almost unaffected (economies of scale are further discussed in 9.5).

There is no need to set out the method of calculating the accounting ratio from the analysis of long-run marginal costs, since it is just the same as for traded goods. There are, of course, generally many more different kinds of inputs to consider, as may be seen by looking at the N-items in Table 10.2. Some of these are traded goods or other non-traded goods and services, but some are labour and capital inputs. Labour inputs are discussed in 1.2.6 and capital inputs in 1.3, and both more fully in Chapters 4, 6 and 9.

In two cases we depart from the above set of assumptions, namely, non-traded agricultural products and urban rents. In each of these cases it seems likely that increased demand would, in the long run, tend to raise prices and have substantial effects on consumption as well as production. This greatly complicates matters, for not only must we consider the accounting ratios of the goods and services to which consumers switch their purchases when prices rise, but also we must allow for the transfer of incomes from consumers to producers which results from the same price rise. We shall not attempt to summarize what we have done, but refer the reader to 7.7 and 9.4.

It is difficult to think of any short cuts for non-traded goods and services, beyond the very simple and crude procedure of using a single conversion factor for them all. This would serve quite well in many cases in Kenya. Thus, if one takes the 28 N-items in Table 10.1, the average error made by taking 0.80 for them all, instead of taking our individual estimates, is only 0.05. Both non-traded agriculture and urban rents are important items for which we estimate accounting ratios of 1.00. If these were separately estimated, the errors involved in the other ones would probably not matter for most projects. Of course, this assumes that one's crude estimate *is* 0.80. The advantage of working out a lot of ratios is that it enables one to make a good crude estimate![1]

For non-traded agricultural goods, the best short cut we can suggest is to look at the accounting ratios of two other groups

[1] It is not the *best* one could make. The arithmetic mean of the ratios for all the N-items is 0.77.

of goods, first, traded agricultural goods and, second, other rural consumption goods such as traded foodstuffs and drink and tobacco. The non-traded goods substitute for the first in production and the second in consumption, and we recommend striking an average between the two. In our case we put the ratio for the first at 1.11 and the second at 0.94 and our final best guess is 1.00 for non-traded agricultural goods at the farm gate. For these goods in the town the ratio is lower, because they include large distributive margins with a lower accounting ratio. Our best guess is 0.85.

For urban rents, much depends on the way in which extra urban population is housed. In Kenyan circumstances we argue that an accounting ratio appreciably above those for construction or urban consumption is justified. The latter are about 0.80 and our best guess for rents is 1.00.

1.2.5 *Income gains and losses occurring outside the public sector*

The main ways in which incomes outside the public sector may be affected as the result of purchases made by a public sector project, and which we have taken into account, are as follows.

First, employment of workers in the 'formal' or 'modern' sector, whether in the towns or the countryside, generally increases their incomes. The wages of typical unskilled urban workers in the formal sector in 1969, for example, appear to have been about three times those of regular workers on small farms. However, the real benefit accruing to a worker transferring from the latter to the former job was much less than this ratio suggests, mainly because of the much higher cost of living in the towns (60 per cent higher we estimate, see 8.4), but also for other reasons (see Chapter 4).

Second, wherever a (long-run) rising supply price seems likely, increased demand will tend to transfer incomes from consumers to producers. We have already mentioned the cases of non-traded agricultural goods and urban rents. Other examples are the employment of many kinds of labour, including skilled labour and labour in both the rural and urban informal sectors (see 4.6).

Third, where there are economies of scale, increased demand will lower costs and this will tend to increase profits and/or lower prices, thus increasing the incomes of capitalists and/or consumers (see 9.5).

Fourth, the boards which control the marketing of many of the most important agricultural products in Kenya often charge prices which diverge from long-run marginal costs, and sometimes cross-subsidize products as well. Increased sales by these boards may therefore involve them in additional profits which they pass on to producers (by way of higher prices) or consumers (by way of lower prices) or the reverse where losses are made (see Chapter 7).

Fifth, there are private monopoly profits. For the most part we lacked the information necessary to identify these, but one example of discriminatory pricing appears to have been cement.

Finally, there are the gains which accrue to settlers when they get their new plots of land, and which take several different forms besides that of straightforward increases in money income (see 5.4).

Where the purchase of an input results in an income benefit for any of these reasons we subtract the social value of that benefit from the resource costs of the input in order to get its net accounting cost. Where the benefit accrues to what we have called 'capitalists' (i.e. companies mainly) we assume that this social value is negligible, as the recipients are either foreign or are well off in relation to the mass of the population. We do not, however, regard the whole of any such payments made to 'capitalists' as a cost. Direct taxes must be subtracted and also the present value of future receipts of taxes, or any other benefits, resulting from additional savings they make. It is the benefits accruing to capitalists from their higher consumption which we ignore (see 1.3 below, and also Chapter 6). In order to evaluate benefits accruing to workers, urban consumers or small farmers, however, we need a set of weights by which we can transform them into their equivalent value to foreign exchange in the hands of the Government. We deal with this problem in two stages, first, relative weights for benefits measured at market prices, and, second, the conversion to foreign exchange equivalents. Both are discussed more fully in Chapter 3.

Our method of weighting is very simple, and is depicted in Figure 1.1. We assume that the Government attaches less weight to a given benefit (measured at market prices) accruing to a rich

Fig. 1.1 Weighting income benefits

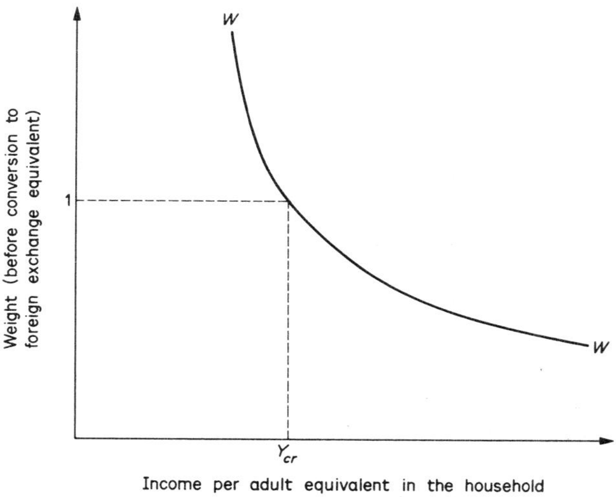

household than to a poor one. There is evidence for this both in the statements made by the Government and in its actions. Hence *WW* slopes downwards to the right as household income rises. Second, we assume that there exists a *critical income*[1] level, Y_{cr}, such that a marginal benefit accruing to households at that level is deemed to be as valuable as if the resources had, instead, accrued to the Government. Marginal benefits at this point are given the weight of one. To determine the weights we therefore need essentially to know two things: the slope of *WW* and the critical income level.

As regards the latter, we can consider certain actions of the Government. A consistent Government which behaved in the way we assume above would not levy direct taxes on households much below the critical income level. Since such taxes inevitably involve a dead-weight loss in the process of

[1] This is similar to the *base consumption* level in Little and Mirrlees, 1974, Section 13.13.

transferring resources from the tax-payer to the Government, it would not be sensible to transfer resources from households as poor as that. Consequently, the minimum income at which people pay direct taxes should provide a rough guide to Y_{cr}. For subsidies the case is stronger. It costs something to transfer resources to poor households, and so the maximum income of those in receipt of direct subsidies should provide a lower limit to Y_{cr}. In Kenya, unfortunately, the data for either of these approaches is non-existent or unobtainable (so far as we can tell)[1]. Nevertheless, we can get some idea of the level of Y_{cr} from these and other considerations, and it does seem to be low.

Figure 1.1 depicts the essentials of what we call 'the fiscal problem'. One would normally expect that the growth of incomes and expenditure through time would shift *WW* upwards and to the right, thus raising Y_{cr}. The shift would be speeded up if foreign aid became more plentiful, or the terms of trade for Kenya improved. Institutional changes leading, for example, to a more efficient tax system would also accelerate the shift. On the other hand, the shift might slow down, or even be reversed, if the budgetary situation suddenly became very tight. There might be a sudden need for famine relief expenditure, or defence expenditure, or the prospects for investment might unexpectedly improve making increased saving very desirable.

As regards the slope[2] of *WW*, it must be admitted that there is virtually nothing to go on. We give some reasons in Chapter 3 for believing that it is probably less steep in Kenya than in some other countries, and also some reasons why it should not be less steep than the slope we finally select, but it must be admitted that our case is weak and that other slopes could reasonably be taken. Despite this, we doubt whether it would make much difference to our estimates of accounting ratios, provided that

[1] It would be much easier to identify Y_{cr} in, for example, the United Kingdom, given Supplementary Benefits which are dependent on income levels. The writer has also made an estimate for Mauritius, based on the system of means-tested sickness benefits which exists here.

[2] Since *WW* is not a straight line, what do we mean by its slope? We mean e, the elasticity of the weight with respect to changes in income, which we assume is constant (see Chapter 3).

the slopes taken lay within limits which would be judged to be reasonable[1].

The second stage in estimating the weights is to convert them to foreign exchange equivalents. We do this by estimating the amount of foreign exchange equivalent required to provide a unit marginal increase in the income of a household at the critical income level. This is a weighted average of the accounting ratios for rural consumption and rural savings (see 8.1). This gives the cost[2] at accounting prices of giving such a household a shilling more, and, by our assumptions, it must also measure the benefit.

The system of weights just described is very flexible. It can be used to evaluate marginal or larger-than-marginal gains accruing at any income level. It is already rather simple. If one wanted to simplify it still further one could reduce it to a few broad categories, such as 'urban consumers' or 'small farmers'. In effect, we have done this (see below and Chapter 9), but we have also retained the continuous system applicable to any income level.

1.2.6 *Shadow wages*

We draw a distinction between 'skilled' and 'unskilled' labour, which is based mainly on the level of earnings. The more highly paid labour is probably more or less fully employed, and if our project employs some it is unlikely to pay it much more than it could have got elsewhere. In that case, there is no income benefit to be taken into account (other than that which arises through bidding up wages). Even where an income benefit does accrue, its social value is rather small because it accrues to someone already relatively well-off. Skilled labour, defined in this way, is an important input into many projects, and much more important in manufacturing, for example, than is unskilled labour. Despite this, we must confess that our estimate of its accounting ratio in 9.1 is subject to a good deal of uncertainty. We end up with a figure of 0.80 which is a typical value for all our accounting ratios (see Figure 1.2).

The main ideas underlying our estimates of the shadow wages

[1] Judged by whom? Ultimately, by the mass of the population of Kenya, we hope, if they could be brought to understand the question!

[2] Ignoring the dead-weight loss of making the transfer, which is irrelevant here.

of unskilled workers in Chapter 4 are as follows. Consider, for example, a worker drawn into the urban formal sector from the rural informal sector. His wage goes up from about £40 a year to about £120 a year (for an unskilled man working full time in both places). To find his shadow wage in his new occupation, let us first assume we *know* his shadow wage in his previous employment–it is estimated to be about £40 in terms of our unit of account. We then need to estimate the *additional* cost involved in employing him for £120 in the urban formal sector. This requires the provision of extra resources to meet the extra expenditures he and his family will incur as a result of his rise in income. Allowing for extra savings they may make (and for the resource costs of the resulting investment expenditures), these extra resource costs are estimated at about £55 in terms of foreign exchange. This must then be added to the £40 we started with, giving £95 so far. Against this, however, we must allow for the fact that the worker and his family have benefited as a result of his getting the job. We have to value this benefit in terms of our unit of account, using the weighting system already described. We return to that below, but for the moment let us complete the calculation by taking the estimated benefit, which is £16 or £11 depending on whether he leaves his family in the countryside or brings it with him into the town (thus incurring more expenditure at the higher urban prices). Taking the second of these two cases, our final estimate of the shadow cost of labour obtained in this way is then £95 – 11 = £84, which is 0.7 times the actual wage.

By way of a digression, it is worth pointing out that this estimate allows for multiplier effects of the increase in wage payments. These are implicit in the way in which we cost the extra resources needed to meet them, and allow for the benefits they produce. We do not demonstrate this here, but refer to the demonstration given by the writer elsewhere[1].

So far we have considered only *one* of the possible sources from which labour for new jobs in the urban formal sector might be obtained. Other possibilities are rural and urban unemployed persons, and workers in the urban informal sector. Furthermore, if increased demand for labour in the urban formal sector led to some bidding up of wages there, some of

[1] Scott, April 1972. Appendix I, Section 5.

the new jobs could be filled from within the sector itself, as labour was released from other jobs in it. In this case, in order to estimate the social cost we have to estimate both the value of the marginal product of the workers released, and the social value of the resulting transfer of incomes from employers and/or consumers to workers when wages rise.

Having estimated the cost of labour drawn from each source, we proceed to estimate in what proportion the labour comes from each of them. We start with the assumption that it comes in the same proportion as existing employment in each (and we give a simple theoretical model to show what this implies). We then modify this assumption in various ways. In particular, we make use of the simplest version of the Harris-Todaro (1970) model to allow for the possibility that, so far from unemployment falling when employment in the formal sector increases, unemployment may actually increase. Although the extent of urban unemployment, and the benefit accruing to workers migrating from the countryside to the town, fit the Harris-Todaro model remarkably well, the writer believes that the simple version of the model probably exaggerates the likelihood that unemployment will increase. After reviewing a number of possibilities, we make our final best guess of the shadow wage.

We started this description of our procedure by assuming that we *knew* the shadow wage in the informal rural sector. In practice, we estimated this *before* estimating the shadow wage of unskilled workers in the urban formal sector. However, two of our estimates of shadow wages were interdependent (i.e. those for workers in the informal rural and urban sectors), and were made by a rather quick and simple process of iteration. In a larger and more complex model one might want to resort to the solution of simultaneous equations using a computer, but that was unnecessary in our case.

We must now retrace our steps to describe how we arrive in our example at the estimated benefit of £11 received by the worker and others as a result of getting the job, the £11 being expressed in our unit of account. For a start, we have to estimate how much of the worker's gain in income is passed on to relatives and how much remains with him. From the latter quantity we must subtract various amounts to allow, for example, for the fact that he now spends most of his income in the town where prices are much higher than in the countryside. In other cases we make allowance for changes in hours of work and some other factors which seem relevant to a final assessment of his gain in real income. In our example we reach the perhaps rather surprising conclusion that, out of a total increase in disposable income of £75 (i.e. 120–41–4 for taxes), all of which we assume accrues to the worker and his family, no less than £55 is needed to compensate him for adverse changes incidental to his change in work, leaving a real gain at rural prices of only £20.

This real gain is then marked down in the two stages mentioned above. First, we mark it down because it is not worth as much as the same amount of money in the hands of the Government. Second, it is marked down because our unit of account is foreign exchange, whereas the £20 gain is expressed at domestic rural market prices. Roughly speaking, the first step reduces the £20 to £13, and the second finally reduces it to £11. The second step is fairly straightforward and uncontroversial. It is the first step which is controversial, since it involves weighting gains accruing to households with different levels of income both in relation to each other and in relation to gains accruing to the Government. It is worth noting that our final estimate of the shadow wage is not particularly sensitive to the outcome, at least in this case. Thus, two extreme possibilities are, first, that we should not have marked down the gains at all, so regarding money in the hands of the worker as equally valuable (in the eyes of the Government) as money in its own hands, and second, that we should have marked down the gains to zero, thus regarding money in the hands of the worker as worthless in the eyes of the Government. There is little doubt that the truth lies between these extremes, and the writer believes that his estimate is nearer to it than either. The first would lower the shadow wage in this example from £84 to £78 and the second would raise it from £84 to £95.

Are there any useful short cuts to this rather lengthy procedure? In the two formal sector cases (i.e. urban unskilled workers and workers on large farms) one would expect the shadow wage to lie between an upper limit set by the market wage multiplied by the accounting ratio for consumption, and a lower limit set by what might be called the supply price of labour, that is, the upper limit minus the apparent benefit accruing to the worker also multiplied by the accounting ratio for consumption (this is rather like the example just given). In default of anything better, one might take half-way between. This gives a fairly close approximation (on the low side) for the urban worker, and is the same as our best guess for the large farm worker[1].

In the two informal sector cases the approach must be different, since wages are not thought to be above the supply price of labour and there is not, therefore, the same benefit accruing to the worker who is given employment. Nevertheless, *some* benefits do accrue to workers as a class through the bidding up of wages and the resulting transfer of incomes from employers to them. For the rural worker we put the accounting ratio for his marginal product at 1.05, and for the urban at 0.82. If we round each of these down to allow something for the above benefits we get, in fact, precisely our best guesses of 1.00 and 0.80.

1.2.7 *Interdependence of the estimates and the use of 'primary inputs'*

We started our description of the method by assuming that we already knew a great many accounting ratios and only wanted to estimate some more. Like any branch of human knowledge, it is easier to build on an existing foundation than to start from the bare ground. In fact, the greatest contribution of the Little-Mirrlees method is to draw attention to the foundation which, in most developing countries, is provided by existing border prices. Without these it would indeed be difficult to make a start. Even with these, however, the problem of interdependence of the estimates must be faced at the beginning. We first describe how we have tackled it, and then

[1] For the urban formal sector, the actual wage is £120 and multiplying by the urban consumption accounting ratio of 0.82 gives an upper limit of £98. The apparent benefit of the worker, allowing only for the higher cost of living of 60 per cent, is £120–1.6 x 41 = £54 at market prices, or 54 x 0.82 = £44 at accounting prices, so the lower limit is £98–44 = £54. Our best guess of £84 is rather higher than the half-way mark of £76. For the large-farm worker the upper limit is £73 x 0.92 = £67, the apparent benefit is £73–41 = £32 at market prices, or 32 x 0.92 = 29 at accounting prices, the lower limit £44 and half-way between them £55, which is also our best guess.

suggest how the various short cuts already mentioned could be put together.

The main device we have used is to create a class of 'primary inputs' (described below), and to convert every cost into these using a technique suggested by input-output analysis. We then make rough estimates of the accounting ratios of the primary inputs, and this gives us at once the corresponding ratios for any good or service. By iteration, we can arrive at a mutually consistent set of ratios for everything.

Since shadow wages depend on the accounting ratio for wage-earners' expenditure, which in turn depends on shadow wages, we start with the list of consumer goods from available family budget surveys and work out the direct inputs into each (items UCF and UCN for urban consumers, RCF and RCN for rural, see Table 10.1 and also Chapter 8). We then take these inputs and analyse each of *them* into their direct cost components, *except* for the primary inputs which we leave as they are. These cost components consist of traded goods (T) and non-traded goods and services (N). If, when we have done this, we have had to introduce some new goods and services, they too must be further analysed in the same way. Eventually we arrive at a list of goods and services whose cost components consist only of two kinds: other goods and services already included in the list, or primary inputs. We have thus provided a means whereby every good on the list can be expressed in terms of its direct and indirect primary input content. To do this we must solve a large number of simultaneous linear equations, which can be done using a computer (see Chapter 10). The solution is given in Table 10.2. The first column of figures in this table gives the direct inputs into each item, and the second the direct and indirect primary inputs.

The choice of primary inputs is to some extent a matter of convenience. Our list is given in Table 1.2. Ultimately we wish to express everything in terms of P 1 and P 10, costs in our unit of account and social surplus, so these two must be included in the list. In between we put items which cannot easily be expressed as linear combinations of other accounting ratios, or about whose value we are particularly uncertain (so that sensitivity analysis is facilitated), or whose value we wish to postpone estimating to a later stage (for example, it may be convenient to have a 'miscellaneous inputs' category which we subsequently estimate in the light of our estimates for particular inputs). Our list includes all the important items for which the problem of weighting benefits arises[1]. It would therefore be relatively easy for someone who disagreed with our weighting system to work out the effects of taking a different one.

The process of iteration is considerably speeded up in two ways. First, we work out the direct and indirect primary input content of consumption-as-a-whole, so that, in effect, it becomes one good (or strictly, two, in our case, rural and urban). Second, we round all the accounting ratios for primary inputs, so that minor changes in other accounting ratios do not lead to revisions in the former.

So much for the method we used. Suppose that we had confined ourselves to the various short cuts which are suggested in the preceding sections, could we have put them together in a relatively simple way and, in particular, without using a computer? The following steps are suggested, and may serve as a summary of the whole of the foregoing.

1. Guess the accounting ratio for the distributive margin (port, transport, wholesaling) on imported goods and then use this and data on tariffs and excise duties and a standard margin of, say, 20 per cent of the wholesale price, to work out accounting ratios for a large number of imported goods. Iterate until the ratio for the margin is 'typical' of the ones found for the goods (or perhaps rather below average, see 1.4). Call this F.
2. Assume that F applies to most non-traded goods and services and to skilled labour, but not necessarily to non-traded agricultural goods or urban rents (nor to heavily taxed consumer goods like beer or cigarettes, for which a separate calculation should be made).
3. Examine some leading traded agricultural products (e.g. maize in Kenya) and estimate their accounting ratios carefully.

[1] We include extra income accruing to large farmers in P 4, although it would be better to have a separate category for this. See Part II, Chapter 15.

4. Estimate accounting ratios for non-traded agricultural products and urban rents in the short way described above.
5. Estimate an accounting ratio for wage-earners' consumption, preferably distinguishing rural and urban, from a weighted sum of ratios for individual consumer goods. Use family budget inquiries or cost of living index numbers to get the weights.
6. Estimate the average difference between consumer prices in the countryside and the towns.
7. Estimate shadow wages for unskilled workers using the short-cut procedures suggested above.

It is not claimed that this short-cut procedure is as reliable as the more lengthy one we in fact adopted. One might need to modify it to suit the particular circumstances of different countries (and it would scarcely apply at all in a quota-ridden country). It would be useful to try it out in several. Nevertheless, in the absence of anything better it should provide one with a sufficient set of accounting ratios for most public sector project inputs, and for those whose outputs consist primarily of traded goods, provided one supplemented it with more careful estimates for particularly important items. It is to be noted that no *explicit* set of weights is required for benefits accruing to those with different incomes outside the public sector. They are probably not needed for a great many projects, but for some they could be fairly crucial. An example is the Settlement Schemes in Part II. The way we have estimated the social cost of family labour on these schemes in Chapter 5 is not covered by the above schema. This is one of the 'particularly important items' which must be estimated more carefully, and it happens to require a weighting system.

1.2.8 *The accounting rate of interest (ARI) and the treatment of inflation*

Let us suppose that we have estimated the net social benefit or cost arising from a project for each year of its life. These benefits or costs are expressed at the relevant accounting prices for each year, and we shall refer to them as estimates at 'current accounting prices'[1]. The problem then is to collapse them all into a single figure, the net present social value, which provides us with our investment criterion: the project being approved if it is positive, and not approved if it is negative[2]. How is this done?

There are two essential steps, first, to correct for inflation and, second, to discount at the accounting rate of interest, or ARI. Both are further discussed in Chapter 2.

The first step, correcting for inflation, arises for any evaluation of *past* projects (or projects partly in the past). For projects which lie wholly in the future it may seem, at first sight, that it is irrelevant, since the estimates can be made on the basis of a constant general level of prices. However, even in this case it makes for clarity of thought if one knows just what one means by a 'constant general level of prices'. Furthermore, it is quite likely that there will be certain amounts which are fixed in *money* and not *real* terms, and whose real value is therefore bound to depend on the future rate of inflation. This applies, for example, to foreign loans or public sector loans to the private sector. Both examples occur in Part II, and are very important items in the analysis.

How, then, should we correct for inflation? We discuss the principles in Chapter 2, here we only summarize the practice. For past years we divide all values at current accounting prices by an index of consumer prices (*not* import or export prices, as might be thought) so as to express them at the prices of some chosen base year (1967-8 in Part II). Had we any evidence of a change in the accounting ratio for consumption, we would have also allowed for that in our index, but as we have not we make the simple assumption of no change. For future years we only correct items which are fixed in money terms. Those denominated in units of Kenyan currency are deflated by the assumed rate of increase of consumer prices in Kenya (3 per cent per annum), while those denominated in any other

[1] The accounting prices in any year depend on the exchange rate at which foreign currencies are converted into Kenyan pounds, since we choose to express our accounting prices in terms of the latter. We use the official exchange rate for convenience, but the choice is essentially arbitrary, and makes no difference to our final decision (see Chapter 2).

[2] We ignore considerations of uncertainty (see Little and Mirrlees, 1974, Ch. 15).

currency are deflated by the assumed rate of increase of consumer prices in the country issuing it. This procedure rests on a simple purchasing power parity theory of exchange rate determination for which there is some evidence[1] so long as it is regarded as one's best guess over a long period (for short periods it can obviously be very mistaken).

The second step is to discount future benefits or costs by the ARI, which we put at 10 per cent per annum. As Kenya is a heavy net borrower from abroad, the ARI should equal the marginal cost of public sector borrowing in this way. Our impression is that, until recently, the Kenyan Government experienced little difficulty in finding foreign finance for projects. In that case, the marginal cost of foreign borrowing may have been little more than 5 per cent per annum in real terms. More recently, however, finance has become more difficult to obtain and so the marginal cost may be higher–and rather hard to estimate. The information we have on social rates of return on public or private sector projects in Kenya is very scanty, but enough to show that very high rates can be earned on some. Our final best guess is the same as the rate of discount used in the Economist Intelligence Unit's East African Transport Study, which we understand was estimated after consultation with the Kenya Government.

An ARI as high as 10 per cent per annum poses a dilemma when it is compared with recent rates of growth of consumption per head of the order of 1 per cent per annum, such scanty evidence as we have on the rate of growth of the critical income level, and our best guess of the elasticity of the weight attached to marginal gains in income, e, which we put at 1. To be consistent, the level of critical income ought to rise at about 10 per cent per annum, divided by e, and *minus* the rate of discount for pure time preference also divided by e. It looks as if *either* our ARI is too high, *or* our value for e is too low, *or* the rate of discount for pure time preference is quite high, *or* some combination of all three applies. We do not attempt to resolve this dilemma.

[1] See Little, Scitovsky and Scott, 1970, p. 468.

1.3 THE PRIVATE SECTOR

Thus far we have confined our attention to public sector projects. Even if we only wanted to appraise such projects, and not projects in the private sector, we would need to tackle the problem of valuing payments made to private 'capitalists' of at least two kinds: those which increase their incomes (before tax) without requiring anything by way of return, and those which, in effect, represent the hire of private capital. In practice, however, there are numerous occasions on which a Government needs to be able to appraise private sector projects (e.g. in approving of foreign investments, or in making loans to private businessmen), and so we must consider how the methods described above can be suitably modified. All these problems are discussed in Chapter 6. As is emphasized there, our estimates and analyses are particularly uncertain in this area, and much more work needs to be done[1].

We have already listed the ways in which surpluses can accrue to capitalists as a result of the implementation of a public sector project. These surpluses may lead to extra consumption or savings by capitalists, or they may be taxed. Taxation has an accounting ratio of zero and for consumption we simply use 0.82, the same ratio as for urban workers (although a separate estimate would be both practicable and desirable). The difficult problem is the treatment of savings. What we have done is to assume that they are multiplied by about $1\frac{1}{3}$ through the addition of bank borrowing and investment allowances, and are reinvested in Kenya to earn about 15 per cent per annum before tax at market prices in real terms. By making assumptions about the proportions of extra profits which are consumed, saved and taxed, we can then work out the net present social value of this investment. We show that it is sensitive to the values chosen for such parameters as the accounting ratio applicable to the profits of the projects in which it is invested, the ARI, and the extent of tax evasion. We consider Kenyan and foreign firms separately. Finally, we take 0.2 as our best guess for the accounting ratio for surpluses accruing to capitalists (P 4), which is consistent with a net present value of capitalists' savings

[1] We have made use of some preliminary estimates by David Newbery, who is currently engaged on research in this field.

of zero. In other words, the social cost of the capital goods bought with those savings about equals the net present value of the future social benefits flowing from them. Consequently, the only cost involved in increasing capitalists' income is their direct extra consumption, which is estimated at rather more than one-fifth of such payments.

It is convenient to take the appraisal of private sector projects next. This proceeds in exactly the same way as for public sector projects with one important addition: earnings received or payments made by the private owners. A simple way of looking at it is to regard the project as *being* in the public sector, with the special feature that capitalists are 'hired' as well. All outputs and inputs, other than profits and private financing, are expressed at accounting prices in the ordinary way. The profits are then the 'hire' whose accounting cost can be worked out in just the same way as for P 4, once we have estimated the fractions of income consumed and saved. Finally, there is the private financing. This is like a negative 'hire', and its value as a receipt or benefit is not easy to estimate. If it all represents capitalists' savings which would otherwise have been invested in Kenya, then our tentative best guess at its value is zero, as above. But if it represents new savings of Kenyan capitalists, its accounting ratio is 0.82, that of capitalists' consumption, while if it represents new foreign exchange from abroad, its accounting ratio is simply 1.00. Which of these alternatives applies makes a tremendous difference to the social rate of return on private sector projects. If the private finance is merely switched from elsewhere in Kenya, the social return is simply the ARI of 10 per cent per annum. But if it represents new savings or foreign exchange, the social return may well be 30 or 60 per cent per annum. On the other hand, these high social rates of return will not be found if the private sector project requires heavy protection, or if the profits flowing from it largely escape tax.

Not surprisingly, the cost of indirect capital inputs into a project (private or public) depends heavily on the same things. These inputs are the gross profit components of non-traded goods or services, and we have to convert them into their accounting costs. We have adopted a short-cut procedure which should give the correct figure if the inputs are provided by the public sector, and which is still a good approximation if they represent investments switched from elsewhere in Kenya, and probably also even if they represent new private savings if the resulting profits largely escape tax. If, however, a project's demands for non-traded inputs lead to new savings or fresh injections of foreign exchange from outside Kenya to provide the capital required, and if tax is successfully levied on the resulting profits, then the cost of this indirect capital requirement is much lower than we have estimated it to be—perhaps only a third as much.

Hirschman's concept of induced investment and backward linkage is very relevant here[1]. His view seems to be that new savings *are* likely to be generated as a result of new demands, and so he stresses the beneficial effect of the latter. If this view is taken, the accounting ratios for some non-traded inputs estimated here must be lowered, perhaps in some cases substantially. The short-cut procedure for estimating them, given in 1.2.7, must also be modified, and some standard deduction must be made to the ratios emerging from it. We have not estimated what that should be—it is one more topic requiring further research.

1.4 THE MAIN RESULTS AND SOME IMPLICATIONS

The main accounting ratios we have estimated are summarized in Table 1.2 and in Figure 1.2, which we consider in turn.

The most obvious point which emerges is that the accounting ratios are generally less than one. In other words, accounting prices are generally less than market prices, and in this sense the currency may be said to be 'overvalued' at the official exchange rate. This is hardly surprising, and probably is true of most countries, developed or underdeveloped. It does, however, carry with it a very important implication: projects which earn or save foreign exchange, for whose outputs demand is highly elastic, and which can cover their costs at market prices, are likely to be socially very profitable. For such projects, the accounting value of their output is close to the market value,

[1] Hirschman, 1958.

Table 1.2

The main accounting ratios

	Item	Accounting ratio	Main reference (pages)
Primary inputs			
P 1	Foreign exchange	1.00	10
P 2	Unskilled urban labour (formal sector)	0.70	99
P 3	Skilled labour	0.80	185
P 4	Extra income accruing to 'capitalists'	0.20	137
P 5	Extra income accruing to urban consumers	0.70	187
P 6	Unskilled rural labour (informal sector)	1.00	91
P 7	Extra income accruing to small farmers	0.50	186
P 8	Non-traded agricultural output, urban retail	0.85	158
P 9	Non-traded agricultural output, farm gate	1.00	158
P 10	Taxes, etc.	0.00	10
Others			
	Unskilled urban labour (informal sector)	0.80	92
	Unskilled workers on large farms	0.75	100
	Urban rents	1.00	192
	Rural consumption, marginal	0.92	168
	Rural consumption, average	0.94	168
	Urban consumption, marginal	0.82	168
	Urban consumption, average	0.82	168
	Critical rural income, f_{cr}	0.87	168
	Critical urban income f_{cu}	0.78	168
	Savings of households, rural and urban	0.40	171
	Savings of 'capitalists'	0.00	138

while the accounting value of their input is appreciably below it. Social profits are then much higher than profits at market prices. Examples of such projects may be found in agriculture (e.g. beef in Part III, or tea in Stern, 1972), and some import substitute industries which have 'natural' protection due to heavy transport costs (e.g. brewing) and possibly tourism (if the elasticity of demand is fairly high).

The accounting ratios for labour are quite high, ranging from 0.7 to 1. This is mainly because the principal source of unskilled labour is thought to be unskilled rural labour, the accounting ratio for its marginal product is thought to be rather more than one, and the benefit accruing to unskilled labour which takes a job in the urban formal sector is not thought to be very great, largely because of the higher urban than rural cost of living. If this is right, the case for a wage subsidy for unskilled urban labour in the formal sector is not as strong as in some other countries[1]. Nevertheless, given a shadow wage 30 per cent less than the market wage, there still is a case, and the writer believes that this may be one of the best ways of promoting manufacturing industry[2].

The accounting ratios for savings, especially those of 'capitalists' (i.e. mainly companies, both Kenyan and foreign), are very low. These are particularly uncertain estimates, but, taken at their face value, they suggest that, *ceteris paribus*, the social profitability of a private project which is financed by *new* savings or injections of capital from abroad is well above its private profitability. This point was made in 1.3. Taken in conjunction with that made in the last paragraph but one, it would seem that some socially very profitable projects, financed by private capital or overseas aid, can probably be found in the sectors mentioned.

Although we estimate that consumer prices in the towns are about 60 per cent higher on average than those in the countryside (Chapter 8), the accounting ratio for urban consumption is not much smaller than that for rural consumption. This suggests that most of the difference in the cost of living is a real one. Part of the explanation lies in the very high urban rents. It should be possible, by suitable policies, to lower substantially the real cost of urban housing[3]. Another part of the explanation lies in the costs of transporting and distributing the food produced in the countryside. Possibly we have overestimated the accounting ratios applicable to these costs, but, if not, the costs are substantial, and measures to reduce them would be very desirable.

[1] For example, the writer has estimated that the accounting ratio for unskilled male labour in Mauritius is about 0.4. The unemployment problem there is much more acute than in Kenya.

[2] See Little, Scitovsky and Scott, 1970, Ch. 4, and Ch. 9 pp. 331-2.

[3] Gordon Hughes, Christ's College, Cambridge, is, at the time of writing, engaged on a study of this question.

Fig. 1.2 Frequency distribution of accounting ratios

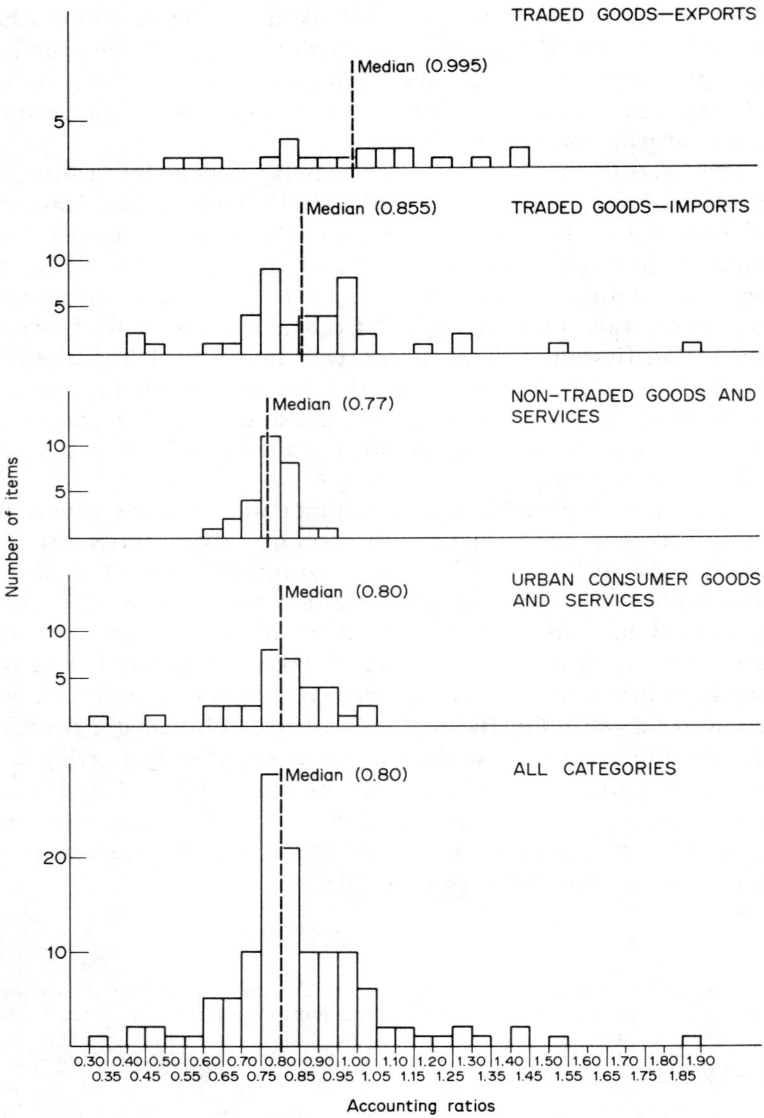

Turning to Figure 1.2[1], there are several rather interesting points to be made. A pattern emerges which will be familiar to those who have studied rates of effective protection in developing countries[2]. Taking the median as our best measure of what is 'typical', 0.80 is the most typical accounting ratio (and is also close to the modal value). In relation to this, export items tend to be high (median of 1.0), but imports only a little higher (median of 0.86). Non-traded goods and services are, by contrast, a bit lower (median of 0.77) and would be lower still if we were to mark down the costs of capital inputs for the reasons discussed in 1.3 above. Urban consumer goods and services are similar to the average. Agricultural products (not shown as a group in Figure 1.2) tend to have ratios around one or more, though there are exceptions (e.g. maize in the years when it is exported). Manufactured goods, by contrast, tend to be below one.

Exports have a wide scatter (standard deviation 0.25), which reinforces the point made in 1.2.3 above that their accounting ratios need to be carefully estimated, especially if they are important items like maize. The three extreme low values are in fact maize in the three years 1966, 1962 and 1967, and are due to the subsidization of maize exports in those years. All the other observations are close to or above the norm of 0.8. Ratios above one show that the commodity concerned is receiving negative protection, and this is typical of exports in many countries. The extreme values, reading from right to left, are pyrethrum in 1962 and 1963, tea in 1967, and pyrethrum in 1964.

Imports also have a wide scatter (standard deviation 0.25), which would show up as well if the short-cut method proposed in 1.2.3 above were used. The three extremely low ratios are, as might be expected, the heavily taxed items: tobacco, motor spirit and gas/diesel oil. Other low ratios are for sugar (wholesale) and tyres and tubes. Close to the lower mode

[1] Exports and imports are drawn from categories T, FO and FI in Table 10.1, non-traded goods and services from category N, urban consumer goods and services from UCF and UCN, and all of these together make the final frequency distribution.

[2] See, for example, Balassa and associates, 1971, and Little, Scitovsky and Scott, 1970, and the associated country studies.

around 0.8 are building materials, inputs into consumer goods (e.g. bottles, flavouring essences, hops, paper for printing, stationery), and some capital goods which are also consumer durables (lorries and Land-Rovers, office machinery, motor spares). Close to the higher mode just below 1.0 are producers' capital goods and agricultural inputs, which are mostly untaxed, with subsidized fertilizers higher still. The two extremely high ratios are for maize as an import substitute in 1963-4 and 1964-5, when imports were, in effect, heavily subsidized.

Non-traded goods and services are much more closely grouped (standard deviation 0.06), reflecting the fact that they are weighted averages of a large number of items. It is this close grouping which suggests the short-cut procedure of taking a single ratio for all of them. If Kenya is typical of other countries, this ratio should be appreciably lower than the median value for imports.

Urban consumer goods and services are also fairly closely grouped (standard deviation 0.14). The two very low ratios are for spirits and for beer and tobacco (combined as one item). These should be carefully calculated, if time permits, as they are clearly atypical. Nevertheless, it is worth noting that our final estimate of the accounting ratio for urban consumption is 0.82 (see 8.1) which is virtually the same as the median for all urban consumer goods or, for that matter, for all categories.

The frequency-distribution for all categories has a marked peak close to 0.80, but quite a wide scatter (standard deviation 0.21).

1.5 EXTERNALITIES

We conclude this chapter with some remarks on externalities. Where these exist, market prices will diverge from shadow prices. Some might say that the reverse also applies, but whether this is or is not the usual meaning of the word does not matter much. It is the divergence of market prices and shadow prices which is the most interesting aspect of externalities from the point of view of project selection. It is sometimes alleged that the Little-Mirrlees method neglects externalities which may be important[1]. No doubt the same accusation will be levelled at

[1] For example, see Stewart and Streeten, 1972.

the estimates given here. This is rather like a spectator, safely planted on the ground, criticizing an early flying-machine because it is noisy, draughty, unsafe and uncomfortable. We have, in fact, made a sustained effort to take account of all the major reasons leading to divergences between market and shadow prices that we could. Let us list them: taxes (probably the most important), institutionally fixed wages, income-distribution effects, multiplier effects, backward linkages, economies of scale, imperfectly elastic demands for exports, prices not related to marginal costs for railways and marketing boards, what we have called 'the fiscal problem', non-pecuniary benefits and costs of settlement farmers and workers, congestion in urban housing, and wear and tear on roads. It is admittedly uncertain whether we have estimated these divergences correctly. Nor do we claim to have allowed for everything. There will inevitably be important factors which can only be properly considered project by project. This may be true, for example, of some environmental effects. Have we, however, omitted any important *general* factors which account for divergences between shadow and market prices?

CHAPTER 2

Numeraire, Accounting Rate of Interest and Inflation

2.1 THE MEANING OF THE NUMERAIRE

Our unit of account, or numeraire, is uncommitted foreign exchange in the hands of the Government 'today'. We express it, however, in Kenyan currency units, and this needs some explanation. At any given moment in time we may regard the border prices which Kenya pays or receives for traded goods as given[1] in terms of any particular *foreign* currency (e.g. dollars—the precise currency does not matter provided it is convertible into others at given exchange rates). Likewise, the actual market prices expressed in Kenyan currency are given[1] for particular goods in particular places. None of these prices is arbitrary—they all exist objectively. We can now arbitrarily choose an exchange rate between our unit of account and, say, dollars. Once this is chosen, all rates of import and export tax or subsidy are determined. If we choose the actual official exchange rate, the tax or subsidy rates will also be the actual ones such as one finds by looking up the Customs and Excise Tariff book. In the case of Kenya, this is obviously the simplest procedure to follow, and we do in fact follow it. For countries with multiple exchange rate systems, however, there is sometimes no obvious single rate to choose. The point we are making here is that this does not matter. It merely means that we have to be careful to ensure that the tax and subsidy rates we use are consistent with the particular exchange rate we select. Given these tax and subsidy rates, and a great deal of other information, we can now work out accounting ratios

[1] By saying that prices are 'given' we only mean that they exist and are not dependent on some arbitrary choice of exchange rates. We do not mean, for example, that they are independent of quantities bought or sold.

which enable us to convert, in principle, the market price of any good into its accounting price in terms of our numeraire. How this is done is described elsewhere in this book, and is not our concern here. The *meaning* of the resulting accounting price, however, *is* our concern. It *means* that, if the Government had at its disposal an amount of foreign exchange (e.g. dollars, or any other currencies convertible into them and each other at given exchange rates) which equalled the accounting price multiplied by the arbitrarily chosen exchange rate, it either

(*a*) could actually buy the good with just that amount of foreign exchange, or
(*b*) could actually pay for all the items necessary to make the good, directly and indirectly, supposing that it was a non-traded good (or had non-traded components, such as transport to a particular locality), or
(*c*) would regard the amount of foreign exchange at its disposal as being as valuable as the good in question.

The numeraire is foreign exchange *or its equivalent value* in this sense. For example, we express benefits accruing to settlers in terms of the numeraire, and some of these are 'psychic', such as shorter hours of work, or the benefit of working for oneself rather than for someone else. No physical good is directly involved, and the benefit certainly does not take the form of an actual increase in foreign exchange in the hands of the Government.

We have also specified that the numeraire is *uncommitted* foreign exchange. Foreign exchange which has already been earmarked for some purpose or other is not necessarily equally valuable.[1]

2.2 INFLATION

So far we have only considered the meaning of the numeraire at a given moment in time. We must extend this to any moment in time. It is convenient to have a numeraire which is, in some sense, 'real', for reasons which may be obvious and are also

[1] For further discussion see Little and Mirrlees, 1974, Section 9.12.

discussed below. We choose our numeraire to be units of Kenyan currency, convertible into foreign exchange at rates of exchange which we shall specify, which have a constant purchasing power over a particular bundle of consumer goods and services. The particular bundle in principle is given by the extra amounts of goods and services bought by a poor rural family with the critical income[1] when their income is increased marginally. In practice, we have to deviate from this, but our reasons for choosing it in principle are given below.

'Purchasing power' is measured at accounting prices, not market prices. Thus the purchasing power of £1 of our numeraire has not changed if the value at accounting prices of the specified bundle of goods has not changed, even if its value at market prices has.

The question then arises as to what price index we should use to convert amounts expressed at accounting prices in different years into units of the numeraire of constant purchasing power. In principle, we need an index with accounting price relatives weighted by values of marginal consumption measured at accounting prices. Since this is not available, we make do with an index of actual consumer prices[2] combined with (in principle) an index of the conversion factor for marginal increases in rural incomes, f_{cr}.[3] This combined price index is:

$$\frac{P_t}{P_o} = \frac{C_t}{C_o} \times \frac{f_{crt}}{f_{cro}}$$

where P_t is the combined price index in year t,
C_t is the consumer price index in year t,
and f_{crt} is the conversion factor in year t.
Suffix o denotes the base year.

We must now specify the exchange rates used in converting our numeraire in any year, at current prices, into foreign exchange. This is covered by the earlier discussion. The exchange rates can in principle be chosen arbitrarily, but their

[1] See Chapter 3.

[2] We use the Wage Earner's Index of Consumer Prices in Nairobi

[3] See Chapters 3 and 8.

choice then determines the conversion factors f_{cr}. The relationship is directly proportional, so that if, say, we double the exchange rate we double the conversion factor. For example, let the exchange rate in year 0 be R_o Kenyan pounds equals one dollar, and that in year t be R_t, and let the corresponding conversion factors be f_{cro} and f_{crt}. Then the combined price index is as above. Now let us arbitrarily choose $2R_t$ in year t, leaving R_o unchanged. Then our new conversion factor will be $2\ f_{crt}$ and our new price index $2\ P_t$. All that has happened is that we have doubled all the accounting prices in year t, and so we must deflate them by twice as much to bring them back to a *numeraire* of constant purchasing power.

In practice, we naturally choose the official exchange rate in Kenya at any given time. This rate has, of course, changed vis-à-vis the pound sterling and many other currencies in the last few years. However, what matters for our price index is not these changes in exchange rates but rather the changes in the conversion factor, f_{cr}. This is determined by changes in import and export tax and subsidy rates, and by changes in quantitative restrictions on imports, and by a number of other factors which influence, for example, the ratio of shadow wages to actual wages. We cannot pretend that none of these things has changed. Nevertheless, as we have no readily available information on which to base an estimate of the change in f_{cr}, and no compelling reason to suppose that it changed very greatly in the years covered by the Settlement Surveys (i.e. 1964-5 to 1967-8, see Part II), we have there assumed that there was no change, and have simply corrected for changes in the consumer price index above.[1]

[1] For further discussion of the treatment of inflation in the Settlement accounts, see Part II, Chapter 13. This also considers the treatment of foreign loans denominated in foreign currencies. It is instructive to consider the effects of an actual devaluation, say, of the Kenyan pound vis-à-vis all other foreign currencies on our combined price index. If the devaluation were accompanied by no changes in import or export taxes or subsidies (or other changes with similar effects), then actual prices in Kenya would tend to rise. The conversion factor f_{cr} would be broadly unchanged, but C would rise and so would P in the same proportion. If the devaluation were accompanied by reductions in tariffs and export subsidies which left domestic prices broadly unchanged, then C would be unaffected but f_{cr} would rise and so would P in the same proportion. In either event, then, devaluation would tend to raise P.

2.3 THE MEANING OF THE ACCOUNTING RATE OF INTEREST (ARI)

The accounting rate of interest simply measures the rate of fall through time of the social value of foreign exchange, once that has been expressed in terms of constant purchasing power in the way just described. It therefore enables us to add together amounts of foreign exchange which accrue in or are disbursed in different periods of time. Thus if the ARI is 10 per cent per annum, £1 of foreign exchange is equal in social value to £1.1 a year hence, and so the social value of foreign exchange has fallen by approximately 10 per cent in a year. Hence we divide all benefits and costs a year hence by 1.1 before adding them to benefits or costs now.

We must now explain why our combined price index refers in principle to the bundle of consumer goods purchased by a poor rural family when its income is marginally increased. In our estimation of shadow wages in Kenya, we make use of the concept of the *critical income* (see 1.2.5 and Chapter 3). It is to be expected that the critical income, in real terms, should rise through time. Consequently, the social value of a given real increase in income to families at this level should fall through time, and, indeed, it should fall at the rate measured by the ARI. Hence, if foreign exchange is measured in units which have a constant purchasing power in terms of what these families buy, then the rate of fall in its social value will be measured by the ARI.

2.4 ESTIMATION OF THE ARI

Ideally, the ARI should equal the real rate of return on marginal projects in the public sector, when they are evaluated using accounting prices. However, unless and until such evaluations are made for a large number of projects, and experience has been gained over a fair length of time, the necessary information is lacking for this approach to the problem of estimation. We have only a few estimates of such rates of return for Kenya. For the Third Expansion Plan of the Kenya Tea Development Authority, N. H. Stern estimated the social rate of return at 39 per cent per annum.[1] For some of the schemes in the Million Acre Settlement Programme, estimates of rates of return are given in Part II of this book. They have a very wide range. The social rates of return on beef fattening, assuming this is done in the public sector, are estimated in Part III of this book. Depending on the different assumptions made, they vary from 25 to 38 per cent per annum.[2] It cannot be said that these rates give much of a guide, although they do show that some projects can be found with very high social rates of return.

An alternative approach is to consider the returns to lending abroad, or the cost of borrowing from abroad. The former would appear to be relevant if Kenya is a net lender, and the latter if she is a net borrower. However, like many countries, Kenya has both lent and borrowed abroad.

The East African Currency Board system was replaced by an independent Central Bank of Kenya issuing its own currency in 1966. From the end of 1966 to the end of 1972, Kenya's foreign exchange reserves rose in every year except 1971, and amounted at the end of the period to between 4 and 5 months' merchandise imports. The marginal rate of return on these assets was almost certainly less than 5 per cent per annum in real terms. However, this does not seem to be particularly relevant to a determination of the ARI, since these foreign assets were accumulated in order to permit an efficient management of the balance of payments, and of macro-economic policy in general, and their marginal social value is not adequately measured by the interest rate they earn. We therefore turn to the other side of the account.

Kenya has been borrowing long-term from abroad, and, indeed, her balance of payments on current account was in deficit in every year from 1966 to 1971 inclusive. The real rates of interest paid on foreign loans varied considerably, some (e.g. from IDA) being close to zero. The relevant rate from our point of view is the *marginal* cost of borrowing, but we have not been able to determine what this was. One difficulty is to estimate the effect of borrowing more from one source on the cost of borrowing from others. Creditors get worried if the ratio of

[1] See Stern, 1972, p. 101.

[2] See Part III, 18.4. However, the range of possible returns is, in fact, wider than this—see, for example, Table 24.3.

debt service to trade increases, and may increase their charges accordingly. This would make the marginal cost greater than the apparent cost on marginal loans, but it is not clear how important this factor is. We rather gained the impression that the Kenya Government had, at least until recently, had little difficulty in obtaining loans from overseas governments or international institutions, and that the problem was rather one of finding projects on which to spend the money. If this was so, it suggests that the marginal cost of borrowing may have been rather low, and perhaps little more than 5 per cent per annum in real terms. This *should* imply an equally low ARI, since if foreign exchange could be obtained on these terms, at the margin, public investment should have been pushed to the point at which its marginal yield was equally low. However, the position may have been changing, with finance becoming scarcer in relation to projects. If the ARI is regarded as an average rate of return ruling over a fairly long period, these more recent developments should be allowed to influence one's view about the appropriate ARI both in the past decade and in the future.[1]

Yet another approach to estimating the ARI is to consider average rates of return realised on investments in the private sector. These are discussed in Chapter 6, where we tentatively conclude that the average marginal rate of return before tax on investment by companies might be of the order of 15 per cent per annum in real terms. However, as we there point out, the ARI would normally be less than this rate of return.

Finally it is worth considering the implications of choosing a particular ARI for the rate of change of the level of critical income. Let us first assume that the Government does not discount future benefits purely and simply because they are in the future, but only because their social value is judged to be less for other reasons. Thus, if £1 at accounting prices were paid to a family with a given income level this year, let us suppose that the Government would regard this as socially equally

[1] In principle, one can and should have an ARI which varies from year to year, the long-term ARI being an average of short-term ones. The short-term ARI may have been low until recently, and may continue to rise for some time if the supply of good projects can be increased in relation to the foreign finance available. In practice, it is simpler to use a single long-term ARI, and to change this only occasionally.

valuable to £1 at accounting prices (after adjusting for changes in purchasing power so that the real quantity of goods is unchanged) paid to a similar family with the same income level next year. In that case it can easily be shown that the rate of increase of the level of critical income should be g, where

$$g = \frac{ARI}{e}$$

and where e is the elasticity of the weight given by the Government to marginal increases in income with respect to changes in income.[1] In Chapter 3 we put $e = 1$, and below we take 10 per cent per annum as our best guess of the ARI. It follows that the critical income level should increase at 10 per cent per annum.

This is certainly a very rapid rate of increase. From 1964 to 1971, real GDP at factor cost per head of population increased at about 3 per cent per annum, and real private consumption per head at only about 1 per cent per annum. Hence, for the above assumptions to be valid, the critical income level in the past would have had to grow much faster than average income levels. This could have come about either through a marked tendency towards equalizing incomes, with incomes of the poor rising much faster than average incomes–for which there is no evidence–or as a result of the Government moving the income level which it regarded as critical upwards much faster than the incomes of poor people were, in fact, rising. If the latter had

[1] By definition, a unit marginal increase in terms of foreign exchange in the income of a family at the critical income level 'to-day' has the same social value as the numeraire. The rate of fall of the social value of foreign exchange is by definition measured by the ARI. On our assumptions, the only change which can reduce the social value of a marginal increase in the income of a family at the critical income level is an increase in that income level. From chapter 3, the weight attached to a margin increase in the income of a family whose income (per adult equivalent) at time t, i.e. Y_t is given by

$$U(1\ ; Y_t) = W \text{ say} = \left(\frac{Y_o}{Y_t}\right)^e, \text{ where } Y_o \text{ is critical income 'today'.}$$

Taking logs, $\log W = e\,(\log Y_o - \log Y_t)$.

Differentiating with respect to time, $\dfrac{d \log W}{dt} = -e\dfrac{d \log Y_t}{dt}$

Or, in words, the rate of fall of the weight (i.e. the ARI) is equal to the rate of increase in income multiplied by e.

been the case, an increasing fraction of the population should have moved into the income groups which were exempted from direct taxation, or were eligible for exemption from school fees, etc. The exemption of those with the lowest incomes from paying Graduated Personal Tax in 1969 is the only example of this that occurs to the writer.

In Chapter 3 we tentatively fix the critical rural income level at the minimum income target for rural households which the ILO recommended should be achieved by 1978. The ILO also recommended that this target should be raised by 50 per cent by 1985, which implies a rate of increase between those years of 6 per cent per annum. Even if these targets are taken to represent the relevant critical income levels, the rate of increase proposed for the future is still well below our figure of 10 per cent per annum.

There are three ways in which one might resolve this dilemma, without departing from the framework of analysis altogether. First, one might take the view that the ARI is less than 10 per cent per annum. This cannot be dismissed out of hand, especially in view of the relatively low apparent cost of borrowing from abroad and the shortage of projects mentioned above. Against this, however, there are the apparently high rates of return earned in the private sector and also in some public sector projects.

Second, one could take a higher value for e. This would also be quite reasonable. Our reasons for putting $e = 1$ are given in Chapter 3. It is certainly at the lower end of the range of plausible values. Nevertheless, a higher value would seem to require rather more powerful attempts by the Government to redistribute income than have been made at least in past years.

Third, one could make some allowance for pure time preference on the part of the Government. Thus if the Government were to discount future benefits and costs simply because they were in the future at, say, p per cent per annum, then our equation for the rate of increase of the level of critical income would become:

$$g = \frac{ARI - p}{e}$$

If p were sizeable, g could be fairly small. It is difficult to decide how great an allowance should be made for p. Some argue that governments are the custodians of future generations, and have no business to weight benefits accruing to them less heavily than those accruing to the present generation. Governments may equally be regarded as representing the present generation, and hence required to reflect their wishes.

Of course, one could take the view that the Kenya Government has never thought about the problem in this way, and so it would not be surprising to find that the average marginal yield on public sector investments was higher than the rate of growth of the critical income level, and that the Government's policies (e.g. on school fees) were inconsistent with such a high return. The question then is, will the Government eventually use this framework and, if so, which of its policies will it change?

Unsatisfactory as it may be, we leave the dilemma unresolved. Our reasons for selecting 10 per cent as our best guess of the ARI are as follows. First, it is somewhere between the high rates of return apparently found in the private sector, and in some public sector projects, and the lower apparent cost of borrowing from abroad. Second, at the time of our original visit to Kenya in 1969, the Economist Intelligence Unit had just completed a massive study of the East African Transport System. They used a discount rate of 10 per cent per annum in this study, and we understood that this was done after consultation with the Kenya Government, amongst others. If a lower ARI were to be used, e.g. 6 or 7 per cent per annum, it would not alter our accounting ratios substantially. It would, however, make an appreciable difference to the estimates of net present social values given in Parts II and III of this book. It is certainly an important magnitude, but its value can probably only be determined with any accuracy by a process of trial and error, and as the result of experience gained in evaluating a large number of projects.

CHAPTER 3

Weighting the Benefits

3.1 SOME FORMULAE

In this chapter we explain how we have estimated a set of weights for the benefits accruing outside the public sector as the result of implementing a project. The problem we discuss can be summed up in the following two expressions, each of which we need to evaluate:

$$\text{(a)}\quad f_{cr} \cdot u\ \{\Delta Y_r\ ;\ Y_r\}$$

$$\text{(b)}\quad f_{cr} \cdot b\ \{Y_J\ ;\ Y_j\}$$

(a) converts an increase in income of ΔY_r accruing to a rural household with income Y_r per adult equivalent into its equivalent social value expressed in terms of the numeraire of foreign exchange in the hands of the Government. (b) performs a similar conversion for a unit transfer from rural households with an income of Y_J to those with an income of Y_j per adult equivalent. It is to be noted that we speak here only of incomes accruing to rural households. We begin by considering only these, and deal with urban households subsequently.

The most important assumptions we make are as follows. First, we assume that there is a *critical income level*, expressed in terms of household income per adult equivalent, such that the Government would be indifferent between using resources costing a unit of foreign exchange equivalent to increase the incomes of households at that level and using resources with the same cost to increase the Government's own expenditure (both increases being marginal).[1] The critical income level may be different for rural households and urban households, and the

[1] Our critical income level is similar to the base consumption level of Little and Mirrlees, 1974, p. 238.

relation between the two is discussed below. In 3.2 we make a tentative estimate of the rural critical income level, but for the present we merely label it Y_{cr} and that for urban households Y_{cu}.

Second, we assume that the value attached by the Government to a unit increase (measured at market prices, not in terms of the numeraire) in incomes falls as the level of income of the recipient increases. Furthermore, to simplify matters we assume that the value or weight falls in a particular way described below and such that the proportionate rate of fall of the weight is a constant multiple of the proportionate increase in income. In economists' jargon, we assume that the elasticity of the marginal utility of income, in the eyes of the Government, is constant.

Finally, we assume that the weight depends *only* upon the income level of the recipient, and not upon other characteristics such as age, sex, tribe, etc.[1].

We attempt to justify these assumptions to some extent in 3.2, where we also try to estimate the rural and urban critical income levels and the rate at which the weight attached to marginal increases in income declines as income increases.

Let us first consider a unit (marginal) increase in income accruing to a rural household with income Y_{cr}. The foreign exchange equivalent cost of the resources needed to meet the resulting extra expenditure is then, by definition, f_{cr}. The social value of this increase in income is, by definition, the same as its foreign exchange equivalent cost, and is therefore f_{cr}.

$$\text{Hence } u \ \{1\,;Y_{cr}\} \equiv 1$$

In order to find the values of the weights attached to increases in income accruing to those with other income levels, we make our second assumption and so derive the utility function:

$$U = B - AY^{1-e}$$

[1] We have not attempted to estimate how far benefits resulting from the payment of wages accrue to foreigners, but have simply assumed that they all accrue to Kenyans or, where they do not, that the Government ignores the difference. We have also failed to make any allowance for concepts of justice. It is likely that the weight given will, in practice, depend on *why* a payment is made to someone, and not merely on his income.

The marginal utility of income is then given by

$$\frac{dU}{dY} = A\ (1-e)\ Y^{-e} = u\ \ \{1\ ;\ Y\}$$

and the elasticity of marginal utility with respect to income is $-e$, which we assume is constant. It is marginal utility which corresponds to the weight given by the Govnrnment to marginal increases in income.

If $e > 1$, increases in income however great cannot increase total utility beyond $U = B$. A is then positive. If $0 < e < 1$, increases in income can increase total utility without limit, and A must be negative.

If $e = 1$ we take the function $U = B + A \log_e Y$, and here again total utility can increase without limit, and

$$\frac{dU}{dY} = \frac{A}{Y}$$

The marginal utility of income to a rural household at the critical income level is by definition 1, so

$$1 \equiv -A\ (1-e)\ Y_{cr}^{\ -e}$$

Hence $A = \dfrac{-Y_{cr}^{\ e}}{1-e}$ (or, if $e = 1, A = Y_{cr}$).

Hence the marginal utility or weight attached to a marginal increase in any income Y is given by

$$u\ \ \{1\ ;\ Y\} = \left(\frac{Y_{cr}}{Y}\right)^{e} \qquad (1)$$

and this also holds if $e = 1$. We thus have a simple formula for deriving the weight to be given to marginal increases in income at any income level.

Where the increases in income are more than marginal, we can find the weight to be given to them as follows. Suppose that, in a household with N adult equivalents, income per adult equivalent increases from Y_1 to Y_2. Then, expressing everything per adult equivalent, we have

$$U_2 - U_1 = -A\left(Y_2^{\,1-e} - Y_1^{\,1-e}\right)$$

$$= \frac{Y^e_{cr}}{1-e}\left(Y_2^{\,1-e} - Y_1^{\,1-e}\right) \qquad (2)$$

$$= u\ \{Y_2 - Y_1\ ;\ Y_1\}$$

If $e = 1$, the above becomes

$$U_2 - U_1 = A\left(\log_e Y_2 - \log_e Y_1\right)$$

$$= Y_{cr} \log_e \left(\frac{Y_2}{Y_1}\right) \qquad (3)$$

The social value of the total benefit is then $N f_{cr}$ times as big.

So far we have assumed that all incomes are rural incomes. How do we evaluate a unit marginal increase in income accruing to an urban household with income per adult equivalent Y_u, say? Suppose that the ratio of urban consumer prices to rural consumer prices is P, so that a rural income of Y_u/P is equivalent, in real terms, to an urban income of Y_u.[1] Consequently, a unit marginal increase in income accruing to the urban household has the same value as an increase of $1/P$ accruing to a rural household whose income is Y_u/P. Then

$$u_u\ \{1\ ;\ Y_u\} = u\ \{1/P\ ;\ Y_u/P\}$$

where we introduce the suffix u on the left-hand side to show that we are dealing with urban incomes, whereas the right-hand side, without suffix, refers to rural incomes as before.

$$\text{But } u\ \{1/P\ ;\ Y_u/P\} = \frac{1}{P}\left(\frac{Y_{cr}}{Y_u} \cdot P\right)^e$$

which gives us the expression we require.

For non-marginal changes between urban income-levels per adult equivalent Y_{u1} and Y_{u2}, the value of the gain is the same as that between rural income levels Y_{u1}/P and Y_{u2}/P

[1] Here, and in what follows, we simplify by assuming that there is a unique price index, P, which applies at all income levels.

Hence $u_u \quad \{Y_{u2} - Y_{u1} \; ; Y_{u1}\} = \left(\frac{Y_{cr}}{1-e}\right)\left[\left(\frac{Y_{u2}}{P}\right)^{1-e} - \left(\frac{Y_{u1}}{P}\right)^{1-e}\right]$

or, if $e = 1$,

$$u_u \quad \{Y_{u2} - Y_{u1} \; ; Y_{u1}\} = Y_{cr} \log_e \left(\frac{Y_{u2}}{Y_{u1}}\right)$$

The relationship between the rural and urban critical income levels may be established as follows. By similar reasoning to that used above, the social value of a unit marginal increase in urban income Y_u, expressed in terms of the numeraire, is

$$f_{cu} \cdot \left(\frac{Y_{cu}}{Y_u}\right)^e$$

where f_{cu} is the conversion factor applying to increases in income of the urban household whose income is Y_{cu}.

The same social value is reached by the method described above, so that

$$f_{cu} \cdot \left(\frac{Y_{cu}}{Y_u}\right)^e = f_{cr} \cdot \frac{1}{P}\left(\frac{Y_{cr}}{Y_u} \cdot P\right)^e$$

Hence $\left(\frac{Y_{cu}}{P \cdot Y_{cr}}\right)^e = \frac{f_{cr}}{f_{cu}} \cdot \frac{1}{P}$ (4)

An interesting conclusion to be drawn from this is that, if $f_{cr} = f_{cu}$, and if $e = 1$, then $Y_{cu} = Y_{cr}$ regardless of P.

We can, however, evaluate the weights for both rural and urban households by reference to Y_{cr} alone, and by expressing all incomes and gains in incomes in terms of rural prices. This is the procedure we generally adopt. In 3.2 we also offer some further comments on the relationship of Y_{cu} to Y_{cr}.

We now turn to expression (b), which is the amount by which a unit of income transferred from those with income per adult equivalent Y_J to those with Y_j must be multiplied in order to calculate the resulting social benefit in terms of the numeraire. It seems reasonable to assume that such transfers as we shall be dealing with are all marginal. In that case the net benefit per unit transferred is simply

$$f_{cr}\ [u\ \{1\ ;Y_j\}\ -u\ \{1\ ;Y_J\}]\ =f_{cr}\cdot b\ \{Y_J\ ;\ Y_j\}$$

$$\text{Hence } b\ \{Y_J\ ;Y_j\}\ =\left(\frac{Y_{cr}}{Y_j}\right)^e-\left(\frac{Y_{cr}}{Y_J}\right)^e \qquad (5)$$

Here again we measure Y_j, Y_J and the income transferred all at rural prices.

3.2 A POSSIBLE SET OF WEIGHTS FOR KENYA

We have already explained why it is necessary to value gains in income accruing to different groups of persons both in relation to each other and in relation to gains accruing to the Government. In this section we make some tentative suggestions as to how this might be done. There is, unfortunately, no agreed procedure for doing it, nor has the Kenyan Government made any such valuations explicit—it would be surprising if it (or indeed any government) had. Nevertheless, if the costs and benefits of a project are to be summed up to give a meaningful total, some valuation must be made. A total which gives the same value to each £1 of benefit, no matter to whom it accrues, implicitly makes the assumption that they are of equal value, which can easily be shown to be implausible if it is meant to represent the Kenya Government's system of values. It is much more plausible to assume that the Government attaches less value to gains accruing to wealthy than to poor persons, and also that the Government attaches less value to gains accruing to better-off persons (e.g. most urban workers) than to itself. This seems clear both from the Government's actions and its statements, as we demonstrate below. Nevertheless, it is not easy to deduce from either just at what point in the income scale the Government would regard a marginal increase in a person's income as being as valuable as an equal increase in its own income, or at what rate the value placed on marginal additions to income falls as income rises. We estimate both these magnitudes, which we refer to in what follows as the '*critical income level*' and '*the rate of fall of the weight*' for short, but our estimates are somewhat arbitrary and open to challenge.

There are numerous official statements of Government policy which imply that the Government attaches more value to increases in income accruing to poorer than to richer persons. Thus in Sessional Paper No. 10 of 1965, on 'African Socialism and its Application to Planning in Kenya', two of the six main features of African Socialism are stated to be (para. 48):

'(v) diffusion of ownership to avoid concentration of economic power;

(vi) progressive taxes to ensure an equitable distribution of wealth and income.'

The objectives of Sessional Paper No. 10 were reiterated in the most recent Development Plan[1].

On the other hand, it seems clear that the Government does not regard the value of increases in income as falling very rapidly as income rises. This is the implication of the emphasis given to economic growth in Sessional Paper No. 10, and of other statements made there.[2] Again, the most recent Development Plan both takes credit for the rapid growth achieved in the previous plan period and proposes an acceleration in the new plan period.[3]

Turning from words to deeds, there is a variety of policies pursued by the Government which are consistent with a higher valuation of income gains to poorer persons. There is the

1 Development Plan 1970-74, p. 1.

2 'The high priorities placed on political equality, social justice and human dignity mean that these principles will not be compromised in selecting policies designed to alleviate pressing and immediate problems. The most important of these policies is to provide a firm basis for rapid economic growth. Other immediate problems such as Africanization of the economy, education, unemployment, welfare services, and provincial policies must be handled in ways that will not jeopardize growth. The only permanent solution to all of these problems rests on rapid growth. .... Growth, then, is the first concern of planning in Kenya ...' *Op. cit.* para. 53. See also paras. 13, 41 and 85.

3 *Op. cit.* p. (iii).

progressive income tax system. There are bursaries and remissions of fees for children with poor parents in Secondary and Primary Schools. Some free medical services are available to destitute persons, famine relief in kind is provided in districts affected by drought or similar calamities, and cash relief payments are made to those in temporary economic difficulties. A National Social Security Fund has been set up. On the other hand, the tax system does not appear to have much effect in redistributing income, at least over a wide range of incomes.[1] Income tax allowances are still quite high in relation to average incomes,[2] and the main direct tax which operates at lower levels of income, the Graduated Personal Tax, is very small and barely progressive.[3] Relief payments are very small[4] and Primary School fees are still charged for the vast majority of children.[5]

It seems fair to conclude from all this that, while the Government attaches greater value to income gains accruing to poorer people, the *rate* at which the weight falls as income rises

[1] The ILO, 1972, Chapter 16, p. 272, quotes estimates of the combined incidence of direct and indirect taxation in 1968/9 by M.J.Westlake, 'Tax Evasion, Tax Incidence and the Distribution of Income in Kenya', Institute of Development Studies Paper, University of Nairobi, Dec. 1971. These show that direct and indirect taxes are a percentage of income which falls from 11.5 per cent for incomes of less than 200 sh. per month to 8.3 per cent for incomes of 400-500 sh. per month rising to 12.7 per cent for incomes over 2000 sh. per month.

[2] In 1967, for example, a married man with two children had allowances totalling £720, which is over double our estimate of average urban African household incomes in 1969 (see Table 4.2). Allowances were substantially higher before Independence, being fixed in relation to typical British incomes.

[3] Thus in 1967 the GPT rate (at the middle of the relevant income bracket) was 3.0 per cent for those with monthly incomes of 200 sh. and rose to 4.3 per cent for those with monthly incomes of 930 shillings.

[4] In 1969-70, according to the Development Plan 1970-74, p. 529, £30,000 was allocated for relief payments which averaged 12,000 a year, or about £2.50 per payment. On the other hand, famine relief in kind has on occasion been much bigger. According to the ILO, 1972, Ch 19, 'conservative estimates of the direct costs in famine relief alone of the 1961 famine and the 1970-71 famine are £600,000 and £1 million respectively'.

[5] 'The Government assists the children of needy parents to get primary education through a system of fee remissions administered at local level by the boards of the individual primary schools. Remissions at present average 5-10 per cent of total fees paid, but it is Government policy that they should rise to 15-20 per cent by 1974. The remission of all primary school fees in areas hit by drought in 1971 was announced this year.' Economic Survey 1971, p. 196.

is not very great, and the critical income level is low. We must now try to quantify these qualitative conclusions, and we take the second one first.

The ILO, 1972, recommended the use of minimum income targets. 'Planners, officials of government departments and local field officers would be required to identify projects and justify their proposals not merely along familiar economic lines but with explicit attention to the effect of projects and programmes on persons with incomes under the minimum target' (*op. cit.*, p. 316). Although the minimum targets should be subsequently determined in the light of detailed household social surveys in different areas, the ILO proposes, provisionally, minimum household target incomes at 1971 prices as in Table 3.1, the dates shown (1978 and 1985) being those by which these minima should be achieved by every household.

Table 3.1

ILO proposed mimum household target incomes

£ p.a. 1971 prices

	Household income		Income per adult equivalent	
	1978	1985	1978	1985
Rural households	72	108	16	24
Urban households	120	150	27	33

Source: ILO, 1972, Chapter 7, pp. 109, 110, monthly figures converted to annual. Income per adult equivalent calculated by the writer by assuming a 'typical' household, as stated by the ILO, of 2-3 adults and 4 children, and so dividing by 2.5 + 4 ÷ 2 = 4.5

These minimum income targets may be compared with the estimates of household incomes in Table 4.2. The latter refer to 1969, when consumer prices were about 5 per cent lower than in 1971. It is clear that the minima for 1978 are well below the estimated average levels of household income per adult equivalent either of the average small farm regular employee (i.e. £21) or of the average self-employed worker in the urban informal sector (i.e. £39).

The ILO do not recommend that incomes below the minimum should simply be supplemented by grants.[1] 'It cannot be emphasized too much that our stategy is based not on permanent transfers of income to the lowest income group through redistribution from the top, but on investment to provide the unemployed and working poor with the basis for earning reasonable minimum incomes the levels of which can be raised over time' (p. 114). Examples of the types of investment which they give are hybrid seed for small farms, credit for the small rural non-agricultural producer, more equipment for the family planning clinics, investment in research on labour-intensive technologies, second-chance educational institutions, and development of processing of agricultural products for export. Some of these investments would yield a direct financial return to the Government as well as to the poor, but some would only yield their return to the poor. In so far as the latter are concerned, the Government is being asked to sacrifice the income it might have received by investing elsewhere in order to benefit the poor. Hence, one could argue, the Government should only undertake investments of this kind if it believes that this sacrifice is worthwhile. Although the argument is not watertight or precise, these minimum income levels are at least one possible estimate of the critical income levels we are seeking, and the case for accepting them is strengthened by the attention given to the ILO Report by the Kenya Government.

It seems unlikely that the critical income level in 1969 can have been much higher than the household income of the average regular employee on a small farm (i.e. £21 per equivalent adult). The head of such a household received about £41 p.a. (Table 4.1, line 2). Until 1969 he would, strictly speaking, have been liable to pay Graduated Personal Tax, but in 1969 those with incomes less than £48 p.a. were exempted. In view of the costs of tax collection, and their effects on

[1] One of the main objections to doing this would be the effect on incentives to work. It is clear that the Kenya Government attaches much importance to the maintenance of incentives to work. Thus in Sessional Paper No. 10 of 1965 we find (paras. 12 and 13): 'Every member of African traditional society had a duty to work. This duty was acknowledged and willingly accepted by members.... African society had the power and duty to impose sanctions on those who refused to contribute their fair share of hard work to the common endeavour. Drawing on this background African Socialism expects the members of the modern State to contribute willingly and without stint to the development of the nation.'

incentives, a consistent Government would not levy direct taxes on incomes much below the critical income level. Hence one could argue that in 1969 this ought to have been below £48 p.a. for a head of household, or, say, below £23 per adult equivalent for his household.

Another argument pointing in the same direction is the levying of primary school fees which, as Sessional Paper No. 10 of 1965 remarks, 'are really a form of tax that is relatively easy to collect'. The fact that only 5-10 per cent of primary school fees were remitted in 1970-71 suggests that the incomes of all but the poorest were being 'taxed' in this way.[1]

We conclude, therefore, that £15 p.a.[2] per equivalent adult in a rural household is a reasonable estimate of the critical income level for Kenya in 1969 at 1969 prices. For an urban household, the critical income level (at urban prices) works out, somewhat surprisingly, at only £17.[3] This is much lower than the same *real* income level as someone with the *rural* critical income level. The latter would be £15 x 1.6 = £24. How can we explain this seeming paradox? The theory behind it is in 3.1, but the essential point is as follows. It costs the Government much more (in terms of foreign exchange equivalent) to give the same real benefit to an urban inhabitant as to a rural inhabitant with the same real income. Each actual £ given to an urban inhabitant costs £0.87 (= f_{cr}). But, since urban prices are 1.6 times rural ones, the benefit secured by the rural inhabitant from his £ is 1.6 times as great as that secured by the urban one. Hence, for almost the same sacrifice in foreign exchange equivalent, the Government secures much less benefit by giving the £ to the urban than to the rural inhabitant. If it is to be indifferent between the two, it must give the £s to the urban

[1] See footnote on p.56. One could argue that the levying of school fees had the additional advantage, compared with ordinary direct taxation of incomes, of reducing family size, and that for this reason fees might be charged to those with incomes below the critical level. This reason has not, however, so far as the writer is aware, been given by the Kenya Government. Sessional Paper No. 10, 1965, *loc. cit.*, only refers to the need to charge fees to finance developmental expenditure.

[2] We take £15 instead of the figure of £16 in Table 3.1 mainly to allow for the rise in prices from 1969 to 1971, but also to allow a little for a general rise in incomes which should raise the critical income level through time.

[3] Using equation (4) in 3.1, and putting $f_{cr} = 0.87$, $f_{cu} = 0.78$ and $e = 1$, we have $Y_{cu} = Y_{cr} \cdot f_{cr} / f_{cu}$, or $17 = 15 \times 0.87/0.78$.

inhabitants who are *poorer* in real terms than the rural inhabitants, and, given our estimates and assumptions, it turns out that the actual money income of the urban inhabitants at the critical income level is not much higher than that of his rural counterpart.

This has interesting implications for the ILO's proposed minimum household target incomes. Instead of the urban incomes in Table 3.1 being much higher than the rural ones, they should, if the above argument and estimates are accepted, be about the same. This is a question which seems to merit further investigation.[1]

We now turn to the estimation of the rate at which the weight declines with rising income. As is shown in 3.1, this may be measured by a concept known to economists as the elasticity of marginal utility, a higher value for the elasticity implying a faster rate of decline of the weight. An elasticity of 1 means that the weight declines in the same proportion as income increases. This would mean, for example, that £2 extra for a person with an income of £200 p.a. would be given the same weight as £1 extra for a person with £100 p.a. Some would think that the weight should decline faster than this, so that plausible values of the elasticity would be greater than one. One argument for this is that there is a maximum benefit anyone can derive from his income—a multi-millionaire is not any happier just because he has a bigger income than a millionaire, nor even appreciably happier than someone with much less who is still comfortably off. Of course there may be many factors other than income which affect happiness, but we abstract from these here. If there is a maximum, then the elasticity of marginal utility must exceed one at least above some income level. It could still, however, be less than one for low incomes. It is hard to think of any satisfactory way of estimating the elasticity empirically, though there are some straws of evidence suggesting values rather greater than one.[2] All this, however, is concerned

[1] The reader might ask why we have based our own value of the critical income level on the ILO's *rural* figure of £16 rather than its urban figure of £27? The latter was rejected because G.P.T. was still, in principle, being levied on families with incomes as low.

[2] Little and Mirrlees, 1974, Section 13.13, remark 'On admittedly extremely inadequate evidence, we guess that most people would put [the elasticity] in the range 1-3 (if they could be induced to commit themselves at all).' In a recent

with the relation between income and happiness, and so is not precisely what we want, namely, the relation between income and the weight given to marginal increases in income by the Kenya Government. We gave some reasons above for thinking that this weight does not diminish very rapidly as income increases. We therefore select as our best guess an elasticity of one, which has the added virtue of simplicity.

In Tables 3.2 and 3.3 we show the weights to be given to marginal increases in income accruing to rural and urban households respectively, with incomes per adult equivalent as estimated in Tables 4.3 and 4.4. It should be emphasized that all incomes and gains in income are measured *at rural prices*. In each case, the weight given to marginal increases in income accruing to households with the critical rural income per adult equivalent of £15 is unity. We show three columns of weights, taking the elasticity of marginal utility as 0.5, 1 and 2 respectively, to illustrate the difference this makes. In subsequent work, however, we confine attention to the weights calculated with an elasticity of one. Two kinds of weighted average are calculated. In the first, in which the numbers of households are the weights, we get the mean expected weight for a marginal increase (or decrease) in income accruing to a household drawn at random. In the second, in which the total incomes of households in each income-group are the weights, we get the mean expected weight for a marginal increase (or decrease) in income which accrues to households in proportion to their expenditures. We use both kinds of weighted average in the subsequent analysis.

---

unpublished paper, Stern, (August 1973), after surveying many attempts to estimate the elasticity, concludes that it probably lies within the range 1-5. However, this refers to the 'social elasticity' (i.e. society's, or the Government's, view of the matter) rather than the individual's elasticity, and allows for a preference for egalitarianism as such, which tends to increase the upper end of the range. The latter half of the 19th century in the U.K. was a long period in which prices were on average remarkably stable and real income per head grew at about 1¾ per cent p.a. The long-term rate of interest on safe investments (Consols) averaged just over 3.0 per cent p.a., and it was remarkably stable, varying only between 2.5 and 3.3 per cent p.a. (averages for each year). Assuming no pure time preference, this suggests an elasticity in the region of 2, but allowing something for pure time preference would make it rather lower (see the formula on p.47). (Estimates of income per head and yield on Consols derived from Mitchell and Deane, 1962, pp. 367 and 455).

Table 3.2

Weights given to marginal additions to African rural incomes at different income levels

Per cent of households	Income per adult equiv. divided by critical income[a]	Marginal value of additions to income as proportion of marginal value of additions to critical income assuming $e = 0.5$	$e = 1$	$e = 2$
(1)	(2)	(3)	(4)	(5)
41.5	1.73	0.760	0.578	0.334
20.9	1.87	0.731	0.535	0.286
14.4	2.13	0.686	0.470	0.221
8.0	2.27	0.664	0.441	0.194
5.8	2.80	0.598	0.357	0.127
5.1	3.53	0.532	0.283	0.080
4.3	6.00	0.409	0.167	0.028
100.0				
Averages wtd. by:				
Households[b]	2.20	0.700	0.497	0.258
Incomes[c]	2.40	0.631	0.414	0.192

(a) I.e. £15 p.a. at rural prices.
(b) The averages are weighted by col. (1).
(c) The entry in col. (2) is simply average income per adult equivalent (i.e. total income divided by the total number of adult equivalents) divided by critical income per adult equivalent. The entries in cols. (3), (4) and (5) are the weighted averages of the appropriate columns using total income for each income group as weights.

Sources: Cols. (1) and (2) from Table 4.3, cols. (2) and (5). Cols. (3), (4) and (5) derived from col. (2) by taking the reciprocal of col. (2) and raising it to the power e. See equation (1) in 3.1.

Table 3.3

Weights given to marginal additions to African urban incomes at different income levels measured at rural prices[a]

Per cent of households	Income per adult equiv. divided by critical income[b]	Marginal value of additions to income as proportion of marginal value of additions to critical income assuming		
		$e = 0.5$	$e = 1$	$e = 2$
(1)	(2)	(3)	(4)	(5)
22.0	0.96	1.021	1.042	1.086
15.0	1.83	0.739	0.546	0.298
11.5	2.13	0.686	0.470	0.221
8.9	2.54	0.628	0.394	0.155
13.1	3.08	0.570	0.325	0.106
10.6	4.08	0.495	0.245	0.060
7.1	4.88	0.453	0.205	0.042
6.4	6.33	0.398	0.158	0.025
5.4	10.75	0.305	0.093	0.009
100.0				
Averages wtd. by:				
Households[c]	3.12	0.672	0.498	0.348
Incomes[d]	3.71	0.490	0.268	0.114

(a) Note that everything is measured at rural prices. Hence cols. (3) to (5) give the marginal value of £1.6 at *urban* prices, or £1 at *rural* prices, received by those whose relative income levels are as in col. (2), divided by the marginal value of £1 at rural prices received by a family whose income per adult equivalent is £15 at rural prices.

(b) I.e. £15 at rural prices.

(c) The averages are weighted by col. (1).

(d) See note (c) to Table 3.2.

Source: Cols. (1) and (2) derived from Table 4.4, cols. (2) and (5). Others as for Table 3.2.

CHAPTER 4

Shadow Wages

4.1 INTRODUCTION

The estimates given in this chapter can be criticized for being unduly laborious and involving a large element of guesswork. In defence of them, the writer can only reply that the subject-matter is important, and that *any* estimates are bound to involve guesswork at some stage. One can take the short-cut method described in 1.2.6, but, if one wants to make use of the wealth of data available, a more complex framework is needed which, it is hoped, is provided here. This still leaves many gaps which have to be filled in by guesswork, but it is capable of further development, and may stimulate others to improve upon it.

The next section gives some basic data on earnings in Kenya. This is followed by a section which summarizes the main ideas in a theoretical framework. The remaining sections explain how we have estimated the different elements which together make the shadow wage. To save space, we have not attempted to explain or justify all our estimates. Instead, we have described the general method and then illustrated its application in a few cases (for a fuller description, see Scott, February 1973).

We confine our estimates to African male unskilled labour in 1969. More work is needed to estimate shadow wages for women. Skilled labour is discussed in Chapter 9.

4.2 ESTIMATES OF INCOMES AND EARNINGS OF AFRICANS IN KENYA IN 1969

This section presents estimates of incomes and earnings of Africans in both rural and urban areas in Kenya in 1969. Data from a number of different sources have been combined with some guesswork by the writer, and the results are correspondingly uncertain. The main source was the ILO, 1972, but the estimates given there often needed to be supplemented or modified in various ways.

Table 4.1 gives estimates of African earnings in various sectors of the economy in 1969. All the estimates for the rural sector are for *regular* employees, and all are derived from the ILO, 1972. The estimate in line 2, for the average small farm regular employee, thus refers, presumably, to a full-time worker hired, typically, by the month, and often living on or near the farm of his employer. Such workers commonly receive free housing and rations as part of their wage, and the value of these (with food valued at rural retail prices) is assumed to be included in the figure given for the wage. Hence, although the adult male wage averages, say, 75 shillings a month for 11 months' work a year, the cash element of this might be only around 40-50 shillings a month.[1] The omission of payments in kind presumably accounts for the much lower average earnings of £25 p.a. for regular employees on small farms and settlement schemes in 1969 given by ILO, 1972 in Table 5, p. 39. The same table gives an estimate of average earnings by *casual* employees of £23 p.a. However, this must be treated with reserve since a footnote to the table in the original source[2] warns against calculating average earnings (as is done here) by dividing the given estimates of total earnings by the given estimates of numbers employed, as the two sets of figures do not refer to comparable time periods. Again, neither the ILO nor the original source state whether the value of payments in kind is included, but it seems reasonable to assume that it is not.

The writer's inquiries from a variety of sources suggested that casual workers and regular workers on small farms typically

[1] A comparison of wages with and without rations paid to workers in small-scale non-agricultural enterprises, given in ILO, 1972, Table 6, p. 39, suggests that for adult males the value of rations is about £20 p.a. or, say, 35 shillings a month for 11 months.

[2] Statistical Abstract 1971, Table 215.

received about the same rate of payment per hour.[1] One would not expect farmers to pay regular workers at an appreciably *higher* rate than casual workers since casual workers could always be hired instead.[2] On the other hand, regular workers might be prepared to work for a lower hourly rate in order to get security of employment. However, we found no evidence to support that hypothesis.

The estimates in Table 4.1 suggest that a combination of minimum wage legislation and trade union pressure maintains wages in both the 'formal' rural and 'formal' urban sectors above the levels of earnings in the respective 'informal' sectors.[3] Thus the average large farm regular employee receives about 80 per cent more than the regular employee on a small farm, and the unskilled employee in the formal urban sector receives about 100 per cent more than the marginal or typical self-employed worker in the informal urban sector.[4]

When comparing rural and urban earnings, differences in the cost of living must be taken into account. In Chapter 8 the urban cost of living is estimated to be about 1.6 times the rural one. This suggests that the urban formal sector wage for unskilled workers (line 5) is roughly comparable, in real terms, to the earnings of the average large farm regular employee (line 1). However, the marginal self-employed worker in the informal urban sector (line 7) earns perhaps 10 per cent less in real terms than the average small farm regular employee (line 2). These

[1] Comparisons are difficult because there is quite a wide variance in rates of pay (not surprisingly, since workers vary greatly in efficiency and rural labour markets are not perfect), because casual workers are often paid, in effect, on piece-rates rather than time-rates, and because of the problem of valuing payments in kind.

[2] However, farmers might want to pay regular workers more to improve their efficiency, or simply because they were relatives.

[3] 'Formal sector' workers are those included in the 'Annual Enumeration of Employees and Self-employed Persons', which covers the whole of the public sector and all large farms and other large-scale enterprises in rural areas. Although all private establishments in urban areas are in principle covered, in practice a substantial 'informal sector' is not.

[4] The relatively high earnings of employees in small-scale non-agricultural rural enterprises (line 3) is, however, rather puzzling, and may be due to higher skills. The earnings of the average self-employed person in the urban informal sector (line 5) are comparable to those of unskilled workers in the urban formal sector, but presumably the former include returns both to skill and to capital (e.g. rents for houses).

comparisons cannot be at all precise, since the estimates are so uncertain.

Table 4.1

Some data on African adult earnings in Kenya in 1969

£ p.a.

	Males	*Females*
Rural		
1. Average large farm regular employee	73	46
2. Average small farm regular employee	41	34
3. Average small-scale non-agricultural enterprise regular employee	67	49
Urban		
4. Average employee formal sector	250	185
5. 'Unskilled' employee formal sector	120	90
6. Average self-employed informal sector	120	100
7. Marginal (typical) self-employed informal sector	60	50

Note: It is assumed that all wages include the value of rent subsidy for employee housing, where this is paid, and also rations valued (for rural employees) at rural retail prices. Direct taxes and remittances are *not* deducted.

Sources: Based on ILO, 1972, Statistical Abstract 1971, Kenya Government May 1971, Mathare Valley Survey, Johnson, September 1971.

In Table 4.2 we move from the individual earnings figures just discussed to estimates of household incomes and incomes per equivalent adult (counting all persons over 14 as one, and children as a half).

For our purposes, it is not sufficient to know the average rural or urban household incomes given in lines 3 and 6 of Table 4.2. We also need to know how these incomes are distributed. We take rural and urban incomes in that order.

The only estimates of rural income distribution known to the writer are those given in the Central Province Survey, which refer to incomes received by rural African households in the Central Province in 1963-4. The two districts which belonged to the former scheduled areas (Thika and Nanyuki), and in which there were large farms owned by non-Africans, were excluded,

Table 4.2

African Household Incomes in Kenya in 1969

£ p.a. (except col. (2))

Occupation of head of household	Total income (1)	No. of equiv. adults (2)	Income per equiv. adult (3)
Rural			
1. Average large farm regular employee	114	4	29
2. Average small farm regular employee	80	3.75	21
3. Average rural households, excluding large farmers and pastoralists	160	4.4	36
Urban			
4. 'Unskilled' employee, formal sector	136	3.25	42
5. Average self-employed, informal sector	118	3	39
6. Average urban household	322	3.6	89

Notes: All households in lines 1, 2, 4 and 5 are assumed to be headed by married workers whose occupations are listed on the left. Households of single workers are, in principle, excluded from these lines, but are included in lines 3 and 6, which are strict averages. For rural incomes, subsistence consumption is valued at rural retail prices by multiplying farm gate values by 1.3 (see p.114). All incomes include remittances (positive for rural, negative for urban) and imputed value of housing provided by employers, and direct taxes have been deducted. In computing adult equivalents, children (i.e. under 15) count a half, adults one.

Sources: Based on ILO, 1972, Central Province Survey, Census of Population 1969, Mathare Valley Survey, and Table 4.1. For details, see Scott, February 1973.

as also were the forest settlements, the Northern Grazing Area and the Meru Game Reserve, and certain villages just outside the Nairobi City boundary. Towns and trading centres were also excluded from the rural part of the survey. Estimates were made of incomes received by each household from all sources, including subsistence output, remittances and wages earned off the family farm. Information was obtained from about 1,000 households.

Although the Central Province included only about 20-25 per cent of the rural African population of Kenya, the Survey is the best guide available to rural income distribution in the whole country. We have, accordingly, constructed Table 4.3 largely from it, but after making certain adjustments, viz:

(i) We subtracted 'enterprise expenditure' from total receipts to get our basic estimate of household income, using p. 44 of the source. It seems that total receipts included some capital receipts and enterprise expenditure included some capital expenditure, but, at least on average for all income groups together, the two roughly cancelled out.[1]

(ii) We increased the value of consumption of farmers' own produce by 30 per cent to express it at the equivalent value in terms of rural retail prices. This had the effect of increasing lower incomes rather more, proportionately, than higher incomes, since subsistence consumption represented about half of the lowest income group's income, but only 20-25 per cent of the highest.

(iii) We multiplied all incomes by 1.98, this being the ratio of average rural household incomes we have calculated in line 3 of Table 4.2 for 1969 to the average derived from the Survey after adjustment as in (i) and (ii).

It is not clear why such a large adjustment was necessary under (iii). From 1964 to 1968 the total income of small farmers increased by 23 per cent,[2] and, although there was some further increase in 1969, the growth from 1963/4 to 1969 can only explain a fraction of the gap. The need for such a large adjustment naturally casts doubt on whether the income distribution in Table 4.3 does give a good representation of that of all rural Kenya (excluding large farmers and pastoralists). If anything, it probably puts too many households into the lowest income groups, but we have no firm basis on which to correct it.

[1] Due to an oversight, we failed to deduct direct taxes, but the amounts involved were very small (8 shillings a year for the lowest income groups, and 17, 28, 27, 46, 45 and 116 shillings a year for subsequent groups).

[2] Development Plan 1970-74, p. 67.

An interesting feature of the estimates is that income per adult equivalent is rather equally distributed. Two important factors making for equality which are commonly omitted in calculations of this kind are the much smaller size of the poorer households, and the greater importance of subsistence consumption for them than for richer households. It must be remembered, however, that the figures on which Table 4.3 is based refer to the Central Province, and it is uncertain how far they represent rural Kenya as a whole, even excluding the large farms and pastoralists.

Table 4.3

Distribution of African rural household incomes (excluding large farms and pastoralists) in 1969

Unadjusted gross income groups (as in Source)	Percentage of households	Average size of household, adult equiv.	Adjusted average income per household	Adjusted average income per adult equiv.
£ p.a.	(%)	No.	£ p.a.	£ p.a.
	(1)	(2)	(3)	(4)
up to 50	41.5	2.9	76	26
50-75	20.9	4.4	124	28
75-100	14.4	5.3	169	32
100-125	8.0	6.2	212	34
125-175	5.8	6.5	270	42
175-250	5.1	6.7	355	53
over 250	4.3	7.2	650	90
Total or weighted average	100.0	4.4	160	36

Source: Based on data given in the Central Province Survey, pp. 39, 44.

Turning to the distribution of African urban household incomes, the main source available is an official survey of about 1,100 households in Nairobi, Mombasa and Kisumu which was conducted in 1968-9, and is reported in ILO (1972), Technical Paper 4. The survey excluded non-African households, which suits some of our purposes, though not others, and also omitted most of the urban shanty areas from the sample frame. The latter omission leads to underrepresentation of poorer Africans,[1] and we have tried to correct for this by using data from the Mathare Valley Survey. In principle, the estimates relate to income after deduction of both direct taxes and remittances, and include the value of income in kind, mainly housing. The value of this may be appreciably understated.

Once again, income per adult equivalent is more equally distributed than income per household. Bearing in mind that urban consumer prices are roughly 60 per cent higher than rural ones, a comparison of Tables 4.3 and 4.4, the latter being at

Table 4.4

Distribution of African urban household incomes in 1968-9

Income groups* £ p.a. (1)	Percentage of households (%) (2)	Average size of household, adult equiv. No. (3)	Income per household* £ p.a. (4)	Income per adult equivalent £ p.a. (5)
up to 120	22.0	2.5	57	23
120-180	15.0	2.8	121	44
180-240	11.5	3.2	166	51
240-300	8.9	3.2	218	61
300-420	13.1	3.9	287	74
420-600	10.6	4.2	411	98
600-840	7.1	4.9	573	117
840-1200	6.4	5.3	802	152
over 1200	5.4	5.7	1,462	258
Total or weighted average	100.0	3.6	322	89

* Income per household is sometimes below the lower limit of the corresponding income group because the latter refers to income *before* deduction of direct taxes and remittances, whereas income per household is *after* deduction of both.

Sources: The main sources used were the official survey of urban households in 1968-9, as reported in ILO, 1972, Technical Paper 4, and the Mathare Valley Survey, p. 40.

[1] The omission of African domestic servants in non-African households also biases the sample in this direction. We have, however, been unable to take this into account.

urban prices, shows that, although average African urban incomes per adult equivalent are about 55 per cent higher than rural ones (*after* correcting for price differences), about a half of urban households have real incomes per adult equivalent which are below the average for all rural households.

4.3 A GENERAL FORMULA FOR THE SHADOW WAGE

In this section we derive a general formula for the shadow wage which can be used in a wide variety of cases. The main points have already been made in 1.2.6, but here they are expressed both more precisely and more generally.

Consider a worker in occupation i who is drawn into occupation j by the offer of employment at a wage W_j. The social cost of employing him can then be subdivided into four parts.

(i) The social cost of employing him had he been employed at the same wage and under the same conditions as in occupation i;
(ii) the social cost of providing the resources needed to meet the extra expenditure resulting from any excess of W_j over W_i, and from any bidding up of W_j as a result of increased employment in j;
(iii) the social benefit accruing to the worker and to others resulting from any excess of W_j over W_i, from any difference in the conditions of work between i and j, and from any bidding up of W_j as a result of increased employment in j;
(iv) the 'external cost (or benefit)' of employing one more man in occupation j.

The total social cost, or shadow wage, is then

$$W^*_{ij} = (i) + (ii) - (iii) + (iv).$$

Each of the four parts distinguished above must be expressed in terms of our numeraire, which is foreign exchange in the hands of the Government. We consider each in turn below.

The simplest is (i), since this is by definition the shadow wage in i, W^*_{ii}. Notice that this takes into account any bidding up of wages in occupation i which occurs as a result of removing a worker from there to j. If 'occupation i' is simply unemployment, then W_i is zero, and we can conventionally put W^*_{ii} as zero as well. When an unemployed man becomes employed, there will generally be some cost to him in extra effort, loss of leisure, travel costs, etc. These are all taken into account in part (iii), since they are offsets to the benefits he gets from the wage he earns. They are accordingly dealt with below.

When the worker moves from i to j, his disposable income after tax increases by $h_jW_j - h_iW_i$, where h is the ratio of post-tax to pre-tax income. To begin with we shall assume that there is no bidding up of W_j, but we relax this assumption later. The gain in disposable income may accrue to the worker's household, but some of it may accrue to other households. For example, the worker may send remittances to relatives, or, if he was previously unemployed and supported by relatives, they may gain when he becomes employed. We also want to consider the *average* worker drawn into occupation j, and he might come from a variety of possible households, each with different levels of income per adult equivalent. To cover all these possibilities, we assume that a fraction k_n of the increase in disposable income accrues to household n (whose income before receiving this gain is Y_n per adult equivalent). Some of this increase in income will be saved and some consumed. The social cost of providing the necessary resources in each case per unit of increase in income is s_nf_{ns} for the part which is saved, and $(1-s_n)\,f_{nc}$ for the part which is consumed, where s_n is the marginal propensity to save and f_{ns} and f_{nc} are accounting ratios for household savings and consumption respectively. Consequently, the social cost of all the resources required for (ii) is given by

$$\text{(ii)} = (h_jW_j - h_iW_i) \sum_n k_n(s_nf_{ns} + (1-s_n)f_{nc}) \;.$$

This formula can be used straightforwardly when the gains in income accrue to households who are located in the same place before and after receiving it. We can then assume that they are confronted by the same prices before and after receiving it, and we can apply the appropriate accounting ratio, f_{nc}, weighted by their *marginal* consumption expenditures. For rural households we apply a rural accounting ratio, and for urban households an urban one. Where, however, the worker (and possibly other members of his household) migrates from the countryside to the town to get a new job, a substantial part of the gain in money income may be needed to cover the higher prices of food and rents in the town. In this case it is preferable to calculate the cost of the extra resources needed by applying separate urban and rural accounting ratios (weighted by *average*, rather than *marginal*, expenditure patterns) to the values of urban and rural consumption respectively, and then take the difference between them. However, as it turns out in Kenya, this point is not important because the average and marginal accounting ratios are virtually the same.

Turning, thirdly, to the benefit accruing to the worker's household and to others, we can express this as follows, ignoring for the moment any difference in conditions of work between i and j. Household n, with income beforehand of Y_n per adult equivalent, benefits through an increase in income at market prices of $k_n(h_jW_j - h_iW_i)$. Let us call the social value of this benefit b_n for short. Its evaluation in terms of our unit of account is discussed in Chapter 3. There is, however, one qualification to be added before we simply sum the b_n to give (iii), and that is to allow for differences in the conditions of work between i and j. Such differences might arise, for example, through differences in the nature of the work (more or less physical effort, or danger, etc.), or in the hours of work, or in the cost of travel to work, or in the cost of living if, for example, the worker has moved from the countryside to the town. All these differences accrue to the worker himself or his own household and must be allowed for in evaluating the benefit he receives. With this qualification, we can then put

$$(iii) = \sum_n (b_n).$$

Finally, there is part (iv) of the shadow wage, which we have called the 'external cost (or benefit)' of employing one more man in occupation *j*. One example might be the provision of additional roads, sewerage, schools, etc., at a greater cost than would otherwise have been necessary, and with additional benefits which do not compensate for the extra cost, as a result of greater employment in towns. In practice, we ignore this possibility as we have no evidence to show that there *is* an additional *net* cost of this kind. Some effects of extra employment which might be regarded as external costs are, in our framework, included elsewhere. Thus we deal with the effects resulting from bidding up wages below. Another effect, which has been stressed by some writers,[1] is the possibility that greater employment in the urban formal sector will *increase* urban unemployment. We discuss this further in 4.7.3. It is allowed for in our framework by making estimates of the extent to which persons who are unemployed are prepared to forgo income in order to search for formal sector jobs, and by estimating how far the numbers unemployed increase as a result of increasing formal sector employment.

In short, we do not in practice make any allowance for the external costs (or benefits) of employing one more man in occupation *j*. They are either assumed to be negligible or else are allowed for elsewhere in our framework. Nevertheless, as a reminder of possible omissions, if nothing else, we may formally put the external cost, in terms of the numeraire as:

$$(iv) = E_j.$$

We have now derived a formula for the shadow wage of a man drawn from occupation *i* into occupation *j*. Let us call this W^*_{ij}, where

$$W^*_{ij} = W^*_{ii} + (h_j W_j - h_i W_i) \sum_n k_n \; (s_n f_{ns} + (1-s_n) f_{nc}) - \Sigma(b_n) + E_j.$$

In practice, the average worker drawn into *j* could come from a variety of different occupations. We must also allow for the possibility that wages in *j* will be bid up as a result of the offer of extra employment there, so that some of the extra workers given employment in *j* may have been provided through a fall in

[1] See references given on p.93.

the demand for j-workers elsewhere. Let us call the proportion of workers drawn into occupation j which come from occupation i, P_i, where i represents any of the occupations from which workers are drawn *except* j. Let us call the proportion drawn from j, P_j, so that

$$P_j + \sum_i (P_i) = 1.$$

So far as the workers drawn from i are concerned, if we can determine the relevant proportions (which is in practice difficult), we can simply derive $\sum_i (P_i W^*_{ij})$, and the above formulae hold. We now proceed to derive formulae to cover the case of workers drawn from j.

Suppose that, as the result of the employment of one extra worker in j, wages in j are bid up by ΔW_j and demand for j-workers elsewhere falls by P_j. Suppose that total employment of j-workers beforehand was N_j. Then the price elasticity of demand for j-workers is given by

$$d_j = \frac{P_j}{N_j} \cdot \frac{W_j}{\Delta W_j}$$

The effect of bidding up the wage is then to transfer an income amounting to $\Delta W_j \cdot N_j$ approximately to workers in j and away from their employers or from consumers of their output (or both). As well as that, these employers or consumers will be left with an extra amount available for expenditure elsewhere equal to the wages of the P_j workers who have been absorbed in the new employment, and they will have lost the marginal product of those workers. Finally, the P_j workers must be provided in their new employment with a wage which we assume is approximately the same as they were getting before, and hence with the resources on which to spend that wage.

In the absence of any evidence to the contrary, we make the following additional simplifying assumptions: first, that employers or consumers only lose the transfer of income amounting to $\Delta W_j \cdot N_j$ because the value of the P_j workers' marginal product is equal to their wages; and second, that the conversion factor applicable to employers' and consumers' marginal incomes is the same as that applicable to workers in j, so that the transfer of income from one to the other involves no net resource cost or benefit.[1]

Given all these assumptions, there are only two components of the shadow wage of the P_j workers to be estimated. The only resource cost is the loss of their marginal product whose market value is $P_j W_j$. If the appropriate conversion factor for this is f_J, then the only resource cost is $P_j f_J W_j$. The only benefit arises from the income transfer of $\Delta W_j \cdot N_j$ if workers in j are on average poorer than the relevant employers or consumers. Let us call the average household income per adult equivalent of workers in j Y_j, and that of the relevant employers and consumers Y_J. Let us call the social benefit resulting from the transfer of £1 from employers and consumers to workers

$$f_{cr} \cdot b\,\{Y_J\,;\,Y_j\}\,.$$

We show how to estimate this expression from known values of Y_J and Y_j in Chapter 3. Then the total benefit resulting from the transfer is

$$\Delta W_j \cdot N_j \cdot f_{cr}\, b\,\{Y_J\,;\,Y_j\}\,.$$

which may be expressed as follows, using the formula for the elasticity of demand, d_j, given above:

$$\frac{P_j \cdot W_j \cdot f_{cr} \cdot b\ \{Y_j\,;\,Y_j\}}{d_j}\,.$$

Consequently the social cost of the P_j workers is

$$P_j W_{jj}^* = P_j W_j \quad \left[f_J - \frac{f_{cr} \cdot b\ \{Y_J\,;\,Y_j\}}{d_j} \right]$$

Hence, finally, the shadow wage in j is

$$W_j^* = P_j\ W_{jj}^* + \sum_i (P_i W_{ij}^*).$$

[1] However, in some cases we relax this assumption; see 4.6.

4.4 ESTIMATES OF THE RESOURCE COSTS OF WORKERS DRAWN FROM ONE OCCUPATION TO ANOTHER

In this section we estimate the resource costs in terms of foreign exchange equivalent of meeting the extra expenditures which result when a worker is drawn into one occupation from another. This is part (ii) of the shadow wage cost in terms of the general formula described in 4.3. There are five steps in the calculation:

1. We estimate earnings in each occupation.
2. We deduct direct taxes.
3. We divide the remainder between amounts accruing to rural households and to urban households.
4. We divide these in turn into extra savings and extra consumption.
5. We convert each component into foreign exchange equivalent costs.

The results of the whole calculation are set out in Table 4.5, the notes to which give details of the various estimates involved, and further explanations are given below.

To use the table, one simply takes the *difference* between the resource costs of the two occupations involved as given in col. (7). An example is given just below the table. The other figures in the table are merely steps leading to this final calculation, and should not be interpreted in any other sense. For example, we do *not* assume that workers on small farms save 10 per cent of their pay, but only that their *marginal* propensity to save is 10 per cent.[1]

[1] To elaborate this point a little more, consider an unemployed rural worker who obtains employment on a small farm. As a result of this transfer we assume that *total* savings rise by £4 p.a., but *not his* savings, since some of the increase in his income of £41 accrues to relatives who have hitherto been supporting him. Furthermore if, as is likely, his savings were negative while he was unemployed, his total savings when he gets employment could be quite small.

Table 4.5

Resource costs of African male adult workers drawn from one occupation to another

£ p.a.

Occupation (for explanation of R & U see notes to sources below)	Earnings	Direct Tax	Disposable income accruing to rural savings	rural consumption	urban savings	urban consumption	Resource cost in foreign exchange equiv.
	(1)	(2)	(3)	(4)	(5)	(6)	(7)
1. Small farm	41	0	4	37	0	0	36
2. Large farm	73	2	7	64	0	0	62
3. Rural unemployed	0	0	0	0	0	0	0
4. Urban unemployed	0	0	0	0	0	0	0
5. Urban informal (R)	60	0	1	9	5	45	48
6. Urban informal (U)	60	0	0	0	6	54	47
7. Urban formal (R)	120	4	4	35	8	69	94
8. Urban formal (R/U)	120	4	2	13	10	91	91
9. Urban formal (U)	120	4	2	13	10	91	91

Note: The resource cost of a worker drawn from line i in the table to line j is the entry opposite line j in col. (7) minus that opposite line i. For example, the resource cost of a worker on a large farm coming from a small farm is £62 − 36 = £26.

Sources: col. (1) is from Table 4.1. Col. (2) is Graduated Personal Tax. Cols. (3) and (5) are 10 per cent of the respective totals of cols. (3) + (4) and (5) + (6). See text for explanation. The division between rural and urban accruals of disposable income was made as follows:

Lines 1 and 2: all accrue to rural households.

Lines 3 and 4: receipts from relatives and expenditure by unemployed cancel out. Rural relatives support the rural unemployed, urban relatives support the urban unemployed.

Line 5 refers to a worker in the urban informal sector whose family and relatives are in rural areas, and who remits £10 p.a. to them. The figure of £10 was chosen partly for simplicity, since it makes an urban informal job yield the same real pay net of remittances as a small farm job. It is also not implausible in the light of such evidence as is available on remittances.

Line 6 refers to a worker in the informal urban sector whose relatives are in the town, and who does not remit anything to the countryside.

Line 7 refers to a worker in the formal urban sector who has left his family in the countryside and who remits a third of his disposable income to them. This is a large fraction, but it is plausible in view of the worker's family circumstances and in the light of such evidence as is available on remittances.

Line 8 refers to a worker in the formal urban sector who has migrated with his family from the countryside to the town. He is assumed to remit £15 p.a. to relatives in the countryside, principally to compensate them for looking after some of his own children whom he has left there (see p.82).

Line 9 refers to a worker in the formal urban sector whose family is in the town (and was there before he got the job). He is also assumed to remit £15 p.a. to relatives in the countryside.

Col. (7) is calculated by multiplying the entries in cols. (3), (4), (5), and (6) by the appropriate accounting ratios given in Table 1.2.

4.5 ESTIMATES OF THE BENEFITS ACCRUING FROM EXTRA WAGES PAID TO WORKERS DRAWN FROM ONE OCCUPATION TO ANOTHER

When a worker transfers from one occupation to another he or his family may benefit from higher earnings. If he was formerly unemployed, and supported to some extent by relatives, they too may benefit. In this section we try to estimate those benefits, that is, part (iii) of the shadow wage in 4.3.

We start by considering the transfer of a worker from regular employment on a small farm to each of six other occupations set out in the upper part of Table 4.6. We have already estimated the total increase in disposable income which accrues to the worker or his relatives as the result of this. It is shown in col. (2) of Table 4.6, and is derived from Table 4.5 in the way explained in Table 4.6. Where the worker moves to other employment, as in lines 3 to 6 of Table 4.6, we assume that the whole of the increase in disposable income accrues to him or his household, so the entries in col. (3) showing the gain accruing to 'relatives' (i.e. outside his household) are all zero. Where, however, the worker becomes unemployed, we have assumed that he is usually able to get some help from relatives. Generally speaking this will be food or lodging, i.e. help in kind rather than in cash. The figures of £10 p.a. for a rural unemployed worker and £16 p.a. for an urban one represent the same real amounts, and are guesses. They are rough estimates of the bare minimum needs of an adult male.[1]

Table 4.6

Benefits from extra wages paid on transfer of African male adult workers

£ p. a.

Occupation to which worker goes	Increase in disposable income total	rela-tives	worker and family	Compensation for change in conditions of work	Net gain of worker and family[a]	Total net gain in terms of numeraire
(1)	(2)	(3)	(4)	(5)	(6)	(7)
Small farm worker to:						
1. Rural unemployed	-41	-10	-31	-11	-20	-18
2. Urban unemployed (R)	-41	-16	-25	- 5	-20	-18
3. Urban informal (R)	19	0	19	19	0	0
4. Large farm	30	0	30	0	30	16
5. Urban formal (R)	75	0	75	45	30	16
6. Urban formal (R/U)	75	0	75	55	20	11
Urban informal worker (U) to:						
7. Urban unemployed	-60	-16	-44	-12	-32	-13
8. Urban formal (U)	56	15	41	0	41	16

[a] For the small farm worker, the gain is expressed at rural prices, while for the urban informal worker it is at urban prices (i.e. 1.6 times as great as rural).

[1] The Mathare Valley Survey, p. 40, states that unemployed heads of households received on average 122 shillings a month, or £73 p.a. However, this probably includes rental income received by unemployed landlords, which could amount to 40 shillings a room per month.

Sources: Col. (1) refers to the same occupations as in Table 4.5.

Col. (2) is derived from Table 4.5 by subtracting £41 (in the upper part of the table) and £60 (in the lower part) from disposable income of the appropriate occupation (i.e. col. (1)-col. (2) in Table 4.5, less £41 or £60).

Col. (3) assumes that relatives outside the immediate family of the worker give him £10 (for rural unemployed) and £16 (if urban unemployed). In line 8, we assume that an urban informal worker, on getting formal employment, remits £15 to relatives in the countryside. See text for discussion.

Col. (4) = col. (2)-col. (3).

Cols. (5), (6) and (7) are explained in the text. Col. (4) = col. (5) + col. (6).

Col. (4) thus shows the change in the worker's disposable income, and in cols. (5) and (6) we subdivide this into two parts. The first, in col. (5), is the amount of any change which is required to compensate him for a change in the conditions of work. The remainder, in col. (6), is the real gain accruing to himself and his household.

For the sake of illustration, we take the estimate in line 6 which refers to a worker on a small farm who obtains a job in the urban formal sector and brings his family with him to town. The calculation of his net gain then depends on what changes occur in the earnings of other members of his family, as well as the fact that he must pay higher urban prices for most of his expenditure. There is obviously a range of possibilities, out of which we have merely selected one which may, hopefully, be typical. We have assumed that the worker has the same income and household size as the small farm worker in line 2 of Table 4.2, before moving, and as the unskilled employee in the formal urban sector in line 4 of the same table after moving. The latter has a smaller household than the former, and we assume that the difference consists of a child who is left with relatives in the country and to whom remittances of £15 are sent (perhaps to pay for education). In this way we calculate that £55[1] is needed to compensate for changes in earnings and higher urban cost of living, and this is entered in col. (5).

[1] The increase in household income is from £80 to £136, i.e. £56, but, in addition, £15 is remitted from the town, so that the total increase is £71. Hence we are assuming a drop in earnings (including a drop in remittances received) of £75 − 71 = £4 of other family members. £136 is spent in the town, so the loss here through higher urban prices is 136 − 136/1.6 = £51, making a total loss of £55.

The estimate in line 5 is similar, except that the worker is assumed to leave his family in the countryside and remit a third of his urban earnings to them. We also allow something (very impressionistically) for the cost of separation. The estimates of net gain in col. (6), lines 1 and 2, are little better than guesswork, but are based on a calculation of the amount of income which an unemployed man would be prepared to sacrifice in order to increase the probability of his getting a formal sector job. We also implicitly assume that the reduction in effort and increase in leisure is worth something for a man becoming unemployed. The other cases are relatively straightforward.

It now remains to express the benefits received by relatives (in col. (3) of the table) and those received by the worker and his family (in col. (6)) in terms of the numeraire of foreign exchange in the hands of the Government. This is done in col. (7) of the table, and involves the following further steps:

1. We assume that the benefits accruing to relatives who live in the countryside (i.e. lines 1 and 8 of col. (3)) accrue at random to all African households in the countryside (excluding pastoralists and those on large farms), and hence to families whose marginal income has an average value of 0.497 in relation to that of a family with the critical income level, assuming $e = 1$ (see Table 3.2, col. (4)). To express their benefits in terms of the numeraire we therefore multiply the sums in col. (3) by 0.497 and then by f_{cr}, the conversion factor for marginal income accruing to a family with the critical income level, which is 0.87. We make a similar calculation for benefits accruing to relatives in towns (i.e. lines 2 and 7 of col. (3)), using Table 3.3.
2. We assume that the benefits accruing to the worker from the small farm (lines 1 to 6, col. (6)), which are all measured at rural prices, accrue to a household with the income given in line 2 of Table 4.2. Since the change in his income is more than marginal, we express its value in terms equivalent to that of marginal gains accruing to the critical income family by means of the formula given in 3.1. We then multiply by f_{cr}. For lines 7 and 8, col. (6),

we make a similar calculation, assuming that the benefits accrue to African urban families drawn at random from the six lowest income groups shown in Table 3.3.

The estimates in col. (7) of Table 4.6 refer, strictly speaking, to the net benefits which accrue when a worker from a small farm transfers to each of the six other occupations shown in lines 1 to 6, or, in lines 7 and 8, when a worker in the urban informal sector transfers to the two other occupations shown. We have, however, used these same estimates for much more than this. Consider, for example, an unemployed man in the countryside who becomes unemployed in the town. This is a transfer from the occupation shown in line 1 to that shown in line 2 of the table. We shall assume that the resulting net benefit is given, in terms of the numeraire, by the difference between the respective net gains shown in lines 1 and 2 of col. (7), which in this case is zero. While recognizing that this procedure may not always be correct, it does not appear to introduce an obvious bias and, as it greatly simplifies matters, we have followed it throughout.

4.6 THE SOCIAL COST OF LABOUR OBTAINED BY BIDDING UP WAGES

In this section we take our estimates for the large-farm sector to illustrate how we have estimated the social cost of obtaining workers from a given sector by bidding up wages in that sector. For two of the other sectors (regular workers on small farms and workers in the formal urban sector) our estimates are approximately equal to the estimated value of the marginal product of a worker (expressed in terms of our numeraire) in each sector. This implies that the net social value of the transfer of income resulting from bidding up wages is approximately zero. In the small farm case, most of the transfer is, in effect, from the farmer as employer or consumer to himself (or his family) as worker, since most labour on small farms is family labour. The social value of *this* transfer clearly is zero. In the formal urban sector case, part of the resulting transfer could be socially beneficial (e.g. from employers' or rich urban consumers' consumption expenditure to workers) but part could be socially costly (e.g. from the Government as employer to workers). Our assumption of zero net benefit is here only a guess. For the remaining sector, urban informal workers, we assume that the transfer is mainly from urban consumers to workers and is beneficial. For them, we estimate a social cost which is thus appreciably less than the value of their marginal product. All our estimates are given in the first lines of Tables 4.8 to 4.11.

4.6.1 *Workers on large farms*

We confine our attention to male employees on large farms. Their average wage is estimated at £73 in Table 4.1, and, assuming that this equals the value of their marginal product at market prices, we need to multiply it by a suitable accounting ratio to express it in terms of foreign exchange. We take the weighted average of traded agricultural outputs used in Chapter 7 for A_t (see p.163), i.e. 1.11, although this was calculated for small farms rather than large ones.[1] Our value of marginal product is then about £80.

As a large part of output from large farms is exported, or marginally exported, an increase in wages is likely to be at the expense of employers rather than consumers. We may neglect the social value of any resulting fall in employers' consumption, since their average incomes are high. However, lower incomes for them also affect their income-tax payments and their savings, neither of which can be neglected. In fact, this is a case in which we cannot plausibly assume that the losers and gainers from the transfer have similar expenditures from marginal changes in their incomes. We must therefore consider afresh the resource costs of the transfer.

In 6.1.2, we estimate the social cost of £1 paid to 'capitalists' at £0.2. 'Capitalists' here refers principally to industrial companies; many large farms are owned by companies who probably account for much of their employment and output. Even where farms are owned by private individuals, rather than

[1] The marginal product of labour does not necessarily consist only of extra output. It might also consist of economies made in co-operating factors of production: capital, land, materials, or management. We have stuck to the simple-minded view that it consists of output, but this needs further consideration and investigation. See also 9.1.

by companies, these individuals are subject to an appreciable rate of tax on marginal income. In default of a better alternative, we therefore take this estimate as applying to all large farm employers. Hence for each £ transferred from employers there is a resource cost saved of only £0.2.

Each £ transferred to an employee increases his consumption expenditure and savings, and the accounting ratio is $f_{cr} = 0.87$. Hence on each £ transferred there is a net resource cost of £0.87-0.2 = £0.67.

The benefit on each £ transferred is simply that received by employees. The average large farm employee's household is estimated in Table 4.2, line 1, to have an income per adult equivalent of £29, and the marginal value of its receipts per £ in terms of our numeraire is thus (see Chapter 3), 0.87 x 15/29 = 0.45 (putting $e = 1$ and $f_{cr} = 0.87$ and with a critical income of £15).

It follows that each £ transferred from employers to employees involves a *net cost* in terms of the numeraire of £0.67-0.45 = £0.22.

We have no estimate of the elasticity of demand for labour, and merely assume that it is one. The total transfer then equals the wage, i.e. £73. Hence the social cost of labour obtained by bidding up wages on large farms is:

$$£80 + 73 \times 0.22 = £96.$$

4.7 THE SHADOW WAGES OF LABOUR IN CERTAIN OCCUPATIONS

4.7.1 *Estimating the proportions of labour drawn from different occupations*

We are now in a position to draw together the various strands to make estimates of the shadow wages of adult male African 'unskilled' labour in certain occupations. Looking back at the general formula for the shadow wage in 4.3, we have estimated parts (ii) and (iii) (resource costs and net benefit) for labour drawn from each and to each occupation and, for labour obtained within each occupation by bidding up wages, we have estimated the total cost. We estimate part (i) in this section–it is, in fact, the end product of the whole exercise, being the shadow wage in each source from which labour comes. We neglect externalities, part (iv). Hence, the only remaining gap in our information is the proportion of labour coming from each source, and we must begin with a discussion of how to fill that in.

Fig. 4.1 Competitive labour supply and demand

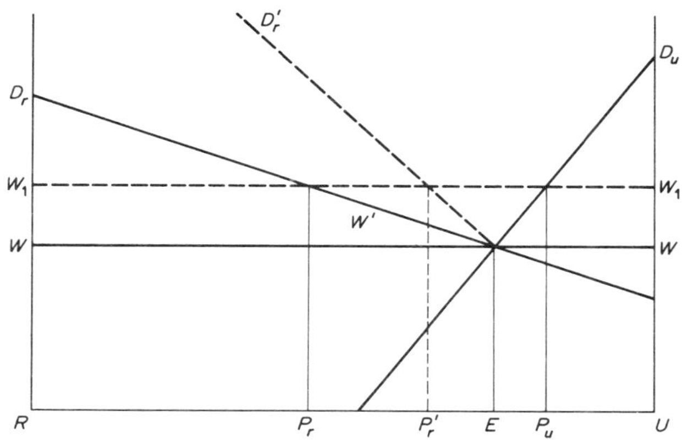

RE = numbers employed on small farms in initial equilibrium.
UE = numbers employed in urban informal sector in initial equilibrium.
RW = *UW* = wage in both country and town in initial equilibrium.
D_r = rural demand curve for labour on small farms.
D_u = urban demand curve for labour in informal sector.
W_1W_1 shows higher level of wage in new equilibrium when P_rP_u of labour has been absorbed in new employment, of which P_rE is drawn from rural and P_uE from urban employment.
D_r' = 'effective' demand curve for rural labour so far as supply to urban sector is concerned (see text).

Figure 4.1 illustrates the model we use in the simplest case in which wages are flexible and labour markets are reasonably competitive. To fix our ideas, we consider only one source of labour, which is employment on small farms, and one destination for it, which is employment in the informal urban sector. The analysis can easily be extended to cover more than one source of labour supply. The meaning of the various magnitudes is explained beneath the diagram. We have, for simplicity, assumed that the rural wage equals the urban informal 'wage' (including self-employed earnings), although this is not essential. It would be sufficient if, say, the proportionate difference between rural and urban wages was fixed (for example, it might equal the difference in the cost of living). We relax this assumption later on.

Now consider what happens when demand for labour in the informal urban sector increases by P_rP_u. How much of this extra demand will come from the rural sector and how much from within the informal urban sector? The answer, according to Figure 4.1, depends on the slopes of the demand curves for labour in the respective sectors. Wages rise in both sectors from W to W_1, thus reducing demand for labour in each. P_rE men are thus released from the rural sector and P_uE from the urban informal sector. If the slope of the rural demand curve, D_r, is given by $\frac{dN_r}{dW}$, etc., then for small changes in demand we have, approximately:

$$\frac{P_rE}{WW_1} = \frac{dN_r}{dW} = \frac{N_r}{W} \cdot e_{dr}$$

and

$$\frac{P_uE}{WW_1} = \frac{dN_u}{dW} = \frac{N_u}{W} \cdot e_{du},$$

where e_{dr} and e_{du} are the elasticities of demand of the rural and urban demand curves respectively (defined so as to be positive). Consequently:

$$\frac{P_rE}{P_uE} = \frac{N_r \cdot e_{dr}}{N_u \cdot e_{du}}.$$

Or, in words, the amounts of labour drawn from each sector are in direct proportion to the numbers employed in each multiplied by the corresponding elasticity of demand in each. In the absence of a better assumption, we take the simple one that the elasticities are the same. Hence the amounts of labour drawn from each sector are in direct proportion to the numbers employed in each—and this holds for any number of sectors.

Now let us relax the assumption that wages rise in the same proportion[1] in the two sectors. It seems plausible to expect wages in the urban sector to be bid up by more than on average in the rural sector, if only because information about wage changes in the urban sector would not percolate to the remoter rural areas. Thus wages in rural areas around the towns might rise about as much as in the towns, but the rises would get smaller and smaller the further one was from a town. Consequently, rural wages would, on average, rise less than urban wages, and a smaller fraction of the increased labour supply would come from rural areas.

To allow for this possibility, we have shown an 'effective' demand curve for rural labour in the diagram, D'_r. It might be better to call this the supply curve of rural labour to the towns. It slopes upwards more steeply than the rural demand curve. When urban wages rise from W to W_1, a smaller quantity, P'_rE, of rural labour is released and, on average, rural wages only rise from W to W'. Although this is true of *actual* average rural wages, our previous analysis can still be used. Provided we frame our estimates (or guesses, at this stage) in terms of the elasticity of the 'effective' demand curve, D'_r, it is still true that

$$\frac{P'_rE}{WW_1} = \frac{N_r}{W} \cdot e'_{dr} .$$

It is convenient to do this in what follows. We give estimates of the fractions of labour drawn from the rural to the urban sector

[1] As already pointed out, this is sufficient for the above conclusion to hold. Thus if the wage increase in the rural sector is dW_r on a wage W_r it follows that $P_rE = \frac{dW_r}{W_r} \cdot N_r \cdot e_{dr}$, and similarly that $P_uE = \frac{dW_u}{W_u} \cdot N_u \cdot e_{du}$, whence the conclusion follows so long as $\frac{dW_r}{W_r} = \frac{dW_u}{W_u}$.

assuming that the 'effective' rural demand curve has an elasticity which is one-fifth that of the actual rural demand curve. This, of course, greatly reduces the fraction of the labour supply drawn from rural areas. The 'one-fifth' has no empirical basis, but is merely to test whether this reduction makes much difference to our estimate of the shadow wage–in most cases, as it turns out, it does not.

The argument above is in terms of rural to urban migration, and one might expect the reverse movement to be roughly symmetrical. When we are considering an increase in the demand for labour in the countryside, we therefore take, as one possibility, an 'effective' *urban* demand curve with an elasticity one-fifth that of the rural one.

Both the possibilities described (i.e. with equal elasticities and with rural (or urban) elasticities one-fifth of the others) are set out in Tables 4.8 and 4.9. These are preceded by our estimates of the numbers employed in each occupation, relevant to our calculations, which are given in Table 4.7 and explained in the note which follows it.

Table 4.7

Adult male African unskilled workers in certain occupations (used for weighting different sources of labour supply)

	Source	*Thousands*
1.	Workers on small farms	500
2.	Workers on large farms	100
3.	Rural unemployed	30
4.	Urban informal	40
5.	Urban formal	180
6.	Urban unemployed	30

Note: The basic sources were ILO (1972), Census of Population 1969, Statistical Abstracts, and Central Province Survey. Although there were about 2,050 thousand rural African adult males in 1969, it is estimated that only about a quarter of these were in households with real income per adult equivalent below that of the unskilled worker in the urban formal sector. Total African male employment in the urban informal sector is estimated at around 80-90 thousand, but about half of these are excluded as being skilled, or petty capitalists. The estimate for rural unemployed is a guess, and all the figures are rounded and very approximate.

4.7.2 *Shadow wages of workers in the rural and urban informal sectors*

The estimates of shadow wages in Tables 4.8 and 4.9 are interdependent, since each is needed for the other. They could be estimated by solving simultaneous equations or (as was done here) by a rather easy process of iteration. In selecting the final estimates of shadow wages of £41 p.a. for a regular worker on a small farm, and £48 for one in the urban informal sector, we chose figures which gave a close approximation to rounded percentages of the respective market wages. These percentages are 100 per cent for the worker on the small farm and 80 per

Table 4.8
Shadow wage of a regular worker on a small farm

Source of labour	Components of shadow wage, £ p.a.				Weights: thousand males: elasticities assumed	
	(i)	(ii)	(iii)	Total	All equal	Urban $\frac{1}{5}$ of col. (5)
	(1)	(2)	(3)	(4)	(5)	(6)
1. Other workers on small farms	..	..	..	42	500	500
2. Rural unemployed	0	36	18	18	30	30
3. Urban unemployed	0	36	18	18	22	4
4. Urban informal (R)	48	-12	0	36	30	6
Weighted averages of col. (4), using weights as in col. (5),				40		
col. (6)				40		

Final estimate £41 = 1.00 times market wage (see text).
Notes: Cols (1), (2) and (3) refer to the first three components of the shadow wage as set out in 4.3. The figures in cols. (2) and (3) are from Tables 4.5 and 4.6 respectively. Col. (1), line 4 is based on Table 4.9. Col. (5) is derived from Table 4.7, but the entries in lines 3 and 4 here are only three-quarters of the totals there given, assuming that only three-quarters have families in the rural sector and would be willing to move back there.

cent for the worker in the urban informal sector (market wages being £41 p.a. and £60 p.a. respectively, see Table 4.1).

Table 4.9
Shadow wage of worker in the informal urban sector

Source of labour	Components of shadow wage, £ p.a.				Weights: thousand males: elasticities assumed	
	(i)	(ii)	(iii)	Total	All equal	Rural $\frac{1}{5}$ of col. (5)
	(1)	(2)	(3)	(4)	(5)	(6)
1. Other workers in informal urban	..	..	..	35	40	40
2. Urban unemployed (U)	0	47	13	34	8	8
3. Urban unemployed (R)	0	48	18	30	22	22
4. Rural unemployed	0	48	18	30	30	6
5. Worker on small farm	41	12	0	53	500	100
Weighted averages of col. (4), using weights as in col. (5),				50		
col. (6)				44		

Final estimate £48 = 0.80 times market wage (see text).
Notes: Cols. (1), (2) and (3) refer to the first three components of the shadow wage as set out in 4.3. The figures in cols. (2) and (3) are from Tables 4.5 and 4.6 respectively. Col. (1) line 5 is based on Table 4.8. Col. (5) is based on Table 4.7, the distribution of urban unemployed between those with urban (U) and those with rural (R) families being guessed.

4.7.3 *Shadow wages of workers in the rural and urban formal sectors*

We first apply the same procedure as for the informal sector. This is unsatisfactory, however, inasmuch as wages in the formal sectors are not competitively determined, but are determined by a combination of minimum wage legislation and collective and individual bargaining. The levels so determined are, it seems, appreciably higher than the levels ruling in the informal sectors, and this affects the impact which increased demand for labour in the formal sector will have on the supply of labour from other sectors. Hence, as well as the two estimates of shadow wages derived by following our previous procedures (called Estimates 1 and 2), we present three further estimates (called Estimates 3, 4 and 5), which are described in increasing degree of complexity below.

Estimate 3 simply assumes that new workers are recruited to the formal sector without any bidding up of wages there, and come in direct proportion to the numbers in each occupation, as in Estimate 1.

Estimate 4 is similar, but assumes that unemployed workers have a bigger chance of getting jobs than employed workers, and that workers in the same locality have a bigger chance than other workers. As a rough guess, the weighting given to the unemployed is doubled as compared with Estimate 3, and the weighting given to the rural (urban) occupations is divided by five for recruiting to the urban (rural) formal sector.

Estimate 5 makes use of the simplest version of the Harris-Todaro model of rural-urban migration.[1] Let us take an increase in employment in the urban formal sector first, since the model was devised with that in mind. The important idea underlying the model is that it is the level of urban unemployment which equilibrates the demand for and supply of jobs in the urban formal sector. Job-seekers equate the rural wage to the *expected* urban wage, the latter being the actual urban wage multiplied by p, the probability of getting a job (the alternative to getting a job being unemployment and a zero wage). Hence, if W_{eu} is the expected urban wage, W_u is the actual urban wage, and W_r is the rural wage, in equilibrium

$$W_{eu} = pW_u = W_r.$$

On certain simplifying assumptions,[2] the probability of getting a job, p, is given by

[1] Harris and Todaro, 1970. Others who have discussed the same phenomenon are Knight, March 1971; Harberger, 1971; Rempel, 1970, and Stiglitz, April 1972.

[2] Harris and Todaro, 1970, pp. 128, 129. Stiglitz, April 1972, has shown that the probability is given by this formula, provided there is no growth in total

$$p = \frac{N_{uf}}{N_{uf} + N_{uu}},$$

where N_{uf} is the number employed in the urban formal sector and N_{uu} is the number of urban unemployed.

Now let us assume that there is an increase of employment in the urban formal sector of dN_{uf}, with no bidding up of wages there. Assume also that there is a negligible effect on wages in the rural sector, so that W_r is constant. It follows that the expected wage, W_{eu}, must also remain constant, and hence that p must remain constant. For this to happen, the number unemployed must increase in the same proportion as the number employed. Hence

$$\frac{dN_{uu}}{dN_{uf}} = \frac{N_{uu}}{N_{uf}}$$

Consequently, unlike all the estimates considered thus far, urban unemployment actually *increases* when demand for urban formal labour increases.

We can make a rough estimate of the size of this increase from the data we have. We put[1]

$$N_{uf} = 180 \text{ th.}, N_{uu} = 30 \text{ th., hence} \frac{dN_{uu}}{dN_{uf}} = \frac{1}{6}.$$

employment in the formal sector, if labour is hired on either of two methods: first, if there is random selection from the unemployment pool, the probability of being hired in any period being given by the number of 'hires' divided by the number of job seekers; and second, a queue model, in which individuals are hired in order of time of arrival in the urban sector.

[1] It is interesting to consider the other magnitudes as well. p = 180/210 = 0.86. Putting W_u = £120 we have W_{eu} = 0.86 x 120 = £103. This is far higher than the rural wage of £41 multiplied by 1.6 to adjust to urban prices, which gives £66. However, it is perhaps more meaningful to look at *household* incomes for workers getting urban formal sector jobs who migrate to the town. We estimated the benefit accruing to such workers at £20 to 30 (depending on whether they took their families or not) in Table 4.6, measured at rural prices. Their income as a rural worker's family is put at £80 in Table 4.2. Hence we could put W_u = 80 + 25 = £105, which would give W_{eu} = 0.86 x 105 = £90, all at rural prices, which is not all that different from £80. Given the uncertainty of all these estimates, it is remarkable how well the simple Harris-Todaro model appears to fit the facts.

Hence, in Estimate 5, we give urban unemployment a negative weight of $\frac{1}{6}$, and all the other sources of labour together (excluding, however, the urban formal sector itself, since we assume no bidding up of wages) a positive weight of $\frac{7}{6}$. The allocation of this positive weight between the sectors is made in direct proportion to the numbers occupied in them, as in Estimate 1.

For the rural formal sector's Estimate 5 we proceed in just the same way, except that the corresponding negative weight for rural unemployment is larger, namely 30/100.

The simple version of the Harris-Todaro model makes it appear inevitable that unemployment will increase when urban formal sector employment increases. The only factor which might prevent this is a rise in the rural wage as more people are drawn out of the rural sector. However, given the size of that sector, it seems unlikely that a big enough rise would occur, and Harris and Todaro themselves believe that in many African economies unemployment *would* increase. In the writer's view this conclusion gives insufficient weight to the factors making for an inelastic supply of labour to the towns. We argued above that a rise in urban wages would not, for a variety of reasons, much influence rural wages in the remoter areas. In just the same way, an increase in the probability of getting a job would not draw in many workers from there. Indeed, Rempel's econometric study of rural-urban migration in Kenya found that, while both distance from an urban centre and 'clan contacts' were significant explanatory factors, the ratio of (or difference between) expected urban and rural wages was not.[1]

To elaborate this point we suggest the following modification of the Harris-Todaro hypothesis, which has the advantage of making it rather more dynamic.[2] Consider a man who is deciding whether to become unemployed in the town for a given period in the hope that he can thereby obtain a job in the formal sector. We suppose that he estimates the present value of the net benefit which will accrue to him if he succeeds, and the probability that he will succeed within the period, and sets this

[1] Rempel, 1970.

[2] See Scott, July 1967, for an attempt to present a general dynamic theory of supply and demand in which a trade-off between financial gain and unemployment is allowed for.

off against the sacrifice in income which he will incur in looking for the job. If he is a marginal man, the expected value of a successful outcome will just equal the sacrifice. The latter can, in fact, be regarded as the investment made in the expectation of this gain. Hence we may write, for a marginal man,

$$s = k\,p\,(V_f - V_i),$$

where the sacrifice per period is s, the probability of getting the job for the *average* applicant in the period is p,[1] the present value of a job in the formal sector for an *average* worker in it is V_f and that for a job in the informal sector is V_i, while k is a factor which varies from individual to individual and modifies the average values used for p, V_f and V_i so as to yield that individual's valuation of the benefit from getting the job. k could allow, for example, for an individual's different wage-earning capabilities in the formal and informal sectors, or for different preferences between countryside and town, or for different family circumstances, or for different risk aversions or probabilities of getting a job. It must be realized that s will also vary from individual to individual, depending, for example, on his preference for leisure and freedom as an unemployed man, on his savings, on the generosity of his relatives, and on the earnings he might have made had he remained in employment.

Now suppose that the number of jobs in the formal urban sector is increased so that p increases while V_f and V_i remain unchanged. Our marginal man will become intra-marginal, and men who were formerly extra-marginal, because their k's were too small or their s's too big, will join the ranks of the unemployed. But there is no guarantee that the number who do so will exceed the number who have been lucky enough to get the newly created jobs. The total number of unemployed might therefore rise or fall, and unless we know how k and s vary as more men are pulled into the ranks of the unemployed, we cannot say which is likely to happen. Hence, unlike in the simple Harris-Todaro model, there is no necessity for unemployment to increase even if rural wages (V_i) remain unchanged.

[1] This is not the same probability as in the previous exposition of the simple Harris and Todaro hypothesis. The probability here depends on the length of the period, whereas the previous probability has no time dimension.

We can also allow for the possibility that an increase in demand for labour in the formal sector will raise wages there to some extent. Although at first sight this might seem unlikely, since with excess supply of labour employers have no need to pay more to get more workers, it is nevertheless possible that there might be some such effect. Thus trade unions might press harder for wage increases since their membership and political power would be increased by the new jobs, and they might be prepared to trade off some of the increased employment against higher wage rates.[1] Hence, V_f might increase, and p might increase rather less than in the constant wage case (since employment in the formal sector would be less), leading to an inflow into the unemployment pool which could be bigger or smaller than in that case. Since the outflow from the pool would be smaller, it seems more likely that there would be a net increase in unemployment if V_f rose than if it were constant. However, it must be borne in mind that about a half of the non-agricultural formal sector employment is in the public sector, and that the Government exercises considerable influence over the level of wages there. Hence, if the Government were reasonably determined to keep wages constant, there seems little reason to expect formal sector wages to rise very much on account of an increase in the demand for labour.

Bearing these points in mind, we may consider the five weighted averages, corresponding to the five estimates described above, which are given in Tables 4.10 and 4.11. We take the formal urban sector first.

The most important point is that all five are reasonably close together. Estimate 2 is probably on the high side since it allows for a good deal of bidding up of wages in the formal urban sector which, as we have argued, is not very likely. On the other hand, Estimates 3 and 4 are probably low, in that they allow for no bidding up at all and also assume appreciable falls in urban unemployment, thus making no allowance for what we may call the Harris-Todaro phenomenon. Estimate 5, which does allow for the latter, is on the one hand too high in that it probably assumes too big an increase in unemployment, and on the other hand too low in that it allows nothing for bidding up wages in

[1] The writer is indebted to Paul Collier for this point.

the formal urban sector. In conclusion, we take as our final estimate £84 p.a. (which is close to Estimates 1 and 5), as it gives a rounded percentage, namely 70 per cent, of the actual wage (£120 p.a.).

Very similar remarks apply to the estimates for workers on large farms in Table 4.11. Our final estimate is £55 p.a., which gives a rounded 75 per cent of the actual wage (£73 p.a.).

Table 4.10

Shadow wage of worker in the formal urban sector

£ p. a.

	Source of labour	Components of shadow wage, (i) (1)	(ii) (2)	(iii) (3)	Total (4)
1.	Other workers in formal urban sector	..	..	..	98
2.	Urban informal sector (R)	48	46	16	78
3.	Urban informal sector (R/U)	48	43	11	80
4.	Urban informal sector (U)	48	44	16	76
5.	Urban unemployed (R)	0	94	34	60
6.	Urban unemployed (R/U)	0	91	29	62
7.	Urban unemployed (U)	0	91	29	62
8.	Small farm worker (R)	41	58	16	83
9.	Small farm worker (R/U)	41	55	11	85
10.	Rural unemployed (R)	0	94	34	60
11.	Rural unemployed (R/U)	0	91	29	62

Source of labour (as above)	Weights used to multiply col. (4) above. Thousand males 1	2	3	4	5
1.	180	180	0	0	0
2.	15	15	15	15	15
3.	15	15	15	15	15
4.	10	10	10	10	10
5.	11	11	11	22	-30
6.	11	11	11	22	-30
7.	8	8	8	16	-20
8.	250	50	250	50	250
9.	250	50	250	50	250
10.	15	3	15	3	15
11.	15	3	15	3	15
Weighted average shadow wage £ p.a.	85	88	81	76	86

Final Estimate: £84 = 0.70 times market wage (see text).
Notes: The upper part of the table shows the first three components of the shadow wage as set out in 4.3. The figures in cols. (2) and (3) are from

Tables 4.5 and 4.6 respectively, and those in col. (1) are based on Tables 4.8 and 4.9.

In the lower part of the table, col. (1) is derived from Table 4.7, assuming that one quarter of those coming from the urban informal or urban unemployed have urban families (U) and the rest rural, and that half of those with rural families (both here and in lines 8 to 11) migrate with the families (R/U) while the others do not (R).

The other columns correspond to the Estimate numbers in the text, and their derivation is explained there. In col. (5) the total negative weight given to urban unemployed is 80, which is roughly $\frac{1}{6}$ of the sum of the weights (490).

Table 4.11

Shadow wage of worker on a large farm

£ p.a.

	Source of labour	Components of shadow wage (i) (1)	(ii) (2)	(iii) (3)	Total (4)
1.	Other workers on large farms	..	..	..	96
2.	Small farm worker	41	26	16	51
3.	Rural unemployed	0	62	34	28
4.	Urban informal sector (R)	48	14	16	46
5.	Urban unemployed (R)	0	62	34	28

Source of labour (as above)	Weights used to multiply col. (4) above. Thousand males 1	2	3	4	5
1.	100	100	0	0	0
2.	500	500	500	500	500
3.	30	30	30	60	-127
4.	30	6	30	6	30
5.	22	4	22	4	22
Weighted average shadow wage £ p.a.	56	57	49	48	56

Final Estimate: £55 = 0.75 times market wage (see text).

Notes: As for Table 4.10, but the negative weight given to the rural unemployed in col. (5) in the lower part of the table is 30 per cent of the sum of the weights (425).

4.8 CHANGES IN SHADOW WAGES THROUGH TIME

As time passes, one would expect various elements in the shadow wage to increase in real terms. The critical income should rise as Government revenue and expenditure per head of population increase with increasing national income per head. As this happens, the marginal value of Government expenditure should fall, so that the Government should be willing to raise the lower limits for liability to direct taxes (such as G.P.T.), to increase the proportion of pupils at primary schools whose fees are remitted, to raise minimum income levels which would qualify for famine relief or other relief, etc., etc. At the same time, real wage levels and the marginal productivity of labour in different occupations should also increase. It seems intuitively clear that if all these elements were to increase in the same proportion, and if certain parameters, such as the accounting ratios for consumption, the marginal propensities to save, and rates of direct taxation, were to remain constant, the ratios of shadow wages to market wages would remain constant.

Although it is unlikely that things would work out in just this way, at least one can say that there is no very obvious reason to expect the ratios to change rapidly in the near future. There may be some factors tending to make the ratios increase, but there are probably others tending to make them fall. Pending further research, we therefore conclude that the assumption of constant ratios is both plausible and convenient.[1]

[1] See Little and Mirrlees, 1968, p. 169, for a similar argument and conclusion. They recommend that the ratio of shadow to market wages should be worked out, ideally, for a period in the future (say, 5 years ahead), which would thus be representative for the whole life of projects currently being examined.

CHAPTER 5

Family Labour on Settlements

5.1 INTRODUCTION

In this chapter we estimate the social cost of family labour on settlement farms forming part of the Million Acre Settlement Programme in Kenya and evaluated in Part II. What do we mean by this 'cost'?

In evaluating the Settlement Schemes it is convenient to treat them, in the first place, as if they were entirely public sector projects. Some important receipts (e.g. foreign aid) and expenditures (e.g. surveying, extension services, settlement officers, etc.) accrued to or were made by the Government. Much of the benefit, however, has accrued to the settlers,[1] and not to the Government. To allow for this we proceed as follows. All receipts from sale of output or expenditures incurred to produce that output are treated as if they were Government transactions, and are converted into foreign exchange equivalents by the use of the appropriate conversion factors. This leaves a net income which, in reality, accrues to the settlers, but is treated so far as if it accrued to the Government. Its social value, in terms of our numeraire, is less than the value emerging from the calculation so far for two reasons. First, the net benefits are less than the net income accruing since we must deduct from the latter the income which the settlers would have received had they not been settlers. Second, the Government is assumed to place a lower value on net benefits accruing to settlers than on the same foreign exchange equivalent value accruing to itself. Both of these points can be allowed for by subtracting from the net income an amount which we shall call

[1] By 'settlers' we mean both those to whom the plots were transferred and the rest of their households.

the cost of family labour. This cost is calculated in just the same way as for any other shadow wage, which makes this procedure especially convenient. After subtraction of this cost, the remaining net income measures the social profit of settlement.

Another point which must be made is that we confine our attention to *small* changes in the number of settlers. The question we are trying to answer may be posed as follows. If there were a small increase in the number of families settled on farms in some of the Million Acre Settlement Schemes, what would be the social cost of this in terms of our numeraire? We consider a *small* increase partly because the resulting estimate of cost is relevant to decisions about, for example, the best density of settlement or the case for Government intervention in the rural labour market. The *direction* in which policy needs to change can often be seen from calculations of this kind. Another reason is that the cost of a small change is easier to measure than that of a large one, and yields a unique estimate of cost, whereas with large changes the cost per family or per worker would depend on the size of the change.[1]

In this chapter, to illustrate the method, we only estimate the cost of the average High Density and Low Density Settlement farmer in 1967-8, using the data provided in Kenya Government, November 1971 (hereafter referred to as Settlement Appraisal). Estimates are given in Part II for other years and for particular schemes using the same method. The basic data available consist of the estimated income of the farmer, and the number of men, women and children in the family living on the farm. We have no data of hours or days worked in 1967-8. We have, however, information on the amount of non-farm income received by the family, and use this as a rough guide to the amount of time spent by family members in non-farm activities. Our aim is to exclude these activities altogether, both the income received and the cost of the labour involved in earning it. We thus, in effect, assume that non-farm activities have not been affected by settlement. While this is certainly untrue, it is not clear *how* they have been

[1] In relation to the total number of small-holders, about 1.2 million in Kenya in 1969, the total number of plots settled by mid-1969 was in any case not that large, viz: 34 thousand (Kenya Government, November 1971, p. 2). Each settlement *scheme* considered in Part II is even smaller, the maximum size being about 700 plots.

affected, and whether it is a net benefit or net cost we should be bringing into the reckoning. We have therefore thought it best to try to exclude them.

The remainder of this chapter deals with the estimation of the three parts of the shadow cost of family labour similar to those of any other labour, viz:

(i) the social cost of employing the family labour in the occupations from which it is drawn;
(ii) the social cost of providing the resources needed to meet the extra expenditure resulting from the family's increase in income on becoming settlers;
(iii) the social value of the benefit accruing to the family as a result of becoming settlers.

The social cost of family labour is then (i) + (ii)-(iii).

5.2 THE SOCIAL COST OF EMPLOYING THE FAMILY LABOUR IN THE OCCUPATIONS FROM WHICH IT IS DRAWN

Let us first consider where the labour might come from. We want to know, in some sense, the *ultimate* source, rather than the immediate source. For example, a settler may have come from the original large farm which was subdivided into settlement plots. Had he not been chosen, however, he would very likely have joined the pool of landless[1] labourers so that, in a sense, it is that pool which is the ultimate source. For all the High Density Schemes, the plots were meant to go to landless unemployed men (or women):

> ... applications were made to the provincial authorities who selected settlers on the basis that they were both landless and unemployed and were able to pay the legal costs of land transfer which were not more than £10. In practice, priority was often given to labourers on the former mixed farms. This may have been an advantage since they could be expected to

[1] We shall refer to 'landless' labourers, although some may have owned, or been able to work on, small plots. The point is that they would *also* want to work for hire.

possess some knowledge of the enterprises and farming methods which were planned for the new farms.[1]

Table 5.1 summarizes information on the origins of plot-holders from one settlement scheme. Since it is only one, and happens to be very near Nairobi, it may not be typical. However, it is the only information of this kind we have. It is consistent with the view that plot-holders were drawn marginally from the pool of landless workers in the countryside, although there were also a few self-employed workers from

Table 5.1

Origins of plot-holders on the High Density Settlement Scheme at Lari

	Origin	Number of plot-holders
1.	Worker on the original Lari Farm (or wife of worker)	61
2.	Casual labourer in the Reserve	19
3.	Non-agricultural worker in the Reserve or small town	7
4.	Worker in Nairobi	5
5.	Freedom fighter	4
6.	Political or governmental work	8
7.	Other	3
	Total	107

Notes: 1. e.g. milker, pigman, casual worker, woodcutter, watchman, poultry-keeper, tractor-driver.
3. e.g. sawmill-hand, butcher, barber, second-hand clothes seller, carpenter.
4. e.g. vegetable seller, plumber.
6. e.g. area council member, elder, 'politician'.
7. e.g. squatter in another area, casual worker at a vetinary research organization.

Source: Information kindly provided by Mr Peter Mehren at Lari in 1969.

Nairobi, and the status of those in 'political or governmental' work is unclear.

For the Low Density Schemes:

[1] Settlement Appraisal, p. 10.

> ... the criteria applied for the selection of settlers was more rigorous than for the High Density Schemes, reflecting the applicants' previous experience and the importance of having a financial stake in his farm. Applications were made to a committee composed of representatives of the provincial authorities and the Ministries of Agriculture and Settlement. The committee chose settlers on the basis that they came from an area in which the farms were situated; they had a certain amount of farming experience; were able to pay 10 per cent of the purchase price of the land and could also provide some working capital.[1]

These plot-holders were clearly *not* drawn from the pool of casual labour in the countryside. In many cases they had, and continue to have, other jobs such as running small businesses (shops, taxis, hiring tractors), or in Government employment (teachers, policemen, settlement officers). Some own more than one plot, and land elsewhere. Insofar as these various activities lead to non-farm income (i.e. income from a source other than the settlement farm), we exclude that income from our calculations altogether. We also exclude (in a very rough and ready way) the corresponding time of the income-earner.[2] Hence, insofar as the plot-holder's ability to earn non-farm income is what differentiates him from those drawn from the pool of landless labour, we have allowed for this difference by excluding both the relevant benefit and the relevant cost. However, the fact that Low Density plot-holders were meant to have had a certain amount of farming experience should have increased the opportunity cost of the time they spent on their plots. We have not allowed for this and, to that extent, may have over-stated the net benefits of Low Density schemes vis-à-vis High Density schemes.[3]

1 Ibid.

2 See p.108. The same procedure is followed for non-farm income in High Density schemes. These estimates are very rough, and in addition it is quite likely that non-farm income was understated on the surveys.

3 Whether this is a material overstatement is uncertain. Some Settlement Officers expressed the opinion that the average farm on the Low Density schemes was not better managed than on the High Density schemes. This may have been due to the more frequent absence of the plot-holder who pursued off-the-farm activities of one kind or another. On the other hand, we also heard the opinion that farmers on Low Density schemes were definitely better than those on High Density schemes.

We thus consider that *all* settlers come at the margin from the pool of landless labour, and we cost them at the shadow wages of regular employees working on small farms, which are estimated in Chapter 4. Two objections might be made to this. First, it could be argued that some of the settlers might have been unemployed (either in the countryside or the towns), or might have been employed in the informal sector in the towns. In reply to this, we point out that the shadow wage for regular employees on small farms allows for all these possibilities. We have no reason to suppose that the sources from which regular employees are drawn differ appreciably from those from which the settlers were drawn. The second objection is that settlers might have been casual, rather than regular, employees on small farms, and so their hours of work might have been less. Furthermore, such evidence as we have suggests that small farmers probably work shorter hours than their regular employees do. This is a material objection, but this is not the most convenient place to deal with it. We allow for the fact that the farmers' families probably work shorter hours than regular employees when we come to estimate the change in conditions of work below, as this is relevant to estimating the benefits accruing to settlers. Apart from that, there is no need to make any other allowance.[1]

For the average farm family on High Density schemes in 1967-8 the total value of their earnings as regular employees is put at £95 p.a. at actual prices and the same in terms of the numeraire. For Low Density schemes, the corresponding estimate is £50 p.a. The derivation of these figures is set out below.

High Density Schemes 1967-8

1. Size of family: 1.8 men, 1.6 women, 3.6 children. (Source: Settlement Appraisal, p. 123).
2. Allowance for non-farm income: this was 621 shillings p.a. (Settlement Appraisal, p. 130). The only directly relevant information available is a small sample of 40

[1] The fact that settlers might have been casual rather than regular farm workers before they became settlers, and might then have worked shorter hours for less pay than regular workers, does not materially affect our estimates, so long as workers are free to choose whether to work on a casual or a regular basis, and the shorter hours of the casual worker just compensate him for his lower pay.

cases collected on the survey of High Density Settlements in 1964-5. Earnings per man-month ranged from 40 to 900 shillings per month, with a median value of 300 shillings per month. We therefore assume that about 0.2 man-years per farm on average was required to earn the non-farm income.

3. Numbers employed and total earnings. In the case of the regular employee's household in Table 4.2, line 2, we assumed that all the adult men, and rather less than half the adult women,[1] worked for wages of £41 and £34 p.a. per adult respectively. We ignored children's earnings, but added on £5 p.a. for subsistence output (at rural retail prices). Making corresponding assumptions here we get:

Working men 1.6 (i.e. 1.8-0.2) @ £41	= £66
Working women 0.7 @ £34	= £24
Subsistence output	= £ 5
Total	£95

4. Conversion to numeraire. We multiply £95 by the ratio of shadow to actual wages for a regular male worker on a small farm, i.e. by 1.00 (see 4.7.2).

Low Density Schemes 1967/8

1. Size of family: 1.3 men, 1.3 women, 3.4 children. (Source: Settlement Appraisal, p. 123).
2. Allowance for non-farm income: this was 3,552 shillings p.a. (Settlement Appraisal, p. 130). Again, the only directly relevant information was an even smaller sample of 14 cases collected on the survey of Low Density Settlements in 1964-5. Earnings per man month ranged from 90 to 2,500 shillings, with a median value of about 400 shillings. We therefore assumed that about 0.7

[1] We assume that 45 per cent of the women worked for wages. According to the Central Province Survey, p. 15, man-days worked by hired women in the Central Province approximately equalled half of those worked by hired men. If this was true of a typical regular worker's household consisting of 1.2 male and 1.3 female adults (i.e. as in line 2 of Table 4.2, with 2.5 adults and 2.5 children, or 3.75 equivalent adults), and if all the men worked for hire, then 0.6 of the female adults would work for hire, which is about 45 per cent of the female adults in the household.

man-years per farm on average was required to earn the non-farm income.

3. Numbers employed and total earnings. Making similar assumptions as in the High Density case we get:

Working men	0.6 (i.e. 1.3–0.7) @ £41	=	£25
Working women	0.6 @ £34	=	£20
Subsistence output		=	£ 5
	Total		£50

4. Conversion to numeraire: as for High Density.

5.3 THE RESOURCE COST OF THE SETTLERS' EXTRA INCOMES

To estimate the resource costs incurred when landless workers become settlers we need to estimate their extra consumption and extra investment expenditures. The data we have enable us to calculate only the following:

1. The extra money incomes of the settlers. This is the gross farm profit, less interest payments on loans, i.e. net farm profit, as given in Settlement Appraisal[1], less earnings as regular employees calculated as above. So we get:
   High Density £108–95 = £13
   Low Density £119–50 = £69
2. The investments on the farm consisting mainly of increases in the values of livestock and, to a lesser extent, of maize. These are[2]:

[1] See p. 130. However, the net farm profit for Low Density given there is £113 (instead of £119) and is based on a figure of livestock costs on p. 129 of £53. The latter compares with a total of £47 for livestock costs given on p. 37. We have taken this lower figure (and hence profits £6 greater). There is no way of telling which is correct.

[2] Settlement Appraisal, p. 127, gives valuation changes as percentages of output, which we multiplied by the value of output as given on p. 130.

High Density £54
Low Density £69

3. The *net* amounts repaid to the Government. These consist of two parts, amortization of old loans minus new borrowings. Settlement Appraisal (pp. 130, 132) only gives the repayments on old loans which *should* have been made in each period. In practice, settlers have typically been meeting only about one half of their loan 'billings',[1] which include interest as well as amortization. We have therefore calculated two figures. The first, net theoretical repayments, assumes loan billings are met in full. The second, net effective repayments, assumes that only half of billings are met (the balance being added to settlers' debts). Thus we get:
High Density £12 (theoretical), –£7 (effective).
Low Density £17 (theoretical), –£11 (effective).

The increase in settlers' income equals the increase in their consumption plus the increase in their savings or net investment. The last can be sub-divided into a real and a financial component. We assume that, as landless workers, they would have had zero net savings. We also assume that net financial savings, other than net loan repayments, are zero when they become settlers. Finally, since we have no data on their net real investments other than the valuation changes in 2 above, we combine the rest of their net real investments with their consumption (the accounting ratios for both are probably close to each other, i.e. 0.92 for rural consumption). Given all these assumptions we are therefore left with three components of the resource cost, for which we apply the accounting ratios shown in Table 5.2 and explained in the notes to it.

The negative figure for extra consumption and 'other' real investment by High Density settlers, even when we assume 'effective' rather than 'theoretical' loan repayments, requires some comment. There are several possible explanations, of which we may mention the following. First, our estimate of

[1] At 31 Dec. 1970, all 'normal' schemes had paid 51.0 per cent of amounts billed or, if certain special schemes are included, 53.4 per cent. The latter percentage has fluctuated from a low of 41.3 per cent to a high of 59.6 per cent since 1964-5, see Department of Settlement Annual Report 1970, p. 59.

Table 5.2

Calculation of the resource cost of settlers' extra incomes

Item	Market prices £ High Density	Market prices £ Low Density	Accounting Ratios	Accounting prices £ High Density	Accounting prices £ Low Density
1. Extra consumption and 'other' real investment					
(a)	-53	-17	0.92	-49	-16
(b)	-34	11	0.92	-31	10
2. Valuation changes on farm	54	69	1.25	67	86
3. Net loan repayments					
(a) 'theoretical'	12	17	0.45	5	8
(b) 'effective'	- 7	-11	0.45	- 3	- 5
4. Total resource cost					
(a)	13	69		24	78
(b)	13	69		33	91

Notes: Lines 1 + 2 + 3 = 4 = extra money income of settlers (at market prices). Line 1 is a residual, line 2 is as in item 2 of the text, and line 3 as in item 3.

The accounting ratio for line 1 is that for rural consumption. That for line 2 is an average of the ratios for cows (FO 2) and maize (FO 4.1) with most of the weight given to the former. That for line 3 treats net loan repayments as the equivalent of savings which earn 6.5 per cent per annum interest (i.e. the rate charged on most loans to settlers). Applying the formula given in 8.2 then gives an accounting ratio of 0.065 x 0.92/(0.10 + 0.03) = 0.46, which we round to 0.45.

earnings before, as landless workers, may be too high. Some of the settlers might have worked shorter hours as casual workers than the regular employee to which our estimates refer. Insofar as this is the case, our final estimate of the cost of family labour is not appreciably affected.[1] However, in some areas it may not just be a question of shorter hours and *therefore* less pay, but of lower *rates* of pay for a given number of hours. Thus for settlers in Kabisi we allow for lower rates of pay as regular workers, and this does appreciably reduce our estimate of the net social cost of family labour (see Part II, Chapter 16). Hence, if the negative

[1] See footnote on p.107.

figure for High Density settlers in Table 5.2 is due to our having overestimated their average rates of pay as regular workers, the implication is that we have also overestimated their net social cost. Second, although the money value of settlers' consumption may have fallen in the way shown, its real value will have fallen by less because of the saving on retail margins on subsistence output (see 5.4.1 below). Third, we estimate that the settlers benefited in other ways which are not included in their money incomes and have no resource cost (see 5.4.2 and 5.4.3). Finally, it is, of course, possible that the incomes of High Density settlers were understated in the economic surveys. If so, our estimate of the cost of family labour is also understated, but so then is our estimate of profits at accounting prices before deducting this cost. These errors would to some extent offset each other, but on balance would lead to an understatement of the net social profit.

5.4 THE BENEFITS ACCRUING TO SETTLERS

We distinguish, and estimate, the following benefits accruing to regular farm workers who become settlers:

1. Gains in money income.
2. Savings in retail margins on subsistence consumption.
3. Shorter hours of work.
4. Various benefits from working for oneself or one's family instead of working for hire.

Estimates of the first are in 5.3, and we consider the others below. It is to be noted that we ignore any benefit settlers may get through their loan transactions with the Government. Implicitly, we assume that the net present value of future interest payments, and repayments of principal, equals for them the net present value of whatever they buy with a new loan (and *mutatis mutandis* for loan repayments). In 1967-8 net loan repayments were fairly small (see Table 5.2), so that it is unlikely that we are making an important error for that year. Since this is also the year on which, in Part II, we base our future projections of income, this is comforting. However, there may be an appreciable error in earlier years when new borrowings were sometimes heavy, if settlers derived an appreciable net benefit from them, as seems probable.

5.4.1 *Saving in retail margins on subsistence consumption*
The main source of information is the 1967 Survey of Non-Agricultural Enterprises in Rural Areas[1] which estimates the mark-up for food, tobacco and drink retailers at 37.9 per cent of the cost of goods sold, and for all retailers at 40.3 per cent. This seems high, but the only other evidence we have relates to just the margin on maize, which in certain markets is 20 per cent.[2]

If we estimate the benefit accruing to settlers simply by multiplying their subsistence consumption by the average retail margin, we overstate the benefit. We should allow for differences in the pattern of expenditure between farmers and landless labourers induced by differences in the prices which confront them. Farmers will tend to buy relatively more subsistence goods as they are relatively cheaper. If we then value the gain farmers make by reference to *their* pattern of expenditure (as we do) we exaggerate the gain in the following sense. The extra amount of wages, which a man would need to earn as a hired labourer to bring him to the same real level of satisfaction as he has when he is a farmer, is less than the value of the distributive margins on his subsistence consumption. For, if we gave him that amount, he could buy exactly the same bundle of goods as he does in fact buy as a farmer. However, since he would, as a hired labourer, be confronted by different prices (i.e. dearer subsistence goods than if he were a farmer) he could do better by altering the pattern of his expenditure so as to buy fewer subsistence goods.

[1] Statistical Abstract, 1969, p. 107.

[2] Alvis and Temu, March 1968, p. 101, report that in certain markets without permanent stalls 'retail sellers sell maize at the same price per debe [a square metal container which in an unmodified state holds about 5 U.S. gallons of liquid] as the price they pay per debe. The retailer's income is derived from the fact that when he is buying, a debe for measuring is used which has been expanded into a cylindrical shape so that it holds about 20 per cent more than an unmodified square debe used to measure his sales. Thus the mark-up is roughly 20 per cent of the buying price. This method of calculating mark-up was found in only certain markets'.

For this reason, and also because the estimate of the mark-up on maize cited is lower than the average of 38 per cent found by the Survey (and maize is an important subsistence food), we have chosen a lower figure, i.e. 30 per cent, to estimate the benefit accruing to settlers through saving retail margins on their subsistence consumption.[1]

5.4.2 *Shorter hours*

We were told in 1969 by one Settlement Officer that regular workers, usually hired on monthly contracts, normally worked six full days a week and 'at planting time they may work all the time'. The same officer said that casual workers typically worked 6 hours a day. This suggests that regular workers might normally work about 300 days a year, or 1,800 hours.

Rates of pay for casual workers vary appreciably, and seemed to be appreciably lower in the settlements in Bungoma and Kakamega in Western Province than in those in Nyandarua in Central Province, or in the Rift Valley Province. Because of this variation, and also because casual workers are often paid by the piece rather than by time, it is difficult to establish a typical daily rate, but our impression is that a figure of 2.75 shillings a day for an adult male would be fairly representative for the higher paid areas mentioned above. It is unlikely that regular workers are paid much more than this, since the farmer could always substitute casual for regular workers. In that case, if the ILO (1972), p. 77, figure of £41 p.a. in 1969 is taken for a typical adult male regular worker,[2] the implication is that he must work for at least 300 days a year.

The information available on work done by small farmers is that it is typically much less than this, perhaps only half as much for adult male farmers. We quote three sample surveys which are relevant.

First, the Nyeri District Survey, p. 63, estimated family

[1] M. P. Cowen, in a careful survey of farmers in Nyeri, found that the average margin was about 30 per cent.

[2] This figure seems consistent with our own information on monthly rates for regular workers. If one assumes 12 months' work, it implies a rate of 68 shillings a month, but one might expect rather less than 12 months' work, so the rate per month could be rather higher. Payment in kind (e.g. food, a hut and use of a small plot) might amount to about 25 shillings a month, so cash wages would be about 45 shillings a month.

labour inputs per adult for full-time farmers at 945 hours per annum. This understates the total work done, however, since 'the amount of labour used on tasks which were not directly concerned with any of the crop or livestock enterprises, i.e. such things as maintenance of hedges and fences, repairing buildings or supervision of employees, was not recorded' (op. cit., p. 57).

Second, Clough's (June 1965) survey of some of the settlement schemes in 1963-4 yielded the information on hours worked by adult male family workers given in Table 5.3. Farmers with regular employment off the farm were not included. One can assume that there was at least *one* adult male providing this labour, and conceivably there could have been more.

Table 5.3

Hours per year worked by adult male family workers on certain settlement schemes in 1963-4

Scheme	Hours per year
Ainabkoi East	1,049
Keben	692
Ndalat	541
Mautuma	1,428
Unweighted average of above	928

Source: Clough, June 1965, pp. 37, 61, 81, 103.

Third, the Central Province Survey gives the estimates of work done on the family enterprise shown in Table 5.4.

The Central Province Survey estimates *under*state the *total* work done by family members, since no allowance is made for work done off the family enterprise. The lower figure for men in Kiambu thus probably reflects the opportunities for work in Nairobi. Against this, however, the system of recording work probably led to a bias in the opposite direction.[1]

[1] Work for more than half a day was taken as work for a day. Work for half a day or less, but more than one hour, counted as work for half a day. Work for less than one hour was ignored. (op. cit., p. 14).

Table 5.4

Average number of days worked by each household member on the family enterprise in the Central Province, 1963-4

District	Men	Women	Children
Kiambu	78	165	23
Fort Hall	147	179	37
Embu	208	227	25
Nyeri	225	205	45
Meru	136	185	8
All Districts	154	188	26

Source: Central Province Survey, p. 16. 'Family enterprise' appears to mean family farm, but includes other activities besides farming (see note to Table 5.5).

On the basis of the evidence quoted, one might assume that adult male settlers work only half as much as regular workers. However, since there are reasons for thinking that family members' work has been underestimated in some cases, it seems better to assume that adult male settlers work two thirds as much as regular workers. We value their increased leisure at the regular worker's rate of pay,[1] and we assume that there is no increased leisure for females.[2] These assumptions yield the following estimates for the benefits accruing to average settlers in 1967-8 from increased leisure:

High Density: $1.6 \text{ men} \times \frac{1}{3} \times £41 = £22$ p.a.

Low Density: $0.6 \text{ men} \times \frac{1}{3} \times £41 = £\ 8$ p.a.

5.4.3 *Benefits from working on the family farm*

Family workers on very small farms in Kenya are apparently prepared to work for a rate of 'pay' which is less than they

[1] If they were regular workers, increased leisure would be worth this at the margin, but would be worth less than this for a large increase in leisure. However, the settlers are richer, and so increased leisure is presumably worth more to them. Since many of them hire labour, it seems reasonable to take the rate they pay for hired labour as a measure of the value of their leisure at the margin, and intra-marginal amounts should, in fact, be more highly valued.

[2] This is rather arbitrary. It is difficult to interpret data relating to women's work, since it is not clear how housework, cooking and care of children have been treated.

would receive if they were to hire themselves out to other farmers. A similar phenomenon has been observed in other countries, notably in India, and the explanation put forward here is that family workers derive more benefits (or incur less costs) as a result of their work than they would if they hired themselves out. By comparing their earnings as family workers with their earnings as hired workers we can estimate these benefits, albeit only very approximately. They are quite significant.

Table 5.5

Earnings per man-day worked on farms in the Central Province in 1963-64

District	Meru		Nyeri		Fort Hall		Kiambu	
Gross Income group sh/year per farm	Acres per farm	Earnings sh. per man-day	Acres per farm	Earnings sh. per man-day	Acres per farm	Earnings sh. per man-day	Acres per farm	Earnings sh. per man-day
Up to 1,000	4.4	1.3	1.3	1.8	5.3	1.1	1.5	0.7
1.001-1,500	5.3	1.7	2.6	1.4	9.1	1.2	3.5	1.4
1,501-2,000	8.0	2.1	3.5	2.0	7.0	1.2	5.0	1.9
2,001-2,500	11.1	1.6	4.5	2.5	11.0	1.8	4.5	1.6
2,501-3,500	12.7	2.4	4.0	2.7	11.4	1.7	6.9	1.9
3,501-5,000	14.5	3.7	7.2	2.2	10.3	1.7	5.7	1.8
Over 5,000	14.7	4.2	12.5	4.6	22.6	2.3	11.3	1.6
Average wage for hired labour, sh./day		1.95		2.05		2.35		2.35

Notes: *Gross income* is equal to gross receipts per household (i.e. per farm) from agriculture (including value of non-marketed output), manufacturing and crafts, trade (net), transport, services (including working for wages), and ownership of dwellings. Cost of materials, wages, rent, interest and miscellaneous expenses are *not* deducted (except for trade, which is net). However, *earnings per man-day* consist of gross income (excluding income from services and ownership of dwellings) *less* costs and *less* imputed rent on land all divided by equivalent man-days worked in the 'family enterprise' (i.e. excluding man-days worked in employment elsewhere). Earnings therefore measure the return to family labour on the family farm, and it is assumed here that the 'family enterprise' includes manufacturing and crafts, trade (net), and transport. A day's work by a woman counted ¾, and that by a child ½, of that by a man.

Source: Based on Central Province Survey, pp. 16, 40-43, supplemented by the writer's estimates.

Table 5.5 gives estimates of family workers' earnings in the Central Province in 1963-4 compared with those of hired workers. They are subject to many uncertainties, but there does seem to be an unmistakeable tendency for earnings on small farms to be below the average wages paid for hired labour (given at the foot of the columns in the table, and derived from the same basic source).

An implication of this tendency is that, if family labour is valued at the same wage as that paid for hired labour, and if allowance is made for imputed rent, small farms all appear to be making losses. It is interesting to note that the same appears to be true of small farms in India.[1] The explanation which has been suggested by Professor A. K. Sen is that family labour is applied to the family farm until its marginal product falls more or less to zero. Consequently, if it is valued at the same wage as that paid to hired labour, the farm may well appear to show a loss. On larger farms where labour is hired, the marginal product of all labour equals the wage and the farm therefore shows a profit if *all* labour is valued at that wage. This also explains why output per acre is lower on large than on small farms in India, since the latter are worked more intensively. The farms which were surveyed in Kenya and provided the data for Table 5.5 revealed the same tendency for agricultural production per acre to decrease with increases in farm size.[2]

Professor Sen assumed that the marginal product of labour on small farms in India was about zero. In Kenya, it seems unlikely that it would be so low, since the farmer whose own land was limited could always seek work on larger farms, or in non-agricultural pursuits. In fact, one might ask why there should be *any* difference in the marginal product of labour on small and large farms, given reasonably competitive conditions in the rural labour market. There are several possible explanations:

1. There are costs involved in working for hire as compared to working on the family farm. These consist of, for example, time spent in looking for work or in getting to

[1] Sen, February 1962.

[2] Central Province Survey, p. 24. The same tendency was also noted in the Nyeri District Survey, p. 62. See also Dorner, 1972.

and from work. They may also include, for many workers in varying degrees, a preference for working for oneself over working under supervision.[1]

2. Where there are marked fluctuations in seasonal requirements for labour, the observed average of daily wages paid to hired labour may overstate the actual average *annual* wage that could be earned by landless labour working for hire.
3. There may be institutional rigidity of wages for hired labour such that, again, the observed average daily rate exaggerates the actual wage which someone looking for work could expect to get. The relevant wage is the observed daily rate multiplied by the probability of getting it, and the latter may be well below one.
4. A quite different kind of explanation relates to the way in which subsistence output is valued. In the Central Province Survey, on which Table 5.5 is based, agricultural output, whether for sale or for subsistence, was valued at current farm sale prices (op. cit., p. 21 and tables on pp. 22, 23, 28, 30 and 31). An employee who wanted to *buy* the same goods, however, would have to pay the higher prices ruling in rural markets (except in so far as he received wages in kind). Consequently, the real value of the employee's wage is less than that of the same money income accruing to a subsistence farmer.

Let us now consider these various explanations to see how far they are consistent with the data available, and what their implications are for benefits accruing to settlers.

5.4.4 *First reason why small farmers' earnings are less than wage rates*

The first reason seems to be consistent with the data, and implies that hired workers who become settlers receive a benefit. This is also in line with Sen's explanation, although not so extreme in as much as the marginal productivity of labour on

[1] The preference for self-employment, or family employment, probably applies most strongly to male heads of families or to females. Sons might well prefer to work away from the family farm, but yet might work for low wages on it. There may be a thin line between 'preference' and 'exploitation'.

small farms may be below that on large farms without actually sinking to zero. The large farms hire labour,[1] and so, for them, the wage sets the opportunity cost of *both* family *and* hired labour. Consequently, marginal productivity is higher on the large farms and output per acre is lower. This is all illustrated in Figure 5.1, which also shows how we propose to estimate the benefit accruing from family employment as opposed to working for hire.

Fig. 5.1 Wage rate and marginal product of labour on farms

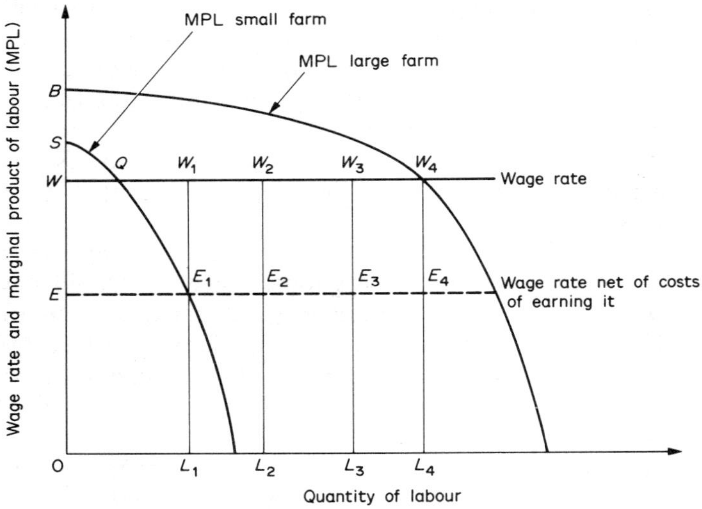

Figure 5.1 shows the marginal product of labour for two different types of farm: a small one, SE_1, and a large one, BW_4, similar to those in the Central Province Survey. For a given labour input the marginal product of labour is higher in the latter than the former, not only because there is more land but

[1] The small farms also hire labour, but in their case it is a very small proportion of total labour input (less than 5 per cent for farms with less than 4 acres, see Central Province Survey, p. 15), and so may refer to only a small proportion of such farms and/or to certain times of the year. For the largest category of farms (8 or more acres), hired labour accounts for 10 to 20 per cent of total labour input depending on the district.

also because there are more other inputs (fertilizer, cattle, dips, etc.) which the richer farmer can finance while the poorer cannot.[1]

The horizontal line W shows the prevailing wage rate for hired labour of a given quality. Beneath it is another horizontal line E which shows the rate of earnings for family labour which is equal in value to the wage, after allowance has been made for the cost of travel to work, of time lost in looking for work, and after allowing too for any preference there may be for family over wage employment. The distance WE thus measures the net difference in value per unit of labour input between working for a wage and working on a family farm.[2] Let us now consider the equilibrium employments for each type of farm.

The small farm employs OL_1 of family labour whose marginal product is E_1L_1. In addition, L_1L_2 of family labour works outside the farm for a wage OW which, however, yields it the same effective wage rate as family labour, namely, OE, once the net cost of this outside work has been deducted. If we value the labour input on the farm at the market wage, total costs are OWW_1L_1, whereas the value of total output is OSE_1L_1. The latter is smaller than the former, so that the farm appears to be making a 'loss'—all the more so if we allow something for imputed rent.

The large farm employs OL_3 of family labour on the farm (it has more family labour available than the small farm[3]) and, in addition, hires L_3L_4 wage labour. Both have a marginal product equal to the wage, OW. Consequently, when labour inputs are valued at this wage, the farm appears to be making a profit. Furthermore, the profit is likely to be greater than the imputed rent of land since it includes a return on working capital (livestock, fertilizer, equipment, etc.) as well as a return to 'management'. It is interesting to note that families on large farms *also* earn a large proportion of their incomes from

[1] See Gwyer, October 1971, and Desai and Mazumdar, February 1970.

[2] We have assumed that this is constant, regardless of the quantity of labour input. This is a simplifying assumption which has some plausibility in so far as the difference represents time lost in travel to work, or in looking for work, which might be expected to vary in direct proportion to the quantity of time spent in wage employment. It is not too clear how the other factors might be expected to vary, nor what their relative importance might be.

[3] See Central Province Survey, pp. 11 and 14.

'services', which includes wage employment off the farm. Indeed, the data in the Central Province Survey shows that in some districts they earn a larger proportion of their (net) incomes in this way than do the very small farm families.[1] This seems to be contrary to what is implied in Figure 5.1. However, the explanation may be that members of such families hold relatively well-paid positions, for example in Government employment of one kind or another. They may have got these jobs partly because they have more 'influence' and partly because they are better-educated, which, in turn, is partly due to their ability to pay for better education. No doubt there is a complex of factors involved, which are to some extent self-reinforcing, and which explain simultaneously these families' greater wealth, earning power and size. Finally, we may note that the large farm is farmed less labour-intensively than the small farm. Against this, it is likely to have more non-labour inputs per acre. The net result, however, is that output per acre is lower on the large farm.[2]

The analysis so far has shown that our model of family employment is broadly consistent with the data in the Central Province Survey. We can also employ the model to work out what benefit accrues to a family, which would otherwise have been forced to rely on wage employment, when it is given a High Density settlement farm. Let us assume for simplicity of exposition that the family is given the large farm BW_4 in Figure 5.1, and that its members work an amount OL_3, hiring L_3L_4 other labour. We assume that the difference between the wage rate for hired labour and what we have called, in Figure 5.1, the wage rate net of the costs of earning it, is constant (i.e. that EE_4 in Figure 5.1 is a straight line so that the distance $WE = W_1E_1 = W_2E_2$ etc.). Consequently, the family which works an amount OL_3 on its own farm benefits by an amount equal to the area WW_3E_3E over a similar family working the same amount as hired labour. To estimate this area, we have to

[1] Central Province Survey, pp. 40-44.

[2] Gwyer, October 1971, pp. 15, 16, argues that within the range of farm size from 1 to 10 acres, large farms are more labour intensive than small ones, because they can afford the complementary inputs needed to raise labour productivity. However, he gives no data to support this view, and it is contradicted by that given in the Central Province Survey and also by that given in the 1964 Nyeri District Survey.

estimate the amount of family work (OL_3) and the net advantage of family over hired work (WE).

5.4.5 *Other reasons why small farmers' earnings are less than wage rates and estimation of benefit from family work*

Before proceeding to the further stages of estimation just mentioned, we must first see how far our analysis needs modification in the light of the other possible explanations for the difference between small farmers' earnings and wage rates which were given in 5.4.3.

There are seasonal fluctuations in the demand for labour in Kenyan agriculture, although for some important farm activities they are fairly small (e.g. livestock and tea), for others they are important (e.g. maize and coffee).[1] One might expect that, in these circumstances, wage rates for hired labour would fluctuate seasonally, and they would be positively correlated with the amount of labour hired. Consequently, the observed average wage rate (which is what is given in the Central Province Survey) would overstate the average wage rate which a landless labourer could expect to earn if he worked more or less uniformly throughout the year.

Unfortunately, we have no data on the seasonal pattern of wage rates. There is data on the seasonal pattern of employment of hired labour in some areas for particular crops, and it does show, as might be expected, some marked fluctuations. Nevertheless, it does not appear to lead to any marked seasonal fluctuation of wage rates. The ILO (1972), Chapter 1, p. 42, remarks 'The limited indirect evidence we have on this seems to suggest that labour shortages at peak times are not very important in Kenyan agriculture . . . we could discover no unambiguous evidence of a farmer's losing crops owing to shortage of labour, or of high rates of pay being offered to recruit labour for the harvest.' Looking at it from the worker's point of view, even for seasonal crops such as maize and coffee grown on small farms, there is *some* hired labour in every month of the year, according to some surveys.[2] This suggests

[1] See Gwyer, October 1971, for coefficients of variation of labour inputs for different crops and for livestock in Nyeri and Kakamega. See also ILO, 1972, Ch. 1, and Technical Paper 2.

[2] See the histograms in Gwyer, October 1971.

that landless labour at least has the *opportunity* to find work throughout the year, but it does not altogether rule out the possibility of an upward bias in the average wage rate mentioned above. Of course, if landless labour did not work evenly throughout the year, but worked more at the seasonal peaks, so that fluctuations in total man-days hired corresponded exactly to fluctuations in man-days worked by the typical landless labourer, then the observed average wage would, when multiplied by actual man-days worked, correctly measure the typical landless labourer's annual earnings. There would then be no bias.

We shall assume that such bias as exists is small, and will largely neglect it. Our reasons for this neglect are, first, the point just mentioned as regards casual labour; second, the fact that some landless labour is more or less permanently employed at a constant monthly wage (so here again there is no bias); and third, the fact that there is no clear evidence that employees on monthly terms are paid at higher or lower rates than casual labour, whereas one might expect them to be paid at lower rates if the observed casual rates overstated the expected annual earnings of a casual worker.

Turning now to the explanation in terms of an alleged institutional rigidity in wages, we again propose to neglect this factor. Reported daily wages differ markedly from farm to farm (we were given estimates on one settlement scheme ranging from 1.5 to 3 shillings a day), which makes an institutional wage (e.g. 2 shillings a day) implausible. This is quite consistent with reports that 'work is difficult to get', because the worker has his own reservation price and the market clearly is not *perfect*. The loss of time involved in looking for work is something which we have, in any case, already allowed for in our earlier discussion and proposed measure. If wage rigidity were important, one might expect that the gap between small farmers' earnings and the average wage paid to hired labour would be greatest in those districts where employment opportunities off the farm were least. However, the data in Table 5.5 suggest the contrary. In Kiambu, which is near Nairobi, and where, as one might expect, income from 'services' is relatively much more important than in the other districts, the gap between farm earnings and the average wage is *more* marked than elsewhere. Nor is it plausible to suppose that there is surplus labour due to wages being down at the minimum level consistent with efficient work (as is probably the case in parts of India). Real wages, at least in most of the settlement areas, are higher than that.

Finally, we have the explanation in terms of the distributive margins which landless labourers must pay on food purchased in rural markets and which farmers avoid paying on their own subsistence output. We want to know how much of the gap between small farmers' earnings and the wage rate shown in Table 5.5 can be explained by this factor. The remainder of the gap can then be attributed to the first explanation and handled in the way already discussed. In Table 5.6 we have therefore calculated the value of retail margins saved per man-day worked in the Central Province. By adding this to earnings per man-day worked we can see what gap remains between this total and the average wage of hired labour per day.

It is clear that allowing for distribution costs saved eliminates the gap between average earnings and wage rates for hired labour on nearly all but the smallest farms. One could argue that the biggest remaining gap measures the other net advantages of working on the family farm as compared with working for hire. A family would be content with a smaller gap, but the net advantages must at least amount to the biggest gap if we are to explain why the families concerned did not work for hire. However, this argument neglects the errors of measurement in the basic data, which make it desirable to take the average of a large number of observations. There could also be temporary factors, such as unexpected crop failures, or illness, which reduced the earnings of particular families in the particular year surveyed. This also makes averaging desirable. We have therefore taken the unweighted average earnings plus the distribution costs saved for the two lowest income groups in each district and compared it with the average wage paid for hired labour. The former average is 1.7 shillings and the latter 2.2 shillings per man-day, the difference being 0.5 shillings per man-day worked.

This difference may appreciably understate the advantages of family employment over employment for hire in 1969, since earnings in the Central Province Survey seem low in relation to

Table 5.6

Distribution costs saved and earnings per man-day on farms in the Central Province Survey in 1963-4

District	Meru		Nyeri		Fort Hall		Kiambu	
Gross income group sh./year per farm	Dist. costs saved	Ditto plus earn-ings	Dist. costs saved	Ditto plus earn-ings	Dist. costs saved	Ditto plus earn-ings	Dist. costs saved	Ditto plus earn-ings
	shillings per man-day worked							
Up to 1,000	0.3	1.6	0.4	2.2	0.3	1.4	0.4	1.1
1,001-1,500	0.4	2.1	0.3	1.7	0.3	1.5	0.3	1.7
1,501-2,000	0.4	2.5	0.4	2.4	0.3	1.5	0.4	2.3
2,001-2,500	0.3	1.9	0.5	3.0	0.4	2.2	0.3	1.9
2,501-3,500	0.4	2.8	0.5	3.2	0.4	2.1	0.4	2.3
3,501-5,000	0.5	4.2	0.4	2.6	0.3	2.0	0.5	2.3
Over 5,000	0.6	4.8	0.7	5.3	0.4	2.7	0.5	2.1
Average wage for hired labour, sh. per day		1.95		2.05		2.35		2.35

Source: As for Table 5.5, with distribution costs saved calculated as 30 per cent of 'consumption of own produce'. These savings are then added to earnings per man-day as given in Table 5.5 to obtain the second column of figures for each district.

other estimates relating to 1969; 0.5 shillings per day is rather less than a quarter of the average wage per man-day given in the Survey, which is 2.19 shillings. Our own estimate of the typical daily wage for an adult male in 1969 is 2.25 shillings a day in the settlements in Western Province and 2.75 shillings a day in those in the Rift Valley and Central Provinces. Hence there is a case for increasing the estimated benefit in the latter areas. For the sake of simplicity, however, we decided to take a uniform 0.5 shillings a day everywhere.[1] Taking the numbers of working men and women for average High and Low Density schemes in 1967-8 given in 5.2, assuming that each works 200 days a year (see 5.4.2), and that the gain for women is three-quarters of

[1] However, in Part II we allow for lower wages in the Kabisi settlements, which are in Western Province.

that for men, the total gains per farm per annum work out at £11 and £5 respectively.[1]

5.4.6 *Total benefits accruing to settlers*

We can now bring together our estimates of the four different components of the total benefits accruing to regular workers who become settlers, and this is done in Table 5.7. All estimates refer in principle to average settlers in 1967-8. Although there is considerable uncertainty about the individual components, there is less uncertainty about the total. For example, had we taken a smaller saving on retail margins than 30 per cent, we would have reduced the second benefit but we should have increased the fourth one, since this was estimated from the gap between actual earnings on small farms and rates of pay for hired workers, in so far as this gap was not explained by a saving on retail margins. Or, again, had we assumed that settlers worked more than 200 days a year, the third benefit (shorter hours) would have been smaller, but the fourth would have been greater.

It is clear from the table that the unadjusted gains in money income are not an accurate guide to total benefits. The adjustments are more important for the High Density schemes since, for them, subsistence consumption is relatively more important, and labour inputs are greater.

To express these benefits in terms of the numeraire we must perform the following operations:

1. We divide total benefits by the number of equivalent adults in the household, i.e. by 5.2 for High Density and by 4.3 for Low Density schemes. This gives benefits per adult equivalent of £11.8 and £23.5 respectively.
2. Applying the formula for discrete changes in income,[2]

[1] i.e.

High Density:	1.6 x 200 x 0.5/20	=	£ 8
	0.7 x ¾ x 200 x 0.5/20	=	£ 3
	Total		£11
Low Density:	0.6 x 200 x 0.5/20	=	£ 3
	0.6 x ¾ x 200 x 0.5/20	=	£ 2
	Total		£ 5

[2] See 3.1, equation (3), assuming $e = 1$.

Table 5.7
Total benefits accruing to average settlers in 1967-8

£ p. a.

	Source of Benefit	Value of Benefit: High Density	Value of Benefit: Low Density
1.	Gain in money income	13	69
2.	Saving in retail margins	16	18
3.	Shorter hours of work	22	8
4.	Benefits from working on family farm	11	5
5.	Total at market prices	62	101
6.	Total at accounting prices	27	21

Source: see text.

we can express these benefits in terms of equivalent marginal benefits to those at the critical income level. Income (including non-farm income) 'before' is £126 for High Density and £227 for Low Density settlers. Per adult equivalent these are £24.2 and £52.8. Adding on the benefits, incomes 'after' per adult equivalent are £36.0 and £76.3 respectively. The formula then gives the following benefits per family, assuming $e = 1$ and a critical income of £15 per adult equivalent:

$$\text{High Density:} \quad 5.2 \times 15 \log_e \frac{(36.0)}{(24.2)} = 31.0$$

$$\text{Low Density:} \quad 4.3 \times 15 \log_e \frac{(76.3)}{(52.8)} = 23.7$$

3. Finally, we multiply these benefits by the accounting ratio for income accruing to poor rural families, f_{cr}, which is 0.87. This gives the estimates at accounting prices shown in Table 5.7.

5.5 CONCLUSION: THE SOCIAL COST OF FAMILY LABOUR ON SETTLEMENT FARMS

We can now put together the three elements in our calculation of the social cost of family labour on settlement farms, and this is done in Table 5.8 (see also Part II, Tables 16.1 and 16.2 for figures for particular settlement schemes and other years). It is interesting to note that the weighting of these three elements is very different for High and Low Density settlers. As compared with the Low Density settlers, the High Density ones have a bigger labour input (hence part (i) is bigger) and, largely because of this and because they are poorer, the social value of their benefits is greater (part (iii)). At the same time, as a large part of these benefits takes the form of shorter hours, better working conditions, and a saving of retail margins, the resource cost of providing them is much smaller (part (ii)). Consequently, although there are, physically speaking, more family labour inputs into High than into Low Density settlement farms, their social cost per farm is smaller.

Table 5.8

Social cost of family labour on settlement farms in 1967-8

	Components of social cost, £ p.a.								
	(i)	+	(ii) (a)	(ii) (b)	−	(iii)	=	Total (a)	(b)
High Density	95	+	33	(24)	−	27	=	101	(92)
Low Density	50	+	91	(78)	−	21	=	120	(107)

(a) assuming 'effective' loan repayments; (b) assuming 'theoretical' loan repayments, see 5.3.

Sources: (i) see 5.2; (ii) see Table 5.2; (iii) see Table 5.7.

CHAPTER 6

Private Profits

In this chapter we consider three problems; first, our estimate of the accounting ratio for extra income accruing to 'capitalists' (i.e. P 4), second, how to appraise the private sector projects of 'capitalists', and third, our procedure for estimating the accounting ratios of indirect inputs of private capital. These problems are closely linked to each other, and a satisfactory solution of them requires much more research than we have been able to undertake. Some major uncertainties underlie our estimates, and there is little doubt that further work in this area is badly needed.

6.1 EXTRA INCOME ACCRUING TO 'CAPITALISTS', P 4

In this section we explain our estimate of the accounting ratio for payments which increase company profits (before tax). The extra profits which result are essentially surpluses, and not payments made in the ordinary way in return for goods and services, since the latter include a compensation for loss of output from the capital had it been employed elsewhere. It is only in so far as the capitalist's income is increased as a result of the project that the payments with which we are concerned here arise. Examples of the different ways in which this can happen are given in Chapter 9.

Both the basic model and the empirical values inserted into it are derived from David Newbery,[1] who is, at the time of writing, undertaking research into this and related matters. As

[1] He is not responsible, however, for any errors in the calculations nor for the final guess at the accounting ratio. The writer was also helped by an earlier model devised by Nicholas Stern (see Stern, August 1973).

this research is still in a preliminary stage, both the estimates and the model are highly provisional. We explain and illustrate some of the major uncertainties in the section on empirical values below. We first describe the model.

6.1.1 *Description of the model*

We start by asking what happens when extra profits of £1 accrue to a company which is privately owned. To simplify exposition we assume that this £1 is paid out by the Government. It is then either consumed by the owner (c), saved (s), or taxed (t). We do not distinguish company from personal savings or taxation, and so put

$$c + s + t = 1. \tag{1}$$

We assume that all the savings are reinvested in the company, or in similar companies. The resulting extra private investment is, however, greater than s for two reasons. First, the act of investment in fixed capital entitles the company to an investment allowance which saves it tax. It is, in fact, allowed to write off a fraction a of the eligible investment (which we assume is a proportion v of the total) on which it saves tax at the rate t_1.[1] This is over and above the normal depreciation allowance. Hence, if the extra investment is k, the tax saved is $kvat_1$ and to that extent k can exceed s. Second, the act of investment and saving enables the company to borrow more from the banking system (and so, we assume, indirectly from the Government, to whom the banks either belong or else would lend). Let the fraction of investment financed by bank borrowing be b. Then

$$k\ (1-b-vat_1) = s, \tag{2}$$

which we may re-write

$$k = ms$$

where $$m = \frac{1}{1-b-vat_1} \tag{2A}$$

[1] t_1 is not the same as t. The former is the rate of tax on corporate profits, the latter includes, in addition, income tax on dividends.

could be called a 'savings multiplier'.

As a result of the extra investment k the companies concerned make extra profits, net of depreciation, which are $r\,k$. We assume, for simplicity, that 'true' depreciation and depreciation for tax purposes coincide, and that these extra profits, after deducting interest on bank loans of $i\,b\,k$, are dealt with in the same proportions between consumption, saving and tax as in (1). Consequently, they lead to extra private savings $s\,k\,(r - i\,b)$ and extra private investment of $m\,s\,k\,(r - i\,b)$. If all rates of return and earnings are expressed as annual rates, then the above process, if continued indefinitely, leads to a rate of growth in the initial investment k of $m\,s\,(r - i\,b)$ per unit per annum. It should be noted that r and i in the above expressions are *real* rates of return and interest respectively. They approximately equal the corresponding *money* rates minus the rate of increase of the general price level (measured, in our case, by the index of consumer prices).

So far we have been concerned only with market values. We now turn to values at accounting prices. Let the accounting ratios for the capital goods purchased be f_k, that for consumption of capitalists be f_c, and that for extra profits be f_p. This last one is the ratio of the extra profits flowing from the extra investment, measuring all outputs and inputs (including labour, but allowing nothing for interest or *net* return to capital) at accounting prices, to their actual value at market prices.

It follows that, as a result of the extra investment k, the *social* benefit which accrues in that year is

$$B = r\,k\,f_p - c\,k\,(r - i\,b)\,f_c - m\,s\,k\,(r - i\,b)\,f_k \qquad (3)$$

That is, the benefit accruing in that year is what remains from the extra profit at accounting prices after extra capitalists' consumption and extra private investment have been deducted from it, both valued at accounting prices.

This benefit grows at the same rate as k, that is, it grows at a rate of $m\,s\,(r - i\,b)$. Consequently, its net present value, if we discount it at the accounting rate of interest, R, is

$$V \triangleq \frac{B}{R - m\,s\,(r - i\,b)}\,. \qquad (4)$$

We can now bring together the various elements of the total cost of paying an extra £1 to a company, measured at accounting prices. This cost is the accounting ratio we seek to determine. Hence

P 4 = direct extra consumption of capitalists
plus cost of direct extra private investment
less net present value of social benefits
flowing from that extra investment

$$= cf_c + kf_k - V$$

$$= c\,f_c + m\,sf_k - \frac{m\,s(rf_p - c(r - i\,b)f_c - m\,s(r - i\,b)f_k)}{R - m\,s(r - i\,b)} \qquad (5)$$

6.1.2 *Empirical values*

Ideally, equation (5) could be used to determine the accounting ratio for profits accruing to various different types of 'capitalists' (e.g. large farms, manufacturing companies, companies engaged in distribution, or in transport, with subdivisions depending on whether they are predominantly in Kenyan or foreign ownership, and distinguishing large and small firms). Their characteristics probably differ in important respects (e.g. proportion of income saved, or taxed, accounting ratios applicable to their profits, rates of return on reinvestment). Unfortunately, it has not been possible in this study to collect and analyse the necessary data. In what follows, we use some very preliminary estimates of Newbery's to derive rough orders of magnitude, and to show which are the crucial items. Our final estimate for P 4 is merely our best guess at this stage. Its precise value is not important for the bulk of our estimates of accounting ratios, as can easily be seen from inspection of Table 10.2. It is, however, quite important in certain cases (e.g. bread, butter, tea at retail, wheat flour, milk as a substitute for butter for export, milk distribution, and cement) and the estimates leading to it are very relevant and important in any evaluation of a private sector project.

The first four parameter values given in col. (1) of Table 6.1, as well as r, the private rate of return before tax, are derived

Table 6.1

Values of parameters needed to estimate P 4 using equation (5), and resulting values of P 4

	Standard case, r = average return	Standard case, r = marginal return	As for col. (2) but Lower f_p	Higher R	No bank borrowing	Tax evasion	Foreign firm
	(1)	(2)	(3)	(4)	(5)	(6)	(7)
Fraction of profits consumed,	0.22	–	–	–	–	0.36	0.25
Fraction of profits saved, s	0.22	–	–	–	–	0.36	0.30
Fraction of profits taxed, t	0.56	–	–	–	–	0.28	0.45
Fraction of investment financed by banks, b	0.20	–	–	–	0.00	–	–
Bank interest per unit, i	0.05	–	–	–	–	–	–
Fraction of capital eligible for investment grant, v	0.70	–	–	–	–	–	–
Rate of investment grant, a	0.20	–	–	–	–	–	–
Tax rate on corporate profits, t_1	0.40	–	–	–	–	0.20	–
Accounting ratio consumption, f_c	0.82	–	–	–	–	–	1.00
Accounting ratio capital, f_k	0.90	–	–	–	–	–	–
Accounting ratio profits, f_p	0.85	–	0.75	–	–	–	–
Private rate of return, r	0.20	0.15	–	–	–	–	–
Accounting rate of interest, R	0.10	–	–	0.15	–	–	–
P 4	−0.13	0.12	0.19	0.27	0.14	0.35	0.23
Accounting ratio savings, f_s	−1.41	−0.27	0.04	0.41	−0.18	0.15	−0.07

from the accounts of typical firms whose shares are registered on the Nairobi Stock Exchange, supplemented by other information. They refer, in principle, to Kenyan-owned firms (foreign-owned firms being dealt with in col. (7)). The average rate of return of such a firm (that is, the ratio of profits net of depreciation but before deduction of interest and tax to total assets at book values) is in the region of 20 per cent. If the private *marginal* rate of return were indeed as high as this, then, as may be seen from the table, P 4 would be negative. In other words, the Government would benefit more from payments made to increase the profits of such companies than by spending the money itself. However, it seems unlikely that the *real* marginal rate of return is as high as this average for a variety of reasons, including the existence of inflation, and we have accordingly taken 15 per cent, rather than 20 per cent, as our best guess of the real marginal rate of return in col. (2) (it would not be difficult to justify an even lower figure). In that case P 4 works out at 0.12, which shows how sensitive it is to this parameter.

The accounting ratio used for profits, f_p, explained above, is one which could vary widely. It could, for example, be negative, and in some instances it almost certainly is where excessive protection is given. The estimate of 0.85 is an average for a subset of the manufacturing industries covered by Phelps and Wasow (undated). They estimated value-added at domestic and world prices for numerous branches of industry, as well as wage costs. The latter were converted by Newbery to world prices using an average of P 2 and P 3, and subtracted to leave estimated profits at world prices. Industries which seemed to be producing mainly non-tradeables (e.g. brewing) were excluded. The figure of 0.85 also seems a reasonable guess at what the ratio would be for various service industries. However, it is quite possible that for *marginal* investments in manufacturing the accounting ratio is lower, as protection is increased in order to foster more costly import substitution. The effect of reducing the ratio is to increase P 4 to quite a marked extent, as may be seen from col. (3).

If we are right in guessing that the average marginal private real rate of return is 15 per cent, it could be argued that the ARI ought to be higher than 10 per cent. It does not follow that it should *equal* 15 per cent, however, since one could well expect the private rate of return to exceed the ARI even in a well-managed economy. This would happen because the Government could only increase private investment by lowering profits taxes or income taxes, or by lowering interest rates charged on loans to the private sector, and any of these actions would involve it in intra-marginal costs which would offset the gain from a marginal increase in private investment.[1] However, in order to illustrate the effect of choosing a higher ARI we have taken one of 15 per cent in col. (4). It increases our estimate of P 4 appreciably.

In col. (5) we show the effect on P 4 of assuming no bank borrowing. This increases it, but not by very much.

Our estimates in cols. (1)-(5) assume that taxes are successfully levied at existing rates on all profits and dividends.[2] While this may be a close approximation to the situation for the larger companies, it is probably not true for a number of smaller firms, who may manage to escape the tax net by one means or another. To show the effect of this we have arbitrarily assumed in col. (6) that taxes are only levied at half the rates in col. (2). This substantially increases P 4.

Finally, in col. (7) we estimate P 4 for a typical foreign company. The main differences between this column and col. (2) are the allowances for differences in tax treatment (only a withholding tax on dividends) and the assumption that all 'consumption' is equivalent to profits remitted abroad with a conversion factor of one. We have also assumed a higher marginal savings rate. Again, P 4 is a bit higher than in col. (2).

Our estimates do not, unfortunately, relate at all closely to the circumstances of companies in agriculture. For many of these, f_p could be well above one. On the other hand, their marginal rates of return, r, may be lower than 15 per cent, and

[1] This argument could be expressed as follows. The Government in effect hires private enterprise to undertake investment. Because the supply of enterprise is almost certainly not infinitely elastic, the Government should pay enterprise a 'wage' which is less than the value of its social marginal product, i.e. it should tax it. This leaves a situation in which, if private investment can be increased in other ways (e.g. through project selection) social profits can be increased.

[2] We have guessed that dividends bear tax at an average marginal rate of 40 per cent. A married man with two children has allowances of £720. On the first £1,000 of income above this he pays 12.5 per cent tax, on the next £1,000, 27.5 per cent, on the next 52.5 per cent, and beyond that higher rates still.

these differences have opposite effects on P 4.

In conclusion, our final best guess of P 4 is 0.2. There is obviously a good deal of uncertainty about this.

6.2 THE APPRAISAL OF PRIVATE SECTOR PROJECTS OF 'CAPITALISTS'

The preceding section has important implications for the appraisal of private sector projects of 'capitalists'. As pointed out in Chapter 1, this is done in just the same way as for public sector projects, except that one must deduct the social cost of payments made to the private owners and add the social benefit of receipts from them. To estimate these at accounting prices, we need to distinguish between payments which return to the Government by way of tax, payments which are saved, and payments which increase capitalists' consumption. The same applies to receipts. We first consider the accounting ratios for each of these components, and then how the latter may be estimated.

The accounting ratio for taxes is, as usual, zero. That for capitalists' consumption we put at 0.82. This is the same as the accounting ratio for urban workers' consumption, and assumes that the social value of the benefit accruing to capitalists is negligible. It would have been better to have calculated a special ratio for higher income consumers, the data for which exist.

The accounting ratio for savings can be deduced from the preceding section, and is equally uncertain and provisional. Using the same notation, the net present social cost of a unit *invested* by a capitalist is

$$\frac{k f_k - V}{k}$$

Each unit *saved*, given bank borrowing linked to saving, leads to m units invested. Consequently, the net present social cost of a unit *saved* is

$$f_s = \frac{m}{k}(k\,f_k - V)$$

$$= \frac{P\,4 - c\,f_c}{s} \text{ (using (2A) and (5)).} \qquad (6)$$

If we work this out for each of the columns of Table 6.1 we get the values shown in its last line. These are clearly sensitive to the assumptions made. If one had to make a guess at this stage one could put f_s at zero, which is approximately consistent with our best guess of P 4 = 0.20 (see cols. (3) and (7)).

Let us now consider the estimation problem, first for the operation of the project and secondly for its financing. So far as the first is concerned, all we have to do is to subtract from the net profit at accounting prices (as it would be for a public sector project) an amount per unit of net profit at market prices before tax equal to

$$\frac{(r-ib)}{r}\,(c\,f_c + s\,f_s).$$

Hence the net social profit, after subtracting the social cost of payments to capitalists, per unit of net profit at market prices before tax, is

$$f_p - \frac{(r-ib)}{r}\,(c\,f_c + s\,f_s) = f_n\,. \qquad (7)$$

For example, if we take col. (3) of Table 6.1 and put $f_s = 0$, we get a social profit per unit of 0.58. For col. (7) (the foreign firm) with $f_s = 0$ it is 0.62.

Turning now to financing, the problem is relatively simple if it is all either foreign or from the public sector. In the first case the accounting ratio is one (unless we think the finance would otherwise have gone to some other project in Kenya), while in the second case it is zero, as *this* receipt is like a transfer within the public sector. Finance provided by Kenyan capitalists is not so easily dealt with. If we think that it would all have otherwise been invested elsewhere in Kenya, then f_s is the appropriate accounting ratio for all of it. But some might otherwise have been consumed and some might *indirectly* have been borrowed from (or not lent to) the public sector, or possibly from abroad, and the accounting ratios for these are much larger than f_s.[1]

The following is a short-cut method of estimating the *social* rate of return on private sector projects. Suppose that the total capital required to provide net profits before tax of 1 is K. Then, since the ratio of profits to capital is r, we have $K = 1/r$. The social cost of this capital is the accounting cost of the capital goods *less* the accounting value of the private financing, i.e.

$$K f_k - \frac{K}{m} f_f = \frac{f_k - \frac{f_f}{m}}{r} ,$$

where f_f is the accounting ratio applicable to the private financing. The social rate of return on the investment is then

$$r_s = \frac{r f_n}{f_k - \frac{f_f}{m}} \qquad (8)$$

For the sake of illustration, we take three possible cases from cols. (3) and (7) of Table 6.1. We choose these columns since they are approximately consistent with our provisional best guess of P 4 = 0.20 and with the simple assumption that $f_s = 0$. In case 1, we take col. (3) parameters and assume that all the private financing comes from savings which would otherwise have been invested in similar projects elsewhere, so that $f_f = f_s = 0$. Then $r_s = 0.10$. In case 2, we take the same data but assume that all the private financing comes from capitalists' consumption, and represents new savings, so that $f_f = f_c = 0.82$. Then $r_s = 0.30$. In case 3, we take col. (7), the foreign firm, and put $f_f = 1$. Then $r_s = 0.59$.

These are rather striking results. Taken at their face value they suggest that Kenyan (or for that matter foreign as well) private investment by 'capitalists' which is switched from similar investment elsewhere in Kenya has a rate of return equal to the ARI (not surprisingly so, see Appendix A.6 for a proof);

[1] For further discussion, see Little and Mirrlees, 1974, Chapter XI.

that Kenyan private investment which is accompanied by new Kenyan savings of 'capitalists' has a very high social return, around 30 per cent per annum; and that new foreign investment in Kenya has an even higher social return, around 60 per cent per annum. The reason for the high returns in the last two cases is that the public sector puts up very little of the original capital but gets a large slice of the subsequent profit through taxation. Both results are, however, very sensitive to the parameters chosen and should be treated with caution. In particular, the value of f_p could vary widely. For a heavily protected industry, f_p could easily be negative. There is no social advantage in getting a large slice of the profits of a company which makes those profits, in effect, at the expense of taxes (i.e. tariffs) which the Government would otherwise have received. Where, however, there is little or no protection (e.g. agriculture and tourism) the social rates of return may be very high indeed. Another important parameter is the extent to which taxes are paid. Our results refer essentially to companies which pay tax at the going rates. Where there is widespread tax evasion, as may be the case for small firms, the social returns would be much lower. There is really no good substitute for a careful examination of particular projects using, if possible, a discounted cash flow analysis.

6.3 INDIRECT PRIVATE CAPITAL INPUTS

In working out the accounting ratios for non-traded goods and services, we analysed their long-run marginal costs of production. We mostly used data from the Censuses of Industrial Production and the Surveys of Distribution, supplemented by other information. The treatment of current inputs such as wages, materials and fuels was straightforward, but how were we to estimate the accounting ratios applicable to the 'operating surplus' of manufacturing industries or building and construction and the 'net profit' of retailers and wholesalers and other service trades covered in the various surveys, which include depreciation, interest, profits and the earnings of the self-employed?

The importance of the operating surplus in total costs

depends very much on whether one is considering *value-added* (as we do, for example, with transport and distributive margins or some processing margins, e.g. N 1, 4, 7, 8, 9, 10, 11, 12, 13, 14, 16, 18, 21, 22, 23, 25, 26, 27, 28) or *sales* (as we do, for example, with all the other N-items). For all manufacturing industries in 1967 the operating surplus was 44 per cent of value-added and only 14 per cent of total output. For all building and construction, the operating surplus was 7 per cent of total output, but for private building and construction alone it was 11 per cent.

For companies, the earnings of self-employed are presumably nil, and this was assumed to apply to all manufacturing firms. Earnings of the self-employed were also assumed to be zero for public enterprises (railways, post office and ports) and for the various marketing boards and their agents. For most remaining activities (building and construction, cinemas and theatres, restaurants, retail and wholesale distribution) various estimates were made based mainly on statistics of the numbers of people in this category and assumed average earnings as workers rather than as 'capitalists'. The accounting ratio for skilled labour was then applied.

Leaving aside the question of the earnings of the self-employed, how should the other inputs, which mainly refer to capital, be dealt with? Ideally, a full discounted cash flow analysis would show each input at the time at which it occurred. There should be no special category of capital inputs, merely inputs which occur sooner or later. For the *direct* inputs into a project, this treatment is practical, but it is hardly so for the *indirect* inputs. We can say when the buildings required for the project itself will be built, but it would be impossibly tedious to date the extra buildings required to distribute the project's outputs, or inputs, or to house the workers who built the buildings required for this purpose. Consequently, we must fall back on approximations. The usual one, which was adopted here, is to treat all such inputs like current inputs, i.e. as if they were simultaneous with the outputs they help to make. We wanted to do this without distorting project selection and as simply as possible. Our procedure was as follows. First, we obtained what information we could on the *percentage composition* of the assets involved, i.e. the capital inputs, dividing them into five categories for which we assumed the following lives and hence arrived at the following annuities, discounting at the ARI of 10 per cent per annum:

	Life in years	Annuity % p.a.	Code
Buildings and construction	40	10.2	N 3
Machinery and equipment	14	13.6	T 14
Vehicles	6	23.0	T 12
Stocks	infinite[1]	10.0	[2]
Furniture (where available)	14	13.6	UCN 7

We then multiplied the percentage of each asset by its annuity rate and so calculated a notional percentage composition of gross profits. The annuity for each asset was multiplied by an accounting ratio for that asset, as indicated by the code number, and this then gave us a weighted average accounting ratio which we applied to total gross profits. Is there any reason to believe that this procedure gives a good approximation to the 'truth' for indirect private capital (it should be correct for indirect capital provided by the public sector)?

To simplify matters, we put aside the question of the composition of the assets[3] and suppose that all capital consists of a single kind of asset whose accounting ratio is f_k and life T years. Let the net profit (before tax) at market prices be 1 with depreciation allowances d so that gross profits are $1 + d$. Denote the net present value of an amount 1 for T years discounted at

[1] The infinite life assumed for stocks is undoubtedly an exaggeration, since stocks of most goods deteriorate to some extent, and their rate of deterioration ought to be added to the interest cost. Our neglect of this point can only be justified if the rate of deterioration is small during the period most goods are kept in stock. For example, if a good deteriorates at 0.5 per cent per annum for the first six months it is in stock, but then its rate of deterioration increases, the error in our annuity rate will only be 0.5 per cent so long as goods typically remain six months or less in stock.

[2] No single category was applied to stocks. Wherever possible we subdivided them into stocks of finished goods and work in progress (which were netted out with the output of the industry) and stocks of materials, for which the appropriate accounting ratio was used. Wholesale and retail distributors' stocks were treated in the special way described in Chapter 9.

[3] We argue below that the private net-of-tax return is probably close to 10 per cent per annum. Hence our procedure for dividing up the gross profit stream is probably a fairly good approximation.

the ARI of R per unit per annum by $P(T, R)$. Let f be the 'true' accounting ratio which we should apply to gross profits. Then we want to choose f so as not to distort project choice. Consequently we want to make the true net present social value of the costs involved in hiring this capital asset for T years equal to the net present value of paying $f(1 + d)$ for T years. Using our previous notation, the true social cost of hiring each year is $\frac{(r-ib)}{r}\,(c f_c + s f_s) + d f_s$, assuming all depreciation allowances are saved, and to its net present social value we must add the social cost of the original capital investment, which we put at K at market prices. Its social cost is given in the preceding section and is

$$K f_k - \frac{K}{m} f_f \,.$$

Consequently, we want to choose f such that

$$f(1+d)P(T,R) = \left(\frac{(r-ib)}{r}\,(cf_c + sf_s) + df_s\right) P(T,R) + K\left(f_k - \frac{f_f}{m}\right).$$

Now if the private capitalist's rate of discount is r_d, we can assume that

$$\frac{K}{m} = \left(\frac{(r-ib)}{r}\,(c+s) + d\right)P(T,r_d) \,.$$

Furthermore, we can put

$$\frac{P(T,r_d)}{P(T,R)} = \frac{R}{r_d} \cdot \frac{\left(1 - \dfrac{1}{(1+r_d)^T}\right)}{\left(1 - \dfrac{1}{(1+R)^T}\right)} = q, \text{ say (clearly } q = 1 \text{ if } r_d = R).$$

By substitution and rearrangement we then get

$$f = \frac{1}{(1+d)}\left\{\frac{(r-ib)}{r}\,(cf_c + sf_s) + df_s + q\left(\frac{(r-ib)}{r}\,(c+s) + d\right)(mf_k - f_f)\right\} \tag{9}$$

If we now insert the values of the parameters given in cols. (3) and (7) of Table 6.1,[1] and if we put $d = \frac{1}{3}$,[2] it turns out that f_k is a reasonable approximation to f *provided that* the investment is regarded as being switched from other similar uses in Kenya. If it is so regarded, then f_f is approximately zero in both cases. But if the private financing represents new savings by 'capitalists' (col. (3)) or new foreign exchange provided from abroad (col. (7)) then f_f is 0.82 in the first case and 1.00 in the second, and in either event f is much lower than f_k. These results are summarized in Table 6.2, together with the value of f when $f_k = 0.90$ for the sake of illustration.

The short-cut procedure we have followed to deal with indirect capital inputs amounts to using f_k instead of f as the accounting ratio by which the market value of these inputs is multiplied. Lines 1 and 2 above show that, provided f_k is in the region of 0.9 (as it is for most items) and provided the capital provided is switched from investment elsewhere in Kenya, this short-cut gives a reasonably good approximation. It also gives a good approximation if the indirect capital input comes from the public sector, and it may well be a good approximation even when the capital comes from new private savings, provided that the resulting profits bear little tax (as may be the case for small firms in retailing, for example). Lines 3 and 4 show, however, that, if the capital represents new savings of Kenyan 'capitalists' who pay tax, or fresh foreign exchange from abroad (belonging to foreign companies who also pay tax), this is no longer true. Our short-cut then substantially *overstates* the indirect capital costs.

[1] The value of q can be worked out once we know r_d, the private rate of discount. We assume that this is given by the ratio of profits net of tax, interest and depreciation to the market value of that part of the capital subscribed by the capitalist, that is

$$r_d = (r - ib)\,(c+s)m.$$

For col. (3), $r_d = 0.083$ while for col. (7), $r_d = 0.103$. In Table 6.2 we show the six different values of q corresponding to these two values of r_d combined with three values of T as on p.142.

[2] Depreciation allowances are about 20 per cent of gross profits of large quoted companies, i.e. 25 per cent of net profits. If we reduce net profits by a quarter to convert them from average to marginal profits, as in Table 6.1, col. (2) et seq., and if we leave depreciation allowances unchanged, then they come to one-third of net profits.

Table 6.2

Accuracy of short-cut method to calculate indirect capital inputs

	Parameter set in Table 6.1	f_f	T years	q	Eqn. for f	Value of f $f_k = 0.90$
1.	Col. (3)	0	6	1.05	$f = 0.13+0.79f_k$	0.84
			14	1.10	$f = 0.13+0.83f_k$	0.87
			40	1.18	$f = 0.13+0.89f_k$	0.92
2.	Col. (7)	0	6	0.99	$f = 0.18+0.84f_k$	0.94
			14	0.98	$f = 0.18+0.84f_k$	0.93
			40	0.97	$f = 0.18+0.83f_k$	0.92
3.	Col. (3)	0.82	6	1.05	$f = -0.36+0.79f_k$	0.35
			14	1.10	$f = -0.38+0.83f_k$	0.37
			40	1.18	$f = -0.42+0.89f_k$	0.38
4.	Col. (7)	1.00	6	0.99	$f = -0.45+0.84f_k$	0.31
			14	0.98	$f = -0.45+0.84f_k$	0.31
			40	0.97	$f = -0.44+0.83f_k$	0.30

Note: the short-cut method involves using f_k instead of f. Its accuracy for the fairly typical case when $f_k = 0.90$ can thus be gauged by the closeness with which the last column above approaches 0.90. For the meaning of the symbols, see equation (9) and discussion in the text.

Appendix A.6[1]

To show that $r_s = R$ if $f_f = f_s$ (see p.139), equation (5) may be re-written

$$P\,4 = \frac{(1-\tau)R}{R-g} - \frac{msrf_p}{R-g},$$

where $\tau = 1 - cf_c - msf_k$ = the 'effective tax'

and $g = ms(r-ib)$ = the growth rate.

From equation (6), sf_s = $P\,4 - cf_c$

and hence using equation (7), $f_n = f_p - \frac{(r-ib)}{r} P\,4$.

Hence, substituting in equation (8) after multiplying numerator and denominator by ms we have

$$r_s = \frac{m\,r\,s\,f_n}{msf_k - sf_s} = \frac{m\,r\,s\,f_p - m\,s(r-ib)\,P\,4}{m\,s\,f_k + c\,f_c - P\,4}$$

$$= \frac{m\,r\,s\,f_p\,(R-g) - g(1-\tau)\,R + g\,m\,s\,r\,f_p}{(R-g)\,(1-\tau) - R(1-\tau) + m\,s\,r\,f_p} = R\;.$$

[1] This proof was provided by David Newbery.

CHAPTER 7

Farm Outputs

In this chapter we consider some special problems which arise in estimating the accounting ratios for farm outputs. The main problems are: the determination of whether a good is exportable, importable or non-tradeable (or all three); fluctuations in accounting ratios from year to year; the difference between average f.o.b. export prices and the marginal revenue from exports; the treatment of marketing boards' profits and losses; the use of discounting techniques to obtain the accounting ratio for cows, i.e. regarding them as 'projects', and the analysis of supply and demand for non-traded outputs. We illustrate these, and some other, problems by reference to maize, pyrethrum, butterfat, coffee, wheat and cows. The value of cattle as beef is discussed in Part III, and the value of tea in Stern (1972). If milk, poultry, vegetables, potatoes and fruit, which we class as non-traded, are included, all the most important agricultural outputs in Kenya are covered except for sisal and sugar.

7.1 MAIZE

Maize is the most important food grain in Kenya, so we start with it. Total production is not known accurately, but was estimated at about 1.4 million metric tons in 1968-9.[1] In 1969, deliveries to the Marketing Board, which has had a legal monopoly of exports and of inter-district sales, were about one fifth of this and exports were half of deliveries. However, deliveries, exports and imports have varied widely from year to year as Table 7.1 shows.

[1] Development Plan 1970-1974, p. 237.

Table 7.1

Maize deliveries, exports and imports and accounting ratios

	Deliveries	Exports	Imports	Accounting ratios
	Thousand metric tons			
1962	153	60	26	0.58
1963	210	87	0	1.87
1964	136	1	0	1.50
1965	104	0	81	1.15
1966	134	0	143	0.52
1967	249	80	0	0.64
1968	353	278	0	n.a.
1969	280	141	0	n.a.
1970	206	0	14	n.a.
1971	257	0	29	n.a.
1972	393	n.a.	n.a.	n.a.

Note: '*Deliveries*' means deliveries to the Marketing Board. *Exports and Imports* refer only to trade in unmilled maize outside East Africa. Recorded trade in milled maize, or with other East African countries, was small. *Accounting ratios* refer to output of settlement farmers at the farm gate.
Sources: Statistical Abstracts for 1972 and 1969, and Table 10.1.

These wide variations were due to fluctuations in the harvest combined with the Marketing Board's fixed price system under which it stood ready (in principle) to buy and sell at fixed (and widely separated) prices, which were normally only changed once a year. In good years, maize was unloaded on to the Board which, in turn, exported a large part of its purchases in order to prevent prices in the towns from falling too far. These exports involved it in losses which were recouped by a subsidy from the Government. In bad years, deliveries to the Board fell away and it imported maize in order to prevent an acute shortage from developing. Imports were also subsidized on occasion.

The effect of subsidizing both exports and imports in this way was to stabilize internal prices. It also led to bigger fluctuations in accounting prices than in market prices, and hence to big fluctuations in accounting ratios from year to year, as may be seen from the last column of the table.[1] When maize was being exported, both the export parity price and the accounting price at the farm were well below the price the farmer received. When maize was being imported, the reverse was true. An illustration of the calculations underlying the estimates of the accounting ratios is in Table 7.2. This gives, in effect, the raw data from which the coefficients in Table 10.2 were derived[2] for two years, one in which maize was an import and one an export.

Several points are worth noting. When maize was being exported, we took the average export price as our measure of marginal revenue from exports. In 1967, for example, 95 per cent of exports went to the United Kingdom and Japan, both large markets in relation to Kenya's sales to them (for butter, see below, we adopted a different procedure). When maize was being imported, we needed to know at what place it competed with domestic production. We assumed that this was Nairobi, so that the import parity price was given by adding freight and distribution from Mombasa to Nairobi to import costs and then subtracting freight and distribution from Nairobi to the farm gate to get the price there. Freight and other handling costs were large in relation to port or farm gate prices, and so it made a big difference to the latter whether maize was being imported or exported (and this was accentuated by the tendency for import c.i.f. prices to be higher than export f.o.b. prices). Rail charges were split into marginal costs and the excess of price over marginal cost in the way described in 9.6. Marketing Board

[1] The timing of these needs some explanation. The crop in the important maize-producing settlement schemes to which the ratios refer (i.e. near Eldoret) is harvested mainly from November to January, and there is a delay of some weeks before it can be sold to the Board to allow the grain to dry out, and there is a further delay before the maize is actually exported. It was therefore assumed that, for example, maize produced in the year ending 30 March 1963 (which is shown as 1962 in the table) was exported in 1963, while maize produced in the year ending 30 March 1965 (1964 in the table) competed with imports brought in in 1965. Maize produced in 1963-4 was treated as an import substitute on the grounds that it became available to the Board around March 1964, which was about when the Board first realised that a shortage was developing and that imports would be necessary (see 'Report of the Maize Commission of Inquiry', June 1966, p. 52).

[2] The transition from the figures in Table 7.2 to those of 'direct inputs' in Table 10.2 is effected by dividing through by the price received by the farmer (hence the entry of 1.00 in Table 10.2 for FO4) and adding together items with the same code numbers. Care is needed with regard to signs.

Table 7.2

Data used in estimating accounting ratios for maize in 1965-6 and 1967-8

shillings per bag of 200lb.

Maize as an import 1965-6	Code	sh/bag	*Maize as an export 1967-8*	Code	sh/bag
1. Imports c.i.f.	P 1	46.7	1. Exports, f.o.b.	P 1	31.2
2. 25 per cent grant PL480	P 10	11.7			
3. Port handling	N 13	6.1	2. Port handling	N 13	6.1
4. Rail freight, M'basa-Nairobi, marginal cost	N 18	2.6	3. Rail freight, Eldoret-M'basa, marginal cost	N 18	3.5
5. Price minus marginal cost	N 19	1.3	4. Price minus marginal cost	N 19	2.9
6. Marketing Board costs	N 8	3.9	5. Marketing Board costs	N 8	3.9
7. Cost at Nairobi (1-2+3+4+5+6)		48.9	6. Cost of bag (net of second-hand value)	T 1	1.5
8. Rail freight, Eldoret-Nairobi, marginal cost	N 18	2.6			
9. Price minus marginal cost	N 19	0.7			
10. Marketing Board costs	N 8	3.9			
11. County Council cess	P 10	1.0	7. County Council cess	P 10	1.0
12. Marketing Board profit	P 10	4.8	8. Marketing Board loss	P 10	13.0
13. Price received by co-operative (7-8-9-10-11-12)		36.0	9. Price received by co-operative (1-2-3-4-5-6-7+8)		25.3
14. Co-op. margin, road transport	N 22	1.9	10. Co-op. margin, road transport	N 22	1.9
15. Ditto, contribution to overhead	N 23	1.2	11. Ditto, contribution to overhead	N 23	1.2
16. Price received by farmer (13-14-15)	FO4.4	33.0	12. Price received by farmer (9-10-11)	FO4.2	22.3

Sources: Annual Reports of the Maize and Produce Board; Alvis and Temu, 1968; Annual Trade Reports of Tanzania, Uganda and Kenya; East African Railways Tariff Book No. 5, 1968; Report of the Maize Commission of Inquiry, June 1966; Economist Intelligence Unit, 1969; Settlement Co-operatives' accounts.

costs make some allowance for economies of scale. In this case we assumed marginal costs were 90 per cent of average costs (see also 9.5). The profits and losses of the Marketing Board were treated as the equivalent of Government taxes and subsidies. We did not treat other marketing boards in this way (see below), but in the case of the Maize and Produce Board it seemed to be the best assumption. Large subsidies were, in fact, received by the Board from the Government in 1967-8, for example.

For a commodity with as variable an accounting ratio as maize, it is important to use different estimates for each year in the past, and we have done this in Part II. But what about projections for the future? It is clearly impracticable to forecast the situation each year, and so we must fall back on an average. The most important mistake to avoid is that of taking the accounting ratio for, say, the most recent year and projecting that forward without considering whether it is likely to be a sensible average. In the case of maize, our estimate for 1967-8 would almost certainly not be a sensible average, since it would be tantamount to assuming that the Government would continue to export maize with a heavy subsidy. This is not what has happened on average in the past, nor does it correspond to the intentions expressed in the latest Plan.

If the future were to repeat the experience of the past, both the accounting price and accounting ratio would average considerably more than their values in 1967. The arithmetic average of the ratios in Table 7.1, for example, is 1.04 compared with 0.64 for 1967-8. The Plan, however, envisages a substantial reduction in maize production costs due to major technological improvements, accompanied by the installation of bulk storage facilities both at Mombasa and up-country, the use of bulk handling methods on the railways and a reorganization of the operations of the Maize and Produce Board.[1] The cost of getting maize from the farm to the port would thus be

[1] Development Plan 1970-1974, pp. 237-8.

substantially reduced,[1] and it would be possible *both* to pay farmers sufficient to call forth a large increase in output *and* to export without the need for a subsidy. At the time of writing, this Plan has not yet materialized. It is still uncertain whether maize production will expand sufficiently to ensure a satisfactory utilization of bulk handling facilities, should they be installed. We have, nonetheless, based our estimated accounting ratio for maize in the future on assumptions similar to those made in the Plan. The accounting ratio for FO 4.1 therefore assumes a substantial reduction in farm-to-port costs and no export subsidy. The resulting figure of 1.10 is, as it turns out, little different from the past average.[2]

In the above analysis, maize is treated either as an importable or as an exportable, or as an average of both. One could argue that *some* maize is non-tradeable, and *some* is partially tradeable. Most maize that is grown is probably consumed on the farm where it is produced. Some of these farms may be so remote that fluctuations in output are simply matched by fluctuations in farm consumption, leaving sales to the Marketing Board unaffected. This maize would be non-tradeable. Maize is *partially* tradeable if an expansion in output leads *both* to effects on local consumption *and* to effects on trade. For example, a farmer who has hitherto been just self-sufficient in maize, with no surplus for sale, might expand his output by the introduction of new varieties of seed, etc., so that he now sells part of it to the Marketing Board, or its agents. Because of the existence of large distributors' margins, this farmer would sell his grain for substantially less than he would have to pay for it.[3] Consequently, its marginal value to him would be lower if he were a net seller than if he were just self-sufficient and, *a fortiori*, than if he were a net buyer. An increase in his output

[1] By about Sh. 76 per metric ton (or Sh. 8 to 9 per bag) according to the Plan, p. 238.

[2] We have used the accounting ratio of 1.10 also in calculating other ratios which depend upon it, e.g. for non-traded agricultural goods, for maize grain and flour in the towns, and for consumption in general. As we found it impracticable to estimate these other ratios year-by-year, this seemed the best alternative. See also the discussion in Part III, Chapter 21.

[3] See 5.4.1 for estimates of distributive margins on maize and other foodstuffs in the countryside (20 per cent for maize and 30 per cent for other products).

would therefore be accompanied by an increase in his consumption as well as an increase in sales to the Marketing Board. This would be reinforced by the income effect of increased production. All this suggests that the accounting ratio for maize should be a weighted average of its ratio regarded as a traded good and its ratio as a non-traded good. As our estimate for the accounting ratio for non-traded goods at the farm gate (P 9) is 1.00, it is probably unnecessary to modify our estimate of 1.10 for maize on this account, particularly where it is used for farms which are as relatively well integrated into the marketing system as are the settlement farms where maize is important.

7.2 PYRETHRUM

Pyrethrum is a flower from which pyrethrins are extracted, for use as an active ingredient in insecticides. Virtually all Kenya's output is exported, and Kenya accounts for a substantial part of world exports.[1] The Pyrethrum Board, together with the Pyrethrum Marketing Board which it controls, buy all the flowers and have a monopoly of exports and of the extraction of pyrethrin. As the Board appears to be financially independent of the Government, and is a non-profit-making organization, we have assumed that any extra profits or losses made accrue to small or large farmers (i.e. P 7 and P 4) in proportion to their sales to the Board in 1967 (i.e. 0.865 to small and 0.135 to large farmers). This would happen if, for example, the Board adjusted its pay-out price so as to keep its own profits at some 'normal' or 'target' level. We have not allowed for the effects of such changes in pay-out price on the level of output, and have thus implicitly assumed that the *net* social costs or benefits of any resulting changes in output are negligible.

Since Kenya dominates the world market for pyrethrum, it seemed reasonable to assume that she could influence its price, even in the fairly long run. We were unable to estimate the elasticity of demand for her exports, and failed to obtain any

[1] Over 60 per cent of 'world supply' in 1961-2 according to 'Development Plan 1966-70', p. 181.

indication of the extent to which, in the Board's view, marginal revenue fell short of the export price. However, since some allowance was clearly called for, we made one in two ways. First, we arbitrarily assumed that marginal revenue from exports was 15 per cent less than the export price. Second, we allowed for some marginal selling costs.[1]

In estimating the marginal cost of processing and distribution incurred by the Board, we took average costs as stated in the Board's Report for 1966-7 after deducting laboratory costs, half of administrative and sales and sales promotion expenses, and half of Board expenses, altogether deducting about 15 per cent of average costs. Our reasons for deducting some selling costs are given in the footnote.[1] The other cost deductions were made partly to allow for economies of scale and partly because the items referred to could be regarded as capital expenditure to some extent. In earlier years average costs were much higher mainly because of a big promotional campaign and of abnormally large stocks (which raised interest costs). It did not seem appropriate to include either of these in marginal costs, and so we assumed the latter were the same as in 1966-7. This meant that, on our reckoning, the Board made a sizeable profit on *marginal* sales in 1962-3 to 1964-5, which was then converted into a loss in 1965-6 to 1967-8. It is this which accounts for the decline in the accounting ratio from 1.40 in 1962-3 to 1.12 in 1967-8 (see Table 10.1).

7.3 BUTTERFAT

As we refer to the possible effects of increased domestic sales of milk or butterfat on exports of butter in 9.2, and explain there how we have treated the resulting changes in profits accruing to the Kenya Dairy Board and Kenya Co-operative Creameries, there is no need to repeat the explanation here. The only special

[1] However, we assumed that these were only a half of average selling costs. In effect, we assumed that marginal sales were made partly as a result of price cutting and partly through incurring selling costs. Had we assumed that *only* price cutting was involved, our implicit elasticity of demand for exports would have been about 6 (consistent, for example, with a world price elasticity of demand of 2 and a price elasticity of supply by competitors of Kenya of 4). However, the implicit elasticity of demand for exports is lower than 6, since extra sales partly result from incurring extra selling costs (see Scitovsky, 1952, Ch. XI).

points we mention relate to the valuation of exports and changes in accounting ratios through time.

In 1967, rather more than 70 per cent by quantity of Kenya's butter exports went to Tanzania and Uganda at an average price of 3.7 shillings/lb. Exports to countries outside East Africa were sold at an average price of 2.9 shillings/lb. Of the latter, exports to the United Kingdom were sold at 2.0 shillings/lb. We took the view that it was the last of these prices which measured the marginal revenue from butter sales. The markets in East Africa and in other countries near at hand (e.g. Aden, Burundi, Ethiopia, Rwanda, Zambia) were limited, and demand for Kenyan exports was probably less than perfectly elastic. On the other hand, Kenya's exports to the United Kingdom were a tiny fraction of butter consumption there, and more could have been sold without appreciably affecting the price. Consequently, instead of taking the average export price for sales to all markets of 3.5 shillings/lb, we took as our marginal revenue the much lower figure of 2.0 shillings/lb.

Maize and pyrethrum are the only items for which we give accounting prices for more than one year. For butter and butterfat, as for other items, our estimates refer only to 1967-8. However, in an earlier paper[1] the writer made some estimates on a slightly different basis for the years 1962-3 to 1967-8 inclusive. Over this period the accounting ratio was comparatively stable and tended to rise moderately. It has probably risen further since then (see footnote on p.164).

7.4 COFFEE

Only two points will be mentioned here. First, we have taken the unit value of exports to non-quota markets as a measure of marginal export revenue. In 1967 Kenya's exports of coffee to quota markets were limited by the International Coffee Agreement and amounted to 41 th. tons at an f.o.b. price of £334 per ton. She also exported 7 th. tons to non-quota markets at £233 per ton. Second, since all exports were channelled through the non-profit-making Coffee Marketing Board, which based its price to producers on its average (and

[1] Scott, August 1970.

not marginal) receipts, additional exports involved it in a loss.[1] This loss was assumed to accrue to small and large farmers (P 7 and P 4) in proportion to their sales of coffee in 1967. We ignored any effects there may have been of changes in producer prices on production, assuming that their net social cost or value was very small.

7.5 WHEAT

Wheat raises many of the same issues as maize. In recent years, it has been exported to both Tanzania and Uganda but not much to other countries. In a few years (e.g. 1962, 1966, 1971) there have been shortages and sizeable imports from outside East Africa. Exports outside East Africa have involved the Wheat Board in losses, but, at least up to September 1969, no subsidy was received from the Government except for the crop year 1968-9.[2] The Government's policy as outlined in the Development Plan 1970-1974 has been 'not to export wheat except to Uganda, and to bring production into line with market requirements in Kenya and Uganda.'.[3] In the longer run, however, the hope was expressed that production costs could be reduced sufficiently to export wheat on a larger scale without need of a subsidy. Although exports of unmilled wheat were therefore discouraged, the Wheat Board stated its intention in 1969 of encouraging flour exports to other African countries and around the Indian Ocean.[4]

Wheat is much less important on the settlement schemes examined in Part II than is maize. We therefore did not devote the same attention to it, but merely contented ourselves with estimating its accounting ratio in 1967-8. As with maize, however, this may be a misleading guide to its accounting ratio in other years, past or future. We assumed that marginal wheat production would increase exports of flour, and we distributed

1 The loss was mitigated by the fact that exports to quota markets were subject to an export tax (£20 per ton to 1 July 1967 when it was reduced to £10 per ton), while those to non-quota markets were not.

2 Report of the Kenya Wheat Board, September 1969, p. 5.

3 Op. cit., p. 239.

4 Report of the Kenya Wheat Board, September 1969, p. 4.

the resulting loss on marginal production half to urban consumers and half to producers, sub-dividing the latter again between small and large farmers in proportion to production in 1967.[1] We ignored the effects of any resulting changes in prices on production and consumption.

7.6 COWS

The increase in the value of livestock, principally dairy cattle, on settlement farms has been a very important component of their total output. For the years 1964-5 to 1966-7 covered in the economic survey of settlement schemes, it accounted for 11 to 32 per cent of output on High Density Schemes and for 13 to 29 per cent on Low Density Schemes. To evaluate the schemes we therefore needed to estimate the value at accounting prices of these increases in value. We therefore undertook a fairly elaborate analysis of the net present value of a typical cow at successive points in its life, both at market prices and at accounting prices. The main outputs allowed for were milk, calves, and carcases. The main inputs were land, labour, feed, salt, dip, A.I. and veterinary services. Unfortunately, the accounting ratio turned out to be very sensitive to the accounting ratios used for the main inputs and outputs, and for this reason the method cannot be regarded as satisfactory. In the absence of a better estimate, we took 1.30 as the accounting ratio for cows, as this was approximately in the middle of the range of estimates. This figure refers to 1969, since when there have been big changes in the price structure for milk, and big increases in the average prices received by farmers for both milk and maize (affecting the cost of feed). More work on this whole matter is thus badly needed.

7.7 NON-TRADED AGRICULTURAL PRODUCTS, P 8 AND P 9

In this section we explain how the accounting ratios for two primary inputs (as defined in 1.2.7) were estimated, that for

[1] See Report of the Kenya Wheat Board, September 1968, p. 21.

non-traded agricultural products bought at retail in the towns (P 8) and that for similar products sold at the farm gate (P 9). As the detailed explanation is somewhat technical, we confine it to Appendix A.7, and only give here a briefer one which may be sufficient for some readers, and which conveys the main ideas. The products included are listed on p.164.

Let us suppose that the project we are considering leads to an increase in the demand for such things as milk, fruit and vegetables in the town (e.g. by increasing employment and wages there). We want to know the cost at accounting prices of meeting this extra demand, which, we assume, increases the prices of non-traded agricultural products in both town and countryside with the following effects:

(a) Other urban consumers buy less of them, because their prices have risen, and more of other consumer goods and services. In fact, we assume that they switch to other *foodstuffs* only (plus drink and tobacco). We estimate the market value of these extra purchases and, from our other estimates of accounting ratios, their cost at accounting prices.

(b) Rural consumers (who are also producers) also tend to switch to other foodstuffs, drink and tobacco because of the relative price increase of non-tradeables, and we estimate the accounting cost of this as well.

(c) Rural producers switch output in the opposite direction, that is, they produce fewer tradeable goods like maize and pyrethrum, and more non-tradeable goods whose prices have risen. We estimate the accounting cost of the fall in tradeables output.

(d) There is a transfer of incomes from urban consumers to rural producers. This has to be allowed for in two respects. First, there are income effects on the demand for non-tradeable foodstuffs and substitutes for them (we ignore effects on other goods for simplicity). These are allowed for in the estimates of (*a*) and (*b*) above. Second, as urban consumers are richer than rural producers, on average, there is a net social benefit which we allow for (but which we estimate is rather small).

The cost at accounting prices of meeting the extra urban demand is then (*a*) + (*b*) + (*c*)–the benefit mentioned at (*d*). By making various simplifying assumptions, as explained in Appendix A.7, the accounting ratio P 8 can be expressed as a weighted average of four other accounting ratios: that for other urban foodstuffs, drink and tobacco; that for other rural foodstuffs, drink and tobacco; that for other tradeable agricultural products; and that for the distribution costs involved in getting extra output of non-tradeables from the countryside to the town. In addition, there is a term which allows for the net social benefit of the income transfer. The formula which expresses this result is equation (15) in Appendix A.7, the weights used being given in subsequent equations, and the empirical magnitudes necessary to calculate them in Table A.7.1.

Once P 8 is determined in the way just described, it is a simple matter to find P 9, the accounting ratio for non-tradeables at the farm gate. The relation between the two is set out in equation (23) in Appendix A.7, which merely states that the accounting cost of non-tradeables in the town is the sum of their cost at the farm gate and the accounting cost of getting them from the farm gate to the urban consumer.

The accounting ratios P 8 and P 9 depend, *inter alia*, on the *extent* to which consumers and producers switch their patterns of consumption and production in response to relative price changes, or, in technical language, on the magnitude of the relevant elasticities of substitution. As we had little or no evidence, we conducted a sensitivity analysis to determine whether the ratios were much affected by differences in these elasticities. It turned out that they were not, provided that the elasticities were arithmetically larger than about 0.2, as we believe that they are. Our final best guesses at the magnitudes of P 8 and P 9 were then 0.85 and 1.0 respectively.

Appendix A.7

Let the total quantity of non-traded foodstuffs produced (all in the countryside) $= N$

of which the quantity consumed in towns $= N_u$

and the quantity consumed in the countryside $= N_r$

So

$$N = N_u + N_r \,. \tag{1}$$

Let the urban retail price of N be P_u
and the rural farm gate price of N be P_r
and the distributive margin between them be M
So

$$M = P_u - P_r \,. \tag{2}$$

Let the value of substitutes for N consumed in the towns = S_u
and in the countryside = S_r
Let the value of substitutes in production for N in the countryside be T

We assume that T consists of tradeable goods whose prices are given independently of output in Kenya, while S and M consist either of tradeable goods or of other goods and services produced under constant cost conditions. Hence the prices of T, S and M are held constant throughout the analysis.

Now assume that there is a small increase in the demand for N in the towns = $\Delta_1 N_u$
The problem is to determine the accounting cost of this.
As a result of the increase in demand, the price of N in the town rises by ΔP_u
and demand elsewhere in the towns increases by $\Delta_2 N_u$
(which will be negative).
Hence the total change in urban consumption of N is

$$\Delta N_u = \Delta_1 N_u + \Delta_2 N_u \,. \tag{3}$$

The rise in the price of N in the towns leads to an equal absolute increase in its price at the farm gate (since M is constant), which we henceforth call $\Delta P = \Delta P_u = \Delta P_r$, and this in turn reduces its consumtpion in the countryside and increases its output. The total change in output equals the total change in consumption, so that from (1) we have:

$$\Delta N = \Delta N_u + \Delta N_r \,. \tag{1A}$$

Let us now consider the total resource cost resulting from the increase in demand for N. In the towns, we assume that consumers' total money income and expenditure is unchanged elsewhere (i.e. excluding the project's increase in demand for N). There is therefore the cost of providing them with the substitutes, S_u, to which they switch when the price of N rises. If the accounting ratio for these is A_{su}, this part of the resource cost at accounting prices is

$$
\begin{aligned}
C_1 &= A_{su} \cdot \Delta S_u \\
&= -A_{su} (P_u \cdot \Delta_2 N_u + N_u \cdot \Delta P) \\
&= A_{su} \cdot N_u \cdot \Delta P\,(e_{ud} - 1)
\end{aligned} \tag{4}
$$

where e_{ud} is the Marshallian price elasticity of demand for N_u, defined so as to be positive. That is $e_{ud} = \dfrac{-\Delta_2 N_u}{N_u} \cdot \dfrac{P_u}{\Delta P}$ (5)

In the countryside, consumers' (who are also producers) total money incomes have increased by $\Delta P \cdot N$, as we assume that the switch in the pattern of rural output has no effect on its money value (i.e. the marginal rate of transformation of T into N is equal to their relative farm gate prices), so that the only gain is through the rise in the price of N. The second part of the resource cost is then given by the accounting value of the substitutes on which rural consumers increase their expenditure as the combined result of this rise in their money income and the rise in the price of N. This is

$$
\begin{aligned}
C_2 &= A_{sr} \cdot \Delta S_r \\
&= A_{sr} (\Delta P \cdot N - P_r \cdot \Delta N_r - Nr\,\Delta P) \\
&= A_{sr} \cdot N_r \cdot \Delta P \left(\frac{N}{N_r} + e_{rd} - y_r \cdot \frac{P_r \cdot N}{Y_r} - 1 \right),
\end{aligned} \tag{6}
$$

where A_{sr} is the accounting ratio for S_r, e_{rd} is the Marshallian price elasticity of demand for N_r, defined so as to be positive, y_r is the income elasticity of demand for N_r, and Y_r is total rural incomes. Equation (6) is obtained by considering the total change in demand for N_r as consisting of two parts, that due to the rise in price of N without the rise in money income of rural producers which we may call

$$\Delta_p N_r = -e_{rd} \cdot N_r \cdot \frac{\Delta P}{P_r} \tag{7}$$

and that due to the rise in money income of rural producers which we may call

$$\Delta_y N_r = y_r \cdot N_r \cdot \frac{N \cdot \Delta P}{Y_r}\,. \tag{8}$$

and putting these two parts together we have

$$\Delta N_r = \Delta_p N_r + \Delta_y N_r\,. \tag{9}$$

The third part of the resource cost is the accounting value of the fall in output of tradeable agricultural goods from which farmers switch in order to produce more N. This is

$$\begin{aligned} C_3 &= -A_t \cdot \Delta T \\ &= A_t \cdot P_r \cdot \Delta N \\ &= A_t \cdot N \cdot \Delta P\, e_s , \end{aligned} \tag{10}$$

where A_t is the accounting ratio of T, and e_s is the elasticity of supply of N, so that

$$e_s = \frac{\Delta N}{N} \cdot \frac{P_r}{\Delta P} . \tag{11}$$

The fourth and final part of the resource cost is the accounting value of the distribution costs on the extra quantity of N moving from the countryside to the town, which is

$$\begin{aligned} C_4 &= A_m \cdot M \cdot \Delta N_u \\ &= A_m \cdot M \cdot (\Delta N - \Delta N_r) \\ &= A_m \cdot M \cdot \frac{N}{P_r} \cdot \Delta P \left(e_s + e_{rd} \cdot \frac{N_r}{N} - y_r \cdot \frac{N_r}{N} \cdot \frac{N \cdot P_r}{Y_r} \right) \end{aligned} \tag{12}$$

Besides leading to these resource costs, the increased demand for N leads to a transfer of income from urban to rural consumers equal to $\Delta P \cdot N_u$. If each shilling at urban prices given to urban consumers of N is given a social value at accounting prices of W_u, while each shilling at rural prices given to rural producers of N is given one of W_r, the net social benefit resulting from the transfer is

$$B = N_u \cdot \Delta P\,(W_r - W_u) . \tag{13}$$

The accounting ratio of non-traded agricultural goods in the town, A_{nu} = P 8, can now be worked out. It is the sum of the four parts of the resource cost minus the net benefit from the transfer divided by the value at market prices of the increased demand for N. Hence

$$A_{nu} = \frac{C_1 + C_2 + C_3 + C_4 - B}{P_u \cdot \Delta_1 N_u} \tag{14}$$

Using (1A), (3), (5), (7), (8), (9) and (11) we can eliminate all the Δ terms except $\Delta_1 N_u$ and ΔP, thus expressing the latter in terms of the former. If we then substitute for ΔP in (4), (6), (10), (12) and (13) we can finally eliminate all the Δ terms in (14). We are then left with the following equation for A_{nu}:

$$P\,8 = A_{nu} = \frac{w_1 A_{su} + w_2 A_{sr} + w_3 A_t + w_4 A_m - \frac{N_u}{N}(W_r - W_u)}{w_1 + w_2 + w_3 + w_4} \qquad (15)$$

This equation shows that A_{nu} is a weighted average of the accounting ratios for the goods and services which substitute for it in consumption (A_{su} and A_{sr}) or in production (A_t) or which are complementary to it in production (A_m), *less* a term which gives the social value of the net benefit resulting from the transfer of income from consumers to producers which occurs when the demand for N is increased. The weights are given below in two forms. In the first, the various elasticities of demand and supply are given in their Marshallian form, as in (5), (7), and (11) above. In the second, elasticities of substitution are given instead since it could be argued that these are more likely to be invariant with respect to changes in the proportion of expenditure on N relative to that on substitutes for N, or to total expenditure, while the Marshallian elasticities would depend upon such proportions. The relation between these elasticities is as follows:

$$e_{ud} = \frac{\sigma_{ud}}{1 + P_u \cdot N_u/S_r} + y_u \cdot \frac{P_u \cdot N_u}{Y_u} \qquad (16)$$

$$e_{rd} = \frac{\sigma_{rd}}{1 + P_r \cdot N_r/S_r} + y_r \cdot \frac{P_r \cdot N_r}{Y_r} \qquad (17)$$

$$e_s = \frac{\sigma_s}{1 + P_r \cdot N/T} \qquad (18)$$

where σ_{ud}, σ_{rd}, σ_s are the elasticities of substitution, and y_u and y_r are income elasticities of demand, and Y_u and Y_r are total urban and rural incomes respectively.

The weights are:

$$w_1 = \frac{N_u}{N}(e_{ud} - 1) = \frac{N_u}{N}\left(\frac{\sigma_{ud}}{1 + P_u \cdot N_u/S_u} + y_u \cdot \frac{P_u \cdot N_u}{Y_u} - 1\right) \qquad (19)$$

$$w_2 = \frac{N_u}{N}\left(e_{rd} \cdot \frac{N_r}{N_u} - y_r \cdot \frac{P_r \cdot N_r}{Y_r} \cdot \frac{N}{N_u} + 1\right)$$

$$= \frac{N_u}{N}\left(\frac{\sigma_{rd}}{1 + P_r \cdot N_r/S_r} \cdot \frac{N_r}{N_u} - y_r \cdot \frac{P_r \cdot N_r}{Y_r} + 1\right) \qquad (20)$$

$$w_3 = e_s = \frac{\sigma_s}{1 + P_r \cdot N/T} \qquad (21)$$

$$w_4 = \frac{M}{P_r}\left(e_s + e_{rd} \cdot \frac{N_r}{N} - y_r \cdot \frac{P_r \cdot N_r}{Y_r}\right)$$

$$= \frac{M}{P_r}\left(\frac{\sigma_s}{1 + P_r \cdot N/T} + \frac{\sigma_{rd}}{1 + P_r \cdot N_r/S_r} \cdot \frac{N_r}{N} - y_r \cdot \frac{P_r \cdot N_r}{Y_r} \cdot \frac{N_u}{N}\right) . \qquad (22)$$

Having found A_{nu} (P 8), the accounting ratio for non-traded agricultural goods in the towns, it is easy to find A_{nr}, (P 9), the corresponding ratio for these goods at the farm gate, by using the equation

$$A_{nu} \cdot P_u = A_{nr} \cdot P_r + A_m \cdot M \ , \qquad (23)$$

i.e. the accounting value of these goods in the town is the sum of their accounting value at the farm gate and the accounting value of the distributive margin between farm gate and town. This gives their accounting value both as rural output and as rural consumption.

Table A.7.1

Values of parameters needed to estimate A_{nu} and A_{nr} (i.e. P 8 and P 9) using equations (15) and (23)

1.	*Accounting ratios*			
	A_{su}	= 0.83	A_{sr}	= 0.94
	A_t	= 1.11	A_m	= 0.75
2.	*Weights for income gains*			
	W_u	= 0.06	W_r	= 0.32
3.	*Expenditure and output ratios etc.*			
	N_u/N	= 0.10	N_r/N	= 0.90
	$P_u \cdot N_u/Y_u$	= 0.07	$P_r \cdot N_r/Y_r$	= 0.20
	$P_u \cdot N_u/S_u$	= 0.28	$P_r \cdot N_r/S_r$	= 0.48
	M/P_r	= 1.50	$P_r \cdot N/T$	= 0.80
	P_u/P_r	= 2.50		
4.	*Income elasticities*			
	y_u	= 0.90	y_r	= 1.25

Empirical magnitudes
All the estimates required to calculate A_{nu} and A_{nr}, using (15) and (23), are given in Table A.7.1, with the exception of the three elasticities of substitution, σ_{ud}, σ_{rd} and σ_s. As explained below, it was unnecessary to make spot estimates of them since A_{nu} and A_{nr} are not sensitive to the different values that might be chosen, provided they are greater than about 0.2, as seems likely.

We assumed that the principal non-traded agricultural goods were foodstuffs, namely, potatoes, other vegetables, fruit,[1] eggs, poultry and milk. We were in some doubt as to whether to treat maize as non-tradeable, but decided in the end to treat it as exportable in the future, and as either exportable or importable in the past (see 7.2). There was some doubt also over the best treatment of milk, since one could regard it as marginally used to make butter, which is exported. In 1967-8, the period to which our estimates principally refer, milk for consumption in the towns as liquid milk was sold through the K.C.C. mainly at the relatively high prices for 'quota' or 'contract' milk (i.e. in the region of 2.5 or 2.0 shillings a gallon at the farm gate), while milk sold for conversion to butter or ghee fetched a much lower price in the region of one shilling a gallon. We were told, in 1969, that milk sold locally in the countryside (i.e. not through the K.C.C.) fetched about 1.8 shillings a gallon. The marginal value of milk to a farmer in this situation could be any one of three or four different prices, ranging from one to 2.5 shillings a gallon. It is clear that our model of supply and demand at a unique farm gate and urban retail price is too simple for this situation. As milk is an important commodity, both in production and consumption, further research into its accounting prices in different situations would be worthwhile. We, however, confined our attention to two estimates.

First, we treated milk as a non-tradeable good selling at the farm gate at the 'contract' price (i.e. the second-highest price applicable to milk sold for liquid consumption in the towns). This applied reasonably well to milk sold for liquid consumption both in towns and in the countryside. Second, we treated milk as marginally exportable as butter. The accounting ratios for these were fairly close to each other (i.e. 1.00 for the former and 0.84 for the latter), but of course the farm gate prices to which these ratios should be applied were very different, so that the accounting price per gallon of milk was much higher for milk as a non-tradeable than for milk as an exportable. In Part II and in deriving the accounting ratio for all non-tradeable agricultural goods we adopted the first assumption.[2]

[1] Some fruit (e.g. pineapples and passion-fruit) is traded. However, it is thought that most fruit grown on small farms (to which we confine our attention—see below) is non-traded.

[2] This could be justified partly on grounds of simplicity and partly by the fact that exports of butter outside East Africa have dwindled. By 1971 they were nil or negligible to the U.K. Hence there has probably been a tendency for the accounting ratio of exported butter to rise as exports have been increasingly confined to the higher priced markets in neighbouring countries. 1.00 may therefore be a better

We assumed that the main substitutes in consumption for non-traded foodstuffs were traded foodstuffs, beverages and tobacco. The accounting ratios for these were derived in the ways described elsewhere and separate weighted averages were calculated for urban (A_{su}) and rural (A_{sr}) consumers using (for simplicity) the same marginal expenditure weights as those used in deriving the accounting ratios for marginal increases in consumption of urban and rural consumers (see Chapter 8).

Non-traded agricultural products are produced both by small farms and by large farms. However, small farms account for most of the output, and we decided to simplify the analysis by assuming that they produced it all. It would have been better to have had two production sectors, one for small farms and one for large farms, instead of the single sector of our model.

Although large farms account for a minor part of total output, they account for a large part of *marketed* output of milk,[1] and an increase in demand for milk could be expected to affect their output as well as that of small farms. Their existence should, therefore, be allowed for, though whether it would make much difference to the final estimate of the accounting ratio is unclear.

We assumed that the main substitutes in production for non-traded foodstuffs were maize, beans, tea, pyrethrum and wheat (omitting coffee because of the restrictions on its output). The accounting ratios for these products were weighted by their estimated values of output in 1969 to obtain the average accounting ratio A_t.

The accounting ratio for the distributive margin, A_m, was worked out for potatoes and milk, with rather similar results, and a simple average was taken. Potatoes and milk were also used to estimate the average ratio of urban retail to rural farm gate prices.

The weights used for income gains accruing to urban consumers (W_u) and rural consumers and producers (W_r) were derived from those given in Tables 3.2 and 3.3, using income weights and assuming $e = 1$, and making an allowance for non-African urban consumers (given zero weight).

The ratios of non-traded agricultural products consumed to traded foodstuffs, beverages and tobacco and to total income in towns and countryside were estimated on the basis of the various family expenditure surveys available, and the Central Province Survey was used to estimate the ratio of output of non-traded agricultural products to traded agricultural products.

The income elasticities of demand for non-traded agricultural products

estimate of the post-1968 accounting ratio for milk converted into butter than is 0.84, and it is this post-1968 ratio which is most important for the estimates of net present values in Part II.

[1] In 1967, according to the Statistical Abstract for 1968, p. 76, large farms' cash revenue from all dairy products was £3,940 thousand compared to £2,440 thousand for small farms. On the other hand, marketed milk production around 1969 was only 290 million litres out of a total production of about 730 million litres (Development Plan 1970-1974, p. 258).

in town and countryside (y_u and y_r) were estimated from the same sources as those used in 8.1.

It only remains to explain the estimates for the two elasticities of substitution in demand and the elasticity of substitution in production (σ_{ud}, σ_{rd} and σ_s). Values of A_{nu} were computed for a large number of different possible values of these elasticities. It was clear that, over a wide range of values, the result was not sensitive to the particular elasticities chosen. It was only if they were low, and lower than seemed at all likely, that A_{nu} varied appreciably. The final value of A_{nu} selected was 0.85, and the corresponding value of A_{nr} was 1.0.

CHAPTER 8

Household Expenditure and Saving

We deal with four topics, all related to the title of this chapter. First, we explain how we have estimated accounting ratios for the whole of rural and urban consumers' expenditures. Second, we explain our accounting ratio for household savings (both rural and urban). Business savings are discussed in Chapter 6. Third, we consider the scanty evidence available on households' marginal propensity to save. Finally, we estimate the average difference in consumer prices between the countryside and the town.

8.1 ACCOUNTING RATIOS FOR RURAL AND URBAN CONSUMPTION AND f_{cr} AND f_{cu}

In our estimates of shadow wages, we needed to estimate the accounting cost of marginal increases in the consumption of wage-earners and their families. Since patterns of consumption, prices and accounting ratios differ considerably between the countryside and the town, we estimated two accounting ratios for this purpose. The first refers to marginal increases in the consumption of poor families in the countryside and the latter to poor families in the towns. It would be possible, given the available information on family expenditures, to estimate accounting ratios for higher-income families, in both countryside and town, and this would be useful in deriving certain other estimates. However, we made do with just two accounting ratios.

Table 8.1 sets out our average and marginal expenditure weights for rural consumers, and also gives the code numbers and accounting ratios we allocated to each head of expenditure.

We prepared a similar (but more detailed) table for urban consumers, which is omitted here to save space. Some of the accounting ratios used need explanation. For rural consumption, we used urban accounting ratios for some items where we lacked alternative estimates or where we thought that the rural ones would be little different (e.g. clothing). Such items only account for 17.5 per cent of total expenditure. For school fees, which are an important component of rural expenditure on 'services', and which are available separately for urban consumers, we assumed that all expenditures were equivalent to taxes. This is how they are regarded in one important pronouncement of Government policy,[1] and it seemed the simplest way to deal with them. It is more appropriate for *poor* rural and urban consumers than for wealthier ones, since the latter may spend money on private schooling, which can hardly be regarded in this way.

The weighted average accounting ratios for rural and urban consumption are summarized below. It makes little or no difference whether average or marginal weights are employed:

	Average weights	Marginal weights
Rural	0.94	0.92
Urban	0.82	0.82

The accounting ratio for marginal increases in income accruing to poor rural or urban families, f_{cr} and f_{cu}, can easily be worked out from the above figures, together with the accounting ratios for rural and urban household savings of 0.4 estimated in 8.3 and the marginal propensity to save of 10 per cent estimated in 8.4. We have:

$$f_{cr} = 0.9 \times 0.92 + 0.1 \times 0.4 = 0.87$$

$$f_{cu} = 0.9 \times 0.82 + 0.1 \times 0.4 = 0.78$$

[1] Sessional Paper No. 10 of 1965 on 'African Socialism and its Application to Planning in Kenya'. We assume, in effect, that the supply of education is independent of the amount collected in fees.

Table 8.1

Accounting ratio for rural consumption

	Average expenditure	Expenditure elasticity	Marginal expenditure (adjusted)	Code number	Accounting ratio
	(1)	(2)	(3)	(4)	(5)
Cereals	150	0.59	92	RCF 2	1.10
Pulses	97	0.79	80	RCF 1	1.09
Roots	104	0.53	57	P 9	1.00
Fruit and vegetables	61	0.79	50	P 9	1.00
Oils and fats	20	1.22	25	UCF 11	0.82
Meat	35	1.20	44	RCF 3	1.16
Eggs	14	1.20	18	P 9	1.00
Milk	72	2.34	174	P 9	1.00
Sugar	42	1.06	47	UCF 17	0.63
Other food	11	1.00	11	UCF 11	0.82
Tobacco and beverages	38	1.12	45	RCF 5	0.55
Fuel and light	170	0.69	121	P 9	1.00
Other non-durables	15	1.09	17	UCN 10	0.80
Clothing	56	0.89	52	UCN 3	0.68
Durables	22	0.99	23	UCN 10	0.80
Housing	30	2.34	73	RCN 1	0.90
Services	63	1.08	71	RCN 2	0.61
Total	1,000		1,000		

Sources: Col. (1), from Table 8.3. Col. (2) from Massell, May 1969, except for 'eggs' and 'other food', which were guessed. Col. (3) = col. (1) × col. (2), divided by 0.962 in order to adjust the sum of the marginal components to 1000. Cols. (4) and (5), see Table 10.1.

8.2 SAVINGS OF HOUSEHOLDS

When workers are employed, their incomes may increase and part of the increased incomes may be saved. We estimate the marginal propensity to save in 8.3. In this section we estimate the accounting ratio which, when multiplied by the actual value of the extra savings, gives their resource cost. We do not allow for any benefits accruing to the saver, as these are taken into account elsewhere. We are only concerned with the resource cost here.

To estimate the accounting ratios for savings, we need to know how they will be invested. The only available information known to the writer is that given in the Central Province Survey, which is reproduced in Table 8.2.

Table 8.2

Capital account of the average rural household in the Central Province in 1963-4

Receipts		Expenditure	Shillings per annum
Savings	34	Land purchased	8
Repayment of loans	15	Buildings (incl. construction,	7
Borrowing	19	Vehicles purchased	18
Dowries (cash)	15	Tools purchased	3
Less money lent out	- 6	Livestock purchased	30
		Less Livestock disposed of	-31
		Less assets sold	- 5
		Increase in cash holdings or deposits	47
Total	77	Total	77

Source: Central Province Survey, p. 38.

In principle, we need *marginal* and not *average* capital transactions, but only the latter are available. Furthermore, inspection of Table 8.2 makes it clear that savings are only one component in the financing of investment. In principle, one should relate the other components (e.g. borrowing) to income and then work out accounting ratios for each component of financing and each component of investment. Thus it is quite likely that an increase in income will result in an increase in both saving and borrowing, and so an increase in investment which is larger than the increase in saving alone.[1]

Unfortunately, we have neither the basic information nor the time to undertake such an analysis. It is one more example of

[1] We make some allowance for this when we consider company savings in Chapter 6.

further research which is required. We adopt, instead, a short-cut procedure which, it is hoped, does not do too much violence to reality. We assume that marginal increases in savings lead to increased investment in buildings, vehicles, tools and cash or deposits in the same proportions as the average shown on the right-hand side of Table 8.2. We ignore investment in land and livestock on the grounds that these largely cancel out, one man's purchases being another man's sales.[1] We apply an accounting ratio of 0.80 to the 'real' component of investment (i.e. 37 per cent of the total), and one of 0.14 to the rest. The resulting weighted average is then about 0.4 for all savings. We use this for urban as well as for rural savings, having no information which would enable us to differentiate between them. We must now explain these accounting ratios.

The accounting ratio for the real component of investment is the rounded weighted average for building and construction (0.80), lorries, etc. (0.79) and tools (0.95).[2] That for cash and deposits is arrived at as follows. We first assume that these savings represent a *permanent* increase in holdings of these assets. Of course, an individual may draw down his cash holdings, for example, when he gets older and his income falls. His case might still be covered by our assumptions, as his negative savings could be attributed to the fall in his income. However, savings are a function of age as well as income, and we neglect the former. It is not clear that this biases our results in any way. Individual income receivers age, but income receivers as a whole may not. We arbitrarily guess that one third of cash and deposits saved consist of cash, for which the accounting ratio is zero. For deposits, taking the typical savings bank interest rate of i per unit per annum and assuming that the banks are, in effect, within the public sector, the social cost is

[1] All the same, one might expect there to be some net investment in livestock, despite the figures in Table 8.2. The latter reflect the procedure adopted in the Survey of regarding half of livestock sales as capital and half as current account transactions. The increase in value of livestock on the farm appears to have been omitted.

[2] By taking the accounting ratio for the assets on which the savings are spent, we implicitly assume that all the future net benefits flowing from these investments accrue to the saver, and to no one else, and that he equates their net present value to him with the cost of the assets to him. We assume, for example, that direct tax payments on future extra income are negligible.

the net present social value of future interest payments. Assuming that all interest received is consumed and that tax paid is negligible, we have

$$\text{NPSV of interest payments per unit saved} \doteq \frac{i \cdot f_c}{R + p}$$

and we put $i = 0.03$, f_c = rural consumption accounting ratio 0.92, R = ARI of 0.1 and p = rate of increase of consumer prices of 0.03 per unit per annum. With these values, the accounting ratio for deposits works out at 0.21.

8.3 MARGINAL PROPENSITY TO SAVE OF HOUSEHOLDS

We have, for simplicity's sake and because we have little data to go on, assumed that the marginal propensities to save of *all* African households, rural and urban, are equal to 10 per cent. The only relevant information the writer is aware of is that given in the Central Province Survey (pp. 39, 44) and the Mathare Valley Survey (p. 40). It must be recognized that the accuracy of such information is open to question. It is notoriously difficult to get accurate data on savings.

Linear equations of the form

$$S = a + b\,Y$$

fitted to this data give the following results:

Central Province Survey Data
(a) $S = -299 + 0.198\,Y$ $(R^2 = 0.96)$
(b) $S = -198 + 0.143\,Y$ $(R^2 = 0.87)$

Mathare Valley Survey Data
(a) $S = -22.2 + 0.156\,Y$ $(R^2 = 0.92)$
(b) $S = -\ 7.2 + 0.094\,Y$ $(R^2 = 0.81)$

In each case, (a) is fitted to all the observations, while (b) omits the last observation relating to the highest income group. The

(b) equations are preferable, despite their lower R^2, since the last observation is unreliable (especially for the Mathare Valley Survey) and tends to dominate the regression.

Our estimate of 10 per cent for the marginal propensity to save is approximately the same as that given by equation (b) for the Mathare Valley. The Central Province data do not in fact relate to saving at all, but to cash (or bank deposit) surpluses or deficits, and the marginal propensity to invest in these could be higher or lower than the marginal propensity to save. There is some reason to expect that cross-section data exaggerate the marginal propensity to save which we are looking for, since lower income families, for example, may include many whose incomes are depressed by temporary factors and who therefore dissave more than they would if they expected their current incomes to be longer lasting. Likewise, higher income families may include those who are temporarily rich and who save more than would be normal for that income level. This is a further reason for selecting an estimate which lies at the lower end of the range of those available, as we have done.

8.4 A COMPARISON OF CONSUMER PRICES IN RURAL AND URBAN AREAS IN 1967-8

8.4.1 *Summary*

In this section we estimate the extent to which prices of consumer goods and services in urban areas on average exceeded those in rural areas in Kenya in, or around, 1967-8. We need this estimate in order to compare *real* wages in the countryside with those in the town. Our estimates of urban prices relate to Nairobi, and this probably exaggerates the difference, particularly for house rents which are an important item. Apart from this, all the estimates are rather uncertain because, for example, of unknown quality differences, and there is the usual index-number problem involved in making any such comparison. Thus with weights derived from the rural pattern of expenditure we estimate that urban prices are 1.80 times rural prices on average. With weights derived from the urban pattern of expenditure, however, we estimate that urban prices are only 1.60 times rural prices on average. The difference is due to the tendency of consumers to buy relatively less of those goods whose prices are relatively high. There is no uniquely correct average price index, but we may take the geometric average of the two mentioned, which is approximately 1.7. This is a very large rural/urban price differential. Apart from the fact that it relates to Nairobi prices, rather than to all urban prices, we know of no reason to suspect that it is biased upwards. Since prices in Mombasa are probably about as high as in Nairobi, and since Nairobi and Mombasa together account for about three-quarters of the urban adult population, the upward bias on this account is unlikely to be very great, and so we finally take a figure which is only a little lower, namely, 1.6, for our average.

8.4.2 *The ratio of urban to rural prices for certain foodstuffs and charcoal*

The basic data for foodstuffs and charcoal were obtained as follows. Nairobi retail prices in 1963, as given in the Statistical Abstract, were compared with 'current farm sales prices' obtained from the Central Province Survey, pp. 22, 23, by dividing values by quantities of output. Comparisons were also made of Nairobi retail prices in 1967 with prices received by settlement farmers in 1967-8, using the same sources as for our estimates of accounting ratios. Using this data, we estimated 'typical' ratios for the various items, and, after adjustment to rural retail prices as explained in 8.4.4, they are shown in col. (4) of Table 8.3.

8.4.3 *Rural and urban rents for dwellings of low-income families*

According to the Economic Survey 1971, p. 2, ownership of dwellings outside the monetary economy contributed £9.58 million to the Gross Domestic Product at factor cost in 1969, and that inside the monetary economy £16.25 million. If we can take the former as the imputed rent on houses in the rural sector, and the latter on houses in the urban sector, then, dividing by the 1,460 thousand rural households in the one case, and by the 256 thousand urban households in the other,[1]

[1] Based on the Census of Population in 1969, and excluding an estimated 220 thousand households of pastoralists from the rural total of 1,680 thousand households.

we arrive at estimates of average annual rents per household of £6.6 in rural areas and £63.5 in urban areas. These, however, are averages, and what we really need are rents applicable to low-income families in rural and urban areas. The Mathare Valley Survey (pp. 40, 64) estimates an average rent per room[1] in the squatter settlements of 40 shillings per month in 1969. If we assume that the ratio of rural/urban average rents is the same as that of rents for low-income families, then the rent of a rural dwelling for a low-income family would be (6.6/63.5) x 40 = 4.2 shillings per month. A low-cost hut in a rural area probably costs 60 to 200 shillings to construct (imputing a cost to family labour and to land) depending on whether it has a thatched roof or a corrugated iron roof. The lower end of this range is more representative of low-income family housing, given that four-fifths of rural houses in the Central Province had thatched roofs in 1963-4.[2] Such houses may have short lives or need, relatively speaking, a high annual expenditure on repair and maintenance.[3] Even allowing for this, a rent of much more than 4 shillings a month would be hard to justify for a hut costing, say, 80 shillings, in a rural area where land is cheap. On the other hand, a rent much below 4 shillings a month would not accord with our own enquiries. Consequently, we estimate the typical rent for a low-income rural family at 4 shillings per month, and for an urban family at 40 shillings per month. In both cases the accommodation provided is more or less the minimum tolerable, and no adjustment for quality differences seems called for.

8.4.4 *Adjustment to rural retail prices and calculation of a weighted average*

The price comparisons in 8.4.2 are not quite what we need,

1 Typically, each room was occupied by a household, although they averaged only about 10 ft. by 10 ft. However, the average size of households was only 3.5, which is much smaller than for rural households in the Central Province Survey (i.e. 5.5) or than rural households in the 1969 Census of Population (i.e. 5.9) and appreciably smaller than the average urban household in the 1969 Census of Population (4.2).

2 Central Province Survey, p. 17.

3 Ibid., p. 58, gives estimates of average expenditure per household on housing, which covers, in the main, expenditure on maintenance and repair. The figures are 6, 26 and 39 shillings per year for the three lowest income groups. These must exclude the cost of family labour.

since they refer to prices received by farmers and not to prices paid by rural consumers. For a farmer consuming his own produce, the prices he receives are indeed as good a measure as we can find of the marginal value of that produce to him. However, a rural worker who is paid a money wage and buys these products in rural markets will have to pay, in addition, the dealer's margin. Of course, many rural workers receive some payments in kind, but it is more convenient to allow for this separately, if necessary. The same is true of farmers' incomes. We discuss these separate allowances elsewhere (see especially 5.4.1). Since the relative importance of own-produced output varies, as does the importance of payments in kind, the most convenient and simple procedure is to adjust all rural incomes to a rural retail equivalent, and then to compare that with urban incomes by using an appropriate price index. It follows that we must adjust prices to rural retail levels before comparing them with urban prices.

The adjustments (described in the note to Table 8.3) were made only to products for which subsistence output was important, that is: cereals, pulses, roots and tubers, fruit and vegetables, eggs, milk and milk products, and fuel and light. For all these items the share of subsistence consumption in total consumption averaged about 50 per cent or more in the Central Province Survey, and was frequently much higher (around 90 per cent). For oils and fats, meat and fish, sugar and sugar products, and other foods, the share of subsistence was much smaller (often zero), and we made no adjustment.

In constructing a weighted average, two further steps were required. First we derived weights from sample surveys of rural and urban expenditure, and second, we filled in the gaps for those goods and services for which we had no direct information on relative rural and urban prices. The results in each case are set out in Table 8.3.

Column (4) of Table 8.3 gives the price ratios finally adopted. For any group for which we had an estimate of the price ratio for a major component (e.g. maize for the cereals group) we used that component, after adjustment to rural retail, as opposed to farm gate, prices. This only approximates the result which would be obtained if information were available on all the items involved, but it is as good as we can do with the

Table 8.3

Calculation of a weighted average of urban/rural price ratios

Item	Weight in rural expenditure	Weight in urban expenditure	Urban/rural price ratio
(1)	(2)	(3)	(4)
Cereals	15.0	13.6	2.25
Pulses	9.7	1.9	1.21
Roots and tubers	10.4	2.0	1.78
Fruits and vegetables	6.1	4.6	2.18
Oils and fats	2.0	3.0	1.00
Meat and fish	3.5	10.9	1.34
Eggs	1.4	0.7	1.75
Milk and milk products	7.2	7.3	2.40
Sugar and sugar products	4.2	4.2	1.05
Other food	1.1	3.1	1.00
Tobacco and beverages	3.8	4.3	1.00
Fuel and light	17.0	4.5	1.23
Other non-durables	1.5	1.9	1.00
Clothing	5.6	5.6	1.00
Durables	2.2	2.6	1.00
Housing	3.0	19.9	10.00
Services	6.3	9.9	1.00
Total	100.0	100.0	(a) 1.80 (b) 1.60 (c) 1.69

(a) = Weighted average using col. (2) weights = $\Sigma(p_u q_r) \div \Sigma(p_r q_r)$

(b) = Weighted average using col. (3) weights = $\Sigma(p_u q_u) \div \Sigma(p_r q_u)$

(c) = Geometric average of (a) and (b).

Sources: Col. (2) derived from the expenditure pattern of households with less than 1,000 shillings a year gross income in the Central Province Survey, using data given there on pp. 48, 50, 58 and 60, but with three adjustments (a) subsistence consumption multiplied by 1.3 to adjust to rural retail price equivalent; (b) all consumption multiplied by 1.98, this being the factor used to adjust rural incomes in the Central Province Survey to get the estimated 1969 average for all rural Kenya (see p. 69), and (c) a figure of 48 shillings p.a. was used for housing for the reasons given in 8.4.3. *(continued overleaf)*

Col. (3) weights used in the lower income index of consumer prices in Nairobi as given in 'New Lower and Middle Income Cost of Living Indices, 1971', Statistics Division, Ministry of Finance and Economic Planning, January 1972. These are based on a family expenditure survey of employees earning up to 400 shillings per month, undertaken in 1969. The weight for 'bought meals' was split half for 'other food' and half for 'services', and the latter also included hospital and maternity charges, recreation and entertainment, transport and school fees.

Col. (4) is based as far as possible on the figures mentioned in 8.4.2 but with adjustment of farm prices to rural retail prices by adding 20 per cent to the price of maize at the farm gate and 38 per cent to all other farm gate prices. The maize mark-up is from Alvis and Temu, March 1968, p. 101. The other mark-up is the average for food, drink and tobacco retailers covered in the 1967 Survey of Non-Agricultural Enterprises in the Rural Areas (Statistical Abstract 1969, p. 107). Apart from the above items and housing (for which see text), it was assumed that there was no difference between rural and urban prices. This is obviously incorrect for particular items, but errors on opposite sides may cancel out.

data available. Indeed, it is not evident what the best procedure to follow is when, for example, baker's bread is an important item in the towns but is hardly eaten at all in the countryside. It may be more useful to try to measure the relative prices of satisfying particular wants rather than to try to measure the relative prices of two very different and precisely defined baskets of goods.[1] Where no direct price comparisons could be made, we assumed that urban and rural prices were the same. For some imported manufactured goods, rural prices may well be higher, and indeed some goods of this kind may only be available in towns so that the rural consumer has to buy at the same price level as the urban consumer and, in addition, has to bear the extra cost of transport to the countryside (which may be zero, however, if he makes the journey in any case). Against this, some of the goods and services we have not covered probably are cheaper in the countryside. Hopefully, errors on opposite sides cancel out, more or less.

[1] For a good discussion of this point, see Dan Usher, 1968, Chapter 3.

CHAPTER 9

Miscellaneous

9.1 SKILLED LABOUR, P 3

In this section we first explain what we mean by skilled, as opposed to unskilled, labour, and how the total wage and salary bill for each activity was divided between payments to skilled and to unskilled labour. We then consider the various sources from which skilled labour may be obtained, and attempt to estimate its accounting cost. The biggest gap in our estimates is the cost of producing more skilled labour by training and education, but, even apart from this, our estimates are very rough. According to our definition of skilled labour, it is a more important input into many activities than is unskilled labour (probably twice as important in manufacturing, for example). Better estimates of its accounting cost would thus be very desirable, but, as we show below, there are formidable difficulties in producing accurate estimates.

By skilled labour we mean labour which is relatively well paid. It may be more or less fully employed, in which case its income in different jobs will be more or less the same so that, if it moves from one job to another, it will not gain very much. Alternatively, even if it is not fully employed, so that hiring some of it to work on a project does increase its income appreciably, that increase will have a very small social value because it accrues to people who are relatively well off. However, we attach importance to the first criterion (i.e. full employment), and have tried to draw the dividing line between skilled and unskilled labour accordingly.

We made the division between the two types of labour for each industry in the following way. From East African Statistical Department, *Reported Employment and Earnings in*

Kenya in 1959, June 1960, we calculated the proportion of the total wage and salary bill in the relevant industry paid to African employees in 1959 (the remainder going to Europeans and Asians). We assumed that the same proportion of the wage and salary bill in 1967-9 accrued to unskilled workers, and the rest to skilled workers.

This is a very uncertain estimate. Many things have changed since 1959. From the Statistical Abstract 1969 it can be calculated that, for private industry and commerce as a whole, the proportion of the wage and salary bill paid to Africans was 34 per cent in 1959 and 51 per cent in 1967. It seems probable that 51 per cent is an overstatement of the proportion going to unskilled labour in 1967, since a fair proportion of the African labour in that year was not in surplus supply, while very little of the European or Asian would have been. On the other hand, the figure of 34 per cent for 1959, regarded as an estimate of the proportion going to unskilled labour in 1967, could be on the low side. A rough calculation based on the frequency distribution of earnings of African males in regular employment in private industry and commerce in 1967 (Statistical Abstract 1969, p. 171) suggests that the cut-off point of 34 per cent would come at a wage of about £200-250 per annum. The legal minimum wage in Nairobi in 1967 was £105 per annum (op cit., p. 172), so our cut-off wage is about double the legal minimum, and would put about 75 per cent of African male employees in private industry and commerce into the unskilled category. As we had no clear reason to believe that this cut-off point was too low or too high, and as the only detailed industry figures we had related to the 1959 Report mentioned above, we decided to leave the estimates as they stood.

It is worth noting that the 1959 Employment and Earnings Survey puts the wage bill accruing to Europeans and Asians in private manufacturing industry and repairs at nearly double that accruing to Africans. Phelps and Wasow (undated) also estimate that wages in manufacturing paid to skilled workers are double those going to unskilled. Their estimate refers to 1969 and treats all workers earning more than 500 shillings per month (£300 p.a.) as skilled.

Some idea of the sources from which skilled labour may be drawn is given by the Employment and Earnings Surveys, which show earnings of Europeans and Asians in different employments. The largest sectors are public service, commerce, manufacturing, other services and agriculture. Two other sources which must be important are expatriates and education and training.

If skilled labour is more or less fully employed, it can be induced to work on a particular project by bidding it away from other employments. To estimate its shadow cost, using the method described in 4.3, we then need to know its shadow cost in each of these other employments, and the proportions in which it is drawn from each. The latter may be regarded as being directly proportional to existing employment multiplied by the elasticity of demand for skilled labour in the relevant sector (see 4.7.1). If, however, the supply of skilled labour coming from expatriates, or from education and training, is very elastic, marginal increases in the demand for it will be satisfied from these sources and there will be little need to bid up its wages to draw it away from other employments.

To estimate the shadow cost of skilled labour drawn from any existing employment we can again, in principle, use the method described in 4.3. We need to know the value of its marginal product at accounting prices, and we have to estimate the net social benefit or cost resulting from the transfer of incomes which occurs when its wages are bid up. Unfortunately, we are not in a position to estimate the value of its marginal product at accounting prices except in two sectors: agriculture and manufacturing industry. For the important commerce and services sectors we can only make a very crude guess, and for the public sector we cannot do even that. As already mentioned, we have no estimate of the marginal social cost of 'producing' skilled labour through education and training. We do, however, give a rough estimate of the marginal cost of expatriate skilled labour. To these various estimates of accounting ratios we now turn.

Let us first of all assume that the private employer (not necessarily the public sector employer) equates the cost to him of skilled labour with the value of its marginal product to him, and let us assume that he regards the supply of such labour to him as being more or less perfectly elastic. Even so, if he is selling in an imperfect market with marginal revenue typically below price, the value of skilled labour's marginal product to him will be less than the value of its physical marginal product times the price of that product. This consideration may not be very important, however, in large-scale agriculture (where most output is sold to marketing boards, or directly exported), and may not even apply to a fair proportion of manufacturing where the main competition is with imported substitutes, although where protection is given by quota the Kenyan manufacturer *is* likely to be a monopolist or oligopolist. Where this consideration does not apply, we might estimate the accounting value of skilled labour's marginal product by multiplying its wage by the accounting ratio of the output of the relevant industry. Where it does apply, the estimate should be higher than this.

There are, however, other possibilities which should be considered. The marginal product of skilled labour may simply be the output of the relevant industry, but it may equally be the saving of other inputs into that industry. Skilled labour may substitute for unskilled labour, for capital, or for materials or purchased services. Furthermore, some of these inputs could be complementary to, rather than substitutes for, skilled labour. In other words, if more skilled labour is employed to produce more output it might require, say, more capital and less unskilled labour. Hence the possible complications in estimating the accounting value of skilled labour's marginal product are rather formidable!

Turning now to specific cases, we may note that Phelps and Wasow (undated) have estimated the average degree of nominal protection received by manufacturing industry in Kenya in 1968[1] at 18 per cent, and the average effective rate of protection at 34 per cent.[2] If employing more skilled labour directly increases gross output, so that the value of its marginal physical product times its price equals the wage, we could

[1] That is the date of the survey of industry they used to derive input-output coefficients. However, they do not state what period or periods their price and tariff data refer to. They may well be more recent.

[2] This is the '*U*' measure of effective protection, i.e.

$1 - \dfrac{\Sigma WVA}{\Sigma DVA}$, where WVA = value-added at world prices and DVA = value-added at domestic prices.

estimate the accounting value of its marginal product at 0.85 times its wage.[1] If, on the other hand, employing more skilled labour directly increases value-added, we could estimate the accounting value of its marginal product at 0.66 times its wage.[2] Since the accounting ratios for unskilled labour and for typical capital goods (machinery—not buildings or vehicles) are respectively 0.7 and 0.95, these give the corresponding ratio for skilled labour which substitutes for either. However, one could estimate a much lower accounting ratio by assuming, for example, that skilled labour combines with machinery to replace unskilled labour. All ratios should be raised somewhat to allow for the probability that employers pay skilled labour less than the value of its marginal physical product times its price. At a guess, the average accounting ratio for skilled labour's marginal product in manufacturing is around 0.7 to 0.8.

For agriculture, the typical accounting ratios for most outputs produced by large farms, with the exception of coffee and wheat, are around one or even greater. Coffee may be regarded as irrelevant, since output is restricted by quota. The accounting ratios applicable to most large-farm inputs are close to one, though less than it. Fertilizers and feeding stuffs are the main exception with accounting ratios above one (see Table 10.1). It seems reasonable to put the accounting ratio for skilled labour's marginal product in agriculture at close to one.

For commerce and services it is hard to give any estimates. The frequency distribution of accounting ratios for all goods and services we have estimated given in Figure 1.2 suggests that a typical ratio in Kenya is 0.8, and this may serve as the best we can do.

Finally, we may consider the marginal social cost of expatriate labour. It seems likely that most expatriates earn sufficient income to make them liable for income tax.[3] The most recent report of the East African Income Tax

[1] I.e. 1/1.18 = 0.85.

[2] I.e. 1-0.34 = 0.66.

[3] The married allowance in 1967 (and also up to 1972 at least) was £480 p.a., and there was a child allowance of £120 per child up to four. The single allowance was £216 p.a.

Department.[1] shows that the average resident employee in 1969 assessed for tax earned an income of £2,644 on which he paid tax of £526, i.e. an average rate of 20 per cent. If we assume that this represents the situation for the average expatriate,[2] and if we further assume that he (or she) remits on average 20 per cent of his gross income (25 per cent of the net), then the accounting cost may be put at about two-thirds of the gross income.[3]

It thus seems likely that the accounting ratio for skilled expatriate labour is rather less than that for skilled labour drawn from employment. At a guess, the accounting ratio for skilled labour 'produced' by education and training is probably also lower—at least if social rates of return to such education and training are more than the accounting rate of interest, as we guess they are. Consequently, if we were to ignore the cost of any transfer of income resulting from the bidding up of skilled wages, we could put the accounting ratio for skilled labour at less than, say, 0.8. It is true that the cost of labour drawn from agriculture is almost certainly higher than this, but the data in the Employment and Earnings Surveys suggest that only a small proportion of such labour would come from this source.

What about the social cost of the transfer? It is very likely that there *is* a cost. It is likely to be highest in so far as wages in the public sector are bid up, for then the transfer is from the Government to the skilled labour, and the accounting cost of each (urban) pound so transferred is around £0.6.[4] If the

[1] East African Community (1970/71), Schedule 2.

[2] The report, loc. cit., states that 19,000 resident employees were assessed for tax in 1969. In that year there were some 14,000 European non-citizens enumerated in the Earnings and Employment Inquiry, which leaves a surprisingly small number of non-Europeans for assessment. Possibly some expatriates were not assessed.

[3] We apply the urban consumption accounting ratio for that part of income spent in Kenya, although it relates to low-income consumers. At a guess, the ratio for high-income consumers would be rather smaller, but perhaps not very much. Against this, expatriates cost something to hire and may get tax-free gratuities. We thus get $0.2 \times 0 + 0.2 \times 1 + 0.6 \times 0.82 = 0.69$.

[4] If the average marginal rate of direct tax on all skilled labour is put at 20 per cent (this is the marginal rate from 1 Jan. 1972 for those with chargeable income from £601 to £1,200 p.a.), and if 10 per cent of marginal incomes are saved, the resource cost of marginal increases in income is $0.2 \times 0 + 0.1 \times 0.4 + 0.7 \times 0.82 \triangleq 0.6$. We allow nothing for the social value of the benefit to the recipient.

transfer is from companies, the accounting cost falls to £0.4,[1] while if it is from consumers, there might be a small benefit.[2] It is difficult to know how much to allow for this, since it depends on the extent to which skilled wages are bid up and on the relative elasticities of demand in the various sectors. On the whole, we think *some* allowance should be made, though not very much, and by way of conclusion arrive at an estimate of 0.8 for the accounting ratio for skilled labour.

9.2 EXTRA INCOME ACCRUING TO SMALL FARMERS, P 7

In this section we estimate the accounting ratio of extra income accruing to small farmers. The need for this ratio arises because of Kenya's system of marketing boards. These finance themselves by various levies on the produce they handle, and some of them, in effect, tax domestic consumers in order to subsidize exports (e.g. the Kenya Dairy Board has taxed liquid milk sales in order to subsidize exports of butter). The result is that an increase in domestic demand for, say, milk, can lead to substantial gains to milk producers as well as to milk consumers. In the first place, overheads of the Kenya Dairy Board and Kenya Co-operative Creameries are spread over a larger volume of sales. In addition, exports of butter, for example, may be reduced. Hence the average price paid to producers can be increased and/or the average price charged to consumers reduced. For lack of a better assumption, we have generally estimated that half of the benefit accrues to urban consumers and half to producers.[3] The latter benefit has in turn been subdivided into benefits accruing to large and small farmers in proportion to their estimated values of sales to the marketing board concerned. This is why our estimates of direct and

1 Against the cost of £0.6 estimated above, we set off the saving of £1 no longer accruing to 'capitalists', for which the accounting cost (P 4) is £0.2.

2 The saving at accounting prices of £1 (urban) transferred from urban consumers is £0.7 (i.e. P 5), so that the net cost of the transfer is

$-0.7 + 0.6 = -0.1$, i.e. a small net benefit.

3 We have ignored the effects of changes in prices on patterns of consumption and output, assuming that their *net* social cost or benefit is very small.

indirect inputs into butter, coffee, milk (regarding it as a substitute for exported butter), wheat flour, tea, and pyrethrum in Table 10.2 all show substantial 'inputs' of items P 4 (extra income accruing to 'capitalists', or large farmers in this context), P 5 (extra income accruing to urban consumers), or P 7. A similar 'input' is allowed for in settlement co-operatives' overheads (N 23), since the distributive margin charged by the co-operatives for handling settlers' milk, maize, pyrethrum, etc., generally includes a substantial contribution towards overheads, and it is assumed in this case that extra sales lead to benefits all of which accrue to the members of the co-operative.

The accounting ratio applicable to such payments to small farmers can be estimated as follows. We first assume that it leads to extra consumption and savings in the same proportions, and of the same accounting cost, as in our estimate for income gains accruing to poor rural families (i.e. f_{cr}). From this resource cost we must subtract the social value of the benefit. It is likely that individual farmers will gain in proportion to their incomes, so that we need an average which is weighted by income. From Table 3.2, the average weight, assuming $e = 1$, is 0.414 for all rural incomes excluding large farmers and pastoralists, and we take this estimate. Again, this weight must be multiplied by f_{cr} to get its social value in terms of the numeraire. Hence, finally, the accounting cost of £1 paid to small farmers is

$$f_{cr}\,(1-0.414) = 0.87 \times 0.586 = 0.51$$

which we round to 0.5.

9.3 EXTRA INCOME ACCRUING TO URBAN CONSUMERS, P 5

In this section we estimate the accounting ratio of extra income accruing to urban consumers. The need for this ratio arises, in the first place, for the same reasons as for the ratio applicable to extra income accruing to small farmers, P 7 (see 9.2). Second, and less importantly, we have estimated that extra income accrues to urban consumers because of price changes resulting from the existence of economies of scale in manufacturing industries which produce non-traded outputs (e.g. baking, soft drinks, beer and tobacco, milling, furniture, printing and publishing, tea-packing and coffee-roasting). These are discussed in 9.5.

The gains made by consumers are the result of lower prices for the goods and services they consume. They therefore do not lead to any extra direct tax payments, but we may assume that they do lead to extra savings and extra consumption. Making our usual assumption that 10 per cent of extra incomes are saved (see 8.3) and applying the accounting ratios set out in Table 1.2, the resource cost of consumers' gains per £ is

$$0.1 \times 0.4 + 0.9 \times 0.82 = 0.78.$$

From this we should subtract the social value of the benefit they get. It is reasonable to expect that consumers gain in proportion to their incomes. We estimate that the average weight given to gains accruing to urban consumers, using income weights, is 0.134 per *rural* pound of gain.[1] This must be divided by 1.6 to get the gain per urban pound, and multiplied by f_{cr} to express it in terms of the numeraire. It then becomes 0.07. If this is subtracted from the resource cost it leaves a net social cost of 0.71, which we round to 0.7.

9.4 RENT OF URBAN HOUSES

We confine our attention to rents paid by unskilled urban workers when more of them are employed. We need to estimate the accounting value of these rents as part of the accounting cost of extra consumption resulting from the employment of unskilled urban labour.

What happens when the demand for urban housing by unskilled workers increases? According to the Development

[1] The gain probably accrues roughly in proportion to incomes, so the average weight given to it, as far as *African* households are concerned, is 0.268 with $e = 1$ (see Table 3.3). We assume that the weight given to non-African households (including expatriates and tourists) is negligible, and that they account for about one-half of urban consumers' expenditure. Hence our average weight is one-half of 0.268 = 0.134.

Plan 1970-74, there has been very little extra public sector housing provided for such workers.[1] Nor has the private sector (as defined in the Plan) filled the gap.[2]

> The shortfall of up to 7,500 urban dwelling units a year has been met by individual families themselves, who have squatted on public and private land and built whatever poor form of shelter was within their means, usually fashioned of mud, wattle, cardboard and tin. Where even this was not possible, they have doubled up or tripled up with other families . . . a partial survey in 1962 showed that in Nairobi some 100,000 persons were living in only 28,387 rooms, and two households out of every three had an occupancy ratio of four or more persons per room. Overcrowding is now even more severe, causing serious health hazards and discomforts. Not only is this unfortunate for those involved, but it creates social problems which affect the social and economic environment of the entire urban population. There is an imperative need to accelerate the creation of inexpensive urban housing for the low income groups, to provide them with shelter of an acceptable standard at a monthly cost within their means. The Government's basic housing policies and programmes are directed to that objective.[3]

In what follows we do not attempt to evaluate the impact of any new Government policies, but merely try to estimate the accounting cost of expenditures on rent on the assumption that extra house room is provided in the way described in the above quotation. This at least describes the situation as it was until recently. Gordon Hughes is, at the time of writing, engaged on a study of the accounting costs of different ways of meeting the demand for low-cost housing, and the estimates given here will need revision in the light of his work. Because of this, and

[1] Op. cit., p. 506. The demand for urban housing is said to have been rising from 7,000 to 10,000 dwelling units a year, with public sector housing averaging 1,900 a year, mostly for those in the middle income range, although 70 per cent of the demand was by the lowest income groups.

[2] 'Private sector activity has catered almost entirely to the higher income market', op. cit., p. 506.

[3] Op. cit., p. 507.

because of our lack of information, we do not claim much for the following estimates.

The marginal supply of low-cost housing, as the above suggests, has been provided in squatter villages such as those surveyed in the Mathare Valley survey. The rents paid have been extraordinarily high. In 1969 the average rent for a single room (typically 130 sq. ft.) was 40 shillings per month, with 3.5 persons per room. These were in 'self-built' houses. Private companies also built rather more substantial houses in the Mathare Valley, and in 1970 the average rent per room for these was 70 shillings per month for a room of 120 sq. ft. with 4.4 persons per room. These rents represented much more than a normal return on the cost of construction of a house. For a rather better than average 'self-built' house, with a corrugated iron roof, the cost of construction was about 250 shillings per room. For a company house, the cost was around 1,000 shillings per room. Hence the cost in the first case was about 6 months' rent, and in the second about 14 months' rent. It is clear that the rents mainly reflected a scarcity premium. The scarcity, in turn, was due to the lack of land for housing near the city centre. The land in the Mathare Valley is said to have risen in price from 3,000 shillings per acre in January 1968 to 30,000 shillings per acre in January 1971. The land shortage does not appear to have been due to a physical shortage, but rather to a failure to organize land use around Nairobi so as to provide more suitable sites for dwellings.[1]

In this situation, a marginal increase in the demand for low-cost urban housing has the following effects.

(a) It leads to a rise in rents which tends to reduce demand by others. This reduction in demand may mean increased crowding together in existing accommodation or moving out further from the city centre (or not moving in). In either case, less is spent on accommodation near the city centre and more on other things—presumably consumption goods in general and urban transport in particular.

(b) It leads to more houses being built in places like the Mathare Valley. This involves a construction cost, which

[1] Mathare Valley Report, p. 79.

is, however, as we saw above, only a small part of the marginal cost of providing these houses if we assume that the price charged for accommodation is anywhere near its marginal cost. Thus, to take the 'self-built' houses, if we assume a life of only two years and an interest charge of 10 per cent, a rent of 12 shillings a month for a room costing 250 shillings would be appropriate, which compares with an average rent of 40 shillings. For company houses, if we assume a life of 5 years and an interest charge of 10 per cent, a rent of 22 shillings a month for a room costing 1,000 shillings would be appropriate, which compares with an average rent of 70 shillings. Hence only about a third of the marginal cost can be accounted for by the cost of the building. What does the other two-thirds of the marginal cost consist of? It does not seem plausible that the difference between rent and construction cost is mainly due to monopoly profit, since there are very many individual landlords, as well as several companies. It seems more plausible that the difference is due, on the one hand, to a loss of amenity by existing residents as more houses and people are packed into a limited area, and, on the other, to the need to pay high rates of profit to get a rapid increase in the stock of houses and also, perhaps, to compensate for the risk that they will be destroyed by the local authorities (though this may be already adequately covered in the short lives assumed in the calculations above).

(c) It leads to a transfer of income from tenants to landlords.

We can express the above considerations in a formula which is analogous to that used for non-traded agricultural goods, and can, in fact, be derived from it quite simply. The formula is:

$$A_h = \frac{A_d \cdot e_d + A_s \cdot e_s - \frac{H_t}{H} (W_l - W_t)}{e_d + e_s},$$

where A_h = accounting ratio for low-cost urban housing rents.

A_d = accounting ratio for expenditures to which consumers switch when urban rents rise (i.e. (*a*), above).

A_s = accounting ratio for marginal cost of extra housing (i.e. (*b*), above).

W_l = weight given to income gains accruing to landlords.

W_t = weight given to income gains accruing to tenants.

H_t = housing stock occupied by tenants.

H = total housing stock.

e_d = compensated price elasticity of demand for housing (defined so as to be positive).

e_s = elasticity of supply of housing.

The formula shows that A_h, the accounting ratio we wish to determine, is a weighted average of the accounting ratios A_d and A_s, together with a term which represents the net social cost resulting from the transfer of incomes when rents go up.

The accounting ratios A_d and A_s are probably rather similar. Thus the main components of A_d are urban consumers' expenditure on goods and services other than rents, and road passenger transport, for which our estimates of accounting ratios are 0.78 and 0.75 respectively. For A_s, we have three elements: construction cost, for which the accounting ratio is about 0.80, higher-than-normal profits, which we could class as a payment for a particular kind of skilled labour in this context, with an accounting ratio of 0.80, and amenity costs. The last is the most difficult to deal with, and may, in fact, have a much lower accounting ratio than the others. There is no obvious resource cost, only a loss of welfare. We might take the accounting ratio for urban consumers' expenditure multiplied by the weight given to income gains accruing to average households in squatter villages, say 0.82 times 0.35 = 0.29. Nevertheless, it seems unlikely that the weighted average of A_d and A_s can differ much from, say, two-thirds.

Unfortunately, we still have to reckon in the social cost of the transfer of incomes when rents go up. We have no estimate of the average incomes of landlords and tenants. It is virtually certain that the former are richer than the latter. There are some grounds for arguing, all the same, that the transfer involves only a small social cost. First, the ratio H_t/H is probably about 0.8.[1] Second, the landlords (especially the companies?) may pay more direct taxation than the tenants. Third, the landlords may save and invest a larger fraction of their incomes, which may lead to employment and increases in tax revenue in the future. All this is, however, very speculative. Furthermore, even a fairly small value for $W_l - W_t$ may make a large difference to A_h if e_d and e_s are small, as they may well be. Finally, in fixing the accounting ratio for rents we ought to make some allowance for externalities of the kind mentioned in the quotation given above from the Development Plan 1970-74. Bad health and crime are partly the consequence of overcrowding, and are therefore part of the social cost of increasing the demand for housing.

In the light of these considerations, and without pretending that our estimate is more than an informed guess, we choose an accounting ratio of one,[2] which is appreciably above the average of A_d and A_s. It should be possible to organize matters so that low cost housing is provided at a much lower social cost than this implies. However, that is for another study.

[1] The Mathare Valley Survey estimates that 60 per cent of heads of households (the Survey, p. 36, talks of the proportion of the *population*, but it seems clear from what follows that it means heads of households) in the squatter villages were tenants, and 90 per cent in company housing (op. cit., p. 63). Company housing probably accounts for rather more than half the total in the Mathare Valley (op. cit., p. 57).

[2] The following calculation may serve for purposes of illustration. Assume that landlords represent the top two income groups (i.e. 23 per cent of households) in the estimates of income distribution for the Mathare Valley made for Table 4.4, while tenants represent the lower ones. The social loss per urban £ transferred from tenants to landlords, making no allowance for tax or saving differences, is then about £0.175, weighting by incomes (in fact, as rents represent a higher proportion of incomes for poorer than richer families, see Mathare Valley Survey, p. 40, the loss is bigger than this. However, the error here is partly or wholly offset by the error involved in neglecting savings and tax of landlords). If the weighted average of A_d and A_s is, say, 0.67, and if external costs for health, crime, etc., are 10 per cent of rent expenditures, say, then we have

$$A_h = 1 = 0.67 + 0.1 + \frac{0.175}{e_d + e_s}$$

whence $e_d + e_s = 0.76$. It is quite possible that the sum of the elasticities is as low as, or even lower than, this.

9.5 ECONOMIES OF SCALE

In general, for non-tradeable manufacturing industries (e.g. milling, baking, brewing) we have assumed that long-run marginal costs are lower than average costs by an amount equal to 10 per cent of value-added. This is equivalent to assuming that, when output expands by x per cent, labour and capital costs together expand by 0.9 x per cent, while materials costs per unit remain constant. Denison assumes in his study of economic growth in various developed countries that there are economies of scale associated with market size which, in effect, increase output per unit of input by about 10 per cent of any increase in input.[1] This is an average for the whole economy, and would be consistent with greater economies of scale in manufacturing industry. The work of Silberston, Pratten and Dean in Cambridge suggests that *potential* economies of scale in British manufacturing industry, expressed as a percentage of value-added as above, may range widely and could perhaps be typified by a figure of 25 per cent.[2] These estimates are based on engineering studies, and may represent a maximum in that potential economies are not always realised for a variety of reasons. On the other hand, the typical figure could well be higher in Kenya, where the market is much smaller.[3] Denison, for example, uses a figure of 10 per cent for the U.S.A., but 11 per cent for the larger North West European Countries, rising to 13 per cent for Norway. It seems likely, therefore, that the assumption of 10 per cent economies of scale for non-tradeable manufacturing industries which is made here is a conservative one. We have allowed for much greater economies of scale in railway transport, often assuming marginal costs are only a half of prices charged (see 9.6). However, in road transport, ports and wholesale and retail distribution we have made no allowance for economies of scale at all, and have simply assumed that long-run marginal costs equal average costs. This, again, errs on the conservative side, although it may be the case

[1] Denison, 1967, pp. 226-35.

[2] See Silberston, 1972, p. 369.

[3] Silberston's figures relate to the range of output between 50 per cent and 100 per cent of minimum efficient scale, and he takes the view that economies may well be more important for smaller scales.

that in distribution, at least, potential economies of scale are not realised because the number of establishments increases as fast as demand.[1]

Although we have allowed for economies of scale in some cases by assuming that marginal cost is less than average cost, we have dealt with the resulting surplus in a very rough and ready manner. We have assumed, in the first place, that the surplus is simply equal to the difference between price and marginal cost. This implies that price does not change, despite the fall in average cost resulting from increased output, or, if price is reduced, that this makes no difference to sales. The error here is likely to be very small as a general rule, although it could be appreciable in particular instances.[2] Second, we have

[1] From 1960 to 1966 the number of establishments covered by the Surveys of Distribution in these years increased by 47 per cent while the value of their sales increased by 51 per cent. Over the same period, retail prices probably increased by over 12 per cent, so the number of establishments increased faster than the *volume* of their sales (see Statistical Abstract, 1969, p. 105). On the other hand, the number of employees fell by 12 per cent, and, although this was partly offset by a rise in the number of self-employed, the total work force fell. Hence the increased volume of sales was handled by fewer people. Wages rose sharply over this period, and it is not possible to draw any firm conclusions about economies of scale in distribution from this evidence. There is evidence for *potential* economies, and economies have been realised in other countries, see for example Hall, Knapp and Winston, 1961, Chapter 7; McClelland, 1966, Chapter 7; and Jefferys and Knee, 1962, Chapter 2.

[2] Let the elasticity of the costs included in value-added (labour and capital) be e with respect to output, so that a 1 per cent increase in output causes these costs to increase by e per cent. The assumption mentioned in the text is that, generally, $e = 0.9$ for non-tradeable manufacturing. Long-run marginal cost is then 10 per cent of value-added less than average cost (average material cost being assumed constant, and so equal to marginal material cost). Let the ratio of value-added costs to total costs be R. Then, we assume that the additional surplus per unit value of extra sales of the non-tradeable is $R\ (1-e)$. For example, if $R = 0.5$, $e = 0.9$, we assume that the additional surplus is 0.05 of the price, since marginal cost is then 0.95 of the price (0.5 for materials plus 0.45 for value-added). This, however, allows nothing for the fact that a consequent fall in price may induce extra sales. If we assume that price always equals average costs, and if the price elasticity of demand for the non-tradeable is d (defined so as to be positive), then it can be shown that, as a first approximation, the surplus per unit value of extra sales to our project, allowing for surplus on induced extra sales elsewhere, is

$$\frac{R\ (1-e)}{1-dR\ (1-e)}.$$

With the values for R and e given above, and putting $d = 1$, for example, the surplus works out at 0.0526 of extra sales instead of 0.05, and this difference is negligible.

to decide who gets this surplus, and our assumption is that half goes to the owners of the non-tradeable activity being considered or to other 'capitalists' (i.e. P 4), while the other half benefits urban consumers (P 5). This is just a guess. If average cost pricing were the rule, all the benefit should eventually accrue to consumers (assuming that materials are in perfectly elastic supply, as we do—otherwise some would accrue to the suppliers or, if materials were also produced under conditions of falling average costs, the total benefit would be larger than we have allowed for). However, it seems likely that in practice some of the benefit will not be passed on, or passed on only with a considerable lag, and so some will accrue to 'capitalists'.

9.6 TRANSPORT

For rail transport we were able to use the East African Transport Study carried out by the Economist Intelligence Unit. This estimated long-run marginal costs of rail transport for certain items, and it appeared from these estimates that there were often wide and variable discrepancies between long-run marginal costs, as defined in that study,[1] and freight charges. Consequently, for a number of items we used these estimates, and this necessitated showing marginal rail transport costs as one input (N 18), and the difference between price and marginal costs as another (N 19). Subsequently, we added more items to our list and, since the Study's estimates were not readily available, we simply assumed for them that marginal costs were half of freight charges, as this appeared to be a fairly typical ratio for the items for which we had estimates. The difference between price and marginal cost for rail transport (item N 19) is assumed to consist of one-third of 'tax' (P 10) and two-thirds of foreign exchange (P 1). This is on the somewhat arbitrary assumption that one-third of any extra profits made by the East African Railways accrues to the Government of Kenya, and two-thirds to the Governments of Tanzania and Uganda.[2]

[1] The writer's impression is that marginal costs did not include such items as the capital cost of the track, but did include engine and wagon costs.

[2] We thus allow nothing for effects on rail freight rates and we take a nationalistic rather than a cosmopolitan point of view.

To estimate rail transport costs we generally used the published schedule of freight rates[1] (East African Railways (1968)) together with estimates of unit values of imports or exports, or wholesale prices. For some (mainly consumer) goods, however, we made use of Dahl (1969), who estimated the share of rail transport costs in the retail value of various groups of consumer goods in Kenya in 1963-5. For maize, we used data given in the Reports of the Maize and Produce Board, and we assumed that freight charges for wheat and beans were similar.

Port handling costs were estimated very crudely. It seemed likely that these costs, expressed as a fraction of the import or export price of a particular product, would depend on the same characteristics of the produce as rail transport costs. Thus for bulky, low value products, both port and rail costs would be high in relation to the import or export value of such products. For high value products, such as machinery, both kinds of costs would be low. For maize, the Reports of the Maize and Produce Board showed that port and rail costs per bag were of the same order of magnitude. We therefore assumed, in the absence of better information, that ports costs equalled rail costs for all commodities.

For road transport, we again used the East African Transport Study. Our estimates for both passenger and goods transport include allowances for wear and tear on the roads, and this accounts for the positive entries for P 10 (tax) in both UCN 16 and N 22 in the direct inputs in Table 10.2. Positive entries here mean a Government subsidy, which is simply the cost of the extra road maintenance needed. Not surprisingly, this positive entry is converted into a negative one when indirect as well as direct inputs are considered. In other words, the taxes levied on the vehicles and fuel (and other items) more than offset the direct subsidy. The final accounting ratios, 0.75 and 0.74 respectively, are remarkably close to the general average.

[1] The rates charged depend on whether the goods are shipped in small quantities or wagon loads. Generally speaking, we took the (lower) wagon load rates, although in some cases, where the quantities moving were small, we took the (higher) small quantity rates.

9.7 WHOLESALE AND RETAIL MARGINS AND STOCKS

Wherever possible, we estimated distributive margins by making direct comparisons of prices at different points (e.g. unit values of petroleum imports with wholesale and retail prices in Nairobi). However, we could only do this for a few goods, as one could not use the published trade statistics in most cases because the commodity analysis was not fine enough. Except for homogeneous goods, such as petroleum, one could not usefully compare unit values from the trade statistics with wholesale or retail prices obtained by direct inquiry. In a few other cases we were able to obtain prices from traders, but, generally speaking, they were (not surprisingly) reluctant to disclose their margins on particular goods.

As a result, we were compelled to rely on average distributive margins derived from the published Surveys of Distribution for 1960 and 1966 (for the former we used the actual Survey, for the latter the summary published in the Statistical Abstract for 1969). For consumer goods we also used the estimates given by Dahl (1969), who, in turn, relied mainly on the Survey of Distribution. From the few cases where we could make comparisons with our direct estimates, we gained the impression that the margins in the Surveys were on the low side. As pointed out in Chapter 1, our general method did not enable us to allow for abnormal profits of distributors holding import quotas. For some urban consumer goods we used the estimates of average retail prices in Nairobi published in the Statistical Abstracts as a check on the wholesale and retail margins derived from other sources. We could do this for bread, butter, coffee, milk, beans, maize flour and grain, wheat flour and paraffin. For maize flour and grain, it seemed clear that the officially controlled margins were not observed—not surprisingly, since they were extraordinarily small. Generally, however, the margins were reasonably consistent with those given in the Surveys of Distribution. Where they differed, we used the margins which could be deduced from the average price data.

For some goods passing through marketing boards (butter, coffee, maize, meat, milk, pyrethrum, tea) we made use of published reports to estimate their distributive margins and/or processing costs. These margins are treated separately as non-traded activities (N). Likewise, the distributive margins of settlement farmers' co-operatives are treated separately.

We made an adjustment to the wholesale and retail margins derived in the way just described to allow for the cost of distributors' stocks. This adjustment is not important, but it was not difficult to make, and so we made it. From the figures available, it appeared that, on average, roughly 10 per cent of distributors' costs (including profits) consisted of interest (at 10 per cent per annum) on stocks. These stocks consisted of the various products being distributed, and hence the social cost of holding them depended on the particular product concerned. This is a case, therefore, where extra consumption of a particular product as an input into a project leads to a *further* input of that product in the form of extra stocks in the hands of distributors. To allow for this, we assumed that for each good for which wholesaling or retailing was an input one-tenth of these inputs consisted of the good itself. We therefore obtained the *net* 'output' of the good by subtracting 10 per cent of the distributive margins from the gross 'output'. To illustrate, we take the case of bottles which is given in Table 1.1. The inputs given there are *after* adjustment for stocks, the adjustment being made in the manner shown in Table 9.1.

Table 9.1

Illustration of the adjustment made for distributors' stocks

Input	Proportion of wholesale price as originally estimated	Adjustment for stocks	Adjusted inputs	Ditto normalised (as in Table 1.1)
	(1)	(2)	(3)	(4)
Imports, c.i.f.	−0.584		−0.584	−0.592
Duty	−0.195		−0.195	−0.198
Port handling	−0.040		−0.040	−0.040
Rail marginal cost	−0.020		−0.020	−0.020
Rail price— marginal cost	−0.020		−0.020	−0.020
Wholesaling	−0.142	+0.014	−0.128	−0.129
Total	1.000	−0.014	0.986	1.000

CHAPTER 10

Data and Results

10.1 DATA

We have referred to many of the sources used in obtaining our data at various places in earlier chapters. A considerable part of the time required for this study was, in fact, spent in assembling data. If the production of good estimates had been our only concern, we should have spent even more time in this way, and there is little doubt that a government planning office could do much better than we have done. Results are no better than the data on which they are based. We are, however, primarily concerned with showing how a method can be applied in practice, and with developing and improving that method. We have therefore spent less time on our data than would otherwise have been desirable, and we have omitted detailed references and explanations of most of our estimates. Nevertheless, a few comments here may be in order.

First, the time required to produce estimates of the kind made here should not be exaggerated. We have been working on Part I of this book for four years, but four man-years grossly exaggerates the time needed as it has been part-time work and, also very important, a pioneer attempt. To illustrate the importance of both points, we visited Mauritius for one month in January 1972 and, after about one more month's work in Oxford, had completed a set of estimates of accounting prices which had a similar coverage to that given here. Mauritius is probably an unusually favourable place to make these estimates. Nevertheless, if one knows what one wants, and can devote all one's time to it, the period required to produce a fairly comprehensive set of estimates should be measured in man-months rather than man-years. A preliminary set of estimates using the short-cuts described in Chapter 1 could probably be produced in a matter of days. These remarks do not apply, however, to countries where import quotas are important, or where it would be appropriate to regard a great many inputs as non-traded.

Second, a complete input-output table for the economy is not required. The writer did not have access to one either for Kenya or Mauritius. For some non-tradeable items (e.g. building and construction) such a table could be useful, but in many cases one needs estimates which are more detailed or in a different form. For example, one needs the freight and distributive margins, and taxes, on imported clothing and textiles, not the cost structure of the domestic textile industry. Or one needs data on maize, say, separately, and not combined with all other agricultural outputs. In some cases, detailed Census of Production data would be more useful than a more aggregated input-output table.

Third, information on taxes is particularly important. A brief description of our main sources is therefore given. For importables, import taxes were obtainable from two main sources. One was the East African Customs and Excise Annual Trade Report for 1967, which shows the duty levied alongside the value of imports for each commodity group distinguished. The other was East African Customs and Excise Tariffs, October 1968, which showed the rates of duty on each item. In almost all cases, both sources gave the same figure, or near enough the same figure allowing for heterogeneity in the trade statistics. Where both specific and *ad valorem* rates applied, we used only the first source to obtain an average *ad valorem* equivalent. We assumed that the marginal source of supply for importables was outside East Africa, and we therefore used the tariff rates applicable to such imports. Goods from Tanzania and Uganda are duty-free (apart from excise). For certain consumer goods produced in Kenya, which we assume are non-tradeable (beer, manufactured tobacco, soft drinks) there are important excise duties. These were estimated from total revenue receipts in 1967 given in the Statistical Abstract for 1969 relative to gross output of the relevant industries in 1967 as given in the same source. For direct taxes, we used the Reports of the East African Income Tax Department.

10.2 THE MAIN TABLES AND THE ESTIMATION OF DIRECT AND INDIRECT PRIMARY INPUTS PER UNIT OF OUTPUT OR EXPENDITURE

Our results are shown in Tables 10.1 and 10.2. Table 10.1 lists our final estimates of accounting ratios for each item. Table 10.2 shows, for most items, two columns of figures. The first gives the direct inputs into the item concerned, the item itself being shown with a positive entry of 1.000. It can be regarded as an output made up of the negative inputs in the column. Where other positive items appear in the column, they are complementary outputs (or savings of inputs, see 1.2.3 for further explanation). The sum of each column is therefore zero (apart from rounding errors).

The second column of figures in Table 10.2 shows the direct and indirect primary inputs into each item. The sum of each column is therefore minus one (apart from rounding errors). Once these inputs are known for many items, it is easy to see how they can be worked out for more. One has merely to take each *direct* input into the item in question and resolve it into its known direct and indirect primary inputs, and then add these up. The procedure to be followed when one starts without this information is to obtain a list of items whose direct inputs consist either of each other or else of primary inputs. In our case, the list involved about 100 items, but it could easily have been made smaller. We then proceed as follows.

The inputs into the 100 (say) items, excluding the primary inputs (P 1-10, which are listed in Table 1.2), are arranged as a square matrix 100 x 100. For any column j of the matrix, the entry in row i shows the value of direct inputs of item i per unit output of item j. Let us call this entry a_{ij} and the whole matrix of entries A. The matrix is normalized so that the entries in all the diagonals are unity, so $a_{ii} = 1$ for all i.

Now we construct another matrix in which the entry in column j, row i shows the value of the direct plus all indirect inputs of item i per unit of item j. Let this entry be $\bar{a}_{ij}$. It can be shown[1] that the required matrix is the inverse of A, which is written A^{-1}. In general, the diagonal elements in this matrix will be close to, but greater than, one.

[1] See for example Allen, 1956, pp. 354-8.

In order to obtain the direct and indirect *primary* inputs per unit output of any item j, we must multiply the direct and indirect inputs of each other item, such as i, into j, by the direct primary inputs into i. We must then add up the totals for each primary input. Thus suppose that we have arranged the ten primary inputs in a matrix with 100 columns and 10 rows, which we will call B, where the entry in column j row p is b_{pj}, then the sum of the direct and indirect inputs of primary input p into j, which we will call $\bar{b}_{pj}$, is given by:

$$\bar{b}_{pj} = \sum_i (b_{pi} \cdot \bar{a}_{ij}) \, .$$

It is to be noted that this sum includes the direct primary inputs into j, as well as the indirect ones, since we sum over all i, including j itself.

The sum of the direct and indirect primary inputs for any item must be minus one, i.e. for any j

$$\sum_p (\bar{b}_{pj}) = -1.$$

This provides a useful check.

The matrix of the $\bar{b}_{pj}$ (which we may call $\bar{B}$) is thus given by post-multiplying the B-matrix by the inverse of the A-Matrix, that is

$$\bar{B} = B \cdot A^{-1} \, .$$

In our case, a computer program was available which, first, normalized the A-matrix, checking that the columns added to zero when added to the columns in the B-matrix, and that the rows added to totals worked out by hand (these checks ensured that the entries had been punched in correctly); second, inverted the A-matrix; and third, post-multiplied the B-matrix by this inverse. The columns of the resulting $\bar{B}$-matrix added up to -1.

Subsequently, we added many other items (most of F 0 and F I) and we also made some revisions in our original estimates. The latter may have resulted in some minor inconsistencies in the figures, as we did not attempt to recompute the original matrix inversion.

Table 10.1

Estimates of accounting ratios for Kenya

Code	Item	Acc. ratio	Code	Item	Acc. ratio
UCF 1	Beans	0.96	RCF 1	Beans (as FO 1)	1.09
2	Beer and tobacco	0.45	2	Maize (as FO 4.1)	1.10
3	Bread	0.77	3	Meat	1.16
4	Butter	0.80	4	Milk (as FO 6 and P 9)	1.00
5	Cocoa	0.85	5	Tobacco and beverages	0.55
6	Coffee	0.79	RCN 1	Rent	0.90
7	Maize flour	0.91	2	Services	0.61
8	Maize grain	0.94	N 1	Baking margin	0.77
9	Meat	1.04	2	Beer and tobacco manufacture	0.71
10	Milk (as substitute for butter)	0.70	3	Building and construction	0.80
11	Miscellaneous food-stuffs	0.82	4	Butter manufacture	0.76
12	Non-traded food-stuffs (incl. milk) P 8	0.85	5	Cinemas and theatres	0.80
13	Salt	0.77	6	Furniture	0.84
14	Soft drinks	0.61	7	Green tea distribution	0.62
15	Spices	0.71	8	Maize distribution	0.87
16	Spirits	0.33	9	Meat processing to CCB	0.81
17	Sugar	0.63	10	Milk distribution	0.69
18	Tea	0.89	11	Milling margin	0.78
19	Wheatflour	0.78	12	Misc. office services	0.76
UCN 1	Building materials	0.84	13	Ports	0.77
2	Charcoal and firewood	0.91	14	Post, telegraph, telephone	0.81
3	Clothing	0.68	15	Printing and publishing	0.80
4	Electricity	0.91	16	Pyrethrum processing	0.76
5	Footwear	0.76	17	Quarrying	0.77
6	Fuel and light	0.88	18	Rail transport: marginal cost	0.90
7	Furniture	0.83	19	Rail transport: p–m.c.	0.67
8	Household utensils	0.77	20	Restaurants	0.70
10	Miscellaneous non-food (excl. rent)	0.80	21	Retail distribution	0.77
11	Newspapers and journals	0.79	22	Road transport (goods)	0.74
12	Paraffin	0.69	23	Settlement Co-op. overheads	0.73
13	Personal care and hygiene	0.83			
14	Petroleum gases	0.81			
15	Rent	1.00			
16	Road transport (passenger)	0.75			

Code	Item	Acc. ratio
24	Soft drinks manufacture	0.76
25	Tea manufacture	0.78
26	Tea packing and coffee roasting	0.81
27	Wholesale distribution	0.78
28	Meat processing, first stage	0.82
T 1	Bags	0.95
2	Bitumen	0.88
3	Bottles	0.75
4	Cement	0.80
5	Construction machinery	0.95
6	Flavouring essences	0.74
7	Fuel oil	0.80
8	Gas/diesel oil	0.45
9	Glass	0.77
10	Hops	0.85
11	Iron and steel	0.90
12	Lorries, etc.	0.79
13	Lubricating oil	0.80
14	Machinery (industrial, etc.)	0.95
15	Machinery (other, e.g. office)	0.77
16	Maize (into mill)	0.98
17	Malt	0.77
18	Metal products	0.90
19	Misc. materials (excl. fuels and foods)	0.82
20	Misc. petroleum fuels	0.56
21	Motor spares	0.76
22	Motor spirit	0.43
23	Non-ferrous base metals	0.97
24	Other construction materials	0.75
25	Paint	0.72
26	Paper and packing materials	0.86
27	Paper for printing	0.84
28	Stationery	0.76
29	Sugar (wholesale)	0.61
30	Textile fabrics for furnishings	0.71
31	Timber	1.01
32	Tobacco (unmanufactured)	0.43
33	Tyres and tubes	0.69
34	Uniforms	0.71
35	Wheat flour (wholesale)	0.78
36	Cars	0.70
FI 1	A.I.	0.79
2	Barbed wire	0.95
3	Dips and sprays	0.90
4	Feed (FO 4.1)	1.10
5	Fertilizers	1.11
5.1	Superphosphates (excl. FI 5.2)	1.28
5.2	Single superphosphate (from Uganda)	1.27
5.3	Sulphate of ammonia	1.01
5.4	Ammonium sulphate nitrate	1.01
6	Machinery service	0.82
7	Milk cans:	
7.1	Milk cans—aluminium	0.95
7.2	Milk cans—steel	0.95
8	Nails	0.86
9	Pangas	0.95
10	Piping—galvanised	0.93
11	Salt—rock salt	0.77
12	Seeds	0.92
13	Tractors and implements	0.95
14	Tractor spares	0.94
FO 1	Beans (as RCF 1)	1.09
2	Dairy cattle—net sales and valuation change	1.30
3	Coffee	0.87
4.1	Maize (after 1967-8—export bulk handling)	1.10
4.2	Maize (1967-8—export)	0.64

Code	Item	Acc. ratio	Code	Item	Acc. ratio
4.3	Maize (1966-7–export)	0.52	6	Non-traded agriculture (incl. potatoes, veg., eggs and poultry, other, and milk) (as P 9)	1.00
4.4	Maize (1965-6–import)	1.15	7.1	Pyrethrum (1967-8)	1.12
4.5	Maize (1964-5–import)	1.50	7.2	Pyrethrum (1966-7)	1.04
4.6	Maize (1963-4–import)	1.87	7.3	Pyrethrum (1965-6)	1.09
4.7	Maize (1962-3–export)	0.58	7.4	Pyrethrum (1964-5)	1.21
5	Milk and butterfat (as substitutes for butter exports)	0.84	7.5	Pyrethrum (1963-4)	1.42
			7.6	Pyrethrum (1962-3)	1.40
			8	Tea	1.34
			9	Wheat	0.84

Table 10.2

Direct inputs (col. (1)) and direct and indirect primary inputs (col. (2)) per unit of output or expenditure

Code No.	(1)	(2)
UCF 1	**Beans**	
UCF 1	1.000	–
N 13	0.062	–
N 18	0.009	–
N 19	-0.039	–
N 21	-0.108	–
N 27	-0.060	–
T 1	0.006	–
P 1	-0.871	-0.902
P 2	–	-0.006
P 3	–	-0.073
P 10	–	-0.019
Total	-0.001	-1.000

Code No.	(1)	(2)
UCF 2	**Beer and tobacco**	
UCF 2	1.000	–
N 2	-0.465	–
N 21	-0.114	–
N 27	-0.047	–
P 1	–	-0.176
P 2	–	-0.119
P 3	–	-0.219
P 4	–	-0.013
P 5	–	-0.012
P 10	-0.374	-0.461
Total	0.000	-1.000

Code No.	(1)	(2)
UCF 3 Bread		
UCF 3	1.000	—
N 1	-0.264	—
N 13	0.024	—
N 18	0.011	—
N 19	0.012	—
N 21	-0.091	—
N 27	-0.034	—
T 1	0.013	—
T 19	-0.032	—
T 20	-0.043	—
P 1	-0.361	-0.472
P 2	—	-0.080
P 3	—	-0.159
P 4	-0.108	-0.118
P 5	-0.118	-0.128
P 7	-0.009	-0.009
P 10	—	-0.034
Total	0.000	-1.000
UCF 4 Butter		
UCF 4	1.000	—
N 13	0.021	—
N 18	0.008	—
N 19	0.005	—
N 21	-0.147	—
P 1	-0.525	-0.537
P 2	—	-0.023
P 3	—	-0.073
P 4	-0.112	-0.112
P 5	-0.181	-0.181
P 7	-0.069	-0.069
P 10	—	-0.005
Total	0.000	-1.000
UCF 5 Cocoa		
UCF 5	1.000	—
N 13	-0.028	—
N 18	-0.014	—
N 19	-0.014	—
N 21	-0.111	—
N 27	-0.061	—
P 1	-0.670	-0.729
P 2	—	-0.051
P 3	—	-0.103
P 10	-0.101	-0.117
Total	0.001	-1.000
UCF 6 Coffee		
UCF 6	1.000	—
N 13	0.008	—
N 18	0.003	—
N 19	0.005	—
N 21	-0.113	—
N 26	-0.275	—
N 27	-0.029	—
P 1	-0.394	-0.542
P 2	—	-0.078
P 3	—	-0.135
P 4	-0.081	-0.091
P 5	—	-0.009
P 7	-0.125	-0.125
P 10	—	-0.019
Total	-0.001	-0.999
UCF 7 Maize flour		
UCF 7	1.000	—
N 11	-0.071	—
N 13	0.035	—
N 18	0.011	—
N 19	0.011	—
N 21	-0.204	—
N 27	-0.050	—
T 1	-0.020	—
P 1	-0.686	-0.749
P 2	—	-0.055
P 3	—	-0.153
P 4	—	-0.003

Code No.	(1)	(2)
P 5	–	-0.003
P 10	-0.026	-0.037
Total	0.000	-1.000

UCF 8 **Maize grain**

UCF 8	1.000	–
N 13	0.041	–
N 18	0.013	–
N 19	0.013	–
N 21	-0.158	–
N 27	-0.049	–
T 1	-0.024	–
P 1	-0.805	-0.836
P 2	–	-0.026
P 3	–	-0.102
P 10	-0.031	-0.036
Total	0.000	-1.000

UCF 9 **Meat**

UCF 9	1.000	–
N 9	0.626	–
N 13	0.006	–
N 18	0.003	–
N 19	0.006	–
N 21	-0.166	–
N 27	-0.018	–
N 28	-0.218	–
P 1	-1.239	-1.087
P 2	–	0.080
P 3	–	-0.009
P 10	–	0.016
Total	0.000	-1.000

UCF 10 **Milk**

Code No.	(1)	(2)
UCF 10	1.000	–
UCN 1	0.002	–
N 4	0.038	–
N 10	-0.420	–
N 13	0.007	–
N 18	0.004	–
N 19	0.004	–
N 21	-0.195	–
N 22	-0.030	–
N 23	0.002	–
P 1	-0.163	-0.315
P 2	–	-0.079
P 3	–	-0.161
P 4	-0.036	-0.086
P 5	-0.057	-0.137
P 6	0.002	0.002
P 7	-0.157	-0.187
P 10	–	-0.036
Total	0.001	-0.999

UCF 11 **Miscellaneous foodstuffs**

UCF 1, 3, 4, 7, 8, 9, 10, 13, 15, 17, 19 each	-0.091	
UCF 11	1.000	–
P 1	–	-0.637
P 2	–	-0.042
P 3	–	-0.114
P 4	–	-0.045
P 5	–	-0.058
P 7	–	-0.025
P 10	–	-0.080
Total	-0.001	-1.001

UCF 13 **Salt**

UCF 13	1.000	–
N 13	-0.133	–
N 18	-0.050	–
N 19	-0.092	–
N 21	-0.183	–
N 27	-0.183	–
P 1	-0.275	-0.476

Code No.	(1)	(2)
P 2	–	-0.141
P 3	–	-0.240
P 4	–	-0.002
P 10	-0.083	-0.141
Total	-0.001	-1.000

UCF 14 Soft drinks

UCF 14	1.000	–
N 21	-0.112	–
N 24	-0.685	–
P 1	–	-0.267
P 2	–	-0.174
P 3	–	-0.229
P 4	–	-0.017
P 5	–	-0.016
P 9	–	-0.021
P 10	-0.202	-0.275
Total	0.001	-0.999

UCF 15 Spices

UCF 15	1.000	–
N 13	-0.022	–
N 18	-0.011	–
N 19	-0.011	–
N 21	-0.113	–
N 27	-0.060	–
P 1	-0.538	-0.591
P 2	–	-0.048
P 3	–	-0.101
P 10	-0.246	-0.260
Total	-0.001	-1.000

UCF 16 Spirits

UCF 16	1.000	–
N 21	-0.113	–
N 27	-0.060	–
P 1	-0.196	-0.230

Code No.	(1)	(2)
P 2	–	-0.036
P 3	–	-0.093
P 10	-0.631	-0.641
Total	0.000	-1.000

UCF 17 Sugar

UCF 17	1.000	–
N 13	-0.075	–
N 18	-0.037	–
N 19	-0.037	–
N 21	-0.112	–
N 27	-0.048	–
P 1	-0.392	-0.490
P 2	–	-0.073
P 3	–	-0.112
P 4	–	-0.001
P 10	-0.298	-0.323
Total	0.001	-0.999

UCF 18 Tea

UCF 18	1.000	–
N 13	0.007	–
N 18	0.002	–
N 19	0.005	–
N 21	-0.112	–
N 26	-0.066	–
P 1	-0.742	-0.787
P 2	–	-0.035
P 3	–	-0.074
P 4	-0.093	-0.096
P 5	–	-0.002
P 10	–	-0.007
Total	0.001	-1.001

Code No.	(1)	(2)
UCF 19	**Wheat flour**	
UCF 19	1.000	–
N 13	0.037	–
N 18	0.018	–
N 19	0.019	–
N 21	-0.103	–
N 27	-0.049	–
T 1	0.020	–
P 1	-0.572	-0.550
P 2	–	-0.011
P 3	–	-0.068
P 4	-0.171	-0.171
P 5	-0.186	-0.187
P 7	-0.015	-0.015
Total	-0.002	-1.002

Code No.	(1)	(2)
UCN 1	**Building materials**	
UCN 1	1.000	–
N 13	-0.009	–
N 18	-0.004	–
N 19	-0.004	–
N 21	-0.141	–
N 27	-0.097	–
P 1	-0.643	-0.697
P 2	–	-0.053
P 3	–	-0.132
P 10	-0.102	-0.117
Total	0.000	-0.999
UCN 2	**Charcoal and firewood**	
UCN 2	1.000	–
N 21	-0.165	–
N 22	-0.124	–
N 27	-0.072	–
T 1	-0.031	–
P 1	–	-0.124
P 2	–	-0.082
P 3	–	-0.154
P 9	-0.608	-0.608
P 10	–	-0.032
Total	0.000	-1.000

Code No.	(1)	(2)
UCN 3	**Clothing**	
UCN 3	1.000	–
N 13	-0.009	–
N 18	-0.005	–
N 19	-0.005	–
N 21	-0.213	–
N 27	-0.051	–
P 1	-0.464	-0.521
P 2	–	-0.062
P 3	–	-0.147
P 10	-0.253	-0.269
Total	0.000	-0.999
UCN 4	**Electricity**	
UCN 4	1.000	–
N 3	-0.480	–
P 1	-0.520	-0.737
P 2	–	-0.122
P 3	–	-0.102
P 4	–	-0.007
P 10	–	-0.032
Total	0.000	-1.000

Code No.	(1)	(2)
UCN 5 Footwear		
UCN 5	1.000	–
N 13	-0.010	–
N 18	-0.005	–
N 19	-0.005	–
N 21	-0.214	–
N 27	-0.051	–
P 1	-0.540	-0.598
P 2	–	-0.063
P 3	–	-0.147
P 10	-0.175	-0.191
Total	0.000	-0.999

Code No.	(1)	(2)
UCN 6 Fuel and light		
UCN 2	-0.344	–
UCN 4	-0.436	–
UCN 6	1.000	–
UCN 12	-0.058	–
UCN 14	-0.161	–
P 1	–	-0.474
P 2	–	-0.105
P 3	–	-0.152
P 4	–	-0.004
P 9	–	-0.209
P 10	–	-0.055
Total	0.001	-0.999

Code No.	(1)	(2)
UCN 7 Furniture		
UCN 7	1.000	–
N 6	-0.837	–
N 21	-0.163	–
P 1	–	-0.528
P 2	–	-0.134
P 3	–	-0.245
P 4	–	-0.014
P 5	–	-0.012
P 10	–	-0.066
Total	0.000	-0.999

Code No.	(1)	(2)
UCN 8 Household utensils		
UCN 8	1.000	–
N 13	-0.009	–
N 18	-0.005	–
N 19	-0.005	–
N 21	-0.168	–
N 27	-0.153	–
P 1	-0.503	-0.576
P 2	–	-0.069
P 3	–	-0.176
P 10	-0.158	-0.178
Total	-0.001	-0.999

Code No.	(1)	(2)
UCN 10 Miscellaneous non-food		
UCN 1-8, 11-14, 16 each	-0.077	–
UCN 10	1.000	–
P 1	–	-0.514
P 2	–	-0.104
P 3	–	-0.197
P 4	–	-0.004
P 5	–	-0.003
P 9	–	-0.051
P 10	–	-0.127
Total	-0.001	-1.000

Code No.	(1)	(2)
UCN 11 Newspapers and journals		
UCN 11	1.000	–
N 15	-0.858	–
N 21	-0.142	–
P 1	–	-0.349
P 2	–	-0.136
P 3	–	-0.411
P 4	–	-0.022

Code No.	(1)	(2)
P 5	–	-0.020
P 10	–	-0.062
Total	0.000	-1.000

UCN 12 **Paraffin**

UCN 12	1.000	–
N 13	-0.108	–
N 18	-0.021	–
N 19	-0.086	–
N 21	-0.203	–
N 27	-0.203	–
P 1	-0.222	-0.402
P 2	–	-0.132
P 3	–	-0.250
P 4	–	-0.002
P 10	-0.157	-0.213
Total	0.000	-0.999

UCN 13 **Personal care and hygiene**

UCN 13	1.000	–
N 13	-0.025	–
N 18	-0.012	–
N 19	-0.013	–
N 21	-0.239	–
N 27	-0.074	–
P 1	-0.552	-0.633
P 2	–	-0.081
P 3	–	-0.178
P 4	–	-0.001
P 10	-0.085	-0.106
Total	0.000	-0.999

UCN 14 **Petroleum gases** (propane butane)

Code No.	(1)	(2)
UCN 14	1.000	–
N 13	-0.049	–
N 18	-0.024	–
N 19	-0.024	–
N 27	-0.439	–
P 1	-0.390	-0.536
P 2	–	-0.101
P 3	–	-0.250
P 4	–	-0.002
P 10	-0.073	-0.111
Total	0.001	-1.000

UCN 16 **Road transport** (passenger)

UCN 16	1.000	–
N 12	-0.076	–
N 17	-0.051	–
T 2	-0.019	–
T 5	-0.019	–
T 8	-0.215	–
T 12	-0.247	–
T 13	-0.025	–
T 21	-0.101	–
T 33	-0.139	–
P 1	–	-0.471
P 2	-0.146	-0.215
P 3	-0.044	-0.166
P 4	–	-0.001
P 10	0.082	-0.147
Total	0.000	-1.000

Code No.	(1)	(2)
RCN 1 **Rent**		
RCN 1	1.000	–
N 13	-0.020	–
N 18	-0.008	–
N 19	-0.008	–
N 27	-0.067	–
T 31	-0.349	–
P 1	-0.278	-0.668
P 2	–	-0.017
P 3	–	-0.037
P 6	-0.147	-0.147
P 9	-0.040	-0.040
P 10	-0.083	-0.091
Total	0.000	-1.000

Code No.	(1)	(2)
RCN 2 **Services**		
UCN 16	-0.260	–
RCN 2	1.000	–
N 14	-0.030	–
P 1	–	-0.132
P 2	–	-0.061
P 3	-0.140	-0.197
P 6	-0.280	-0.280
P 10	-0.290	-0.330
Total	0.000	-1.000

Code No.	(1)	(2)
RCF 3 **Meat**		
RCF 3	1.000	–
N 9	0.850	–
N 13	0.008	–
N 18	0.063	–
N 19	-0.004	–
P 1	-1.917	-1.527
P 2	–	0.282
P 3	–	0.206
P 10	–	0.039
Total	0.000	-1.001

Code No.	(1)	(2)
RCF 5 **Tobacco and beverages**		
UCF 2	-0.780	–
UCF 6	-0.020	–
UCF 14	-0.020	–
UCF 18	-0.050	–
RCF 5	1.000	–
P 1	–	-0.193
P 2	–	-0.100
P 3	–	-0.182
P 4	–	-0.017
P 5	–	-0.010
P 7	–	-0.003
P 9	-0.130	-0.130
P 10	–	-0.366
Total	0.000	-1.000

Code No.	(1)	(2)
N 1 **Baking margin**		
UCN 7	-0.010	–
N 1	1.000	–
N 3	-0.096	–
N 12	-0.247	–
T 12	-0.066	–
T 14	-0.163	–
T 19	-0.008	–
T 35	-0.001	–
P 1	–	-0.304
P 2	–	-0.231

Code No.	(1)	(2)
P 3	-0.186	-0.344
P 4	-0.036	-0.039
P 5	-0.037	-0.037
P 10	–	-0.045
Total	-0.002	-1.000

N 2 **Beer and tobacco manufacture**

UCN 4	-0.001	–
UCN 7	-0.008	–
N 2	1.000	–
N 3	-0.066	–
N 12	-0.199	–
T 10	-0.014	–
T 12	-0.016	–
T 14	-0.093	–
T 17	-0.099	–
T 19	-0.023	–
T 20	-0.007	–
T 26	-0.023	–
T 29	-0.008	–
T 32	-0.189	–
P 1	–	-0.373
P 2	-0.073	-0.144
P 3	-0.131	-0.264
P 4	-0.025	-0.027
P 5	-0.025	-0.025
P 10	–	-0.169
Total	0.000	-1.002

N 3 **Building and Construction**

UCN 7	-0.024	–
N 3	1.000	–
N 12	-0.081	–
N 22	-0.100	–
T 4	-0.107	–
T 5	-0.048	–
T 9	-0.002	–
T 11	-0.124	–

Code No.	(1)	(2)
T 12	-0.024	–
T 18	-0.034	–
T 20	-0.010	–
T 23	-0.009	–
T 24	-0.053	–
T 25	-0.011	–
T 28	-0.006	–
T 31	-0.060	–
P 1	–	-0.452
P 2	-0.192	-0.253
P 3	-0.114	-0.213
P 4	–	-0.015
P 10	–	-0.066
Total	0.001	-0.999

N 4 **Butter manufacture**

UCN 4	-0.030	–
N 3	-0.037	–
N 4	1.000	–
N 12	-0.421	–
N 13	0.000	–
T 12	-0.009	–
T 14	-0.057	–
T 19	-0.043	–
T 20	-0.030	–
T 26	-0.151	–
P 1	-0.006	-0.373
P 2	-0.054	-0.160
P 3	-0.057	-0.282
P 4	-0.032	-0.035
P 5	-0.053	-0.053
P 7	-0.020	-0.020
P 10	–	-0.077
Total	0.000	-1.000

N 5 **Cinemas and theatres**

UCN 1	-0.071	–
UCN 4	-0.011	–

Code No.	(1)	(2)
N 3	-0.200	–
N 5	1.000	–
N 12	-0.101	–
T 14	-0.018	–
P 1	-0.280	-0.470
P 2	-0.184	-0.260
P 3	-0.081	-0.181
P 4	–	-0.003
P 10	-0.055	-0.086
Total	-0.001	-1.000

N 6 Furniture

UCN 4	-0.005	–
N 3	-0.066	–
N 6	1.000	–
N 12	-0.119	–
T 9	-0.014	–
T 12	-0.013	–
T 14	-0.021	–
T 18	-0.069	–
T 19	-0.112	–
T 20	-0.007	–
T 25	-0.021	–
T 30	-0.072	–
T 31	-0.286	–
P 1	–	-0.597
P 2	-0.068	-0.116
P 3	-0.096	-0.186
P 4	-0.015	-0.017
P 5	-0.015	-0.015
P 10	–	-0.069
Total	0.001	-1.000

N 7 Green tea distribution

Code No.	(1)	(2)
N 7	1.000	–
P 1	-0.063	-0.063
P 2	-0.315	-0.315
P 3	-0.111	-0.111
P 7	-0.499	-0.499
P 10	-0.012	-0.012
Total	0.000	-1.000

N 8 Maize distribution

UCN 4	-0.004	–
N 3	-0.241	–
N 8	1.000	–
N 12	-0.038	–
N 14	-0.014	–
N 22	-0.042	–
N 27	-0.146	–
T 14	-0.016	–
T 19	-0.002	–
T 28	-0.029	–
T 34	-0.002	–
P 1	-0.247	-0.459
P 2	-0.067	-0.175
P 3	-0.191	-0.356
P 4	–	-0.004
P 10	0.037	-0.005
Total	-0.002	-0.999

N 9 Meat processing into canned corned beef

N 9	1.000	–
P 1	-0.412	-0.412
P 2	-0.314	-0.314
P 3	-0.227	-0.227
P 10	-0.046	-0.046
Total	0.001	-0.999

N 10 Milk distribution

UCN 4	-0.014	–
N 3	-0.022	–
N 10	1.000	–

Code No.	(1)	(2)
N 12	-0.153	–
N 18	-0.036	–
N 19	-0.036	–
N 22	-0.040	–
N 27	-0.044	–
T 12	-0.005	–
T 14	-0.034	–
T 19	-0.009	–
T 20	-0.014	–
T 26	-0.161	–
P 1	–	-0.306
P 2	-0.020	-0.088
P 3	-0.021	-0.150
P 4	-0.121	-0.123
P 5	-0.195	-0.196
P 7	-0.075	-0.075
P 9	-0.001	-0.001
P 10	–	-0.063
Total	-0.001	-1.002

N 11 **Milling margin**

UCN 7	-0.012	–
N 3	-0.117	–
N 11	1.000	–
N 12	-0.239	–
T 12	-0.013	–
T 14	-0.203	–
T 19	-0.012	–
P 1	–	-0.311
P 2	-0.144	-0.231
P 3	-0.181	-0.341
P 4	-0.039	-0.042
P 5	-0.039	-0.039
P 10	–	-0.037
Total	0.001	-1.001

N 12 **Miscellaneous office services**

UCN 4	-0.019	–
UCN 7	-0.020	–

Code No.	(1)	(2)
N 3	-0.201	–
N 12	1.000	–
N 22	-0.010	–
T 12	-0.030	–
T 15	-0.092	–
T 20	-0.008	–
T 28	-0.098	–
P 1	–	-0.269
P 2	-0.125	-0.193
P 3	-0.375	-0.448
P 4	–	-0.004
P 10	-0.022	-0.086
Total	0.000	-1.000

N 13 **Ports**

N 3	-0.448	–
N 12	-0.027	–
N 13	1.000	–
N 22	-0.075	–
P 1	-0.013	-0.255
P 2	-0.305	-0.442
P 3	-0.131	-0.253
P 4	–	-0.007
P 10	–	-0.043
Total	0.001	-1.000

N 14 **Post, telegraph telephone**

UCN 4	-0.022	–
N 3	-0.198	–
N 12	-0.213	–
N 14	1.000	–
N 21	-0.086	–
T 12	-0.047	–
T 14	-0.124	–
P 1	–	-0.314
P 2	-0.040	-0.161
P 3	-0.270	-0.474

Code No.	(1)	(2)
P 4	–	-0.004
P 10	–	-0.047
Total	0.000	-1.000

N 15 Printing and publishing of newspapers and journals

Code No.	(1)	(2)
UCN 4	-0.005	–
UCN 7	-0.009	–
N 3	-0.010	–
N 12	-0.193	–
N 15	1.000	–
T 12	-0.005	–
T 14	-0.084	–
T 19	-0.052	–
T 20	-0.005	–
T 27	-0.264	–
P 1	–	-0.378
P 2	-0.061	-0.121
P 3	-0.265	-0.389
P 4	-0.024	-0.025
P 5	-0.023	-0.024
P 10	–	-0.064
Total	0.000	-1.001

N 16 Pyrethrum processing

Code No.	(1)	(2)
UCN 4	-0.014	–
UCN 7	-0.024	–
N 3	-0.104	–
N 12	-0.130	–
N 13	-0.012	–
N 16	1.000	–
N 18	-0.005	–
N 19	-0.019	–
N 27	-0.172	–
T 12	-0.026	–
T 14	-0.067	–
T 15	-0.002	–
T 19	-0.005	–

Code No.	(1)	(2)
T 26	-0.044	–
P 1	-0.081	-0.360
P 2	-0.029	-0.126
P 3	-0.097	-0.293
P 4	-0.023	-0.026
P 7	-0.145	-0.145
P 10	–	-0.050
Total	0.001	-1.000

N 17 Quarrying

Code No.	(1)	(2)
N 3	-0.064	–
N 12	-0.054	–
N 17	1.000	–
N 22	-0.180	–
T 8	-0.043	–
T 12	-0.008	–
T 14	-0.111	–
T 19	-0.259	–
T 28	-0.003	–
P 1	–	-0.421
P 2	-0.239	-0.328
P 3	-0.036	-0.147
P 4	–	-0.003
P 10	-0.002	-0.100
Total	0.001	-0.999

N 18 Rail transport (marginal cost)

Code No.	(1)	(2)
N 3	-0.053	–
N 18	1.000	–
T 4	-0.016	–
T 11	-0.019	–
T 18	-0.005	–
T 23	-0.001	–
T 24	-0.008	–
T 25	-0.002	–
T 31	-0.013	–
P 1	-0.566	-0.641
P 2	-0.158	-0.174
P 3	-0.158	-0.174

Code No.	(1)	(2)
P 4	–	-0.003
P 10	–	-0.008
Total	0.001	-1.000

Code No.	(1)	(2)
N 19	**Rail transport (price minus marginal cost)**	
N 19	1.000	–
P 1	-0.667	-0.667
P 10	-0.333	-0.333
Total	0.000	-1.000

Code No.	(1)	(2)
N 20	**Restaurants**	
UCF 2	-0.228	–
UCF 3	-0.066	–
UCF 4	-0.026	–
UCF 6	-0.007	–
UCF 9	-0.099	–
UCF 10	-0.049	–
UCF 12	-0.053	–
UCF 16	-0.025	–
UCF 17	-0.020	–
UCF 18	-0.010	–
UCN 3	-0.013	–
UCN 6	-0.036	–
UCN 7	-0.013	–
UCN 8	-0.013	–
UCN 10	-0.011	–
N 3	-0.088	–
N 20	1.000	–
P 1	–	-0.326
P 2	-0.154	-0.223
P 3	-0.086	-0.208
P 4	–	-0.021
P 5	–	-0.023
P 6	–	0.000
P 7	–	-0.012
P 9	–	-0.030
P 10	-0.007	-0.155
Total	-0.004	-0.998

Code No.	(1)	(2)
N 21	**Retail distribution**	
UCN 4	-0.003	–
N 3	-0.077	–
N 12	-0.040	–
N 14	-0.022	–
N 15	-0.022	–
N 21	1.000	–
N 22	-0.053	–
T 12	-0.062	–
T 15	-0.036	–
T 26	-0.003	–
T 27	-0.022	–
T 34	-0.004	–
P 1	–	-0.173
P 2	-0.177	-0.228
P 3	-0.471	-0.546
P 4	–	-0.002
P 5	–	-0.001
P 10	-0.008	-0.050
Total	0.000	-1.000

Code No.	(1)	(2)
N 22	**Road transport (goods)**	
N 12	-0.113	–
N 17	-0.038	–
N 22	1.000	–
T 2	-0.015	–
T 5	-0.015	–
T 8	-0.105	–
T 12	-0.210	–
T 13	-0.015	–
T 21	-0.113	–
T 22	-0.105	–
T 33	-0.113	–
P 1	–	-0.425
P 2	-0.173	-0.241
P 3	-0.053	-0.183
P 4	–	-0.001
P 10	0.068	-0.150
Total	0.000	-1.000

Code No.	(1)	(2)
N 23	**Settlement farmers' co-operatives' overheads**	
UCN 16	-0.017	–
N 3	-0.040	–
N 12	-0.095	–
N 14	-0.005	–
N 22	-0.018	–
N 23	1.000	–
T 12	-0.140	–
T 14	-0.030	–
T 28	-0.025	–
P 1	–	-0.200
P 2	–	-0.044
P 3	–	-0.077
P 4	–	-0.001
P 6	-0.240	-0.240
P 7	-0.390	-0.390
P 10	–	-0.048
Total	0.000	-1.000

Code No.	(1)	(2)
N 24	**Soft drinks**	
UCF 12	-0.073	–
UCN 7	-0.008	–
N 3	-0.043	–
N 12	-0.237	–
N 24	1.000	–
T 3	-0.037	–
T 6	-0.044	–
T 12	-0.064	–
T 14	-0.056	–
T 19	-0.063	–
T 20	-0.012	–
T 26	-0.044	–
T 29	-0.060	–
P 1	–	-0.362
P 2	-0.134	-0.216
P 3	-0.079	-0.245
P 4	-0.023	-0.025
P 5	-0.023	-0.023
P 8	–	-0.031
P 10	–	-0.098
Total	0.000	-1.000

Code No.	(1)	(2)
N 25	**Tea manufacture**	
UCN 4	-0.090	–
N 3	-0.046	–
N 13	-0.001	–
N 19	-0.001	–
N 25	-1.000	–
T 8	-0.105	–
T 14	-0.123	–
T 26	-0.210	–
P 1	-0.180	-0.568
P 2	-0.045	-0.086
P 3	–	-0.056
P 4	–	-0.002
P 7	-0.204	-0.204
P 10	–	-0.085
Total	-0.001	-1.001

Code No.	(1)	(2)
N 26	**Tea packing and blending, coffee roasting**	
UCN 4	-0.004	–
UCN 7	-0.008	–
N 3	-0.085	–
N 12	-0.060	–
N 13	0.001	–
N 19	0.001	–
N 26	1.000	–
T 12	-0.029	–
T 14	-0.155	–
T 19	-0.025	–
T 20	-0.007	–
T 26	-0.208	–
P 1	-0.077	-0.473
P 2	-0.138	-0.188
P 3	-0.138	-0.220
P 4	-0.034	-0.036
P 5	-0.034	-0.034
P 10	–	-0.050
Total	0.000	-1.001

Code No.	(1)	(2)
N 27	**Wholesale distribution**	
UCN 4	-0.006	–
N 3	-0.081	–
N 12	-0.079	–
N 14	-0.043	–
N 15	-0.044	–
N 22	-0.068	–
N 27	1.000	–
T 12	-0.062	–
T 15	-0.037	–
T 26	-0.006	–
T 27	-0.044	–
T 34	-0.007	–
P 1	–	-0.231
P 2	-0.100	-0.171
P 3	-0.414	-0.531
P 4	–	-0.003
P 5	–	-0.001
P 10	-0.008	-0.062
Total	0.001	-0.999

Code No.	(1)	(2)
N 28	**Meat processing, first stage only**	
N 28	1.000	–
P 1	-0.370	-0.370
P 2	-0.361	-0.361
P 3	-0.244	-0.244
P 10	-0.025	-0.025
Total	0.000	-1.000

Code No.	(1)	(2)
T 1	**Bags (e.g. for maize)**	
N 13	-0.076	–
N 18	-0.061	–
N 19	-0.015	–
N 27	-0.102	–
T 1	1.000	–
P 1	-0.746	-0.888
P 2	–	-0.061
P 3	–	-0.084
P 4	–	-0.001
P 10	–	-0.015
Total	0.000	-0.999

Code No.	(1)	(2)
T 2	**Bitumen**	
N 13	-0.169	–
N 18	-0.055	–
N 19	-0.114	–
N 27	-0.159	–
T 2	1.000	–
P 1	-0.502	-0.694
P 2	–	-0.111
P 3	–	-0.137
P 4	–	-0.002
P 10	–	-0.056
Total	0.001	-1.000

T 3	**Bottles**	
N 13	-0.040	–
N 18	-0.020	–
N 19	-0.020	–
N 27	-0.129	–
T 3	1.000	–

Code No.	(1)	(2)
P 1	-0.592	-0.659
P 2	–	-0.043
P 3	–	-0.082
P 4	–	-0.001
P 10	-0.198	-0.214
Total	0.001	-0.999

T 4 Cement

N 18	-0.093	–
N 19	-0.152	–
N 27	-0.191	–
T 4	1.000	–
P 1	-0.438	-0.642
P 2	–	-0.049
P 3	–	-0.117
P 4	-0.127	-0.128
P 10	–	-0.063
Total	-0.001	-0.999

T 5 Construction machinery

N 13	-0.010	–
N 18	-0.005	–
N 19	-0.005	–
N 27	-0.191	–
T 5	1.000	–
P 1	-0.789	-0.842
P 2	–	-0.038
P 3	–	-0.105
P 4	–	-0.001
P 10	–	-0.014
Total	0.000	-1.000

T 6 Flavouring essences

N 27	-0.133	–
T 6	1.000	–

Code No.	(1)	(2)
P 1	-0.635	-0.666
P 2	–	-0.023
P 3	–	-0.071
P 10	-0.232	-0.240
Total	0.000	-1.000

T 7 Fuel oil

N 13	-0.240	–
N 18	-0.074	–
N 19	-0.166	–
N 27	-0.355	–
T 7	1.000	–
P 1	-0.165	-0.466
P 2	–	-0.180
P 3	–	-0.262
P 4	–	-0.003
P 10	–	-0.089
Total	0.000	-1.000

T 8 Gas/diesel oil

N 13	-0.096	–
N 18	-0.021	–
N 19	-0.075	–
N 27	-0.156	–
T 8	1.000	–
P 1	-0.189	-0.313
P 2	–	-0.073
P 3	–	-0.111
P 4	–	-0.001
P 10	-0.462	-0.502
Total	0.001	-1.000

T 9 Glass

N 13	-0.048	–
N 18	-0.024	–
N 19	-0.024	–

Code No.	(1)	(2)
N 27	-0.122	–
T 9	1.000	–
P 1	-0.598	-0.670
P 2	–	-0.046
P 3	–	-0.081
P 4	–	-0.001
P 10	-0.183	-0.201
Total	0.001	-0.999

T 10 Hops

Code No.	(1)	(2)
N 13	-0.061	–
N 18	-0.031	–
N 19	-0.031	–
N 27	-0.051	–
T 10	1.000	–
P 1	-0.719	-0.787
P 2	–	-0.041
P 3	–	-0.048
P 4	–	-0.001
P 10	-0.107	-0.124
Total	0.000	-1.001

T 11 Iron and steel

Code No.	(1)	(2)
N 13	-0.066	–
N 18	-0.012	–
N 19	-0.054	–
N 27	-0.119	–
T 11	1.000	–
P 1	-0.710	-0.799
P 2	–	-0.052
P 3	–	-0.082
P 4	–	-0.001
P 10	-0.038	-0.066
Total	0.001	-1.000

T 12 Lorries and Land Rovers

Code No.	(1)	(2)
N 13	-0.010	–
N 18	-0.005	–
N 19	-0.005	–
N 27	-0.154	–
T 12	1.000	–
P 1	-0.655	-0.699
P 2	–	-0.032
P 3	–	-0.085
P 4	–	-0.001
P 10	-0.171	-0.183
Total	0.000	-1.000

T 13 Lubricating oil

Code No.	(1)	(2)
N 13	-0.044	–
N 18	-0.009	–
N 19	-0.036	–
N 27	-0.358	–
T 13	1.000	–
P 1	-0.458	-0.582
P 2	–	-0.082
P 3	–	-0.203
P 4	–	-0.001
P 10	-0.095	-0.131
Total	0.000	-0.999

T 14 Machinery, industrial or agricultural

Code No.	(1)	(2)
N 13	-0.020	–
N 18	-0.010	–
N 19	-0.010	–
N 27	-0.189	–
T 14	1.000	–
P 1	-0.771	-0.833
P 2	–	-0.043
P 3	–	-0.107

Code No.	(1)	(2)
P 4	–	-0.001
P 10	–	-0.016
Total	0.000	-1.000

T 15 Machinery, non-industrial and non-agricultural (e.g. office machinery)

N 13	-0.020	–
N 18	-0.010	–
N 19	-0.010	–
N 27	-0.189	–
T 15	1.000	–
P 1	-0.591	-0.653
P 2	–	-0.043
P 3	–	-0.107
P 4	–	-0.001
P 10	-0.180	-0.196
Total	0.000	-1.000

T 16 Maize (into mill)

N 13	0.052	–
N 18	0.016	–
N 19	0.016	–
T 1	-0.030	–
T 16	1.000	–
P 1	-1.015	-1.006
P 2	–	0.024
P 3	–	0.014
P 10	-0.039	-0.032
Total	0.000	-1.000

T 17 Malt

Code No.	(1)	(2)
N 13	-0.033	–
N 18	-0.016	–
N 19	-0.017	–
N 27	-0.051	–
T 17	1.000	–
P 1	-0.680	-0.721
P 2	–	-0.026
P 3	–	-0.038
P 10	-0.204	-0.214
Total	-0.001	-0.999

T 18 Metal Products

N 13	-0.020	–
N 18	-0.010	–
N 19	-0.010	–
N 27	-0.125	–
T 18	1.000	–
P 1	-0.775	-0.822
P 2	–	-0.032
P 3	–	-0.073
P 4	–	-0.001
P 10	-0.060	-0.072
Total	0.000	-1.000

T 19 Miscellaneous Materials (excl. fuels and food-stuffs)

T 1-6, 9-15, 18, 21, 23-28, 30, 31, 33, 34 each	-0.040	
T 19	1.000	–
P 1	–	-0.723
P 2	–	-0.042
P 3	–	-0.088
P 4	–	-0.006
P 10	–	-0.141
Total	0.000	-1.000

T 20 Miscellaneous Petroleum Fuels

T 7	-0.333	–
T 8	-0.333	–

Code No.	(1)	(2)
T 20	1.000	–
T 22	-0.333	–
P 1	–	-0.354
P 2	–	-0.108
P 3	–	-0.165
P 4	–	-0.002
P 10	–	-0.372
Total	0.001	-1.001

T 21 Motor Spares

N 13	-0.010	–
N 18	-0.005	–
N 19	-0.005	–
N 27	-0.238	–
T 21	1.000	–
P 1	-0.559	-0.623
P 2	–	-0.046
P 3	–	-0.130
P 4	–	-0.001
P 10	-0.183	-0.200
Total	0.000	-1.000

T 22 Motor Spirit

N 13	-0.084	–
N 18	-0.017	–
N 19	-0.067	–
N 27	-0.182	–
T 22	1.000	–
P 1	-0.162	-0.281
P 2	–	-0.071
P 3	–	-0.121
P 4	–	-0.001
P 10	-0.488	-0.525
Total	0.000	-0.999

T 23 Non-ferrous base Metals

Code No.	(1)	(2)
N 13	-0.010	–
N 18	-0.005	–
N 19	-0.005	–
N 27	-0.127	–
T 23	1.000	–
P 1	-0.853	-0.892
P 2	–	-0.027
P 3	–	-0.071
P 10	–	-0.010
Total	0.000	-1.000

T 24 Other construction Materials

N 13	-0.020	–
N 18	-0.010	–
N 19	-0.010	–
N 27	-0.125	–
T 24	1.000	–
P 1	-0.626	-0.673
P 2	–	-0.032
P 3	–	-0.073
P 4	–	-0.001
P 10	-0.209	-0.221
Total	0.000	-1.000

T 25 Paint

N 13	-0.020	–
N 18	-0.010	–
N 19	-0.010	–
N 27	-0.125	–
T 25	1.000	–
P 1	-0.596	-0.643
P 2	–	-0.032
P 3	–	-0.073
P 4	–	-0.001
P 10	-0.239	-0.251
Total	0.000	-1.000

T 26 Paper and Packing Materials

N 13	-0.020	–
N 18	-0.010	–

Code No.	(1)	(2)
N 19	-0.010	–
N 27	-0.098	–
T 26	1.000	–
P 1	-0.753	-0.794
P 2	–	-0.027
P 3	–	-0.059
P 10	-0.109	-0.119
Total	0.000	-0.999

T 27 Paper for Printing

N 13	-0.060	–
N 18	-0.010	–
N 19	-0.050	–
N 27	-0.094	–
T 27	1.000	–
P 1	-0.682	-0.759
P 2	–	-0.044
P 3	–	-0.067
P 4	–	-0.001
P 10	-0.103	-0.129
Total	0.001	-1.000

T 28 Stationery

N 13	-0.020	–
N 18	-0.010	–
N 19	-0.010	–
N 27	-0.143	–
T 28	1.000	–
P 1	-0.618	-0.669
P 2	–	-0.035
P 3	–	-0.083
P 4	–	-0.001
P 10	-0.199	-0.212
Total	0.000	-1.000

T 29 Sugar (wholesale)

Code No.	(1)	(2)
N 13	-0.084	–
N 18	-0.042	–
N 19	-0.042	–
N 27	-0.054	–
T 29	1.000	–
P 1	-0.441	-0.530
P 2	–	-0.054
P 3	–	-0.057
P 4	–	-0.001
P 10	-0.336	-0.358
Total	-0.001	-1.000

T 30 Textile Fabrics for furnishing

N 13	-0.004	–
N 18	-0.002	–
N 19	-0.002	–
N 27	-0.088	–
T 30	1.000	–
P 1	-0.636	-0.659
P 2	–	-0.017
P 3	–	-0.048
P 10	-0.269	-0.275
Total	-0.001	-0.999

T 31 Timber

N 18	0.080	–
T 31	1.000	–
P 1	-1.080	-1.029
P 2	–	0.014
P 3	–	0.014
P 10	–	0.001
Total	0.000	-1.000

T 32 Tobacco unmanufactured

N 13	-0.022	–
N 18	-0.011	–
N 19	-0.010	–
N 27	-0.051	–
T 32	1.000	–
P 1	-0.354	-0.386

Code No.	(1)	(2)
P 2	—	-0.020
P 3	—	-0.035
P 10	-0.551	-0.559
Total	0.001	-1.000

Code No.	(1)	(2)
T 33	**Tyres and tubes**	
N 13	-0.010	—
N 18	-0.005	—
N 19	-0.005	—
N 27	-0.163	—
T 33	1.000	
P 1	-0.544	-0.591
P 2	—	-0.033
P 3	—	-0.090
P 4	—	-0.001
P 10	-0.272	-0.285
Total	0.001	-1.000

Code No.	(1)	(2)
T 34	**Uniforms**	
N 13	-0.010	—
N 18	-0.005	—
N 19	-0.005	—
N 21	-0.220	—
N 27	-0.046	—
T 34	1.000	—
P 1	-0.489	-0.547
P 2	—	-0.063
P 3	—	-0.148
P 4	—	-0.001
P 10	-0.224	-0.240
Total	0.001	-0.999

Code No.	(1)	(2)
T 35	**Wheat flour** (wholesale)	
N 13	0.042	—
N 18	0.025	—
N 19	0.016	—
N 27	-0.054	—
T 1	0.023	—
T 35	1.000	—
P 1	-0.637	-0.593
P 2	—	0.015
P 3	—	-0.012
P 4	-0.190	-0.190
P 5	-0.208	-0.208
P 7	-0.016	-0.016
P 10	—	0.004
Total	0.001	-1.000

Code No.	(1)	(2)
FI 1	**Artificial Insemination**	
N 23	-0.100	—
FI 1	1.000	—
P 1	—	-0.020
P 2	—	-0.004
P 3	-0.900	-0.908
P 4	—	-0.000
P 6	—	-0.024
P 7	—	-0.039
P 10	—	-0.005
Total	0.000	-1.000

Code No.	(1)	(2)
FI 2	**Barbed Wire**	
N 13	-0.034	—
N 18	-0.013	—

Code No.	(1)	(2)
N 19	-0.013	–
N 27	-0.164	–
FI 2	1.000	–
P 1	-0.776	-0.840
P 2	–	-0.045
P 3	–	-0.098
P 4	–	-0.001
P 10	–	-0.016
Total	0.000	-1.000

FI 3 **Dips and Sprays**

N 3	-0.006	–
N 13	-0.012	–
N 18	-0.006	–
N 19	-0.006	–
N 23	-0.261	–
N 27	-0.077	–
FI 3	1.000	–
T 14	-0.030	–
P 1	-0.483	-0.592
P 2	–	-0.034
P 3	–	-0.069
P 4	–	-0.001
P 6	-0.119	-0.182
P 7	–	-0.102
P 10	–	-0.021
Total	0.000	-1.001

FI 5 **Fertilizers** (weighted average)

Code No.	(1)	(2)
N 13	-0.070	–
N 18	-0.048	–
N 19	-0.032	–
N 21	-0.058	–
N 22	-0.022	–
N 27	-0.167	–
FI 5	1.000	–
P 1	-0.799	-0.927
P 2	–	-0.086
P 3	–	-0.151
P 4	–	-0.001
P 10	0.196	0.166
Total	0.000	-0.999

FI 5.1 **Superphosphates** (excl. single Superphosphate from Uganda)

N 13	-0.070	–
N 18	-0.041	–
N 19	-0.028	–
N 21	-0.048	–
N 22	-0.018	–
N 27	-0.168	–
FI 5.1	1.000	–
P 1	-0.985	-1.103
P 2	–	-0.082
P 3	–	-0.144
P 4	–	-0.001
P 10	0.358	0.330
Total	0.000	-1.000

FI 5.2 **Single Superphosphate (from Uganda)**

N 18	-0.048	–
N 19	-0.032	–
N 21	-0.086	–
N 22	-0.032	–
N 27	-0.168	–
FI 5.2	1.000	–
P 1	-0.983	-1.102
P 2	–	-0.064
P 3	–	-0.151
P 4	–	-0.001
P 10	0.349	0.318
Total	0.000	-1.000

Code No.	(1)	(2)
FI 5.3	**Sulphate of Ammonia**	
N 13	-0.086	—
N 18	-0.055	—
N 19	-0.036	—
N 21	-0.064	—
N 22	-0.024	—
N 27	-0.145	—
FI 5.3	1.000	—
P 1	-0.690	-0.826
P 2	—	-0.093
P 3	—	-0.148
P 4	—	-0.001
P 10	0.100	0.068
Total	0.000	-1.000
FI 5.4	**Ammonium Sulphate Nitrate**	
N 13	-0.074	—
N 18	-0.047	—
N 19	-0.030	—
N 21	-0.054	—
N 22	-0.020	—
N 27	-0.188	—
FI 5.4	1.000	—
P 1	-0.691	-0.821
P 2	—	-0.090
P 3	—	-0.160
P 4	—	-0.001
P 10	0.104	0.073
Total	0.000	-0.999
FI 6	**Machinery Service**	
T 8	-0.280	—
T 14	-0.460	—
FI 6	1.000	—
P 1	—	-0.471

Code No.	(1)	(2)
P 2	—	-0.040
P 3	—	-0.080
P 4	—	-0.001
P 6	-0.260	-0.260
P 10	—	-0.148
Total	0.000	-1.000
FI 7.1	**Milk Cans—Aluminium**	
N 13	-0.031	—
N 18	-0.004	—
N 19	-0.004	—
N 27	-0.173	—
FI 7.1	1.000	—
P 1	-0.788	-0.841
P 2	—	-0.044
P 3	—	-0.100
P 4	—	-0.001
P 10	—	-0.013
Total	0.000	-0.999
FI 7.2	**Milk Cans—Steel**	
N 13	-0.030	—
N 18	-0.008	—
N 19	-0.008	—
N 27	-0.155	—
FI 7.2	1.000	—
P 1	-0.799	-0.853
P 2	—	-0.041
P 3	—	-0.091
P 4	—	-0.001
P 10	—	-0.014
Total	0.000	-1.000
FI 8	**Nails**	
N 18	-0.024	—
N 19	-0.024	—
N 27	-0.123	—
F 18	-1.000	—

Code No.	(1)	(2)
P 1	-0.723	-0.783
P 2	–	-0.025
P 3	–	-0.070
P 4	–	-0.001
P 10	-0.106	-0.122
Total	0.000	-1.001

FI 9 Pangas

N 13	-0.022	–
N 18	-0.013	–
N 19	-0.013	–
N 27	-0.199	–
FI 9	1.000	–
P 1	-0.753	-0.822
P 2	–	-0.046
P 3	–	-0.114
P 4	–	-0.001
P 10	–	-0.018
Total	0.000	-1.001

FI 12 Seeds

N 12	-0.244	–
N 27	-0.146	–
FI 5.1	-0.051	–
FI 5.3	-0.112	–
FI 12	1.000	–
T 14	-0.163	–
P 1	–	-0.384
P 2	–	-0.094
P 3	–	-0.228
P 4	–	-0.002
P 6	-0.203	-0.203

Code No.	(1)	(2)
P 9	-0.081	-0.081
P 10	–	-0.008
Total	0.000	-1.000

FI 10 Piping (galvanised)

N 13	-0.028	–
N 18	-0.033	–
N 19	-0.033	–
N 27	-0.213	–
FI 10	1.000	–
P 1	-0.693	-0.792
P 2	–	-0.055
P 3	–	-0.126
P 4	–	-0.001
P 10	–	-0.026
Total	0.000	-1.000

FI 11 Salt (Rock Salt)

N 13	-0.166	–
N 18	-0.060	–
N 19	-0.112	–
N 27	-0.226	–
FI 11	1.000	–
P 1	-0.336	-0.544
P 2	–	-0.122
P 3	–	-0.172
P 4	–	-0.002
P 10	-0.100	-0.159
Total	0.000	-0.999

Code No.	(1)	(2)
FO 1	**Beans**	
N 8	0.025	–
N 13	0.102	–
N 18	0.059	–
N 19	0.048	–
N 22	0.040	–
N 27	0.105	–
FO 1	1.000	–
T 1	0.025	–
P 1	-1.428	-1.258
P 2	–	0.089
P 3	0.023	0.134
P 4	–	0.001
P 10	–	0.034
Total	0.001	-1.000

Code No.	(1)	(2)
FO3	**Coffee**	
N 12	0.015	–
N 13	0.019	–
N 18	0.011	–
N 19	0.008	–
N 27	0.083	–
FO 3	1.000	–
T 1	0.011	–
P 1	-0.883	-0.834
P 2	–	0.028
P 3	–	0.059
P 4	-0.106	-0.106
P 7	-0.159	-0.159
P 10	–	0.010
Total	-0.001	-1.002

Code No.	(1)	(2)
FO 4.1	**Maize (after 1967-8, export, bulk handling)**	
N 8	0.122	–
N 13	0.078	–
N 18	0.097	–
N 19	0.097	–
N 22	0.091	–
N 23	0.057	–
FO 4.1	1.000	–
P 1	-1.532	-1.279
P 2	–	0.097
P 3	–	0.101
P 4	–	0.001
P 6	–	0.014
P 7	–	0.022
P 10	-0.010	0.044
Total	0.000	-1.000

Code No.	(1)	(2)
FO 4.2	**Maize (1967-8, Export)**	
N 8	0.173	–
N 13	0.275	–
N 18	0.158	–
N 19	0.129	–
N 22	0.084	–
N 23	0.053	–
T 1	0.069	–
FO 4.2	1.000	–
P 1	-1.402	-0.961
P 2	–	0.205
P 3	–	0.184
P 4	–	0.003
P 6	–	0.013
P 7	–	0.021
P 10	-0.540	-0.466
Total	-0.001	-1.001

Code No.	(1)	(2)
FO 4.3	**Maize (1966-67, Export)**	
N 8	0.132	–
N 13	0.209	–
N 18	0.120	–
N 19	0.088	–
N 22	0.064	–
N 23	0.040	–
T 1	0.053	–

Code No.	(1)	(2)
FO 4.3	1.000	—
P 1	-1.090	-0.761
P 2	—	0.156
P 3	—	0.140
P 4	—	0.002
P 6	—	0.010
P 7	—	0.016
P 10	-0.614	-0.561
Total	0.002	-0.998
FO 4.4	**Maize (1965-6, Import)**	
N 13	-0.186	—
N 19	-0.020	—
N 22	0.057	—
N 23	0.035	—
FO 4.4	1.000	—
P 1	-1.063	-1.092
P 2	—	-0.066
P 3	—	-0.034
P 4	—	-0.001
P 6	—	0.008
P 7	—	0.014
P 10	0.176	0.172
Total	-0.001	-0.999
FO 4.5	**Maize (1964-5, Import)**	
N 13	-0.222	—
N 19	-0.022	—
N 22	0.068	—
N 23	0.042	—
FO 4.5	1.000	—
P 1	-1.394	-1.429
P 2	—	-0.080
P 3	—	-0.041
P 4	—	-0.002
P 6	—	0.010
P 7	—	0.016
P 10	0.528	0.523
Total	0.000	-1.003

Code No.	(1)	(2)
FO 4.6	**Maize (1963-4, Export)**	
N 13	-0.277	—
N 19	-0.026	—
N 22	0.085	—
N 23	0.053	—
FO 4.6	1.000	—
P 1	-1.741	-1.782
P 2	—	-0.100
P 3	—	-0.050
P 4	—	-0.002
P 6	—	0.013
P 7	—	0.021
P 10	0.907	0.902
Total	0.001	-0.998
FO 4.7	**Maize (1962-3, Export)**	
N 8	0.134	—
N 13	0.212	—
N 18	0.122	—
N 19	0.058	—
N 22	0.065	—
N 23	0.041	—
T 1	0.053	—
FO 4.7	1.000	—
P 1	-1.132	-0.819
P 2	—	0.159
P 3	—	0.142
P 4	—	0.002
P 6	—	0.010
P 7	—	0.016
P 10	-0.552	-0.509
Total	0.001	-0.999
FO 5	**Milk and butter-fat (as substitute for butter exports)**	
UCN 1	0.011	—
N 4	0.226	—
N 13	0.043	—

Code No.	(1)	(2)
N 18	0.021	–
N 19	0.021	–
N 22	0.011	–
N 23	0.194	–
T 14	0.011	–
FO 5	1.000	–
P 1	-0.979	-0.795
P 2	–	0.071
P 3	–	0.098
P 4	-0.183	-0.174
P 5	-0.290	-0.278
P 6	0.032	0.079
P 7	-0.118	-0.038
P 10	–	0.039
Total	0.000	-0.998
FO 7.1	**Pyrethrum (1967-8)**	
N 16	0.333	–
N 22	0.026	–
N 23	0.152	–
T 20	0.051	–
FO 7.1	1.000	–
P 1	-1.527	-1.348
P 2	–	0.061
P 3	0.017	0.140
P 4	-0.009	0.000
P 6	0.017	0.053
P 7	-0.058	0.049
P 10	–	0.047
Total	0.002	-0.998
FO 7.2	**Pyrethrum (1966-7)**	
N 16	0.244	–
N 22	0.019	–
N 23	0.111	–
T 20	0.037	–
FO 7.2	1.000	–
P 1	-1.299	-1.168
P 2	–	0.045
P 3	0.012	0.101
P 4	-0.018	-0.012
P 6	0.012	0.039
P 7	-0.119	-0.041
P 10	–	0.034
Total	-0.001	-1.002
FO 7.3	**Pyrethrum (1965-6)**	
N 16	0.243	–
N 22	0.019	–
N 23	0.111	–
T 20	0.037	–
FO 7.3	1.000	–
P 1	-1.385	-1.255
P 2	–	0.045
P 3	0.012	0.101
P 4	-0.007	-0.001
P 6	0.012	0.039
P 7	-0.043	0.035
P 10	–	0.034
Total	-0.001	-1.002
FO 7.4	**Pyrethrum (1964-5)**	
N 16	0.292	–
N 22	0.022	–
N 23	0.133	–
T 20	0.044	–
FO 7.4	1.000	–
P 1	-1.662	-1.505
P 2	–	0.053
P 3	0.015	0.122
P 4	0.019	0.027
P 6	0.015	0.047
P 7	0.121	0.215
P 10	–	0.040
Total	-0.001	-1.001

Code No.	(1)	(2)
FO 7.5	**Pyrethrum (1963-4)**	
N 16	0.431	—
N 22	0.033	—
N 23	0.197	—
T 20	0.066	—
FO 7.5	1.000	—
P 1	-2.179	-1.948
P 2	—	0.078
P 3	0.022	0.180
P 4	0.055	0.066
P 6	0.022	0.069
P 7	0.354	0.493
P 10	—	0.061
Total	0.001	-1.001

Code No.	(1)	(2)
FO 7.6	**Pyrethrum (1962-3)**	
N 16	0.450	—
N 22	0.035	—
N 23	0.205	—
T 20	0.068	—
FO 7.6	1.000	—
P 1	-2.166	-1.924
P 2	—	0.081
P 3	0.023	0.188
P 4	0.049	0.061
P 6	0.023	0.072
P 7	0.314	0.459
P 10	—	0.063
Total	0.001	-1.000

Code No.	(1)	(2)
FO 8	**Tea**	
N 7	0.552	—
N 12	0.018	—
N 13	0.025	
N 18	0.014	—
N 19	0.036	—
N 22	0.009	—
N 25	0.482	—
FO 8	1.000	—
P 1	-2.136	-1.779
P 2	—	0.233
P 3	—	0.106
P 4	—	0.001
P 7	—	0.373
P 10	—	0.064
Total	0.000	-1.002

Code No.	(1)	(2)
FO 9	**Wheat**	
N 3	0.045	—
N 11	0.438	—
N 12	0.004	—
N 13	0.071	—
N 18	0.060	—
N 19	0.062	—
N 22	0.041	—
N 27	0.009	—
T 1	0.064	—
T 19	0.039	—
T 20	0.032	—
FO 9	1.000	—
P 1	-1.086	-0.720
P 2	—	0.175
P 3	0.026	0.241
P 4	-0.305	-0.284
P 5	-0.328	-0.309
P 7	-0.026	-0.026
P 8	-0.146	-0.146
P 10	—	0.068
Total	0.000	-1.001

PART II

EVALUATION OF LAND SETTLEMENTS IN KENYA

by
J.D. MacArthur

CHAPTER 11

Background to the Study and Summary of Results

This Part of our book has a close affinity to Part I. As part of the research programme for applying the Little-Mirrlees method a number of Kenya settlement schemes were studied. For this purpose, a comprehensive set of Accounting Prices for Kenya were calculated.

The general methodology of the study was discussed in Part I, and details were given of the basis of the accounting ratios which were presented mainly in Chapter 10. Data for the settlements are presented in this Part and the schemes are appraised at market and social values. In Part I basic principles were discussed, the principal relationships were formulated, and available information was applied to them. This called for much theoretical discussion and relatively few figures. In Part II there are many more figures and only a limited amount of theoretical discussion.

11.1 THE CHOICE OF THE STUDY TOPIC

The study covered here concerns four schemes from the very big settlement programme undertaken in the early 1960s as part of the arrangements for transferring to African ownership land which, until 1959, had been reserved for immigrant European farmers. This topic was selected for a number of reasons.

First, the Kenya settlement programmes are of considerable intrinsic interest. Production from the land concerned, both before the schemes were undertaken and after, was of no little importance to the Kenyan economy. The different approaches to land development embodied in the programmes are of interest in the general field of rural development strategy for low-income tropical countries. Much could potentially be learnt from comparative studies of different approaches to settlement which might involve comparing small-scale farming settlements with larger forms of land use units. All of these are still relevant questions both in Kenya and outside. The diversity of different approaches to settlement there continues to increase, and the 1972 ILO Mission recommended subdivision of large farms to allow more settlement to take place. Study of the two main types of scheme may help to guide future policy.

A second reason for choosing this topic was the practical one that usable information was known to exist, relating both to the plans for individual schemes and to their development in practice. The incipient availability of processed information from comprehensive economic surveys of settlement farms was a major factor affecting the choice. This information was eventually forthcoming. Much of it was presented in summary form in the report that we refer to as the Settlement Appraisal,[1] a most important basic information source.

The third major reason for choosing settlement schemes arose from their distinctive features as projects involving a complete change in land use pattern. They embody a type of agricultural situation with special features not found in the other agricultural projects evaluated in the same research programme. In the main, those studies were based on projects affecting single enterprise types of farming, as in the Malaysian Oil Palm Estate Study (Little and Tipping, 1972), the Kenya Tea Study (Stern, 1972), and the study of Beef Fattening that is presented in Part III of this book. All were concerned with forms of agricultural production that had much in common with the relatively simple features of industrialized processes. Farming in the settlements has features which make it more typical of agricultural development situations in developing countries than situations covered in the other studies. The type of farming being developed in the schemes is a mixture of subsistence and production for sale. Within each farm, different crop and livestock enterprises can be combined in systems whose composition can fluctuate markedly from year to year. Furthermore, settlements were developed in many ecologically different parts of the country. Consequently some settlement farming systems contained enterprises that were not feasible in

[1] Kenya Government, 1971, Farm Economic Survey Report No. 27.

other areas. Many of these enterprises require little or no fixed farm investment, involving mainly the production with unspecialized equipment of annual or peri-annual crops. Thus, as is very typical of mixed farming systems anywhere, settlement farmers were able to change from year to year both the number and types of enterprise which comprised the farm system, whilst the balance between enterprises could easily be shifted. As a result, a study of settlements in different parts of the country presented the need that we sought for valuing a wide variety of different types of farm input and product. Moreover, being concerned with small-scale partial-subsistence agriculture in a land-shortage situation, both labour and land were particularly important costs. They presented special problems of evaluation which called for more detailed treatment in this work than the companion studies required.[1]

11.2 SOME FEATURES OF SETTLEMENT FARMING

Sub-divisional settlement of the types administered by the Department of Settlement[2] led to the creation of small family farms designed to be worked mainly or entirely by the members of a 'typical' rural household. It was expected that the settlers would produce both for subsistence and for sale, and that they would receive an income per family which, whilst not generally particularly high, would compare well with incomes obtainable in other small-scale farming areas, and would be attractive to unemployed landless people, a group for whose partial accommodation the programmes were designed.

The settlement programme comprised almost 120 separate schemes, basically of two different types with substantially different levels of resource availability and production intensity. High Density schemes, which were the most numerous, allowed for a relatively low-level provision of development assets when farmers embarked on their new farming operations. Their farms were relatively small in terms of total income capacity at full development, and were mainly designed for landless,

[1] Summary details of the main features of and differences between the five agricultural projects studied are given in MacArthur, 1973.

[2] Hereafter referred to as 'the Department'.

unemployed people. Family labour was a major input, and an important implication of the programme was the introduction of around 30,000 families to relatively modern market-orientated farming.

Low Density settlements were designed to have a greater 'development' effect. Settlers in these schemes had to have previous experience of modern farming. They were given relatively large farms with considerable development potential, for whose operation a generous amount of development assets were available, and technical advice was provided at a very intensive level. Production for sale was far more important than subsistence, and family labour was complemented by far more material and service inputs than on High Density farms.

Both programmes were implemented on land that had already been in use for many years. The purchase of this land at market-based prices was a fundamental objective of the two programmes, which brought important financial implications, both for flows of foreign aid into Kenya, and for loan financing of the settlers by the Department. Because of the special nature of these schemes, finance flows at these two levels have been taken into account in our appraisal.

Both programmes encompass schemes developed in a wide range of ecological conditions, involving many different mixed-farming enterprises. Because of the diversity of each programme, no single scheme is typical of either main type. However, the ecologies in which they are developed can be broadly divided into low and high altitude types (LA and HA). One long established High Density (HD) settlement at each altitude level was selected for study together with two corresponding groups of contiguous Low Density (LD) settlements. The total size of each Low Density group was roughly equal to that of each High Density scheme.

11.3 SITUATIONS STUDIED, AND ORGANIZATION OF THIS PART

For each of the four settlements, two basic situations were studied: the plans for each scheme, and their actual development, particularly during the first four to six years up to

1967-8. In both cases it was necessary to place a social value on the land concerned. This should in principle be based on the social profitability of the best alternative use. Partly because it was the only alternative farm situation for which data was available, the alternative use considered was large-scale farming of the type that the land transfer settlements displaced.

These three associated studies of land use in four settlement areas make up the greater portion of this Part. Before they are considered in detail, Chapter 12 outlines the main features of the two settlement programmes, and of the schemes chosen for detailed study.

Chapter 13 presents the plans for each of the four schemes. In this first main chapter, basic features of the planning and operation of a settlement are outlined, before the apparent planned levels of cost, output and finance flows are presented. In a final section, the plans for the four schemes are compared in summary form. Chapter 14, the second main chapter, is concerned entirely with the settlements in operation. Farming systems, costs and output values are discussed at current market prices for the years up to 1967-8, the last period for which comprehensive data is available. A final section of the chapter contains a comparative summary.

Estimating the profitability of large-scale farming is the subject of Chapter 15, where estimates are made of the social cost of land. These estimates and material from earlier chapters are incorporated in the appraisal of the settlement plans and the schemes in practice, which is the subject of Chapter 16. This involves both a forward-looking *appraisal* of what appeared from the plans to have been expected, and an *evaluation* of the ongoing projects which looks back over past experience as well as forward, with alternative views of how the position might be projected from the last period for which comprehensive figures are available.

These chapters allow three main objectives of the study to be fulfilled. Most important, they allow experience to be obtained of the problems encountered in extending the Little-Mirrlees method of social cost-benefit appraisal. Second, they allow further experience to be obtained of methodological questions raised in appraising in terms of any set of values agricultural projects of the type with which we are here concerned.

Particular problems and the treatment given to them, are mentioned at several places in Chapters 13 to 16. Third, this work has allowed the plans and the actual operation of four of the most representative types of established settlement scheme to be assessed in market and social value terms.

Fulfilling the last of these objectives is intrinsically interesting, and is possibly of value in a wider sense. However, it does not allow the fulfillment of what might be regarded as a fourth main opportunity, namely a comparative assessment of the general performance and potential of each of the two main types of settlement. For various reasons, particularly the diversity of the different types of farming situation covered by each programme and special features of the actual development of the schemes concerned, a study of four settlements does not provide an adequate basis for any general conclusion to be drawn. Consequently a final chapter contains available information put together in the best way possible for evaluating the actual development of typical composite High and Low Density settlements.

11.4 A SUMMARY OF THE RESULTS

This study led to the derivation of many sets of results. For each of the four settlement areas the pre-settlement, planned and actual situations were considered, while the actual development of the 'average' Low and High Density schemes were also studied.

The most important conclusion from these results is that, with the exception of one High Density scheme (Kabisi), the Net Present Value (NPV) at accounting prices of the schemes studied was positive, indicating that, in social terms (and apart from wider political considerations), settlement was preferable to large-scale farming. This was also true of the average High Density settlement. The average Low Density scheme appeared to be approximately as socially profitable as large farms.

Summary results covering all of these situations are presented in Table 11.1. For each settlement area, vertical comparison indicates the implications of planned and actual changes in land use. Horizontal comparison allows different situations to be compared at the same level. In each of the first three sets of figures, output and costs are related for the most relevant 'stability' year, when farming situations can be regarded as having 'stabilized'. For large-scale farming, this was the level of operation estimated for 1959; for the settlement plans, it was the maturity year of the farm plans; and for settlement actuals, it was the level of operation in 1967-8, the last year for which comprehensive data is available. All are given in 1967-8 values.

For the settlement plans and the actuals, the NPV of a perpetual net income flow was calculated using the Accounting Rate of Interest (10 per cent). This calculation took account of the finance flows associated with the development of each settlement, the view being taken that these finance flows would not have been available to Kenya for use in alternative projects. The NPVs also take account of an increase in the value of the operating margins from the maturity level for 25 years, which allows for expected increases in productivity. The Rate of Return (ROR) has also been calculated, being that discount rate that would give a zero NPV on the basis of the values used.

The planned conversion from large-scale to settlement farming allowed for a higher per acre operating margin at market values on Low Density settlements, but a lower margin than before on the High Density schemes. However, at accounting values, the planned change in land use was always shown to lead to an improvement. In all four areas, settlement as planned appeared to be socially profitable, and preferable to large-scale farming.

With the single exception of Kipipiri (HD, HA) settlement in practice was less profitable than was planned, actual production being lowest in relation to the planned levels in the two low altitude schemes. Kabisi (HD, LA) settlers never had the opportunity to fulfil the plans for their scheme, and in practice that settlement was less profitable at both market and accounting values than large-scale farming. However, in every other case the operating margin was higher than for large farms. Settlement has led to an intensification of production and an improvement in profitability.

Conversion from market to accounting prices had effects that varied between schemes. By far the most important items from the viewpoint of revaluation were the social costs of land and

TABLE 11.1

A summary of the main results 1967-68 prices

£ per acre

Settlement Name:	Kabisi		Lessos		Kipipiri		Passenga		'Average' LD		'Average' HD	
Settlement Type:	HD	LA	LD	LA	HD	HA	LD	HA				
	MP	AP	MP	AP	MP	AP	MP	AP	MP	AP	MP	AP
1. Large-scale farming												
Output	5.80	6.15	4.65	4.59	8.07	7.56	7.74	7.09	-	-	-	-
Costs	3.73	4.23	3.55	3.54	7.37	6.47	6.82	6.06	-	-	-	-
Operating margin	2.07	1.92	1.10	1.05	0.70	1.09	0.92	1.03	-	-	-	-
2. Settlement Plans												
Output	7.83	8.12	10.79	11.36	4.71	5.04	8.15	8.33	-	-	-	-
Costs	6.67	5.50	6.36	6.66	4.21	3.40	5.75	5.98	-	-	-	-
Operating margin	1.17	2.62	4.42	4.70	0.50	1.64	2.40	2.35	-	-	-	-
NPV	5.35	13.41	30.92	37.49	0.63	22.76	17.22	29.33	-	-	-	-
ROR %	28	18	INF	INF	13	INF	INF	INF	-	-	-	-
3. Settlement Actuals												
Output	6.07	6.53	9.23	10.11	7.55	8.60	9.18	9.72	7.94	8.64	6.42	7.11
Costs	9.31	6.36	5.72	8.47	5.72	6.09	6.84	8.37	6.50	8.43	5.63	5.95
Operating margin	-3.24	-0.18	3.87	1.64	1.83	2.51	2.34	1.35	1.44	0.21	0.79	1.16
NPV	-15.64	4.56	25.31	17.11	6.81	20.75	10.83	13.55	7.06	0.00	1.32	9.63
ROR %	% 4	9	57	INF	INF	INF	INF	INF	INF	3	13	INF
4. Labour Costs[a]												
Large-scale Farming	0.96		0.72		1.33		1.14					
Settlement plans	3.04		2.42		2.80		1.73					
Settlement actuals	7.18		3.08		4.17		2.67		2.84		3.93	

[a] Market Prices. See text for detail of items included.

Note: Output, Costs and Operating Margin refer only to the 'stability' year; 1959 for large-scale farming; the 'maturity' year of the budgets; and 1967-8 for the settlement actuals. Finance flows are not included.

Output covers all production, including subsistence. Costs include farm costs (including the value of settlers' family labour), the marketing costs of co-operatives and Department costs at all levels.

NPV and ROR values are based on the full cost and output flows (including finance) from the initiation of each scheme, assuming that it will last indefinitely at a long-term stabilized level.

settlers' family labour. These two items were valued individually for each settlement. There was no systematic relationship between land values and the estimated net product of land. In one instance, its social value was higher than the market price, but otherwise it was lower. The cost of family labour varied according to settlers' incomes. On Low Density schemes, where farms were larger and more profitable, family labour was more costly at accounting than at market prices[1] but this factor had a much smaller effect on High Density settlements. Naturally the results were sensitive to the treatment of land and family labour, as they also were to the inclusion in the evaluation of finance flows. However, in general alternative treatments of finance flows and the application of an expansion factor to the last known annual operating surplus had little effect on the results.

The lower part of Table 11.1 shows the value at market prices of unskilled labour brought into account at each level of study. In every case this includes the cost of wages actually paid, as well as the imputed value of settlers' family labour. In the settlement schemes, this was always by far the biggest labour item. The figures suggest that settlement led to a great intensification of labour utilization. This was especially true of Kabisi, the imputed cost of the large post-settlement families there being one reason for the poor 'actual' result. Family size in that scheme appears to have been exceptional, the other three schemes being more representative in this respect.[2]

[1] The market price cost of family labour is taken as its alternative earnings.

[2] The figures relate to the cost of labour. In the absence of figures on wage rates at all levels, reliable figures of numbers supported cannot be estimated. However, preliminary estimates of numbers of adults employed per 1,000 acres gave the following figures:

As a final stage, aggregated average figures for Low and High Density schemes were prepared for settlement in practice. These are shown in the last four columns of Table 11.1. With the same assumptions as elsewhere, it appears that, whereas at market prices Low Density showed up as the most profitable form of settlement, at accounting prices the order was reversed. While High Density as a whole looked very attractive, Low Density seemed barely profitable in social terms. Probably available data under-rates the value of output in both cases, and both programmes were probably socially profitable as a whole. However, there is a strong implication that the Low Density programme may contain individual settlements that are not socially profitable. On such schemes unprofitability generally arises either because the plans for these settlements were not socially profitable, or because, in actual development, the settlers followed paths that differed from the plans. The major cause of the poor outcome at Kabisi—the non-availability of cattle—would almost certainly not apply to Low Density settlements.

11.5 THE APPLICABILITY OF THE LITTLE-MIRRLEES METHOD

For the great majority of inputs and products, the application of the Little-Mirrlees method presented no very unusual problems. The settlements were chosen for study because they contained a wide range of inputs and products. Consequently accounting prices were calculated for a fairly large number of major items and, as was shown in Part I, several called for special treatment. The most relevant features of the application to the settlements is the very great importance of one cost item—Settlers' Family Labour—and the need for and problems of adjusting land prices to reflect social values.

	Before settlement	*After settlement*
Kabisi	23	213
Lessos	-45	109
Kipipiri	33	166
Passenga	38	96

11.5.1 *Family Labour*

The cost of family labour at 'market prices' presents important problems of definition. This major input into small-scale family farming is not paid a wage. Our estimates of its market price cost have been based on what family members' alternative earnings might have been, but there is no very satisfactory way of knowing what these would have been for all family members; how many adult family members would, without settlement, have been available for other productive employment and for what period; and how time that settlers spent earning non-farm income should be handled. To obtain realistic and acceptably accurate estimates of these things would require more field-work than we could contemplate. Although we have made the most realistic assumptions in the circumstances, these are obviously crude and the treatment of this item, to whose variation the appraisals are obviously very sensitive, could undoubtedly have been improved if more information on local earnings opportunities in each area had been available, together with a more complete picture of the detailed composition of and income-sharing relationships within settlement families.

These same difficulties apply to the estimation of the social cost of family labour, which is based on the same starting point of alternative earnings, but which incorporates other factors which themselves present problems, many of which were explained in Chapter 5. However, a fundamental feature of the method outlined there—and used in all estimates of unskilled labour costs—is the use of income-based weightings for valuing extra benefits received by private individuals. The use of weights had little effect on the evaluation of High Density settlements, since the extra benefits thought to be enjoyed by settlers were relatively small. However, the social profit of the Low Density schemes was sensitive to the weights used, as settlers' incomes there increased substantially. As a result, our method of valuing family labour had a big effect in altering the relative attractiveness of the two types of settlement considered.

The important point here is that the outcome of our study depends a lot on the treatment of this cost item, whose calculation contains this important but uncommon element. We feel that income-based weightings of some kind should be used in the social valuation of labour and we have been bold in choosing a basis for determining these weightings. This is, however, a particularly 'normative' feature of the study. No doubt the principle and the form of the weighting function will occasion comment, and the Kenya Government may not completely accept our particular judgement on this matter. Whenever rural development involves giving a fairly substantial lift in income to family farmers, the form of the weighting function used will be very important to social appraisal.

These two aspects of labour valuation (alternative earnings and progressive income weights) are, amongst the agricultural projects to which the Little-Mirrlees method has so far been applied, peculiar in their significance to this study. However, they are aspects of social appraisal that will be important in the great majority of rural development projects, where change is introduced through family farming and farm families are the principal beneficiaries.

11.5.2 *Land*

Our experience of valuing land as the capitalized value of the stream of net social or market value benefits obtainable from a particular form of land use suggests that the agreed purchase prices (which were based on market values) were a very imperfect guide to either. The settlement land was bought on the basis of valuations that should have reflected the profitability of large-scale farming by Europeans. That was the 'normal' situation to which the values were related. Whether it was realistic to regard this as the proper alternative to settlement or not, our method allowed capitalized profitability estimates to be compared with the valuations. This approach, despite crudeness in the estimation procedure, showed that there was a substantial difference in three of the four cases between valuation and residual values based on capitalized profit. The difference was not systematic, although at market values actual purchase prices tended to be above the calculated residual values when the latter were based on 'realistic' private discount rates. This may have reflected the situation common in agriculture that farmers accept unusually low returns on their own funds, although the rate of return implied by the market values varied between cases from 3 to 12½ per cent. Almost certainly, land values were influenced by considerations other than profitability.

This experience suggests that existing free market values for land may not be a suitable basis to which to apply a standardized accounting ratio to convert from market to social values. If widely different land-use projects are being compared, it may often be necessary for the profitability and capitalization of alternative uses to be calculated separately for each. Here again, more evidence from different situations could give a clearer indication of the extent and nature of distortions in free land markets in developing countries. However, the need to make a detailed valuation of land for project appraisal will generally arise only when a major change in land-use structure and practice is contemplated.

11.5.3 *Finance flows*

Another feature of the settlement study calling for special treatment is the inclusion of external money flows connected with individual schemes. There are likely to be many project situations where this practice will be appropriate. These finance flows are very simply handled in the Little-Mirrlees method, foreign exchange in the hands of government being the numeraire. External finance flows are, at 'market prices', expressed exactly in these terms and thus need no adjustment for conversion to social prices.

11.6 SOME POLICY IMPLICATIONS

This study, and the methodology which it employs, may help throw light on some important policy questions. A few merit brief consideration.

11.6.1 *Alternative major forms of land use*

Whether land in the Kenya Highlands should best be farmed in small or large units is a question that has been argued for many years. One of the principal difficulties in this debate has been the resolution of conflicting objectives, namely productivity of land or labour on the one hand and labour absorption on the other. Although it is often argued that small farms are almost always more intensively farmed than large ones,[1] this does not imply necessarily that smallholder farming is the most profitable in the full social sense. Through our method we have sought to combine all factors in a single set of measures, and so to avoid problems associated with multiple criteria.

It appears that both for the four areas studied and for the 'averages' of the two types of scheme, small-scale farming of the types represented is preferable. It would be wrong to generalize too far from this, but our study suggests that, at relative prices applying at the time, the change to smallholder crops (pyrethrum and milk especially) from large-scale holdings based on those enterprises requiring management in large units—sheep, small grains, beef cattle breeding and rearing—may be a change for the better, and that the continuing sub-division of large holdings recommended by the ILO Mission may be justifiable. This would certainly be the case unless very high levels of technical efficiency were obtainable only in large-scale farming. However, even then, those types of large-scale farming based on the intensive use of undervalued inputs—fertiliser and sometimes farmers themselves, who may have abilities that are in short supply—to produce overvalued products like wheat could seldom be socially profitable.

11.6.2 *Alternative forms of settlement*

This study has shown that, whereas at market prices Low Density settlement appears to be more profitable than High Density, in social terms the latter will generally be the case. This suggests that the decision to follow in the 'Harambee' settlement programme a pattern similar to that for High Density may have been wiser than copying Low Density.

Two further points can be made. First, without using a method which aims to take account not only of true opportunity costs and efficiency in resource use but also of governments' implicit income distribution objectives, the relative social profitability of the two types of scheme would almost certainly have been misjudged. Second, our study has covered only two types of settlement. Other land sub-division approaches were followed in Kenya. It is quite likely that

[1] Dorner, 1972, largely bases his case for distributive land reform on this argument.

applying our methods to the 'Squatter' or 'Haraka' settlement schemes might show them to have been even more socially profitable than High Density. The major inputs are land of low value, and family labour, whose social cost is likely to be very close to its alternative earnings. Although less intensively productive than much land in the other settlement programmes (and consequently sometimes castigated for being 'uneconomic'), these settlements may prove to have been the most socially profitable of all. The question should not be prejudged, but our method shows that a high level of output does not necessarily imply social profitability, especially if the surplus generated is not widely distributed to low-income people. The method of this study could be applied to all forms of land transfer in the Kenya Highlands to indicate which was the most 'appropriate' in the widest sense.

11.6.3 *The value of the method for guiding policy decisions in settlement planning*

The valuation method used, and the general approach that underlies it, could be adopted to help guide several important policy questions.

(1) The social suitability of different farming structures

In principle, a given stretch of land, especially one involved in an orderly ownership-transfer programme, might be suitable for use in a number of ways, from large-scale mechanized units[1] through smaller mechanized units, 'large' peasant farms, smaller cash-and-subsistence farms, to those producing subsistence only. In the Kenya Highlands, all of these land-use types were developed during the 1960s. Given the availability of data, the relative merits of each could be determined. In general, the outcome might have been that, where productivity was not related to scale of operation, the smaller the farms, the higher the social profit. However, the management of some areas with difficult soils, or the production of certain crops or types of stock may call for forms of organization and levels of management that are scarce and can only be obtained if management were paid competitive (and consequently relatively

[1] The largest such unit in Kenya, the Ol Kalou Salient, is run by the Department of Settlement.

high) wages. Without a systematic evaluation that embraces alternative levels of inputs, outputs and income distribution effects, clear indications of the best choice from alternative land-use strategies may not be obtained. The relative social merits of each type may never be established, with the consequence that, as in Kenya during the 1960s, all types operate simultaneously and emphasis shifts from one to another according to fashion rather than changes in underlying conditions and objectives.

(2) Land valuation

Our method for valuing land is that normally employed in economic analysis, which attributes to it the residual value after operating balances are capitalized and the value of other assets is deducted. This approach can be used to estimate the profitability of any pattern of use for a particular piece of land. It could also be used to determine, for any given planned land-use system, the maximum land price that would allow a particular project to remain profitable. In Kenya land can be purchased only on the basis of free negotiation. This valuation approach would not necessarily indicate what price government *should* pay for any suitable piece of farming land, irrespective of the interests of the seller or other buyers. However, if (as our experience suggests) land values are not directly related to profitability in use, this approach would indicate which farms (distinguished according to market price) of a similar quality should be sought for purchase for a particular use. There is more to commend such an approach than the practice in the 1960s of purchasing farms purely because of their location, the circumstances of their ownership, or other factors unrelated to future use, and then planning as best one can within the constraint of a separately determined land cost.

(3) The distribution of settlement benefits

Within any planned land-use system, our general method, and especially the weighting of income benefits, can help to indicate those aspects of settlement administration affecting the distribution of the social benefits generated. Important policy questions arise in settlement planning regarding *inter alia* product and input price policy; the allocation of production quotas; the prices at which land may be sold to incoming farmers; and loan repayment terms and conditions. These and other important planning questions can be dealt with systematically in our method to arrive at the most appropriate arrangement for each form of settlement. Thus, the distribution of costs and generated benefits between settlers and government that loan repayment and settlement charges specifically allow for could be optimally determined. However, the same general conditions should not be expected to be most appropriate in all types of settlement. Different land charges or loan repayment schedules might be optimal for each type of scheme. Moreover, using this approach would free these important questions from the consideration of purely financial requirements that were so dominant in the planning of the High and Low Density programmes during the early 1960s and since. As a result, land-use policy could be more firmly based on social objectives.

CHAPTER 12

The Kenya Settlement Programmes

12.1 INTRODUCTION: THE DIFFERENT APPROACHES TO LAND TRANSFER

Land settlement projects of different kinds have been developed in various parts of Kenya since 1939, particularly during the early 1960s. Those begun before 1961 were largely of an *ad hoc* nature. None was large, and each settlement was specially designed to meet the needs of a particular situation. However, in the early 1960s a new form of settlement was begun which became embodied in a large new programme whose size and speed of implementation has attracted much attention.

This study concerns four of the settlements developed as part of the new programme of the 1960s. The programme concerned, known (albeit inaccurately) under the general title of the 'Million Acre Settlement Scheme', arose out of special features of Kenya's land history. Until its revocation in 1960, an Order-in-Council provided that much of the highland parts of the country should be reserved exclusively for occupation by European farmers. The revocation of the Order was soon followed by constitutional developments which made it a political necessity that substantial portions of the area popularly known as the 'White Highlands' should quickly be transferred from European to African ownership. Several programmes were begun for the transfer to local people of the 3,500 or so individual properties which these areas contained. The settlement schemes considered here were elements in one of these land-transfer programmes.

The White Highlands were ecologically very heterogeneous. This gave rise to a wide range of different types of farming systems. In some areas, the land-use economy was based on plantation crops, especially tea, sisal and coffee. For a variety of reasons, land in these areas was not transferred quickly to new ownership. Nor, in the main, were the extensive areas of semi-arid ranching land that the Highlands contained. Most of the land transfer that the Government prompted and assisted took place in the mixed-farming areas, where wheat, maize, barley, oats and pyrethrum were the main crops, their production being associated with the keeping of various types of stock, particularly dairy and beef cattle, and woolled sheep.

Land in these areas was typically farmed in units of 800 to 1,000 acres, although size varied enormously. The transfer programmes for mixed farm areas mainly involved two types of arrangement. Under the first, individual farms were sold on a willing-buyer, willing-seller basis to individuals, partnerships, companies or co-operatives who could raise sufficient capital for a small deposit and for working capital, but who received considerable financial support from the Land Bank and other public financial institutions. The structure of ownership and land use was in principle unchanged, and large-scale mechanized mixed farming of the kind that had previously been practised generally continued. Transfers of this kind have gone on steadily since 1962. By 1969, about 1,200 farms had changed hands in this way, involving around one million acres.[1]

The second type of arrangement was quite different. It envisaged the purchase of the land by the Government and its planned sub-division for occupation by small family farmers. They would obtain some input services from co-operative societies to whom they would also sell produce, all with the assistance of Government services provided at a comparatively intensive level. This kind of change generally increased significantly the numbers of people living and owning land in the areas transferred. Often whole new communities were created. For planning and administrative convenience, this operation of 'settling' new farmers on an area was carried out in a series of 'Settlement Schemes', each of which had its own boundaries, administration and, eventually, its own community identity.

Settlement programmes of different types have been implemented in the former White Highlands since 1961. To administer these schemes, new Government Departments were

[1] Development Plan 1970-74, p.200

established. Most important was the Department of Settlement.[1] Sub-divisional settlement programmes were its main function in these areas. However, the Department also administered some other land-transfer arrangements, partly for reasons of 'historic accident' and partly because they were financed in a way similar to the sub-divisional settlements. These included 8 co-operative mixed farms, 9 co-operative ranches, 129 Assisted Owners, 119 Compassionate Case farms, and the Ol Kalou Salient. There, some 80 large farms were first brought into a single massive farming unit. It has since been sub-divided into 19 operational units with an average size of 6,500 acres which it is planned will eventually be operated by semi-independent co-operatives as large extensive farms.

These non-subdivisional programmes are not the subject of further consideration here. However, all reflect the basic philosophy of credit-financed land transfer by purchase for continuous intensive operation that characterizes all of the Department's operations.

The Department has to date (mid-1973) carried out four separate settlement programmes. Between 1961 and 1968, it mainly concentrated on the High and Low Density programmes which are considered in more detail below. In 1969 a third, small programme, the Harambee Scheme, was carried out, whose style was broadly similar to that of middle-income High Density. Finally, in 1972, a fourth programme was begun, the Shirika settlements. These schemes, which combine sub-divisional settlement with large-scale operation of part of the land concerned, are very new, and little is known about them.

In addition to the four sub-divisional programmes operated by the Department, a fifth was operated in the late 1960s by a separate, specially created agent, the Special Commissioner for Squatters. This officer, using technical staff from other Departments, arranged for abandoned or run-down farms and some forest reserve land to be sub-divided for allocation to landless, unemployed people who, at settlement, received no material assistance and very little advisory support. These

[1] The Department grew out of an earlier new body, the Land Development and Settlement Board (LDSB), which ceased to exist on 31 July 1962, when the new Department was created.

low-cost schemes, which could at first give rise to little more than subsistence farming, were taken over by the Department in 1971. It is not known how many families they affected, but the Development Plan 1970-74[1] refers to 13,000 farmers having been settled in this way by 1968.

These outline details of land transfer operations (which began in 1961 and are still going on), and of the different types of settlement programme, emphasize the great variety of approaches that were taken to the joint problems presented by the need (i) to change rapidly the land ownership pattern that existed in the White Highlands in 1960, and (ii) to continue the development on this land of a modern farming sector. This study looks at only one of the types of strategies employed. Although the settlements studied represent the major programmes, three points should be emphasized:

(1) the High and Low Density schemes are only two of the five different types of settlement with which the Department has been concerned;

(2) sub-divisional settlements were only part (albeit the major part) of the responsibilities of the Department, and

(3) the land transfer programme outside the orbit of the Department was also very substantial.[2]

12.2 THE HIGH AND LOW DENSITY SETTLEMENT PROGRAMMES

These two programmes, which were amongst the most important features of Government economic activity in the 1960s, have been the subject of many papers and reports.[3] Only the most salient details need be considered here.

[1] P.207.

[2] Illustrating this point, the land on which was situated the Beef Research Station that is the subject of Part III of this book, was also included in the land transfer programme. In this case, as with several others, the transfer was to the Government.

[3] Main sources include: Carey-Jones, 1965; Department of Settlement, *Annual Reports*; Etherington, 1963; LDSB, 1963; MacArthur, 1968; Maina and MacArthur, 1970; Nottidge and Goldsack, 1966; Odingo, 1967 and 1971 (Ch. 9); Storrar, 1964; Whetham, 1968; Kenya Government, Van Arkadie Mission, 1966.

The rationale of their development stems largely from the financial arrangements made. The objects of the programme were not limited to a rapid but orderly transition in land ownership between immigrant and indigenous owners. Other main purposes were the maintenance and intensification of previous land-use patterns; an increase in the numbers of people supported on the land; and the restoration of confidence amongst the immigrant farming community as a whole. During a period of obvious political uncertainty, the continuation of intensive farming by other Europeans would be required for several years. To meet the latter point especially, it was accepted that all land should be purchased from outgoing farmers at prices based on market values. This arrangement implied the commitment of large sums of money, much of which was available from the British Government as long-term normal-interest-bearing loans.

So that the land purchase cost should not become a general exchequer burden, the settlement farms were to be sold to incoming settlers through 30-year mortgage loans from the Settlement Fund Trustees[1] carrying interest at 6½ per cent. So as to allow farmers to generate funds to service these loans, it was important that development assets should be made available from the outset in fairly large amounts, financed through development loans to farmers, to co-operative societies, to machinery contractors and for water supply. Thus, both to meet the development objectives and to make the programme viable financially within the stipulated conditions, a fairly high level of farming intensity had to be attained through the supply of large amounts of credit as quickly as possible after settlers entered their farms. Furthermore, both to meet the rigorous planning standards set, to permit the large amount of associated administration to be carried out, and to try to ensure that farmers quickly reached high levels of production, heavy land development and administrative costs had to be incurred by the Department.

These two settlement programmes began in 1962. By December 1970, expenditure on them by the Department of Settlement was as follows:

[1] The Trustees (SFT) were the three Ministers of Agriculture, Finance, and Lands and Settlement. All finance and assets in the programme were vested in them, and the Department of Settlement operated basically as agents of the SFT.

	High Density[1]	*Low Density*	*Total* (£'000)
Land Purchase	10,751	1,902	12,653
Development Loans	4,778	2,027	6,805
Administrative Expenses[2]			9,270
Totals	15,529	3,929	28,728

Although the figures overstate the costs of land purchase and development loans for High Density schemes, and administrative costs attributable to the two programmes, most of these costs are due to the sub-divisional schemes. They indicate expensive forms of settlement.

The High Density programme was much bigger than the Low Density. Table 12.1 shows that, by 1970, nearly 29,000 settlers had been placed in some 84 schemes. This was nearly six times the number placed in the Low Density programme. The essential difference between the two types was the target income expected for each settler, and allowed for in the planning of farm sizes and available development loans. Most High Density farms were planned to allow a cash surplus (after loan repayment and excluding the value of subsistence foods) during the years of maximum loan repayment of only £25 or £40. Low Density farms were planned to allow cash surpluses of £100 or more.

Other important differences existed between the two types. The Low Density schemes were to be developed on land with considerable unrealized development potential. No such stipulation was made for the High Density settlements. Consequently, the latter were often located on land of poor quality, a fact which is reflected in the table: despite the big differences in target incomes per plot, the average area per settler in the two programmes is not wildly different. A further difference is that Low Density settlers had to be able to show on application that they had experience of modern farming, whilst they had to deposit cash or farming assets of a fairly high value—£100 or more. High Density settlers on the other hand

[1] Includes co-operative farms and ranches.

[2] Includes all Department activities.

Table 12.1

Summary details of settlements in the High and Low Density programmes

Target Income[a]	No. of Schemes	Total area (acres)	No. of plots	Acres per plot
(1) **High Density**				
A. *Low income schemes*				
25	10	79,011	3,649	21.7
25-40	17	208,657	6,710	31.1
25-70	22	229,790	8,716	26.4
25-75	2	21,627	675	32.1
25-100	1	2,273	35	64.9
Total £25 schemes	52	541,358	19,785	27.4
40	13	127,882	4,845	26.4
40-50	5	41,875	1,181	35.5
40-80	1	10,146	409	24.8
Total £40 schemes	19	179,903	6,435	28.0
Total low income schemes	71	721,261	26,220	27.5
B. *Middle income schemes*				
60	1	1,782	180	9.9
70	10	77,788	2,223	35.0
70-100	1	4,436	54	62.1
100	1	10,482	253	42.4
Total middle income schemes	13	94,488	2,710	34.9
Total High Density	84	815,750	28,930	28.2
(2) **Low Density**				
100	34	173,627	4,946	35.1
250	1	4,890	35	139.8
Total Low Density	35	178,517	4,981	35.8
Total High and Low Density Settlements	119	994,267	33,911	29.3

Source: Appendix G of the Annual Report of the Department of Settlement for 1970.

a. The ranges shown are those referred to in the source report. In each settlement the farms would typically have target incomes of the lowest value shown. Generally only abnormal plots were budgeted for incomes at the top of each income range.

were mainly to be recruited from people who would otherwise be landless and unemployed. An incidental feature of this programme was the need to create a very large number of new small-scale modern farmers. However, the relative farming abilities of the two types of farmer were not reflected in the levels of intensity of administrative and advisory support. Each scheme in both programmes had a supervisory team of roughly similar size (see below, Table A.13.2). However, both in terms of acreage and numbers of settlers, the High Density schemes were almost twice the size of the Low Density settlements. High Density settlers had to learn from experience much more than their better-endowed Low Density fellows.

Naturally the distribution of large areas of land was surrounded by local political interests, many of which concerned the tribal allocation of the settlement areas. To meet these needs in selecting areas to be purchased for settlement, land of a suitable type was sought for each main tribal group whose land was contiguous with the Highlands. In the event, it was possible to arrange that each tribe concerned that needed land had at least one High and one Low Density settlement in its 'sphere of influence' area. This arrangement, which called for no little ingenuity in planning, gave rise to a very scattered pattern of settlements along the fringes of the Highlands, as the Map shows. Given this need to spread their occurrence, and the wide range of ecological conditions throughout the whole area, many different types of farming system were planned for, including new crops in some areas, like sugar production on schemes in Nyanza Province, and tea in four separate places. However, the settlement programmes as a whole are dominated by two main types of area: the cool, high land to the West and North of the Aberdares, where pyrethrum, small-grains, dairying and sheep offer the main farming possibilities; and the lower, warmer areas West of the Rift Valley, where maize production and dairying are the main operations.

12.3 THE SETTLEMENTS CHOSEN FOR STUDY

The main purpose of this study was to gain experience in the application of the Little-Mirrlees method of shadow pricing to small-scale mixed farming of the types that the settlement programmes contain. Another objective was to try to say something useful about the relative social profitability of different types of settlement project. Consequently settlements of different but interesting kinds were sought for which usable information was known to be obtainable. To get some idea of how settlement was working out in practice, it was also desirable to select schemes that had been in operation for several years.

Given these considerations it was decided that four schemes would be selected, covering the four main settlement situations. Two of each of High and Low Density, one of each at high altitude and one at low altitude. Some of the Low Density schemes, especially the earlier ones, are very small, and in the economic surveys from which much data was obtained the size of sample from them was also small. To overcome problems stemming from these causes, it was decided to study as a group sets of basically similar contiguous Low Density schemes. As it happened, the High Density schemes selected were larger than average. Studying groups of three Low Density schemes at each altitude meant that all of the four 'settlements' studied were fairly similar in total size.

Identifying details of the chosen settlements are given in Table 12.2. The three Low Density schemes at low altitude share a single co-operative society. These three are referred to below as the Lessos Settlements. The three at high altitude, referred to as the Passenga Settlements, each have their own society. All of the settlements considered are amongst the oldest in the two programmes. Taken together, they not only contain the range of situations that was sought, but allow estimates to be made of the social values of the planned intentions and the actual experiences of the four major types of scheme being developed in 1962 and 1963. Farm Survey data for the two schemes in Western Kenya,[1] Kabisi and Lessos are available in a continuous series up to 1967-8. This particular data source is less complete for the high altitude settlements, Passenga and Kipipiri. Implications of this situation are discussed in Chapter 14, where an account is given of how a picture was built up of the operation of the settlements in practice.

[1] The location of the settlements is shown in the Map, where the scheme numbers identify each one.

TABLE 12.2

Particulars of the four 'settlements' chosen for study

Scheme number and name	Scheme type	Target Income (£ p.a.)	Altitude (metres a.s.l)	Area (acres)	Final no. of settlers	Date of first land purchase	Name of Co-operative Society	Coverage in economic surveys 1963-4	1964-5	1965-6	1966-7	1967-8
12 Kabisi	High D	25–40	1,650	12,277	701	Jan. 1963	Farmers C.S.	-	X	X	X	X
The Lessos Group												
47 Lessos	Low D	100	2,050	5,679	130	Dec. 1962	Kabisi		X	X	X	X
48 Keben	Low D	100	1,980	3,716	147	April 1961	Lessos	X	X	X	X	X
53 Koylat	Low D	100	2,150	4,749	88	March 1963	Farmers C.S.		X	X	X	X
The Passenga Group												
210 Nyairoko	Low D	100	2,680	4,913	99	Dec. 1962	Nyairoko Farmers C.S.		X	X	-	-
213 Passenga	Low D	100	2,750	4,774	125	Feb. 1963	Passenga Farmers C.S.		X	X	-	X
214 Silanga	Low D	100	2,650	3,890	89	Feb. 1963	Silanga Farmers C.S.		X	X	X	X
229 Kipipiri	High D	25	2,440	12,338	525	June 1962	Kipipiri Farmers C.S.		X	X	-	-

CHAPTER 13

The Plans for the Four Settlements

13.1 INTRODUCTION

In this chapter an account is given of the way in which the complete picture of planned development for each settlement was built up from various data sources, and necessary assumptions are explained. First a general account is given of the basic planning elements of the settlement process. The next sections explain how detailed estimates were obtained of the planned value of these elements for one settlement, Kabisi. Much of the detail of cost calculation is to be found in Appendix A.13. After the general features and the Kibisi plan have been considered in some detail, the plan for each other settlement is briefly discussed. Finally the four sets of plan figures are brought together in summary form. All values referred to and derived in this chapter are at market prices.

For appraisal, each settlement is defined as embracing all activities contributing to and arising from the development and operation of farming on the land identified as a particular scheme. All costs directly attributable to this purpose are considered relevant, including the administration costs of the Department. Sale produce is valued as it leaves the settlement area. In many cases this is after handling and processing by the co-operative. By valuing production at this stage, the market prices used are the same as apply to other agricultural producers in Kenya delivering more than small quantities. Defining each scheme in this way means, however, that the costs of establishing and operating the co-operatives have to be included. Taking account of these and other off-farm expenses essential to the operation of the settlements allows a comprehensive picture to be built up for each scheme that covers virtually all cost and output items analagous to those that might be taken into account in building up a picture of any other kind of farming, including large-scale operation of the land as it was used before purchase, as described in Chapter 15.[1]

The settlement programme as a whole, and the individual schemes within the programme, were the subject of relatively detailed planning, and the actual plans are the main source of our estimates of planned costs and production. Much of this planning information is available in published documents, including particularly Nottidge and Goldsack, (1966), and the Annual Reports of the Department of Settlement, its predecessor the Land Development and Settlement Board (LDSB), and the Central Land Board (CLB), which was responsible for the purchase of land on which the settlement programmes were implemented. Additional material was obtained directly from the Department and this has in some cases been supplemented by unpublished information from other Kenya Government sources. These sources, which are discussed in Appendix A.13, collectively cover plans for almost every aspect of these relatively complex types of settlement. However, two important elements of the programme were never the subject of detailed cost estimates: first, the marketing operations of the co-operative societies through which settlers sell much of their surplus produce; and second, the opportunity cost of the settlers and their families. Our planning estimates for the societies were based on the analysed accounts of each scheme's Co-operative in the manner described in Appendix A.13. The cost of family labour was discussed in Chapter 5, and further details are given in this chapter.

13.2 THE OPERATIONS ASSOCIATED WITH THE DEVELOPMENT OF A SETTLEMENT PROJECT

The processes involved in preparing for, establishing and operating a settlement project extend over several years, dating from the time when the decision is made to prepare for a particular scheme. The types of expense that arise are of four basic kinds.

[1] This is not quite true, in that the estimates for both the plan and actual costs of settlements include the costs of administering the different credit programmes. No analagous costs item is taken account of in Chapter 15 for large-scale farming, but for that type of farming this cost is likely to have been very small.

1. Change in land use of the kind that all settlement projects involve requires incurring once-and-for-all expenditures on *planning and preparation of the settlement site*, to provide the framework for orderly allocation and occupation of the land. For the settlements considered in this study, inescapable expenses additional to these pre-settlement costs were incurred in transferring to Government ownership the land on which the settlements were developed.

2. Although not an essential feature of every settlement programme, *permanent improvement in the land structure* is a common preliminary to the establishment of a settlement project. Thus, roads may be constructed, water storage and supply installations put in, soil conversion and protection works built, and other permanent improvements of this kind constructed, either before settlers are admitted, or in the first few years after occupation.

3. *Establishment and initiation of the prepared settlement* as a viable form of continuous productive land use is the third main type of cost. This stage, in which the community is created and the land-use processes got going, involves such things as the transportation of settlers and their assets to the settlement site; the issue to them and associated agencies of the moveable assets required to begin farming; and, where necessary, the distribution to new arrivals of food or cash to tide them over the period until the harvest of their first crops. Necessarily associated with many of these initiating processes will be administrative costs for documentation and financial recording, the organization of group activities, and the instruction of farmers in the new technologies required for the systems of farming being developed.

4. The fourth type of expense is for the long-term *operation of the settlement project* as a continuing productive activity. Costs of this kind can usually be further divided into three groups, according to who incurs them.

(i) Farm expenses incurred by settlers in the production processes.

(ii) Costs incurred by multi-farm agencies like co-operatives and machinery contractors, which allow advantage to be taken of scale economies in different processes, particularly in the handling of farmers' produce through the early marketing stages of grading, bulking and processing, and in supplying input services that individuals could not provide for themselves.

(iii) The cost of administration and advisory personnel outside the farms, whose continuing presence is required for the management of the settlement project at a planned level of intensity. They are provided and paid for by the Government.

The sequence of processes in settlement operation does not necessarily exactly follow the order in which they have been considered. For cost-benefit analysis, particulars of the time sequence of operations is required. Different cost items in the planned development of High and Low Density settlements are considered below in order of their position in the time sequence of events, which is mainly based on the account given in Nottidge and Goldsack. This chapter indicates what it was *planned* would happen, not the sequence and timing that actually occurred.

Operations would begin with the *valuation* of each large farm within the indicative boundary of a proposed settlement. We estimate that this valuation process, negotiation of the price, payment and the handover of the farm would take six months on average. This stage would end with the payment on the day of takeover of the full *Land Purchase Price* for the land and fixed assets concerned.

On takeover, in practice, many properties had growing crops on them, including perennial crops like pyrethrum. In a number of cases, livestock were also purchased from outgoing farmers and others, and held by the Department before re-sale to settlers. Thus, whilst the area was being prepared for settlement the property would be managed, and to an extent 'farmed' by the Department; unissued live-stock would be maintained, and growing crops tended and harvested. This was especially important where production quotas had to be maintained. This stage, '*Interim Farming*', might generally have been expected to last about a year, before all productive operations were taken over by the settlers. During this period, attempts were naturally made to run these enterprises on a business-like basis, but in the event incomes from these farming operations (which included the maintenance of Livestock Holding Grounds) were generally less than expenses, and losses arose. Realistic planning would have anticipated the need for finance to cover losses of this kind.

During this interim phase, the settlement area would be surveyed for the *Preparation of Planning Maps*. This process would generally be completed within six months from the date of farm takeover.

When the maps were available *Planning and Demarcation* of the settlement farms could be carried out, in which the structural pattern to be laid out was determined, agreed and marked on the ground. This stage would be quickly followed by the installation of *Roads and Soil Conservation Works*. Both planning and installation would normally be completed within six months of the completed planning maps becoming available. Thus, generally by twelve months after takeover (eighteen months after valuation began), each scheme would be laid out and ready for settlement.

The introduction of settlers, which constitutes the main act of 'settlement', would then occur. With the arrival of settlers and the allocation of farms, each scheme would become subject to a typical pattern of *Supervision and Administration* by the Department. Supervision costs have been identified at three levels: on the scheme itself; at Field Headquarters level (i.e. at Senior Settlement Officer and Area Controller levels);[1] and at Settlement Headquarters in Nairobi.

It was originally planned that intensive administration, particularly at field level, would be required only during the first 30 months after settlement, during which time the principal functions of the administrative and advisory personnel would be: the allocation of farms; the issue and recording of all development loan materials; initial documentation; the organization and development of co-operative societies and other farm input supply or marketing agencies; and the

[1] At different periods, the structure of settlement administration outside headquarters varied to meet changing needs, but in the mid and late 1960s there were four Area Controllers, each of whom serviced an average of three Senior Settlement Officers, who typically were each responsible for around ten settlement schemes.

instruction of settlers in the ways of the new style of farming. At the end of this period, it was intended that the intensity of staffing would be reduced, and supervision expenses would be incurred at a lower level. However, experience showed that withdrawal of staff as early as two and a half years after the date of settlement could not be undertaken without seriously risking the progress of the schemes. Consequently, the original plans were amended to allow for a second thirty-month period of 'Extended Supervision' to end five years after the date of settlement. It has been assumed that this period of extended supervision was a feature of the plan to be evaluated. What it was planned should happen after the periods of original and extended supervision was not, to the best of our knowledge, ever defined. Consequently, assumptions had to be made about what might have been expected to happen beyond that stage. Alternative possibilities are considered in Chapter 16.

When settlers were allocated their plots, a number of essential processes would begin almost simultaneously with supervision, all of which give rise to significant expenditure. These costs are mainly of the type (3), referred to above. First, although this is peculiar to High Density settlements, each settler would receive a daily allowance to cover the cost of *Subsistence* for six months, after which it was assumed that he would be able to feed his family either from farm production or through purchases covered by farm produce sales. During this time, at the discretion of the Settlement Officer, each settler was required to spend some time on work connected with the development of the scheme, although usually this would not seriously reduce the amount of time during which settlers could work on their farms.

A second important activity at this time is the issue to settlers of assets and materials paid for from the *Development Loans* to which all were entitled. Each settler would receive in kind basic assets required for the farm to become operational at the level envisaged in the Budget. In general, it was expected that these loan-financed assets would usually be issued during each settler's first year of occupation.

Third, at (or soon after) the time of settlement, co-operatives would be formed in each scheme. *Co-operative Loans* could then be drawn to permit each society to acquire property and assets needed for its operations, particularly for marketing. Co-operatives were expected to build up their assets and activities over time, so these loans would be drawn upon over a fairly long period. For the plans, we have assumed that they would be drawn during the first two years after settlement.

Fourth, *Contractor Loans* would become available to individuals, co-operatives or other agencies for use in the purchase of tractors and implements required for cultivation work on settlement farms. These were required very soon after settlement occurred, so it has been assumed that they would be taken up during the first six months after settlement.

Fifth, loans would be available for the development of piped *Water Supply* systems in each settlement. It is unclear when it was planned that these would be installed, but, since they necessarily involve detailed planning and construction, they would not normally be constructed until some time after settlement had taken place. It has been assumed that work on water supply systems was planned to begin eighteen months after settlement occurred, and required two years for completion.

These five processes that established the settlement scheme, and the supervision processes, would all require expenditure by the Department. However, the introduction of settlers would be accompanied by processes funded from other sources. First is the payment of *Legal Fees* and stamp duty that each settler would have to make for the completion of allocation, registration and mortgage processes, etc. On some schemes, payment would also have to be made by in-coming farmers for the purchase of milk quotas, whilst in a number of cases farmers would have to provide some of the *Productive Assets* (livestock especially) necessary for the budgeted operation of the farms.[1] In Low Density settlements, in-coming farmers would also have to deposit with the Department sums equal to roughly 10 per cent of the land purchase charge as an advance on loan repayment, and a sum which varied between £50 and £250 in respect of working capital. Sometimes high quality livestock brought to the farm could be counted at valuation towards the working capital deposits.

[1] These applied to most Low Density farmers but also a few High Density settlers. At Kipipiri, for example, settlers on the sheep plots had to provide money for the purchase of some of the sheep needed for their farms.

When the main establishment processes were completed, productive activities on the farms would get under way and steadily build up. From the moment of settlement, farmers would begin meeting the *Recurrent Costs of Farm Operation.* At the same time, as farmers began to produce surpluses for sale, recurrent expenses would be incurred for the *Operation of the Co-operative.* Both types of expense would continue indefinitely.

The last item of planned expenditure for a typical settlement process was *Survey for Title for the Registration of Ownership.* This process mainly involved aerial photography of the area after farm boundary marks had been established, so it could not begin until some years after settlement had taken place, although scheme regulations generally required settlers to mark their boundaries within a year of allocation. No precise timing for this process was planned, but it has been assumed that it would occur during the third and fourth years after settlement.

The processes described so far are those normally planned for every sub-divisional settlement in the High and Low Density Programmes. However, tea on the Lessos settlement required two additional expenditure processes. Smallholder tea grown in any part of Kenya is normally controlled by the Kenya Tea Development Authority (KTDA). This authority carried out a succession of expansion plans since the late 1950s, one of which was the subject of a social appraisal (Stern, 1972) analagous with this study. The development of tea in settlement areas[1] was not an integral part of KTDA's development programmes, but arose from a separate initiative by the Department of Settlement. However settlement tea development was managed by KTDA for the Department on an agency basis. The development of this crop thus involved expense both for the supply (on credit) to farmers of the required *Tea Planting Material*, and for KTDA Management Costs for (i) the supervision of growers *ab initio*; (ii) the collection and delivery of harvested green leaf once production had begun; and (iii) for overhead costs of the Authority. Planting material would be required only when the tea was being established, but the other KTDA costs would be incurred indefinitely.

[1] Tea was planned as a settlement crop on ten schemes in four separate parts of the Highlands, mainly on Low Density settlements.

The processes considered above cover all of those planned sources of expense that would arise because the settlement programme was undertaken. Although they constitute a long list, all refer to expenditure arising either within the settlement areas themselves or within the Department of Settlement and KTDA. To carry out its comprehensive and complex programme in the necessary time, the Department was created from scratch to provide a wide range of technical, administrative and social services for the settlements whose provision elsewhere was the responsibility of several separate central or local Government departments. The cost of these services, which were mainly provided by personnel seconded from other Ministries, is included with other items in the cost of settlement administration. However, settlers also enjoyed the 'normal' support provided by Government departments in such fields as health, education and police duties,[1] but the cost of these services has not been included.

The treatment of road costs in the settlement areas should be mentioned. Major roads through or outside the settlement areas are maintained by the Ministry of Works or the County Councils, but responsibility for road maintenance within schemes was apparently never assigned, and little work on them was carried out after construction during the pre-settlement phase. In the late 1960s it became apparent that this situation was unsatisfactory. Many were in poor condition and a foreign loan was obtained specifically for the improvement of settlement roads. We have taken the view that the settlement programme as planned in the early 1960s could have been operated without this new investment eight or ten years after settlement began, and that the road improvement programme is a separate project whose purpose is to raise settlement production above the levels allowed for in the budgets. The costs and benefits of the settlement road programme are thus ignored.

[1] They also received a degree of 'normal' coverage from the Department of Agriculture over and above the extension service provided by the Department of Settlement.

13.3 PLANNED COSTS, OUTPUT AND FINANCIAL FLOWS FOR THE KABISI SETTLEMENT

In this section, a detailed account is given of the planned cost and output values for this High Density settlement. This is presented in full detail to show the pattern used for all of the four schemes. Later sections summarize the planned development of the other three settlements.

13.3.1 *Costs*

To evaluate each settlement scheme as an individual project marginal to the settlement programme, a comprehensive time-series of expenses of every kind was built up to reflect the way in which plan information for a settlement might have been submitted as an individual project for appraisal before it was undertaken. For the model plans an April to March financial year has been adopted. This corresponds to the normal cropping season for farming in those areas where the Department developed schemes in the 1960s. It has, furthermore, been assumed that the plan for Kabisi was to purchase the land at the beginning of the 1963-4 financial year; to prepare it for settlement during that year; and to admit all of the settlers in one group at the beginning of April 1964 so that they could begin farming in the crop year 1964-5.[1] The timing of all other activities stems from these basic assumptions. Thus, expenditure attributable to the settlement would begin in 1962-3. The last establishment process, Survey for Title Registration, would be completed in 1967-8, the year in which all farms should have reached the 'maturity' levels of the planning budget. 1968-9 would be the last year of extended supervision, and the pattern of planned expenditure would be expected to stabilize at the level applying to 1969-70.

Table 13.1 shows the planned pattern of expenses. Details are given in Appendix A.13 of the way in which the unit costs for this settlement were calculated for the processes listed in the Table.

Kabisi contains 701 farms, of three different basic types. 640

[1] Starting times for each settlement plan were chosen to correspond closely with practice. In the purchase of Kabisi farms, the first land was taken over in January 1963. By July of that year, all but 40 acres had been acquired.

Table 13.1

Summary of costs for processes in the development and operation of the plan for the Kabisi Settlement, and of output

1962 Market Prices (£)

701 farms	1962-3	1963-4	1964-5	1965-6	1966-7	1967-8	1968-9	1969-70 et seq.
I. *Cost Processes*[a]								
1. Land Valuation	530	—	—	—	—	—	—	—
2. Land Purchase	—	73,198	—	—	—	—	—	—
3. Interim Farming	—	6,139	—	—	—	—	—	—
4. Survey for Planning	—	3,683	—	—	—	—	—	—
5. Planning and Demarcation	—	3,683	—	—	—	—	—	—
6. Roads and Soil Conservation	—	9,208	—	—	—	—	—	—
8. Payment of Legal Fees	—	—	3,533	—	—	—	—	—
9. Scheme Supervision	—	—	4,550	4,550	3,825	3,100	3,100	2,100
10. Field Overhead Supervision	—	—	2,653	2,653	1,990	1,326	1,326	663
11. Headquarters Overhead Supervision	—	—	3,580	3,580	2,983	2,386	2,386	1,193
12. Settler Subsistence	—	—	12,618	—	—	—	—	—
13. Development Loan Assets[b]	—	—	52,994	1,350	—	—	—	—
14. Co-operative Assets	—	—	3,505	3,505	—	—	—	—
16. Water Supply	—	—	—	3,069	3,070	—	—	—
18. Recurrent Costs of Farming	—	—	22,212	26,052	30,922	30,922	30,922	30,92
19. Recurrent Costs of Co-operatives	—	—	3,832	4,798	5,623	6,300	6,300	6,30
20. Survey for Title	—	—	—	—	—	2,455	—	—
21. Settlers' Labour	—	—	31,961	31,961	31,961	31,961	31,961	31,96
Annual Totals	530	95,911	141,438	81,518	80,374	78,450	75,995	73,13
II. *Output*								
Maize	—	—	15,612	19,515	23,418	27,300	27,300	27,30
Butterfat	—	—	21,240	27,060	29,970	32,880	32,880	32,88
Cull Cows	—	—	—	—	—	10,620	10,620	10,62
Calves	-	-	1,051	1,143	1,154	1,154	1,154	1,15
Subsistence	—	—	14,020	14,020	14,020	14,020	14,020	14,02
Annual Totals	—	—	51,923	61,738	68,562	85,974	85,974	85,97

a. Processes are numbered according to the system used in Appendix A.13.

b. During the first year, some recurrent farm costs were paid for from Development loans. These amounts (£16,176 in 1964-5) have been included in line 18. Line 13 understates the total planned value of development loans by this amount.

are of budget type II (A), which were planned to have an average size of 15 acres of arable equivalent land,[1] with the main emphasis of the farm programme on maize and dairy cattle. 54 farms are of type II (B). They are the same size as type II (A), but were planned to concentrate for cash production entirely on dairy cattle, because they contained no arable land. Finally, seven farms were of the type V, which were very much larger, being planned to have an average size of 37 acres of arable equivalent land, with both maize production and dairy cattle as major activities. The first two types of budget were respectively expected to give a net cash income at maturity of £36 and £32 plus subsistence, whilst the third was expected to provide £74 plus subsistence. The first of these budgets is copied for illustration in Appendix Table A.13.3.

The budgets used for evaluating the Kabisi plan are not those that were first drawn up. The original budgets, prepared in or after September 1963, envisaged the production of sisal on many farms. However, in 1965 it was decided that sisal was not a suitable crop for settlements, and new budgets were drawn up for those schemes where it featured in the planned system. The new budgets provided for the expansion of maize, and an increase in the number of cows from two to three per farm. The revised budgets are more directly comparable with the actual experience of farming discussed in the next chapter.[2]

The last item in Table 13.1, *Settlers' Labour*, was not taken into account in scheme planning, but is of course one to which social appraisal must give regard. Each settler and his family was

[1] For planning purposes, stereotype budgets were drawn up on the assumption that each farm would contain only good arable land. As part of the process of Planning and Demarcation, all land in a settlement area was inspected and classified into three main classes. The best was given an arable equivalent rating of 1.0. Poorer land was given a weighting of either 0.5 or 0.25. In the design stage, all farms were planned to have a total weighted area equal to the planned arable equivalent acreage. Farms on poor land were thus larger than others on good land which had the same budgets. If all Kabisi farms had been of the planned arable equivalent size, the 701 would have required 10,669 acres, an average size of 15.2 acres. The average number of acres per farm in the settlement is 17.5. When allowance is made for settlement land outside farms, these figures indicate that most of the Kabisi land was graded in the best class. It has been assumed that it was known at the time of planning that the settlement would eventually contain 701 farms of the types mentioned.

[2] So far as we know, this is the only instance of rebudgeting in the schemes being studied.

expected to find whole-time occupation within the farm, so from a national viewpoint an item must be introduced for the opportunity cost of each family had it not been engaged in running a settlement farm.

Valuing the opportunity cost of a settler family involves determining the size and composition of a typical family and the value of the marginal product of productive family members had they not become settlers. For all settlements, it has been assumed that each household contained only one man and one woman who would otherwise have been able to find employment and make a contribution to the national economy. A typical family with a labour force of only two adults is smaller than average. According to Nottidge and Goldsack (1966), it was assumed for planning that each family would be able to provide the equivalent of three adult workers. Since settler selection was mainly directed towards choosing relatively young married people, it may be expected that a work contribution equivalent to that of a third adult would, where necessary, be provided by children.

As was explained in Chapter 5, settlers' family members were assumed to have alternative earning opportunities of £41 for men and £34 for women. These values are based on the averages for all rural areas in Kenya. Evidence collected during our visits to the settlements in 1969, and figures given in various survey reports, indicates that the wages of small-farm employees in Western Province were significantly lower than in other parts of the country. Reflecting this situation, a reduction factor based on daily wage rate was applied which gives estimates for Kabisi of £34 for men and £28 for women.

Allowing for the time for which women were not available for work,[1] and for the net value of subsistence production, the cost at 'market prices' of the average Kabisi settler family can be summarized as:

	£
1 man	34
1 woman	12
Net value of subsistence production	5
	51

[1] See 5.2

These figures are in 1967-8 value terms, and a factor (0.894) has been applied to convert them to 1962-3 values, which makes them comparable with the other planning values.[1]

Our estimates of family size, composition and alternative net income opportunities may be subject to error; these are not points about which much relevant data is available. In view of the importance of this particular item, other possible values are considered when the figures for each settlement are brought together for appraisal in Chapter 16, but the figures shown in Table 13.1 reflect our best estimates for this item.

The development of planned costs reflected in Table 13.1 follows a pattern typical of settlement projects. Large expenses would be incurred during the first few years on land preparation and the issue of the basic stock of productive assets. However, untypically for settlement programmes elsewhere, but characteristically in this programme, land purchase is the largest single item at this stage. After a few years, the establishment processes would be completed, and expenditure would settle down to a much lower level than in the earlier years, with supervision, the recurrent costs of farming, and the cost of settler labour the main continuing items. The estimated cost of supervision and administration would fall as the settlement matures, from an initial level of over £15 per farm in the first period to almost £10 in the extended supervision phase, and £5.6 in the period of final supervision. At this 'maturity' stage, the imputed value of settlers' labour would be by far the largest expense, accounting for 44 per cent of all costs taken into account from 1969 to 1970 onwards. At that level, total costs per acre would amount to Sh. 119. This is a lot higher than the cost per acre of Sh. 67 (in 1962 values) estimated for large-scale farming in the area.

Further analysis of each cost process, as described in Appendix A.13, allows a re-presentation to be made of the cost items listed in Table 13.1. This permits comparison between the settlement plans and large-scale farming in the same area. At the assumed plan maturity level of 1969-70 the different classes of unskilled labour, including settler families, together account for 51 per cent of all annual expenses brought into account. No

[1] See 16.1.3

other single item in the table accounts for more than 9 per cent of total expenditure in that final year. This fact particularly emphasizes the labour-intensive nature of the types of farming being planned. The change from large-scale farming to the style envisaged in the settlement plans would involve the direct employment of unskilled labour costed at nearly four times the value of payments to workers on large farms.[1] Since settler labour has been valued at less than the minimum wage on large farms in 1962-3 (Sh. 65 per month), the plans for settlement appeared to envisage the direct employment of more than four times the number of people on the land as were involved in large-scale farming.[2]

13.3.2 *Planned Output*

The budgets give details of the quantities and values of production expected in the maturity year. However, while Low Density budgets always show a year-by-year build-up, no details are generally given for High Density farms of how farming system would develop before the maturity year, as crop acreages, livestock numbers and production grow to the anticipated levels. Consequently, assumptions had to be made on the way in which production would expand each year. The output figures presented in Table 13.1 allow for the gradual development of farming systems and increases in crop and livestock yields to the levels planned for the maturity year. Although the point is not explicitly made in any report, the introduction of farmers to new enterprises and the planned levels of intensity should be reflected in a gradual improvement in performance during a learning period. The full budgeted levels of production could not be expected to be attained from the outset.[3]

[1] This comparison involves an adjustment to bring the large farm figures from 1959 to 1962 values.

[2] This comparison may not seem quite fair, in that the settlement evaluation includes the imputed cost of settlers' wives whilst the large-farm estimates do not have a specific item of this kind. However, the wage bill on large farms includes payments to women, who were frequently employed on some tasks, especially (where relevant) pyrethrum picking and weeding, and maize harvesting. Furthermore, many men working on large farms were not accompanied by a wife, either because they were single or because their families were living elsewhere, and almost certainly growing their own subsistence crops or doing other work.

[3] This assumption does *not* apply to Low Density settlements, where planned yields for annual crops and livestock products were the same every year. In view of the

The budget for every type of settlement farm contains an item 'subsistence' whose composition is not specified. A fundamental planning assumption for all High and Low Density schemes was that settlers would produce most of their subsistence crops. It was obviously difficult to estimate the composition and value of subsistence for a typical household, and the simple device was wisely adopted in planning farms of all kinds of setting aside in the farm plan two acres[1] for this purpose, and to assume production of £10 per acre. No improvement on this practice has been attempted here.

The value of planned annual production at Kabisi stemming from these assumptions is shown in Table 13.1. Planned production would stabilize by 1967-8, and, if there were no further improvement in yields beyond the maturity year, the output pattern for 1967-8 would continue indefinitely. At that level, subsistence accounts for 16 per cent of the total value of output. The main budgeted sale commodities were maize and butterfat, the only other products being slaughter cattle, a by-product of the dairy enterprise. This pattern of sales is very similar to that for large-scale farming in the area, although the latter included a number of minor enterprises not included in the settlement plans. At the level of 1967-8, budgeted production in the settlement would be Sh. 140 per acre, which is nearly 40 per cent higher than the estimated per acre output level (in 1962 values), for large scale farming of Sh. 105 when the value of workers' cultivation is included. The change of land use to settlement was thus expected to lead to considerable intensification.

13.3.3 *Financial arrangements for the settlement programme*

For a total appraisal of a particular scheme, we feel that account should be taken not only of costs and output but of the special external financial arrangements made particularly

farming experience that Low Density settlers were expected to possess, it must have been assumed that no learning period was required. No such expectation could realistically have been applied to High Density settlers, whose selection required no evidence of previous farming experience.

[1] An exception to this general rule occurred at Passenga, where 1 and 1½ acres of subsistence were budgeted for two types of farm. See 13.6

with the British Government for settlements of this kind. As was explained in Chapter 12, because of the strong political motivation underlying the High and Low Density settlement programmes, finance was made available which might not otherwise have been available to the Kenya Government. It is not customary in project appraisals for finance to be taken into account, on the grounds that the external funds used in a particular project would have been available for use in other projects. The High and Low Density settlements differed from this general situation. Loans and grants made to the Kenya Government for this programme would not otherwise have been available. To regard all finance involved in this programme as having this special nature is almost certainly an overstatement, though it is not, in our opinion, a gross one. In Chapter 16, the results of each appraisal and evaluation are presented with and without finance in such a way that the implication of any assumption about finance can be estimated.

Under the terms of the programmes, the following items were entirely covered by grants from the British Government: Valuation; Preparation of Planning Maps; Planning and Demarcation; Roads and Soil Conservation; Supervision at all levels up to the end of the period of normal supervision; Settler Subsistence; and Survey for Title. It is not known whether Interim Farming losses were also planned to be covered by grants (if indeed they were envisaged in planning), but it has been assumed that this was so.[1]

Land purchase was financed partly by grants and partly by loan. In both programmes, all land was purchased with British Government funds. Over the programmes as a whole, grants could cover one-third of all costs for land and permanent improvements. It was not essential that this grant be applied at the same level to land purchased for every individual settlement, but it has been assumed here that for planning purposes a one-third grant was expected to apply to each scheme.

That part of the land purchase cost not covered by grants was covered by loans repayable by the Kenya Government over 30

[1] In the event, they were covered by 'savings' in the grants earmarked for settlement administration.

years, generally at an interest rate of 6.5 per cent per annum.[1] Loans for High Density settlements were available from the British Government[2] to cover the full cost of loan issues made to a variety of agencies involved at the scheme level: to settlers for farm development assets; to co-operative societies for operating assets; to contractors for the purchase of tractors and cultivating machinery; and to co-operatives or other agencies for the establishment of water schemes. Money spent on these activities was also loaned to the Kenya Government for 30 years, but for the first four years only interest was payable, typically at 6.5 per cent. Thereafter principal and interest were repayable in equal instalments over 26 years.

The inflow and outflow of grant and loan finance associated with the Kabisi scheme are shown in the three penultimate columns of Table 13.2. In calculating these flows, it is assumed that external finance would be drawn in the accounting period during which expenses were incurred. They are shown in the Table in Kenya pounds at 1962 prices. Adjustment to allow for changes in exchange rates is made in Chapter 16 as part of the appraisal.

13.3.4 *The overall plan situation for Kabisi*

Estimates of planned values for output, costs and financial flows for the Kabisi Settlement are brought together in Table 13.2. For the first five years operating deficits would arise annually, particularly during the second and third years, when land purchase, preparation of the settlement site and loan issues to settlers gave rise to high levels of expenditure. An annual surplus from settlement operations would first be expected in the sixth year, and would stabilize in the eighth at just less than £13,000 per annum. When external finance is taken into account, there would be no deficit for the first two years, all expenditure in those years being covered by inflows. Only in

[1] The interest rate on all U.K. loan drawings was the Treasury Bill rate payable on the day that the loan was drawn. Details of individual drawings up to 1966 are given in Appendix G of the Report of the Mission on Land Settlement, 1966. They ranged from 5½ to 7 per cent.

[2] A limited amount of money from the West German Government was used for development loans in the High Density settlement programme. Easier terms applied to this money than to the loans drawn from London, but this has not been allowed for in this study.

Table 13.2

A Summary of output, costs and financial flows for the plan for the Kabisi Settlement

1962 Market Prices (£)

Year	Output	Costs	Operating surplus	Grants drawn	Loans drawn	Loans repaid	Final surplus
1962-3	–	530	-530	530	–	–	–
1963-4	–	95,911	-95,911	47,113	48,798	–	–
1964-5	51,923	141,438	-89,515	23,401	79,685	3,708	9,863
1965-6	61.738	81,518	-19,780	10,783	7,924	8,888	-9,961
1966-7	68,562	80,374	-11,812	5,392	3,070	9,403	12,753
1967-8	85,974	78,450	7,524	2,455	–	9,603	376
1968-9	85,974	75,995	9,979	–	–	9,603	376
1969-70	85,974	73,139	12,835	–	–	10,814	2,021
1970-1	85,974	73,139	12,835	–	–	10,935	1,900
1971-2 to	85,974	73,139	12,835	–	–	10,981	1,854
1993-4	85,974	73,139	12,835	–	–	10,981	1,854
1994-5	85,974	73,139	12,835	–	–	7,273	5,562
1995-6	85,974	73,139	12,835	–	–	882	11,953
1996-7	85,974	73,139	12,835	–	–	246	12,589
1997-8 et seq.	85,974	73,139	12,835	–	–	–	12,835

1965-6 would a small deficit remain after financial flows were taken into account. Small surpluses arise each year thereafter. Until 1993-4, the thirty-third year, when repayment of the loans would end, the Final Surplus is very small, only 2 per cent of the value of output.

13.4 THE PLAN FOR THE LESSOS SETTLEMENTS

The group of three schemes considered here as the Lessos Settlements occupied 14,144 acres. One of these, Keben, was the first scheme in the High and Low Density programmes to be started, the land being purchased in April and May of 1961. The other two, Koylat and Lessos, were developed during the next three years by building on to Keben. The scheme individuality usually reflected in a specific co-operative society for each settlement never developed in this isolated group of settlements. For this study, it has been taken that all of the schemes might have been planned together, with the land purchased in 1962-3. This compromise 'average' starting date allows a fair comparison to be made in Chapter 16 between the settlement plan and its actual development.

The Lessos group of settlements occupy gently sloping land. At the highest point pyrethrum can be grown, although yields are lower than on higher land, as found, for example, at Kipipiri or Passenga. Some of the middle land is suitable for tea, whilst throughout the area maize can be grown on arable land. Reflecting the differences in basic ecology and soil quality, each of the three schemes had its own budgets, and the 365 farms laid out were of seven different types. In size they ranged from 22 to 57 acres Arable Equivalent, and the planned net cash incomes at maturity were between £147 and £202 per annum. 26 farms were budgeted for pyrethrum, and 220 were expected to have tea. Maize and dairy cattle featured in all budgets. Had all farms been of exactly the planned size, their total area would have been 13,064 acres, 92 per cent of the total settlement size. The balancing area would be required for roads and other publicly owned land. In this area variation in soil type appears to have been accommodated by drawing up a diversity of farm budgets, rather than by planning farms of different actual size with the same basic farming system and budget. More detailed planning of this kind was a characteristic feature of the Low Density programmes.

Using the budgets for each type of plot and other basic planning information, a detailed year-by-year summary of costs was prepared similar to that shown in Table 13.1. Settler Subsistence was not a cost, but farm assets planned to be provided by settlers as part of their qualifying capital was a significant item. Part of the development loans on farms budgeted for tea was for land preparation in the second year, so the issue of loan assets would extend over more than one year.

Settlers' family labour was valued in the same way as at Kabisi, but national average values were used for alternative earnings.

With the exception of the yield-related portion of KTDA expenses (which were planned to stabilize in the ninth year after the first tea was planted), all other costs would stabilize in 1968-9, the eighth year of expenditure. Supervision costs in this group of settlements, where farm sizes are relatively large, would begin at an annual level of over £86 per farm, but would fall to £52 during the 'extended supervision' stage and £30 in the maturity year. By then, all costs attributable to the schemes would be running at a level of Sh. 114 per acre, which is slightly less than the level of planned costs at Kabisi, but was a lot more than the large-scale farming cost level of Sh. 64 per acre.

Despite the higher level of supervision and the presence of the high-value crop tea, the Lessos area would not be farmed particularly intensively. However, as was found at Kabisi, settlement was planned to lead to an intensification of production over large-scale farming.

Itemization of the costs of the different processes listed to the level of their 'scheme boundary' composition shows that, at the maturity level, unskilled workers of different kinds accounted for 37 per cent of all costs. Skilled Labour, Superphosphates and Lorry Transport each accounted for between 8 and 10 per cent; no other item accounted for more than 6 per cent of costs.

The basic economy of the Lessos Settlements is, like Kabisi, dominated by the production of maize and dairy produce. Calculation of the value of planned output was based directly on the budgets with the single exception of the planned value of tea which, for the reasons explained in Appendix A.13, has been valued at 45 cents per lb. According to the scheme plans, pyrethrum would always be a product of minor importance, while at maturity, tea would account for only 27 per cent of the value of all planned output. Subsistence production would also be relatively unimportant, accounting for only a little more than 5 per cent of output in the maturity year. By then, planned production per acre would be Sh. 193 per acre (at 1962 values), 38 per cent more than planned production at Kabisi and more than twice the output value (at 1962 prices) of Sh. 85 estimated in Chapter 15 for large-scale farming in the area. One reason why planned production at Lessos is higher than at Kabisi is because the High Density scheme was not expected to be able to sell whole milk,[1] thus losing the opportunity to

[1] The reservation for Low Density settlements of available milk quota was a general feature of settlement planning, partly designed to ensure that these schemes met the 'development' criteria on which part of their financing depended, but mainly because it was felt that whole milk marketing could not be easily organized from the one or two cow herds planned for High Density farms.

obtain a price more than twice as great as for butterfat sales. Were all Lessos milk also to be sold as butterfat, the maturity value of planned production would be only Sh. 179 per acre.

The same items as at Kabisi were financed by external grants and loans. All grants and the land purchase loans were received from the British Government, under the same conditions as described above. Finance for the different kinds of development loan in Low Density schemes came from two different sources. Two-thirds was provided by IBRD. Interest only would be charged on this loan up to mid-1968, at a general rate of 6 per cent per annum, but thereafter constant annual payments should be paid for 13½ years.[2] The remaining development loan finance came from the Commonwealth Development Corporation (CDC), whose general terms were: 8 per cent interest only for four years after drawing, followed by the payment over eleven years of equal annual sums.

The British Government, IBRD and CDC were the only external donors of finance for Low Density settlements. However, apart from the Kenya Government contributions to pay for supervision after the first 2½ years (which applied to every settlement) the Low Density schemes also involved a financial contribution from the settlers themselves. At Lessos this amounted to £100 apiece. However, over and above this, the presence of tea at Lessos involved the Kenya Government in making further finance available to cover the advances to KTDA made through SFT for the cost of tea stumps and for agency work carried out by the Authority. It is difficult to assess the sums concerned, since the financial arrangements between KTDA and SFT are obscure, and are not discussed in published reports. Eventually, the normal cesses charged against tea deliveries would be sufficient to cover these items. This position should have been reached by 1967-8, when a total sum attributable to Lessos of over £18,000 would have been advanced to KTDA.

The planned values of output and costs are brought together in the first three sections of Table 13.3. With planned production in the early years at a high level, substantial operating deficits would arise only in the second and third

[2] This is a slightly simplified account. The actual loan agreement (KE303) stipulates repayment sums that vary slightly and irregularly from year to year.

Table 13.3

Summary of costs, output, finance flows and surplus for the plan for the Lessos Settlements

1962 Market Prices (£)

365 Farms	1961-2	1962-3	1963-4	1964-5	1965-6	1966-7	1967-8	1968-9
I. *Costs*								
Establishment Processes[a]	1,166	26,168	2,921	–	–	1,414	1,415	–
Land purchase	–	130,529	–	–	–	–	–	–
Supervision	–	–	31,449	31,449	25,203	18,936	18,936	11,043
Productive assets[b]	–	–	105,297	15,141	7,779	7,779	–	–
Recurrent farming costs	–	–	31,392	32,586	34,819	34,819	34,819	34,819
Recurrent co-op costs	–	–	7,371	7,619	7,619	7,619	7,169	7,619
Settlers' family labour	–	–	19,905	19,905	19,905	19,905	19,905	19,905
Other Costs[c]	–	–	1,825	2,700	2,700	3,245	4,235	5,224
Total Costs	1,166	156,697	200,160	109,400	98,025	93,717	86,929	78,610
II. *Output*								
Butterfat	–	–	28,500	30,060	30,060	30,060	30,060	30,060
Milk	–	–	20,221	20,221	20,221	20,221	20,221	20,221
Pyrethrum	–	–	1,040	1,560	1,560	1,560	1,560	1,560
Maize	–	–	32,334	30,037	30,037	30,037	30,037	30,037
Tea[d]	–	–	–	–	–	4,455	12,555	20,655
Cattle	–	–	1,224	1,224	4,464	10,794	10,794	10,794
Subsistence	–	–	7,300	7,300	7,300	7,300	7,300	7,300
Total output	–	–	90,619	90,402	93,642	104,427	112,527	120,627
III. *Operating surplus*	−1,166	−156,697	−109,541	−18,998	−4,385	10,710	25,598	42,017
IV. *Net financial inflow*[e]	1,166	156,697	138,625	21,539	9,019	−5,810	−14,106	−21,953
V. *Final surplus*	–	–	29,084	2,541	4,636	4,900	11,492	20,064

a. Includes Land Valuation, Interim Farming, Survey for Planning, Planning and Demarcation, Roads and Soil Conservation, Legal Fees, Settler Subsistence and Survey for Title.

b. Includes Settlers' Development Loan Assets, Co-operative Assets, Water Supply and Assets provided by Settlers.

c. KTDA costs only.

d. Planned tea output would stabilize in 1971-2 at £36,450.

e. Outflow increases to a maximum of £22,351 from 1971 to 1972.

years. By the tenth year the overall Operating Surplus would exceed £150 per farm or Sh. 79 per acre. When the associated finance flows are taken into account, the Final Surplus is positive in every year. Loan repayment costs build up rapidly, but the early repayment of development loans means that the outflow would fall substantially from 1980 to 1981, the eighteenth year after settlers entered their farms. Viewed simply as a financial operation, the Lessos Settlement plan would clearly be an attractive proposition.

13.5 THE PLAN FOR KIPIPIRI

The Kipipiri settlement is a high altitude scheme of 12,338 acres which were purchased between June 1962 and May 1963, so the time series of planned events assumes purchase of the whole area during the accounting year 1962-3. Structural planning allowed for the creation of 525 farms. 482 were of a Standard type, requiring 7 acres of good land and allowing an annual net cash income at maturity of £38. Farming systems in these plots were based on the production for sale of pyrethrum, potatoes and milk, although each farm was planned to have only one cow. The remaining 43 farms contained no arable land, and their budgets included only subsistence, dairy cattle and sheep. The 32 Small Sheep plots (expected size 40 acres) were planned to give a net cash income at maturity of £47, whilst the 11 Large Sheep farms (70 acres or more) were expected to provide a net income of £70. Had all farms been of their planned size on soil of the best type, they would have occupied 5,424 acres. The fact that this is only 44 per cent of the total settlement area reflects the relatively poor general quality of land in the Kipipiri area.[1]

The planned cost of each process at Kipipiri was generally calculated in a straightforward way. A particular feature of the Standard plot budgets was the provision for almost 30 per cent of the available sum for Development Loans to be used for cultivation. This amount was more than all budgeted cropping

[1] Nearby land of almost similar type was rejected for transfer through the settlement programmes. Eventually it was incorporated in the Ol Kalou Salient and farmed extensively on a very large scale.

costs in the first year, so some was carried over to the second. Settlers' family labour at Kipipiri was valued in exactly the same way as for Lessos. In the maturity year, this item constituted nearly 62 per cent of the costs of all processes taken into account. At Sh. 17 per acre, planned recurrent farming costs were exceptionally low, reflecting the low intensity of farming possible on this land. Planned supervision costs per farm were higher than at Kabisi, the same costs being incurred for fewer families. They would fall from £20 per farm in the earliest years to £7.50 in the maturity year.

With costs further analysed in the way described for Kabisi and Lessos, Unskilled Labour of different kinds would account for two-thirds of all expenses in the maturity year. The next most important items would be Skilled Labour, Superphosphate and Potato Seed, but each would account for only between 4 and 5 per cent of all costs. This pattern of expenses is very different from that estimated for large-scale farming, where in 1962 values, of a total cost per acre of Sh. 132, only 18 per cent was for labour. The change in land use would lead to the employment of workers valued at just over twice the cost of those estimated for large-scale farming.

The level and pattern of production envisaged in the budgets was very stable from year to year, increasing only as pyrethrum was established and came into full production. In the maturity year, this crop accounted for 35 per cent of the value of all output. A small amount of whole milk sales was planned for the Small Sheep plots. Milk produced by the single cow on each Standard plot would be separated, and the skim used for home consumption. The low potential of this area is again reflected in the fact that subsistence accounts for 20 per cent of all output.[1] Total planned output per acre at maturity would be Sh. 84, considerably less than the Sh. 155 (in 1962 terms) estimated for large-scale farming in this area.

The estimated values of planned costs and output are shown in Table 13.4. Not until the fifth year after land purchase would the value of production exceed costs. When everything stabilized, the operating surplus would be only Sh. 9 per acre. This would be less than the value of external loan repayments until the land loan was paid off, when a positive final surplus

[1] At Kabisi, subsistence was 16 per cent of total output at maturity.

Table 13.4

Summary of costs, output, finance flows and surplus for the plan for the Kipipiri Settlement

1962 Market Prices (£)

525 farms	1961-2	1962-3	1963-4	1964-5	1965-6	1966-7	1967-8	1968-9
I. *Costs*								
Establishment processes	954	22,825	11,722	–	–	1,254	1,254	–
Land purchase	–	93,756	–	–	–	–	–	–
Supervision	–	–	10,783	10,783	8,798	6,812	6,812	3,956
Productive assets	–	–	30,642	7,842	3,085	3,084	–	–
Recurrent farming costs	–	–	10,522	11,221	10,686	10,686	10,686	10,686
Recurrent co-op. costs	–	–	2,223	3,038	3,178	3,178	3,178	3,178
Settlers' family labour	–	–	28,630	28,630	28,630	28,630	28,630	28,630
Total costs	954	116,581	94,552	61,514	54,377	53,624	50,540	48,450
II. *Output*								
Butterfat	–	–	7,758	7,895	7,936	7,936	7,936	7,936
Milk	–	–	745	993	993	993	993	993
Pyrethrum	–	–	7,230	15,665	18,075	18,075	18,075	18,075
Potatoes	–	–	9,640	9,640	9,640	9,640	9,640	9,640
Cattle	–	–	–	–	310	310	310	310
Sheep	–	–	1,944	1,944	2,484	2,484	2,484	2,484
Wool	–	–	2,030	2,030	2,030	2,030	2,030	2,030
Subsistence	–	–	10,500	10,500	10,500	10,500	10,500	10,500
Total output	–	–	39,847	48,667	51,973	51,973	51,973	51,973
III. *Operating surplus*	−954	−116581	−54,675	−12,847	−2,404	−1,651	1,433	5,523
IV. *Net financial flow*[a]	954	116,581	59,611	10,793	362	−3,997	−7,281	−9,186
V. *Final surplus*	–	–	4,936	−2,054	−2,042	−5,648	−5,848	−3,663

a. Maximum outflow is £9,395 from 1971-2 to 1992-3.

would arise in the thirty-second year of the project. Clearly the Kipipiri plan was not an attractive proposition when valued at market prices. However, the overwhelming importance of the cost of settler labour should be remembered for its relevance to overall 'profitability'.

13.6 THE PLAN FOR THE PASSENGA SETTLEMENTS

With the exception of one very small property, all 13,577 acres of land in these three high altitude schemes were purchased between December 1962 and August 1963. The assumed planned date for land purchase was thus taken to be 1963-4. Due to basic similarities in land type and situation the same three farm plans were used for each settlement. 313 farms were laid out. 225 were of type A, where, on a planned holding of 32 acres, wheat, pyrethrum and milk (much of it sold whole) were planned to give a net cash income at maturity of £156. On the 83 type B plots, whose planned size was 40 acres, neither wheat nor dairy cows were planned for. From growing pyrethrum and rearing purchased calves for sale as in-calf heifers, these farms were expected to give an income at maturity of £140. The 5 type C farms were similar to type A, but were expected to be larger (45 acres each), and to grow more wheat but no pyrethrum. This would yield a maturity income of £168. Had all farms been of the planned size, they would have occupied 80 per cent of the settlement area.

The estimated cost of each process in the plan for this settlement has only one unusual feature. Unlike the budgets for all of the other schemes, those for the Passenga farms allowed nothing from development loans to be used for cultivation or crop establishment. Pyrethrum was the most important planned crop, and it is likely that a large productive acreage was available for allocation to farmers when settlement began.[1] Wheat, it seems, was planned to be grown entirely with resources provided by the settlers.

Supervision costs in these schemes have been taken to be the same as at Lessos. With fewer settlers, the cost per farm would be greater, ranging from an annual cost of £100 apiece at the outset to £60 during the 'extended supervision' stage, and £35 after the first five years. Settlers' family labour was costed at the same level as for Lessos and Kipipiri and accounted for

[1] It is unlikely that the requisite acreage would have been located at the outset on every farm budgeted for pyrethrum. Frequently, when productive pyrethrum was taken over, settlers were first allocated part of an existing block of the crop, which might at the time be growing on another farm. Generally they would be allowed a year or two to establish the crop on their own farm, before having to give up rights elsewhere.

almost 25 per cent of all costs in the maturity year. Annual recurrent farming costs of Sh. 52 per acre reflected a farming system that was fairly extensive, but the total planned expenditure of Sh. 103 per acre was a little less than the sum (Sh. 122 in 1962 values) estimated for large-scale farming in the area.

First-round analysis of the cost of each process showed that, as elsewhere, Unskilled Labour was the most important item, accounting for one-third of all costs in the maturity year. Skilled Labour absorbed 10 per cent, while Diesel Fuel (for cultivating tractors), Superphosphate, Artificial Insemination, Livestock Medicines and Veterinary Costs, and Lorry Transport each took roughly 5 per cent of all costs.

Planned production was expected to be at a high level (80 per cent of the maturity level) in the first year. Dairy produce sales were most important, with pyrethrum, wheat and dairy cattle the other main items. Subsistence production would be of only minor importance—only 4 per cent of total output—because two of the Passenga budgets were unique in anticipating less than 2 acres per farm to be used in this way. At maturity planned production would be valued at Sh. 146 per acre, Sh. 19 of which is attributable to some of the milk being planned for sale as whole milk, not as butterfat. Obviously this land was expected to be much more productive than was Kipipiri, but planned production per acre was little more than the value (in 1962 terms) of estimated total production under large-scale farming of Sh. 140.

The financial arrangements for the Passenga schemes are closely analagous to those for Lessos. Settlers provided from their own resources the finance needed for some productive assets, and to establish the first crops of wheat.

The overall position in these schemes is summarized in Table 13.5. With production planned to begin at a fairly high level, significant operating deficits arise only in the first three years. During the next two, a break-even position would be expected, with a surplus building up quickly to a maturity level of £93 per farm. The finance flows are such that, after a zero Final Surplus in the first two years, a positive amount remains in every year but the first year of full development loan repayment. Like the Lessos settlements, the Passenga group were planned to be profitable Low Density settlements.

Table 13.5

Summary of costs, output, finance flows and surplus for the plan for the Passenga Settlements

1962 Market Prices (£)

313 Farms	1962-3	1963-4	1964-5	1965-6	1966-7	1967-8	1968-9	1969-70
1. *Costs*								
Establishment processes	1,749	25,118	3,130	–	–	1,357	1,358	–
Land purchase	–	151,316	–	–	–	–	–	–
Supervision	–	–	31,449	31,449	25,203	18,936	18,936	11,043
Productive assets	–	–	104,904	–	7,467	7,468	–	–
Recurrent farming costs	–	–	33,418	33,603	35,058	35,058	35,058	35,058
Recurrent co-op costs	–	–	6,612	7,471	8,220	8,220	8,220	8,220
Settlers' family labour	–	–	17,069	17,069	17,069	17,069	17,069	17,069
Total costs	1,749	176,434	196,582	89,592	93,017	88,108	80,641	71,390
II. *Output*								
Butterfat	–	–	14,860	14,860	14,860	14,860	14,860	14,860
Milk	–	–	25,368	25,368	25,368	25,368	25,368	25,368
Pyrethrum	–	–	10,700	15,105	17,595	17,595	17,595	17,595
Wheat	–	–	13,736	13,736	13,736	13,736	13,736	13,736
Cattle	–	–	7,605	7,605	7,605	14,505	14,505	14,505
Sheep	–	–	–	5,478	5,229	5,229	5,229	5,229
Wool	–	–	3,418	3,418	3,418	3,418	3,418	3,418
Subsistence	–	–	4,305	4,305	4,305	4,305	4,305	4,305
Total output	–	–	79,992	89,875	92,116	99,016	99,016	99,016
III. *Operating surplus*	-1,749	-176,434	-116,590	283	-901	10,908	18,275	27,626
IV. *Net financial flow*[a]	1,749	176,434	136,949	16,237	7,980	-6,885	-18,828	-22,453
V. *Final surplus*	–	–	20,359	16,520	7,079	4,023	-453	5,173

a. Net outflow increases to £22,753 in 1972-3 to 1980-1.

13.7 A SUMMARY COMPARISON OF THE FOUR SETTLEMENT PLANS

Some figures for the four settlement plans have been brought together in Table 13.6, to allow comparisons to be made between the schemes.

Land costs per acre in the two Low Density settlements were higher than in the others, although whether this reflects potential productivity is questionable (see Chapter 15). The Low Density farmers would not only have bigger farms, but each would receive between three and four times as much assistance through development loans than would High Density settlers. Given the apparent advantage of better land and clearly preferential positions regarding development loans and the support of technical and supervisory staff, it is not surprising that the Low Density farms were expected to be the most productive. The value of planned production per acre at Kipipiri was exceptionally low, and the operating surplus there seems scarcely compatible with the price at which the land was purchased. However, none of the four settlements was planned to be particularly intensive.

The composition of recurrent costs varies substantially between schemes. Farming and co-operative costs per acre were similar in all cases except Kipipiri, but the per acre value of settlers' labour would naturally be much higher in the High Density schemes. This factor outweighed lower supervision costs, with the result that all costs per acre at Kabisi would actually be higher than at Lessos. However, the higher value of production at Lessos (partly attributable to whole milk sales and tea) would give a higher surplus there than at Kabisi, and a much higher surplus per farm. Both planned output and estimated surplus per acre on the low altitude schemes were higher than in the analagous settlements at high altitude.

To summarize the position, it is clear that, in planning, the Low Density schemes were given the opportunity to pursue farming systems that were both more productive in terms of land use and more profitable to the settlers. When all costs and outputs are taken into account, the Low Density settlements were also planned to have, at maturity, the highest surpluses. However, this is only what was planned. We shall consider how these settlements developed in practice in the next chapter.

TABLE 13.6

Summary details for the four settlements of capitalization and the operating situation in the maturity year

1962 Market prices (£)

	Kabisi		Lessos		Kipipiri		Passenga	
	per farm	per acre	per farm	per acre	per farm	per acre	per farm	per acre
1. *Capitalization*								
Land cost	104	5.96	358	9.23	179	7.60	483	11.15
Development loans:								
Settlers	101	5.74	290	7.48	79	3.34	268	6.18
Co-operative	10	0.57	39	1.00	10	0.43	43	1.00
Contractors	10	0.57	50	1.29	10	0.43	50	1.15
Water Supply	9	0.50	43	1.10	12	0.50	48	1.10
Total development loans	130	7.38	422	10.87	111	4.70	409	9.43
Settlers' assets	–	–	33	0.86	3	0.14	24	0.54
Total Capitalization	234	13.34	813	20.96	293	12.44	916	21.12
2. *Recurrent costs and output values at maturity year*								
Supervision	5.64	0.32	30.25	0.78	7.54	0.32	35.28	0.81
Recurrent farm costs	44.11	2.52	89.77	2.32	20.35	0.87	112.01	2.58
Recurrent co-operative costs	8.99	0.51	20.87	0.54	6.05	0.26	26.26	0.61
Settlers' labour	45.59	2.60	54.53	1.41	54.53	2.32	54.53	1.26
Other	–	–	25.22	0.65	–	–	–	–
All expenses	104.34	5.96	220.66	5.69	88.48	3.76	228.08	5.26
Sale produce	102.64	5.86	353.76	9.13	79.00	3.36	302.59	6.97
Subsistence	20.00	1.14	20.00	0.52	20.00	0.85	13.75	0.32
Total output	122.64	7.00	373.76	9.65	99.00	4.21	316.35	7.29
Surplus	18.30	1.05	153.10	3.95	10.52	0.45	88.26	2.03
Acres per farm	17.46		38.75		23.38		43.38	

APPENDIX A.13

ESTIMATING COSTS FOR THE SETTLEMENT PLANS

In this appendix an outline is given of the way in which cost estimates were derived for each settlement process, following the sequence in Table 13.1, and how the costs for each activity were sub-divided into different items, as a basis for shadow pricing (see Table A.13.1). Full particulars are not given of the basis for deriving every planning figure; where appropriate, illustrations are given from Kabisi.

1. LAND VALUATION

Valuation was undertaken by professional valuers working first for LDSB and then for CLB before it was wound up in October 1965. By that time virtually all land for the High Density, Low Density and associated purchase programmes had been valued. All valuation costs incurred up to October 1965 have therefore been related to the valuation of land purchased in the settlement programme.

No explicit figures of planned or actual valuation costs are available, but details of personnel involved and expenditure are given in different reports. Total salary costs are estimated from these sources as follows:

Period	*Cost £*	*Source*
Jan. 1961-July 1962	13,623	LDSB Report App. II
Aug. 1962-June 1963	16,394	D. of S. Report 62/3 p. 7
July 1963-June 1964	37,201	CLB Report 53/4 p. 16
July 1964-Oct. 1965	29,804	CLB Report 64/5 p. 20
Total	97,022	

Taking into account the cost of vehicles and 'other charges', the overall estimated cost of valuation is £116,000.

This expenditure covered the valuation of 1,094 properties which contained 1,421,257 acres valued at £12,589,051. The cost of valuation is likely to be related to each of these measures, but the cost per property valued has been taken as the basis for allocation. This indicates a cost per property of £106. The number of separate properties purchased for each settlement were: Kabisi 5; Lessos 11; Kipipiri 9; and Passenga 16½.

The greater part of the valuation cost is for professional services, categorized as skilled labour. The itemized analysis of this process is shown on the first line of Table A.13.1.

2. LAND PURCHASE

Details for each settlement of the actual prices paid for the land and permanent improvements were supplied by the Department.

3. INTERIM FARMING LOSSES

From various sources it appears that the final *balances* in the Farming Operations Account of the Department each year up to June 1967 (by which time most of the sub-divisional settlements had been long begun) were as follows (in pounds):[1]

1961	6,730	1964	(-200,000)
1962	32,613	1965	-154,176
1963	-220,765	1966	- 16,365

Total -551,963

The figure for 1964 is an author's estimate. The loss that year was described as 'considerable'.

There is no clear basis on which this amount may be attributed to a particular settlement. The view has been taken that it can reasonably be regarded as a charge against *all* sub-divisional schemes in the High and Low Density programmes. Nottidge and Goldsack give a final acreage for all schemes of this kind of 950,015 acres, indicating an average per acre farming losses figure of Sh. 11/62. Because of uncertainty about the true value of these losses, a per acre value of Sh. 10 has been used. No attempt was made to sub-divide this cost for shadow pricing.

4, 5, and 6. SURVEY FOR PLANNING; PLANNING AND DEMARCATION; AND ROADS AND SOIL CONSERVATION

According to Nottidge and Goldsack, these processes were planned to cost Sh. 6, Sh. 6 and Sh. 15 per acre respectively. The composition of these figures is not given anywhere, so assumptions about their likely make-up were made, as shown in Table A.13.1.

8. PAYMENT OF LEGAL FEES AND STAMP DUTY

The amounts payable on each type of farm are shown in the budgets. Although part of the total cost is a fee, the major part is a duty, which could be regarded as a tax. However, it is likely that documentation and

[1] These figures are mainly derived from the Annual Reports of the Settlement Fund Trustees.

other related costs incurred outside the department could equal the whole of the combined amounts paid. The sums concerned are relatively small, and it was assumed that the whole charge was for resources employed, itemized as shown in Table A.13.1.

TABLE A.13.1

The basis for itemized sub-division of the cost of various planned settlement processes

Percentages

	Skilled labour	Unskilled labour	Vehicles	Vehicle spares	Imported equipment	Petrol	Diesel	Other Charges
Land Valuation	84	–	4	2	–	7	–	3
Survey for Planning	20	65	5	2	3	5	–	–
Planning and Demarcation	70	30	–	–	–	–	–	–
Roads and soil Conservation	15	10	–	10	40	–	25	–
Legal fees	90	–	–	–	–	–	–	10
Water loans	20	20	–	–	60	–	–	–
Survey for title	70	–	–	–	10	–	–	20
Overhead supervision:								
Field level	72	6	5	2	–	6	–	9
Headquarters	71	4	–	1	–	3	–	21

9, 10 and 11. SUPERVISION AT SCHEME, FIELD AND HEADQUARTERS LEVELS

A paper on the cost of scheme supervision was prepared in July 1969 by the Financial Controller (Settlement). His figures, which are the basis for all supervision costs, provided estimates of the actual costs of scheme supervision. In the absence of any other information, it has been assumed that, except where referred to below, planned costs were exactly equal to actual costs. This assumption is likely to be realistic. A unit staffing structure for teams in the different kinds of settlement was adopted for both the periods of normal and extended supervision. Their composition is shown in Table A.13.2. During the early years of the settlement programme, the Department was given priority in staffing, and the field teams were probably staffed very closely to establishment.

No detailed plans were made early in the settlement programme about the level of staffing at scheme and other levels after the period of intensive supervision. Consequently, an assumption about staffing levels in the long term had to be made. The staff we expect would be required during the 'final' period of scheme supervision are also shown in Table A.13.2. These reflect the assumption that technical staff could not be reduced beyond the level of the extended supervision period, but that the settlement officers, with their clerks and vehicles, would be spread more thinly. This assumption implies that the complete withdrawal of government officers is unlikely ever to be possible, although the nature of their functions would change over time.

Itemized cost analyses for scheme supervision is shown in the lower part of Table A.13.2. These figures, based on information from the Financial Controller, imply that all employees, except Settlement Officer, Clerk, Agricultural Assistants, Animal Health Assistants, Headman and Co-operative Assistant, are unskilled labour.

Figures for overhead supervision at field and headquarters levels were given by the Financial Controller. Field overhead costs during the period of extended supervision were shown to fall to half their previous level, while headquarters costs fell in this phase to two-thirds of the previous level.[1] What might have been planned at these levels during the phase after extended supervision is not known, so it has been taken as a first assumption that costs at these two levels would be further reduced by 50 per cent, but that these cost levels would continue indefinetly. Estimates for the Department for 1966-7 were used to obtain an analysis of costs for the higher levels of supervision. These gave rise to the percentage breakdowns shown in Table A.13.1. Vehicles are included only at the field level in accordance with a convention adopted in the paper by the Financial Controller.

12. SETTLER SUBSISTENCE

This item applies only to High Density schemes, and provides for the payment of Sh. 2 per day to each settler for roughly the first six months after the allocation of his farm. A planning figure of £18 per settler has been used.

13. DEVELOPMENT LOANS

Particulars of the planned disposal of money available to each settler as development loans are contained in the budget for each type of plot. The budget for the most important type of farm at Kabisi is shown for illustration in Table A.13.3. The most important use of development loans in all schemes was the purchase of dairy cows. It is assumed that these cattle and the other items covered by development loans would be issued very soon after settlement occurred. However, where large numbers of

[1] This judgement on relative costs was the informed opinion (in 1969) of the Financial Controller, who supplied the information. With a large number of different settlements, all at different stages of development at any one time, the accurate apportionment to each scheme of costs at these levels was impossible.

Table A.13.2

The composition and cost of the settlement administration team within schemes at different supervision stages

	High Density			Low Density		
Supervision Stage	Normal	Extended	Final	Normal	Extended	Final
Level of staffing per scheme						
Settlement Officer	1	1/3	1/10	1	1/3	1/10
Clerk	1	1	½	1	1	½
Agricultural assistant	2	2	2	2	2	2
Junior agricultural assistant	1	1	1	1	1	1
Animal health assistant	1	1	1	1	1	1
Junior animal health assistant	3	3	3	1	1	1
Health assistant	½	0	0	½	0	0
Headman	½	0	0	½	0	0
Administrative policeman	1	0	0	1	0	0
Co-operative Assistant	½	½	½	½	½	½
Itemized cost of each scheme unit. (£ p.a.)						
Skilled labour	2,390	1,378	1,043	2,466	1,154	1,044
Unskilled labour	947	832	832	671	556	556
Vehicles	250	200	50	250	200	50
Vehicle spares	216	173	45	216	173	45
Petrol	647	517	130	647	517	130
Total	4,550	3,100	2,100	4,250	2,600	1,825

Source: Department of Settlement.

cows were involved it has been taken that some would not be issued until the second year.

The loan schedule in each budget gives an itemized breakdown. Housing and fencing have been itemized into different types of material. Amounts shown for the establishment of crops have been taken to be entirely for mechanized cultivation. These have been broken down into different items on the basis of tractor running costs found in large farm surveys of the most similar area.

Table A.13.3

The full budget for Type II(A) farms at Kabisi

Date: September 1965[a]

Western Province Complex Scheme Kabisi No. 12

BUDGET

Plot category	II(A) (Maize) Average size 15 acres A.E.[b]
Target income	£25—40 Plus subsistence
Settlement charge	Shs. 2,300/-
Land loan	Shs. 2,300/- (30 years @ 6½%), annual repayment 176/-
Development loan	Shs. 2,000/- (10 years @ 6½%), annual repayment 276/-

Loan Schedule	*Shs.*	*Qualifying capital*	*Shs.*
Cattle	1,400	Stamp duty	60
Housing and fencing	100	Legal fees	40
Establishment of crops	500		
	2,000		100/-

Farm Plan at Maturity (4th year)	*Livestock Inventory*	L.U.
0.50 acre homestead	3 cows	3
2.00 acre subsistence	1 heifer	
3.50 acre maize	1 yearling	1.5
1.00 acre fodder crops		4.5
8.00 acre grazing		
15.00	= 2 acres A.E. per L.U.	

Income	*Shs.*
3 cows 120 lb. butterfat @ 2/50 per lb.	900
1 surplus calf, @ 30/-	30
3.5 acres maize @ 8 bags p.a. @ 30/- per bag.	840
1 cull cow @ 300/-	300
	2,070
Expenses	
3 cows @ 70/- per head	210
1 heifer @ 70/- per head	70
1 yearling @ 35/- per head	35
3.5 acres maize @ 143/-	500
1 acre fodder — crop @ 90/- per acre	90
	905
Loan Repayments: Land and Development Loans	452
Gross Margin: Plus subsistence	713

Source: Department of Settlement

a. This budget was revised in 1965, using 1962 prices, after it had been shown that previous budgets incorporating Sisal were unsound.

b. Arable Equivalent. See 13.3.1.

14. CO-OPERATIVE LOANS

Nottidge and Goldsack state that in High Density settlements £10 per member was provided for loans to co-operatives, whilst in Low Density settlements the corresponding sum was £1 per acre. It has been assumed that 75 per cent of this sum would be spent on equipment and the balance on buildings.

15. CONTRACTOR LOANS

In High Density settlements, £10 per settler was provided for these loans, while £50 per settler was allowed in Low Density schemes. These sums would be used entirely for the purchase of tracters and cultivating machinery. No item for contracter loans is shown in Table 13.1 because the full cost of contractor services is included in item 18. However, contractor loans are accounted for in the financial projections.

16. WATER SUPPLY LOANS

Provision for piped water supplies within schemes was made at the notional rate of Sh. 10 per acre for High Density and Sh. 22 per acre for Low Density schemes. No details are available on how these sums might be spent. The assumed itemized breakdown is shown in Table A.13.1.

17. SETTLER PURCHASE OF ASSETS

On High Density schemes, settlers were not normally expected to provide from their own resources any of the assets needed to make the budgeted farm programmes workable, although this item occurred in the budgets for the 43 sheep plots at Kipipiri. On Low Density schemes, all budgets show in full detail what part of the settlers' qualifying capital was planned to be spent on specific items of this kind.

18. RECURRENT COSTS OF FARMING

Planned operating costs for each enterprise in the maturity farm plan are detailed in every settlement budget. For High Density settlements these are shown only for the maturity year. Farms at Kabisi and Kipipiri were expected to take three or four years to reach maturity. Both to calculate costs and to estimate production, assumptions had to be made on the ways in which the farm systems in these two schemes would develop before the maturity year. Budgets for all years for all types of farm in Low Density schemes were individually prepared during planning. On tea plots at Lessos, these covered eight separate years.

Itemized breakdowns of each enterprise costs were given in working papers drawn up for use in budgeting by the Planning Officer of the Department of Settlement. These were made available for this study, and itemized unit costs for each enterprise were built up from this source.

19. RECURRENT COSTS OF CO-OPERATIVES

Co-operatives were not budgeted for in any of the settlements. To fill this gap, actual co-operative operating costs were used as a guide to what might have been planned for the marketing services that they provide. Accounts were obtained from the Assistant Commissioner for Co-operative development (Settlement) for the co-operative in each settlement for each accounting period up to 1968-9. Although in these accounts costs are allocated to specific marketing and other operations, there was irregularity between one year and the next in the number of items listed and the levels of expenditure for each product handled. In all cases the accounts for 1967-8 have been taken to represent the 'normal' level of direct costs for marketing maize, pyrethrum, milk and other products. Estimates of the overhead costs of operating each society were based on the general pattern for all of the full accounting periods.

In using actual records as the basis for estimating plan costs, difficulty arose because, although it was usually a major item of budgeted output, the societies actually handled very little butterfat, sales of whole milk being the principal disposal of dairy produce. The pattern of costs for milk marketing is different from that of butterfat. Both require handling within the settlement, but transportation off the scheme is very much more expensive for whole milk than for butterfat. Consequently, adjustments to the actual accounts had to be made to derive an estimate of planned handling costs for butterfat.

The composition of marketing expenses for the handling of each commodity was also based on 1967-8 figures. The same accounts were also used to express direct co-operative expenses as a percentage of the value of sales, this being the basis used for calculating the total handling cost for each commodity in a particular year. At Kabisi, direct expenses on butterfat were 6.5 per cent of the value of butterfat sales, whilst handling expenses on maize equalled 12.5 per cent of realization. It has been assumed, on the basis of evidence in the accounts, that overhead expenses would rise to a fixed level in the third year of each society's existence, and would then stabilize.

20. SURVEY FOR TITLE

According to Nottidge and Goldsack, Sh. 4 per acre were provided for to cover this expense. The assumed itemized composition of this item is shown in Table A.13.1.

21. SETTLERS' FAMILY LABOUR

This important item is considered in detail in Chapter 5 and in Chapter 16.

22. TEA STUMPS

This and the following two items arose only at Lessos. As grown on smallholdings in Kenya, tea is planted at a density of around 3,500 stumps per acre. Although since 1968 all new smallholder planting material was grown by Vegetative Propagation (see Stern, 1972) the tea planted in settlements was grown from seed. This was supplied for settlers by KTDA, who obtained stumps from two sources. Most came from their own nurseries. Figures taken from KTDA annual reports 1963-4 to 1967-8 indicate that over this period some 56 million stumps were produced at an average cost of 16¼ cents per stump.[1] The second source was purchases from private growers. Every year up to 1968-9, KTDA reported purchases of tea stumps, at average prices that ranged from 26½ to 37¼ cents per stump. This is much more than the cost of stumps produced by the Authority, probably because they were grown at greater cost in smaller nurseries.

Since the tea planted on settlements was outside the KTDA development programme it has been taken that the stumps planted at Lessos increased KTDA's need for purchase, and so should be costed as though purchased. In principle, our view of tea at Lessos as a marginal addition to all other tea production could require costing these seedlings at the highest purchase price each year, but this is not known. An average price must be used, and we assume that 30 cents per stump is correct. This is the sum normally charged by KTDA to smallholders for tea stumps delivered to their farms. The following cost composition was taken for the cost of producing a tea stump:

Seed	4 cents
Superphosphates	4 cents
Sulphate of ammonia	5 cents
Unskilled Labour	15 cents
Lorry Transport	2 cents
	30 cents

23. FARM EMPLOYEES

The budgets for all types of farm at Lessos provided for the employment of non-family workers who were required to operate the planned farm system. These were treated for shadow pricing as workers in the rural informal sector, as discussed in Chapter 4.

[1] This is calculated by dividing the unweighted sum of all expenditure reported as nursery costs over the period by the total reported number of stumps produced. Tea seedlings are normally in the nursery for up to 2 years. This figure refers to direct nursery costs only, and contains nothing for KTDA overheads.

24. KTDA SERVICES

The supervision of tea planting, cultivation and harvesting in the settlements was undertaken by KTDA as agents for SFT. The Authority also purchased the green leaf and transported it for processing.

Charges for these services were raised against SFT by KTDA under three item headings. *Field Development Costs* covered arrangements for planting and culture of the crop, and general extension work. *Inspection and Collection Costs* were incurred when tea was purchased from growers and transported for processing, while *Administration and Overhead Costs* referred to other costs, particularly accounts and other records. The first and last items were charged to SFT on an average per acre basis. The method apparently used each year was to express the settlement tea acreage as a proportion of the total acreage supervised by KTDA, and to apply this percentage each year to the total sums allocated under these headings in the Authority's final accounts. Inspection and Collection costs were similarly calculated, the proportion of all KTDA costs for this purpose charged to SFT being that for tea collection from settlement schemes expressed as a proportion of all tea purchases.

To the extent that tea in settlement schemes is marginal to KTDA's operations as a whole, and that economies of scale might be expected to occur in all of these operations, especially the first and third, it is arguable that only the marginal cost to KTDA should be taken note of. This would be less than the amounts actually charged. However, in many of the settlement areas, and at Lessos in particular, the settlement is some distance from adjacent blocks of KTDA tea. The marginal costs of these processes at Lessos would be higher than marginal costs elsewhere. The use of unadjusted average costs is thus justifiable.

So far as is known, the costs of these processes were not separately estimated for in settlement planning. Settlement budgeting followed the KTDA practice for non-settlement growers, which is eventually to cover these costs from cesses deducted from the value of green leaf deliveries.[1] Growers are paid the value of deliveries net of cess deductions. However, in the long term, cess income should more than cover the cost of these processes,[2] and their true cost will be less than the cess deductions. To get both the amount and the timing of KTDA costs correct, they must be separately determined. The corresponding relevant value of tea produced on the schemes is that which applies before cess deductions are considered.

Details of expenditure under each of the three relevant cost headings are published in the KTDA annual reports. On the basis of those figures, and information given elsewhere of acreages and deliveries, the actual annual costs assignable to Lessos were calculated and used as the basis for estimating planning costs.

1 Until sales reach such a level that cess income covers annual KTDA expenditure, these costs are covered by external lending, and money for this use is a major feature in the financing of KTDA's development programmes.

2 The surplus should become a major source of new KTDA finance, unless cesses are steadily reduced.

CHAPTER 14

The Development of the Settlements in Practice

14.1 INTRODUCTION

In this chapter an attempt is made to depict, to the extent that available data allows, the actual development of each scheme up to March 1968. This is done in such a way that comparisons can be made between the settlement plans discussed in the last chapter and the way that things worked out in practice. In building up a picture of how expenditure occurred, the basic pattern of successive processes discussed in Chapter 13 was largely adhered to. A completely analogous approach was not possible since available information did not allow items to be separately identified in the same way, but the ensuing figures are very comparable. Data from a variety of sources were drawn upon. The records and published accounts of the Department were an important primary source. A second main source, particularly for production and sales from each scheme, was information collected in the economic surveys of settlement farms.

In this chapter each settlement is considered individually, Kabisi in full, and the other three in summary style. Attention is given to the development of farming systems within the scheme; the patterns of expenditure and production for each year for which there is data; and the financial flows associated with each settlement. In a final section, some summary figures for the four settlements are brought together. Details are given in Appendices A.14 and B.14 of how information on costs and output was put together.

14.2 ACTUAL DEVELOPMENT IN THE KABISI SETTLEMENT

The first positively identifiable event in the actual development of Kabisi was the purchase of the first farm in late January 1963. All of the land was purchased before July of the same year. The settlement was planned to accommodate 701 families: 690 were allocated farms before the end of March 1964. One more farm was occupied in the following year, and the remaining ten farms were allocated during 1965-6. Thus, for the farming year 1964-5 all but ten of the farms had been allocated in time for a full year's operation.

14.2.1 *The development of farming and production*

Information on selected aspects of the development of farming in all schemes is given in appendices to the annual reports of the Department. These do not give a full picture of farming systems, but the tables show the numbers of livestock estimated to be on each scheme at 30 June or 31 December each year,[1] the acreage of pyrethrum grown where this crop occurred, and the volume of milk and pyrethrum sales to co-operatives during the reporting period. Livestock numbers and acreages published in these appendices were estimated by extension workers, and are probably based more on impressions than actual observation. Data on sales to co-operatives are taken from society records. Both milk and pyrethrum are the subject of monthly statements from the purchasing organization, so these should be accurate.

The only figures from this source relevant to Kabisi are cattle numbers and milk sales. Figures taken from each annual report up to 1971 are shown in Table 14.1. They show that the budgeted cattle numbers were never anywhere near being reached before the end of 1971. In June 1967, when the reported cow population was at its highest, it was only 36 per cent of the budgeted number of roughly 3 per farm.[2]

[1] The Department of Settlement reporting period was changed from July to June to a calendar year after a half-year period from July to December 1969.

[2] Experience in the whole settlement programme showed that the numbers of cows budgeted for exceeded the numbers available by a wide margin, and even in December 1971 there was a shortfall of 13 per cent of the planned levels. As one of

A shortfall of this degree in the achievement of planned targets obviously had severe implications for the attainment by settlers of the planned production and income targets. Table 13.1 showed that, at the maturity level, sales of butterfat were expected to amount to almost 40 per cent of the value of output. Not surprisingly, the actual volume of milk sales through the co-operative was substantially below the budgeted amount. However, the shortfall was far greater than could be accounted for by the cow shortage. The budgets expected sales of 300 gallons per cow. Table 14.1 indicates sales of 63 gallons per cow in the three years to June 1967. By 1970 this had declined to 38 gallons. The highest volume of sales was in the year to June 1967, when cow numbers were at their peak. However, during that year, when available cows were 36 per cent of the budgeted number, co-operative sales were only 7.7 per cent of the budgeted volume.

Table 14.1

The development of dairy production in the Kabisi Settlement

Date	Cow Nos.[a]	Co-op milk sales (gallons)	Date	Cow Nos.	Co-op milk sales (gallons)
Maturity budgets[b]	2,178	653,400	June 1968	761	32,108
June 1964	231	0	June 1969	743	45,813
June 1965	757	47,701	Dec. 1969	734	18,081[c]
June 1966	777	49,379	Dec. 1970	725	27,796
June 1967	790	50,132	Dec. 1971	767	32,259

Source: Annual Reports, Department of Settlement.

a. The 1964 and 1965 reports gave only numbers of mature cattle. All would probably be cows.

b. Calculated from the scheme budgets and expected to arise first in 1967-8.

c. Six months' production only. See footnote on p. 304.

the earlier settlements, Kabisi ought not to have been badly affected by the developing 'shortage' of cows, but this situation may have arisen because rebudgeting in 1965 implied an increase in numbers which could not be supplied. However, Kabisi was not the scheme worst affected in this way. The Department's report for 1971 shows that on 12 other settlements a smaller percentage of the budgeted number were on the schemes than was the case at Kabisi.

A number of factors may have contributed to this very low volume of sales. Some relevant points may be mentioned.[1] First, the average number of cows per farm was, according to Table 14.1, never much more than 1.0. As Table 14.4 shows, the size of each farm family steadily increased during the first four years of the settlement. Whatever the sale price of milk, farmers would be likely to give first priority in the disposal of available milk to household consumption. With only one cow per farm, it is understandable that most of the milk produced was consumed on the farms. Had increased numbers of cattle been available, production in most months might have been well beyond the subsistence requirements of each family, thus increasing more than proportionately the amount available for sale.

A second factor to which the low volume of sales may be attributed was the low price for milk delivered to co-operatives who eventually sold it for butterfat.[2] After handling cost deductions,[3] the amount remaining for credit to settlers' accounts was only 70 or 80 cents per gallon. This price might easily not provide a sufficient inducement for farmers whose plots were far from the milk collecting centres to bring in daily the small quantities they had available for sale.

A third factor may stem from the further disincentive applying to sales through the society, where substantial but arbitrary deductions for loan repayments could be made from amounts credited to settlers' accounts. Repayment through the co-operative was a thing that the settler could not avoid, if he had to use that channel for sales, but it had the net effect of reducing further the value of milk sold in this way.[4]

[1] The following discussion does not touch on the technical problems associated with managing one-cow herds, especially those of ensuring regular calving, but these were also probably important contributing factors.

[2] Although the Kabisi Co-operative was able to secure a quota to sell a limited amount of whole milk, only morning milk could be sold in this way. All evening milk delivered to the society had to be separated. Separate accounts were kept for morning and evening milk, and settlers received a lower price for the latter.

[3] During the four accounting periods up to and including 1968-9, deductions made by the society from the net sales value on the scheme of all milk handled were 28, 25, 32 and 22 per cent respectively.

[4] During the period of extended supervision, co-operatives were increasingly encouraged to act as agents in the collection of loan repayments, for which they

Poor incentives may have induced farmers to consume a lot of milk or sell it through other channels rather than deliver it to their co-operative. However, possibly the sales opportunity never arose. A fourth explanation of low sales might simply be low levels of production. Milk yields in the early years were probably below those assumed in the budgets, High Density settlers being unfamiliar with the husbandry requirements of high grade cattle. Certainly the production systems envisaged in the budget were not followed, since the Kabisi farm surveys record no instance of the purchase of fodder crop seeds, although one acre or more was envisaged in every budget. There may have seemed no need for such crops, since cattle numbers were far below those anticipated, and plenty of other grazing was available. Whether low sales are attributable to husbandry failure or lack of incentives cannot be determined from available data. Several factors were probably important.

A fuller indication of farming systems is obtainable from the economic surveys. Figures from the four years of survey at Kabisi are shown in Table 14.2. These figures show that, while there was undoubtedly a substantial shortfall in the number of grade cows available, it was less severe than the Department's figures suggested. The reason for the marked difference between the two estimates are not known but the farm survey figures are likely to be the more reliable, being based on actual counts at least twice a year.

On the cropping side Table 14.2 indicates that here again there was substantial underfulfilment of the planned levels. During the first three years, sisal was still occupying much land, though it was of no commercial value and was steadily being removed. At Kabisi, the main subsistence crop would be maize, and if the budgets had been fulfilled practically all the cropped area would be in maize. By 1967-8 it appears that almost all of the cropped land was in fact growing maize, but by then only 84 per cent of the maturity planned acreage was being grown.

received a 1 per cent commission. Often it was decided by a majority vote at a general meeting that a certain percentage (sometimes as much as 30 or 40) of all sums credited to members' accounts should obligatorily be assigned to loan repayment while they had outstanding debts. In such cases, the individual had no choice of how this portion of his sales revenue should be applied. It is not known whether this practice applied at Kabisi. However, wherever it did apply it must have been a strong incentive to settlers to seek sale outlets other than the society, especially to those whose debts were large in relation to production.

Tables 14.1 and 14.2 clearly indicate that by 1967-8—the 'maturity' year of the plans—settlers were not following the farming systems which the budgets envisaged would by then be in operation. However, Table 14.2 shows that the unbudgeted enterprise poultry was relatively popular. Large numbers of birds were recorded, especially in 1965-6, although thereafter their popularity declined.

14.2.2 *Actual costs in the Kabisi Settlement*

The levels of annual expenditure for each item up until 1967-8 are shown in Table 14.3. Many of the processes listed are completely analogous with those described in detail in 13.2. However, some are different, as is explained in Appendix A.14. The item *Pre-Settlement Development* includes the plan cost items Interim Farming Losses, Survey for Planning, Planning

Table 14.2

Actual patterns of farming in the Kabisi Settlement as indicated by the survey of settlement farmers

Farm Survey Means — per farm

Land Use in acres	Maturity Budgets	1964-5	1965-6	1966-7	1967-8
Maize	3.34	2.85	3.00	3.92	4.43
Sisal	-	0.97	0.14	0.15	-
Potatoes and vegetables	-	0.15	-	0.14	-
Other crops	-	1.22	0.04	0.42	0.07
Subsistence	2.00	-	-	-	-
Total Crops	5.34	5.20	3.18	4.63	4.50
Other Land	9.88	11.14	12.17	10.43	10.50
Total Farm Area	15.22	16.34	15.35	15.06	15.00
Livestock numbers					
Grade cows	3.11	0.52	1.86	1.95	2.2
Other cattle	2.04	0.21	0.62	0.65	0.9
Poultry	5.15	70.29	205.51	140.17	41.1
No. of farms		28	47	30	55

and Demarcation, and Roads and Soil Conservation. The item *Farmers' Assets* refers to the purchase or construction of buildings and other fixed improvements on the farm and the cost of large tools and implements that settlers acquired, irrespective of the source of their funding.[1] This item does not include livestock purchases. Their initial cost is shown only for 1964-5. Purchases in later years are included in the output item 'net sales'. By the end of March 1968 no expenditure had been incurred on two of the processes listed, namely Water Supply and Survey for Title. Expenditure on both items would arise before it could be said that settlement establishment was complete. Their cost is discussed in Appendix A.14, whilst the possible timing of their execution is considered in 14.2.6.

The valuation of settlers' labour is not explained in Appendix A.14. Details of the approach used were outlined in Chapter 5. The numbers of people resident on each farm were recorded in the economic surveys, and are shown in the first lines of Table 14.4. Average farm household size increased steadily during the four years covered. As in the costing of the settlement plan, a problem arises as to what might be meant by the actual cost of family labour valued at 'market prices'. Following the practice of Chapter 13, it has been taken that only the 'opportunity cost' of adult workers should be taken into account, as reflected in alternative earnings. For adult residents at Kabisi these were taken to be £34 for men and £12 for women, together with net subsistence production of £5 per family. People available for work can therefore be valued at these rates. However, as was explained in Chapter 5, adjustment is required to allow for time spent earning 'non-farm income'. The relevant figures are shown in Table 14.4.

The pattern of expenditure shown in Table 14.3 differs fairly substantially from that for the settlement plan given in Table 13.1. In particular, the recurrent costs of farming and of co-operative operations are much less than were planned, whilst settlers' labour is a very much bigger item, accounting in 1967-8 for 72 per cent of all costs. The lower level of co-operative costs reflects the low volume of milk sales referred to, and the relatively small amounts of maize handled by the society. With the substantial shortfall in the number of cows, recurrent farming costs would be expected to be below the planned levels, and this they certainly were. In 1967-8, when all costs

[1] The financial implications of the acquisitions of assets from different sources are considered in 14.2.4.

Table 14.3

Actual Costs in the Kabisi Settlement until 1967-8

Current Market Values (£)

	1962-3	1963-4	1964-5	1965-6	1966-7	1967-8
Current Values:						
31. Valuation	106	318	–	–	–	–
32. Land purchase	28,800	44,398	–	–	–	–
33. Pre-Settlement development	–	18,514	–	–	–	–
34. Legal fees	–	3,478	5	50	–	–
35. Scheme supervision	–	1,137	4,550	4,550	3,462	3,100
36. Field overhead supervision	–	663	2,653	2,653	1,658	1,326
37. Headquarters overhead supervision	–	895	3,580	3,580	2,685	2,386
38. Settler subsistence	–	12,420	18	180	–	–
39. Farmers' assets	–	–	578	1,870	2,135	2,339
40. Co-operative assets	–	–	145	149	382	405
41. Water scheme	–	–	–	–	–	–
42. Recurrent costs of farming	–	–	22,516	18,218	8,803	20,452
43. Recurrent costs of co-operatives	–	–	444	1,331	1,363	1,486
44. Survey for title	–	–	–	–	–	–
45. Settlers' labour	–	–	35,089	51,257	53,374	82,760
46. Cows	–	–	19,200	–	–	–
Total	28,906	81,823	88,778	83,838	73,862	114,254

Sources: see Appendix A.14.

amounted to £9.23 per acre,[1] recurrent farming costs were only 66 per cent of the planned level, but in that year they were more than double their level in 1966-7, when a very low level of farm expenditure was recorded. No explanation of that startingly low figure can be found in available sources. The possibility of faulty enumeration cannot be dismissed, but the figures shown in Table A.14.1 indicate that reduced

[1] Corresponding values (in 1967-8 terms) for large-scale farming and the maturity plan were £3.72 and £6.81 respectively.

TABLE 14.4

Farm residents, non-farm income and the cost of settlers' labour in the Kabisi Settlement

	1964-5	1965-6	1966-7	1967-8
Residents per farm				
Men	1.00	1.47	1.51	2.70
Women	1.18	1.54	1.65	1.80
Children	3.89	3.15	4.03	4.05
Total	6.07	6.16	7.19	8.55
Non-farm income per farm Sh.	246	40	20	48
Men-equivalent reduction for non-farm income	0.07	0.01	0.00	0.01
Cost of Settlers' Family Labour (current values £)				
Men	21,849	34,798	35,689	64,113
Women	9,785	12,954	13,880	15,142
Subsistence	3,455	3,505	3,505	3,505
Total	35,089	51,257	53,374	82,760

Sources: Residents and non-farm income are taken from the economic surveys. Men-equivalent reduction for non-farm income, as explained in Chapter 5. Cost of family labour for different types of worker based on per caput values given in text.

employment of non-family workers, and the complete absence on any survey farm of cultivations by hired tractors, account in some degree for the very low cost level in that year.

Annual expenditure figures in disaggregated form were prepared through the analysis of individual process costs, as explained in Appendix A.14. When considered at this level, the overwhelming importance as a cost item of unskilled labour is even more clearly emphasized. In 1967-8 all forms of unskilled labour taken into account at this level of analysis (Government employees, co-operative workers, hired farm labourers and settler families) accounted for over 77 per cent of all costs. The next most important item, superphosphates, accounted for slightly less than 8 per cent.

14.2.3 *The development of production in the settlement*

Information on production from Kabisi farms is obtainable from two sources, the economic surveys and the co-operative accounts. The use of these sources in determining the pattern and value of production is described in Appendix B.14.

Figures are shown in Table 14.5 of the value of all output, including sales through the Kabisi Society. They reflect not only the declining volume of milk sales but a similar decline in the value of maize handled each year. As a result, the total value of produce marketed by the society fell steadily.

The annual value of output other than sales through the co-operative is also shown in Table 14.5. These figures bring out a number of interesting points. The value of crops consumed on the farm increased steadily over successive survey periods, in line with the increase in household size. In 1964-5, when farmers were only becoming established on their holdings, the value of crops consumed was Sh. 82 per farm, but by 1967-8 it had risen to Sh. 746. It is notable that in the last two years covered the consumption of vegetables was valued more highly than maize. The basis for valuing vegetables of different kinds is not known, but it is possible that home consumption was over-valued. As Wilson, 1972, has shown, the price of different kinds of fresh vegetables in Kenya varied substantially during and between seasons, and untypically high prices may have been used.

On the livestock side, the figures reflect an erratic pattern in the value of net output from dairy and beef cattle. The latter probably consists of male animals from the dairy herd. In 1964-5, a net output of cattle per farm of Sh. 270 arose, possibly because the cattle were purchased for less than the standard prices used in the surveys. In 1966-7, the value of cattle declined over the year, possibly reflecting some deaths.

Production from poultry was recorded only in the last of the four survey years; Table 14.2 showed relatively large numbers of birds on these farms; and it must be assumed that the recording of egg and poultry sales was omitted during the previous three years. No adjustment to the figures has been made to take account of this apparent omission.

Comparison of the consolidated picture of actual output in the settlement for each of the four years up to 1967-8 with the planned figures given in Table 13.1[1] shows that in none of

[1] Table 13.2 has figures expressed in 1962-3 values. To compare them with Table 14.5, Table 13.2 values should all be divided by the inflation index factor, discussed in 16.1.3.

those four years did the total value of production reach the budgeted levels. This is scarcely surprising in view of the shortfall in livestock numbers and the underfulfilment of crop acreages. The total value of production from the scheme in 1967-8 was 77 per cent of planned output for that year, when the latter is adjusted to 1967-8 prices.[1] Production per acre was £6.08, as compared to £5.79 and £7.83 for large-scale farming and planned maturity respectively.

Further comparison of the two tables shows that practically all of the difference between planned and actual output is attributable to the shortfall in milk production. At constant prices the value of co-operative sales and consumption in 1967-8 was only 24 per cent of the planned value of butterfat sales. In the same year, the value of crop production exceeded the planned level by over 75 per cent; the value of household consumption was almost two-thirds more than planned subsistence. Maize sales were only 49 per cent of the planned level, although if all of the maize in stock at the end of that period had been sold at its valued price, the value of maize sales would be 90 per cent of the planned sum.

Table 14.5 shows that output from the Kabisi Settlement increased fairly steadily during the last three years covered by the survey, albeit from the very low level of 1965-6. Settlers appeared to be compensating for the shortfall of milk production by producing substantial quantities of vegetables for home consumption, and through poultry production.

14.2.4 *Financial arrangements for the settlement in practice*

Financial arrangements for the settlements were discussed in Chapter 13. In this section an outline is given of the inflow and outflow *to Kenya* of external finance attributable to the development of the Kabisi Settlement as actually developed.[2] The total value of all inflows up to 1967-8 and the consequential outflow to that year, are given in Table 14.6.

The same values for land purchase loans and grants are used

[1] In this chapter, comparisons of the kind made here all involve bringing values to their 1967-8 levels.

[2] At this stage, settlement finance flows within Kenya are not considered. The important questions of finance flows between Government and settlers, and the problems of loan defaulters are touched on in Chapter 16.

Table 14.5

Value of actual output in the Kabisi Settlement up to March 1968

	Current Market Values (£)			
	1964-5	1965-6	1966-7	1967-8
Maize: Co-operative sales	1,895	4,129	3,223	2,997
Other sales	7,009	3,888	23,777	12,115
Consumption on farm	1,938	8,846	8,839	11,363
Stock increase	12,877	-	-	12,409
Potatoes and Vegetables: Co-operative sales	-	-	44	57
Other sales	39	971	844	301
Consumption	886	3,267	11,801	14,770
Milk: Co-operative sales	2,116	4,232	4,882	3,416
Consumption on farm	4,651	3,761	6,061	5,286
Dairy Cattle: Net sales	-19,200	-	403	45
Value increase	28,528	3,803	-4,323	5,413
Beef Cattle: Net sales	-220	209	183	-29
Value increase	3,455	-	-	3,244
Sheep	-	89	-	63
Poultry	-	-	-	3,122
Total	43,974	33,195	55,734	74,572

Sources: See Appendix B.14.

in both plan and actual cases, though with different timing. The value of settlers development loans drawn each year were obtained from the Department for each farm studied in the surveys. With the shortage of available cattle, the development loan issues by the end of 1967-8 had not reached the permitted level of Sh. 2000, although by the end of March 1968 the average value of development loans issued on farms of Types II(A) and II(B)[1] was Sh. 1,919. The major part of development loan issues were made during 1964-5, although small new drawings were recorded in each subsequent survey.

Particulars of loans to the Kabisi Co-operative (and all other co-operatives) were taken from their accounts. The value of contractor loans had to be calculated in an *ad hoc* manner, since they were not particularly associated with individual schemes. It was the intention that contractors would each operate in several settlements, possibly removed from each other by many miles.

[1] No type V farms were covered in the surveys.

Table 14.6

A summary of output, costs and financial flows for the Kabisi Settlement in practice, up to 1967-8

Current Market Values (£)					Current Market Values (£)		
Year	Output	Costs	Annual surplas	Grants drawn	Loans drawn	Loans repaid	Final surplas
1962-3	-	28,906	-28,906	9,706	19,200	0	0
1963-4	-	81,823	-81,823	48,746	30,665	1,459	-3,871
1964-5	43,973	88,778	-44,805	10,801	52,781	3,778	14,999
1965-6	33,195	83,838	-50,643	10,963	7,092	7,209	-39,797
1966-7	55,734	73,862	-18,128	2,697	5,258	7,670	-17,843
1967-8	74,572	114,254	-39,682	-	2,874	8,012	-44,820

Note: Grants and loans drawn and loans repaid refer only to drawings and payments by the Kenya Government from or to foreign sources. It is assumed that grants and loans were drawn in the same year as that in which the relevant expenditure was made, and that (unlike settlers) the Kenya Government made full loan repayments on time.

Great difficulty was experienced by the Department in finding individuals or organizations to take up these loans, and enormous under-issue arose; contractor loans made by June 1968 were just over 15 per cent of the sum available. For calculating the sum attributable to a particular settlement, this actual percentage fulfilment rate has been applied to the sum available for its settlers. These loans would be made immediately before the bulk of settlers were introduced: at Kabisi this was in 1963-4.

14.2.5 *Summary of the overall position up to March 1968*

A summary is given in Table 14.6 of the year-by-year values of output, costs and financial flows associated with the actual development of Kabisi up to 1967-8. Every year costs exceeded output, leaving substantial annual deficits. During the earlier years, this deficiency was ameliorated by a net financial inflow but by 1967-8 outflows exceeded inflows, and the final surplus showed an even greater deficit than the annual surplus for that year. Only in 1964-5 was there a positive final surplus. In terms of total output and costs, Kabisi was a serious drain on resources up to 1967-8. However, the overwhelming importance in costs of family labour should be remembered. Removing this item from costs and subsistence consumption from output indicates an 'operating surplus' in 1967-8 of £11,659.

14.2.6 *Changes at Kabisi after 1967-8*

In Chapter 16 evaluations are made of the settlements as planned and as operated in practice. For the latter purpose, as in all evaluations of ongoing projects, assumptions have to be made about developments after the last date for which information is available. Three possibilities are envisaged, namely (i) that things would proceed after 1967-8 at the level of that year (adjustment being made on the cost side to remove once-and-for-all establishment expenses occurring in 1967-8); (ii) that the 1967-8 levels would persist, but with uncompleted establishment expenses and known relative price changes after 1967-8 taken into account together with increasing yields of long-maturing crops; and (iii) with known changes after the last full data period taken into account, and with net output expanded for several years at a constant rate to reflect increases in productivity that could be expected to occur. For the last two possibilities, estimates must be made of known or expected changes after 1967-8. It is convenient to discuss them here. They almost always concern only costs.

For evaluation of the post-1967-8 period, the first adjustment required is to remove all non-recurring items included as costs in 1967-8. At Kabisi, there were no costs of this kind, but they were quite important at both Lessos and Passenga. However, costs of this kind were planned for and expected to arise. At Kabisi such costs were quite important, establishment of the settlement not having been completed by March 1968. Further capital expenditure is known to have since been made. The co-operative drew a loan in 1968-9 for new buildings and another between 1970-1 and 1972-3 for its share of the cost of a comprehensive water scheme. These are known costs. Although the completion of Survey for Title has not yet[1] been reported, it is assumed below that it was carried out during 1971-2.

New expenses of this kind are specific to each settlement. So also are changes in post-1967-8 finance flows arising from both earlier loan drawings and these items. However, a further known

[1] I.e. in the Annual Report for 1971.

change affecting all settlements was the salary increase awarded from July 1969 to all junior Government employees.

Known post-1967-8 cost changes taken into account in the Kabisi evaluation were as follows:

	1968-9	1969-70	1970-1	1971-2	1972-3	1973-4 et seq.
Co-operative building loan	1,350	-	-	-	-	-
Water supply	-	-	12,852	12,852	12,851	-
Survey for Title	-	-	-	3,683	-	-
Salary Increase	-	505	673	673	673	673
Totals	£1,350	505	13,525	17,208	13,524	673

14.3 ACTUAL DEVELOPMENT IN THE LESSOS SETTLEMENTS

Development in these three isolated settlements took place over several years. Keben,[1] historically the first of the High and Low Density settlements, took in its first settlers in 1961-2. Lessos was mainly settled in 1962-3 and Koylat in the following two years.

As planned, the farming systems developed were based mainly on cattle, maize and tea. After the completion of settlement in 1966, cow numbers were below the budgeted level, but this was exceeded by mid-1969. However, milk sales through the co-operative never reached the planned level. These had envisaged three-quarters of milk sales as butterfat, a product in which the society showed little interest. During the years up to 1969, its efforts and funds were devoted to acquiring quota and contracts for whole-milk sales, and the volume of milk sales rose more or less in line with the acquisition of quota. However, sales outside the co-operative were always important at Lessos, labour on nearby tea estates offering a more attractive outlet than the butterfat price.

The area planted to maize increased steadily from a low level, and only in 1967-8 did its acreage equal that budgeted for maize and subsistence. Tea planting also occurred more slowly than was planned[1] but eventually the area established exceeded the planned amount by 16 per cent. Tea yields were, on the

[1] Keben was originally called Lessos. The name was changed in 1962.

whole, lower than expected. Allowing for the different ages of tea growing at the time, yields during the four years 1967-8 to 1970-1 were between 78 and 55 per cent of these expected, the weighted average level being 65 per cent.

By 1967-8 all of the main enterprises had been developed roughly to the levels envisaged in planning. Average household size also increased steadily over the four years of survey to 6.72 members in 1967-8. However, its composition changed, with a reduction in the number of men after 1965-6 to 1.08 per farm. This affected the cost of family labour, which was at its highest in 1965-6. Non-farm income at Lessos was not a very important item in any year.

A sample of farms in each of the three schemes was studied in all four economic surveys, while Clough, 1965, had earlier studied Keben. Cost estimates are thus based on actual observations to the fullest extent possible. Despite the increasing intensity of the farming systems being developed, recurrent farming costs fell from 1965 to 1966, no doubt partly reflecting increasing efficiency on the part of the settlers as farmers and managers. The imputed cost of settler labour was not such an overwhelming item as at Kabisi, being only 27 per cent of all costs in 1967-8, when unskilled labour of all kinds accounted for 44 per cent of costs analysed to the 'scheme-gate' level. At 15 per cent, skilled labour was the next most important item. No other input accounted for more than 7 per cent of all costs. In 1967-8, costs per acre at £6.68 were more than the equivalent planned sum of £6.62. However, deducting non-recurrent items (water scheme and tea stumps) leaves £5.69, a little less than the planned 'maturity' level. The main source of cost difference between plan and actual is the much lower level of recurrent farm costs, although this is partly offset by higher settler labour costs, which reflect household sizes larger than were planned.

Itemized figures of the value of production each year are shown in Table 14.7. They depict the typical production pattern for 'low altitude' areas of heavy dependence on maize, milk and cattle. Despite the long-term potential importance of

[1] Partly because of settlers' resistance to a change in policy by the Department regarding the balance between deposits by settlers and SFT credit for the second acre of tea budgeted for many tea farms.

Table 14.7

Summary of costs, output, finance flows and surplus for the Lessos Settlements as actually developed up to 1967-8

Current Market Prices (£)

365 farms	1961-2	1962-3	1963-4	1964-5	1965-6	1966-7	1967-8
I. *Costs*							
Establishment processes	6,438	9,485	7,303	2,139	26	9	8
Land purchase	45,127	48,360	29,620	7,480	–	–	–
Supervision	873	10,483	26,860	29,016	24,743	18,936	18,936
Productive assets	–	13,938	36,105	18,590	16,083	18,645	18,794
Recurrent farming costs	–	2,862	11,676	21,873	29,702	24,577	20,222
Recurrent co-op. costs	–	216	1,952	2,605	4,228	5,524	8,087
Settlers' family labour	–	4,451	16,157	19,876	32,933	25,985	25,392
Other costs	–	997	1,331	2,330	2,771	2,832	3,086
Total costs	52,438	90,792	131,004	103,909	110,486	96,508	94,525
II. *Output*							
Milk and butterfat	–	4,351	18,182	24,299	33,157	45,552	59,106
Pyrethrum	–	–	–	–	91	318	817
Maize	–	2,623	9,786	17,265	21,447	25,142	31,866
Potatoes and vegetables	–	–	223	910	1,414	59	17
Cattle	–	580	4,114	11,686	-4,638	23,698	35,308
Tea	–	–	138	245	651	1,178	3,323
Other products	–	843	1,736	62	–	–	59
Total output	–	8,397	34,179	54,467	52,122	95,947	130,396
III. *Operating surplus*	-52,438	-82,395	-96,825	-49,442	-58,364	-561	35,971
IV. *Net financial inflow*	51,922	78,613	95,415	50,482	24,841	7,134	9,538
V. *Final Surplus*	-516	-3,782	-1,410	1,040	-33,523	6,573	45,509

tea, the three main products accounted for 97 per cent of the value of all production in 1967-8. Milk sales were most important, sales outside the co-operative having by then become worth more than half the value of sales through the society. The value of maize production also increased pretty steadily year by year during a period of relatively stable producer prices.[1] Tea sales were, by the last year shown, only beginning to pick up. The 'farm gate' value of the crop in 1967-8 was (for the first time) only slightly greater than the associated KTDA costs.

At the 1967-8 level, actual production was still 15 per cent below the final maturity planned level of £10.79 per acre. However, despite the planting delay and poor yields of tea actual output in 1967-8 was almost 4 per cent higher than the adjusted value of planned production for that year shown in Table 13.3.

With land purchase and the introduction of settlers stretched over four years, grants and loans for establishment expenses were drawn over a long period. However, all IBRD loan funds had to be drawn before mid-1968. With the completion of the water schemes in that year, this target was fulfilled. With new loans being drawn up to the end of 1967-8, a net financial inflow continued until then. In 1968-9, full repayment of the IBRD loans began, and net outflows would apply thereafter for 27 years until land loan repayments were completed.

The finance flows up to 1967-8 are shown in the lower part of Table 14.7. By 1966-7, these costs and output were almost equal, and in the following year a substantial operating surplus arose. During previous years, the net financial inflow had roughly covered the annual deficit (except in 1965-6) and by 1967-8 the undiscounted cumulative final surplus was over £13,000.

Quite a number of further changes after 1967-8 were either known or could be expected to occur, including not only uncompleted establishment costs and other things referred to above for Kabisi, but also KTDA expenses. These would increase in parallel with the value of tea production from both established (but immature) and newly planted tea. Changes of these kinds would increase for several years, but could be expected to stabilize in 1977-8.

[1] Index numbers of producer maize prices (1967 = 100), were: 1962, 90.6; 1963, 93.1; 1964, 102.6; 1965, 100.8; 1966, 113.6. (Source: Statistical Abstract, 1970.)

14.4 THE DEVELOPMENT OF THE KIPIPIRI SETTLEMENT

The first land at Kipipiri was purchased in June 1962, and a quarter of the final number of settlers were admitted before April 1963. During the following twelve months, all but three of the remaining plots were allocated, and almost all land was in use during 1964-5.

The main budgeted enterprises were dairy cattle and pyrethrum. From the outset, more cows were kept than had been budgeted for, possibly because settlement began before the full extent of the cow shortage was appreciated. However, milk sales through the co-operative never reached the planned levels. After 1964-5, they stabilized at around just over half the expected quantity. Unlike the position at Kabisi and Lessos, this probably does not reflect any unwillingness on the part of settlers to sell at the low butterfat price. Low yields are a more likely cause. The Kipipiri co-operative obtained quota and contract rights far beyond the planned level, and, between 1964 and 1966, in almost all months except those immediately after the rains, they were unable to supply milk up to the full permitted level.[1]

Sheep numbers increased from a low level to the budgeted number by mid-1967, but fell away soon after, and became of little general importance. Sheep have not been a successful enterprise in any settlement scheme. Pyrethrum, however is an ideal smallholder crop. Reacting to steadily increasing prices,[2] Kipipiri settlers increased acreage and production, and exceeded the budgeted levels by a long way in 1966-7 and 1967-8. However, in 1968 and 1969 prices were cut drastically[3] and this led to a sharp fall from which recovery began only in 1970.

Due to variations between years in the coverage of schemes, Kipipiri was covered in only two of the four years of economic survey. This obviously inhibits our consideration of the scheme over a longer period, but it appears that, apart from the pyrethrum situation, a fair degree of stability in the farming

[1] See footnote in Appendix B.14.

[2] Index numbers of producer prices, (1967 = 100) rose each year from 71.7 in 1963 through 95.7 in 1965 and 104.8 in 1966.

[3] 1969 price index 81.9.

system had been reached by 1966, when survey coverage ended. Cropping probably had not reached the expected levels by 1967-8; land planted in 1965-6 to vegetables and subsistence crops in particular was only 67 per cent of budgeted acreage.

Typically for a High Density settlement, the imputed cost of family labour is the largest single long-run cost item. Its year-to-year value after 1965-6 is taken to be constant, because information on household size and composition is available for only two years. Figures for those years were extrapolated forwards and backwards to cover the whole period up to 1967-8, as is shown in Table 14.8. Non-farm income was surprisingly high, at Sh. 707 per farm in 1965-6, when the number of adults was similar to that for Kabisi before household size in the latter scheme increased rapidly. Assuming a constant family size at the 1965-6 level probably does not imply serious undervaluation.

Estimates of actual costs at Kipipiri are given in Table 14.8. By 1967-8, most establishment expenses had been completed or were under way. Survey for Title was finalized in 1968-9. No reference to a water supply scheme being developed for this area is made in the Department's annual reports up to 1971 and it seems unlikely that there will ever be one.

Because of the limited availability of farm survey data the same levels of recurrent farming costs have been taken for the last three years shown.[1] This may not seriously misrepresent the situation. In 1965-6, farm costs had three main components: dairy cattle expenses; potato and vegetable seeds; and hired workers. Sales through the co-operative of dairy produce, potatoes and vegetables did not increase in the next two years. It is possible that the increased production of pyrethrum in 1967 and 1968 may have led to a higher cost of hired workers, although the recorded level of £9.34 per farm in 1965-6 is remarkably high when the low level of these settler's earnings is considered.

Recurrent costs per acre brought into account in 1967-8 were £5.98, which, although a relatively small amount, is more than the planned cost for that year of £4.58 per acre in 1967-8 values. Recurrent costs of farming and of the co-operative are both higher than planned, but the main source of difference is

[1] The figures in the table differ slightly because of inflation adjustments.

the imputed cost of family labour, which accounts for 59 per cent of all long-run costs. At the level of disaggregated cost analysis adopted for shadow pricing, unskilled labour of all kinds accounted for 69 per cent of all costs. Only one other item accounted for more than 3.5 per cent of all costs; skilled labour (almost 7 per cent).

Like certain aspects of costs, the pattern of output depicted in Table 14.8 depends heavily on the two years of economic survey. The only other source of output data is the records of the co-operative, through which most marketed production passed, especially pyrethrum. In each of the last two years, this crop accounted for more than half of the total value of output. However, for subsistence consumption, non-co-operative sales, and stock value increases, the survey figures for 1965-6 have been used for the following two years, corrected only for changing money values.

Estimated output in 1967-8 of £7.55 per acre exceeded the equivalent planned figure by a very wide margin. The difference was mainly attributable to the high level of pyrethrum production, but the value of all products save sheep and wool exceeded the planned level.

In this relatively simple scheme, almost all grants and loans were quickly drawn, and the build-up of loan repayments led to a net financial outflow annually from 1966-7, as Table 14.8 shows. However, after four years of net annual deficit, output exceeded costs in 1966-7 and a fairly high annual surplus arose then and in the next year.

Known changes after 1967-8 were very few: in 1968-9, one more settler was in operation, while survey for title was completed. From 1969-70, settlement supervision costs increased, in the way described earlier.

14.5 THE ACTUAL DEVELOPMENT OF THE PASSENGA SETTLEMENTS

These three schemes were developed almost simultaneously. Almost all of their land was purchased in the first half of 1963, and by the following March 90 per cent of all plots had been settled.

TABLE 14.8

Summary of costs, outputs, finance flows and surplus for the Kipipiri Settlement as actually developed up to 1967-8

Current Market Prices (£)

525 farms	1962-3	1963-4	1964-5	1965-6	1966-7	1967-8
I. *Costs*						
Establishment processes	13,301	17,665	384	—	—	1,873
Land purchase	83,206	8,700	1,850	—	—	—
Supervision	—	1,197	10,783	10,683	8,136	6,812
Productive assets	—	21,072	6,673	4,394	2,985	3,128
Recurrent farming costs	—	3,572	14,343	13,042	13,627	13,919
Recurrent co-op. costs	—	580	2,249	4,819	4,912	6,347
Settlers' family labour	—	7,450	29,916	43,592	43,592	43,592
Total costs	96,507	60,836	66,198	76,530	73,252	75,671
II. *Output*						
Milk and butterfat	—	4,487	12,693	18,827	18,251	18,269
Pyrethrum	—	457	4,935	12,487	45,727	51,505
Maize	—	—	—	5,557	5,806	5,931
Potatoes and vegetables	—	3,994	16,040	10,246	9,508	10,748
Cattle	—	1,064	4,272	5,787	6,080	6,211
Sheep and wool	—	87	418	-413	614	497
Total output	—	10,089	38,358	52,491	85,986	93,161
III. *Operating surplus*	-96,507	-50,747	-27,840	-24,039	12,734	17,490
IV. *Net financial inflow*	96,142	61,296	9,761	5,306	-4,108	-5,374
V. *Final surplus*	-365	10,549	-18079	-18,733	8,626	12,166

Farm development in these schemes reflected a pattern not dissimilar to that found elsewhere. As one would expect in a Low Density settlement, cow numbers were brought close to the budgeted levels soon after settlement, and from 1967 they exceeded the planned maturity level. However, milk sales in any year were never more than 75 per cent of the budgeted level.

This was probably for the same main reason as at Lessos, namely unwillingness on the part of farmers and co-operatives to sell milk at the low butterfat price. Actual milk sales were thus fairly closely related to the amount of milk quota and contract obtained by the three societies.

The experience with sheep was similar to that at Kipipiri: an early increase to near the planned level was followed by a quick decline with stabilization at a flock size well below what was budgeted. Pyrethrum, on the other hand, was grown until 1969 on a scale beyond that planned for, and sales in the peak years 1966 to 1968 were correspondingly high. However, with falling producer prices, production fell sharply in 1969 and 1970.

Survey figures showed that wheat was not grown at anything like the planned level. Furthermore, while cow numbers were high, a shortfall in the numbers of other cattle suggested that the calf-rearing enterprise planned for the 83 Type 'B' plots had not become well established by 1967-8.

Apart from fluctuations in the numbers of children, the surveys showed family composition to be fairly stable. However, recorded non-farm incomes (which were in every year higher than recorded in the other schemes) increased by 1966-7 to the very high average level of Sh. 3,539 per farm. As a result the cost of the residual part of family labour regarded as a settlement liability declined after 1965-6. By 1967-8, this item accounted for only 15 per cent of all costs taken into account.

The overall cost picture is shown in Table 14.9. By 1967-8, recurrent farming costs had become the dominant item. At £3.39 per acre they exceeded the planned cost by nearly 20 per cent, mainly because of a very high level of expenditure on cattle food, but also because of the unbudgeted employment of farm workers, who were no doubt required to handle the pyrethrum crop, especially where settlers were occupied on non-farm work.

By 1967-8 all recurrent scheme expenses were running at a level of £8.83, substantially more than the planned cost (in 1967-8 values) of £7.15. Disaggregation of costs shows that unskilled workers accounted for 32 per cent of all recurrent costs. Cattle Food (13 per cent) and Skilled Labour (10 per cent) were the only other recurrent cost items covering more than 5 per cent of the total.

Output figures of production each year are also shown in Table 14.9. They further reflect the extent to which the economy of these schemes came to rely increasingly on pyrethrum and milk sales. The importance of wheat declined towards 1967-8, and it was substantially exceeded in value by

Table 14.9

Summary of costs, output, finance flows and surplus for the Passenga Settlements as actually developed up to 1967-8

Current Market Prices (£)

313 farms	1962-3	1963-4	1964-5	1965-6	1966-7	1967-8
I. *Costs*						
Establishment processes	3,296	21,673	737	–	10	–
Land purchase	58,597	91,525	1,194	–	–	–
Supervision	–	15,723	31,449	30,305	19,979	18,936
Productive assets	–	22,312	29,495	16,839	13,069	20,427
Recurrent farming costs	–	24,190	50,475	38,054	42,738	45,969
Recurrent co-op. costs	–	1,445	5,735	8,958	9,892	11,529
Settlers' family labour	–	9,384	19,183	23,715	16,758	16,401
Total costs	61,893	186,252	137,904	117,871	102,446	113,262
II. *Output*						
Milk and butterfat	–	12,126	35,601	46,354	52,484	54,665
Pyrethrum	–	5,321	8,746	26,134	39,317	45,224
Maize	–	29	57	1,235	2,879	1,342
Wheat	–	3,020	5,635	5,577	3,852	1,930
Potatoes and vegetables	–	2,723	5,877	8,046	13,249	10,008
Cattle	–	2,796	18,137	17,050	5,941	9,849
Sheep and wool	–	170	4,645	64	914	1,645
Total output	–	26,185	78,696	104,460	118,636	124,663
III. *Operating surplus*	-61,893	-160,067	-59,208	-13,411	16,190	11,401
IV. *Net financial inflow*	61,593	160,932	65,975	31,930	-6,266	-2,006
V. *Final surplus*	-300	865	6,767	18,519	9,964	9,395

potatoes and vegetables, which were grown primarily as subsistence crops. Increases in the value of cattle were also an important form of output, although these were mainly retained on the farms and were not reflected in a large volume of net sales.

By 1967-8, output per acre had risen to £9.18 per acre, which exceeded the maturity budget output value of £8.16 in 1967-8 terms by 11 per cent.

Reflecting timing, volume and conditions of the development and other loans, there was a substantial inflow of funds until 1965-6. These exceeded each year the amount by which costs exceeded output, so that a positive final surplus remained. In 1968-9 the volume of loan repayments increased substantially but if the 1967-8 level of production were maintained, a positive final surplus would remain indefinitely. As they worked out in practice until 1967-8, the Passenga settlements promised to be an attractive investment.

With the water supply system being completed in 1968-9, the only other outstanding establishment process after 1967-8 was Survey for Title, which was finished in 1969-70. In the latter year, the increased cost of settlement supervision also came into effect. However, a further adjustment for the post-1967-8 period has been made at Passenga that was not made elsewhere. This applied to the recurrent costs of farming. The 1967-8 economic survey in one of the schemes (Passenga) recorded very high expenditure on Cattle Food which was not related to either a sharp increase in cattle numbers or extra milk production. The view has been taken that the recorded cost level was exceptional, and a lower figure was used for later years, based on the average levels recorded in the surveys.

14.6 A SUMMARY COMPARISON OF THE FOUR SETTLEMENTS IN OPERATION

To permit a comparison to be made between the four settlements in practice, summary details have been brought together in Table 14.10.

The first part of the table gives an approximate summary of those aspects of 'capitalization' that differ between settlements.

They have been calculated by adding the undiscounted values of expenditure on the items listed whenever they occurred. They do not reflect the total value of all processes that could be classed as 'investments'. For example, since it was taken to have the same per acre cost in every scheme, Pre-Settlement Development is not included, although clearly most of these costs were of an investment nature.[1] Nor, for the same reason, is any part of the cost of settlement administration included, although it is arguable that part of it could be. Furthermore, the figures underestimate the value of investment made by settlers' themselves. However, the partial figures of capitalization that are shown bring out differences in the basic capital-based opportunities in each settlement. They underline the extent of the differences between the High and Low Density schemes that were noted in section 13.7. Development loans per farm were far higher at Lessos and Passenga than in the other two schemes, although the relatively small size of farms at Kabisi means that loans per acre there were second only to those at Lessos. The form of the available data does not allow reasonable estimates to be made of investments financed from sources other than loans. However, the figures for Passenga are interesting. Farmers there appear to have invested fairly large amounts in durable assets from their own resources. The co-operative societies (for which the table covers all actual investments up to 1967-8) also invested large amounts in buildings and plant.

The lower half of Table 14.10 gives comparative figures of recurrent costs and output for the settlements as operated in 1967-8. In general, the figures reflect points made earlier in this chapter, especially the overwhelming significance in costs of settlers' family labour at Kabisi and Kipipiri; the high level of recurrent farm costs at Passenga; and the low level of co-operative activity at Kabisi. Not surprisingly, because of their higher levels of capitalization, output per acre was highest on the two Low Density schemes, but not by a very large margin. Nevertheless, operating surplus per farm there was much greater than on the High Density schemes. However, the difference is less marked when viewed as the return to family labour. Excluding family labour as a cost item gives the following values

[1] The cost *per farm* for this collection of processes (which cost Sh. 30/16 per acre) was: Kabisi £26, Lessos £58, Kipipiri £35 and Passenga £65.

Table 14.10

Summary details of actual capitalization in the four settlements, and the operating situation in 1967-8

Current market prices (£)

	Low Altitude				High Altitude			
	High Density		Low Density		High Density		Low Density	
	Kabisi		Lessos		Kipipiri		Passenga	
	per farm	per acre	per farm	per acre	per farm	per acre	per farm	per acre
1. *'Capitalization'*								
Land cost	104.42	5.96	357.77	9.23	178.58	7.60	483.44	11.15
Development loans:								
Settlers	95.97	5.48	294.22	7.59	84.09	3.58	268.18	6.18
Co-operatives	1.04	0.06	1.78	0.05	0.97	0.04	18.28	0.42
Contractors	1.52	0.09	7.62	0.20	1.52	0.06	7.50	0.17
Water Supply	55.00	3.14	90.23	2.33	–	–	72.44	1.67
Total	153.53	8.77	393.85	10.17	86.58	3.68	366.40	8.44
Other durable farm assets	n.a.	n.a.	n.a.	n.a.	17.47	0.74	111.07	2.56
Other co-operative assets	2.09	0.12	8.95	0.23	6.78	0.29	48.83	1.13
Total	260.04	14.85	760.57	19.63	289.41	12.31	1009.74	23.28
2. *Recurrent cost and output values in 1967-8*								
Supervision	9.72	0.55	51.88	1.34	13.00	0.55	60.50	1.39
Recurrent farm costs	29.17	1.67	55.40	1.43	26.56	1.13	146.87	3.39
Recurrent co-op. costs	2.12	0.12	22.16	0.57	12.11	0.51	36.83	0.85
Settlers' labour	117.06	6.68	69.57	1.80	83.19	3.53	52.40	1.21
Other	–	–	8.45	0.22	–	–	–	–
All expenses	158.07	9.02	207.46	5.36	134.86	5.72	296.60	6.84
Sale produce	44.82	2.56	198.67	5.13	126.00	5.35	318.88	7.35
Stock value increase	30.05	1.72	114.09	2.94	14.94	0.63	31.51	0.73
Subsistence	31.51	1.80	44.76	1.16	36.85	1.57	47.89	1.10
Total output	106.38	6.08	357.52	9.23	177.79	7.55	398.28	9.18
Operating value surplus	-51.69	-2.94	150.06	3.87	42.93	1.83	101.68	2.34
Acres per farm	17.46		38.75		23.38		43.38	

of operating surplus per farm: Kabisi, £65; Lessos, £220; Kipipiri, £126; Passenga, £154. Viewed in this way (a relevant viewpoint for social evaluation), Kipipiri compares relatively well with Passenga.

The figures of Table 14.10 also allow rough estimates to be made of farmers' cash incomes. Making such estimates is hampered by the fact that sale produce is valued in this table and elsewhere as it leaves the co-operative. However, if we assume (arbitrarily) that co-operatives charged margins that were 20 per cent more than their costs[1] the following figures remain as the difference per farm between sales income and recurrent farming and co-operative costs: Kabisi, £13; Lessos, £110;[2] Kipipiri, £85; Passenga, £128.

These crude figures, which allow nothing for loan repayments, emphasize the very great difference that existed between the two High Density schemes in practice. Farmers in the two Low Density settlements appeared to benefit to roughly the same extent. The figures offer no explanation as to why there were such large differences in non-farm income between Lessos and Passenga. In the latter case, income from other sources was higher than that obtained from farming. Its level is probably to be explained in terms of the local opportunities for off-farm work and the peculiar abilities of Passenga settlers.

APPENDIX A.14

ESTIMATING COSTS IN THE SETTLEMENTS AS ACTUALLY DEVELOPED

An outline is given here of how the pattern of expenditure on settlements was built up from different records and sources, illustrations being given from experience at Kabisi. The numbering of different expenditure items used here follows the order used in Table 14.3.

1 This can be regarded as a high estimate.

2 This figure also allows a deduction for KTDA cesses.

31. LAND VALUATION AND PURCHASE

Each settlement had previously constituted between four and sixteen large farms. Details are available of the date of purchase and the cost of each property. As with the plans, a financial year April to March is used. The actual cost of land valuation is calculated in the same way as for the planned cost (see A.13.1), and its timing determined in relation to the purchase dates.

32. THE INTRODUCTION OF SETTLERS

Information of the number of settlers introduced each month is not available. However, the annual reports of the Department up to 1969 give details of the numbers of plots allocated at 30 June each year, and this is some guide. The paper on settlement supervision prepared by the Financial Controller (Settlement) shows the month by which 60 per cent of the plots in each scheme were allocated. From this information new allocations could be determined. The same information allowed estimates to be made of the number of farms operated each season for a full year. At Kabisi, for example, the pattern seems to have been:

	1963-4	1964-5	1965-6
New settlers allocated farms	690	1	10
Total number of settlers at year's end	690	691	701
Settlers farming	-	691	701

33. PRE-SETTLEMENT DEVELOPMENT

Settlement accounting did not allow for the recording of separate figures for each of the four processes covered by this item, namely Interim Farming, Survey for Planning, Planning and Demarcation and Roads and Soil Conservation. However, annual expenditure on Pre-Settlement Development as a whole is itemized in Appendix D of the Department's annual report for 1967-8. This shows a total expenditure to June 1968 of £1,677,616. According to Appendix B of the same report, 1,122,387 acres had by then been settled. This indicates an average cost per acre for all processes covered by this item of Sh. 30/16. In the absence of any other basis for calculation, a per acre cost of Sh. 30/16 has been assumed right across the board for all land prepared for settlement. The combined planned cost of these processes was Sh. 37 per acre.

Itemizing Pre-Settlement Development expenditure has been done by combining the assumed itemization for each one as described in Appendix A.13 except Interim Farming losses. For reasons given there, this was taken to have cost Sh. 10 per acre, and an equal percentage saving in operating cost has been assumed for each other process. The percentage breakdown of the combined item is thus:

Skilled labour	15	Petrol	1
Unskilled labour	16	Diesel	7
Equipment	27	Financial loss	33
Vehicles	1	*Total*	*100*

Timing this expenditure was arranged in relation to purchase dates and settler admissions.

34. LEGAL FEES

It has been taken that the legal fees itemized in the budgets were in fact paid, and that their itemized composition was the same as estimated in Appendix A.13. They were paid when settlers entered their farms.

35, 36 and 37. SUPERVISION AND ADMINISTRATION AT SCHEME AND OTHER LEVELS

Actual annual costs of supervision and administration at the three different levels were given in the Financial Controller's paper. Supervision was regarded as an activity separate from Pre-Settlement Development from the month in which 60 per cent of farms had been allocated. This starting date, and expenditure at each level during each accounting period, were given in the paper, which was prepared during July 1969. Although they are averages for each main type of scheme, his figures represent actual expenses to the end of 1968-9. Figures for 1969-70 were based on expenditure estimates for that year. No reduction in the intensity of staffing beyond the level of extended supervision was envisaged for that year, but a general salary award to all Civil Servants increased the cost of supervision at all levels.

The itemized breakdown of actual supervision costs used for shadow pricing was the same as for the plan for all years except 1969-70, when increased salaries were allowed for.

38. SETTLER SUBSISTENCE

Appendix D of the annual report of the Department for 1967-8 shows expenditure up to June 1968 on Settlers' Wages and Subsistence of £440,343. Appendix L of the same report shows that by the same date, 26,481 people had been settled in sub-divisional High Density schemes. It is not known whether settlers in co-operative farms also received these payments, but excluding them indicates an average cost per settler to that date of £16.63. However, 1,602 High Density settlers had been allocated new plots during the previous financial year, and may have still been in receipt of subsistence payments. The average figure is sufficiently close to the planned figure of £18 per settler to justify using it. The time pattern for this item follows the pattern of farm allocations.

39 and 42. ASSETS PURCHASED BY FARMERS AND RECURRENT COSTS OF FARMING

Figures for both items were taken from the results of the economic surveys of settlement schemes carried out by the Statistics Division since 1963-4. The surveys have been the subject of a number of publications, in which coverage, methodology and results have been discussed.[1] Results from these surveys in the two major reports (the last two listed) were presented at a highly aggregated level, and do not give details for individual schemes. For this study, computer records were obtained of the original summarized information for each farm in the 1964-5, 1965-6 and 1966-7 surveys. Individual farm figures for the 1967-8 survey were not available in as much detail as for the preceding three years. Examination of individual farm figures permitted changes to be made to ensure consistency, particularly in the valuation of output referred to in Appendix B.14, but these did not involve significant departures from any of the cost figures recorded in the survey. Figures for the Lessos settlement in 1963-4 were obtained from an earlier economic survey by Clough, 1965.

In the use of these figures, total values for each scheme were based on the mean results for all farms covered by each year's sample. For each scheme survey, the sample was never less than ten farms, and samples of this size occurred only in Low Density settlements, where a number of schemes have been aggregated for this study. In one year, the Kipipiri survey covered 80 farms, so the unweighted mean should be a good estimate.

Estimates of the value of Assets Purchased by Farmers from their own resources were based on the depreciation values in the survey figures for Buildings and Fixed Assets, Tools and Implements. These long-term assets have been covered.by the use of an annuity value for each item based on the assumed life of the asset and a 10 per cent discount rate. At Kabisi approximately 30 per cent of all farmers' assets were tools and small equipment, but in the other settlements buildings were of greater relative importance; on the Low Density schemes they accounted for 87 to 89 per cent of all assets. For this study, the items 'buildings' or 'buildings and fencing' were divided into timber, wire and nails, etc., in the percentages 60, 33 and 7 respectively.

Average levels of expenditure each year on each recurrent expenditure item in the Kabisi samples is shown in Table A.14.1. These figures reflect year to year variations in total amount and composition that occurred in every settlement. For Table 14.3 these average per farm figures were multiplied by the number of farms in the settlement thought to be operational for a full cropping season during the year in question. For Lessos and Passenga, these details were calculated on an individual scheme basis before amalgamation.

[1] See: Kenya Statistical Digest, 1966; MacArthur, 1968; Kenya Government, 'Settlement Appraisal', 1971; von Haugwitz and Thorwart, 1972.

40 and 43. CO-OPERATIVE SOCIETY ASSETS AND RECURRENT COSTS OF CO-OPERATIVE OPERATION

Information on these two classes of expense was obtained directly from the annual accounts of each society. The actual price of all assets purchased could be seen from the accounts, and, with assumptions about the expected life of each asset, correct annuity values were calculated.

Insofar as they cover buildings, the expense category Co-operative Assets covers only the cost of new structures built by the society. Co-operatives were allowed to purchase existing houses and other buildings at 10 per cent of their valuation, on the normal terms for Co-operative Loans. These purchases have not been included in Table 14.3, since they are included in the land purchase price.

In calculating the Recurrent Costs of Co-operative Operation, account has been taken only of direct costs incurred in the marketing of settlers' produce, and society overheads. Many societies occasionally carried out other functions including the operation of retail shops, the sale of producer inputs and the supply of group services for mechanical cultivation and cattle cleansing. These were supplied to farmers at a price which it is assumed was generally expected to cover only direct supply costs. These costs would be taken into account as recurrent cost of farm operation, so they have been excluded from co-operative expenses. However, some activities separately identified in societies' accounts had elements of both marketing and producer services. An example is tractor services, which may be used both for farm cultivation work on a repayment basis and for the transportation of milk and other tasks associated with marketing. In such cases, where the tractor operating account shows a deficit, the balancing sum has been regarded as a recurrent marketing expense. In some cases, the accounts showed that societies had bought tractors but were not carrying out cultivation work on a repayment basis. In these cases the tractor was counted as an asset used only for marketing work.

Itemized costs of co-operative operation brought into account at Kabisi are shown for illustration in Table A.14.2. The society was first registered in April 1964, soon after the arrival of the settlers. The first accounts cover 18 months to 31 March 1966. Accordingly, 25 per cent of the operating costs for this period were attributed to 1965-6, and the remainder to 1966-7. The society's accounting period 1967-8 covered 15 months, so 80 per cent of the costs for that period have been taken as applying to 1967-8. Adjustments of a similar kind were required for all sets of co-operative accounts, to get figures coincident with the accounting periods used.

41. WATER SUPPLY

Water supply schemes were planned and constructed separately for each settlement, or group of adjacent schemes. Details of progress with these

Table A.14.1

Average per farm recurrent expenses recorded in sample surveys of Kabisi farms

Sh.

	1964-5	1965-6	1966-7	1967-8
Purchased foods	29.15	45.72	21.17	35.93
Minerals	2.07	12.64	25.10	18.82
Artificial insemination	3.21	8.30	8.70	4.00
Dip	28.93	15.70	2.43	29.35
Vet. and med.	5.18	26.26	7.70	4.05
Sundry Stock Items	0.36	0.21	-	-
Maize Seed	83.25	41.79	55.63	49.31
Superphosphates	99.46	27.34	66.80	242.49
Crop chemicals	0.07	1.13	2.37	5.18
Diesel	52.88	23.69	-	6.84
Tractors and implements	48.81	21.87	-	6.31
Tractor and implement spares	48.81	21.87	-	6.31
Sundry crop items	3.25	34.60	17.00	21.23
Lorry transport	28.21	1.94	-	-
Tools, etc.	107.29	110.87	8.97	2.96
Other costs	30.57	47.23	-	14.03
Unskilled Labour:				
Hired farm workers	26.75	54.96	35.30	129.85
Tractor drivers	52.88	23.69	-	6.84
Total	651.25	519.81	251.17	583.50

Source: Economic survey of Kabisi farms.
Note: To obtain an itemized picture analagous with that used for settlement plans and large farms, the recorded cost of cultivations has been divided into tractor, fuel and driver costs on the basis of cost composition found in the large farm surveys for the areas most similar to each settlement.

installations are given in the Department's Annual Reports. Work on them began only some years after settlement, but the Low Density schemes had priority, to allow all expenditure to be completed before June 1969, the last date for drawing the loans concerned. Consequently the full cost of water supply at Lessos and Passenga is accurately known. No plans had been made by December 1971 for a water supply scheme at Kipipiri. There are several perennial streams in the area, and we have assumed that no special investment of this kind will be made there.

No expenditure on water supply for Kabisi was made before the end of March 1968. However, the settlement is one of those covered by the Little Nzoia Water Project which has been constructed to cover from a single source most of the settlements in Western Province. This scheme supplies water to 4,770 farms through a gravitational supply system. According to Appendix A of the 1970 annual report, the cost of this system will be £262,350, or £55 per settler supplied. This per settler figure was the basis for calculating the water supply cost. The 1970 report lists this water scheme as being installed in 1970. Water became available to the first farms supplied in mid-1972. Accordingly, the water supply cost is spread evenly over the three years 1970-1 to 1972-3. The same itemized composition of total costs has been assumed as was shown in Table A.13.1.

Table A.14.2

Itemized details of actual operating costs brought into account for the Kabisi Co-operative

£

	1964-5	1965-6	1966-7	1967-8
Skilled labour (manager's salary)	50	150	127	80
Unskilled labour	78	236	225	328
Bank charges	4	11	10	13
Repairs and maintenance (machinery)	11	33	1	38
Audit	25	75	50	96
Lorry transport	155	464	392	549
Bags	35	104	243	-
Diesel	52	158	159	136
Sundry items	34	100	156	110
Tractor spares	-	-	-	136
Total	444	1,331	1,363	1,486

Source: Audited accounts of the Kabisi Farmers' Co-operative Society.

44. SURVEY FOR TITLE

Survey for Title is one element in the administrative process called 'finalization' carried out in the first schemes in the late 1960s. According to the annual report for 1971, Kabisi was not one of the settlements where these processes had been either completed or was in progress. However, by that date all other study settlements had completed 'finalization', so the date of this process was known.

Those parts of the finalization process other than survey for title are normal administrative costs of the Department, and are included in items 35 to 37. However, aerial photography, survey and mapping will not have been included there. It is not known what the mapping cost per acre was but the Mission on Land Settlement in Kenya 1966 suggested Sh. 6 per acre. This cost has been used here with the itemized composition shown in Table A.13.1.

45. SETTLERS' LABOUR

The treatment of this very important cost item is explained in full in 14.2.2.

46. COWS AND OTHER LIVESTOCK

The method used for estimating output takes account of the net value of sales (i.e. sales minus purchases) and the increase in values of each type of stock between the beginning and end of each accounting period. Under this method stock purchases do not appear as a cost, but as negative output. Change over the years in the value of stock reflects only natural increase and changes in type.

This treatment covers adequately all animals that are the subject of cash transactions. However, many animals on the schemes were issued against development loans, for which payment would be made over ten years. In this case, their cost is covered in the item 'Net Sales', but there is a corresponding large increase in stock values whenever they are issued. These cancel out, and the original purchase does not appear as a cost. The value of all other issues financed from development loans is covered in items 39 and 42, but a separate entry for the purchase price of cows and sheep is required. The figures shown in line 46 of Table 14.3 are based on recorded information on the numbers of cows or sheep, and assumed values of £25 to £30 per cow.

47. TEA STUMPS

This item occurred only at Lessos. General features of the cost of tea planting material were considered under item 22, Appendix A.13. Tea was planted at Lessos in every year from 1961-2 to 1968-9. The average price paid each year by KTDA for purchases from private growers has been used. The composition of tea stump costs used for the Lessos plan was also used for the actuals.

48. KTDA EXPENSES

As was also explained in Appendix A.13, costs were incurred by KTDA and recovered from SFT in connection with the Authority's work amongst growers of this crop. Estimates of actual charges of these kinds attributable to the Lessos Settlements were discussed in Appendix A.13.

APPENDIX B.14

ESTIMATING OUTPUT IN THE SETTLEMENTS AS ACTUALLY DEVELOPED

This appendix is briefly concerned with sources for the estimation of actual production, and the way that output estimates were made.

Production on the settlement farms could be disposed of in five separate ways.

(1) Sales through the settlement co-operative.
(2) Sales direct to a statutory marketing agency.
(3) Sales to private individuals buying in the rural areas.
(4) Consumption in settlers' households.
(5) Retention on the farm, to give a change in stocks.

CO-OPERATIVE SALES

Information on disposals in all of these ways was recorded in the economic surveys of settlement farms. However, the surveys probably under-estimated the value of output. There are several reasons why this might be so, but it is particularly true of co-operatives sales, which present difficult recording problems. Payments to settlers (who are the basic source of the survey information) is often made by co-operatives several months in arrears, and net of deductions for inputs and services provided by the society, for loan repayment, and for other reasons. Often the settler receives only one payment for deliveries of several products. Consequently, it is often difficult to tell what value should be attributed to sales of a particular commodity in a specified period. Checking individual settlers' co-operatives records (as was done in the surveys) does not always allow full elucidation. Because of this, and because our definition of the settlement includes the marketing functions of the societies, co-operative records were used as the source for sales particulars. Although co-operative accounts present their own uncertainty problems,[1] the values of sales by societies should be reliable since they were in the main to a small number of marketing agencies whose records were checked by the co-operative auditors. The accounting periods of the seven societies involved seldom coincided with the April/March year, while the period covered by each set of accounts was not always twelve months, especially that for a society's first set of accounts, which covered in some cases as much as 20 months. Adjustments to a standard timing had to be made on an *ad hoc* basis.

[1] At least one year's figures (before 1967-8) for one of the societies with which we are concerned remained unaudited in spring 1973, and adverse comments were made by the auditors about most of the sets of accounts with which we are concerned.

DIRECT SALES TO STATUTORY MARKETING AGENCIES

Sales of this kind arose only with tea at Lessos, which was all brought by KTDA, who give in their annual reports details of purchases and prices for each settlement. This source of information was used for every year.[1] The accounting period of the authority is July to June: adjustment to our accounting year was made on the basis of the quarterly pattern of tea deliveries as a whole experienced by KTDA. In line with the treatment as a separate item of KTDA costs (see item 24, Appendix A.13), tea production has been valued at its full producer price, both first and second payments, before cesses or other deductions are made.

STOCK CHANGES AND PRODUCE CONSUMED ON THE FARM

Estimates of the value of production disposed of in the three other ways were based on the economic surveys, the only possible source. For 1964-5, 1965-6 and 1966-7 records, access to the original farm data (which, *inter alia*, showed separately sales to the co-operatives and other sales)[2] was particularly valuable in the case of crops like maize, milk and, in some years at Kipipiri and Passenga, wheat and potatoes, all of which could be sold both through the co-operatives and outside. The value of non-co-operative sales could thus be separately identified. This access also allowed a check (and sometimes an adjustment) of the prices used for the valuation of stock increases and farm use, which includes mainly household consumption, but also covers food issues to workers, use for seed and livestock food. For changes in cereals stocks, it was taken that all stocks held were of saleable quality and that they could or would be sold at the price ruling in that season. Subsistence consumption of all commodities except milk was valued at the sale price in each scheme. Milk differed from that of other products. All of the scheme co-operatives sold some milk at the relatively high quota price, and the remainder as butterfat. The amount that individual settlers could sell to the society at the high whole-milk price was generally limited.

Beyond this limit, further deliveries would receive much less, if indeed the society would accept it at all. The small amounts of butterfat sold by most societies suggests that most farmers preferred to consume milk at home rather than sell it at the low net realisation to them.[3] Consequently,

[1] Purchases from Lessos in 1968-9 were wrongly reported in the Authority's Annual Report for that year. Correct figures were obtained direct from KTDA.

[2] For the 1967-8 survey, data with these two types of sales shown separately was never put on to a computer record.

[3] In some instances, the preference not to sell milk as butterfat may have been that of co-operative management rather than settlers. Frequently societies would not accept milk delivered in the evening, preferring not to open their dairies twice each day. Generally farmers have no option but to milk cows twice daily. In such circumstances they have to consume milk, even if they would have preferred to sell it for cash at the low butterfat price.

for all settlements except Kipipiri, the price of milk delivered to the society for sale as butterfat was the basis for valuing farm-consumed milk. At Kipipiri there is evidence[1] that the society was often unable to deliver milk up to the level of its quota. In this case, milk consumed on the farm was valued at a level between the whole milk and butterfat prices.

LIVESTOCK PRODUCTION

The valuation of livestock production is always a problem in farm surveys. In the settlement farms surveys simple but 'safe' procedures were adopted for valuation and these we have followed. All cash transactions affecting animals were recorded at actual prices and consolidated to give a value of 'Net Sales', which was negative if sales were less than purchases. Negative values of 'Net Sales' are usually associated with positive values of 'Value Increase'. This item is simply the difference between the value of the stock on each farm at the beginning and end of each year. If purchases exceeded sales, the closing value should be higher than the opening value.

Changes in the value of stocks are a source of considerable difficulty in single-year farm surveys like those on which this study is largely based. Problems particularly arise through animals being priced differently at each valuation when there is no change in their condition, size, etc. In the settlement surveys, standard values were adopted for each class of animal for use right across the board for every valuation. In this case, changes during the year in stock values reflect only changes in numbers and/or the transfer of animals of different kinds from one value class to another as they grew and matured. Changes due to short-term price variations or the subjective judgement of different valuers is thus removed.

[1] In the statistical appendix to the report of the Mission on Land Settlement in Kenya, 1966.

CHAPTER 15

The Valuation of Land

15.1 IDENTIFYING THE ALTERNATIVE USE OF LAND

Land purchase was an important element in the settlements, both in the financial arrangements for the programme as a whole, and in the cost projections for each of the schemes studied. Its social valuation is a matter of considerable significance. If potential productive capacity were the only source from which land derived value, and other privately valuable factors (amenity, tax advantages, etc.) were ignored, the social cost of changing land use would be the net social profitability of the land involved, in its best or most likely alternative use. Determining this social profitability involves deciding what the alternative use of the land would be; estimating what inputs, outputs and surplus would be under this alternative system; and finally, expressing these things in terms of the numeraire. Valuation along these lines of the land on which the four settlements were developed is the subject of this chapter.

The areas developed for the settlements were previously farmed on a large scale by expatriates. Were there substantial areas of unused but easily developed land elsewhere in Kenya to which the displaced farmers might have moved, it could be argued, as was done by Little and Tipping, 1972, for West Malaysia, that using particular areas for settlement would simply have led to the development of unused land elsewhere, so the effect on the economy would have been small or negligible. However, this was emphatically not the case in Kenya. Land hunger has for long been a serious problem and its relief through the displacement of foreign farmers was a principal motive behind the settlement programme. After land purchase, displaced farmers did not move on to other land.

Using land for settlement thus reduced the area available for other uses and had a real social cost stemming from the 'opportunity cost' of possible alternative uses.

Deciding what was the relevant alternative use to evaluate is not a straightforward matter. Although, in the light of subsequent political developments the view may seem unrealistic, it could be argued that one opportunity facing the Government in the early 1960s was to make no change in the large-scale farming areas, and to permit farming of the type that had been developing there for up to 50 years to continue uninterrupted. From an appraisal point of view, this would be the 'no-change' situation. An alternative, more realistic view would be that sooner or later the land would be transferred to African ownership under one of the land-transfer programmes of the period 1961-75, of which, as was explained in Chapter 12, the High and Low Density settlement programmes were only two. However, alternative forms of land transfer took many forms, from State Farms to private operation on a large scale by individuals, partners and co-operatives; and at a different level, through alternative forms of sub-divisional settlement, Harambee, Squatter, Shirika or even Low and High Density types. Which of these alternatives would have applied to the four areas considered, and when the change in land use would have been made, could not be easily determined. Even if these points could be determined, the problem would remain of obtaining usable data relating to particular relevant alternatives. With the single exception of a report on large-scale farming by new African owners in the Trans Nzoia area (Kenya Government, 1972) no data on any alternative form of post-transfer land use is known to exist other than for the High and Low Density settlements.

In the circumstances, the only alternative use that could be studied was the farming system that applied before transfer. Despite the element of unrealism in taking this as the alternative to settlement, pursuing this course allows the methodology to be explored of valuing this type of farming, and allows the different types of settlement to be compared with the form of land use that preceded sub-division. Comment is made below on the extent to which valuing the land in this particular use gives a distorted idea of the social cost of the settlement land.

15.2 LARGE-SCALE FARMING IN THE FOUR AREAS IN 1959

To assess the economics of pre-settlement farming, a reasonable estimate is needed of how land of the kind taken for each scheme was used before purchase. The relevant situation is that which applied when farm operation and development last followed a 'normal' pattern. This would be before, firstly, uncertainty about national political developments affected the outlook and mode of operation of large-scale farmers as a whole, and, secondly, the later time when the knowledge that land in particular areas was included in a dated purchase programme introduced short-term factors whereby farmers followed 'abnormal' patterns of operation as they wound up their businesses. A 'normal' situation was last considered to exist in the European farming areas in 1959. At the end of that year it was decided at a constitutional conference that Kenya should make a rapid move towards independence. This induced uncertainty amongst large-scale farmers which affected both the values of farm land and assets, and the patterns of farming that were subsequently followed. Thus, in the settlement purchase programme, the land was to be valued at its 'fair purchase price', and 1958-9 market values were adopted as the basis for valuation in all parts of the country, it being argued that this was 'the last period in which there was an untrammelled market in land'.[1]

Building up a picture of the economics of large-scale farming in these four areas in 1959 was tackled in three parts. First, the system of farming being followed was determined. Next, the volume and value of output to which this farming system would give rise was estimated, whilst the third stage was the estimation of the associated levels of operating costs. Output and expenses needed to be calculated in analysed form, to facilitate the application of accounting prices. Details are given in Appendix A.15 of how the different calculations were made, and of the data sources used.

A summary of the estimated values of output and costs in the four areas in 1959 is given in Table 15.1. Wheat and maize were the main crops produced, and milk was the most important

[1] Quotations taken from Central Land Board, 1963-4, p.10.

livestock product. Surprisingly, pyrethrum was not a very prominent crop in either of the two high altitude areas. Amongst costs, unskilled labour was by far the most important item, accounting for between 18 and 26 per cent of all estimated costs. The only other input that accounted for more than 10 per cent of all expenses in any area was superphosphate, a variety of other items being of relatively similar importance just below this level. The costs patterns reflect the degree of mechanization used in these types of farming, and the relatively high level of material inputs used for the fairly intensive production methods employed. However, there was a marked difference in land-use intensity between High and Low Altitude areas. Despite this, margins per acre in the High Altitude farms were lower than in the other two groups. Much higher costs led to less than correspondingly high levels of output.

15.3 ESTIMATING LAND VALUES AT MARKET PRICES

The calculated values of operating margin can be used for calculating land values. Had no consideration other than farming profitability affected their judgement, it could be argued that farmers might have valued the land in 1959 by assuming that they could obtain, for an indefinite period, a net margin per acre of at least the amounts shown in Table 15.1. In that case, the present value of the business (assuming for simplicity that all land subsequently taken for one settlement can be regarded as a single farm business) would be equal to the annual net margin (viewed as the surplus obtainable indefinitely) divided by the appropriate discount rate. Given adequate long-term security, farmers of the kind being considered might be expected to discount future earnings at at least 12 per cent, and probably at 15 per cent per annum. This very simplified basis would provide a first estimate of the value of each area if taken over as a going concern. Such an approach would imply, however, that farmers would not anticipate any change in long-term growth in profitability stemming from greater efficiency and the application of new technology. This is unrealistic. Allowance should be made for increasing

Table 15.1

Summary of output and costs on large farms in 1959 in the four settlement areas

	Market Prices (£)			
	Low Altitude		High Altitude	
	Kabisi	Lessos	Kipipiri	Passenga
1. *Output*				
Wheat	-	20,845	36,919	50,848
Maize	22,682	9,175	1,117	398
Pyrethrum	-	4,094	4,374	6,278
Other crops	2,268	1,474	11,516	11,082
Milk	17,056	12,578	10,748	8,332
Cattle	13,864	5,368	5,400	3,666
Sheep and wool	495	418	4,876	3,686
Pigs	3,680	1,556	9,099	4,414
Total output	60,045	55,508	84,049	88,704
(per acre)	(4.89)	(3.92)	(6.81)	(6.53)
2. *Costs*				
Direct enterprise costs	27,038	32,658	61,057	61,988
Overheads	11,584	9,678	15,726	16,222
Total costs	38,622	42,336	76,783	78,210
(per acre)	(3.15)	(2.99)	(6.22)	(5.76)
3. Operating margin	21,423	13,172	7,266	10,494
(per acre)	(1.75)	(0.93)	(0.59)	(0.77)
Acres	12,277	14,144	12,338	13,577

profitability. In a recent paper, Price, 1972, gave estimates of year-to-year changes in a productivity index for the main inputs into large-scale farming, using census data for his calculations. He estimated that the index of productivity increased from 79 in 1954 through 100 in 1958 (the base year) to 134 in 1966. This indicates an annual compound rate of increased factor productivity of 4.5 per cent. Clearly improvements in the efficiency of large-scale farming were taking place rapidly over the relevant period. The benefits of adopting new techniques would have been clearly discernable, and farmers would have expected to benefit from their continuation, and would have taken them into account in land valuation.

This definite, sizeable trend in productivity growth would be reflected in the annual net operating margin that farmers would look forward to. For this calculation to allow for the downward movements over time in relative product prices that would probably occur to offset productivity increases, it has been assumed that, without important increases in fixed capital, farmers could expect an annual increase of 3 per cent in the value of net surplus per acre.

The discounted value of the stream of annual operating surplus would show the value of the whole business as a going concern. To arrive at a residual valuation of the land and permanent improvements, deductions need to be made for the value of the moveable assets (livestock, machinery and working capital) required to operate each 'business'.

The value of livestock tied up in farming of this kind has been estimated from the figures for capitalization in 1959 given in the Farm Economic Survey reports. The value of investment in machinery was estimated from the same source, whilst the working capital requirement was taken as 40 per cent of total recurrent annual expenses.

Figures relating to these calculations are shown in Table 15.2, together with the actual purchase value of the land. They suggest that the market value of moveable assets in the two High altitude areas was particularly high, and exceeded the capitalized value of the net operating margin under any of the capitalization assumptions made. This gave rise to negative residual land values. For the Lessos land[1], the actual purchase price is also far above any of the capitalized estimates, although the purchase price at Kabisi is roughly consistent with capitalization at 15 per cent of the estimated operating margin, when expanded at 3 per cent per annum for 20 years.

Negative or low capitalization values are not completely surprising results. The capitalized value depends on the discount rate used and fairly high rates were used in Table 15.2. The fact that land of the type occurring in each area appears to have

[1] It is notable that despite the requirement that land for such schemes should be 'undeveloped', the highest prices amongst this group of four settlements were paid for the Low Density settlements. This was not typical of all land in the High and Low Density programmes.

changed hands in or around 1959 at the prices actually paid,[1] must be explained in other ways. Various alternative explanations may be suggested, including hopes of land value appreciation, tax advantages and others. However, an important explanation may be that the purchasers of land were prepared to accept a return on capital tied up in farming below the capitalization discount rate used. The implicit rate of return on farming capital suggested by the purchase prices can be simply calculated by relating the land price and the value of other necessary assets to the annual margin. These implicit rates are shown in the last line of Table 15.2. They are pessimistic estimates, since for ease of computation they assume that no increase in productivity will occur, whilst realistically this should have been allowed for. Nevertheless, the figures suggest that farmers in three of the four areas were obtaining a low rate of return on capital tied up in farming.

Farmers' acceptance of such a situation, which is not uncommon in many forms of agriculture, could be explained through the substantial non-monetary benefits from land ownership that farmers receive, particularly location-based amenity benefits. Benefits of this kind were particularly associated with the two High Altitude areas which were both well located with regard to Nakuru, the main social centre for European farmers in the Central Rift Valley area, and Nairobi. This kind of consideration applied much less to the Lessos area, and least of all to Kabisi, which, from the viewpoint of European farmers, was not well placed either climatically or for social congeniality.[2]

Whatever the force of these different factors, the figures in Table 15.2 suggest that land values, as reflected in actual purchase prices, were a poor guide to the relative profit-creating capacity of farms when run along typical operating systems for

[1] Actual prices for recorded sales were the basis of the valuation system used in the purchase of the settlement land, as carried out by LDSB and CLB.

[2] For low rates of return to be accepted for long periods, unless farms are very large, a necessary condition is that some farmers must have received incomes additional to those from farming. Personal impressions of visiting farmers in all of these areas in the early 1960s were that between the four, this appeared to be most true of farmers in the Kipipiri area, and was least true of farmers in Western Kenya, especially at Kabisi.

Table 15.2

The capitalization of net margins, and residual land values, at market prices, for large-scale farming in the four settlement areas

1959 Prices (£)

	Kabisi	Lessos	Kipipiri	Passenga
1. Net margin	21,423	13,172	7,266	10,494
2. Market values of moveable assets:				
Livestock	59,500	33,039	56,877	39,010
Machinery	25,900	21,938	49,442	61,274
Working Capital	12,700	16,934	30,713	31,284
Total	98,100	71,911	137,032	131,568
3 a. Residual land values with capitalization at 12% assuming:				
(i) no increase in productivity	80,425	37,856	-76,482	-44,118
(ii) 3% annual increase in productivity for 20 years	134,390	71,127	-59,093	-18,562
b. Capitalization at 15% assuming:				
(i) no increase in productivity	44,720	15,092	-88,592	-61,608
(ii) 3% annual increase in productivity for 20 years	81,255	38,327	-76,181	-44,698
4. Actual purchase price	73,198	130,529	93,756	151,316
5. Implicit rate of return, assuming no increase in productivity	12.5%	6.5%	3.1%	3.7%

their area. For social evaluation, the application to the market price of a Standard Conversion Factor for mixed farming inputs and products would not be a satisfactory type of adjustment to find the true social value of the land in this particular alternative use. As often appears to be the case, land prices are a poor guide to true commercial values. A more thorough procedure for estimating the social value of a particular form of land use is required where this is a major project cost.

15.4 ACCOUNTING PRICES FOR LAND OPERATED ON A LARGE SCALE BY EUROPEAN FARMERS

The information derived in the last sections provides the basis for estimating the social value of land used for the four settlements. The first step is to apply accounting ratios to itemized output and costs in 1959. For this purpose, the accounting ratios presented in Table 10.1 have mainly been used, especially those in the series FI and FO. However, a number of small variations were made from the ARs for general use. For superphosphates, the AR for 1967 was not appropriate for application to 1959, since in the earlier year subsidies on fertilizers had not been introduced. Using the figures for this item given in Table 10.2, an adjusted AR of 0.94 was calculated.[1] For pyrethrum and maize the long-run ARs of 1.2 and 1.1 were used, in preference to those for a particular year.

Applying ARs to farm output and expenses, gives the values at accounting prices shown in the first two lines of Table 15.3. Two adjustments to the consequent 'farmers' margin' are required to arrive at the true social value of farm operation in each area. The first takes account of production from land used for growing food crops by regular farm workers. It has been estimated that in each area 100 acres of land might have been used in this way. Taking an estimated net product value of £10 per acre (the budgeted output in settlement plans for 'subsistence' land) indicates an additional net product of £1,000 per annum.

The second adjustment is to take account of the social value of incomes received by large farmers.[2] Details of this

[1] This is one example of how revised ARs can be quickly calculated when information is available of the kind given in Table 10.2.

[2] It is assumed in what follows that the farms are owned by those who farmed them. If they were tenants, it can be argued that the same adjustments should be made in respect of the receivers of land rents. All of the land for these settlements was in private ownership before take-over.

calculation are shown in Table 15.4. The first step is the calculation of the farmers' operating margin at market prices. Two deductions are then made from this margin, for interest payments and for income tax. Interest is estimated at 2 per cent of the value of total output [1] and for income tax a deduction was made of 20 per cent of the remaining sum.[2] The balance after these two deductions is the market value of the net disposable income accruing to farmers. It can be assumed that the farmer would not become a Kenyan citizen so no allowance has been made for any benefit he receives; in any case, such benefit would have been given a low value weighting (see Chapter 4) because farmers of this kind are relatively well-off. Consequently, the social cost of the farmers is the accounting cost of the expenditure from disposable income that they make. It can fairly be assumed that all savings (which we estimate at 10 per cent of net disposable income) would be remitted abroad, so to this element a conversion factor of 1.0 is applied. The remaining 90 per cent represents local consumption to which the AR for marginal urban consumption is applied.[3] Figures for this adjustment are shown in the second part of Table 15.4.

Taking account of workers' production and the social cost of farmers allows the calculation at accounting prices of the annual surplus arising from the use of the land in large-scale farming. Comparison between Tables 15.2 and 15.3 shows that in all four areas the net margin at accounting prices is greater than at market prices, the accounting ratios for inputs being generally lower than for products.

[1] This estimate is based on information given on pp.40 and 41 of the Large Farm Census Report for 1960.

[2] The Report of the East African Income Tax Department for 1970 to 1971 (which gives statistics for income earned in 1969) states that, for Kenya, the average rate of income tax assessed on individuals whose principal source of income was agriculture was 20.4 per cent of actual income. The Report for 1960 to 1961 (which we also looked at and which refers to income earned in 1959) does not distinguish between individuals, companies and employees, as does the later Report. For those taxpayers whose principal source of income was agriculture, the ratio of gross tax to actual income then was 23.6 per cent.

[3] This conversion factor may be on the high side, since large farmers might be expected to purchase goods with rather lower ARs on average than those bought by African workers in towns, whose consumption pattern was used to get this conversion factor. However, the error is probably only slight, and no other appropriate factor is available for use for this singular conversion.

TABLE 15.3

Calculation of the residual land values at accounting prices for the four areas under large-scale operation

1959 prices (£)

	Kabisi	Lessos	Kipipiri	Passenga
Farm output	64,045	54,754	78,369	81,233
Farmers' expenses	31,543	35,076	64,343	64,574
Net margin	32,502	19,678	14,026	16,659
Workers' production	1,000	1,000	1,000	1,000
Cost of farmers	13,577	8,086	3,744	5,846
Annual Surplus	19,945	12,592	11,282	11,813
(per acre)	(1.625)	(0.890)	(0.914)	(0.870)
Capitalized annual surplus[a]	268,216	169,334	151,718	158,859
Less: Value of moveable assets:				
Livestock	70,805	40,638	65,977	46,032
Machinery	23,828	19,964	45,981	57,598
Working capital	12,700	16,934	30,713	31,284
Residual Value of Land	160,883	91,798	9,047	23,945
(per acre)	(13.10)	(6.49)	(0.73)	(1.76)

a. Based on a 10 per cent discount rate and an expansion of the annual surplus at 3 per cent per annum for 20 years.

To calculate the social value of the residual attributable to land and fixed assets, the annual surplus is first capitalized using the ARI of 10 per cent. As before, an increase in productivity of 3 per cent per annum for 20 years has been assumed. From this value of the whole business as a going concern is deducted the social cost of movable assets.[1] Because of the relatively high conversion factors for livestock, movable assets are valued in social terms more highly than at market prices. This is one reason why the residual social values of land are in two cases very low.

In all cases, the social value of land is substantially different

[1] To allow for the different composition in each area of the livestock investment, individually derived composite ARs were used of from 1.16 to 1.23. ARs for machinery similarly varied between 0.91 and 0.94, reflecting the assumed balance between cars and other farm machinery. Working Capital was given an AR of 1.0.

Table 15.4

Calculating the social cost of large-scale European farmers in the four areas in 1959

£

	Kabisi	Lessos	Kipipiri	Passenga
1. *Market Prices*				
Total output	60,045	55,508	84,049	88,704
Cash inputs	38,622	42,336	76,783	78,210
Farmers' margin	21,423	13,172	7,266	10,494
Interest payments	1,201	1,110	1,681	1,774
Income tax	4,044	2,412	1,117	1,744
Farmers' disposable income	16,178	9,650	4,468	6,976
2. *Accounting Prices*				
Remittances	1,618	965	447	698
Consumption	11,939	7,121	3,297	5,148
Total Social Cost	13,557	8,086	3,744	5,846

from its market price. Except at Kabisi, the social value is less than the purchase price. At Kabisi, however, the market price seriously underestimates the social value of using this land for large-scale farming. Despite the relatively high income accruing to farmers, farming at Kabisi produced socially valuable products (maize and milk) with great efficiency, through the use of inputs many of which had social values significantly below their market prices. The residual land values at accounting prices shown in Table 15.3 are those used in the next chapter in the social appraisal of the settlement schemes, adjusted where necessary to bring them to inflation-corrected values for a particular year. In the social appraisals a single land cost item has been applied in only one year. An alternative way of dealing with land would be to use an annual cost, which would be incorporated in the calculation of the annual surplus before discounting. For discounting at the ARI of 10 per cent, either method of bringing land into account will give the same NPV since the capitalized figure is a single sum that has the same discounted effect as a series of annual values. Dealing with land in this way for social appraisal means giving an analagous treatment to land as in appraisal at market prices, for which only the single purchase price is available.[1]

15.5 LAND VALUES UNDER OTHER FARMING SYSTEMS

What might residual land values have been under other farming systems? As was suggested earlier, this question cannot be answered through lack of information. However, there is some evidence that where land was taken over from Europeans but retained in large-scale operation, working capital shortages and the inevitable early difficulties of management gave rise to less intensive and less profitable results than had previously been the case.[2] They would probably have given land values a little lower than these referred to in this chapter. Furthermore, one can only speculate on what the valuation would have been if some kind of sub-divisional settlement had been the alternative. It would certainly have varied between different forms of settlement, a point on which further comment is made below in Chapter 16. The estimates of an accounting price for land shown in Table 15.3 give an estimate of social value suitable for use in this study, in that they allow the social profitability of settlement land to be compared with the land-use method that preceded it. However, land values are a point where alternative values are considered in the settlement appraisals.

1 This treatment means, however, that the capitalized value used is correct only for discounting at the ARI. Using capitalized values to calculate true Internal Rates of Return is invalid. See footnote 2 on p. 362.

2 See for instance Kenya Government, Farm Economics Survey Unit *Report No. 28*, 1972, and Development Plan 1970-74, p.415.

APPENDIX A.15

SOURCES AND CALCULATION METHODS USED TO ESTIMATE THE PATTERN OF LARGE-SCALE FARMING IN 1959 IN THE FOUR SCHEME AREAS

1. THE FARMING SYSTEMS

Census data were used as indications of the farming systems followed in the four areas in 1959. Summary information is given in reports published by the Statistics Division of the Census of Large Farms conducted annually since the early 1950s. Each census provided for the collection (at a date in the middle of the cropping season) of information on acreages under different crops and numbers of different types of livestock. Many particulars are reported only as totals for each Production Sub-Committee Area, which typically covered relatively small areas of 50 or so farms.[1]

Three alternative data sources were considered: (i) Individual census returns for the farms concerned. These returns (being confidential) were not available for use. However, the intention is not to compare the operation of a *particular* group of farms and the actual settlement that was implemented on the same land, but to compare representative types of settlement with the *types* of farming that they succeeded. Information for particular farms might not help meet this end. (ii) Information on farming systems in 1959 followed in samples of large-scale farms studied by the Farm Economics Survey Unit. These studies which covered four ecologically distinct parts of Western Kenya, are not by themselves a suitable guide to farming systems outside the narrow areas that they covered. Kabisi is the only settlement studied that lay near an area covered by these surveys. (iii) Detailed estimates of pre-settlement production given in papers submitted to the agencies providing development finance for Low Density schemes to show that they would give rise to an increase in production over previous levels. The source of these details is unknown but they were thought to be unreliable.

In view of their almost complete cover, the census reports provide good data on actual farming systems. Figures for the four areas in 1959 are given in Table A.15.1. The patterns of land use and stocking reported for that year were the basis for land value calculation. Thus, so far as cropping patterns are concerned, the same percentage pattern of land use as applied in each Sub-Committee Area was assumed to apply to the farms taken for the settlements under study.[2] So far as grazing livestock were concerned, it was assumed that the same ratios existed in the settlement farms and in each Area between numbers of different types and the area of land not under crops.[3]

[1] Full details of these Sub-Committees and a map, can be found in Odingo, 1972.

[2] The settlement farms accounted for from 13.5 to 23.4 per cent of the full Sub-Committee Areas.

[3] Pig numbers were calculated on the basis of sow numbers per 1,000 acres of land.

Table A.15.1

Land use in the Sub-Committee Areas where the four settlements were developed, as given in the annual census reports

	Low Altitude		High Altitude	
	Kabisi[a]	Lessos[b]	Kipipiri[c]	Passenga[d]
Land use				
('000 Acres)				
Crops: Wheat	-	6.0	18.2	14.3
Maize	6.6	2.0	0.5	0.1
Barley	-	0.3	4.1	1.6
Oats	0.1	0.3	2.2	1.3
Pyrethrum	-	0.5	0.6	0.6
Sunflower	1.8	-	-	-
Linseed and others	-	-	0.3	0.1
Coffee	0.6	-	-	-
Wattle	1.4	6.5	-	0.1
Plantation crops	-	1.1	-	-
Total crops	10.5	16.7	25.9	18.1
Other Uses	75.1	71.1	66.1	34.1
Total Area	85.6	87.8	92.0	52.2
Livestock				
('000 Head)				
Dairy cattle	11.8	8.2	7.4	3.8
Beef cattle	8.5	2.9	3.7	1.4
Sheep	3.2	4.1	10.8	5.4
Pigs ('000 sows)	1.4	0.1	0.8	0.2

a. Production Sub-Committee Area: Trans Nzoia S.S.W.
b. Production Sub-Committee Area: Lessos.
c. Production Sub-Committee Area: Ol Bolossat/Wanjohe.
d. Production Sub-Committee Area: Ol Kalou.

Although farming systems for the four areas were in general determined on this basis, a number of departures were made from the 1959 figures.

(i) The settlement land contained little or no wattle and coffee, although the 'Plantation Crops' referred to at Lessos partly consisted of young tea planted on an experimental basis and purchased with the settlement land. Wattle and coffee thus had to be excluded. Both crops are grown on arable land. In determining cropping systems, it was assumed that the same proportion of the land was under crops as in the census but that only annual crops and pyrethrum were grown, in the same proportions to each other as reported.

(ii) For no obvious reason, the maize acreage in the Area where Kabisi was located was in 1959 well below the level of earlier and later years. This reduction was not general and may have been caused by temporary factors on a few farms. A maize acreage between the 1958 and 1960 acreages was assumed.

(iii) Much land in the Ol Bolosat/Wanjohe Sub-Committee Area (where Kipipiri is situated) was of such poor quality that it was rejected as being completely unsuitable for settlement.[1] The area used for the scheme was almost certainly of better quality than the average for the Area as a whole, and would therefore have been farmed more intensively. Consequently a farming system was assumed at Kipipiri 20 per cent more intensive than that in the Area as a whole.

The patterns of farming taken for the four settlement areas in 1959 are shown in Table A.15.2. Livestock numbers are expressed there in terms of Livestock Units (L.U.) of each type of stock. This unit provides a means for converting livestock—especially grazing types—into a common measure on the basis of food requirements. Here the standard of measurement is a grade milking cow, which is taken as 1 L.U.[2]

2. OUTPUT

No completely satisfactory basis exists on which crop and livestock yields in the late 1950s can be estimated for any particular part of the large farm area. The annual census was held in the middle of the normal crop year, when crops were established but not harvested, and no questions were asked about crop production during the previous year. Information was collected on numbers of livestock sold and some livestock products, but this information is reported only on a highly aggregated basis.

Estimates of the yields of certain crops in each Sub-Committee were made annually in the 1950s and early 1960s by the Board of Agriculture (Scheduled Areas) in connection with its short-term crop finance programmes. These figures were thought at that time to be somewhat inaccurate, since they referred only to approved plantings under the crop

[1] In 1964 this land was incorporated in the Ol Kalou Salient, where large-scale operation by the Department of Settlement has been undertaken.

[2] See in the List of Abbreviations p. xxv. The following overall conversion factors were used: Dairy cattle and Beef cattle 0.8 L.U. per head; Sheep 0.135 L.U. per head; Pigs 2.50 L.U. per sow.

Table A.15.2

Patterns of farming, yields and output (at market prices) for large-scale farming in 1959 in the four settlement areas

Crops (Acres)	Kabisi No.	Kabisi Sh. per unit	Kabisi Output value (£)	Lessos No.	Lessos Sh. per unit	Lessos Output value (£)	Kipipiri No.	Kipipiri Sh. per unit	Kipipiri Output value (£)	Passenga No.	Passenga Sh. per unit	Passenga Output value (£)
Wheat	-	..	-	1,774	235	20,845	2,685	275	36,919	3,698	275	50,848
Maize	1,461	310.5	22,682	591	310.5	9,175	73	306	1,117	26	306	398
Barley	-	..	-	88	174	766	605	247.5	7,487	414	247.5	5,123
Oats	12	172.5	104	88	161	708	324	189	3,062	337	189	3,185
Pyrethrum	-	..	-	149	550	4,094	108	810	4,374	155	810	6,278
Other Crops	307	141	2,164	-	..	-	45	430	967	129	430	2,774
Total Crops	1,780	..	24,950	2,690	..	35,588	3,840	..	53,926	4,759	..	68,606
Livestock (L.U.)												
Dairy cattle: Milk	1,312	260	17,056	1,057	238	12,578	1,014	212	10,748	786	212	8,332
Cattle		70	4,592		63	3,330		54	2,738		54	2,122
Beef cattle	951	195	9,272	374	109	2,038	507	105	2,662	294	105	1,544
Sheep: Wool	60	20	60	89	31	138	250	131	1,638	189	131	1,238
Sheep		145	435		63	208		259	3,238		259	2,448
Pigs	92	800	3,680	40	778	1,556	268	679	9,099	130	679	4,414
Total Livestock	2,415	..	35,095	1,560	..	19,920	2,039	..	30,123	1,399	..	20,098
Total all products			60,045			55,508			84,049			88,704

finance arrangements (which could be more or less than the number of acres actually planted), whilst the treatment in these figures of produce consumed on the farms was unsatisfactory.[1]

In the absence of a suitable data source, output figures were estimated from three sources. The first was yield levels for enterprises covered in the Farm Economic Surveys. This is the only available source of livestock output figures. A second source was information contained in the settlement budgets, which generally relate to the actual land on which the schemes were developed. These budgets were drawn up by Agricultural Officers with local knowledge who were well qualified to estimate likely levels of production. The third source was personal impression, gained from knowledge of production in the early 1960s in the areas taken for settlement. Obviously none of these sources is entirely satisfactory, but the yield levels adopted are considered to be realistic.

The yield levels used are shown in value terms in Table A.15.2. For crops they are based on estimates of physical yields and the sale prices of produce of normal quality, but livestock yields can only be expressed in money terms, in the way used in the Farm Economic Survey reports.[2] Using observed money yields implies assuming that the produce sold from farms in the settlement areas was of the same quality and composition for each particular type of livestock as was observed in the surveys. This is probably a fair assumption for all types of livestock product, although it may be less true of milk than of other products. The ability to sell in the preferential whole-milk market was partly associated with location. For example, farms in the Kabisi area, being on the edge of the large farm area, were probably able to sell less whole milk than would others in central parts of the Trans Nzoia district. However, in the absence of information on the relative importance of alternative milk disposals it has been assumed that the balance there was the same as in the farms included in the Trans Nzoia survey. The same principle was applied to the three other areas.

The crop output levels shown in Table A.15.2 all relate to the crop year 1959. Cereals have been valued at the prices for that year shown in Table A.15.3. The assumed levels of output per Livestock Unit for different kinds of stock are those found in the Economic Surveys for the three years 1959-61. Experience in the surveys showed that the estimated per unit value of production from certain types of stock varied fairly markedly from year to year, particularly with beef cattle and pigs, where the annual valuation of immature and breeding stock can introduce short-term errors in production estimates. The output calculations were made using the three year average levels of production for each type of stock, deflated by price changes over the three years to bring them back to 1959 levels. The

[1] Despite these drawbacks, records of these yields could not be traced in Nairobi.

[2] Livestock yields and the value of production from 'Other Crops' were based on FES surveys in 1959 for the areas ecologically most analogous to the settlement areas. These were: Kabisi-Trans Nzoia (FES Report No. 22); Lessos-Uasin Gishu (Report No. 16); Kipipiri and Passenga-Molo/Mau Narok (Report No. 19).

figures in Table A.15.2 thus indicate 'typical' levels of livestock and crop yields that could have been expected in 1959. They are not necessarily those obtained in that particular season.

Under large-scale farming in the four areas, maize or wheat were the most important products, with milk and beef cattle the main livestock items. Surprisingly, pyrethrum was not a very prominent crop in either of the two high altitude areas.

Table A.15.3

Producer prices of the main products of large farms[a]

Sh.

	1958-9[b]	1959-60	1960-1
Wheat: Grade 1, per bag of 200 lb[c]	52.33	48.62	46.62
Maize: Grade 2, per bag of 200 lb[c]	27.00	32.00	35.50
Pyrethrum: per lb.	169.71	180.10	186.69
Milk: Pool 1, per gall.	2.18	2.18	2.22
Butterfat: Grade 1, per lb.	2.50	2.51	2.84
Cattle: Standard 'A' per lb. C.D.W.	1.10	1.10	1.15
Sheep: Grade 'A', per lb. C.D.W.	1.56	1.56	1.50
Baconers: Grade 'A', per lb. C.D.W.	1.75	1.50	1.60

a. Milk prices applies only to sales to the K.C.C. Creamery for North West Kenya at Eldoret, to which sales from Kabisi and Lessos would have been made. All other prices applied throughout the large farm area.

b. Prices are the average of those applying in the 12 months from April to March of the years shown.

c. Net of producer cesses, without bag.

Sources: Statistical Abstract 1967, Tables 70 and 73. FES Reports Nos. 2 and 22.

3. OPERATING COSTS

There is only one reliable contemporary source of information on the composition and levels of operating costs for large-scale farming, namely the Farm Economic Surveys. These studies give details for 1959 that are quite suitable for estimating production costs in the four areas, since

Table A.15.4

Itemized direct production costs for enterprises on large farms in the Kabisi area

Sh.

	Crops costs per acre			Livestock costs per L.U.			
	Maize	Oats	Sun-flower	Dairy Cattle	Beef Cattle	Sheep	Pigs
Tractors	41.05	29.76	39.39	9.17	—	—	—
Field machinery	17.19	11.94	16.49	2.30	—	—	—
Combines	—	22.87	—	—	—	—	—
Seed	3.72	14.10	3.40	5.73	—	—	—
Superphosphates	25.44	12.20	8.23	5.72	—	—	—
Crop chemicals	2.98	—	—	—	—	—	—
Bags	20.47	0.84	11.65	—	—	—	—
Lorry Hire	6.62	—	2.48	10.19	—	—	—
Railage	—	—	—	—	—	—	16.02
Water supply	—	—	—	5.51	1.82	2.90	—
Unskilled labour	40.77	5.59	24.32	45.46	9.33	61.47	60.00
Minerals	—	—	—	10.00	4.66	4.56	20.00
Compound foods	—	—	—	16.73	—	—	386.78
Farm-grown cereals	—	—	—	9.21	—	—	197.15
Vet. and Med.	—	—	—	8.96	2.89	19.49	2.92
Dip	—	—	—	5.37	5.34	—	—
Sundries	—	—	—	5.42	0.85	4.13	6.33
Total	158.24	97.30	105.96	139.77	24.89	92.55	689.20

Sources: All columns except Oats: FES Report 22.
: Oats: FES Report 16.

production methods in each are likely to have been very similar to those on surveyed farms in the analogous ecological zone.

Enterprise Direct Costs

The survey reports give itemized figures of per unit costs incurred on each major enterprise. Figures from the relevant sample surveys can be used as they stand to provide estimates of total direct expenses incurred in the operation of each enterprise. Taking these figures at face value implies accepting that cultivation practice and the input levels of fertilizers, purchased feed, etc., were the same on the farms concerned as in the areas surveyed. In general this is consistent with the assumption that production in the area was roughly similar to that found in the comparable survey farms. In the case of maize at Kabisi a rather lower yield has been assumed than was generally found in the surveys,[1] but there is no clear basis for reducing the corresponding survey cost figures to allow for lower yields, and they have been adopted unchanged.

Overheads

Estimating overhead expenses is less simple than determining direct costs. Overheads are those expenses which are not directly attributed to individual enterprises, and whose total level is not related in a simple way to farm size, output or direct costs. There is no obvious way in which their total level can be determined. However, expenditure on overhead items is likely to be loosely related to the intensity of farm operation, as reflected in both the levels of total direct enterprise expenditure and total output. The simplest method of calculating the total cost of overhead items, and the one used, was to assume a directly proportionate relationship between overheads and these two separately determined quantities. The percentage composition of overhead expenses for the farms in each area was taken as being identical to that found in the corresponding FES report.

1 The three-year average for the Trans Nzoia sample was 11.6 bags per acre, while an assumed yield of 9 bags has been used here. At the time of the surveys, the comment was made that recorded yields on the survey farms were untypically high, and Kabisi had no outstanding characteristics regarding maize production.

CHAPTER 16

Appraisal of the Four Settlements as Planned and as They Actually Developed

The results of the appraisal of the four settlements are presented in this chapter. Planned and actual situations are considered separately in the two main sections, while a final section draws together some general points.

16.1 FEATURES OF THE APPRAISALS

For each settlement and situation considered individually, appraisal is based on the detailed particulars presented in Chapters 13 and 14. Basically, the appraisals involve calculating the Net Present Value (NPV), at the Accounting Rate of Interest (ARI)[1] of 10 per cent, of the cost and output flows identified as having been planned or as having actually arisen in each settlement when viewed as an individual project marginal to the settlement programmes as a whole. NPVs are calculated at both market and accounting prices. The Rate of Return (ROR)[2] that would, as a discount rate, give a NPV of zero was also calculated for most situations, although the main emphasis of the presentation is on NPV effects.

16.1.1 *Basic assumptions*

For appraisal, some assumptions had to be made to complement available information, while a few adjustments to the existing figures were required. These can usefully be summarized at this point.

[1] See 2.4.

[2] The RORs calculated are not always true 'Internal Rates of Return'. The difference arises because some inputs are valued as a single capitalized figure which itself represents a stream of values over time discounted at a single discount rate. Land and cows are examples. To calculate a true IRR, these should be brought into the calculation as annual values, not as a single sum.

Wherever available, figures prepared in settlement planning and records of actual occurrences are the bases for each appraisal. In large part the data sources discussed in earlier chapters were sufficient to build up a complete schedule of costs and output, and changes in them over time. However, some aspects required assumptions to be made about what might have been expected, or of what actually occurred. For example, in both the planned and actual situations, estimates of the cost of family labour depend heavily on the assumed alternative earnings that the settlers would have obtained. This was not estimated in planning by the Department of Settlement, nor for settlement in practice were standard values for use in evaluation suggested to us by Kenya officials. We had to make our own estimates, as discussed in Chapter 5. For the planned situations, we also had to make assumptions about scheme supervision by the Department in the long run, and the development of production beyond the maturity years. The latter problem also applies to the settlement actuals, since their evaluation has to include assumptions about how production might develop after the years for which we have information.

These are the most significant areas where appraisal has to rely on our own assumptions. The results could be sensitive to these assumptions, so the analysis allows the importance of each assumption to be assessed, and alternative values are given.

16.1.2 *Conversion from market to accounting prices*

The main price adjustments made were conversions from market to accounting prices. For this, the Accounting Ratios given in Tables 10.1 and 10.2 were used. The same AR was used for every cost item in whatever year it occurred, with the single exception of maize seed. Where, as with certain types of output, the cost and price structure of a commodity varied significantly from year to year, different ARs were separately calculated. Amongst all prices in a relatively free economy, variation between years and the need for re-estimation is likely to be most true of the prices of agricultural products, where intervention in pricing is very common.[1] This is reflected in this

[1] An example of the need to adjust for intervention in the pricing of a farm *input* arises with regard to superphosphates used on large farms in 1959, when the fertilizer subsidy embodied in the general AR for this item did not apply. This point was allowed for in Chapter 15.

study in the use of year-specific values for maize and pyrethrum, which were used for the settlement actuals. However, long-run ARs for these two crops (which were taken as the mean values of ARs for the individual years) were used in the appraisal of the settlement plans and large-scale farming.

Accounting prices for two major costs items were individually calculated for each settlement, namely land and the cost of settlers' family labour. How land was dealt with was discussed in Chapter 15.

16.1.2.1 *The social cost of family labour in the settlement plans*

The method for calculating the social cost of family labour was described in Chapter 5, where, for illustration, the method was applied to estimate the cost of 'average' High Density and Low Density farmers in 1967-8. This cost has three elements: (i) the social opportunity cost of workers in alternative employment; (ii) the social value of the resource cost of settlers' income; and (iii) the social value of new benefits enjoyed by settlers. The social cost is (i) + (ii) - (iii).

The first element depends on the number of people in each family, the net earnings of each adult as a small-farm employee, and the value of any other production that they may have undertaken while employed in this way. Standardized procedures and figures were adopted for all of these items. The 1969-value annual earnings rate for full-time farm workers were given in Chapter 5. As explained in Chapter 13, lower values were applied for Kabisi, but in the other three cases the general values were used unchanged.

Family composition for the planned situation was taken from our interpretation of the recorded planning assumptions (i.e. one adult of each sex and two children per farm), and for the actual situation from the numbers of people per farm recorded in the sample surveys, adjusted for time spent earning non-farm income. In all cases, it was assumed that family women would, if not settlers, have been available for employment for 45 per cent of their time.[1] It was also assumed that, as landless workers, each *family* would have produced subsistence foods to the net value of £5.

[1] See 5.2.

To calculate element (ii), the item was broken down into component parts, along the lines depicted in Table 5.2. In every case, the basis for estimating family incomes after settlement was the profit per farm of the budgets or the farm surveys. Income from other sources was ignored.

In calculating element (iii), account is taken of four types of benefit: gains in money income; savings in retail margins; shorter hours of work; and other benefits derived from self-employment. These benefits were discussed in detail in Chapter 5.

Components in the last two elements depend on the actual levels of net and money income each year. The value of these elements thus changes whenever income changes, so year-specific family labour costs must be calculated.

Estimates of the social value of family labour for the plans were made for each year up to the 'maturity' level, when it was assumed that incomes would stabilize.

Table 16.1 shows, in analysed form, the net cost of settlers' labour for the full 'gestation' period of each settlement plan. The figures bring out some interesting points. The second and fifth columns show that if the plans for Kabisi were met exactly, settlers' incomes would be expected to fall until the fourth year. At Kipipiri, settlers' net incomes would be permanently lower, at least until the periods of loan repayment were over.[1] This consequence of settlement varies markedly between the High and Low Density schemes, as also do the unadjusted values of settlers' extra benefits. At Lessos and Passenga these mainly take the form of extra money income, but (because changes in money incomes are so small) other benefits are more important at Kabisi and Kipipiri. The extent of these differences is, of course, reduced when the total benefits are adjusted through the application of a factor that combines the AR for rural consumption (0.87) and income

[1] For the appraisal of the settlement plan, eventual changes due to the termination of loan repayments by settlers have been ignored. Loan repayment schedules allow for constant repayments for 10 years at a high level (including both land and development loans) and then constant payments at a lower level for a further 20 years until land loans are repaid. While in principle adjustments for this might have been made, ignoring them is justified on the grounds that (1) the changes will not occur until their discounted values will be very small, and (2) a reduction of this item in element (ii) of the calculation would be offset by an opposite (but, after weighting, less than equal) adjustment in the first component of element (iii).

Table 16.1

Estimates of the social cost of settlers' family labour in the settlement plans, showing their composition

Accounting Prices[a] in 1967-8 Values (£)

		Extra Resource Cost			Settlers' Extra Benefits						Net cost
	Earnings before[b] (1)	△Net income[c]	Amort-ization	Total (2)	△Money income[d]	Retail margins	Hours of work	Self Empl.	Total	Adjus-ted total (3)	(1) + (2) −(3)
abisi											
964-5	51	−30.9	3.9	−27.0	−24.9	6.7	11.3	6.7	−0.2	−0.2	24.2
965-6	51	−23.6	3.9	−19.7	−16.9	6.9	11.3	6.7	8.0	5.7	25.6
966-7	51	−21.9	3.9	−18.0	−15.1	7.1	11.3	6.7	10.0	7.0	26.0
967-8	51	2.7	3.9	6.6	11.6	6.6	11.3	6.7	36.2	21.0	36.6
essos											
963-4	61	27.4	9.9	37.3	51.9	6.7	13.7	6.7	79.0	32.5	65.8
964-5	61	22.7	9.9	32.6	46.8	6.7	13.7	6.7	73.9	31.1	62.5
965-6	61	25.6	9.9	35.5	49.9	6.9	13.7	6.7	77.2	32.0	64.5
966-7	61	51.2	9.9	61.1	77.8	7.1	13.7	6.7	105.3	39.3	82.8
967-8	61	65.5	9.9	75.4	93.3	6.6	13.7	6.7	120.3	42.6	93.8
968-9	61	79.8	9.9	89.7	108.8	6.6	13.7	6.7	135.8	45.9	104.8
969-70	61	94.0	9.9	103.9	124.3	6.6	13.7	6.7	151.3	48.8	116.1
970-1	61	104.3	9.9	114.2	135.5	6.6	13.7	6.7	162.5	50.8	124.4
971-2	61	107.5	9.9	117.4	139.0	6.6	13.7	6.7	166.0	51.4	127.0
ipipiri											
964-5	61	−4.1	3.1	−1.0	2.4	6.7	13.7	6.7	29.5	15.5	44.5
965-6	61	−1.7	3.1	1.4	5.1	6.9	13.7	6.7	32.4	16.7	45.7
966-7	61	−1.7	3.1	1.4	5.1	7.1	13.7	6.7	32.6	16.8	45.6
967-8	61	−1.7	3.1	1.4	5.1	6.6	13.7	6.7	32.1	16.5	45.9
assenga											
964-5	61	8.6	9.4	18.0	30.1	4.6	13.7	6.7	55.1	25.2	53.8
965-6	61	37.6	9.4	47.0	61.7	4.8	13.7	6.7	86.9	34.7	73.3
966-7	61	37.7	9.4	47.1	61.8	4.9	13.7	6.7	87.1	34.7	73.4
967-8	61	60.4	9.4	69.8	86.5	4.5	13.7	6.7	111.4	40.7	90.1

a. In the section covering Settlers' Extra Benefits, all values are at market prices except the Adjusted Total.

b. The calculations in both this table and Table 16.2 of earnings before settlement have in every year been based on the 1969 levels of £41 for men and £34 for women. No adjustment has been made for the changing value of money over time. We could trace no reliable data on wage rates in the informal rural sector in earlier years, on which to base any variation from these figures. We heard in a number of places that 'work was getting more difficult to find', and similar comments. This may be true, as population increased and man/land ratios worsened. The build-up of household size in some settlements (Kabisi especially) is probably a manifestation of this growing problem. Making this assumption implies a falling real wage over time for people of this kind. This implication may be correct.

c. The calculation of this and other figures assumes that all loans were issued in full; all loan repayments were made by settlers in full and on time; and that all income was consumed.
d. This includes the value of subsistence production.

distribution weightings. This adjustment reduces the value of the extra benefits received by the Low Density settlers by much more than applies to High Density farmers. Because of this factor and the high extra resource costs of the Low Density settlers, their net cost at accounting prices increases steadily through the periods of the plan until the maturity levels are reached. Only once (at Passenga in the first year) is the social cost of settler family labour on either Low Density scheme less than the market cost of settlers' alternative earnings. By contrast, family labour on the two High Density schemes has, every year, a social cost less than the market value of alternative earnings, the basis for costing family labour at market values in the plans. Consequently, this divergence between the two types of scheme in the social cost of settler labour will be an important source of divergence at appraisal between the results at market and accounting prices.

16.1.2.2 *The social cost of family labour in the settlements in practice*

Figures detailing the similar calculation for settlement in practice before April 1968 are given in Table 16.2. Variation between the figures merits a little discussion.

Although the net social cost being calculated applies to the average settler's household viewed as a unit, calculating the value of some component parts, especially the first element, is based on the numbers of people living on the farms.[1] Since constant money values have been adopted for per capita earnings elsewhere, changes from year to year in the first column mainly reflect changes in the size and composition of settlement households.[2] At Kabisi family size increased

[1] Also reflecting this effect are Hours of Work and Self-Employment Benefits. It also influences the weighting factor applied to extra benefits, which is calculated on a per capita basis.

[2] Unfortunately, usable farm survey results for Kipipiri were available for only 1964-5 and 1965-6. Identical values in several columns for each of the last three years reflects the assumption that things in 1966-7 and 1967-8 were the same as in 1965-6.

annually, with a big change between the last years. On both Low Density schemes, household size declined after 1965-6.

In calculating the extra resource cost element, changes in stocks were an important feature of income that did not apply to the settlement plans. Stock changes were a major item, especially on the Low Density schemes, where both the opportunities latent in large farms and some departure from the planned farming system gave rise to regular increases in the value (net of purchases) of the livestock carried. Scope for changes of this kind was much more limited at Kabisi and Kipipiri.

The net social cost of settlers' families varied in practice substantially from year to year, and except at Kipipiri, in an erratic manner. At Lessos, where family size varied little, steady increases in the value of livestock and (apart from 1965-6) in the value of extra money income pushed family labour costs far beyond the plan levels. Through a combination of influences, the social cost in 1967-8 was in practice twice the plan level at Kabisi, Lessos and Kipipiri, and one-and-a-half times at Passenga. The implications of these facts are further discussed below.

16.1.3 *The reference time-bases for appraisal*

Data for different situations were prepared on the basis of prices for particular years. Large-scale farming was assessed in Chapter 15 at 1959 values. The settlement plans were priced in 1962-3 values, while data for settlements in practice, being based on actual contemporary records, are expressed in terms of individual years' prices.

For the collective evaluation of settlement actuals, all years' figures were adjusted to 1967-8 values. For this purpose, and to allow comparisons of situations, adjustments were required to allow for changes over time in the value of the money units in which all market and accounting values are expressed. These changes give rise to differences in the general level of prices between particular years and 1967 (or 1967-8).

The question of inflation was discussed in Chapter 2. Adjustments for this factor were made in a very simple way. The Lower Income Index of Consumer Prices in Nairobi was taken as the index of changes in the general price level. Values

Table 16.2

Estimates of the social cost of settlers' family labour during the first few years of the established settlement, showing their composition

Accounting Prices[a] 1967-8 Values (£)

	Extra Resource Cost					Settlers' Extra Benefits						
	Earnings before (1)	ΔNet income	Δ Stocks	Amortization	Total (2)	ΔMoney income[b]	Retail margins	Hours of work	Self empl.	Total	Adjusted total (3)	Net cost (1) + (2) −(3)
Kabisi												
1964-5	50.5	-11.5	81.1	-37.8	31.8	-31.5	3.2	10.5	6.6	-11.2	-10.6	92.9
1965-6	73.0	-58.1	7.0	-5.3	-56.4	-69.4	6.8	16.5	9.9	-36.2	-39.4	56.0
1966-7	75.8	-9.8	-8.1	-4.6	-22.5	-27.2	11.4	17.0	10.3	11.5	9.4	43.9
1967-8	118.2	-77.9	35.6	-2.0	-44.3	-59.1	13.4	30.5	16.4	1.2	0.8	73.1
Lessos												
1964-5	60.5	-46.2	107.9	-17.2	44.5	-3.8	9.6	13.0	6.6	25.4	14.8	90.2
1965-6	91.4	-76.8	52.5	-22.5	-46.8	-87.7	15.0	20.9	10.2	-41.6	-27.5	72.1
1966-7	71.8	11.1	96.7	-12.0	95.8	61.5	11.9	15.2	7.9	96.5	44.8	122.8
1967-8	69.4	49.5	143.1	-4.2	188.4	158.8	13.5	14.2	7.6	194.1	75.1	182.7
Kipipiri												
1964-5	57.2	-28.1	15.3	-4.6	-17.4	-28.9	7.6	12.3	6.2	-2.8	-2.3	42.1
1965-6	80.4	-37.3	18.2	-2.3	-21.4	-31.7	10.4	17.2	8.9	4.8	2.5	56.5
1966-7	80.4	19.0	18.2	-2.3	-34.9	29.4	10.4	17.2	8.9	65.9	28.1	87.2
1967-8	80.4	27.8	18.2	-2.3	43.7	39.0	10.4	17.2	8.9	75.5	31.3	92.8
Passenga												
1964-5	68.9	-116.4	210.2	-36.9	56.9	-46.9	6.5	15.2	7.6	-17.6	-9.2	135.0
1965-6	76.4	18.1	73.2	-11.1	80.2	51.3	10.1	17.2	8.5	87.1	30.1	126.5
1966-7	54.1	96.9	21.3	-11.1	107.1	97.0	15.2	10.4	5.8	128.4	27.7	133.5
1967-8	52.7	75.0	36.8	-5.3	106.5	98.0	14.7	9.2	5.6	127.5	25.3	133.9

a. Note (a) to Table 16.1 also applies to this table.
b. Includes both stock changes and the value of subsistence production.

of the index, converted to give 1967 a value of 100.0, are shown in Table 16.3. All figures were first calculated in market or accounting prices of the years to which they related, and the totals or net figures then adjusted through the application of these index numbers to express them in terms of values for another year. Thus, the residual value of land used for large-scale farming (which is the basis for estimating the social value of land) was calculated in 1959 values. For incorporation in the settlement plan, all of the rest of which is expressed in 1962 values, it was converted to values for that year. To compare the plan appraisal with the evaluation of settlement actuals (which are expressed in 1967 terms), its discounted values were all adjusted to 1967 terms. In preparing summary details of settlement actuals, individual year's adjustment

Table 16.3

Lower income index of consumer prices in Nairobi

1967 = 100

1959	84.4	1964	90.8	1969	101.7
1960	85.6	1965	93.7	1970	102.5
1961	87.5	1966	97.9	1971	107.2
1962	89.4	1967	100.0	1972	112.7
1963	90.6	1968	101.3		

Sources: Statistical Abstracts and Kenya Statistical Digest, various issues. The figures shown for each year are the arithmetic averages of the index numbers for December of the year in question and December of the previous year.

factors were used to express all in 1967 terms, and the years beyond 1967-8 were projected at constant 1967 prices.

16.1.4 *The treatment of grant and loan receipts and repayments from and to foreign governments*
For reasons explained in Chapter 13, it was felt legitimate (as an extreme assumption) to include as integral features of the settlement projects all foreign aid flows to which they gave rise. Although these flows applied to aid from several sources,[1] most came from Britain and for simplicity it has been assumed that all were denominated in Pounds Sterling. Adjustment in the calculations involving these financial flows is required to take account of actual or expected changes in the relative values of sterling and the Kenya Pound.

The original financial arrangements for the settlement programme were made in 1961, when the two pounds were at parity. However, in November 1967 sterling was devalued, and the conversion rate changed to Stg. £1.00 = K£0.86. Since then small changes have occurred in both directions in the rate of exchange, but at the time of writing (mid-1973) the rate of exchange is nearly the same as in December 1967. For simplicity, changes since November 1967 have been ignored.

For the settlement actuals, receipts and repayments have been dealt with as follows:

[1] HMG, IBRD, CDC and the West German Government.

(1) Up to and including 1966-7,[1] the finance values were divided by the consumer price index for the relevant year from Table 16.3 with 1967 = 100.

(2) For 1967-8 it was assumed that drawings and repayments were made uniformly throughout the year. The figures as stated in Stg.£ were therefore multiplied by an average exchange rate for the year of 0.94[2] to convert them to current K£.

(3) For 1968-9 and all subsequent years, the figures as stated in Stg.£ were first multiplied by 0.86, and then divided by $(1.04)^n$, where n = 1 in 1968-9, 2 in 1969-70, and so on. In other words, payments after 1967-8 have been discounted by an interest rate 4 per cent greater than the ARI of 10 per cent. Under certain simplifying assumptions, 4 per cent per annum is our estimate of the long-term trend rate of increase from 1967-8 in the UK general price level.[3] As such, it may be considered to be on the low side. If it is, the NPV of the cost of future loan repayments given below is overstated.

This procedure for dealing with settlement in practice was the guide for accommodating the same factor in the settlement plans. To allow the derivation of analogous figures, external finance flows were reduced in value for the whole of the relevant period from the level of base year (1962) values by the same special discount factor of 4 per cent per annum.

[1] The small discrepancy between calendar years and settlement accounting years beginning 1st April has been ignored.

[2] $0.94 = \{(7 \times 1) + (5 \times 0.86)\} \div 12.$

[3] The simplifying assumptions amount to a purchasing-power parity theory of exchange rate determination. We assume that each extra 1 per cent by which prices rise in the U.K., given the level of Kenya prices, leads to a 1 per cent extra depreciation in the Stg. £ vis-à-vis K£. Likewise, each extra 1 per cent by which prices rise in Kenya, given the level of U.K. prices, leads to a 1 per cent extra depreciation in K£ vis-à-vis Stg. £. Consequently, if prices rise in the U.K. by 0.04 per unit and by P per unit in Kenya the depreciation of the Stg. £ vis-à-vis K£ is approximately 0.04–P per unit. But as prices in Kenya have gone up by P per unit, we must correct for this as well to get the value of loan repayments in terms of our numeraire at constant purchasing power. The total correction then involves division by (1 + 0.04 - P + P), i.e. by 1.04, and this correction applies cumulatively if U.K. prices rise by 0.04 per unit per annum.

Because the finance flows included a substantial grant element and the interest rate on loans (6½ per cent) was less than the ARI, finance flows were important net benefits arising from these settlements. Allowing for a falling real cost of external payments makes the value of this benefit even greater than if constant currency ratios are assumed.

16.1.5 *Project life*

For evaluation, the life of the settlements had to be determined. For simplicity in comparing the different situations studied a life of indefinite length has been assumed. Once a 'stabilized' level of net product was reached, this has been expected to persist indefinitely.

16.2 APPRAISAL OF THE FOUR SETTLEMENT PLANS

The points made above and the data presented in the last three chapters cover all aspects of the basis on which the appraisals were made. These can now be considered, with the plans taken first.

16.2.1 *The Main Results*

Main results from the appraisal of the plans are presented in Table 16.4. For each settlement, eight sets of NPV and ROR values are given, covering the results at market and accounting prices. Within each group the alternative figures shown reflect different major assumptions. The first major division of the results reflects alternative views of how the 'Operating Surplus' of each scheme might develop once the 'maturity' level had been reached. Two possibilities are envisaged: (i) that there would be no further changes in profits, so that the same annual net product would be obtained for an indefinite period; and (ii) that there would be a continuous annual increase of 3 per cent in the value of the settlement's net product for a period of 25 years or so.[1] The latter assumption allows for increased productivity of all resources employed, reflecting continuing

[1] For ease of computation, this expansion was assumed to stop when the financial outflow associated with each scheme came to an end. This was between 30 and 33 years after the year of land purchase, when the first loans were drawn.

Table 16.4

Main results from the appraisal of the four settlement plans

1962-3 Values

	With 3% Expansion				Without Expansion			
	With fin.		Without fin.		With fin.		Without fin.	
	NPV £'000	ROR % p.a.	NPV £'000	ROR % p.a.	NPV £'000	ROR % p.a.	NPV £'000	ROR % p.a.
Kabisi: (HD, LA)								
Market prices	59	28.3	-84	6.9	31	24.5	-112	4.9
Accounting prices	148	17.5	4	10.1	89	16.4	-55	8.3
Lessos: (LD, LA)								
Market prices	391	inf.	167	13.3	306	inf.	82	12.0
Accounting prices	474	inf.	250	15.9	387	inf.	163	14.7
Kipipiri: (HD, HA)								
Market prices	7	12.5	-133	4.1	-6	7.4	-146	2.6
Accounting prices	251	inf.	111	19.2	210	inf.	70	17.6
Passenga: (LD, HA)								
Market prices	209	inf.	-24	9.4	147	inf.	-86	7.5
Accounting prices	356	inf.	123	14.9	294	inf.	62	13.1

Notes:
1. With 3% expansion means that the operating surplus for the planned 'maturity' year was expanded for around 30 years at 3% per annum.
2. With fin. means that the value of external finance flows associated with each scheme was taken into account. The difference between these values and those in the (Without fin.) column is the NPV of the finance flows.
3. ROR = Rate of Return that would make NPV = 0. inf. indicates an infinite rate of return, when the Annual Surplus is positive every year.
4. Market prices include an allowance for the cost of family labour.

land improvement; the application of newly developed technology; learning by settlers of the techniques of modern farming, and improvements in their abilities as enterprise managers; better management and expanded activities by each co-operative; and improving effectiveness of the extension and other advisory personnel. The rate at which such an expansion in net value might occur is not easily determined, but 3 per cent seems reasonable, particularly in view of the evidence of increasing productivity in large-scale farming referred to in Chapter 15 and allowed for in determining the social cost of land.[1]

The second division of each set of results allows external finance flows to be taken into account. The view that most or all of the foreign financing associated with the settlement programmes would not have been available to the Kenya Government if these programmes had not been undertaken is extreme, so the results are presented in terms of the limits of this point, namely with *no* finance flows taken into account and with all finance flows incorporated.[2] In taking finance flows into account, allowance has been made for a steady decline in the real cost to Kenya of the loan repayments, because of world inflation.

This form of presentation has the advantage from a policy viewpoint of indicating what the outcome would have been if the Kenya Government had undertaken these settlement projects using only its own resources. This possibility may still arise: the land transfer programme in the White Highlands is not yet completed. Furthermore, the ILO report, 1972, recommended the continued sub-division of large farms as a sound economic strategy for Kenya, irrespective of whether the land is owned or farmed by Kenyans or foreigners.

Of the four sets of figures given for each settlement at market and accounting prices, those in the first column (i.e. with expansion, with finance) are the most relevant, since they most accurately reflect the opportunity offered in 1962 to decision-makers if, as we are supposing, the question was posed whether any of these settlements should be undertaken as an

[1] The relative merits of this and alternative ways of allowing for increased productivity are discussed below (p. 379). The NPV of a constant expansion obviously depends heavily on the net product in the base year.

[2] Neither assumption may be entirely realistic. An intermediate position may be preferable, but there is no objective basis for making a division. The simple distinction between grants (which could be called specific to the projects) and loans (which might have been available for other uses) would not meet the case. The entire financial arrangements were part of a single package, albeit an exceptional one.

extension to the existing settlement programmes. The figures show that, in every case, adoption would be worthwhile, whether the schemes were appraised at market or at accounting prices. This is in every case an unambiguous outcome, whatever the valuation basis. However, the positive NPV at market prices is small for Kipipiri and so is the expansion effect. Removing it gives a negative NPV even with finance taken into account. This is the most marginal scheme at market prices.

Were associated finance not available, the advisability of adopting these four projects would be less clear-cut. The very important point emerges from the second column of results (with expansion, without finance) that appraisal of three of the projects at market prices would, at a discount rate of 10 per cent, lead to their rejection on straightforward NPV or ROR terms, whereas our method indicates that they would be socially profitable.

On any appraisal basis, Lessos was clearly an attractive project to undertake. At market prices Passenga is far less attractive than Lessos, and the two High Density schemes show up very poorly. However, at accounting prices, the appraisal of Kipipiri is very different. A market price appraisal could have led to the rejection of what appears to be socially a very profitable settlement.

The effects of applying accounting prices to the Kabisi plan were very different from those for Kipipiri. Even at accounting prices and with expansion, Kabisi without finance is very marginal. Whatever it implies about the relative attractiveness of the two High Density schemes, this comparison indicates that, whilst for projects of this kind the direction of change stemming from the use of accounting prices may be constant and predictable, the extent of this change cannot be the subject of generalization. Differences in the composition of costs and outputs and in the ARs for different commodities can give rise to very different outcomes.

16.2.2 *The sensitivity of the results, and the disaggregated effects of using accounting prices*

Figures given in Table 16.5 allow an assessment to be made of: the importance to the results of different cost components; the main assumptions made; and the effects of using accounting

Table 16.5

Disaggregated NPVs for the settlement plans

1962-3 Values £'000

	Kabisi HD, LA		Lessos LD, LA		Kipipiri HD, HA		Passenga LA, HA	
	MP	AP	MP	AP	MP	AP	MP	AP
I. *Present Values at 10%*								
1. Output	796	825	1,118	1,199	531	540	960	980
2. All costs except Settlers' family labour and land	-545	-474	-706	-598	-296	-246	-725	-658
3. Settlers' family labour	-290	-214	-199	-341	-287	-214	-170	-235
4. Land	-73	-191	-131	-97	-94	-10	-151	-25
5. Extended supervision continuing indefinitely	-18	-14	-49	-37	-17	-13	-49	-37
6. Financial flows of constant value	121	121	194	121	121	121	198	198
7. Financial flows declining throughout at 4% p.a.	143	143	224	224	140	140	233	233
8. Annual surplus expanded at 3%	28	59	85	87	13	41	62	61
II. *Rates of return*[a]								
9. Social cost of Land at estimated level	..	8.3	..	14.7	..	17.6	..	13.1
10. Social cost of land halved or doubled[b]	..	11.7	..	11.4	..	15.8	..	11.6
11. Social cost of Land equals market cost	..	13.0	..	13.4	..	9.2	..	8.0
	12,277		14,144		12,338		13,577	

a. Expansions and finance not taken into account.
b. Halved at Kabisi, doubled elsewhere. See p. 378.

values. Study of the table brings out many important points, and indicates differences between the schemes. Only the principal features are discussed.

The four settlements are all of roughly the same area.[1] The total discounted values can thus be compared with each other in

[1] Kabisi, the smallest, is only 13 per cent smaller than Lessos, the largest.

a meaningful way. As was indicated in Chapter 13, the Low Density schemes were planned to produce the most output, while Kipipiri was not expected to be very productive.

16.2.2.1 *Sensitivity to the assumptions made*

Differences in the labour-intensities (settlers' family labour that is) of each settlement were considerable. At market values, family labour at Kipipiri was as big an item as all other costs except land, other inputs being relatively so few. On the Low Density schemes, however, other costs (except land) were over three-and-a-half times as important as settlers' labour. Consequently, the appraisal results for the Low Density schemes were least sensitive to changes in the valuation of settler families. The effect on the NPV of variations in the value of settlers' labour (or any other major item) can be easily calculated from Tables 16.4 and 16.5.[1] Clearly our treatment of this cost item has a very important bearing on the results.

This is less true of other areas where assumptions had to be made about what was planned. Allowing for settlement supervision costs to continue indefinitely at the levels of staffing in the extended supervision stage made only a small difference.[2] The effect of allowing for a declining rather than a constant real cost of external finance flows was also relatively small. So also, in the case of the two High Density schemes, was the effect of allowing for a 3 per cent expansion in the 'maturity year' operating surplus. Because this surplus was higher in the maturity years in the Low Density schemes, the effect of the expansion was much greater at Lessos and Passenga.

16.2.2.2 *The effects of using accounting prices*

The effects of using accounting prices vary between items and between settlements. The aggregate effect on the valuation of output was very slight. Many products, being different forms of

[1] ROR effects cannot be found in this way. Reducing the market cost of family labour by 50 per cent would (without finance or expansion) give the following ROR values: Kabisi 11.8 per cent (28.3); Lessos 14.6 per cent (inf); Kipipiri 9.8 per cent (12.5); Passenga 9.9 per cent (inf). Figures in parentheses are the ROR values when this adjustment is not made.

[2] See 13.2, and Appendix A.13, items 9, 10 and 11.

'Non-traded agricultural products', had ARs of 1.00. Only two products had long-run ARs in excess of 1.10, tea (1.34) and dairy cattle (1.30). Tea was never a prominent crop in any settlement, and dairy cattle did not feature largely as final products in the settlement plans.

Conversion to accounting prices decreased costs for items except settlers' labour and land a little in every case. A fall with adjustment from market to accounting prices is generally to be expected from the nature of the considerations taken into account, and Table 10.1 shows that most ARs for settlement inputs are less than 1.0. At Kabisi, cost items with high ARs were relatively important, namely cows (1.30), superphosphates (1.27) and maize seed (1.10). Although these three inputs were the foundation of the planned farming system, their prominence in the overall cost picture was relatively light.

The effects on the valuation of settlers' family labour of using social costs rather than market prices varies between cases, but is usually quite large. At Kabisi and Kipipiri the social cost is lower than the 'market price' cost, since in both schemes it was expected that settlers incomes would fall when they became settlers. Furthermore, since their incomes as settlers would be close to the threshold level at which extra benefits have a weighting of 1.0, benefits they received are given a high weighting. On the Low Density schemes, however, these two effects work in quite the converse way. As a result of becoming settlers, Low Density farmers' incomes would increase substantially, while the social weighting given to their extra income would be relatively small, even if non-farm income were ignored. Settlement alone would transfer them from the poorer to the richer sections of Kenya society.

Because of the importance of settlers' labour as a cost item and the extent of the difference between its 'market price' and social cost, this item in the two Low Density schemes outweighs the combined adjustment effects of applying ARs to output and 'other costs'. In the main, however, adjustments to all three of these items are systematic and predictable. This cannot be said of land, the other main cost considered individually. The relationships between the market price and the accounting price for these four schemes were very irregular. This may well be true as a generalization for land values in many places, and not just in the Kenya settlements. There, the basis of valuation paid no direct attention to farming profitability, either at the time when the land was valued or for the use to which it was going to be put. For the settlement programmes, the land prices were set at such a level that they gave a 'fair price' to the outgoing farmer, an approach which was probably of more significance (from the viewpoint of maintaining confidence) to farmers *not* being bought out than to those who were.

The differences found in Chapter 15 between the social value of land and the purchase valuation are reflected in line 4 of Table 16.5. On all schemes except Kabisi this adjustment led to a much lower social cost. However, the methods used to value land in social terms were somewhat uncertain. Varying these values (i) by a factor of 2 towards the market values,[1] and (ii) by using an Accounting Ratio of 1.0,[2] so that the social and market values coincided, gave the RORs shown in the lower part of Table 16.5. These relate to the situation without expansion or finance allowed for. Obviously the results are sensitive to the social value of land.

16.2.2.3 *Alternative rates of expansion*

The assumptions made about expansion envisage that the per acre values of operating surplus for the full area of each settlement (not just the land within farms) would, at constant 1962-3 prices, be as follows by around 1993: Kabisi £2.39; Lessos £7.57; Kipipiri £2.99; Passenga £4.50. None of these figures could be regarded as exceptional, and all may be easily attainable. The best way of dealing with productivity changes in the settlements is not easily determined. Assuming a 3 per cent increase from the level of operating surplus in the maturity year may understate what could be expected to happen, especially where the surplus in the base year was very small, as for example at Kipipiri. Alternative rates of expansion were considered. In particular, that rate of expansion was found which would need to be sustained if each settlement were to show a positive NPV at the ARI in market prices when finance

[1] I.e. by either halving or doubling as appropriate.

[2] An AR of 1.0 seems a reasonable figure to use, in view of the average ARs of outputs and inputs excluding settlers' labour.

is not taken into account.[1] This consideration is not relevant at Lessos (see Table 16.4). However, for the other three settlements, the following figures apply:

	Expansion rate to give zero NPV at market values	Operating surplus per acre in finally stabilized year	
		Market Prices	*Accounting Prices*
Kabisi	8 per cent	£9.02	£21.90
Kipipiri	12 per cent	£4.12	£34.94
Passenga	4 per cent	£5.73	£ 5.77

The stabilized values of operating surplus arising from the expansions at Kipipiri and Passenga needed for these projects to become acceptable without associated finance should be attainable. However, under the assumptions made, this is less certain for the Kabisi plans.[2]

16.3 EVALUATION OF THE FOUR SETTLEMENTS IN PRACTICE

The treatment in this section of the results of evaluating the settlements as they actually developed follows a pattern similar to that for the plans. The main results are given in Table 16.6 with disaggregated values in Table 16.7.

In evaluating the settlement actuals, similar problems arose over the valuation of settlers' labour at market prices, and the projection of events beyond the levels of 1967-8, the last year for which we have specific figures. For family labour, a similar procedure to that used for the plans was followed. Constant

[1] In every case, the NPV at accounting prices without finance is positive at an expansion rate of 3 per cent.

[2] An alternative way of looking at the long-term effects would be to consider what level of operating surplus per acre (at constant prices) might ultimately be attainable, and how soon that level might be reached. A more rapid build-up to this level might then be forecast. The exponential increase method used is a slow means of reaching the final levels. More rapid expansion could give the same NPV while stabilizing at a lower long-term level of operating surplus. Our possibly pessimistic approach has been followed because there is no objective means of knowing what level of operating surplus might eventually be obtained.

values equal to the 1969 levels were taken for the alternative earnings of settlers.

For the projection of costs and output beyond 1967-8, three possibilities were considered. The first was that the 1967-8 levels of cost and output would persist indefinitely, adjustment being made only to remove the costs of those once-and-for-all establishment processes (installing water supply, survey for title, etc.) carried out in that year. This would be a very unrealistic view. The second possibility was that the corrected 1967-8 levels would continue indefinitely, but to allow for later cost and output changes that are known to have occurred or for

Table 16.6

Main results from the evaluation of the four settlements as actually developed

1967-8 Values

	With 3% Expansion				Without Expansion			
	With fin.		Without fin.		With fin.		Without fin.	
	NPV £'000	ROR % p.a.	NPV £'000	ROR % p.a.	NPV £'000	ROR % p.a.	NPV £'000	ROR % p.a.
Kabisi[a] (HD, LA)								
Market prices	-192	4.2	-352	3.5	-385	-100[b]	-546	-100
Accounting prices	-56	8.7	-216	6.8	-245	-100	-406	-100
Lessos: (LD, LA)								
Market prices	358	56.8	127	12.3	281	56.3	51	11.1
Accounting prices	242	inf.	12	10.2	198	inf.	-32	9.2
Kipipiri: (HD, HA)								
Market prices	121	inf.	-25	9.1	84	inf.	-62	7.3
Accounting prices	343	inf.	197	21.8	208	inf.	134	20.5
Passenga: (LD, HA)								
Market prices	204	inf.	-42	9.0	147	inf.	-98	7.1
Accounting prices	220	inf.	-25	9.0	184	inf.	-61	7.1

a. Expansions are of gross output, not annual surplus.
b. An ROR of -100 signifies that every year the Operating Surplus has a negative value. At any percentage discount rate below -100, the NPV is positive.

Table 16.7
Disaggregated NPVs for the settlements in practice

1967-8 Values £'000

	Kabisi		Lessos		Kipipiri		Passenga	
	MP	AP	MP	AP	MP	AP	MP	AP
I. *Present Values of major items*								
1. Output at 1967-8 levels[a]	676	711	994	1,080	770	872	1,116	1,181
2. All costs at 1967-8 levels except settlers' family labour and land[a]	−376	−368	−644	−596	−324	−309	−876	−806
3. Settlers' family labour	−736	−507	−223	−513	−392	−414	−168	−399
4. Land	−84	−220	−133	−99	−112	−11	−158	−27
5. Post-1967-8 changes	−26	−22	57	96	−4	−4	−12	−10
6. Financial flows of constant value	130	130	195	195	128	128	210	210
7. Financial flows of declining value	151	151	228	228	146	146	243	243
8. Post-1967-8 additional finance	8	8	2	2	0	0	2	2
9. Annual surplus[b] expanded at: 3%	194	190	76	44	37	63	56	36
5%	385	377	152	85	74	125	113	73
6%	508	497	200	112	99	166	150	87
7%	653	639	257	144	128	215	193	124
II. *NPVs of cost of settlers' labour under various assumptions*								
Settlers' family labour:								
10. At planned size with non-farm income allowed for	−363	3	−203	−574	−303	−268	−183	−329
11. At planned size, assuming no non-farm income	..	59	..	−598	..	−311	..	−367
12. At actual size, allowing for non-farm income, but assuming settlers' loans repaid in full	..	−468	..	−468	..	−390	..	−337
13. As in line 3, but settlers' extra benefits all given a weighting of 1.0	..	−501	..	−299	..	−285	..	−196

a. Recorded items measured as they occurred, but 1967-8 values used for all later years.

b. For Kabisi, gross output.

which adjustments could reasonably be made to individual items without allowing for associated variations in the levels of other costs. Particulars of these changes were given in Chapter 14. They include no changes in the volume of output or sales for anything other than tea, since changes in production (for which co-operative records give partial information) is probably associated with changes in inputs for which there is no matching information.

The third possible assumption is that, once a stable level was achieved, the operating surplus would increase each year at a steady expansion rate. As with the plans, a basic 3 per cent expansion was envisaged up to the year of the final financial outflow. This allows for the anticipated increases in productivity referred to in 16.2.1. Many of these would remain unrealized by 1967-8, especially those associated with water supply systems, which were by then only being planned or installed in the settlements studied.

16.3.1 *The main results*

The figures in Table 16.6 reflect the second and third of these possible situations. The values for 'with expansion' allow for both of the post-1967-8 adjustments mentioned, while those for 'without expansion' incorporate only known post-1967-8 changes.

The figures show that, at every level of evaluation, Kabisi was a most unsuccessful project. The degree of underfulfilment of the plans referred to in Chapter 14, particularly the shortfall in milk production, has led to this scheme (whose plan was only marginally profitable) becoming a very wasteful investment. With finance taken into account, all of the others turned out to be very profitable. However, if finance flows are ignored, the apparent rate of return at market prices on the two high altitude settlements was below the ARI.

Applying accounting values to the figures had a varied effect. Kabisi is shown to be better than the market price figures suggest, though still far from good. Kipipiri is far better in social terms than at market prices. At Passenga, the difference in evaluation between market and accounting prices was small, but at Lessos adjustment to accounting values worsened the result obtained at market prices. As is discussed in more detail in the next section, this was mainly because the sharp apparent increase in settlers' incomes meant that their social cost was far higher than their cost at 'market prices'.

In Table 16.6 there is no single column of figures that contains the most relevant evaluation figures. Those 'with expansion' are the most appropriate for Kabisi[1] and Lessos, but those without expansion are probably the most realistic for Kipipiri and Passenga.[2] As was made clear in Chapter 14, in 1967-8 both high altitude schemes were enjoying a 'pyrethrum boom'. Almost certainly, total output and the value of the operating surplus fell in the next few years. In view of the high levels of output obtained in 1967-8, it would be a significant achievement in both cases (but especially at Kipipiri) if output in the 1970s and beyond were expanded in such a way as to have a discounted effect similar to that of holding constant the 1967-8 levels. However, at this level, Kipipiri appears to have been in practice the most socially profitable of the four settlements studied, a fact that emphasizes the suitability of pyrethrum as a crop on high altitude, High Density settlements.

16.3.2 *The sensitivity of the results, and the disaggregated effects of using accounting prices*

Details of the NPV at market and accounting prices of output and different groups of costs are shown in Table 16.7. In large part, they reflect situations basically similar to those found for the plans. Substantially higher levels of output were obtained in the Low Density projects, being associated with high levels of costs other than labour and land. Family labour was more important absolutely and as a proportion of all costs in the High Density schemes, with land a relatively major cost feature only at Kabisi.

16.3.2.1 *Significance of the assumptions made*

The results are sensitive to only a few of the assumptions made. Taking account of post-1967-8 changes and a declining real value of finance, flows had relatively small effects; small also

[1] For Kabisi, Output has been 'expanded', not the operating surplus, since the latter was negative for every year up to and including the 'stability' level.

[2] The most relevant situation values are underlined in Table 16.6.

(except at Kabisi and Lessos) were the effects of expanding the annual surplus at 3 per cent per annum beyond the stability level of 1970-1 or thereabouts. As Table 16.6 shows, taking finance into account affected the results in an important way, but this factor was much less significant than the valuation of labour.[1]

16.3.2.2 *The effects of using Accounting Prices*

As was the case with the settlement plans, the use of accounting prices made only a small difference to the valuation of output. The same was broadly true of all 'other costs', although at Kabisi, the importance in total costs of superphosphates, maize seed, and cattle food resulted in a cost 23 per cent higher in social terms than at market prices. The effects of using accounting prices for land different from the market valuations are the same as for the settlement plans, the same land values having been used in both cases.[2]

The use of accounting prices had its main effect in influencing the cost of family labour. The effect naturally varied from scheme to scheme. At Kabisi, we estimate that family incomes fell substantially and permanently. So great was the fall that, as Table 16.2 showed, settlers experienced large negative total benefits during their first two years. Moreover, family size grew by 1967-8 to such a size that per capita income levels there were very close to the threshold level, and an income distribution weight close to 1.0 was applied to family benefits. As a result, the social cost was less than market price every year except 1964-5. In 1967-8, it was 40 per cent lower.

In the three other settlements, money incomes by 1967-8 had reached a level far beyond both the settlers' alternative earnings and the threshold per capita income level, so the social cost of family labour was higher than the market price. This

[1] Reducing the cost of settlers' family labour at market prices to 50 per cent of the assumed level, with neither finance nor expansions taken into account, would give the following RORs: Kabisi 1.1 (-100); Lessos 14.7 (11.1); Kipipiri 15.4 (7.3); Passenga 9.8 (7.1). These differ markedly from those obtained when the full cost of labour is taken (shown in parentheses), especially at Kabisi and Kipipiri.

[2] Small differences exist between the values of land at MP and AP in Tables 16.5 and 16.7 for two reasons: (i) Table 16.5 is expressed in 1962-3 values; and (ii) in most cases land purchase in practice was spread over two or three years. Summation for Table 16.7 involved the use of declining discount factors and inflation corrections.

effect was only slight at Kipipiri, but was very marked at Passenga, where high non-farm incomes reduced the social weighting given to extra benefits.

16.3.2.3 *Some further implications of the methods used to value family labour*

It is useful at this point to consider some features of the method used to calculate the social cost of family labour. In this calculation, the following assumptions, *inter alia*, were made.

(i) All people recorded as being resident on the farm were taken to be members of the farm household; all were potentially full-time small farm workers; and all shared in the benefits of the settlers' farming activities.

(ii) Non-farm income is earned by males, and their number is reduced to allow for this in calculating the value of alternative earnings foregone.[1] This makes the cost of settlers' labour less than would otherwise be the case.

(iii) As seems generally to have been true, it was taken that settlers paid only 50 per cent of repayment billings. Their income was thus higher than if they had paid their loans in full, and government's income was lower.

(iv) The weights given to extra benefits decline as income rises. As incomes increase, the extra resource costs are offset by increased benefits which are given a steadily decreasing weight.

The effects on the calculation of these different assumptions is interesting and is here considered for settlement in practice. This is done through reference to figures given in the lower part of Table 16.7.

(1) **Family size.** We have interpreted settlement planning as providing for only one man and one woman in each settlers' household. In practice, average households were often larger than this, especially at Kabisi. After allowing for non-farm

[1] However, all household members are counted in full when calculating and weighting benefits.

income, all remaining adults were regarded as 'costs' to the settlement schemes. This implies that all such people forgo other earning opportunities to devote their time to settlement farming. This may not be true. Some adults counted in the surveys in the farm household may not have been fit for work. The definition of 'farm residents' or 'farm households' is itself complex and unclear. Consequently some people may have been recorded as present on farms who were neither seeking work nor working. If people of this kind congregated on settlement farms, our method would exaggerate settlement costs. Although any alternative view has implications for our assessment of the value of each type of person's alternative earnings,[1] labour costs have been recalculated assuming that families were only of the planned size.

The aggregated PVs of settlers' labour costs calculated in this way (and with no allowance for non-farm income) are shown in line 10 of Table 16.7. Comparison of these figures with those in line 3 shows that this factor was very important at Kabisi, but was much less so on other schemes, where actual family sizes (after adjustment for non-farm income) were much closer to the planned size. At Kabisi the extent of the difference[2] was so great (373 at MP, 510 at AP) that taking this view would transform the main appraisal results, to make this seem a very profitable scheme.

Kipipiri would also look better, but on the Low Density schemes the effect of this factor on the weighting of benefits would outweigh any reduction in the cost of alternative earnings and would worsen their results.

An implication of this finding is that, where family size varies from year to year above a 'normal' level, evaluation should involve enquiring whether 'additional' people were required for farm operation; whether their alternative earnings were the same as those assumed for core members of the family; and whether they enjoyed a share of the benefits that settlement brought. There could be circumstances where to adjust the cost of family labour to allow for these factors would be justifiable.

[1] The values used throughout were designed to apply to settlers and their first wives and not necessarily to other adult members of their households, who may not have had the same earning opportunities open to them.

[2] It was so great at accounting values as to indicate an aggregate 'negative cost' for the NPV of settlers' labour.

(2) **Non-farm income.** It is conceivable that this income might have been obtained from rents or other 'unearned' sources, or that the time spent earning it had no true opportunity cost, in which case the adjustments for non-farm income would be invalid. The effect of ignoring non-farm income could be tested for households of actual or planned size. For illustration, we have used the latter to calculate the figures shown in Table 16.7 on line 11. In all of the three schemes where non-farm income was important the effect (cf. line 10) has been to increase the cost of family labour, but in the other case, Kabisi, the effect has been to increase the 'negative cost' of family workers. Small but higher alternative earnings are outweighed as costs by the higher weighting given to benefits.

(3) **Settlers' loan repayments.** The basic plan for both High and Low Density programmes was that the cost to the Kenya Government of foreign loans for land purchase and development assets should be recovered from the settlers themselves through equal annual payments for up to 30 years, each payment covering interest at 6.5 per cent and a steadily increasing capital repayment sum.

In practice, loan repayments have always been in arrears. Details of loan repayment for each scheme are not available,[1] and in estimating the cost of family labour a 50 per cent rate of repayment was assumed.[2] Actual billings were known.

The effect of under-repayment is to increase settlers' incomes, giving rise to higher consumption resource costs and offsetting benefits that are valued less highly than the numeraire unless incomes are very low. Thus, the higher the level of loan repayment, the lower the social cost of family labour. The strength of this effect will depend primarily on the income level and the associated benefit-weighting effect.

Line 12 of Table 16.7 shows what the cost of settlers' family

[1] Mention of loan repayment in individual schemes or groups of settlements is sometimes fortuitiously made in the Department's annual reports, especially if they are very low. Such a mention was made in the report for 1971 of a 7 per cent repayment for the year in the Lessos group.

[2] For loans with long amortisation periods, 50 per cent of billings in the first years would not cover the interest portion. A permanent repayment rate of 50 per cent implies a steadily rising outstanding capital sum and either a longer repayment period or increased annual billings.

labour would have been if settlers had repaid their loans in full. Comparison with line 3 shows that in every case the cost would be less, but not by much. The greatest difference, at Passenga, is only £62,000. The smallest difference, at Kipipiri, is only £24,000 or £46 per settler. The social appraisal of these settlements is not very sensitive to the level of loan repayment, at least so long as arrears remain at or near the levels of the years up to 1967-8.[1]

(4) **The weighting of benefits according to income.** This is a fundamental feature of our method for estimating the social cost of any type of labour, including particularly settlers' families. Making no income weighting adjustment produces the aggregate figures in Line 13 of Table 16.7.[2] Comparison with line 3 shows that this effect operates in an entirely predictable way. At Kabisi, where settlers' actual post-settlement incomes were lowest, there is practically no difference at all. In the other three schemes the difference is much greater, being most pronounced at Passenga, where weighting doubled the social costs of family workers.

16.3.2.4 *Alternative rates of expansion*

As with the settlement plans, calculations have been made to see what rate of expansion from the 'stability' levels of 1970-1 or thereabouts would give a zero NPV at 10 per cent when finance is not taken into account. As with the plans, this is not relevant to Lessos, nor to Kipipiri in accounting prices, but it is in all other cases. The relevant expansion rates are as follows:

[1] The loan billing and repayment system is such that unpaid arrears and interest on them are added to new billings. Calculation of the extra cost of this factor is based on only the first four years. If debts continued to mount, the cost of this factor would also increase.

[2] If benefits accruing to settlers are given the same weight as benefits accruing to the Government (i.e. 1.0) the social value of extra benefits is found by applying an AR of 0.87 to the market values shown in the last column but two.

	Expansion rate to give zero NPV	Operating surplus per acre in finally stabilized year	
		Market prices	*Accounting prices*
Market prices			
Kabisi[1]	7 per cent	£23.67	£28.76
Kipipiri	5 per cent	£ 5.61	£ 9.37
Passenga	5 per cent	£ 7.51	£ 4.82
Accounting prices			
Kabisi[1]	6 per cent	£16.77	£21.34
Passenga	5 per cent	£ 7.51	£ 4.82

While the final operating surplus values for Kipipiri and Passenga look plausible, those for Kabisi obviously are not!

16.4 COMPARING THE RESULTS FOR THE PLANS AND FOR ACTUAL DEVELOPMENT

Since this study covers four separate but not entirely dissimilar projects, it is interesting for the four schemes to be compared with each other at the different levels of appraisal, and for each settlement in practice to be compared with its plans. These comparisons are briefly made in this section, using figures shown in Table 16.8. They refer to the most relevant set of results for each appraisal.[2]

To remove any differences in NPV stemming from different sizes of project, the figures in the first part of the table are standardized into NPV per acre terms, area being taken as a relevant indicator of project size. This presentation reveals relationships between plans and actuals which may already have become evident. Kipipiri turned out better than was planned, while Kabisi in the event was very much worse than had been

[1] The expansion rates at Kabisi apply to Gross Output, not operating surplus.

[2] In every case this involves taking finance into account. For all scheme plans, and for Kabisi and Lessos actuals, 3 per cent expansions from the 'maturity' or 'stability' levels are also allowed for. For Kipipiri and Passenga, no expansions are considered.

Table 16.8
Summary figures to compare plan and actual situations in the four settlements

	Plans[a]		Actuals	
	Market prices	Accounting prices	Market prices	Accounting prices
1. *NPVs of Final Surplus £ per acre (1967-8 values)*				
Kabisi (HD, LA)	5.38	13.49	-15.64	-4.56
Lessos (LD, LA)	30.92	37.48	25.31	17.11
Kipipiri (HD, HA)	0.64	22.75	6.81	20.75
Passenga (LD, HA)	17.21	29.33	10.83	13.55
2. *NPV/Land Value Ratios*				
Kabisi: Land MP	1.81	3.03	-1.29	-1.95
AP	0.69	1.16	-0.49	0.75
Lessos: Land MP	3.98	4.36	3.69	2.56
AP	5.38	5.89	4.96	3.44
Kipipiri: Land MP	1.07	2.78	1.82	2.59
AP	10.10	26.10	17.00	24.27
Passenga: Land MP	2.38	2.52	1.93	2.16
AP	14.40	15.24	11.30	12.67

a. Plan NPV values were converted to 1967-8 values from 1962-3 values by applying the inflation correction factor of 1÷0.894.

hoped, settlers there having never had the opportunity to fulfil the plans. Neither Lessos nor Passenga were likely to fulfil their plans under the assumptions made. Nevertheless in per acre terms these Low Density settlements were far more productive than the others.

The figures in the top half of the table also provide a first basis for comparing individual settlements with each other. In terms of social profit per acre, there is a clear ranking: Kipipiri, Lessos, Passenga, Kabisi. But it may be asked whether this simple per acre comparison is really valid, since it does not take into account quality of land. This obviously relevant factor should be allowed for.

Since land in the four areas was not of similar quality, how can this element be accommodated? The simplest way would be to assume that market values reflected relative quality. However, as was shown in Chapter 15, actual values in the only situation for which there is a clear indication of a free price (i.e. 1959 values) bore no relation to potential profitability. Use of those values would not provide a fair reflection of land quality, measured in social terms. The alternative values calculated for this study provide a far better indication of possible quality in use. However, they may be open to criticism in some respects.

To accommodate the point, project net benefits have been related to both estimates of land values, which can be regarded as extreme high and low estimates. At Kabisi the accounting price (AP) estimate is the higher of the two values, but in every other case the opposite is true.

This procedure gives the figures in the lowest part of Table 16.8, where the NPVs of the operating surplus without land are related to the two estimates of land value. The ratios should indicate which schemes made the best use of their land. Not surprisingly, the ranking order of the four projects varies between plan and actuals; between different land value estimates; and between market and accounting prices. However, taking an average of the ratios for the two land values gives the following ranking, running down from best to poorest:

Plans		Actuals	
Market Prices	*Accounting Prices*	*Market Prices*	*Accounting Prices*
Passenga	Kipipiri	Kipipiri	Kipipiri
Kipipiri	Passenga	Passenga	Passenga
Lessos	Lessos	Lessos	Lessos
Kabisi	Kabisi	Kabisi	Kabisi

In every ranking, the high altitude schemes show up better than the two at low altitude. Although Kabisi—the High Density, low altitude scheme—shows up in every measure as being the least successful, it must be remembered that settlers there never had the same opportunity of meeting their potential that others enjoyed. The fact that they were never allocated for purchase the planned number of cows must cloud any judgement about the success of that scheme, although the implication of the plan results suggests that allowing for this factor would not have altered any ranking.

CHAPTER 17

An Evaluation of the Low and High Density Settlement Programmes as a Whole

17.1 INTRODUCTION

In Chapter 16 the four chosen settlements were appraised, both as planned and as operated in practice. Although the schemes covered were selected to be typical of the major types being developed in 1962 and 1963, they were not 'average' settlements, and they throw only limited light on the relative virtues of the two main types. Comparison between the two types based on these examples has limited validity, especially in view of the distinctive way that each settlement worked out. Consequently, it seemed worth making an evaluation of the High Density and Low Density settlements as a whole. That is the subject of this chapter.

A comparison of the two programmes might, in principle, be useful in deciding which approach had been the 'best' use of the land in the sense of giving the highest social return. A principal difficulty in using overall evaluations for making such a judgement is the fact that they do not combine different farming situations in the same proportions. There is, to give a simple example, more tea in Low than in High Density settlements, because the Low Density schemes contained more tea land. The differences between the programmes are not just size of farm and level of development assistance to farmers. To some extent, they also cover different farming areas and systems, a difference that is reflected in both the programmes as a whole and in the coverage of the economic surveys, the main data source. But valid as the point is, it is not an overwhelming objection. The comparison of aggregates should allow some interesting conclusions to be drawn.

Schemes in both programmes differ from each other a great deal. The portrayal of an 'average' composite High or Low

Density settlement involves suggesting a combination of enterprises that would not be possible in one place. However, numeric details of an average scheme in practice can be obtained from the average survey results. The extent of variation between schemes and their large number prevented any estimates from being made of the profitability of the plans for the average settlement of each type. Consequently, this chapter is concerned only with the average settlement as actually developed.

This evaluation can be undertaken only because detailed aggregated information is available from the economic surveys of settlement farms, as presented in the Settlement Appraisal Report. These surveys covered the four years 1964-5 to 1967-8. Accordingly, figures have been built up of an imaginary composite settlement of each type, taken to be experiencing its first full farming year in 1964-5. This implies land valuation in 1962-3, and purchase and preparation of the site in the following year.

Information on those items of cost for which details are not given in the Appraisal Report has been taken from the sources discussed in Appendices A.14 and B.14 in ways similar to those for the four schemes. However, there is no information from either source on co-operative society costs and sales, only of farm costs and incomes. Consequently, in this chapter, the co-operatives have been excluded: nothing is counted for their costs, and all sale values are amounts received by the farmers.[1]

17.2 DEVELOPMENT OF THE 'AVERAGE' LOW DENSITY SETTLEMENT

Figures given in the annual reports of the Department and elsewhere show that the average Low Density settlement[2] was developed from four large farms. It was 5,101 acres in extent, which were purchased at an average cost of £10.66 per acre.

[1] The limitations referred to in Appendix B.14 on the accuracy of these records thus apply.

[2] The average figures taken are the simple averages of all schemes of each type covered by each data source. No attempt is made here to calculate averages for the sample of schemes included each year in the economic surveys.

When developed, it contained 142 plots, which allows 35 acres per plot.

The development of farming systems is shown in the first part of Table 17.1. When allowance is made for the land in each settlement outside farms, the average size of farm covered by the surveys each year in 1964-5 and 1966-7 is close to the overall average, although in the second and last years the surveys seem to have given undue coverage to small farms. The area cropped increased steadily up to 1966-7, but in 1967-8 all crops except vegetables and pyrethrum were cut back. Livestock numbers also fluctuated, but the number of cows per farm was always relatively high, and these farms were quite densely stocked.

Recorded family size increased very little over the four years. This is particularly true of the number of adult members, but child numbers were more variable. Non-farm income also increased constantly and steeply until by 1967-8 earnings from this source *averaged* almost £178 per farm. Clearly many Low Density settlers were much more than just farmers! Allowing for time spent earning this income reduces the number of men effectively employed by 57 per cent in 1967-8. As a result the cost of family labour imputed to the schemes was relatively low.

This cost, and all others attributable to the average settlement, is shown in Table 17.2. This table is very similar in composition to Table 14.3; the origins of the figures are explained in the notes to the table. By 1967-8, recurrent costs (i.e. all those shown except Water Supply and Survey for Title) were running at £6.50 per acre, of which 59 per cent were recurrent farming costs.

The annual value of output is shown in Table 17.3. Milk and butterfat accounted for more than half the value of production in 1967-8, with pyrethrum, maize and increases in the value of cattle the other main products. Pyrethrum was particularly prominent that year, but the plantation crops sugar and tea were not important.

The annual values of output and costs up to 1967-8 are related in Table 17.3. Not until the last of the years shown (during which establishment expenditures were still being made) did the value of output exceed costs, and then by only a small

Table 17.1

Farming patterns and family composition in the 'average' Low Density farm

			1964-5	1965-6	1966-7	1967-8
1. *Farming Systems*						
Land Use:	Maize		2.33	3.15	4.28	3.26
(Acres)	Pyrethrum		0.55	0.77	0.42	0.44
	Wheat		0.17	0.19	0.11	0.09
	Potatoes and Vegetables		0.42	0.77	0.28	0.66
	Tea		0.14	0.06	0.28	0.09
	Sugar		-	-	0.81	0.56
	Other crops		0.47	0.28	0.23	0.06
	Total crops		4.08	5.22	6.41	5.16
	Other land		30.22	25.68	28.99	26.14
	Total farm size		34.30	30.90	35.40	31.30
Livestock Numbers:						
	Dairy cows		5.7	3.5	3.8	5.2
	Other dairy cattle		4.8	2.8	3.7	3.4
	Beef cattle		2.3	1.0	1.5	1.3
	Sheep and goats		1.4	1.9	1.4	1.5
	Poultry		7.5	2.8	4.8	8.0
2. *Family Size*						
Residents per Farm:						
	Men		1.1	1.3	1.2	1.3
	Women		1.0	1.0	1.2	1.3
	Children		3.7	2.3	3.3	3.4
	Total		5.8	4.6	5.7	6.0
Non-farm income:		Sh.	967	1,325	2,600	3,552
Non-available men[a]			0.20	0.28	0.54	0.74

Sources: *Settlement Appraisal*, Tables B.13, B.14, B.16 and B.25.
a. Estimated in the way described in 5.2.

margin.[1] Taking finance flows into account does make a considerable difference, however, but even then only a small positive final surplus remained in 1967-8, despite a large inflow that year.

[1] With co-operative marketing activities not taken into account, the operating surplus shown in Table 17.6 gives a lower value than would arise if the methods of Chapter 14 were followed. Normally co-operatives make a small surplus to build up their reserves.

Table 17.2

Costs attributable up to 1967-8 to the 'average' Low Density settlement

Market Values (£)

Current Values	1962-3	1963-4	1964-5	1965-6	1966-7	1967-8
Land valuation	424	-	-	-	-	-
Land purchase	-	54,377	-	-	-	-
Pre-settlement development	-	7,692	-	-	-	-
Legal fees	-	1,420	-	-	-	-
Scheme supervision	-	1,062	4,250	4,250	3,012	2,600
Field overhead supervision	-	663	2,653	2,653	1,658	1,326
Headquarters over-head supervision	-	895	3,580	3,580	2,685	2,386
Water supply	-	-	-	-	-	4,544
Recurrent costs of farming	-	-	18,914	17,849	17,374	19,575
Survey for title	-	-	-	-	-	1,530
Settlers' labour	-	-	8,080	8,778	7,108	6,739
Cows	-	-	24,282	-	-	-
Other costs	-	-	218	386	496	550
Total	424	66,109	61,977	37,496	32,333	39,250

Sources: Land Valuation: Average actual costs, as explained in App.A.13.
Land Purchase: D. of S. Annual Report 1970; average for all Low Density schemes.
Pre-settlement development: Average actual costs, as explained in App.A.14.
Legal fees: 'Typical' Low Density charges.
Supervision: Financial Controller's figures for typical schemes, as explained in App.A.13.
Water supply: D. of S. Annual Report 1970, App. A. Based on cost of water systems installed up to June 1969, and the total area of Low Density schemes.
Farming costs: Settlement Appraisal, Tables 4.7, 4.8 and B.22.
Survey for title:, Details of schemes finalized and mapped given in D. of S. Annual Report 1969.
Settlers' labour: Table 17.1 and alternative earnings; men £41, women £15, subsistence plots £5.
Cows: 1964-5 numbers in Table 17.1.
Other costs: KTDA charges for all settlements each year related to total Low Density acreage.

By 1967-8, the last year for which comprehensive data can be prepared, most establishment costs in these settlements had been completed, or were being made. However, for the years after, allowance has to be made for uncompleted water supply systems, steadily increasing 'other costs' associated with tea development and higher settlement supervision costs after 1968-9.

Table 17.3

Output, finance flows and surpluses up to 1967-8 in the 'average' Low Density settlement

			Market Values		Market Values (£)	
	1962-3	1963-4	1964-5	1965-6	1966-7	1967-8
Output						
Maize	-	-	2,876	2,734	4,359	3,649
Potatoes	-	-	1,598	2,428	1,456	1,214
Pyrethrum	-	-	639	2,428	2,038	5,268
Vegetables	-	-	319	909	582	809
Other crops	-	-	639	2,123	2,329	809
Milk and butterfat	-	-	19,482	13,966	13,959	21,066
Net cattle sales	-	-	-3,515	-1,825	-	-
Stock increase	-	-	9,266	6,681	3,777	6,887
Other livestock	-	-	639	909	575	809
Total	-	-	31,943	30,353	29,075	40,513
Costs	424	66,109	61,977	37,496	32,333	39,250
Operating surplus	-424	-66,109	-30,034	-7,143	-3,258	1,263
Finance flows	424	64,689	58,281	4,178	-3,685	-534
Final surplus	0	1,420	28,247	-2,965	-6,943	729

Source: Output: *Settlement Appraisal*, Tables 4.6 and B.17.
: Finance Flows: Appendix A.15 and Chapter 15.

17.3 DEVELOPMENT OF THE 'AVERAGE' HIGH DENSITY SETTLEMENT

High Density settlements were typically much bigger than Low Density schemes. The average size was 9,863 acres which, before settlement, had made up roughly 7.5 large farms. These were purchased for settlement at an average cost of £10.58 per acre, almost exactly the same as for Low Density land. The average High Density scheme had 352 farms, which gives 28 acres per farm, over 20 per cent less than the average Low Density farm.

Details of the development of farming in the average surveyed High Density scheme are shown in Table 17.4. Mean farm size each year was remarkably constant. The total area under crops increased steadily from 1965-6. Maize was by far the most important crop, despite the large number of high altitude schemes of this kind included in the surveys.[1] Pyrethrum and vegetables were the other most important crops, although some High Density settlers tried wheat in 1967-8. Plantation crops (sisal in the first two years, sugar in the last two) were not very important in the High Density programme by the last year of survey. Dairy cow numbers increased slowly but steadily, but by 1967-8 grazing land in these schemes was far less closely stocked than were the Low Density farms.

The numbers of adults in each farm household increased steadily from year to year reflecting the pattern already observed at Kabisi and Kipipiri. Recorded non-farm incomes were small by comparison with Low Density farms, but in the last two years of survey average income from these sources was higher than the target income from farming for very many High Density farms.

The year-by-year composition of costs for the 'average' scheme is shown in Table 17.5. Unlike the Low Density case, the cost of settlers' family labour was by far the biggest item. In 1967-8, this item constituted 56 per cent of all costs. By then, recurrent farm costs had stabilized. All recurrent scheme expenses[2] were then running at a rate of £5.63 per acre.

Output figures are given in Table 17.6. The importance of milk production and cattle as a whole in the settlement schemes is again emphasized, the latter being especially important in 1967-8. Maize, pyrethrum and potatoes were the most important products of the cultivated land, but crops of all kinds accounted for only 42 per cent of output.

[1] Maize was not a suitable crop for most 'high altitude' areas.

[2] I.e. excluding water supply and survey for title.

Table 17.4

Farming patterns and family composition in the 'average' High Density Settlement

			1964-5	1965-6	1966-7	1967-8
1. *Farming systems*						
Land use:	Maize		1.45	1.70	3.03	2.99
(acres)	Pyrethrum		0.45	0.53	0.61	0.87
	Wheat		0.14	0.15	0.16	0.41
	Potatoes and vegetables		0.83	0.45	0.45	0.49
	Plantation crops		0.02	0.02	0.07	0.14
,	Other crops		0.25	0.27	0.31	0.04
	Total crops		3.14	3.12	4.63	4.94
	Other land		20.66	18.98	18.87	19.16
	Total farm size		23.80	22.10	23.50	24.10
Livestock numbers:						
	Dairy cows		1.7	1.6	2.2	2.4
	Other dairy cattle		1.3	1.3	2.2	2.0
	Beef cattle		0.5	0.6	0.9	0.6
	Sheep and goats		2.7	2.2	1.6	2.4
	Poultry		4.1	3.5	4.2	9.1
2. *Family size*:						
:	Men		1.0	1.4	1.6	1.8
	Women		1.1	1.3	1.5	1.6
	Children		3.5	2.8	3.5	3.6
	Total		5.6	5.5	6.6	7.0
Non-farm income:		Sh.	328	394	625	621
Non-available men			0.09	0.11	0.17	0.17

Sources: *Settlement Appraisal*, Tables B.13, B.14, B.16 and B.25.

Output and costs are related in the lower part of Table 17.6. After years of deficit during the establishment period, a positive operating surplus was achieved in 1967-8, when output exceeded costs by one-eighth, or £0.72 per acre.

The annual operating deficit in the first five years was largely covered by the net financial inflow, and only relatively small negative final surpluses arose. However, by 1967-8 the repayment by the Government of loans drawn to finance the

Table 17.5

Costs attributable up to 1967-8 to the 'average' High Density Settlement

Market values (£)

Current Values	1962-3	1963-4	1964-5	1965-6	1966-7	1967-8
Land valuation	795	-	-	-	-	-
Land purchase	-	104,378	-	-	-	-
Pre-settlement development	-	14,873	-	-	-	-
Legal fees	-	1,760	-	-	-	-
Scheme supervision	-	1,137	4,550	4,550	3,462	3,100
Field overhead supervision	-	663	2,653	2,653	1,658	1,326
Headquarters overhead supervision	-	895	3,580	3,580	2,685	2,386
Settler subsistence	-	6,336	-	-	-	-
Water supply	-	-	-	-	-	596
Recurrent costs of farming	-	-	16,755	15,418	18,638	17,846
Survey for title	-	-	-	-	-	63
Settlers' labour	-	-	18,897	24,957	27,724	30,891
Cows	-	-	17,952	-	5,280	-
Total	795	130,042	64,387	51,158	59,447	56,202

Sources: All items as for Table 17.2 except for Settler Subsistence, which is calculated as discussed in Appendix A.14.

settlements had reached a level that exceeded the operating surplus, and a negative final surplus remained. By then, however, the installation of water supply systems and survey for title were unstarted or uncompleted on the majority of High Density settlements, and it has been taken (possibly optimistically for the purpose of making projections beyond 1967-8) that they would both be completed by 1970-1.

17.4 A COMPARISON OF THE TWO AVERAGE SITUATIONS

Summary figures have been brought together in Table 17.7, which allow the two situations to be compared. Those in the

Table 17.6

Output, finance flows and surpluses up to 1967-8 in the 'average' High Density settlement

Market values (£)

	1962-3	1963-4	1964-5	1965-6	1966-7	1967-8
Output						
Maize	-	-	2,658	3,784	10,120	10,138
Potatoes	-	-	4,435	5,174	5,614	5,702
Pyrethrum	-	-	880	4,822	5,614	7,603
Vegetables	-	-	1,338	1,725	2,253	1,901
Other crops	-	-	1,109	686	563	1,267
Milk and butterfat	-	-	7,533	11,370	24,165	22,158
Net cattle sales	-	-	-3,538	-1,725	563	-
Cattle value increase	-	-	7,093	7,920	6,178	13,939
Other livestock	-	-	651	686	1,126	616
Total	-	-	22,158	34,443	56,197	63,325
Costs	795	130,042	64,387	51,158	59,447	56,202
Operating surplus	-795	-130,042	-42,229	-16,715	-3,250	7,123
Finance flow	795	128,282	39,005	11,803	-43	-7,702
Final surplus	0	-1,760	-3,224	-4,912	-3,293	-579

Source: Output: *Settlement Appraisal*, Tables 4.6 and B.17.
Finance Flows: Appendix A.15 and Chapter 15.

first section show only the value of loans given to settlers, the only part of capitalization for which there is information.[1] Although they probably underestimate total capitalization on Low Density farms more than on High Density, they re-emphasize one of the biggest differences between the two types of scheme, namely the much bigger development loans given to Low Density farmers. High Density settlers carried a similar land loan repayment burden, but were provided with fewer development assets, and were expected to obtain much lower personal incomes from farming.

Further differences are reflected in the lower part of Table

[1] On High Density farms this would be the major portion of all 'capital' sums involved. On Low Density farms, additional investment would have been made from special tea development loans; from settlers' qualifying capital; and from farm profits and other private capital sources.

Table 17.7

Summary details of loans for the average Low and High Density schemes, and the operating situation in 1967-8

Current market values (£)

	Low Density		High Density	
	per farm	per acre	per farm	per acre
1. *'Capitalization' up to 1967-8*				
Land Cost	383	10.66	297	10.58
Development Loans	407	11.33	136	4.85
Total	790	21.99	433	15.43
2. *Recurrent costs and output values in 1967-8*				
Supervision	44.45	1.24	19.35	0.69
Recurrent farm costs	137.85	3.84	50.70	1.81
Settlers' labour	47.46	1.32	87.76	3.13
Others	3.87	0.11	—	—
All expenses	233.63	6.50	157.80	5.63
Sale produce	136.94	3.81	68.36	2.44
Stock value increase	68.47	1.91	57.57	2.05
Subsistence	79.88	2.22	,53.97	1.93
Total output	285.30	7.94	179.90	6.42
Operating value surplus	51.67	1.44	22.10	0.79
Acres per farm	35.92		28.02	

Source: *Settlement Appraisal*, Tables B.13, B.14, B.16 and B.25.

17.7, where recurrent costs in 1967-8 are detailed. Recurrent farm costs per acre (of which 29 per cent was wage payments to employees) were more than twice as high on the Low Density schemes as on the others, and this factor, together with the greater availability of productive assets, gave rise to higher levels of output. Also reflecting the basic nature of each type, the supervision input was higher on the Low Density farms, but the cost of family labour was much less. To a marked degree, these two types of settlement reflect a capital-and-management-intensive approach on the one hand and a labour-intensive approach on the other.

17.5 EVALUATION OF THE AVERAGE SETTLEMENTS

For evaluation, the two average settlements have been treated in the same way as were the four settlement actuals (see 16.3). Each case has been considered at market and at accounting values, with and without finance, and with and without an expansion in the value of the operating surplus beyond the level of 1967-8.

The conversion from market to accounting prices is based on the Accounting Ratios of Tables 10.1 and 10.2 for all items except Settlers' Family Labour and Land. The first of these has been treated in a way analogous to that used for estimating its social cost in the four individual settlements.[1]

Deriving an AR for land was less straightforward. The method used earlier in this study was based on calculations for the most likely alternative use of land of the kind on which particular settlements were located. This method cannot be applied to all land covered by the two programmes, so large and varied is each. But, as Chapter 15 showed, there is no consistent relationship between the cost at market and accounting prices that could be used as a guide. The best that could be done was to take the weighted average relationship between accounting and market prices for the four schemes for which accounting prices were individually estimated. This gives an AR of 0.67, which has been used for both types of settlement.

NPV and ROR results from the evaluation are shown in the first part of Table 17.8. The 'most relevant' results are those shown on the first two lines—with finance and with expansion. These show small positive NPVs for each type of settlement on each value basis. However, if the special financial features of these programmes are ignored, both types show poor results and low RORs at both market and accounting prices.[2]

[1] The cost of this item for the two average settlements in 1967-8 was calculated in detail in Chapter 5 in the exposition of the method.

[2] The extraordinary nature of the RORs for Low Density calls for some comment. For these schemes, the annual operating surplus is very close to zero. Consequently,

Table 17.8

Results from the evaluation of average Low and High Density settlements

1967-8 Prices (£'000)

		Low Density		High Density	
		Market prices	Accounting prices	Market prices	Accounting prices
1. *Main Result*					
With 3% Expansion:					
With finance	NPV	36	0	13	95
	ROR	inf.	3.4	13.4	inf.
Without finance	NPV	-56	-92	-141	-59
	ROR	5.9	1.6	4.6	7.4
Without Expansion:					
With finance	NPV	24	-2	0	73
	ROR	inf.	1.6	9.8	inf.
Without finance	NPV	-68	-94	-154	-81
	ROR	4.3	1.0	3.0	5.6
2. *Disaggregated PVs*					
Output at 1967-8 levels		385	415	571	622
All costs except family labour and land at 1967-8 levels		-315	-300	-322	-295
Settlers' family labour		-72	-164	-294	-331
Land		-54	-36	-104	-70
Post 1967-8 changes		-12	-9	-8	-7
Financial flows of constant value		72	72	112	112
Financial flows of declining value		92	92	151	151
Post 1967-8 addition-al finance		1	1	3	3
1970-1 operating surplus expanded at:	3%	11	2	13	22
	5%	23	4	27	44
	7%	36	7	48	77
	9%	55	10	78	127
3. *PVs of settlers' family labour under various assumptions*					
Families of standard size, with no non-farm income allowance		-87	-148	-197	-301
Families of actual size, but assuming loans repaid in full		..	-146	..	-301

An interesting feature of the main results is that the conversion from market to accounting prices has made the Low Density schemes look worse, while the converse is true of High Density. As may be seen from the second part of the table, this is entirely attributable to the treatment of the cost of family labour. As the earlier examples might lead one to expect, the social cost of 'other' inputs is less than the market value in both cases. Also total output is consistently valued more highly at accounting than at market prices. But both of these changes are slight. So also is the change in value of the cost of settlers' family labour in the High Density scheme, where the extra benefits received by settlers have been given a relatively high social value which largely offsets the extra resource costs. On the Low Density settlements, however, settlers are made a lot better off as a consequence of settlement. Their extra resource costs are high, but incremental benefits are not valued highly, with the result that the PV of their social cost is more than double their 'market price' cost.

The effects of variation in the level of any main item of costs or of output can be gauged from the figures in the second part of Table 17.8. With the NPVs in the most relevant results so close to 0, the result is obviously sensitive to relatively small changes in the valuation or AR used for almost any item. For example, valuing land at its purchase price would reduce the NPV at accounting prices on the average Low Density schemes by £18,000, and so give a negative NPV of that amount.

With such a small operating surplus in both cases in the 'stability' year, expansion at fairly high rates has only small NPV effects. At 9 per cent (the highest expansion rate tested), the situations without finance taken into account would be as follows:

---

a small change in any long-run value (such as applies to the period after 1967-8) can convert an almost continuous stream of small positive undiscounted values to smaller positives or to a continuous stream of negatives. While this has a small effect on NPV, it has a dramatic effect on ROR over a very narrow range of final surplus values. For example, at accounting prices with expansion and finance, the NPV (rounded to the nearest £1,000) is 0, but the ROR is 3.4 per cent, and not a value close to 10 per cent as would be expected. With an expansion rate of 5 per cent, the rounded total NPV is 2, but the ROR is infinite: the final surplus is positive every year, although in most years only by a very small amount. This is another of those circumstances where the ROR can be a very poor guide to the value of a project.

		Low Density	High Density
Market Values:	NPV	£-12,000	£-76,000
	ROR	9.4	8.1
Operating Surplus per acre at final stability level		£ 8.51	£ 9.56
Accounting Values:	NPV	£-84,000	£ 46,000
	ROR	3.9	11.1
Operating Surplus per acre at final stability level		£ 1.66	£ 15.37

These figures suggest that, for them to be judged successful if undertaken without special external finance, each type of average scheme would have to show a rate of progress beyond the stability level whose effect was greater than a steady annual rate of 9 per cent per annum. This especially applies to the evaluation of the Low Density schemes at accounting prices.

The effects of varying some features of the method used to estimate the social cost of family labour are also shown in the final section of Table 17.8. Taking families as being of standard size throughout, and ignoring non-farm income, would make Low Density families most costly at market values,[1] but less costly at accounting values. In view of the larger family size on the High Density schemes, this adjustment would lead to a substantial reduction in 'market prices' cost but a smaller reduction in social value terms.

The effects of assuming that loan repayments would be made at the full rate is shown in the last figures in the table. As was found with the four individual settlements, this change would lead to a reduction in the cost of family labour in both cases, and would thus improve their social profitability, although the extent of the difference is small.

17.6 COMMENT

The comparative results shown in Table 17.8 have interesting and significant implications. Evaluation at market prices

[1] This is because the non-farm income adjustment left 'residual' families whose cost was less than that for the average family.

indicates that, in every situation, Low Density schemes were better than High Density. However, at accounting prices (which we consider to be more relevant), the opposite judgement would be made. The ordering of the results is mainly influenced by the treatment of the cost of settlers' family labour. Obviously a social evaluation of the effects of different patterns of structural design for technically similar types of small-scale farming will be susceptible to the treatment of this item.

A number of possible treatments of this item may be considered from the viewpoint of their effect on ranking the two alternative types of scheme when appraised at accounting prices.

(1) Cost of family workers ignored or set at zero: High Density, Low Density.
(2) Family workers costed at value of alternative earnings, with extra benefits ignored: Low Density, High Density.
(3) All social cost and benefit factors taken into account, but no income-based weightings applied to extra benefits: equal ranking.
(4) The full method used for determining the social cost of family labour: High Density, Low Density.

The method devised for calculating accounting prices for Kenya was designed to reflect our interpretation of the social-value implications of the policy statements and actions of the Government. Accordingly, from the viewpoints both of what we regard as the proper methodology for costing family workers, and of the 'normative' adjustment made on realistic grounds to reflect national income-distribution values, the last ranking is the most relevant.

As a final point, comment should be made on the general levels of social profitability indicated by this evaluation. If the ARI is correct, and the view is also taken that *all* external financial flows should be taken into account as integral features of each project, then both High and Low Density settlements could be regarded as socially valuable, but Low Density is only at the margin of acceptance on a NPV basis. Without finance, both programmes are shown to be socially unprofitable.

However, in view of the uncertain way in which land has been valued at social prices, it is probably unjustified to accept the logical implication of these results and to say that, on the whole, large-scale farming by Europeans was more valuable socially than either form of settlement. A strong conclusion on the social profitability of the settlement programmes as a whole could only be reached after a more exacting study than has been presented in this chapter.

PART III

A FEASIBILITY STUDY OF INTENSIVE CATTLE BREEDING

by
D.M.G. Newberry

CHAPTER 18

Introduction, Summary and Background

18.1 INTRODUCTION: THE BEEF INDUSTRY DEVELOPMENT PROJECT

In the first few years after Independence the Kenya Government gave highest priority in the rural sector to the orderly transfer of land from expatriates to its own people, and started a major settlement scheme which forms the subject of Part II of this volume. By the time of the second Five-Year Plan, published in 1969 for the period 1970-4, the emphasis had changed. Agriculture was still to be accorded high priority, as is appropriate in a country where the majority of the population still live in the country and work in agriculture, but the process of land transfer was to give way to a more productively oriented programme of development. The Second Plan called for an increase in the quantity and quality of inputs into agriculture–more education, extension, fertilizers, new seeds–and the more efficient use of existing resources, particularly the increasingly scarce land. Marketing and handling facilities were to be improved and the economy was to be more export-oriented, with internal prices gradually adjusting to export parity levels. As part of this general programme the government was concerned to increase the efficiency of the livestock industry by reducing the time taken to bring cattle to maturity for slaughter, by improving the transport of cattle from range areas to the slaughter house and by transferring immature cattle from marginal areas to areas of greater potential, reducing the number of premature deaths and increasing the weight of beef produced per animal. To this end the Kenya Government, with the assistance of the United Nations Development Programme and the Food and Agriculture Organization, set up the Kenya Beef Industry Development

Project, 'to determine the optimum intensive stock feeding and management techniques for increasing beef production, both for domestic and export markets'.[1]

In order to gather the necessary information and experience the Project set up the Beef Research Station at Lanet (120 km north west of Nairobi) in 1969. The basic strategy guiding the research is quickly described, and has two strands. Historically, the livestock industry, like much of the agricultural sector, was divided into a traditional and a modern commercial sector. Most of the cattle in the country grazed in the semi-arid areas which comprise some four-fifths of Kenya's land area. These cattle were primarily for subsistence consumption: they put on weight slowly, many died prematurely, and those cattle which were sold were underweight and of poor quality. At the time of the Second Plan they were slaughtered in this condition, and their low value represented a very poor yield on the considerable capital invested in the national herd. The commercial sector mainly consisted of large ranches, mostly managed by European farmers, with higher rainfall and better grazing than the semi-arid range lands. Most have breeding herds, either of crossbreds (European breeds crossed with the native Zebu)[2] or of the native Zebu types which have been improved by selective breeding. Their aim was to produce heavier carcases of higher grade beef for sale and their off-take (the proportion of the herd sold each year) was significantly higher than in the traditional sector. At the same time the country produced in normal years an export surplus of maize, which with the high transport costs both to the port and from there to the world markets yielded a low price to the grower. If the young immature cattle from the pastoral areas could be transferred to the better grazing of the commercial ranches they would put on weight faster and stand a higher chance of survival. They would also reach a higher quality, but as things stood they would compete with breeding herds for the scarce grazing land. However, if cattle could be transferred from these ranches still as immatures and fattened in feed lots the number of cattle passing through the ranches could increase substantially. The logic of the feedlot, which is a small pen holding between 50

1 W. Schaefer-Kehnert, 1971.

2 A glossary of technical terms and abreviations is provided on p. 535.

and 100 head with stall feeding, is that higher rainfall land is used to grow a crop—in this case maize—which can be harvested and fed to the cattle. The feed can be designed to give a high rate of weight gain which results in a fairly heavy carcass of high quality meat from a young animal. This in turn leads to a higher throughput of cattle per hectare of land used. Instead of cattle spending their whole life in the same environment, at each stage they are moved to a place and provided with feed which yields increases in weight at minimum cost or of maximum value.

The other aspect of the research strategy was more speculative. Kenya was devoting considerable resources to operating a Disease Free Area (DFA) centred on the high potential agricultural zone (see Map on pp. xxvi-vii). All cattle movements within the DFA were under veterinary control, and all cattle entering had to be innoculated and screened for contagious diseases, particularly foot-and-mouth. Such freedom from disease is necessary if high yielding exotic and crossbred cattle are to be economic, as many of the endemic cattle diseases lead to a dramatic decline in productivity. Very crudely, it was argued that the indigenous (Zebu) cattle had good disease tolerance, but rather low productivity, whilst exotic cattle, though more productive, were less tolerant, and their productivity was more vulnerable to disease. The solution was to specialize, and the DFA emerged as a further distinction between the traditional and modern commercial sector. The DFA conferred additional advantages in permitting the export of chilled and frozen beef, but in 1970 Kenya was still excluded from the European chilled beef market. At that time prices in Europe were appreciably above those in the markets available to Kenyan exports, and there was considerable incentive to find a means of gaining access to the high price European market. Feedlots offered such a possibility as they would permit very close quarantine control of cattle over an extended period, and it was hoped that the combination of quarantine feedlots within a well-established Disease Free Area would prove adequate to satisfy the European Veterinary authorities. This aspect is discussed in greater detail in 18.7.2.

Thus the hypothesis was that the Kenyan beef industry might derive two advantages from specialization (or stratification in the parlance of the Ministry of Agriculture; increased productivity from the national herd, and access to new and more valuable markets. Specialization would make use of the comparative advantage different areas possessed in the production of different kinds of beef as follows.

The semi-arid areas have a comparative advantage in breeding native Boran cattle (since they are unsuitable for crops and exotic cattle), but the commercial ranches are the only source of crossbred cattle and Improved Borans. Pastures in the Disease Free Area enable immature cattle to be most efficiently fattened to a weight suitable for feedlots and provide the first part of the quarantine requirements, whilst it was hoped that feedlots would both prove the most economic method of finishing cattle, and satisfy the quarantine requirements imposed for beef destined for Europe. It might be that, even without access to Europe, stratification could be economic; or this might be conditional on access to the new market. Either way, if stratification is economic, cattle will move from breeding herds, to graziers or backgrounders, and then finally into feedlots, typically in quite separated places. A further beneficial result would be to transform the bulky low-priced maize exports into the higher valued beef, which is less bulky and incurs lower transport costs, simultaneously increasing the value of exports, the amount of employment generated in processing the maize into beef, monetizing the subsistence pastoral areas and integrating them into the national economy, and perhaps, by reducing the stocking rate in the pastoral areas, improving their productivity.

The Beef Industry Development Project was set up to explore the economics of this proposed stratification, whilst the Beef Research Station was concerned to identify the best feeding regime for intensive feeding, and to see if it was indeed economically attractive to finish cattle. To this end the station grew maize which it harvested as forage and made into silage—and so collected information otherwise unavailable on the costs of producing silage—bought in other feedstuffs, and fed experimental groups of cattle different rations.

18.2 THE PURPOSE AND NATURE OF THIS STUDY

This study is concerned to appraise the economic feasibility in social cost-benefit terms of intensive feeding within this context, and so can be considered as an adjunct to the task of the Beef Research Station. The main difference between this study and others in the same series (such as Stern, 1972, Little and Tipping, 1972, and the settlement scheme of Part II of this volume) is that the project to be evaluated is not well defined before the evaluation, nor can it be assumed that the Government's policies are completely specified.

Perhaps not too much should be made of these distinctions, but we may make one remark. A common criticism of the Manual methodology is that it does not take adequate account of alternatives, and that in any case the proper selection and design of projects depends on a comprehensive approach and cannot be achieved by seriatim appraisal of individual projects. To the extent that this is anything more than a statement that planning involves hunting for projects and examining their interactions (both of which are recognised by the Manual, § 5.3, 5.7) it implies that many perhaps quite good projects could have been improved by a change of design. The suspicion lurking at the back of the critic's mind is perhaps that the choice of technique or mode of production is not best suited to the prevailing factor scarcities in the country. A good feasibility study is intended not just to produce a profitable project or to say whether or not a given project is profitable, but it should produce the *most* profitable project given the information available. The qualification is important—no one believes that subsequent investigations will not in many cases suggest even better formulations—but the only reasonable aim is to achieve the best currently available. If it is felt that further investigation might yield more profitable projects, that is an argument for investing in further research. I shall have some remarks to make in this direction in 24.7 and 24.8.

A good project evaluation will not only say whether or not the project is socially profitable, but what government policies are required to permit the full potential benefits to be realized. This aspect is particularly important in a feasibility study like the one considered here. The viability of the feedlots will depend on, amongst other things, the availability of cattle and maize from elsewhere in the economy, and these will in turn depend very much on the Government's agricultural price policy, its investment in cattle routes, the operation of quarantine regulations and so forth. Moreover, the social value of any profits generated will depend on who receives them. In this case the profits might accrue to the Kenya Meat Commission (an agency of the Government), the feedlot owners (public or private), the original cattle herders, the ranchers, maize growers, or some combination of these.

The Kenya Beef Industry Development Project has been closely involved in advising the Kenya Government on price policy, particularly the setting of the beef producer price schedule, which is the responsibility of the Ministry of Agriculture, and to a lesser extent the price of maize for cattle feed. Indeed, some estimates of the accounting prices of different grades of beef made in the early stages of this study were used in the preparation of this advice, and after lengthy discussions the Ministry of Agriculture has drawn up guide-lines for the management of the Kenya Meat Commission requiring that producer prices be related to export prices.

Another distinguishing feature of the present study is that it involves looking at a wide range of economic activities spanning several sectors of the Kenyan economy. We need to look at the production of the immature cattle, which is itself an industry involving a variety of widely different production techniques and using a variety of inputs; we need to examine the production and marketing of feed grains, again a major industry with a fairly articulated structure; then to examine the feeding operation itself; and finally to follow through the output of the feeding operation, itself an intermediate input which must be processed and then marketed as a bundle of joint products. The proposed method requires that we examine the whole chain of production, not merely the link which comprises the project chosen, and since the chain is in this case quite long, and made up of segments of very different production techniques varying from subsistence peasant herding to modern industrial processing, it provides a searching test of the feasibility of applying the Little-Mirrless method.

A final distinguishing feature of this study is the extensive use of sensitivity analysis as a powerful technique in identifying crucial determinants of the profitability of the project. Compared with other more well-defined projects this study had to deal with greater uncertainty as to the true technical relationships between inputs and outputs, particularly for the cattle themselves (converting feed into beef) but also in the supply of immature cattle for fattening, and in the processing of cattle into end products. This has been handled by calculating the likely error (measured by the standard deviation) of each estimate and presenting confidence limits for the final assessment. Extensive use of sensitivity analysis and the identification of the most significant uncertainties lead to a reduction in the uncertainty of some estimates, and an indication as to which data could usefully be refined.

The main by-product of this sensitivity analysis was the discovery that a theoretical model of cattle fattening behaviour derived from laboratory results and used in designing ration compositions for cattle in Europe appears to give good predictions in Kenya. This suggests that the method used in the present study ought to be almost directly applicable in a number of other countries without the need for much further information.

18.3 AN OUTLINE OF THE METHOD USED IN THE STUDY AND A GUIDE TO SUBSEQUENT CHAPTERS

The intensive fattening of cattle requires inputs of immature cattle and feed (based mainly on maize) to produce beef and related by-products. A variety of different types of cattle are available whilst the ration composition and energy can be varied over a wide range so there are a large number of possible combinations of cattle type and ration to be considered before the most profitable combination can be identified. In addition the opportunity cost of each type of cattle will vary as the supply of and demand for that type changes, which it will do as the various parts of the livestock economy grow at different rates. Since the *relative* prices of different types of cattle can be expected to change through time and as a result of the expansion of the feedlot industry it is necessary to determine the optimum configuration for each stage of development. The feasibility study was substantially finished by Easter 1972 and this provides an appropriate baseline from which to project the development of the feedlot industry, which will take place in three distinguishable stages. In the *short* run, or in the first stage which will only last for at most a few years after 1972, the supply of immatures will exceed the total demand from all sources (both by the small feedlot industry and by other ranchers), so that the opportunity cost of immatures is their slaughter value. In the *medium* run the feedlot industry will expand to the point that it competes directly with other purchasers of immatures from the Livestock Marketing Division (LMD). In the *long* run the feedlot industry is assumed to be larger than the supply of immatures from the LMD, and it therefore has to draw supplies from other parts of the livestock economy. The opportunity cost of the immatures will thus rise to the marginal cost of production in these other sectors.

The absence of an initially well defined project coupled with the changing nature of the best method of fattening cattle dictated the following approach. The accounting costs or values of the inputs and outputs were calculated under a variety of assumptions about the supply and demand situation. Thus Chapter 19 examines the beef processing industry to construct a price schedule for all the different grades of beef and hence for all the different types of cattle to be considered. Chapter 20 determines the supply price of immatures in the short, medium and long run. Chapter 21 deals with the cost of the various constituents of the possible rations which might prove suitable to feed to the cattle. This chapter also describes how the bulk of these rations (maize grain and maize silage) might most economically be produced on a farm adjacent to the feedlot. For all inputs and outputs the same general approach of working back from world prices of exports was followed and proved to be quite straightforward (though rather complicated in the case of beef as so many distinct products and processes has to be considered). Immature cattle are not traded goods in the Little-Mirrlees sense (and in fact there was not a well-established market for them until the LMD started significant cattle movements) but it was quite straightforward to calculate their opportunity cost in terms of the beef they could eventually have produced.

The subsequent chapters use the accounting prices of the inputs and outputs to identify the optimum configuration of the feedlot. Chapter 22 looks at a possible organization of a feedlot and calculates the cost of feeding the cattle the rations described and costed in the previous chapter.

The next step was to identify the production function which relates inputs of feed to outputs of beef. This is done in the second part of Chapter 22, which draws on the theoretical and empirical literature on cattle input-output relations as well as the findings of the Beef Research Station. In many ways this is the core of the study, and raises some of the most interesting methodological points, particularly regarding the applicability of the approach and findings to other countries. Once the production function has been identified it is simple to calculate the profitability of feeding different cattle different rations, and, in particular, the most profitable combination under each supply assumption (for the short, medium and long run). Chapter 23 presents these results and compares the best configuration at accounting prices with the most profitable combination at market prices. Despite considerable differences in the market and accounting prices (and differences in the *ratios* of accounting to market prices) it is interesting to find that the most profitable configuration is the same at both sets of prices in almost all circumstances (though the level of profits differs and is higher at accounting prices). Chapter 23 also assesses the extent to which the results are sensitive to errors in the measurement of, or changes in, the various factors which might be thought to affect profitability.

Finally, Chapter 24 describes the best *project* and determines its profitability at accounting and market prices. Various summary measures such as capital intensity, the capital-output ratios, etc., are presented and their usefulness in describing the project discussed. The treatment of uncertainty, economies of scale and the policy implications are discussed, and the role of the research station in identifying profitable investment opportunities is examined. The final sections draw various conclusions from the study which are discussed in the next two sections of the present chapter, after a brief description of the most profitable project. The main methodological problems and innovations are also dealt with in the present chapter which concludes and completes the introduction by placing the project in its context in the maize and livestock sectors of the Kenyan economy.

18.4 SUMMARY OF THE MOST PROFITABLE METHOD OF FATTENING BEEF

The main conclusion is that it *was* socially profitable to transfer *all* suitable cattle via pastures in the DFA to feedlots. This was true at the world prices for beef expected in 1972 whether or not Kenya was granted access to Europe. By early 1973 the evident *commercial* profitability of feedlots had induced a significant number of farmers to establish feedlots. Conditions under which Kenya could export feedlot beef were agreed in late 1972 and the first feedlot exported beef to Switzerland in early 1973, though almost immediately exports had to be suspended when an outbreak of foot-and-mouth disease occurred in the Disease Free Area. However, this is taking the story somewhat beyond the point it had reached in 1972, and with which we are mainly concerned.

The study has determined the most profitable method of feeding cattle in an ecological environment similar to that of the Beef Research Station, which can be taken as fairly typical of farms suitable for intensive feeding. Any particular farm contemplating intensive feeding would of course have to make the best use of the resources available, and might in consequence look rather different from the plan described here, but it is unlikely that the economic organization would be very different. The best size of farm appeared to be about 700-800 hectares, and it would have to be located in the Disease Free Area within 15 miles of line of rail on land suitable for maize growing–this implies an average rainfall of perhaps 900 mm (compared with 500-700 mm on good ranching land). Later on as experience with sorghums is gained it may be possible to relax this last requirement. About half the farm would be devoted to growing maize, which would be harvested by a forage harvester as greenchop (the whole maize plant chopped finely) and ensiled for subsequent use; the remainder of the farm would consist of Rhodes grass pastures for grazing cattle prior to entering the feedlots. The feedlots would have a capacity of about 3,000 head and an annual throughput of nearly 10,000 head. The most profitable cattle in the short and medium run would be NEP Borans purchased either direct from the Livestock Marketing Division or from graziers in the Disease Free Area, who themselves would purchase the immatures from the LMD and 'background' them for the feedlots to a weight of about 270 kg (that is, they would graze them but sell them as immatures rather than as finished animals). The rations all contain wet ground maize grain or maize germ as the main source of high energy, silage (made from the finely chopped whole green maize plant), as a lower energy, higher roughage constituent, together with supplements of cotton seed cake, minerals, urea and molasses. In the short run the availability of silage is the limiting factor, its opportunity cost is high and the most profitable ration economizes on its use by substituting the higher energy maize grain. If high energy rations can be satisfactorily fed to NEP Borans without their putting on too high a proportion of the weight gain as fat, then the high energy ration fed to NEP Borans will be the most profitable combination not only in the short run, but also in the medium run when silage is no longer a binding constraint and cattle have become more expensive. If, on the other hand, it is not satisfactory to feed the high energy ration to NEP Boran, then the most profitable combination in the short run will be an even higher energy ration fed to crossbred cattle from the commercial ranches, switching in the medium run to NEP Boran on a medium energy ration (containing about 50 per cent by dry matter weight of silage). In the long run it will also be profitable to fatten cross breds and improved Boran from the commercial ranches, and for these more exotic cattle the most profitable ration is again a high energy dominantly maize grain ration. The cattle will spend a minimum of 90 days in the feedlots to satisfy the quarantine requirement. The finished cattle will be walked to the railhead and sent live to the slaughterhouse, where they will be processed into chilled beef for export to European or comparable markets.

It is convenient to assume that the farm is Government owned (directly through one of its subsidiaries such as the Agriculture Development Corporation or indirectly through shareholding) so that profits can be measured as though they accrue to the Government. In principle, even if the feedlot industry were not publicly owned, it ought to be possible to transfer the supernormal profits to the Government by manipulating the producer price schedule for cattle, and by setting reservation prices for the sale of immature cattle by the Government-owned LMD. In practice, it is quite likely that the development of the feedlot industry will be left in the private sector. Indeed, it might quite possibly prove socially more profitable to do this. The argument for calculating the social rate of return on the assumption that the Government owns the feedlots is that it *could* do so, and the decision whether to own and produce in the public sector, or whether to leave it to the private sector, requires us to calculate the social profit under this assumption. This ought (assuming a rational Government) to place a *lower* bound on the *social* profitability of intensive cattle fattening. It is difficult to calculate the social profitability of a private feedlot industry without knowing more about the likely producers and likely Government policy, and to that extent this study is not quite complete. If these gaps in our knowledge could be rectified it should be possible to determine the social profitability of private development using the methods of Chapter 11 of the revised Manual and Chapter 6 of this volume.

On the assumption that the Government owns the farm feedlots the expected rate of return in 1972 for the medium run at accounting prices was 38 per cent (with a standard deviation of 13 per cent) if the high energy ration could be fed to NEP Borans, or 31 per cent if a lower energy ration had to be used instead. This return would fall to 25 per cent in the long run as the industry expands to absorb the entire stock of immatures from the NEP and has to turn to other sources of supply at the margin. The net present social value of the farm feedlot at the ARI of 10 per cent in the medium run would be about £520,000 on the more conservative assumption that NEP Borans would be fed the lower energy ration, with a range of value of ± £300,000. The range of possible values corresponds to uncertainties about the performance of the cattle, the efficiency of the slaughterhouse, the supply price of immatures and fluctuations in the world prices of both inputs and outputs.

18.5 THE APPLICABILITY OF THE LITTLE-MIRRLEES METHOD

This study, like the others reported in this and similar volumes, was intended to test the applicability of the Little-Mirrlees method to agricultural projects. It will be remembered that the first version of the Manual was originally confined to industrial projects, according to one of the authors,[1] for the following reasons:

(i) The calculation of shadow prices should be more straightforward.
(ii) Manufacturing projects can usually be considered in isolation and need not be integrated into sectoral programmes.
(iii) The distribution of income can often be ignored.
(iv) Inputs and outputs are more reliably predictable.

In agriculture, on the other hand, it might be expected that there are more non-tradeables (and ambiguous cases) to value, that the valuation of land would be more important and rather difficult, that labour might both be more important and less homogeneous, that affecting the distribution of income may be a major aim of agricultural projects and that input-output relations are probably more variable (because of weather) and less predictable. It is not very difficult to extend and expand this list of problems, but it is important to realize that agricultural projects encompass a very wide range of different types, and that by no means all of them suffer from all, or, even most, of these problems. Anticipating the conclusion somewhat, it is possible to make the following remarks about the present study.

One of the main problems is that an industrial project is usually highly specific—a single project at a specified location. In agriculture we are often concerned with a general problem—in this case, is intensive beef fattening profitable? The answer in general depends on the location and characteristics of the farms accepting the project. In a feasibility study such as this, one can specify the type of environment likely to be

[1] Little, 1971.

suitable (in terms of rainfall, access to road and rail, disease risk, soil fertility, etc.) and show how the general evaluation can be modified to deal with specific instances. The diversity in possible locations is the root of many of the other problems; especially predicting the input-output relations, and valuing inputs and outputs. Transport costs may even be such as to turn traded into non-traded goods. Most of these difficulties have been avoided (or sidestepped) in this study, by the necessary restriction of possible sites to the Disease Free Area near line of rail.

18.5.1 *Land*

The principles involved are simple; the difficulty lies in assessing the best alternative use of the land, and in computing the allocation of costs, particularly overheads, to different crops. The problems are discussed at some length in Chapter 21. In practice the final result is quite insensitive to different land valuations, and so the problem is not very serious.

18.5.2 *Labour*

Again we have the problem that the opportunity cost of labour will vary with the location, and will probably not be known very accurately. However, in this study wages and salaries were found to comprise a very small part of total value added (total wages and salaries at accounting prices were 10 per cent of gross value added), so that no difficulties arose.

18.5.3 *Other Inputs and Outputs*

With the exception of some parts of cattle (offals, high quality fore-quarters) all the main inputs and outputs were fully traded. Their border price was found without much difficulty, though in common with most agricultural products their price varies substantially over periods of a year or more. An analysis of this fluctuation and of the long term trends in prices revealed that their effect on profitability was not very significant (compared with some of the other factors). The project used the accounting prices derived in Part I of this volume for small items, and used the same methods to calculate some additional minor items recorded in Appendix A.18. None of these items was important enough for the uncertainties in its accounting price to affect the outcome significantly.

18.5.4 *Intersectoral Linkages*

If an agricultural project is profitable it will usually be desirable to replicate it elsewhere. Of course, this may not be possible (one thinks of specific and unique irrigation schemes), and the extent of the expansion or replication will ultimately be limited by the supply of inputs or the size of the market, but certainly in this case a considerable expansion is foreseen (and has already begun). Although it is unlikely to eliminate the projected export surplus of maize, between 5 and 10 optimal size feedlots will absorb the current supply of immature cattle from the NEP, with consequent shifts in the source of supply and the opportunity cost of the immatures. One of the main advantages of a detailed cost benefit approach (as distinct from macro or sectoral planning) is that the implications for the profit of the project of the changing structure of the supplying industries can be taken into account. In this study the profit is calculated for the short, medium and long run as progressively more expensive sources of supply are required at the margin. Chapters 20 and 24 discuss this aspect in some detail, and show that the optimal ration will also change as the industry expands. The criticism that project appraisal is incapable of taking these 'linkages' or intersectoral consequences into account is decisively shown to be false; indeed, a by-product of the study is to give some prediction as to the evolution of the industry and the best path to follow in its development.

18.5.5 *Distribution of Income*

Agricultural pricing policy has a significant impact on the income of farmers, and its distribution between different sectors, as has already been mentioned in 18.2.

The most suitable pricing policy will depend, amongst other things, on whether the feedlot industry is left to develop in the private sector, or whether it will be directly or indirectly owned by the Government, and what policies the Government wishes to pursue with respect to the remainder of the livestock and dairy industry and the maize economy. A thorough examination of the distributional consequences of varying all prices would take us rather far afield, and only a few steps are taken in this direction in 24.4.1. If it is agreed that one of the main decisions facing the Government is the setting of relative agricultural prices (relative to each other and to industry) then a careful social cost-benefit analysis of the different agricultural possibilities will be needed in any case. This would seem to provide an additional justification for the use of scarce resources on project evaluation in agriculture.

18.5.6 *Input-Output Relations*

The main source of uncertainty as to the social profitability of the project lies in predicting the efficiency with which cattle will convert feed into beef, though it is impressive how accurately this can be predicted. The efficiency with which breeding herds produce immatures (particularly the calving rate) is also uncertain and affects the accuracy of the final estimate. For these and other reasons the study presents estimates of the standard deviation of each figure, often derived from a sensitivity analysis designed to identify the most critical parameters and increase the accuracy of their estimate. On the other hand, it appears that the beef-feed production function can be specified fairly well in physical terms, and should be widely applicable in other countries. Again, a single project analysis may have implications for a very large number of individual projects. Furthermore, there is some reason to expect the physical production function to be more stable in agriculture than for industrial production (at least, at the level of detail specified in this report).

Other input-output relations were less critical in this study (response to fertilizer, grazing intensity, yield per acre, etc.). If anything the production efficiency of the slaughter house (or a new slaughter house) i.e. of the *industrial* processing component, is more uncertain than some of the agricultural production functions, though this turns out to be unimportant for the project (this is discussed in Chapter 19).

18.5.7 *Uncertainty*

Price uncertainty has already been mentioned, as has that stemming from ignorance as to the true production functions. Fluctuations in profit due to the weather and disease were not very significant in comparison—if anything the scheme *reduces* uncertainty for other sections of the beef industry and for the country as a whole.

18.5.8 *Was the Analysis Worthwhile?*

The whole study took between three and five man-months. The time taken was probably longer than needed for a fairly accurate analysis, as an attempt was also made to assess the accuracy and to investigate quantitatively unimportant details. Moreover, some of the time spent could have been avoided if more of the experimental results had been available at the start of the enquiry. The delay necessitated almost completely repeating the study as the situation had changed so much in the interim (between July 1970 and March 1972). On the other hand the longer time-period gave a better feel for the effect of changing world and local market conditions on the profitability of the project. The cost of the social cost-benefit analysis was certainly small compared with the cost of collecting the original data at the Beef Research Station, and should have quite wide applicability. My own conclusion is that the Manual has shown itself well suited to at least some kinds of agricultural project evaluation, and to be of considerable use in helping to formulate policy.

This judgement was certainly endorsed by the Beef Research Station, who found that the approach of working consistently in world prices greatly clarified some of the conceptual problems and enabled them to argue their case more cogently. Memoranda from the Ministry of Agriculture concerning the principles to be used in setting the producer prices of beef (and other agricultural crops) suggest that, by 1973, at least some of these arguments had been effective.

18.6 THE RELATION OF THE FEEDLOT INDUSTRY TO THE KENYAN ECONOMY

The main inputs to a feedlot are maize, or maize-based silage, and immature cattle, the output is finished beef, so that the feedlot must be seen in the context of both maize production and the livestock industry. It is interesting that both beef and maize have several features in common. They are both produced as subsistence and commercial products, they both dictate the life-styles of the traditional producers, in both cases a comparatively small proportion of total production enters the marketed sector and an even smaller proportion the foreign trade sector, and, finally, both are handled by Government-controlled marketing boards with producer prices set by the Government. The short summaries that follow are too brief to discuss the wide range of different views held about the likely development of each industry and the reader is warned not to assume that the single view expressed here represents any consensus as to what is most likely to happen.

18.7 LIVESTOCK

In 1969 the livestock industry marketed over £21 millions, or 29 per cent of gross marketed agricultural production, and as such was the single largest agricultural industry. Of course the sector was quite heterogeneous but even if we take sales of beef cattle plus hides and skins the gross marketed output of £12.9 m was second only to coffee (£16.6 m). These figures give only a partial picture of the importance of the industry, for according to land use classifications some four-fifths of Kenya's land area receive on average less than 25-30 inches (600-750 mm) rainfall per year. The vast proportion of this is unsuitable for permanent cultivation and is given over to wild-life and range lands. In detail this low potential land comprised:

(i)	Existing commercial ranches	10,400 sq. km
(ii)	Subsistence range lands	435,000 sq. km
(iii)	National Parks	28,500 sq. km
(iv)	Unoccupied and unallocated public lands mostly in the coastal hinterland	18,100 sq. km

(Source: Plan 70-74: p. 264)

The population of these dry areas was approximately 1½ million people (in 1967 when the total Kenyan population was about 10 million) and roughly half of this number derived their living as pastoralists almost exclusively from meat and milk. A further 300,000 were semi-pastoralists and the remainder were basically subsistence cultivators who kept a small number of cattle in addition to growing crops.[1]

The productivity of these range areas was low and despite their extent they accounted for only half the production of beef. The remainder came from the High Potential Area, where it was produced in competition with dairying and crops and where the bulk of the population lived. The bulk (80 per cent) of the quality beef came from large farms or ranches in this high potential area.

The World Bank, in its 'Study of the availability of fattening beef breeding and dairy breeding stock in East Africa, 1970-75' (1972), estimated the total Kenyan cattle population as 9,080,000 in 1970, of which 8,390,000 were the native Zebu cattle. The estimates given in the Second Plan and by Aldington and Wilson suggested an off-take of about 13.2 per cent in 1967, though the cattle population figures were probably unreliable. Of this total production only 26 per cent by weight was sold to the Kenya Meat Commission (KMC). The overall offtake rate of 13.2 per cent conceals considerable differences between regions and methods of herding, ranging as it does from about 7.5 per cent in some pastoral areas to the 20-25 per cent from commercial ranches.

18.7.1 *The Development of the Livestock Industry*

By 1972, world market prospects for beef probably looked better than for all other Kenyan export industries except tourism. This, together with the importance of the industry in the national economy and its underdeveloped state in the range areas, caused it to be given quite high priority in development plans and in the Ministry of Agriculture's activities. Moreover, the marketed surplus left only a narrow margin for exports and during the last decade planners had frequently expressed concern lest Kenya become a beef deficit country in the near future. Thus the First Plan (1966-70) reported that a survey undertaken by a U.N. Special Fund/FAO team predicted a short-fall by 1970 unless the offtake rate, then estimated at 12 per cent, could be raised. A variety of measures to raise the productivity of the national herd were recommended and funds were spent to improve disease control, stock routes, water

1 Figures taken from Aldington and Wilson, 1968, page 1.

supplies and research. (See e.g.: Development Plan 1966-70, pp. 191-3.)

The World Bank's projections from 1970 to 1975 showed production growing from 174,000 tons to 195,000 tons–an increase of 12 per cent. If 1970 per capita levels of beef consumption were maintained, local demand would rise from 162,000 tons to 190,000 tons, or by 17.3 per cent. Other projections by Aldington and Wilson and in the Plan suggested that unless the productivity of the national herd could be increased Kenya would probably face a beef deficit in the mid-1970s. The significance of this possible deficit is clear–if beef has to be imported its price will be higher. If there is a significant chance that this will happen the profitability of beef production is understated when measured, as in the present study, on its export parity price.

The alternative strategies available for increasing the productivity of the national herd were strictly limited. There is a complex inter-relationship between calving rates, milk withdrawn for human consumption, offtake and stocking rates, so that the range areas, for example, are constrained to have 30-35 per cent of their herd as mature females to meet the human milk requirement (in contrast with commercial ranches with 20 per cent).

There seemed to be two possibilities. Either the standard of husbandry could be improved, by culling, better breeding, improving water facilities and disease control, or the young cattle could be transferred to other areas for fattening, as described earlier. Both strategies were adopted. The Livestock Marketing Division of the Ministry of Agriculture was entrusted with the development of stock routes and the organization of cattle purchases from the North East Province, where the second strategy seemed more appropriate.

At the same time the Range Management Division was acting with a number of organizations (the Kenya Government through the Agricultural Finance Corporation, the World Bank and the Government of Sweden) to establish and develop ranches as part of their range development programme. Water supplies, credit, land surveying and adjudication and the provision of managerial technical services were the basic inputs, and the idea was that the nomadic herdsmen, who would otherwise have little incentive to restrict the cattle population and prevent overgrazing and degradation of the pastures, would manage their cattle commercially. In addition to breeding their own cattle they would purchase immatures from the Livestock Marketing Division to fatten, so that they would also become part of the programme of stratification. The main features of the programme are shown on the Map (pp. xxvi-vii) which also shows the slaughterhouse, rail transport system and the Beef Research Station, and are reported in another social cost benefit analysis (Simpson, 1973).

The IBRD Study quoted above gave figures for the availability of feeder steers (i.e. immature cattle) in 1970, and estimated an availability of 84,000 large Zebu steers and 245,700 small Zebu steers per annum. Until 1972 at least little was known about fattening small Zebu and the majority of them were in any case slaughtered in the subsistence areas. Initially, then, all the proposals related to the large Zebu steers, though it may also prove economic to fatten the more numerous (and at present less accessible) small Zebus.

Demand by the IBRD and AFC for their ranch programme was projected to rise to 20,000 p.a. by 1974, although these were not necessarily lost to the feedlots, as they might be subsequently transferred for finishing. It was difficult to predict what the effect of the improved stock routes and increased sales would be on the future supply of feeder steers, but it would have been optimistic to anticipate a supply greater than 100,000 per annum.

18.7.3 *Disease Control and the Export of Beef*

Cattle in Africa are prone to a wide variety of diseases, amongst which the most well-known are trypanosomiasis, carried by the tsetse fly, rinderpest, East Coast Fever, Contagious Bovine Pleuropneumonia, and foot-and-mouth disease. The last named is particularly important, because the strain endemic to East Africa is exotic (and therefore particularly dangerous) to Europe. Like influenza in humans, vaccination against one of the fifteen or so varieties of foot-and-mouth disease does not confer immunity to other varieties, and for this reason the European countries were naturally reluctant to expose their cattle to any risk of infection by exotic strains. Until 1973 this meant that only canned beef could be exported from Kenya to Europe—chilled beef could only be exported to non-European markets, principally Tripoli, Hong Kong, Saudi Arabia and the Congo. Kenya had for a considerable period pursued a vigorous policy of disease control so that by 1972 her position was considerably in advance of most other countries in Africa. The main feature of this policy was the maintenance of a Disease Free Area centred on the large commercial ranches. This area, the main part of which is shown in the Map on p. , is closed, either by fencing or natural barriers. Any cattle entering the area had to be isolated for three months on the edge of the area and vaccinated twice against foot-and-mouth before entry, whilst all cattle within the area were vaccinated every six months. Movement of cattle was controlled and special regulations covered any outbreaks of disease. In September 1971 a joint working group of the OIE Foot-and-Mouth Disease Commission and the FAO European Commission for the Control of Foot-and-Mouth Disease met in Paris and published criteria under which beef could be imported into Europe.[1] In addition to the regulations governing the operation of a Disease Free Area the relevant requirements were than an abattoir should be established within the Disease Free Area to deal only with beef satisfying the export conditions and that cattle should be kept under quarantine in the Disease Free Area. A feedlot forms an ideal quarantine area, so that intensive fattening might confer an additional advantage in enabling the beef to be exported to the European market. The economic implications of this are discussed in some detail in Chapters 19 and 24.

The important regulations affecting feedlots were:

(i) Movement of animals into the quarantine area should be permitted only after they have been in the disease-free zone for at least six months.

(ii) Animals entering the quarantine area or feedlot should be isolated for one month at entry, during which they will be closely observed and re-vaccinated against foot-and-mouth disease.

(iii) Animals should be held in the feedlots for at least three months before slaughter.

1 FAO/OIE, 1971.

The immediate consequences of this report have been mentioned: Kenya was granted permission to export to Switzerland (the least vulnerable country as her mountains form a natural quarantine boundary) in late 1972, under interim regulations dealing with the operation of the slaughter house (which was *not* in the DFA). Shortly after the first consignment had been despatched an outbreak of the Tanzanian strain of foot-and-mouth was observed in the DFA—this strain is exotic to Kenya and not fully protected by current vaccinations. The final result was not known when this study was written, but at that time no feedlots had had outbreaks.

18.8 MAIZE

Maize is the staple food of Kenya. In the past the country exported an average of 33,000 tons p.a. (1946-64) or rather more than 10 per cent of marketed production which was estimated at an average of 280,000 tons (1968-70) but from 1969 several poor harvests and the demands of a growing urban population led to large imports and concern about the country's ability to feed itself. Fortunately, in 1964 the Maize Research Unit at Kitale produced a hybrid maize which permitted increases in yields of 30 per cent. The area sown to hybrids increased from 12,000 hectares in 1964 to an estimated 200,000 hectares in 1971.

The combination of new varieties which derive substantial benefits from good husbandry and advice provided by the extension service produced a quite dramatic increase in supply, changing an export deficit of 143,000 tons in 1966 to a surplus of 277,000 tons in 1968 (See Table 18.1). The Second Plan projected a marketed surplus of 610,000 tons and an export surplus of 430,000 tons by 1974 and proposed the development of bulk handling and storing facilities to reduce the very high costs of handling between farmer and f.o.b. When this was completed the 1970 subsidized producer price would correspond almost exactly to the export parity price, though this has been far from true since 1952 (in 1962-3 the subsidy was over £1 million).

Instead of exporting the comparatively low value/weight and

Table 18.1

Quantity of Selected Cereals Marketed and Traded Abroad

'000 metric tons

	1966	1967	1968	1969	1970	1971	1972[b]	Plan 1974
1. Wheat								
marketed	128.4	162.2	216.3	241.6	221.5	205.7	174.6	230.0
imported	25.0	4.5	–	–	–	13.0	n.a.	n.a.
exported	32.2	50.7	52.8	24.7	44.0	–	n.a.	53.0
2. Maize								
marketed[a]	134.3	248.8	352.6	280.3	205.7	256.6	392.9	610.0
imported	143.4	–	–	–	14.3	29.1	n.a.	–
exported	–	79.0	277.5	140.9	–	–	n.a.	430.0

[a] Sales to Board only
[b] Estimate

Sources: Statistical Abstract 1972
Development Plan 1970-4

minimally processed maize grain, it could be used up-country (before incurring a large proportion of the handling costs) to feed cattle, which in contrast has a quite high value/weight ratio and is subject to substantial processing. Very roughly, one animal finishing on an intensive maize diet requires 0.4 metric tons of maize, so that by 1974 if the maize projections were correct over 1 million head of cattle could be intensively fed. This is far in excess of the planned increase in immature cattle estimated at 100,000 (Plan 70-74, Table 8.19, p. 272) and it was unlikely that all these cattle could be available for fattening. Even if *all* cattle from the large farms were intensively fed, and this led to an increased offtake of 50 per cent, releasing some 300,000 head per annum, the maize export surplus would remain. It was therefore valid to assume that the Kenyan economy would remain a maize export economy even with a very large intensive feeding operation, provided, of course that the optimism of the Plan was warranted as far as maize production and exports were concerned.

18.9 WORLD PRICES FOR BEEF AND MAIZE

A large fraction of the value of a typical beef carcass was tradable abroad, and with the projected surplus maize would be a fully traded commodity. Thus the value of the main inputs and outputs of the project were dependent on world prices. (Graphs of some of the main prices are shown on pp. 30-1). The world average export value for maize does not appear to fluctuate very substantially from year to year, and over the 15 years to 1970 has shown no upward or downward trend in dollar price. On the other hand, the price of beef fluctuates quite widely over periods of three to four years. Between 1970, when this study was started, and March 1972 Kenyan beef export prices increased between 35 per cent and 50 per cent (depending on the type of export). Longer time-series of beef prices show a rapid rise in price during the period 1935-51, (the peak of the Korean war boom). Since 1953-5 the upward trend has been slight, until the recent rapid rise between 1970 and 1972. These conclusions are based on producer prices in major beef-producing countries such as the U.S. and Australia. If we look at chilled beef export prices their upward trend has been more pronounced over the 15 years for which data is readily available. Kenyan chilled beef export prices have risen rather more rapidly than world prices generally, perhaps reflecting her gradual establishment in export markets. It is also possible that the recent growth of air freighted chilled beef has increasingly linked markets which previously had widely different beef prices so that part of the upward trend is the adjustment to a more uniform set of prices and cannot be expected to continue. Canned corned beef prices appear to move on the same trend (though year to year fluctuations make any statistical comparisons of trends difficult). Hide prices fluctuate even more than beef prices and it is difficult to see any strong trend. Finally the U.S. beef/maize price ratio has risen at 1.63 per cent p.a. over the past 30 years. All the evidence suggests that the terms of trade between beef and other products showed no tendency to deteriorate over long periods, whilst price movements in 1972, which were consistent with the emergence of the world beef shortage forecast by the FAO, suggested that the future export prices for beef were likely to be even more favourable. In particular, it seemed very likely that the beef/maize price ratio would continue to improve as the Green Revolution increases grain supplies.

18.9.1 *The Effect of Access to Europe on Prices*

In 1970 there was a significant gap between the price of beef allowed into Europe and beef exported to non-European markets. The profitability of intensive fattening in Kenya appeared to depend on obtaining access to the European markets. Between 1970 and early 1972 the received price for Kenyan exports of chilled beef rose substantially but European prices did not appear to have moved so markedly. Prices of Argentine beef at Smithfield, London gave no higher prices f.o.a. Nairobi than sales to Tripoli. During the latter part of 1972 European prices continued to drift up, but so did North African prices, and at the time of the first consignment of beef to Switzerland there was again no price differential. Of course this may have reflected a short run scarcity in Tripoli, with buyers there aware of the European prices available to Kenya, but prices continued high after foot-and-mouth closed the European market. If this was a temporary phenomenon, the differential might reassert itself in the future: the marketing manager of the Kenya Meat Commission thought that on an average European prices might be worth an extra Sh.1. per kg CDW, or nearly 20 per cent after averaging over the whole carcass, only a proportion of which is exported as chilled beef. On the other hand the beef deficit seemed to be growing more rapidly in non-European markets than in Europe, which would suggest, if anything, a narrowing of the differential. Argentina and other Latin American countries were exporting to both markets in 1972, which suggested a low differential, if any.

It seemed reasonable to take present non-European export prices as the best indicator of prices for the subsequent few years—although they rose rapidly in 1972, they were expected to remain at their new level. It should, however, be remembered that substantial fluctuations in prices are as likely as ever, and perhaps the main benefit of access to Europe would be in reducing the effect of such fluctuations. The significance of price fluctuations will be discussed in the final summary.

Appendix A.18
Additional accounting prices for minor items

In most cases the prices derived in Part I of this volume have been used, but occasionally a separate calculation for a specific item seemed justified, and these are reported here. Again, some composite items do not warrant a detailed breakdown into their components and the appropriate conversion factor is recorded here.

Table A.18.1
Accounting Prices for Minor Items

Item	Conversion Factor	Notes
Fertilizers		
Urea	1.15	Fertilizers receive a Government subsidy
15-45-0	1.38	
ASN	1.07	
Tractor services		
Large (70HP)	0.704	See Appendix A.21
Small	0.725	
Metal cans for canned beef	0.81	derived from unpublished census data (supplied by the Statistics Division)
Conversion factors for KMC[a]		
First stage direct costs	0.75	
Interest and depreciation	0.88	
Canning Department costs	0.68	
Cans	0.81	as above
Packing	0.88	
Interest and depreciation	0.86	
Cut beef department costs	0.69	
Packing	0.83	
General overheads (factory)	0.73	
Head office	0.70	

[a] Derived from the detailed cost allocation from the KMC 1970 Profit Plan, to be used in Table 19.2

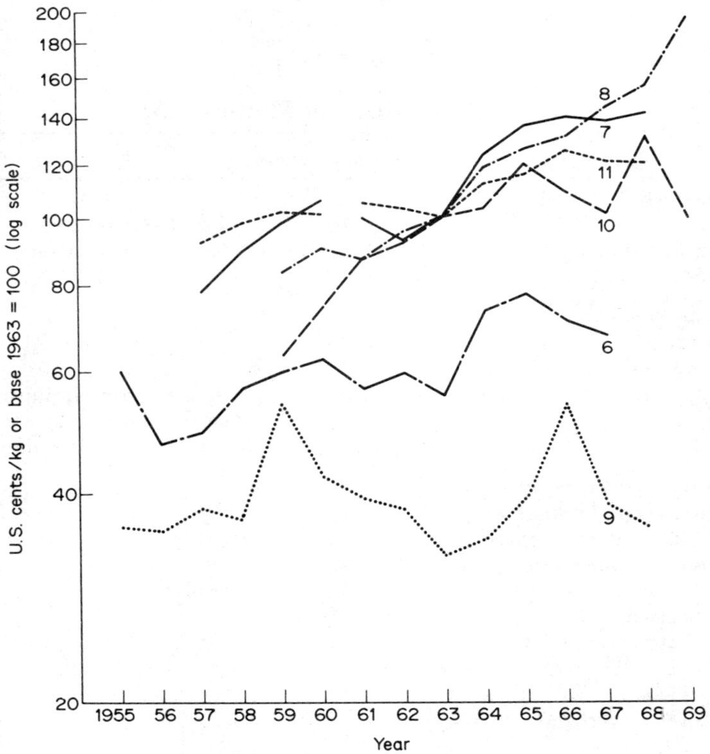

Key 1. Canada wholesale price
2. U.K. wholesale price
3. U.S. producer price
4. Belgium producer price
5. Beef-Maize price ratio

Sources: 1 to 4, FAO Trade Yearbooks. 5, U.S. Department of Agriculture Livestock and meat statistics, 1962 and 1969.

Fig. 18.1 Local beef prices

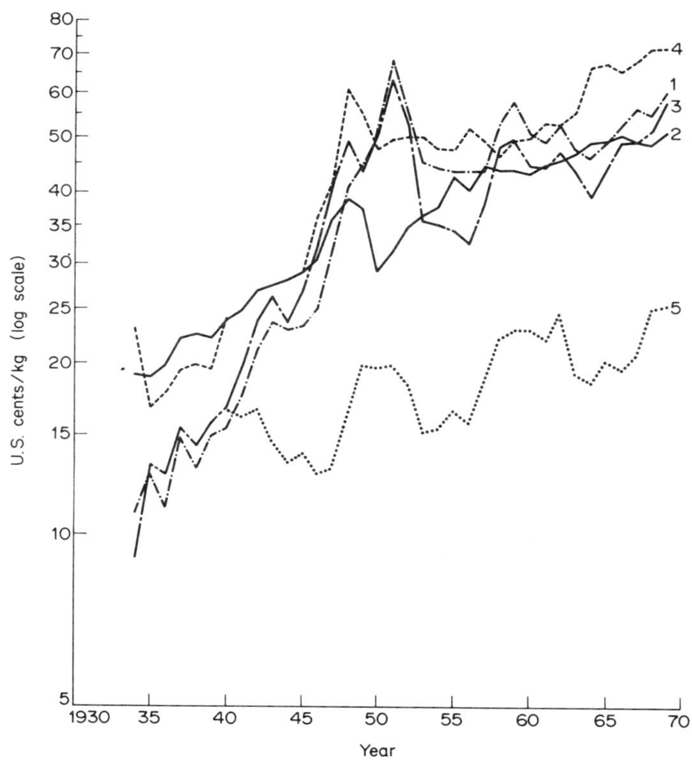

Key
6. U.K. chilled side import price (U.S. cents/Kg)
7. World chilled beef export price (index no.)
8. Kenyan chilled beef export price (index no.)
9. U.K. Cattle hide import price (U.S. cents/Kg)
10. Kenyan canned corned beef export price (index no.)
11. World CCB export price (index no.)

Source: FAO Trade Yearbooks and Production Yearbooks.

Fig. 18.2 World beef product prices.

CHAPER 19

The Value of Finished Beef

We want to devise a method of establishing the social value of any given finished animal (described by breed, live weight, age and past history—origin and feeding regime) as it leaves the farm or feedlot. The past history is particularly important because if the animal can be certified to have been in quarantine and under veterinary inspection for three months prior to slaughter it may be eligible for export to the possibly more valuable European and Israeli markets. The quarantine situation and its implications have been discussed in 18.6.3 and 18.8.1 and need to be kept in mind throughout this chapter.

There are two main difficulties, peculiar to the beef industry, which complicate the recommended practice of working back from the border value. First, the live animal is a bundle of joint products (hide, offals, different cuts of meat, bone, etc.) subject to differing processes and ultimately destined for very different markets, some of which are local, so that part of the output is non-traded, and, second, different qualities of animal produce different mixes of products. The first factor makes it inherently difficult to allocate processing costs and so makes it difficult to predict the value of a given animal if market demand conditions alter; the second need not in principle raise problems but the crude accounting procedures employed by the Kenya Meat Commission makes it difficult to relate inputs to outputs and to relate processing costs to each quality or grade of animal. In fact the absence of a good cost accounting system has obviously led to incorrect processing and marketing so that the value of output less operating costs has not been maximized. This makes it doubly difficult to compute the value of an animal on the assumption that it is directed to its most valuable use, which is the value required in the social cost-benefit calculation. It is worthwhile digressing briefly to examine the consequences of this failure to cost account and organize production efficiently (efficient in the economist's sense of the word; we say more about the wider meanings of efficiency later.

19.1 THE KENYA MEAT COMMISSION AND THE PRODUCER PRICE SCHEDULE

The Kenya Meat Commission (KMC) is a quasi-Government organization regulated by Acts of Parliament, established in 1950, and responsible in the first instance to the Minister of Agriculture, who is also Chairman of the Board of Commissioners. Loan capital was £1,098,298 in December 1968, of which £270,000 was from non-Government sources (Standard Bank, Commonwealth Development Corporation, and Guardian Assurance Company) though the loans are gradually being repaid. There was no equity capital, but the main plant at Athi River (handling 70 per cent by weight) was under a management contract (with bonuses) to an American company of meat packers, who also sold canned corned beef through their distribution system abroad. The Ministry of Agriculture specifies the purchase prices of different grades of cattle, lays down the description of the grades and also grades the cattle at the factory. The KMC is responsible for processing and marketing.

The grading system and associated price schedule is of central importance in determining the structure and evolution of the beef industry, since it transmits the signals which should indicate what type of cattle to produce, where and how. This is the logic behind the Ministry of Agriculture taking responsibility for the schedule. To give a rough idea of the effects of the price schedule we note that the majority of cattle are raised on the semi-arid range lands by traditional minimum cost techniques and if they are sold at all tend to produce underweight low grade (standard grade or below) carcasses. These cattle could be transferred to other ranches which have better grazing and herd management and would then reach heavier weights and higher grades. The extent to which this will happen (and thus the overall level of productivity of cattle production) will depend on the profitability of buying low grade animals and fattening them to reach higher grades, and will thus depend on the *difference* between the high and low grade prices. The *level* of prices affects the profitability of beef production relative to other activities (such as dairying). Finally, the *margin* between the producer price and the local retail price affects the extent to which cattle pass through the KMC and are subject to disease detection and control, or are slaughtered locally with attendant health risks (particularly from the beef tapeworm (*Taenia Saginata*) present in measled beef).[1]

One can distinguish a number of pressure groups potentially able to influence the price schedule. The main export in the past was canned corned beef and the management contract is with a firm specializing in meat canning. The price of canned beef is determined on the world market and will limit the internal price of lower grade (canning quality) meat. The vets in the Ministry of Agriculture wish to encourage good husbandry and to give premium prices for animals that have been tended in the approved manner. The large commercial ranchers want a good profit and thus high prices for the higher grades. Consumers want low price, low-grade meat—the most vociferous relevant consumers being unskilled urban workers. (Other low-income consumers buy non-KMC slaughtered beef.) The Ministry of Agriculture wants to encourage the transfer of immature cattle from the over-stocked low productivity area to the high productivity ranches in order to raise overall beef production and its average quality. Finally, the KMC is a legal monopoly, whose prices are regulated by the Government, and whose management receives bonuses rather than profits. These factors might be expected to lead to relatively low producer prices for low grade meat (which is canned or sold locally) and a wide margin between high and low grade prices. There is no strong pressure to relate prices to production costs or export prices since the profitability of the KMC can be ensured by either lowering purchase prices or raising domestic sales prices, and there is no obvious way of judging the efficiency of the KMC since it is not subject to competitive pressures or comparisons with other plants. A succession of investigations of the KMC (one in 1966, a Systems and Methods Survey in 1967

1 See the discussion in Aldington and Wilson, 1968, pp. 200-4.

and Aldington and Wilson's study in 1968) have confirmed these suspicions and suggested that the Kenya Beef Industry Development Project would need to scrutinize the processing and marketing of beef. To this end FAO installed Mr. G. Beddoes as a Cost Analyst in the Athi River Plant and most of the data used in the valuation of beef in this chapter is based on his detailed and careful studies. I have, however, occasionally made different assumptions about the allocation of costs and the valuation of inputs (such as capital, management, etc.) and so my figures will not necessarily coincide with those issued by the Project (Beddoes, 1971). Nor do they coincide with Aldington and Wilson's figures (pp. 97-100) which were derived from the published accounts of the KMC and did not have the advantage of a reasonable breakdown and allocation of total costs.

19.2 THE METHOD USED TO VALUE BEEF

It soon became apparent that the grading system in operation in 1970 made distinctions that did not appear to be warranted by the subsequent processing and marketing of the meat, and that the price schedule was a poor guide to the relative value of different grades of meat. This ruled out the obvious short cut of deflating average production costs by an overall conversion factor, which would have been easy to calculate from the available information. Instead the method used was first to identify the most profitable destination for each final product, either in export markets or domestically. It was assumed that the *marginal* export revenue was the same as the average for that destination, on the assumption that Kenya is a comparatively small exporter. This assumption appears justified in North African markets which also import from South America, but may be less appropriate for nearby markets like the Congo and Saudi Arabia. However, discussions with the KMC marketing manager suggested that one could meaningfully talk of a world price in Kenya's export markets, and the assumption has been retained. Local sales of effectively non-traded beef cuts were assumed to displace traded beef cuts of equal value, thus making their accounting price bear the same relation to the market price as for traded beef. This assumption is defended in 19.6. Finally, the carcass value was found by adding up the values of its component parts. The costs of processing each product were based on the cost analyst's allocation (Beddoes, 1971), but differ from these figures in a number of respects:

(i) The costs presented here are mainly based on the 1970 Profit Plan, whereas Beddoes' report is based on January-August 1970 actual figures. The Plan ought to correspond to average or expected operating conditions and should therefore be a better guide to the future, particularly as the factory was expected to be at nearly full capacity in 1970.

(ii) Where plant was obviously under-utilized or was about to be adapted I have attempted to correct the average costs to long-run marginal costs. Otherwise there did not appear to be economies of scale and expected average costs were thus equal to expected long-run marginal costs. The main corrections were to the Cut Beef department and the cost of the freezer. Short run marginal costs will differ from average costs if there is a significant seasonal fluctuation in throughput. This is important because different types of cattle had a different seasonal flow, and is discussed in 19.7.1.

(iii) The average costs included a 10 per cent return (the ARI) on capital, so that the presentation here differs from the accounting convention of calculating 'contributions to overheads'. This again reflects a long-run view of production costs. Some of the costs, and particularly transfer prices, have been allocated or determined differently after discussions with Beddoes and the Kenya Meat Commission management.

Whilst some allowance could be made for the higher costs of under-utilization of capacity where this occurred, it should be pointed out that the Athi River Plant of the KMC was considered to be a high-cost inefficient plant,[1] so that the 1970

1 Aldington and Wilson, 1968, pp. 38-46, Beddoes, 1971, pp. 19–25.

production costs may exceed future costs in a reorganized or new slaughter house. It is difficult to assess the extent of this inefficiency but some pointers can be given. From 1961 to 1970 output was roughly constant, total costs including head office rose 31 per cent, whilst head office expenses rose 110 per cent (compared with a rise in wage earners' consumer prices of 13 per cent over the same period, and a rise of 22 per cent in the implicit GDP deflator of 'Manufacturing and Repairing' from 1964 to 1970). Comparisons with comparable factories in Botswana and Rhodesia show that if the canning line (which has high operating costs) is removed the total costs per kg CDW on a comparable basis are:

Processing Costs	K.Sh./kg CDW
Athi River 1970	0.99
Botswana 1969	0.55
Rhodesia 1968	0.45

(Source: Beddoes, p. 23.)

It seemed likely that Kenya would eventually locate a new slaughtering/processing factory in the Disease Free Area to handle high quality animals intended primarily for export, because, quite apart from the need to expand capacity, the European organizations such as WHO and OIE are concerned to maintain quarantine conditions right through to the final processing stages. However, the plans for the future development of the beef industry (which in 1972 were being submitted to various donors) were extremely vague about likely costs. They indicated an investment of £2.25 million over the period 1974-6 which was projected to handle 40,000 head in 1975-6, rising steadily to 200,000 head in 1979-80, compared with about 145,000 head at Athi River in 1970. The factory was planned to yield the same profit per head as existing KMC plants but this gives no guidance as to its anticipated operating costs.

However, the present figures give a good guide to relative accounting prices if the inefficiency of handling different products is more or less uniform, and since relative prices are more important for our purpose than the absolute level of prices it seems reasonable to use the unadjusted figures.

To summarize, it is important to realize the limitations of the figures given here. Beef processing is very complex, and it is difficult to apportion costs correctly. The efficiency with which the plant is operated is not a constant, and the sales prices can fluctuate substantially. All these uncertainties (of sales prices, the correct allocation of costs, etc.) are summarized in an estimated standard deviation of the point estimate. The avoidable errors appear to be sufficiently large to make it very important for the KMC to improve its cost accounts if the Ministry of Agriculture is to promulgate sensible price schedules, quite apart from the obvious point that inefficiency is easier to identify and eliminate with good financial information.

The accounting price of a given grade of beef carcass is found by adding together the sales values of its output (at accounting prices) and deducting processing costs. Figure 19.1 is a simplified flow diagram of the Athi River slaughter house which shows the components of output and the internal transfers of intermediate products. The grading is done by the Ministry, and beef is further categorized Passed free of measles (P) or Retained (R). Retained beef containing measles cysts (*Cysticercus Bovis*), unless kept frozen for 14 days, gives rise to tape worms (*Taenia Saginata*) in humans and cannot therefore be sold untreated. It can, however, be canned or used for *frozen* export cut beef. The grades and the corresponding producer price schedule in use from 1970 to 1972 are shown below in Table 19.1.

19.3 ASSUMPTIONS IN ALLOCATING COSTS

In 1970 the Athi River factory handled 76 per cent by weight of the total throughput of the KMC, so 76 per cent of total Head Office expenses have been allocated to the factory. A detailed cost analysis of the first stage direct costs allocated 89 per cent to beef and the balance to smallstock (sheep and goats). The same proportion has been used for overheads. First stage costs were allocated per head (it takes the same resources to handle a small carcass as a large carcass at this stage); canning

Fig. 19.1 Flow diagram of beef through the slaughterhouse

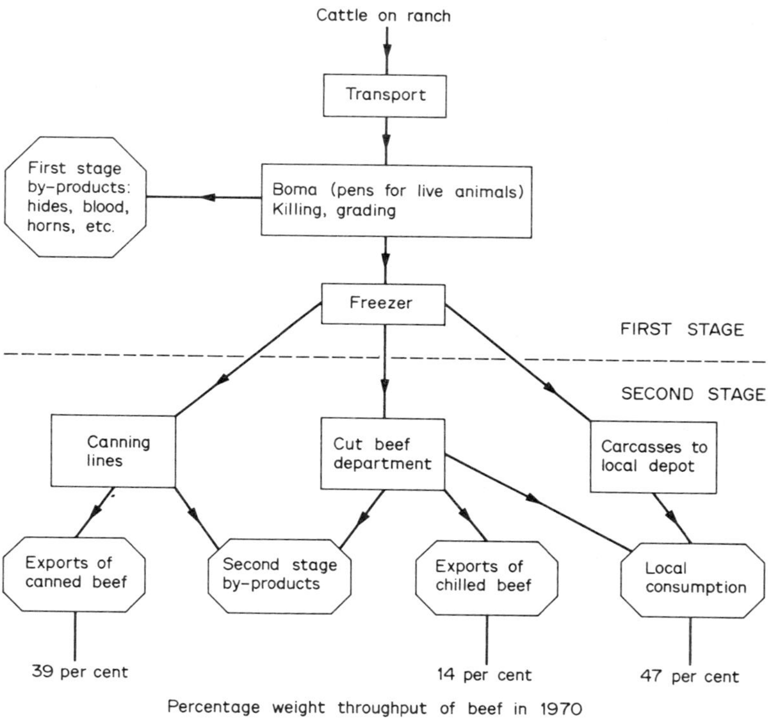

Beef Grades and the Producer Price Schedule

Grade names (July 1970)		Per cent weight (1970)	Grade names (March 1972)		Price Sh /kg CDW July 1970	March 1972
First		<1	Prime		3.85	4.70
GAQ		17	Choice		3.41	4.45
FAQ	P	20	FAQ	P	3.30	4.20
	R	2		R	2.97	3.18
Third	P	22	Standard	P	2.75	3.15
	R	4		R	2.65	2.65
Fourth	P	19	Commercial	P	2.40	2.80
	R	11		R	2.30	2.30
Manufacturing		5	Manufacturing		1.10	1.50
Reject		<1	Reject		Realization[a]	

[a] Value of by-products

costs were allocated per can, and cut beef costs on a weight basis. The value of first stage by-products was assumed to be a constant rate per kg CDW; smaller animals have a higher ratio of by-products to meat, but have hides of lower quality. Overheads were divided between the first stage, canning department and the cut beef department in the ratio 50 : 40 : 10 on the basis of employment and throughput in each department.

Capital costs were more difficult to estimate, although it is clear what is needed. We need to determine that rate of annual expenditure which when discounted at the ARI over the life-time of each department yields the same sum as the present value of investment expenses incurred over the life of that department. The difficulty stems from the fact that the existing capital was old, not ideally suited to the current pattern of production, and was shortly to be considerably modified. The 1970 written down value of all capital was £699,000, prices had not been rising faster than 2 per cent p.a. and both machinery and construction had been written down to about 50 per cent of their purchase cost. The planned expenditures would involve replacing the freezer and reorganizing the flow of meat through the factory (both steps were necessary if the factory was to retain the right to export beef to many of its existing markets), and the estimated expenditure was put at £1 million, though such a major reorganization would increase capacity by 20 per cent and probably reduce processing costs.

In Table 19.2 the items for depreciation and interest are calculated assuming that about £1.5 million of capital at 1970 market prices would be necessary to permit *continued* production at 1970 levels. The actual figures under these headings are 11 per cent of construction capital plus 21 per cent of machinery. The operating costs at accounting prices can be calculated using the conversion factors presented in Appendix A.18; these in turn were based on the detailed profit plan.

19.4 THE VALUE OF CANNING BEEF

The largest single exported product is canned corned beef, which also absorbs many of the by-products of other types of beef, so that it is a main determinant of the value of beef. It is

Table 19.2

KMC Operating Costs at Market Prices

£'000

	First Stage	Canning	Cut Beef
Department costs	..	133	20
Cans	..	265	..
Packing	..	65	23
Subtotal direct costs	208	463	43
Overhead plus head office	187	168	41
Interest and depreciation	157	55	13
Interest on stocks (10 per cent of average value)	30	20	10
Total £'000	582	706	107
per unit	81.8 Sh/head	1.31 Sh/kg CDW	a

[a] See Note to Table 19.5. *Source:* KMC 1970 Profit Plan.

therefore logical to start with the valuation of beef and beef products destined for canning. Table 19.3 below determines the ex-factory value of beef sold in the can in terms of the original carcass weight. The number of cartons which can be produced by 100 kg of CDW meat varies from year to year (from a low of 4.04 in 1966 to 4.86 in 1970) and one suspects that the proportion of by-products used is the main determinant of the relation between cartons and CDW. Some of the variation in the

Table 19.3

Value of Canning Beef in Selected Years at Market Prices

	1965	1966	1967	1968	1970	1972[a]
Carton sales price ex factory (Sh)	49.81	52.71	62.17	68.34	65.65	90.00
Extract price (Sh/kg)	103.7	47.8	30.7	29.4	28.5	60.5
Total sales/kg CDW Sh.	3.49	2.79	3.12	3.55	3.59	4.90

[a] March spot estimate, assuming 4.5 cartons = 100 kg CDW
Source: KMC Annual Reports

value of sales/kg CDW in the table is therefore likely to be spurious, reflecting changes in the amount of uncosted by-products included, but even so, the year-to-year fluctuation in prices is substantial.

Table 19.4

Value of Canning Beef

Cents/kg CDW

Item		Market prices, 1970 budget	Accounting prices, 1970
1.	Sales CCD and Extract f.o.b. Mombasa	364.3	364.3
2.	Factory to f.o.b.	5.3	4.0
3.	Canning costs	131.5	103.2
4.	Second stage by-products	+31.5	+31.5
5.	Value ex first stage	259.0	288.6
6.	First stage by-products	+56.0	+56.0
7.	First stage costs for 115 kg carcass	71.0	55.8
8.	Value of canning beef into factory	244.0	288.4
9.	Standard deviation of estimate	32	35
10.	Value at 1972 estimated prices	375	418

Notes: Line 1 is derived from the 1970 figures from Table 19.3 *plus* transport costs from line 2. Since this is the calculated f.o.b. price it is the same at both market and accounting prices.

Lines 3, 7 are taken from the last line of Table 19.2.

Lines 4 and 6 come from 1970 budgeted input (slightly different from Table 33 of Beddoes.)

Line 7 has been expressed per kg CDW.

Line 9 was derived from estimated fluctuations in export prices of by-products (from Kenya Trade Statistics) of 20 per cent, from the implied fluctuations in Table 19.3, and the uncertainties in the amounts and allocation of processing costs. All these were assumed independent, so that variances (squares of S.D.) could be summed to give the overall variance, of which the figure shown is the square root.

The standard deviation gives a measure of the uncertainty attached to the final estimate, and its derivation is explained in the notes to Table 19.4. It should be noted that fluctuations in the world price have a magnified effect on fluctuations in the value of carcass beef, since process costs will not fluctuate systematically with export prices.

19.5 THE VALUE OF EXPORT CHILLED AND FROZEN BEEF

Appropriate grades of beef can be sent to the Cut Beef department for processing into one of the three main types of chilled beef exports: primal cuts (comprising a whole range of cuts; see Beddoes, Table 50), pistolas (or Gilson cuts) and boneless beef. I assume that only FAQ grade and above hindquarters (H/Q) can be exported as primal cuts and pistolas, but that sides can be exported as boneless beef (though there would be substantial transfers to canning, presumably from the forequarters). Only standard and below will be transferred to boneless beef.

The value of beef destined to be sold as cut beef as it leaves the first stage is the sales price of the main product plus the value of by-products less the processing costs. For convenience and comparability these are all expressed per kg CDW in Table 19.5.

The value of boneless beef can be compared with the value of canning beef as it leaves the first stage, since the same quality of beef can be sent to either destination. The figures suggest that low grade beef is slightly more profitable exported as boneless beef, though the difference is not significant given the difficulty of allocating costs (especially the freezer cost) accurately, and of allowing for different movements in the value of by-products. The approach adopted is to take an average of its value as boneless beef and canning beef to give the value of low grade beef (i.e. standard and below, passed and retained) ex first stage. There seems no reason to distinguish between P and R, nor between the grades *except* insofar as different grades have different carcass weights and attract different first stage costs. This conclusion would be altered if it were found that the carcass composition were significantly different for different grades.

The accounting prices of beef ex first stage computed for some grades are shown in Table 19.6.

19.5.1 *Future Developments*

The possibility of Kenya exporting chilled beef to Europe has already been mentioned. In 1970 the best estimate was that

Table 19.5

Value of Cut Beef ex First Stage at Accounting Prices

cents/kg CDW

	Primal cuts	Pistolas	Boneless Beef	CCB
Sales value of main product				
1. 1970	392	444	193	
2. 1972 estimated	561	590	302	
Sales value of by-product				
3. 1970	68	35	129	
4. 1972	77	35	183	
5. Processing costs	31	29	27	
Value of cut beef ex first stage				
6. 1970 accounting prices	429	450	295	289
7. 1972 accounting prices	607	596	458	420
8. 1970 market prices	417	441	273	259
9. 1972 market prices	595	587	436	390

Notes: The 1970 budgeted throughput of the Cut Beef department was 3.4 m.kg. but at this level the department was significantly under-utilized. Subsequent rises in world prices encouraged KMC to divert a larger proportion of its total throughput through this department at a marginal cost below the average cost. It is assumed that throughout can double with only a 50 per cent increase in departmental costs, 100 per cent in packing costs, and no increase in overheads shown in Table 19.2. Packing costs differ between the three cuts and explain the variations in line 5. Accounting prices are derived from Appendix A.18.

Table 19.6

Accounting Prices of Beef ex First Stage

Sh/kg CDW

Grade	Best destination 1970	Best destination 1972	Accounting price[a] 1970	Accounting price[a] 1972
FGAQ[b] H/Q P	Pistolas	Primal cuts or Pistolas	4.50	6.00
FGAQ[b] H/Q R	Primal cuts	Primal cuts	4.29	6.00
Standard and below	CCB and boneless beef	CCB and boneless beef	2.92	4.38

[a] Market prices can be deduced from Table 19.5 in a similar fashion, identifying best destinations for each grade

[b] FGAQ = both FAQ and GAQ

chilled beef would receive Sh.11. per kg for primal cuts f.o.a. Nairobi airport if she were granted export status. (This was the figure for corresponding cuts from Salisbury, Rhodesia, to Switzerland.) Depending on the assumptions about the proportion of primal cuts in the hind quarter this would give a point estimate of 620 cents/kg CDW for H/Q ex first stage (± 40 cents). As can be seen, this is significantly higher than the best alternative in 1970, but not in 1972. There was an additional suggestion that Israel might be prepared to import forequarters if sufficient supplies could be guaranteed (the figure mentioned was 10,000 tons or 100,000 head p.a.) and provided the cattle were slaughtered in the approved Kosher manner. The price quoted was 493 cents/kg f.o.b., equivalent to 465 cents/kg CDW ex first stage. Again, in 1970 this was a significant improvement on the best alternative (see below) but not in 1972. Of course, in the face of rising prices elsewhere the Israeli export prospects may improve but no firm data was available.

This completes the valuation of beef which is exported. All grades of beef *can* be exported, for anything that cannot be sold as chilled or frozen beef can be canned, but some grades of beef are obviously best sold locally.

19.6 LOCALLY SOLD BEEF

We want to calculate the accounting price of beef which is best sold in the local market and not exported, i.e. beef which is socially more valuable when domestically consumed and which is thus a non-traded good. The general method of valuing non-traded agricultural products has already been outlined in 7.8, and rather than repeat the arguments here we shall ask instead what are the *special* features of non-traded beef which modify or simplify the general formulae given in 7.8.2. These features are listed below:

(i) non-traded beef cuts are supplied in fixed proportions with traded beef, since both come in physically preordained proportions from a single animal;

(ii) all cuts *can* be exported, at worst as canned beef;

(iii) the producer price schedule is fixed by Government and is inflexible in the short run. It is illegal to sell beef except through the KMC and licensed slaughter houses, although this does happen with attendant disease risks. A rise in the wholesale price of beef will tend to make sales to non-KMC butchers more attractive to cattle owners unless the producer price rises.

Given these considerations, the simplest plausible method of calculating the accounting prices of non-traded beef is to assume that it bears the same relationship to the market price as for locally sold traded beef. This would be strictly correct if consumers spent the *same* amount of money on beef and purchased whatever combination of traded and non-traded beef were available, with no change in the average level of wholesale prices. If the KMC adjusted the supply of traded beef to the local market with the object of stabilizing prices there this would happen. A unitary elasticity of substitution between cuts of beef seems plausible when it is realized that both high and low grade beef have traded and untraded cuts.

If, on the other hand, domestic sales of beef from the KMC were restricted, two offsetting tendencies would affect the accounting price. If consumers switched to other consumer goods the accounting price of non-traded beef will be overstated (see below), but if they induced extra sales through the illegal markets this would both restrict supplies of cattle to the KMC and increase disease risks. The first effect reinforces the assumption of treating non-traded and traded beef similarly (both could be withheld from the KMC) whilst the second makes it socially more desirable to keep KMC beef *market* prices low to prevent such a switch, i.e. it tends to raise the ratio of the accounting price to the market price.

We conclude that there is no strong evidence against the simplest (and most obvious) solution of assuming that the ratio of accounting price to market price should be the same for non-traded beef as for traded beef. Table 19.7 is constructed on this assumption, allowing for a handling cost of 8 cents/kg at market prices, or 6 cents at accounting prices.

Table 19.7
Wholesale Prices of Beef

Sh/kg

		Market Prices		Known accounting prices		Remaining accounting prices	
		1970 (1)	1972 (2)	1970 (3)	1972 (4)	1970 (5)	1972 (6)
Choice	H/Q	4.19	5.40	4.56	6.06	—	—
	F/Q	3.42	4.00	—	—	3.69	4.48
	Side					4.14	5.30
FAQ	H/Q	4.11	4.75	4.56	6.06		
	F/Q	3.25	3.85	—	—	3.69	4.48
	Side					4.14	5.30
Standard	H/Q	3.19	3.50	—	—	3.76	5.36
	F/Q	2.53	2.90	2.98	4.44		
	Side	—	—	—	—	3.39	4.92

Notes:

1. Columns (3) and (4) are equal to the accounting prices in Table 19.6 *plus* 6 cents handling.
2. Columns (5) and (6) are derived on the assumption that the ratio of F/Q to H/Q price is the same at market and accounting prices. The figures for Choice and FAQ at APs are the same, and are a weighted average of Choice and FAQ.

The average ratio of accounting to market price for high grade H/Q and standard F/Q is 1.12 in 1970 and 1.31 in 1972 or 1.21 overall. These ratios are significantly different from those for other urban consumer goods, viz:

Maize flour	0.91
Milk	0.70
Wheat flour	0.78
Miscellaneous foodstuffs	0.82
Non-traded foodstuffs	0.85

so that if exports, by making traded beef cuts locally less available, caused consumers to switch into other consumer goods, the non-traded beef accounting prices in Table 19.8 would be slightly too high, as mentioned above. Note that the 1972 high grade forequarters price ex first stage of Sh.4.42 per kg CDW is not far from the price quoted for Israeli exports of

Sh.4.65 so the assumptions lead to a result consistent with export parity. The accounting price of beef ex first stage for all grades is calculated from this table by deducting the 6 cents handling costs.

19.7 THE PRODUCER PRICE SCHEDULE AT ACCOUNTING PRICES

Most of the information has now been assembled to calculate the value of beef on the farm, except for transport costs. The KMC producer price schedule gives the price at the nearest railhead—the KMC bears the transport costs and does not discriminate against more distant producers. This is not quite as illogical as it seems, for the accounting cost of transport does not vary much with rail haulage distance, at least up to about 300 miles, which is the size of the catchment area. The reason for this will emerge in the following calculation of social transport costs.

The difference between the rail tariff and the long run marginal cost (LRMC) accrues as profit to the East African Railways and Harbours, which are jointly owned by the three East African countries. If we assume that only one-third of these profits are available for Kenyan development, and if we suppose that the Government is only concerned with receipts by Kenya, then the social cost is equal to LRMC + two-thirds (price-LRMC). This is the procedure followed by Scott and it will be used here with some reservation—at least as strong a case could be made for using the LRMC.

Figures for the long-run marginal cost are available for the Economist Intelligence Unit's Transport Study. For cattle the Study gives two methods, the simpler of which is to use the formula relating costs to mileage. For 18 head of cattle in a CF wagon the cost per head is Sh. $(18.60 + .0228\, m)$ where m is the number of miles. The second method is to compound up from the system costs using the geographical costings; this is not specific to cattle (except in the assumptions about type of wagon and degree of empty running back) but is specific to station of origin. From Lanet to Athi River, for example, assuming that the unavoidable terminal costs per wagon are

144/-, the total cost is 476/- or 26/40 per head, compared with the estimate by the simple mileage formula of 21/40. From Nanyuki to Athi River the costs by the first method are: 22/30, by the mileage formula 28/-.

In 1970 the actual tariffs were well out of line with LRMC and a new schedule was under discussion. If we take these proposals as indicative of the likely future tariff the situation is shown in Table 19.8.

Table 19.8
Rail Transport Costs for Cattle

Sh/head

Miles	1970 tarrif	Proposed tarrif	Accounting cost	Accounting cost of proposed tarrif
0	2/22	8/–	18/60	9/25
100	11/–	15/–	20/90	14/38
200	19/30	24/30	23/16	20/76
300	25/30	29/30	25/40	24/80
500	35/80	39/80	30/–	32/70

As can be seen, the LRMC varies less with distance than either the 1970 or the proposed tariff, so that the KMC policy of paying transport costs, equivalent to charging all cattle the *same* transport cost, is closer to the accounting price than charging for transport at the market price.

Both the proposed tariff and the accounting cost of transport from Lanet to Athi River is Sh.18 per head. The first stage processing costs are Sh.81.8 per head at market prices, Sh.64.2 at accounting prices. The total of transport and processing costs from the farm to the end of the first stage processing are thus Sh.82.2 per head at accounting prices. The figures in Table 19.7 give the value of standard and higher grades of beef ex first stage after deducting the 6 cents handling between first stage and wholesale. To this must be added the value of first stage by-products (56 cents/kg CDW) and from this is deducted the transport and first stage costs to give the accounting price at the farm. The accounting price of any grade and weight can now be found. Thus for a 200 kg CDW FAQ P animal its accounting price is in 1970 Sh.4.14 (col. 5, Table 19.7) *less* 0.06 handling *plus* 0.56 by-products *less* 82.2/200 transport and processing (=0.41) giving Sh.4.23/kg CDW farm gate accounting price.

The farm gate accounting prices and the market prices (which are already farm gate prices) for cattle of a typical weight for that grade are given in Table 19.9. The accounting prices of cattle of a different weight, W, can be calculated by adding the figure in the third column and then deducting $82.2/W$.

Table 19.9

Accounting and Market Farm Gate Cattle Prices

Sh/kg CDW

Grade	Average carcass weight kg	Costs to first stage	1970[a] AP	1970[a] MP	1970[a] Ratio AP/MP	1972 AP	1972 MP	1972 Ratio AP/MP
(1)	(2)	(3)	(4)	(5)	(6)	(7)	(8)	(9)
Choice	244	0.34	4.31	3.41	1.26	5.47	4.45	1.23
FAQ P	227	0.36	4.29	3.30	1.30	5.44	4.20	1.30
FGAQ R	227	0.36	3.55	2.97	1.20	5.44	3.18	1.71
Standard P	174	0.47	3.42	2.75	1.24	4.95	3.15	1.57
Standard R	174	0.47	3.01	2.65	1.14	4.42	2.65	1.67
Commercial	114	0.72	2.73	2.40	1.14	4.02	2.80	1.44
Manufacturing	100	0.82	2.62	1.10	2.38	3.91	1.50	2.61

a 1970 accounting prices based on existing export markets

These figures must be interpreted with some care. Errors and uncertainties in allocating costs and forecasting price movements give rise to an estimated standard deviation of about 60 cents for the higher grades and 40 cents for lower grades. Further, the assumed weights for animals of different grades are based on the averages for the 1970 throughput. If the weight and grade of an animal can be predicted from other information then a better estimate of the accounting price can be derived directly, and this can be doen for feedlot beef. Finally, it has been pointed out to me that although I have not been able to detect any difference in the eligibility of different cuts of meat going to the same market this does not imply that there is no difference in fact or that there will continue to be no difference. Thus although it appears to be possible to export both Retained and Passed Choice and FAQ hindquarters as primal cuts the average price received *may* depend on the proportion of Choice and Passed grades. Even if this were not true at the present, as the volume of exports increases the market may develop in discrimination and offer a premium for higher quality cuts. However, the information is not yet available to resolve the issue, and in any case the likely difference it would make to the accounting prices is almost certainly less than the underlying uncertainty measured by the standard deviation, so in some sense it could be argued that we have already implicitly allowed for these additional uncertainties.

It is interesting to compare the market and accounting price schedules. The first point that stands out is that accounting prices are in all cases appreciably *above* the market price, in contrast to most accounting ratios. (See 1.4 for a discussion of the values taken by the accounting ratios in general. To a large extent this is understandable because beef is a traded exported good, though Figure 1.1 shows that this is not a sufficient explanation.) The degree of distortion *within* the beef price schedule is not large, and its increase from 1970 to 1972 reflects an incomplete adjustment to a rapidly changing world beef market situation. Given the pressures on the KMC discussed in 19.1, the lack of distortion, and particularly, the relatively higher market prices for low grade beef in 1970, is slightly surprising, but it can be explained by the method of accounting at KMC, which is, roughly speaking, to relate all costs per kg CDW. The average weight of low grade cattle is lower, and both transport costs and first stage costs vary with the number of cattle, rather than their weight, so that processing costs are actually higher per kg for low grade cattle, whereas the KMC assumes they are equal for all cattle.

The 1972 market price schedule should not be criticized as reflecting the long run views of the Government, given the rapid increase of world beef prices. Indeed in December 1972 the prices of low grade beef were raised, and in March 1973 the Ministry of Agriculture in a policy statement on KMC pricing announced its intention of basing the pricing structure on export parity and paying 'the realizable economic value for carcasses which are retained for measles'.

19.7.1 *Seasonal Price Variation*

The throughput of cattle at Athi River shows substantial fluctuations during the course of the year as grazing becomes available. It is difficult to predict the fluctuation in price which would even out this flow, but a substantial variation would be justified by the quite large difference between the average cost (equal to the long run marginal cost, and equal to the total of direct and fixed costs in Table 19.2) and the short-run marginal cost (which can be approximated by the direct costs alone in Table 19.2). This difference amounts to about 50 cents/kg CDW. Athi River at present pays a premium of 20 cents/kg CDW for feedlot beef which is available throughout the year, but gives no seasonal encouragement (though carcasses are said to grade higher during the slack months—a concealed price increase). On the other hand the feedlot industry is likely to use a specific slaughterhouse, in which case no seasonal fluctuation will arise and capacity will be better adjusted and hence overheads will be lower. If the elimination of seasonal fluctuations permitted a reduction in factory overheads including capital of one-third, costs would be reduced by about 10 cents/kg CDW. For lack of a better estimate this figure of 10 cents will be used in the final profit assessment.

19.7.2 *Accounting Price of Feedlot Beef*

Anticipating the results of later chapters we have to distinguish two types of cattle—NEP Boran, sold at 180 kg CDW, and crossbreds, sold at 225 kg CDW. The proportion in the different grades are shown in the top part of Table 19.10.

The incidence of measles is not critical as higher or lower rates will be reflected in different purchase prices paid by the feedlot. The average incidence recorded at the Beef Research Station varied from 6 per cent (crossbreds from medium and low rainfall ranches) to 20 per cent (NEP Boran direct from LMD).

Allowing for the different weights, and the 10 cents seasonal factor at accounting prices or 20 cents special premium at market prices (both discussed in 19.7.1) Table 19.10 gives market and accounting prices of the two types of typical feedlot cattle.

Table 19.10

Farm-Gate Prices of Different Types of Feedlot Cattle

	Sh/kg CDW			
	NEP Boran (180 kg CDW)		Crossbred and Improved Boran (225 kg CDW)	
Average grading pattern				
Choice P	9%		60%	
Choice R	1		0	
FAQ P	69		30	
FAQ R	8		4	
Standard P	10		5	
Standard R	1		1	
Below	2		0	
Measles incidence	19%		5%	
Year	Accounting prices	Market prices	Accounting prices	Market prices
1970	4.04	3.40	4.31	3.52
1970 (exporting to Europe)	4.95	n.a.	5.51	n.a.
1972	5.38	4.19	5.51	4.44

Notes:

1. The average grading pattern is for the surviving cattle sent to KMC, and is derived from the Technical Assumptions of Beef Research Station (1971).

2. The prices are weighted averages using the weights shown of the figures in Table 19.9, *plus* 10 cents at APs, 20 cents at MPs explained in 19.7.1.

Table 19.10 shows that permission to export to Europe would have made little difference in 1972, but would have had a dramatic effect in 1970.

CHAPTER 20

The Supply Price of Immature Cattle

The profitability of the feedlot depends sensitively on the margin between feeder stock and fat stock (finished) prices. Intensive feeding will be profitable only if it is at least as efficient as the (marginal) alternative method of converting feeder stock to fat stock (or at least to cattle destined for slaughter; they might not be technically finished animals).

Immatures can come from three different sources—breeding herds, direct from the Livestock Marketing Division's (LMD) holding grounds at Isiolo, or from graziers who have in turn purchased them from the LMD and held them for some time. The opportunity cost of an immature depends on the source of supply in the following way. If they come direct from LMD they would otherwise have been sold for slaughter—at least for the next few years, during which the supply of immatures from the LMD will exceed the demand from graziers. If they come from graziers then they might otherwise have been finished on pasture. Their price must be such as to yield the same return per hectare of grazing land as keeping fewer animals and finishing them. Finally, the alternative open to the manager of a breeding herd is not to sell immatures but fully grown finished animals. Such breeding herds are the only source of cross-breds and improved Boran, and as the determination of the cost of immatures from this source is the most complex and illustrates more generally applicable methods, it is logical to take this calculation first.

20.1 THE COST OF IMMATURES FROM BREEDING HERDS

We have abundant information on the technical characteristics of breeding herds, and this can be used to design the optimal herd structure of a breeding herd selling matures. The structure of a herd in this context means the number of cattle of each age and sex that gives a herd capable of reproducing the structure year by year using the same quantity of land: it will depend on the fertility of the cows, the pattern of culling or selling and the area of pasture needed by beasts of different age. The optimal herd will depend on the producer price schedule as well as the basic herd parameters, and it is a comparatively simple (if tedious) exercise to determine the optimal herd—an exercise that lends itself to computer programming. Indeed, the Agricultural Finance Corporation use a similar program, designed by one of their staff, R. von Kaufmann, to calculate the profitability of herds which they are considering for loans, and Dr. Klaus Meyn, of the Animal Husbandry Research Station at Naivasha, has published sample calculations in the *Kenya Farmer* (February 1969).

Once the income generated by a given area of land under the optimal herd structure has been determined we can ask what price would have to be paid for immatures such that a herd using the same area (and other facilities) restructured to produce animals of a different age would yield the same net income to the rancher.

20.1.1 *The Optimal Breeding Herd and the Basic Parameters*

The equilibrium state of a herd (or its dynamic evolution) can be determined by a simple algebraic model with the following basic parameters. Here we assume that the area of land available for the herd is constant, which implies that it can support a known number of Livestock Units (LSUs, which are cattle of a standard weight and appetite. For poor range land 1 LSU may need as much as 6 ha. or 15 acres. Further details are given in Appendix A.20).

Parameter	*Description*
Bull Pressure	The number of females to be served (inseminated) by each bull—specifies the number of breeding bulls required. Can be replaced with artificial insemination.

Calving rate (or calving interval)	The percentage of mature females who produce calves in one year (or the inverse, the interval between calves).
Age of first calving	Age of female when first calf delivered.
Culling rate	For breeding cows—the percentage of the breeding herd weeded out for sale each year (because of age, infertility, etc.). For bulls—ditto (to prevent inbreeding, etc.).
LSU equivalents	The feed required for animals of given age and sex in terms of the standard. Dictates the number of cattle of different ages, etc., which can be carried on the given area of land.
Weight and grade gain	The functional relationship between quantity and quality of meat and the age/sex of animal.
Mortality	Mortality rates (percentage p.a.) by age/sex, from natural causes.

In addition we will need to know the price schedule for cattle grades and the marginal running costs per head of a given age/sex. This will dictate the profitability. The decision variable is the number of animals of each age/sex group to sell for slaughter and this is chosen to maximize net revenue.

A simple herd model starts from an assumed number of breeding females (say 1,000). At the end of the year there will be a determinate number of calves, bulls and culls. The calves will become heifers and steers in the next year and these will either be sold or continue for a further period. The equilibrium herd will have animals of different ages in a well defined numerical relationship, and its required area is determined by the LSU equivalents. Finally the actual number of the breeding herd will be found by multiplying the original number by the ratio of land area available to that required to support the calculated number of LSUs.

As an example consider a herd with a bull pressure of 30, a calving rate of 70 per cent (defined as the ratio of calves surviving one year to breeding cows), a mortality rate of 2 per cent p.a., an age of first calving of 3 years, a cow cull rate of 20 per cent and a bull cull rate of 25 per cent. We consider two possible arrangements of the same herd at the same point of time (just before the annual sales of cattle) requiring the same grazing acreage:

	Herd A, Breeding and Fattening	*Herd B, Breeding and rearing immatures*
	1,000 breeding cows	1,479 breeding cows
	33 bulls	49 bulls
	700 calves (1 year old)	1,035 calves
	686 2-year olds	1,015 2-year olds
	672 3-year olds (of which 200 heifers are cow replacements)	296 3-year old heifers for cow replacements
	329 4-year old steers	
	129 4-year old heifers	
Sales:	180 cull cows	266 cull cows
	7.6 cull bulls	11.3 cull bulls
	329 4-year old steers	507 2-year old steers
	129 4-year old heifers	206 2-year old heifers
Herd numbers	3,549	4,144
LSU	2,580	2,580

20.1.2 *The Data*

In principle we want the basic parameters from all potential sources of supply of immatures. In practice it is difficult to establish the basic parameteres with much precision even for quite well documented cattle herds, and they will obviously fluctuate from place to place with changing weather, disease, etc.

The approach adopted was to perform a sensitivity analysis to identify the most important parameters, and then use the best information available on these parameters, correlated as appropriate, to give a point estimate and a standard deviation. The data and technical details of the analysis are relegated to Appendix A.20.

It was discovered that the most important parameter was the calving rate—none of the remaining parameters led to uncertainties in the final price of more than 7 per cent taken individually. The final results are summarized in Table 20.1

Table 20.1

Supply Price of Immatures from Breeding Herds

		Source of immatures			
		Good range land		Poor range land	
1.	Supply price as a function of producer price	0.48 FAQ		0.55 Standard	
2.	Likely measles incidence	5%		20%	
		1970	1972	1970	1972
3.	Accounting prices sh./kg live weight	2.01	2.66	1.77	2.69
4.	Market prices sh./kg live weight	1.58	1.99	1.50	1.68
5.	Standard deviation of estimate	4%		6%	

Notes: Lines 1 and 3: price for full, not shrunk, *live* weight.

Line 2: The percentage of measles gives the percentage of cattle graded either FAQ R (good range land) or standard R.

Line 3: The producer prices used to calculate the supply price are given in Table 19.9, though lower carcass weights were assumed. Adjustments for different carcass weights can be made with the data from column (3) of that table as explained in the preceding text.

As the margin between high and low grade prices narrows, the attractiveness of poor range lands as a source of supply diminishes. Since the distance of these ranches from the feedlots is greater they are further penalized. At market prices, though, the poor range lands appear cheaper, in both 1970 and 1972.

20.2 THE COST OF IMMATURES FROM THE LIVESTOCK MARKETING DIVISION

As a result of a considerable investment in stock routes, holding grounds and stock-handling equipment started towards the end of the 1960s the number of cattle purchased by the LMD has increased from less than 30,000 to nearly 50,000 per annum by 1972. In 1970 it was a fair assumption that the supply of cattle was greater than the demand from graziers and feedlots so that surplus cattle were sold direct to KMC for slaughter—and thus the opportunity cost of cattle from this source was measured by their slaughter value. The average mob of cattle would probably have graded 40 per cent Standard, 59 per cent Commercial, 1 per cent Manufacturing, with perhaps 10 per cent measles, and at a 47 per cent dressing percentage they would have been worth Sh.1.35 per kg live weight at accounting prices (1970) rising to Sh.2.00 per kg at 1972 accounting prices. These prices are both substantially below the opportunity costs of cattle from breeding herds, so that in the short run if we assume that the LMD is committed to marketing cattle in these numbers they will form the cheapest source of supply. There are, however, two important qualifications to this conclusion.

The first and obvious point is that the LMD was concerned to move cattle out of the NEP not just in order to slaughter them but to increase the total quantity of beef produced, and expected that these cattle would be further fattened. Moreover, the costs of moving the cattle from the NEP to the holding grounds have been substantial and it is not clear that they would have been justified if the cattle were merely destined for slaughter. It is difficult to estimate the marginal cost of moving cattle, but in 1972 the average cost (equal to the trading loss on purchases less sales plus direct costs and overheads) per kg live weight at market prices was probably greater than 35 cents. The correct computation at accounting prices would require us to know the opportunity cost of the cattle purchased in the NEP, which would be difficult, although the purchase price may not be a bad guide as there is competition for the purchase of cattle by neighbouring countries at the sales grounds in the NEP. Indeed, in 1972 only 15,000 head were sold direct to KMC, the remaining 35,000 head—and undoubtedly the best

35,000—were purchased by graziers. There is some evidence that the graziers were able to exercise monopsony powers at the auctions and frequently purchased cattle below slaughter value which they then sent to KMC so it is difficult to estimate the true surplus—or what the quality of the marginally slaughtered cattle was—but it does suggest that the opportunity cost of LMD cattle had risen above the slaughter value by 1972. When the demand for immatures by feedlots and graziers rises to absorb the whole supply (which was itself planned to increase significantly for the few years after 1972) then the relevant opportunity cost will be determined by the profitability of grazing.

20.3 THE COST OF IMMATURES FROM GRAZIERS

It is difficult to obtain information on this comparatively recent phenomenon of purchasing immatures from the LMD and fattening them on grass, so we are compelled to make a rather *ad hoc* estimate. Suppose the live weight gain per hectare is independent of the size of the animal (in general it will decline slightly with size) and that the grazier can upgrade an average LMD mob to 40 per cent FAQ, 40 per cent Standard, 18 per cent Commercial P and 2 per cent other grades without changing the measles incidence. At a 49 per cent dressing percentage the accounting value of live weight has increased to Sh.1.75 per kg in 1970 and Sh.2.42 in 1972. If the opportunity cost of the cattle purchased by the grazier were their slaughter value (as we considered above) and if the cattle were purchased at 200 kg live weight and sold at 340 kg the accounting revenue per kg of weight gain would have been Sh.2.32 in 1970 and Sh.3.02 in 1972. If instead of finishing the cattle the graziers sold them to feedlots at 270 kg live weight they would earn the same revenue per kg of weight gain (and therefore by hypothesis per hectare) if the prices were Sh.1.60 per kg live weight in 1970, Sh.2.26 in 1972, where all these prices are accounting prices. (Exactly the same calculation can be performed to find the market prices that would have to be paid to the graziers.) This will give us an estimate of the opportunity cost of immatures in the medium run. In the long run the purchase price of cattle from the LMD will rise, and with it (but by not so much) the price of immatures to the feedlots, presumably until it is no cheaper to purchase from graziers than breeding herds. All this information is summarized in Table 20.2.

Table 20.2

Accounting Prices of Immatures

Source of immatures	Sh/kg full live weight 1970 accounting prices	1972 accounting prices	1972 mart prices
LMD holding grounds (short-run; slaughter value)	1.35	2.00	1.35
Graziers (medium-term)	1.60	2.26	1.52
Poor range breeding herds (eg IBRD ranches)	1.77	2.69	1.68
Good range breeding herds (commercial established ranches)	2.01	2.66	1.99

Notes:

(1) These are the supply prices at the source, delivered prices will be higher by transport costs.

(2) Cross-bred cattle can only come from the last source, the others supply NEP Borans. The three prices give a measure of the extent to which the price will rise as demand rises relative to supply.

(3) The market prices for 1972 are predictions, not observed prices. Earlier predictions made by the same methods gave values close to those subsequently observed and provide a partial validation of the method.

Appendix A.20

The Breeding Herd Simulation Model: Data and Results

In this appendix we bring together all the available data on the parameters which are needed to describe the structure and production of a breeding herd. The general structure of the computer model has been described in 20.1.1; the detailed assumptions and results of running the computer model under these assumptions are described in the following sections.

A.20.1 DATA AND ASSUMPTIONS

The Live Stock Unit (LSU) system adopted in the model is as follows:

Calves	0.2	
1-2 year	0.6	LSU
2-3 year	0.8	
3 +	1.0	

Roughly speaking this is the system adopted by the Range Management Division. A more sophisticated system which relates feed requirements systematically to animal weight and then to sex and age is the Kenya Stock Unit (KSU) proposed by the FAO Range Management Project (Preinvestment Survey Report of Ranching Potential in Kaputiei—1969).

Table A.20.1

K.S.U. System

Age (months)	Females	Steers and Bulls
0 – 12	0.109	0.095
12 – 24	0.244	0.222
24 – 36	0.428	0.405
36 – 48	0.664	0.486
Over 48	0.664	0.605

1 KSU is that animal requiring .09 kg of 90 per cent air dry feed equivalent daily. It will be seen that the difference between this system and the LSU adopted is very slight[1] and the former is retained for convenience of programming.

Weight Gain and Quality Change
This will depend on the breed, quality of the range and its management (and the weather). There are three main sources, referring to different but overlapping regimes. Dr. Klaus Meyn, of the Animal Husbandry Research Station, Naivasha, has published two sets of data (in 'A Breeding Policy for Borans', *Kenya Farmer*, Feb. 1969), one relating to a well-developed ranch with a long established herd in good ranching country (Herd A), the other a less developed ranch in drier country, say in Laikipia (Herd B). Next we have data from tests conducted in 1963[2] and quoted by Peberdy (Head of the Livestock Division of the Ministry of Agriculture). Dietrich Bock has conducted field weighings on a number of ranches but none for animals

1 It is the relative scale that is important. Divide all items in Table A.20.1 by 0.664.

2 I suspect on Borans under a slightly odd regime at a research station but I have not been able to identify the souce of the widely used data.

Table A.20.2

Age, Weight and Grade Data for Different Cattle

Herd	Age months	Liveweight (kg) Steers M	Heifers F	Dressing out fraction of full weight M	F	Grade M	F
A Meyn	24	318	273	0.47	0.49	3.6	3.0
	30	364	309	0.49	0.50	4.0	4.0
	36	409	341	0.50	0.52	4.5	4.5
	42	446	368	0.51	0.52	5.0	5.0
	48	477	386	0.52	0.53	5.0	4.5
	54	496	396	0.52	0.53	4.5	4.0
	60	500	400	0.52	0.53	4.0	4.0
B Meyn	36	323	282	0.47	0.48	3.0	4.0
	42	359	314	0.48	0.49	4.0	4.0
	48	391	341	0.49	0.50	4.0	4.5
	54	423	359	0.50	0.51	4.5	4.99
	60	455	364	0.51	0.51	5.0	4.5
C Peberdy	24	305	259	0.47	0.48	3.0	3.0
	30	352	300	0.47	0.49	3.8	3.8
	36	400	336	0.48	0.50	4.4	4.4
	42	447	368	0.50	0.51	4.8	4.8
	48	505	386	0.51	0.52	4.7	4.5
	54	562	396	0.53	0.54	4.5	4.0
	60	564	400	0.52	0.52	4.0	4.0
D UNDP Study	24	126	138				
	30	155	166				
	36	184	194		n.a.		
	42	215	234				
	48	245	274				
	over	343					
E Kajiado	24	223	200	0.47	0.47	2.5	2.5
	30	272	246	0.47	0.47	3.0	3.0
	36	323	291	0.48	0.48	3.0	3.0
	42	373	336	0.49	0.49	3.5	3.5
	48	418	382	0.50	0.50	3.7	3.7
	54	446	391	0.51	0.51	3.8	3.8
	60	468	400	0.51	0.51	3.6	3.6

Grade definition: 1.0 = Manufacturing; 2.0 = Commercial; 3.0 = Standard
4.0 = FAQ; 5.0 = Choice

Decimals indicate *average* grade

more than 24 months old. The figures give slightly higher weights than Peberdy's—but relate to well-managed ranches, so it will be best to assume that Peberdy's figures are for Borans on good ranges. These are presented as Herd C. Next we have the previously quoted FAO study of Kajiado (Kaputiei) which gives actual weights on 16 group ranches in June 1968 (Herd D). These are clearly in an undeveloped state. Assumed data in planning ranch development is in Herd E.

Calving Rate
This is one of the less well known parameters. If we take the effective calving rate to be the number of calves surviving to age 1 year this could be as low as 45 per cent for poor marginal ranches, 55 per cent for established but dry ranches, and as high as 80-90 per cent for commercial ranches.

Bull Pressure
Anything from 25 to 35, or nearly infinite with artificial insemination. Not very critical.
Cow culling rate: 10 to 20 per cent depending on age at sale.
Bull culling rate: 25 per cent.
Age of first calving: 3 years on good ranches, 4 years on poor ranches.
Mortality: Usually taken as 2 per cent p.a. on good ranches, but it may be as high as 6-7 per cent on poor ranches.
The Running costs can be broken down into two categories—independent of the number of head (but perhaps depending on LSUs), and those dependent on the number, such as herding fees, veterinary attention, dipping etc. The figures vary, as shown in Table A.20.3.

Table A.20.3

Costs Per Head of Herding

Source of data	Health	Labour	Sh/Head Total
Kajiado Commercial ranch	25.0	n.a.	n.a.
Meyn's figures	21.5	15.5	37.0
Peberdy (good ranches)	n.a.		100.0
(other data)	33.0	12.0	47.0
Narok ranch (high grade), 1968	n.a.	n.a.	63.2
Koma Rock Co-operative Ranch, 1968	n.a.	n.a.	33.5
Lukenya Co-operative Ranch, 1968	n.a.	n.a.	40.0
Konza Co-operative Ranch, 1968	n.a.	n.a.	43.0

Some of these figures are misleadingly high, as they include non-number-dependant costs. A good estimate would probably be 30/- to 45/- at market prices, multiplying by the SCF of 0.75 gives a range 22/50 to 33/75.

A20.2 *Sensitivity Analysis*
It is straightforward (though time consuming) to write a computer program to give the required information. The present Fortran program takes less than 1 second to run one specification (of basic parameters and price data) in a sensitivity analysis on an IBM 360-size machine and it is therefore feasible to experiment with a wide range of parameters. The results of the sensitivity analysis are summarized briefly.

The figure we are interested in is the cost of an immature steer, and I have assumed that it would weigh 320 kg live weight at sale from the breeding herd. I compute the cost per kg live weight and also express it as a ratio to the price per kg CDW paid for the mature animals of that herd. (In practice this means a price between standard and choice.) This ratio is a useful summary statistic as it will be independent of the absolute level of the price schedule, and the results given in Table A.20.4 are for variations in this ratio.

Table A.20.4

Sensitivity Results

Parameter varied	Median Value	Variation from this	Maximum variation in ratio[a] (per cent)
Immature sale weight	320 kg	± 25 kg	± 1%
Mortality	2%	to 6%	± 1%
Cow cull rate	20%	to 10%	- 2%
Cow age at first calf	3 years	to 4 years	+ 6%
Calving rate	70%	50% to 80%	±18%
Bull pressure	30	25 to ∞	± 1%
Bull cull rate	25%	20% to 30%	± 1%
Marginal cost Shs	30.0	to 50.0	± 1%
Price schedule	see Note		± 3%
Weight data	see Note		± 6%

[a] ratio is cost/kg live weight/price per kg CDW for mature animals

Notes:

1. Four different price schedules were used in the main simulations, all based on 1970 market and accounting prices, but making different (extreme) assumptions about the ratio of FAQ to Standard prices. A final check with 1972 prices gave consistent results.

2. Weight data A, B, C and E was used. (See Table A.20.2). Two different selling ages for immatures were computed.

3. The minimum number of computations needed for the above table is 9 X 4 X 4 = 144. Rather more were run to test sensitivity away from the median value chosen.

The conclusion to be drawn from this test is that the calving rate is the most sensitive parameter.

A20.3 *Final Estimates of Feederstock Prices*

The results of the sensitivity analysis were used to identify the few parameteres which were both sensitive and not too well established (calving rate and herd weight gain). The range of likely values for each herd type was then used to generate the final estimates given in the table below. The ratio *R* given here is defined to be the ratio of the immature price/kg liveweight to the price per kg CDW which the animals would reach if they were sold at the optimal age. Thus the supply price can be obtained by multiplying this ratio by the expected mature sales price.

Table A.20.5

Best Estimates of the Supply Price of Feeder Stock

Herd	Type of range land	Parameters—range of values: Calf rate (%)	Morta-lity (%)	Cow cull (%)	Heifer maturity years	Sale weight (kg)	*R*	% variation in R as parameters vary
A	Good	70	2	15	3	318	0.48 FAQ	4
		90	3	20	3½	364		
C	Good	70	2	15	3	305	0.49 FAQ	4
		90	3	20	3½	352		
B	Poor	45	7	10	4	323	0.56 Standard	4
		70	5	15	3½	359		
E	Poor	45	7	10	4	273	0.55 Standard	4
		70	5	15	3½	323		

It is encouraging that the final uncertainty about the value of *R* is as low as the table suggests. The fall in the percentage variation of *R* between this table and the previous analysis is the result of correlating likely variations in the basic parameters—for example, a low calving rate is likely to be associated with poor rangeland, low marginal costs, high ages of maturity, etc., and these variations offset each other. The range of values cited is such that it would be unlikely for values to lie far outside the range for the given herd.

CHAPTER 21

Feed Costs

21.1 INTRODUCTION

The experimental work at the Beef Research Station up to the time of writing had been directed to establishing the costs and profitability of maize based rations, although it was planned to broaden its scope in the near future to appraise other crops and possible feedstuffs, particularly sorghums and processing by-products such as pyrethrum marc, etc. The restricted nature of the original research is not as serious as might appear, as the early experimental results suggested that it should be possible to predict how cattle will perform on alternative rations, so that the profitability of alternative rations can in principle be computed from a knowledge of the opportunity costs of their constituents. In this chapter we confine attention to establishing the costs of the constituents of the maize based rations for a farm-feedlot located in maize growing country. Such a farm would almost certainly have a substantial proportion of its arable land down to pasture (this would form part of the crop rotation) and this pasture can also be used for fattening cattle.

The management of these pastures is more closely related to the agricultural side of the farm-feedlot (as opposed to the feedlot side) so the costs and returns of grazing are also considered in this chapter. The rations to be considered will be compounded of ground wet maize grain or maize germ meal as concentrates, silage for roughage (in this case made from the whole maize plant chopped and then ensiled) and a minerals-urea-molasses (MUM) supplement together with cottonseed cake as an additional protein source. Thus the main component of the ration (and its cost) is directly or indirectly maize. We therefore start by determining the accounting cost of the maize based components.

21.2 MAIZE AND SILAGE COSTS

Again the principle is to work back from the world price (at Mombasa) of maize. Silage costs are found by deducting the harvest costs of maize and adding the extra forage harvesting costs, silage making costs and additional management input. As a check the production costs of silage are calculated separately to see if the implied rent per acre is reasonable.

There is a substantial difference between the farm value of maize if Kenya is exporting maize and if it is importing, though in the latter case the maize for feed would be yellow maize rather than the white maize imported for human consumption. In 7.2 Scott gives estimates of the accounting price of maize in the years 1962-3 to 1967-8, during which period Kenya shifted from a maize-import to a maize-export economy as described in Chapter 18. This change has repercussions which go further than the obvious and substantial change in the value of maize, for the transport and distribution system has had to be redesigned. The costs of exporting maize in 1968 were the costs of exporting maize through an inefficient distribution system which it is intended to change in the near future. Table 21.1 presents estimates for the market and accounting price of a bag of maize at Lanet. The figures for the early years are taken from Scott, 1970, and except for the rail costs are identical to those shown in Table 7.2. The figures for 1968-9 are derived from the Maize and Produce Board's accounts using Scott's method, whilst the projected figures assume that the bulk handling facilities projected in the *Report of the Working Party on Storage and Handling of Wheat and Maize* (Ministry of Agriculture, 1969) are installed. In this case the maize is handled naked and rail costs may be even lower than shown, once wagons have been modified to take loose grain.

The world price fluctuates substantially, but is unlikely to be much below Sh.47 without a grant element, and it is unlikely that Kenya would be eligible for food aid for cattle feeding. If maize is imported only for the urban population the accounting price is found by equating local and import prices at Nairobi, in which case Sh.47 per bag is the best estimate. If, however, maize has to be imported to Nakuru, the price will be the import price plus the various projected handling costs in col.

(3), or Sh.55 per bag. These prices can now be used to derive the cost of silage, assuming either that maize is exported or imported.

Table 21.1

Market and Accounting Price of Maize Grain

Sh/bag of 90 kg

	Export Parity			Import Parity		
	1967/8	1868	Future	1966/7	Future	Future
	(1)	(2)	(3)	(4)	(5)	(6)
World price at Mombasa (f.o.b. or c.i.f.)	31.21	32.20	31.50	35.03	47.00	47.00
Port Costs	-6.13	-4.14	-1.61	+6.13	+1.61	+1.61
MPB handling costs	-3.86	-2.97	-2.50	—	—	+2.50
Rail costs (net)	-6.39	-5.03	-4.00	+0.65	0.00	+4.00
Bag cost net	-1.54	-1.54	0	0	0	0
Subsidy less cess	+12.01	+8.48	+0.21	-5.81	0	0
Price at railhead	25.30	27.00	23.60	36.00	48.61	55.10
Price at farm	23.30	25.00	21.60	34.00	46.61	57.10
Accounting price at farm	15.43	19.68	23.50	40.00	46.75	55.00

Notes: All prices except the last line are market prices. The sources and interpretation of the columns are:

(1) Derived from Scott, Aug. 1970. Maize Board costs are 90 per cent average costs to give an estimate of the marginal cost here and for the other columns.

(2) Derived from the Maize and Produce Board's accounts using Scott's method.

(3) The projected price after the installation of bulk handling facilities.

(4) See Table 7.2. The c.i.f. price is net of a 25 per cent grant element under PL480 from the USA. The farm price is calculated on the assumption that grain is imported to feed urban workers in Nairobi, and also exported from the maize areas to Nairobi. The MPB costs cancel out since prices are assumed equated for both sources at Nairobi, and the net rail cost is the excess of the Mombasa-Nairobi cost over the maize area-Nairobi cost.

(5) The projected future import parity price after bulk handling is installed (assuming it can also handle maize imports), similar assumptions to column (4).

(6) A pessimistic projection assuming that maize is imported right to the farm.

If the farm were operated as a commercial maize farm it would produce about 40 bags/ha (16 bags/acre); instead of harvesting the ripened maize grain, the whole maize plant would be chopped by a forage harvester and would yield 40 tons/ha of green chop or about 11 tons/ha of dry matter. The main problem in determining the opportunity cost of the greenchop lies in calculating the *extra* managerial input needed above that required for growing maize grain. Problems of this sort are likely to be quite common and troublesome in evaluating agricultural projects in developing countries where the alternative style of management and farming a given piece of land may be quite different and not readily indentifiable. Putting it another way, managerial inputs are less homogeneous and the optimal farm plan less well defined than in either developed country agriculture or LDC industrial projects, so much of the clarity and precision of the concept of opportunity cost is lost.

A related point is that typically we are not just costing one crop but a whole rotation of crops and related activities where precision in the allocation of costs requires a knowledge of all the different possible rotations. In a stable environment with homogeneous and quantifiable inputs the costs can then be found by linear programming, but under the conditions prevalent in tropical agriculture such precision is pointless and probably misleading. The best that can be hoped for is some reasonable judgement on the allocation of costs. In the case dealt with here the land will be devoted to a rotation of maize and pastures of Rhodes grass, with a second crop sown after the maize is harvested as silage, to be foraged by grazing cattle. For a farm of 750-800 ha (which appears[1] to be the optimum size) the rotation would probably be:

Year	1	2	3	4	5	6	7=1
Land use	Maize, then second crop	Maize, then second crop	Maize, undersown with Rhodes	Rhodes	Rhodes	Rhodes	Maize etc.

325 ha Maize
325 ha Rhodes Grass pasture (year round)
105 ha Rhodes Grass pasture (½ season)
210 ha second crop (Sorghum?) (½ season grazing).

1 See 24.1.1. and appendix A.21.

The management is thus to be allocated over the growing of maize silage, the second crop, grazing cattle on the Rhodes pastures, and, of course, the operation of the feedlot. The direct costs involved in growing the various crops are shown below.

Table 21.2

Crop Costs

Sh/ha

	Crop	Maize	Maize	Second Crop	Rhodes Grass	Rhodes Grass
1.	Previous crop	Rhodes	Second Crop	Maize	Maize	Rhodes
2.	Area: First Crop ha	108	216	—	—	324
3.	Second Crop ha			216	108	
	Item					
4.	Seed	45	45	20	105	0
5.	Fertilizer	260	260	0	280	280
6.	Labour	50	20	0	0	0
7.	Tractor + implements	300	220	130	30	30
8.	Total at market prices	655	545	150	415	310
	Average direct cost/ha					
9.	Maize (324 ha)	582				
10.	Grazing (324 ha)				548	
11.	at accounting prices	550			550	
12.	Rent at accounting prices	150			150	

Notes: Line 1: The previous crop locates the crop described in the rotation, so that e.g. second crop (possible sorgum or some other crop suitable for grazing) is a second crop following a first crop of maize. Sh.90 per ha has been added to the tractor costs for maize to cover interest and depreciation on £7,250 of equipment (3. ploughs, 3 harrows, 4 cultivators, 2 planters, 2 sprayers, 2 fertilizer spreaders, 4 manure spreaders).

Line 10: The second crop (or the undersown Rhodes) is assumed to supplement the semi-permanent Rhodes pastures, permitting higher annual live weight gains.

These figures are best estimates and draw on documents produced at the station (Beef Research Station 1970; Jepsen, 1973; Miles, 1973;) and discussions with the staff. The costs, and the figure for rent discussed in the text, appear to be consistent with available data on good farming practice under similar conditions, as for example given in Allan, 1969; Farm Economics Survey data, 1962, 1971, 1972, accounts of large commercial maize growers and estimates made by the Statistics Division.

The estimate of Sh.150 per hectare for rent at accounting prices was derived as follows. If the land had grown maize grain its value before harvest (i.e. deducting the costs of harvest estimated at Sh.2.25 per bag at accounting prices) would be Sh.850 per acre, Sh.300 more than the direct costs. This figure includes both rent on the land and management, which would be less intensive for grain production than for forage. I assume that half of the Sh.300 is management and half rent.

Total overheads for the whole farm plus feedlot (of 650 hectares arable area) are substantially above Sh.150/ha, they amount to £14,600 at accounting prices (details are given in the farm plan in Appendix A.21). If one-third of the total were allocated to the forage crop this would amount to Sh.300/ha (at accounting prices). At double the rate of overheads attributable to the simpler management task of producing maize grain this is consistent with the observation that contract forage harvesting gives a profit to the contractor over and above direct costs of about Sh.80 per hectare–a measure of the extra management involved in this part of the operation. Allowing about the same again for the other stages (transporting and ensiling) brings the total up to about Sh.300, as assumed. The remaining two-thirds of overheads are allocated to grazing and feeding the cattle.

The costs of producing silage can now be computed as the cost of the maize up to harvest plus harvesting costs, plus handling into the silo, losses in the silo and handling out again (Table 21.3). Details of the equipment needed and its running costs are given in the farm plan in Appendix A.21.

The other main constituent of the ration is moist ground maize grain which is also ensiled, or alternatively maize germ meal (the by-product from milling fine maize flour). Maize germ meal is exported and its accounting price is directly available. It can be stored in bags. The cost of ground maize grain is its cost delivered to the farm (the same as its price at the local Maize Board depot) plus grinding, handling and silage-making costs. Losses in the silo are small for maize grain, and the extra costs are justified by the reduced losses from insects and theft. The costs are summarized in Table 21.4.

Table 21.3

Cost of Silage

		Accounting prices	Market prices
			Sh/ton
1.	Maize grain (1 bag = 1 ton silage) export parity	23.50	21.60
2.	*Less* harvesting costs	-2.25	-3.00
3.	plus extra management costs	3.75	6.25
4.	plus forage harvesting cost	11.08	13.33
5.	plus silage making costs	1.70	2.50
6.	Total costs in	37.72	40.68
7.	after shrinkage of 10%	42.00	45.00
8.	interest at 10% of 1½ years stocks	6.13	6.75
9.	handling ex silo	1.88	2.50
10.	Value at export parity	50.0 (± 15%)	54.25
11.	Formula for price	$1.27p + 20.1$	$1.27p + 26.9$
12.	Value at import parity	79.5	86.1

Notes: Line 3: Equal to one-third total overheads less the management costs on maize grown of Sh.150/ha.

Line 7: The loss in dry matter content of the silage from fermentation, estimated at 10 per cent of initial weight, but could be as high as 15-20 per cent.

Line 8: Average stocks could be as low as half the yearly harvest. The extra stocks provide an insurance against poor harvests and rising prices.

Lines 11 and 12: This gives the silage price per ton where p is the maize price per bag, and is a long run price. If prices rose to import parity levels stocks would be reduced, deferring the data at which prices would rise and saving some interest costs. A better estimate of the import parity price, assuming imports are the exception rather than the rule, would be Sh.75/ton (APs), assuming siz months stocks.

21.3 THE ACCOUNTING COSTS OF SUPPLEMENTS

The main supplments are cottonseed cake (CSC) and Minerals-Urea-Molasses (MUM). All these are traded goods with the possible exception of molasses, and their accounting prices are worked back from foreign trade prices. In the case of CSC export prices are known up to 1970, whilst the intermediate

Table 21.4

Cost of Various Feedstuffs per kg Dry Matter at Accounting Prices

cents/kg

		Maize grain	Maize germ	Silage (greenchop)
Price per kg at farm	(export parity)	32.2	33.0	5
	(import parity)	56.9	a	7.5
Dry matter per cent		87%	87%	28%
Cost/kg Dry matter	(export parity)	37.0	38.0	17.9
	(import parity)	65.4	a	26.8

Note: [a] In years of mild shortage the price would remain the same, but if there was an acute shortage in Kenya and Uganda maize germ would not be produced as the production of fine flour would be suspended.

costs are consistent with the actual price at Lanet, and are similar to the handling costs of maize grain. The 1971-2 costs are given in Table 21.5.

Table 21.5

Cotton Seed Cake Market Prices

cents/kg

	1967	1968	1969	1970	1971-2
Export price f.o.b.	47	49	43	56	47
Handling to f.o.b.	-13	13	13	13	13
Handling to Lanet	+ 7	7	7	7	7
Wholesaler's margin	+ 7	7	6	7	7
Price at Lanet	48	50	43	57	48

The accounting price will be the same as the market price (because the handling charges cancel and the market price is equal to the f.o.b. price) and its cost will be taken as 48 cents/kg or 53 cents/kg dry matter (91 per cent by weight dry matter).

The main constituent of MUM is molasses, which was exported at 10.6 cents/kg in 1968 (the latest date available). The delivered price was 11 cents/kg. whilst handling costs from the factory to Lanet are the same as to the coast (the wagons would otherwise be empty). Market and accounting prices for other items almost coincide, except for mixing costs. The composition and accounting cost of MUM is given in Table 21.6.

Table 21.6

Accounting Price of MUM Supplement

		cents/kg
Ingredients	Composition by weight (per cent)	Cost per kg
Molasses (84% Brix)	74	11
Urea	4	46
Phosphoric acid	1	240
Minerals premix	0.16	285
Water	20.84	–
Total ingredients	100.00	12.8
Mixing and handling at cost		3.2
Total cost per kg		16.0
Total cost per kg dry matter (65%)		25

The handling costs are derived from a knowledge of the equipment and management costs, although the Research Station envisages traders setting up to sell at a delivered price of 27 cents/kg. For a large feedlot it would be cheaper to mix it on the farm—so the production cost is appropriate.

The costs of the various feedstuffs and supplements can now be summarized together with a measure of their energy value, which will be needed to determine the energy of any given combination of ration ingredients (Table 21.7).

21.4 THE COSTS AND PROFITS OF GRAZING

The rotation of maize and Rhodes grass implies the existence of 324 ha of semi-permanent pasture on the optimal size farm of 800 ha. This will be supplemented by the second crop sown after the harvest of the greenchop and by the newly establishing Rhodes grass pastures, so that a substantial number of cattle can

Table 21.7

Costs and Energy Values of Ration Constituents

Item	Metabolizable energy mcal/kg	Digestible protein	Acc. price (cents/kg dry matter)	Mart price (cents/kg dry matter)
Maize grain				
(export parity)	3.29	7.4%	37.0	35.5
(import parity)			65.4	66.0
Maize germ meal	3.29	>8%(1)	38.0	38.0
Silage (greenchop)				
(export parity)	2.53	7.2%	17.9	19.4
(import parity)			26.8	28.6
MUM	3.04	21%	25.0	25.0
CSC	2.82	44%	53.0	53.0

Note: The values for metabolizable energy (ME) are on a dry matter basis and with the figures for digestible protein are taken from Crampton and Harris, 1969.

(1) The estimated value for crude protein is between 10 and 14 per cent, rather higher than for maize. Otherwise it is assumed that maize germ meal is as nutritive as maize grain.

be kept and fattened through the year. The purpose of this section is to determine the return to the farm-feedlot of using these pastures to graze cattle. Amongst other things this will depend on the supply situation of immatures, specifically on the cost of the cattle purchased for grazing and the value of the cattle after grazing. The calculation described below should be considered as illustrative, and measures the return to pastures in the medium run—different assumptions about purchase and sales prices can be substituted to give alternative estimates.

The pastures can be used for fattening underweight steers to a weight suitable for transfer to the feedlots, or for finishing them completely for slaughter. It ought to be more profitable to use the pastures for the former as the ability to transfer cattle from pasture to the feedlots will permit more efficient use of the pasture, whilst the existence of the pasture means that the cattle entering the feedlot can do so at more nearly the optimal age/weight/conformation. In this case the simplest assumption is that the value of the pasture is measured by the revenue it would earn if it were finishing the cattle, whilst the

Table 21.8

Returns to Semi-permanent Pastures at Accounting Prices

Sh/ha

		1970	1972	1972
		Accounting prices		Mart prices
1.	Purchase cost per head (200 kg live) Sh	270	400	270
2.	Sales value (340 kg live, 175 kg CDW) Sh	595	823	582
3.	Income per kg liveweight gain Sh/kg	2.32	3.02	2.31
4.	Income per hectare 640 kg gain (±150kg)	1,485	1,933	1,480
5.	Costs: direct pasture costs	550	550	548
6.	dipping, minerals for cattle	65	65	80
7.	Interest/mortality on cattle ıttle	210	300	210
8.	Total direct costs	825	915	838
9.	Rent	150	150	150
10.	Income less costs and rent	510	868	492
11.	Total gross profits (£)	£8,262	£14,062	£7,970
12.	Profits net of one third overheads (£)	3,395	9,195	1,463
13.	Two-thirds overheads less profits (£)	1,472	4,328	5,037
14.	Standard deviation of gross profits (£)	5,638	7,340	5,640

Notes: Line 1: Purchased direct from LMD at slaughter value, price excludes transport costs which are more conveniently allocated to the feedlot and would amount to between Sh.80-100 per hectare.

Line 4: The *average* stocking rate will lie between 4 and 6 head/ha.

Line 9: Rent is based on the supposition that maize could be grown the whole time and will therefore tend to be a slight overestimate (other crops in the rotation are presumably less profitable). Given the profitability of grazing this seems a reasonable estimate.

Line 12: The allocation of overheads is discussed in the text. This line gives the profits to be carried forward to the total farm profits when one-third of total overheads are allocated to the feedlot.

Line 13: This gives the remaining overheads to allocate to the feedlot when all grazing profits are allocated to feedlot profits.

profitability of the feedlot will be based on the assumption that cattle enter it in the right condition to respond to rations as predicted. This will possibly understate the benefits of the pasture and overstate the profits of the feedlot but give about the right total sum. The exact allocation of profits between the constituents of such a closely integrated system is in any case both arbitary and unnecessary.

The Beef Research Station has gained experience in the stocking rates and liveweight gains possible from pastures over a period of nearly two years on two different farms (reported in Jepsen, 1973, and Miles, 1973). The year-to-year fluctuation in yields was considerable, and depends almost directly on rainfall in the year. In neither case were second crops available to supplement the grazing after the maize harvest. Taking all these factors into account a figure of 640 kg liveweight gain per hectare of semi-permanent pasture p.a. would seem a reasonable average, with a standard deviation of 150 kg.

Table 21.8 gives the return per hectare and to the whole farm. There is no single obviously correct method of allocating overheads and profits between the grazing and the feedlots as they are complementary activities, and it might therefore seem simpler to allocate all grazing profits against outstanding overheads to determine the overheads remaining to be borne by the feedlots—this alternative is shown in the penultimate line of the table. Instead it seemed preferable to deduct a notional one-third total overheads and carry forward grazing profits, if only to emphasize that grazing profits and feedlot profits will change by different amounts as immature supply prices change.

Appendix A.21

Farm Plan for a Typical Farm-Feedlot

The optimum size feedlot appears to be the minimum size that can fully employ two of the critical items of equipment—mixer feeders and forage harvesters. A smaller size farm runs a higher risk that any breakdown of either of these pieces of equipment will stop operations with considerable cost to the farm. Above this size there are no obvious economies, except perhaps a further slight reduction in risk of holdup from breakdown. The farm plan described below is for this minimum optimum size. Both recurrent and capital costs can be either allocated to specific farm activities or as general farm overheads. The only partial exceptions are tractors which are allocated to most operations, but for convenience are grouped with harvesting equipment, as the peak demand for tractor services occurs at harvesting. Their recurrent costs have been allocated to specific operations.

A. Capital costs at market prices

A1 Crop cultivation

3 ploughs	@	£250
3 harrows	@	300
4 cultivators	@	325
2 planters	@	500
2 sprayers	@	150
2 fertilizer spreaders	@	100
4 manure ditto	@	700
Total		£7,250

A2 Harvesting

2 forage harvesters	@	£1,500
6 3-ton trailers	@	330
3 70HP tractors	@	1,700
6 50HP tractors	@	1,100
1 4-wheel drive loader		3,600
Total		£20,280

A3 Pastures

2 slasher/mowers	@	£250
electric fencing		£1,000
water supplies		£500

A4 Silage making

1 silage loader	@	£1,100
silos	@	£1,750

A5 Feedlots

water storage	£1,800
cattle yards (15)	10,500
crush and scale	700
stores	2,250
roller mill	1,300
hammer mill	300
2 mixer feeders =	6,600
2 feed augers =	400
front end loader	250
platform scales	3,000
Total at mart prices	£27,100
at acc. prices	£23,272

A6 General overheads

manager's house	£3,500
offices	700
grade 7 house	1,500
lowgrade housing	3,500
roads	800
electricity	3,600
cement mixers	300
2 pickups	3,000
1 lorry	3,000
2 motor cycles	200
workshop	1,000
Total	£21,100

B. Recurrent costs at market prices, per annum

Manager	£5,000
farm manager	2,500
feedlot manager	2,000
TA's (5)	2,500
mechanic (1)	80
sec/clerk (1)	80
office expenses	500
professional services	400
general tractor	600
transport	1,200
water, rates	1,300
Total	£16,160

Interest and depreciation on overhead capital A6
£3,200

Total overheads £19,360 at market prices
£14,600 at accounting prices

Crop costs have been given in the text; here we give the composition of specific costs:

Tractor costs Sh./hr

	70hp tractor	50hp
fuel, oil, lubricant	5.48	3.00
maintenance	4.00	2.50
driver plus mate	2.00	2.00
depreciation and int.	5.40	3.95
Total at mart prices	16.88	11.45
at acc. prices	11.88	8.30

Harvesting costs	Sh./ton
harvester int. and dep.	2.30
spares and maintenance	2.50
tractor use	5.87
int. and dep. on other equipment	2.50
labour	0.16
Total at mart prices	13.33
at acc. prices	11.08

Silage handling costs	Sh./ton
silo construction	0.31
covering materials	1.01
tractor use	0.78
labour	0.16
Total at mart prices	2.26
at acc. prices	1.70
handling out of silo	2,50
at acc. prices	1.88

In addition to the labour force allocated to recurrent overheads the farm will employ:

4 artisans	@	£15 per month
16 drivers	@	15 pm
39 labourers	@	5 pm
4 herdsmen	@	5 pm
1 recorder	@	15 pm
1 storeman	@	15 pm

CHAPTER 22

Feedlot Costs and Cattle Performance

22.1 INTRODUCTION

The Beef Research Station was instructed to determine the optimum intensive stock-feeding and management techniques, which, for our purposes, requires us to determine the most suitable cattle to fatten, the best ration and the best farm/feedlot configuration. This in turn requires us to calculate the profit of feeding the various types of cattle different rations so that the most profitable combination can be identified. Profit is equal to the increase in value of the cattle (sales value less purchase cost) less the costs of feeding the cattle. There are two different ways of expressing this profit, each relevant in a particular context—profit per head of cattle fattened, or profit per ton of silage. For any given farm the amount of maize that can be grown for silage will be limited, and since the transport costs on silage are very high it will be uneconomic to buy in silage from other farms. Therefore, as far as the farm is concerned, if the other inputs (purchased feed and cattle) are available in adequate quantities with no increase in price the farm will maximize its profits by maximizing its profit per ton of silage. If this leads to supernormal profits, either other farms will set up as feedlots, or, if the Government is the sole producer in the feedlot industry, it will expand until the total demand for cattle by the feedlot industry is constrained by their supply. This will happen in the medium or long run when total profits to the feedlot industry will be maximized when profit per head of cattle fattened is maximized. In the very short run we need to measure profits per ton of silage (and maximize this), whilst in the medium and long run profits should be measured and maximized per head. Both measures, however, require us to know the conversion ratios for different rations—that is, the number of kg of ration required to increase liveweight by 1 kg—so that we can convert the known costs per kg of feed into the costs of increasing liveweight. The main part of this chapter will be concerned to establish the conversion ratios for different rations, in other words to identify the underlying input-output relations or production function for beef fattening. It will then be possible to calculate the total costs of fattening an animal, which is the sum of three distinct components:

(i) throughput related or transaction costs, expressed per head, of which the most important are transport costs and veterinary costs;

(ii) yarding costs, per head per day, which include interest, depreciation, and overheads associated with the feedlot, and

(iii) ration costs, to be expressed per kg of liveweight gain which will depend on the technical efficiency with which the cattle convert feed into beef as measured by the conversion ratio.

Finally, we need to know the rate of liveweight gain per day to calculate the increase in value. This chapter will confine attention to costs and the input-output relations; the profitability of feeding different rations will be left to the next chapter.

The first two costs are readily identified.

22.2 THROUGHPUT COSTS

Transport costs from Lanet to the slaughterhouse have already been netted out of the sales prices. Transport costs to the feedlot will depend on the source of the cattle, and should lie between Sh.12 and Sh.20 per head, at both market and accounting prices. Veterinary costs are put at Sh.7 per head at market prices (Sh.5.25 at accounting prices). A best estimate at accounting prices of average throughput costs would be Sh.20 per head.

22.3 YARDING COSTS

The European export regulations would require cattle to spend a minimum of 90 days in the feedlots. Given the quantity of silage which can be produced by the farm (the limiting factor) this implies a throughput of about 10,000 head per annum.

Fifteen yards each of capacity of 200 head would give an average utilization of 83 per cent and be adequate to handle seasonal fluctuations in throughput. The operating costs are given in Table 22.1 and include the interest cost of holding cattle of different value in the feedlots—this is a substantial item and is given at 1972 prices but can be recomputed for different cattle prices.

It could be argued that the total should include interest on feed eaten by the cattle—amounting to perhaps 4 cents/day—but this has been included in the crop costs. The figure can be compared with the Beef Research Station's rough estimate of 55 cents/head/day at market prices.

Table 22.1

Recurrent Yarding Costs at 1972 Accounting Prices

	Items	Total (£)	Cents/head/day NEP Borans	Crossbreds
1.	Interest and depreciation at 10% on capital excluding cattle	3,477	8.5	8.5
2.	Salaries and wages	2,749	6.7	6.7
3.	Subtotal	6,226	15.2	15.2
4.	One-third of general farm overheads	4,840	11.8	11.8
5.	Interest on stock of cattle at 10% and mortality losses (2%)		18.6	28.4
6.	Total at accounting prices (cents)		45.6	55.4
7.	at market prices		51.0	60.0

Notes: Lines 1, 2: Derived from Appendix A.21, B.

Line 4: See 21.4 and footnotes to Table 21.8.

Line 5: On average accounting value of cattle: NEP 250 kg at Sh.2.26/kg; Crossbreds 325 kg at Sh.2.66/kg.

If we are interested in determining the profit per ton of silage the farm overheads (and grazing profits) should be allocated to the cost of silage, and yarding costs will be reduced by 11.8 cents/head/day. This calculation is deferred to the next chapter.

22.4 FEED COSTS

The previous chapter determined the costs of the component parts of the rations, and also gave the energy and protein characteristics of the different feed stuffs. The Beef Research Station has based almost all of its experiments on six rations, whose composition, energy and costs are given in Table 22.2. (The costs already include the costs of handling the feed.)

The ration costs are better approximated by the export parity price as sufficient stocks of feed should be carried in silos to bridge a temporary scarcity (and hence importation of maize). Further, other roughage sources such as pyrethrum marc from the local pyrethrum factory may be available and could be substituted for silage when maize is scarce. (Pyrethrum marc is the waste product after dried pyrethrum flowers have been ground and the pyrethrins extracted. Its quoted price is 15 cents/kg dry matter, and its alternative use is fuel in the factory or feedstuffs for dairy cattle.)

22.5 ESTIMATING THE CONVERSION RATIO FROM FEED TO BEEF

When this study was started in 1970, the Beef Research Station had only been operating for a short period and had collected very little accurate data on the efficiency with which different breeds of cattle converted the different rations into liveweight gain. Fortunately a great deal of experimental and theoretical work has been done on devising a method of predicting the response of cattle to rations of known metabolizable energy and it was possible to construct a theoretical production function using these published research findings.

In order to predict the profitability of a given ration, whose energy concentration, E, we can either measure or calculate from standard tables, we need to know how fast the cattle will grow (their daily weight gain in kg, g,) and how efficiently they convert feed into liveweight gain, most conveniently measured by the conversion ratio, R (defined as the number of kg of dry matter of feed needed to increase liveweight by 1 kg).

There is a complex relationship between E, R, g and W, the

Table 22.2

Costs and Composition of Rations at Accounting Prices

Ration numbers	Per cent by DM weight of: Silage	Maize	MUM	CSC	Energy E (Mcal/kg)	Cost per kg. DM (cents) Export parity	Import parity
1	83.37	–	9.63	7.0	2.60	21.0	28.5
2	87.95	–	9.40	2.65	2.59	19.5	27.3
3	66.81	20.61	9.93	2.65	2.74	23.5	29.7
4	50.17	36.66	10.52	2.65	2.87	26.6	31.6
5	33.42	52.83	11.10	2.65	3.00	29.7	33.4
6	16.35	69.33	11.67	2.65	3.11	32.9	35.3
Market prices	19.4	35.5	25.0	53.0			
Accounting prices	17.9	37.0	25.0	53.0			

Notes:

1. The last two lines are taken from Table 21.7 and give export parity prices. The ration cost at import parities assumes maize germ meal at 38 cents/kg (AP and MP) substitute for maize, silage is 26.8 cents AP, 28.6 cents MP. Overall ration accounting costs differ from market costs by less than 6 per cent.

2. Ration 1 is a high nitrogen diet for young animals. The ration numbers correspond to those defined at the Beef Research Station, for Trial 9.

3. E is a measure of the energy concentration–metabolizable energy in megacalories per kg of Dry Matter (DM).

weight of the animal, which is described in detail in Agricultural Research Council, 1965, and set out as an algebraic model in Newbery, 1974. Very briefly, theory and experimental observations suggest a relationship between the weight of feed consumed per day, D, the energy of the feed and the weight of the animal. For a given ration, feed is proportional to the metabolic weight of the animal (weight raised to the power of 0.73), at least until it approaches maturity. Given D and E the total energy consumed per day is known, and this determines the rate of weight gain, g, which in turn determines R $(=D/g)$. The weakest link in this chain is the first step of assuming a fairly simple relationship between feed intake, body weight and ration energy. Other factors, particularly the age and previous dietary history of the animal (particularly whether it has been systematically underfed like the NEP Borans from the semi-arid areas), and whether it is adapted to the environment like the indigenous zebu, are known to be important in at least some circumstances.

If, however, we already know the likely daily weight gain for a given animal on a given ration it is then comparatively simple to predict the conversion ratio. The ARC formulae can be combined to give a quadratic expression for R:

$$\frac{(0.11E^2 - 0.418E)g^2 k_m}{AW^{0.73}} \cdot R^2 + (0.89E + 0.418)\, g.\, R$$

$$- \left\{\frac{AW^{0.73}}{k_m} + \frac{1.45 + 0.0035W}{k_f(1/g - 0.23 - 0.0001W)}\right\} = 0$$

where k_m and k_f are respectively the efficiency of using metabolizable energy for maintenance and for fattening and are themselves functions of the ration concentration:

$$k_m = 0.25 + 0.06E$$

$$k_f = 0.20 + 0.08E$$

The only other unknown parameter in the formula is A, which takes a value of about 0.1 mcal/kg$^{0.73}$. $AW^{0.73}$ is the energy required for an animal of weight W to maintain itself at constant weight, including the muscular energy required for standing and walking.

22.5.1 *The Construction and Use of the Prediction Model*

In the early stages of this study (before the Beef Research Station had collected adequate data on cattle performance) the main functions of the model described above were twofold—to provide a first approximation of the as yet unobserved Kenya cattle production function, and to model the dependencies between the economically important parameters g, E, W and R in order to test the overall sensitivity of profit to uncertainties in the original data. When the first experiments were complete the predictions were confronted with observations, which suggested that the ARC formulae were over-optimistic, in that they predicted a lower conversion ratio than was in fact observed. There seemed on the face of it to be three different kinds of explanation for the discrepancy between predictions and observations:

(i) The ARC predictions are based on observations made on grade cattle under temperate conditions, and might not apply to native cattle (and crosses) under African conditions. Moreover, most of the observations were made under laboratory conditions and might not apply to large groups in feedlots.

(ii) The fact that the experiments were conducted on a large scale under commercial conditions rather than close scientific control may have introduced a systematic bias into some of the observations.

(iii) Observations were based on herd average, rather than individual animal performance, and given the non-linear relationship between input and output, predictions which take these averages as describing a single representative animal will be systematically biased.

A comprehensive simulation study of the ARC model using a high speed computer suggested the following conclusions, which are discussed and defended more fully in Newbery, 1974.

(i) The bias mentioned in (iii) above could be quantified given some assumptions about the variability between cattle in the same herd, and turned out to be quite small. This effect by itself was unlikely to account for more than a 4 per cent increase in the observed conversion ratio, and it could, moreover, be quite easily corrected.

(ii) It became apparent that a quite small error in measuring feed intake or in measuring the daily weight gain could have a significant effect on the conversion ratio, whereas errors in the measurements of other parameters (the ration energy, the fasting metabolism, A, or the efficiencies, k_m and k_f, would have a smaller effect. These first measurement errors were particularly likely, since the feed was weighed and then fed. Any spillage or wastage after weighing would lead to an over-estimate of the feed actually consumed. Simularly, there is a difference of up to 8 per cent of body weight between the full and shrunk weight of an animal. This potential source of error (which affects the estimated rate of growth in a magnified fashion) can be partially removed by measuring the final carcass weight, and using this to calculate a standardized final live-weight, but obviously, this will not work for estimating the initial weight. However, this source of error ought not to be systematic, unlike the measurement of feed. (It still makes sense to devise formulae to predict standardized final weight or weight gain, since the sales value of the cattle is based on carcass weight, and so this procedure has been adopted in all the tables presented in this chapter.)

Of course, as we are interested in the economics of fattening cattle, we are concerned to predict the overall relationship between feed and beef production taking likely spillage and wastage into account. Consequently, in the next section we confront prediction with observation and use this to construct a table showing the *effective* conversion ratios for cattle under commercial Kenyan conditions.

The final conclusion, strengthened by subsequent (and rather more reliable) experimental data, suggested that the theoretical model was quite good at predicting cattle performance when the necessary biases had been taken into account. This may turn out to be one of the most important methodological findings of this study, for it has two directly useful implications. The first is that the model can be used to predict the performance of as yet untested rations, and so to predict the optimum (most profitable) ration given the costs of the ration constituents. It can also be used to determine the optimum period to keep the cattle in the feedlot, since the model predicts a decrease in conversion efficiency with increasing body weight.

Secondly, it suggests that the model has general validity, i.e. that it will not be necessary to replicate the whole research project in different countries. Indeed, the model can be used to identify the most promising areas for research and so can increase its cost effectiveness. This aspect is discussed in greater detail 24.7.

22.6 INTERPRETATION OF THE EXPERIMENTAL RESULTS

The experimental results from the two main sets of trials available by late 1972 are combined in Table 22.3. The observations are grouped by breed of cattle rather than type of experiment and to that extent the table is not homogeneous and must be interpreted carefully. The table shows, for each lot of 50 cattle, the ration they were fed (the number identifies the constituents and energy value given in Table 22.2), the average live weight at the start of the trial, the length of the trial, the average daily live weight gain (calculated from the final weight) and the average conversion ratio (total feed consumed divided by total weight gain). The last column gives the predicted herd average conversion ratio using the formulae of the previous section and correcting for the bias which would arise from assuming that all the cattle in the group grow at the same rate (i.e. behave as one single animal). It should be close to the figure given in the previous column if the theoretical model is good.

The first trial was the Breed Characterization Trial of 1971, designed to see if different breeds of cattle responded differently to the two rations (ration 3, a low energy high silage ration, and ration 5, a high energy high grain ration). The four results (two rations for two periods) are shown first for each breed. The trial showed that the only significant difference between breeds of cattle was between the NEP Boran (the native cattle) and the rest (crossbred or Improved Boran), corresponding to two different sources of supply (the NEP and the commercial ranches). Moreover, the latter behaved closely as predicted (the average predicted conversion ratio was 2 per cent lower than the observed value), whilst the NEP Boran

Table 22.3

Experimental Results from the Beef Research Station compared with Predicted Conversion Ratios

						herd averages	
	Breed	Ration	Initial weight (kg)	Daily weight gain *g* (kg/day)	Duration of trial T days	Observed conversion ratio	Predicted conversion ratio
(1)	(2)	(3)	(4)	(5)	(6)	(7)	(8)
1.	NEP Boran	3	309	0.82	68	10.1	7.9
2.		3	309	0.88	110	9.5	8.4
3.		5	309	1.02	67	8.1	6.7
4.		5	309	0.99	109	8.7	6.9
5.		4	286	1.00	68	6.4	8.3
6.	Seq. slaughter	4	286	0.99	90	6.6	8.4
7.		4	286	0.99	112	6.8	8.5
9.		4	257	1.04	67	6.6	6.9
10.		4	257	1.20	81	5.6	7.4
11.		4	257	1.09	95	6.4	7.3
12.		4	257	1.04	109	6.8	7.4
13.	Improved	3	302	0.89	68	9.1	7.9
14.	Boran	3	302	1.10	110	7.9	9.7
15.		5	302	1.30	67	6.9	6.7
16.		3	302	1.260	109	7.4	7.0
17.		4	319	1.00	61	7.8	7.7
18.		4	319	1.00	82	8.3	7.7
19.	Seq. slaughter	4	319	1.11	103	7.3	8.2
20.		4	319	1.03	124	8.3	8.0
21.	Small	3	301	0.80	68	10.5	7.7
22.	crossbreds	3	301	1.09	110	9.1	8.0
23.		5	301	1.38	68	6.7	6.7
24.		5	301	1.38	110	7.2	7.1
25.		5	303	1.53	77	6.5	6.9
26.	Seq. slaughter	5	303	1.63	101	6.5	7.3
27.		5	303	1.63	129	6.6	7.6
28.	Large	3	337	0.87	68	9.6	8.6
29.	crossbreds	3	337	1.06	110	7.9	9.5
30.		5	337	1.30	67	6.7	7.3
31.		5	337	1.39	109	7.1	7.6
32.	Seq. slaughter	5	327	1.08	72	7.9	7.0
33.		5	327	1.25	93	7.8	7.1
34.		5	327	1.20	114	8.0	7.3
35.		5	327	1.27	135	7.8	7.6

Notes: Column (3) gives E, the ration energy 2.74 mcals/kg corresponds to ration 3, 2.87 to 4, 3.00 to ration 5 of Table 21.7.

Column (5) gives the herd average daily weight gain, calculated as the average standardized final weight (defined as cold dressed weight divided by 0.51) *less* the average initial weight shown in col (4), divided by the number of days, col (6).

Column (6) gives the number of days from start of trial to slaughter.

Column (7) is total feed fed during trial divided by total standardized liveweight gain.

Column (8) is predicted from the formula in the text assuming that half the herd grows 25 per cent faster than the average, the other half grows 25 per cent slower than the average. This reflects an attempt to correct for biases arising from using herd average data. Full details are given in Newbery, 1974.

Sources of data Rows 1-4, 13-16, 21-24, 28-31 are from the Breed Characterisation Trials, (Beef Research Station, 1971). For each breed four matched groups were fed two rations for two different periods. The remaining rows are from the Sequential Slaughter Trials (private communication from Dr. M. Creek, 20 September 1971). Each group of rows (e.g. 5-7) refer to the sequential slaughter of one of the initial matched groups.

behaved very poorly (their conversion ratio was an average 22 per cent higher than predicted). One possible explanation was that the NEP Boran had been kept on pasture until they reached a weight comparable to the crossbred cattle (about 300 kg). However, the NEP Boran had experienced a quite different previous history (of slower growth under harder conditions) and were older. On the quite high energy rations they rapidly put on fat, which has a very high energy value per unit weight, and this meant they grew less quickly but needed more feed energy, hence resulting in a higher conversion ratio.

The second set of experiments was designed to test the relationship between growth and weight, and involved slaughtering matched initial groups of cattle fed the same ration at successively later dates. The trial occurred in 1972, took NEP Borans at their normal weight and fed both types of Borans ration 4, the crossbreds ration 5. This time the NEP Borans behaved *more* efficiently than predicted, whilst the rest behaved on average exactly as predicted. It is difficult to account for this satisfactorily, though it might be that these cattle were experiencing 'compensatory growth'. Cattle kept on a low level of nutrition (as these were in the NEP) achieve very high rates of growth when the nutrition level is raised, tending to bring them back onto the 'growth curve' that they would have followed under normal conditions of adequate nutrition. However, this explanation is not completely satisfactory, as the rate of growth is an explanatory variable in the prediction equation and has therefore been taken into account. It is not clear that compensatory growth leads to more *efficient* as opposed to faster growth, which is what is required to explain the present observations.

22.7 CONCLUSIONS FROM THE THEORY AND EXPERIMENTS

Improved Boran and crossbreds behave as predicted by the model described in 22.5.1. NEP Boran tend to grow less rapidly than the other cattle, and experience some difficulty with very high energy rations. At low weights they seem to fatten very efficiently at these somewhat lower rates of growth, but at higher weights (or after a medium period on good rations or pasture) they put on a high proportion of fat with a higher conversion ratio. Theory predicts that the conversion ration will rise with body weight, and fall with faster rates of live weight gain, and this is supported by the observations (see for example lines 17-20 in Table 22.3 and Table 22.6). The theoretical model allows us to construct Table 22.4, which gives the relation between the rate of growth and the conversion ratio for each of the eligible rations (rations 1 and 2 are obviously unprofitable) for cattle of an average weight (the conversion ratios will also vary with weight).

Table 22.4

Predicted Conversion Ratios for Kenyan Cattle

Ration number	Daily weight gain, g = (kg/day) 0.8	0.9	1.0	1.1	1.2	1.3	1.4	1.5	1.6
3	9.3	8.8	8.4	8.1	7.9	7.8	7.7	–	–
4	–	8.2	7.9	7.6	7.4	7.3	7.2	7.1	–
5	–	–	7.4	7.1	6.9	6.8	6.7	6.6	6.6
6	–	–	7.0	6.8	6.6	6.5	6.4	6.3	6.3

Note: These values are calculated for an average value of bodyweight W, and will tend to rise with W. See Table 22.6.

Table 22.5 gives the best estimate and the range of likely values for rates of live weight gain for the different breeds on the different rations, and also the cost per kg of live weight gain including the yarding costs, i.e.

$$y = Rc + b/g$$

where y is the cost per kg of live weight, c is the ration cost/kg of dry matter (given in Table 22.2) and b is the yarding cost/head/day (given in Table 22.1).

Table 22.5

Predicted Costs of Live Weight Gain at Accounting Prices

Sh/kg

	NEP Boran			Crossbred + Imp. Boran			
Ration	3	4	5	3	4	5	6
g kg/day	0.9	1.0	1.2	1.0	1.3	1.4	1.5
range	0.8–	0.9–	1.0–	0.8–	0.9–	1.2–	1.2–
	1.1	1.2	1.3	1.4	1.5	1.6	1.7
Cost y Sh.	2.58	2.56	2.43	2.53	2.38	2.39	2.44
range	2.76–	2.69–	2.66–	2.87–	2.79–	2.51–	2.63–
	2.32	2.35	2.37	2.22	2.27	2.31	2.38

Table 22.5 suggests that ration 5 looks the most profitable ration for NEP Boran, and ration 4 or 5 look almost equally profitable for other cattle, though higher energy rations become progressively more attractive for heavier animals which grow faster, and should be more profitable for crossbreds above 350 kg live weight. The conclusion that ration 5 is the most profitable ration might have to be modified for NEP Boran if it were found that at the weight they entered the feedlot and given the necessary minimum time in the feedlots their final weight had too high a proportion of fat. As not very much information is available on this problem the profitability of fattening NEP Borans on both rations 4 and 5 will be calculated in the chapters that follow.

Parenthetically, it should be noted that the cost of producing beef rises with the weight of the animal, as the calculation in Table 22.6, derived from the theoretical model which gives g as a function of W, demonstrates.

Table 22.6

Cost-Weight Relationship

Weight W kg	Theoretical growth rate g kg/day	Theoretical conversion rate R	Marginal cost Sh/kg $y = cR + b/g$ (Crossbreds)
354	1.26	6.6	2.41
372	1.27	6.8	2.46
389	1.28	7.0	2.50
407	1.28	7.2	2.57
424	1.29	7.3	2.62

Notes: These figures are based on parameters appropriate to crossbred cattle on ration 5, but they are illustrative of a general tendency. The marginal cost rises 9 per cent in 67 days and would rise about 16 per cent over 110 days. In other words, the costs used in the calculations earlier will increase between 5 and 10 per cent towards the end of the period above their average value.

CHAPTER 23

The Profitability of Feeding Different Rations under Different Supply Conditions

23.1 THE DIFFERENT SUPPLY CONDITIONS TO BE CONSIDERED

In Chapter 20 we argued that the opportunity cost of cattle from different sources would change through time as the feedlot industry expanded, and we distinguished three supply conditions. In the very short run there would be an excess supply of NEP Borans from the LMD, so that their opportunity cost was their slaughter value. Feedlots and ranches together would be unable to take all available suitable immatures. In the medium run the two sources of demand would absorb the whole demand, and the opportunity cost of cattle sent to the feedlot would be dictated by the profitability of grazing the cattle to maturity on pasture. In the long run the feedlot industry would expand demand to exceed the supply of immatures from the NEP, in which case the supply price will be the cost of production of cattle on commercial ranches.

In the very short run the excess supply of cattle implies that the profit of the feedlot industry is maximized when the return to the inelastically supplied factor is maximized, and in 22.1 it was argued that this implied maximizing the profit per ton of silage. A considerable number of calculations are therefore needed (one for each breed, ration, and supply condition), but we can simplify matters by dividing profits into two parts: profits that depend on the supply price of the cattle, and profits that depend on the cost of rations.

23.2 THE PROFIT CALCULATIONS

All the accounting prices and costs estimated so far have included interest costs at the ARI of 10 per cent on any capital inputs, including working capital, so that the estimates of profit given in this chapter are supernormal profits; that is, profits above the 10 per cent normal return already allowed for. Zero profits imply the project is on the margin of being socially acceptable. With this proviso we can now express supernormal profits per head of cattle in a simple formula:

$$\pi = [W\,(q\beta - p) - a] + gT\,[q\beta - cR - b/g]$$

where π = supernormal profit per head
W = weight into feedlot (265 kg for NEP Borans, up to 325 kg for others)
q = sales price per kg CDW
p = purchase price per kg liveweight
β = dressing out fraction, standardized to 0.51 (see note below)
a = throughout costs per head (= Sh.20)
b = yarding costs per head per day in feedlot
g = daily liveweight gain (standardized)
T = number of days in feedlot (usually 90)
c = cost per kg dry matter of the ration
R = conversion ratio (standardized)

Note: Weight increases are 'standardized' in that the final live weight is calculated by dividing the CDW by an assumed dressing out fraction of 0,51. It was found that the theoretical model predicted the standardized weight gains more accurately than actual live weight gains, and more importantly, the sales price is paid not on live weight, but on CDW.

The first term can also be considered as the profit on turnover of the cattle, or the profit on improving the quality. The second term is the profit from increasing live weight, and depends on the length of time the cattle are fed, as well as the type of rations. Profits per ton of silage can be found by dividing π by $gTRs$, where s is the proportion of silage in the ration. Clearly this will be maximized when T is minimized. In the long run competition between feedlots would make the opportunity cost p rise to the point where total supernormal profit per head was zero. In effect this means that the first component of profit (which we will describe in shorthand as turnover profit) will be determined by (be equal and opposite to) the second, more fundamental, source of profits (the profit on weight gain). Thus the division of profit into these two components has an underlying economic logic as well as being convenient.

The next step is to assemble all the components. Sales prices are given in Table 19.10, supply price of immatures in Table 20.2 and ration costs (more specifically $cR + b/g$) in Table 22.5. Table 23.1 does not allocate the profits from grazing to the cattle—the correct treatment of these profits is discussed later. All cattle are assumed to spend 90 days in the feedlot (the minimum quarantine period).

Table 23.1 shows clearly the advantage of splitting total profits per head into the two components. The three supply prices for NEP Borans correspond to the very short run, the medium run and the long run and it will be seen that as the supply price rises the turnover profit falls though the profit on weight gain remains the same. The converse is true if we compare the same type of cattle on different rations, the turnover profit remaining the same whilst the profit on weight gain varies.

All these deductions are based on tables which give the best point estimate of prices, costs, profits, etc. Before we come to any definite conclusions about the most profitable mode of operating the feedlot we need to see how robust the profit estimates are to changes in the parameters which are not known accurately, or which can be expected to change over time. Table 23.2 gives an estimate of the standard deviation of profit per head in 1972 resulting from variations in the values taken by different parameters. The standard deviation of total profit assumes that different factors are independent except where obviously causally related as in the case of R and g (whose interdependence is shown in Table 22.4) and the purchase and sales price (the former was derived from the latter). Thus each item in the table represents the standard deviation in the particular category of profit arising from a variation of one standard deviation in that particular parameter (and the causally connected parameters referred to in the same line). The standard deviation in that particular parameter (and the casually and the total standard deviation, allowing for uncertainty in *all* parameters, is the square root of the sum of the squares of the standard deviation of *total* profit. A better estimate of the

Table 23.1

Supernormal Profit Per Head

Sh/head

Ration / Breed / Source of cattle	Turnover profit 1970 AP	Turnover profit 1972 AP	Turnover profit 1972 MP	Profit on weight gain 1970 AP	Profit on weight gain 1972 AP	Profit on weight gain 1972 MP	Total profit 1970 AP	Total profit 1972 AP	Total profit 1972 MP
Ration 4									
NEP Borans									
1. Ex LMD at slaughter value	168	179	187				123	196	143
2. Ex graziers (medium run)	102	110	142	−45	17	−44	57	127	98
3. Ex breeding herds (long run)	57	4	100				12	21	56
Improved Borans and Crossbreds	42	29	66	−20	52	−19	22	81	47
Ration 5									
NEP Borans									
1. Ex LMD at slaughter value	168	179	187				128	214	154
2. Ex graziers (medium run)	102	110	142	−40	35	−33	62	145	109
3. Ex breeding herds (long run)	57	4	100				17	39	67
Improved Borans and Crossbreds	42	29	66	−24	53	−18	18	82	48
Ration 6									
Improved Borans and Crossbreds	42	29	66	−33	50	−22	9	79	44

Source: Tables 19.10, 20.2, 22.5

Notes:

1. NEP Borans start at 265 kg, others at 325 kg.
2. All rations at export parity prices. Import parity prices are given in Table 22.2.
3. The ration which maximizes profit/head is underlined in the column of profit on weight gain.

uncertainty arising from the parameter is the proportion of total variance attributable, which is shown in cols. (3) and (6).

It is interesting to observe that profits are not very sensitive to the existence of an export surplus of maize, though the calculation does assume that maize germ meal will still be available in export surplus. It is also slightly surprising that fluctuations in the world beef price are of no greater significance than uncertainties and variations in the conversion ratio, or of the supply price of immatures. This underlines the characteristic feature of a feedlot which is to make profits on the small margin between buying and selling cattle. Anything that affects this margin will have a large effect relative to movements in the level of beef prices. The exact composition of the ration is also of less importance than, for example, the calculation of yarding costs. The standard deviation of the estimate is likely to be smaller in the short run (as beef and maize prices are likely to move less than allowed for) and with more experience it should be possible to estimate the various parameters with greater precision.

23.3 SHORT RUN PROFITABILITY ECONOMIZING ON SILAGE

The final step in determining the best ration and breed combination requires a calculation of the supernormal profit per kg of dry matter of silage, since this will limit cattle throughput and total profits in the short run. The quantity of silage produced by the farm feedlot is fixed, whilst the number of cattle can vary over quite a wide range (assuming that additional pens can be easily constructed). Total overheads and total profits from grazing are also fixed and for this calculation should all be allocated to silage. Profits per kg of silage will therefore be some fixed amount (equal to grazing profits less all remaining farm overheads) plus profits per head of cattle (excluding overheads allocated to cattle in Table 22.1, which amount to Sh.10.6 at accounting prices, Sh.14.3 at market prices) divided by the number of kg of silage consumed per head. Table 23.3 gives these figures, which are derived by

Table 23.2

Standard Deviation of 1972 Social Profit Attributable to Various Uncertain Factors

Sh/head

Uncertain parameter	Crossbred			NEP Boran		
	Standard deviation of		per cent variation due to	Standard deviation		per cent variation due to
	Turnover profit	Profit on weight gain		Turnover profit	Profit on weight gain	
	(1)	(2)	(3)	(4)	(5)	(6)
1. Conversion ratio *R* (and *g*)	–	38	24	–	20	9
2. Supply price of immatures (5% variation)	33	12	34	27	10	30
3. Yarding cost *b*	–	13	3	–	13	4
4. Throughput costs *a*	5	–	–	5	–	1
5. World beef prices, *p*, *q*	5	35	27	5	30	27
6. Maize exported or imported	–	24	10	–	29	19
7. Different ration	–	5	–	–	18	7
8. Grade	5	2	1	9	4	4
9. Total standard deviation		77	100		67	100
10. Extra profit selling to Europe in 1970	+115	+60		+108	+40	

Notes: Line 1 is derived from line 4 of Table 22.5.

Line 2. The variation in the supply price of immatures is the variation due to uncertainty in the formula, not that from changes in the world price or the source of supply. See Table A.20.5.

Line 3. The variation in the yarding cost reflects different assumptions about the allocation of costs, and will mainly affect the choice of the optimal ration. (Allocating the yarding costs to silage, for example, favours higher energy rations.)

Line 5. Although movements in world beef prices are large, much of their effect is cancelled out by the rise in the cost of immatures. There is thus less uncertainty about profit than about the absolute level of prices. See 19.7 and Table 19.4.

Line 6. If feed costs were evaluated at *import* parity the profit on weight gain would be Sh.6 for NEP on ration 5 (Sh.19 on ration 4) and

Sh.29 for other cattle on the now optimal ration 6. The difference between these figures and the best shown for Table 23.1 gives the SD. It is roughly the same as the effects of a 10 per cent change in world maize prices on profits.

Line 7. The difference between the profit on the optimal ration and the next ration. It is a measure of the error in feeding the wrong ration, either through failure to calculate its costs correctly, or ignorance about cattle response to different rations.

Line 8. This is an estimate of the variation in profit for the likely variation in grade awarded by KMC—and the important uncertainty is the variability in the proportion of cattle grading standard or below.

Line 9. Calculated as the square root of the sum of the squares of the sum of both items in each line (which together measure the SD of total profit arising through uncertainties in that parameter).

Line 10. The extra profit were Kenya to have been given permission to export quarantined cattle to Europe in 1970. In 1972 the advantage of this permission appears to have disappeared, but it *may* re-emerge with a time lag. This item is excluded from the standard deviation of the previous line.

Columns (3) and (6) give the proportion of *variance* attributable to uncertainties in that parameter (variance = square of SD).

adding the overheads per head to the figures for total profit in Table 23.1, and dividing these by total silage consumed by that breed on that ration (*RgsT,* which may be found from Tables 22.4 and 22.5, and *s,* the fraction of silage in the ration, comes from Table 22.2). The standard deviation of the estimate comes from Table 23.2. The table shows that at both market and accounting prices feeding NEP Boran ration 5 is the most profitable, though feeding ration 6 to crossbreds *may* be as socially profitable, and will be more profitable if ration 5 is of too high energy for NEP Borans.

23.4 THE OPTIMAL CONFIGURATION

We can now combine the information of Tables 23.1-23.3 to determine the optimal configuration, which is shown in Table 23.4.

The first point that stands out from these two tables is that the most profitable configuration (under both criteria of profitability) is the same at market prices as at accounting prices, except perhaps in the short run if Boran cannot be satisfactorily fed ration 5. In the short run NEP cattle from the

Table 23.3

Comparative Profits per kg of Silage in 1972

cents/kg

	Silage consumed *RgsT* kg	Profit/kg silage Accounting prices	Market prices
Ration 4			
NEP Boran ex LMD	357	58 ± 19	44
Crossbreds	429	21 ± 18	14
Ration 5			
NEP ex LMD	249	*90* ± 27	*68*
Crossbreds	282	33 ± 27	22
Ration 6			
Crossbreds	139	64 ± 55	42

Note: These figures *exclude* the constant profit per kg from grazing less overheads.
Sources: Tables 22.2, 22.4, 22.5, 23.1.

Table 23.4

Most Profitable Breed and Ration Under Various Supply Conditions

	At accounting prices			At market prices		
Time period	Most profitable breed	Ration	Supernormal profit/head (Sh.)	Most profitable breed	Ration	Supernormal profit/head (Sh.)
1. Short run (silage scarce)	NEP ex LMD	5	214 ± 67	same as at APs	5	154
	(crossbreds	6	79 ± 77)	(NEP ex LMD	4	47)
2. Medium run	NEP ex Graziers	5	145 ± 67	same as at APs	5	109
3. Long run	Crosses	5	39 ± 77	same as at APs	5	48
	NEP	5	(82 ± 67)	same as at APs	5	(67)

Notes: Line 1. If NEP Boran cannot be fed ration 5 the next line shows the most profitable alternative.

Line 3. In the long run both NEP Boran and commercial cattle will be fattened so returns will be equalized between them, presumably either at the lower of the two, or at zero supernormal profits.

LMD will maximize profit per head and per ton of silage at both market and accounting prices; the same is true of NEP cattle from graziers in the medium run. In the long run at market prices it seems more attractive to buy NEP Boran from breeding herds at market prices than to purchase from the commercial ranches. At accounting prices the converse is true. But this is a minor point since it is still profitable to purchase both, and their prices would adjust to make each equally profitable.

We have so far been assuming that NEP Boran can be satisfactorily fed the high energy ration 5 without putting on fat so fast that they are overfat before the end of the 90 days. If this consideration ruled out such a high energy ration, the only change in the previous conclusion would be that in the short run it would be more profitable at accounting prices to purchase nothing but crossbreds and feed them ration 6, whilst at market prices the feedlot would purchase nothing but NEP Boran from the LMD and feed them ration 4.

The second point is that profits at market prices are lower than at accounting prices, which in 1972 is best explained by the lag between changes in the producer prices schedule and the rapid rise of world beef prices during this period.

Table 22.6 at the end of the previous chapter showed that the marginal cost of increasing live weight would rise with the weight of the animal and hence the length of the feeding period. This means that the profit on weight gain will fall, and, assuming that silage is not a short run constraint, this will imply an optimal period for feeding. The average profit on weight gain is lower for NEP Boran than for crossbreds (see Table 23.1) and it will therefore be preferable to sell them earlier. The best estimate suggests that marginal profit per kg of weight gain falls to zero for NEP Boran after about·100 days, compared with 150 days for crossbreds, though these estimates are subject to a fairly wide margin of error.

Finally, it should be remembered that the supernormal profits reported so far exclude the considerable profits derived from grazing cattle on the farm pastures, which, averaged over a total throughput of 10,000 head, would amount to Sh.18 per head at accounting prices, or Sh.3 at market prices. This profit will decrease as the supply price of cattle rises (Table 21.8, which calculates grazing profits, assumed that immatures would remain available at slaughter value). In the long run there will be no supernormal profits from grazing at accounting prices (purchasing crossbreds will allow one-third of total overheads to be covered by income from grazing, as has been assumed in calculating feed costs and profits).

CHAPTER 24

The Results of the Feasibility Study

24.1 THE SOCIAL PROFIT OF THE BEST PROJECT

The previous chapter was concerned to find and measure the profit per head of the best ration fed to the most suitable cattle. In the medium run this was shown to be feeding the fairly high energy ration 5 to NEP Borans, which would yield Sh.145 per head supernormal social profits if maize were in export surplus. If ration 5 were of too high energy then ration 4 fed to the same cattle would yield Sh.127 per head, 12 per cent less. We can now describe the best project and calculate the total profit. The correct method is to discount the flow of outlays and receipts measured at accounting prices at the ARI and determine the net present value, and this is done below. For planning purposes we need merely ask whether the net present value is positive, but for presenting the results of the study it is convenient to have some summary measure of profitability, of which the most obvious is the internal rate of return.

This measure has the attraction and drawback that it is independent of the size of the project and it must be interpreted with caution, as we shall see. In addition to the normal difficulty that the rate of return is sensitive to the time pattern of inputs there is the additional problem that it does not, strictly speaking, measure the return to capital involved in the project. The accounting prices of all inputs and outputs have been calculated assuming an ARI of 10 per cent, which measures the cost of the capital indirectly involved in producing or further processing these goods. Relating the profits of the farm to the capital of the farm alone will overstate the return to all capital directly and indirectly involved in the project.

We shall return to the correct measure of profitability in the next section, after comparing the alternatives available. The social rate of profit (i.e. this internal rate of return) can be calculated by two essentially similar methods. The first rather crude method takes profit per head and relates it to total capital involved—this has the advantage of investigating in what sense, if at all, the project is capital-intensive (or management-intensive) but has the drawback of giving an essentially timeless view of the project. The other considers the project of establishing a feedlot from scratch and finds the internal rate of return. This would be the appropriate way to do a project evaluation and provides a check on the piecemeal evaluation conducted in the previous chapters—necessarily piecemeal, since at each stage we were trying to narrow the range of alternatives down by selecting the best at that stage. Table 24.1 demonstrates the first approach, not for the optimal configuration as calculated, but for the next best project of feeding NEP Borans ration 4 under medium-run supply assumptions. As such it represents a slightly pessimistic estimate, but for a project which is known to be attainable. A comparison between this project and the theoretically most profitable configuration is given in Table 24.2, which handles the time pattern of expenditures and receipts in a more satisfactory manner. The table has the same format as a similar calculation at market prices reported in *Enterprise Costings for Commercial Feedlot Companies* (Beef Research Station, October 1971).

24.1.1 *Economies of Scale*

The profit calculations in the previous section can be interpreted as the rate of return to an 800 ha farm-feedlot, or the average rate of return on this size farm. It is not obvious that unit costs will fall if the size of the farm is increased substantially above 800 ha, but unit costs certainly rise for smaller scale operations, mainly because of indivisibilities. At half scale, for example, machinery will be 58 per cent of full scale, fixed capital 72 per cent, wages and salaries 60 per cent. The decline in the social rate of return might be as much as 5-10 per cent, and the riskiness of the operation will increase as the insurance element of replicating vital pieces of equipment such as harvesters and mixer feeders is reduced. We conclude therefore that 800 ha is the optimal size for the farm and that average and marginal rates of return coincide at this scale.

24.2 COMPARISONS OF THE VARIOUS MEASURES OF PROFITABILITY

Table 24.2 conforms the previous conclusion that ration 5 could be more profitable if it could be satisfactorily fed to NEP Boran. A careful comparison of the two tables shows that the internal rate of return is quite sensitive to the time pattern of building up stocks of feed and silage, and purchasing cattle. Although the rates of return on ration 4 are quite close (31 per cent and 33 per cent), this should not conceal the possibility that they might have been further apart. In Table 24.2 the fixed capital (including machinery) is installed 2½ years before the farm reaches full production, but stocks of purchased feed are lower (and amount to 6-9 months supply). The carried forward costs of establishing the farm are thus larger than suggested in Table 24.1, which, however, allows for greater stocks of silage to account partially for the gestation period. Comparing rations 4 and 5 in Table 24.2 suggests that the purchase of feed may affect the time profile of costs quite considerably. The conclusion must be that the rate of return is an imprecise measure of profitability (in that it may be subject to a greater proportionate standard error than other measures such as profit per head), though it remains true that if it exceeds the ARI the project will be profitable. We cannot guarantee that a higher rate of return will always be associated with a higher net present value, though in this case it is. In the tables that follow we shall continue to present the rate of return as a useful statistic but we shall include profits per head as the most stable and least ambiguous summary statistic.

Other criteria often used in evaluating projects are their capital or labour intensity. The Little-Mirrlees method rejects such measures as likely to ignore other scarce factors, quite apart from the conceptual problem of defining an appropriate measure of intensity. It is, however, interesting to calculate simple summary statistics of factor intensity, if only because the Beef Research Station often attracts the criticism of being

Table 24.1

Summary Evaluation of 800 ha Farm-Feedlot at 1972 Prices (NEP Boran in Medium Run on Ration 4)

Reference to table	Item	Accounting prices £		Market prices £	
	Capital				
A21.1	Structures	23,590		27,050	
	Machinery and vehicles	50,750		53,530	
			74,340		80,580
21.3	Silage (1½ years)	38,377		41,553	
	Other feed (½ year)	25,434		26,750	
21.2	½ crop costs	8,910		9,153	
			72,721		77,456
19.10	Cattle 1,800 grazing				
20.2	2,300 feedlots		131,890		94,406
	Total		278,951		252,442
	of which working capital		204,611		171,862
	Labour				
	Unskilled and semi-skilled labour employed on farm (men)		65		65
	'Fixed' capital/man		£1,144		£1,240
	Total capital/man		£4,291		£3,883
	Return				
21.8	Supernormal Profits from grazing		1,312		-6,753
23.1	Supernormal profits from feedlots		58,420 @ Sh 98		45,080
	Total supernormal profits		59,732		38,327
	Total rate of return		31%		25%
	Confidence interval for rate of return (1. SD)		20% to 41%		14% to 36%
	Value added				
	Rent		6,000		2,560
	Wages/Salaries		14,500		20,000
	Depreciation		8,500		9,000
	Profit		87,627		63,571
	Gross value added		116,627		95,131
	Capital/net value added		2.6		2.9

Notes:

1. The optimal plan at both market and accounting prices is to feed NEP Boran ration 5. This may, however, be of too high energy, and the table assumes NEP Boran will be fed ration 4. This has the advantage that the throughput of 9,200 cattle p.a. is close to that assumed in earlier

calculations, and corresponds to the early assumption of the Beef Research Station. A comparison with ration 5 is made in Table 24.2.

2. The stocks of silage and other feed are put in at the accounting value (excluding any interest on storage costs). For silage, this will include a return on some of the capital used in production, and thus overstates the cost. Against this there is no item for installing productive capital *before* production starts.

3. *All* cattle are purchased at the medium run price, thus reducing the grazing profits as shown.

4. The average value of cattle is 1,800 cattle grazing at an average weight of 225 kg live, and 2,300 cattle in feedlots at an average live weight of 290 kg, and value midway between purchase and sale price.

5. The valuation of capital is rather *ad hoc* since what is required is strictly the present value of a time pattern of inputs. The inclusion of stocks and growing costs is a rather simple reflection of this temporal aspect.

6. The total rate of return = supernormal profits/total capital *plus* the ARI of 10 per cent.

7. Profit in value added is supernormal profit *plus* 10 per cent of the total capital.

too capital-intensive for Kenyan conditions. It is interesting to note that the capital such critics have in mind (the tractors and capital, the great majority of which is working capital, particularly cattle. The figures for 'fixed' capital (i.e. structures, machinery and vehicles) of £1,240 per man at market prices can be compared with the ILO's estimate of £2,000 as the capital stock per worker in manufacturing (ILO 1973, p. 446), though it should be remembered that the variation *between* industries in enormous (thus cord, bags and twine £500/man, tyres £23,000/man). In 1967 the sum of input and output stocks per worker in manufacturing averaged £312 over all establishments of 5 workers and above, though work in progress is not known. On the face of it, then, if we include working capital the total of nearly £4,000 per worker at market prices is comparable to and probably above the industrial average. The capital-output ratio of about 2.9 at market prices is also not high (the *incremental* capital-output ratio for the second plan is 2.30 for manufacturing, or 2.8 including the stock/output ratio of 0.5, and this includes making up a lot of excess capacity. (Plan, 1969, p. 310).)

More to the point, it is difficult to see how the capital-intensity could be much reduced, especially given the

Table 24.2

Pattern of Expenditures and Receipts for 800 ha Feedlot in Medium Run

At 1972 accounting prices (£)

Reference to table in text	Year	1	2	3 and subsequent
A21.1	Structures	23,590	–	–
A21.1	Machinery and vehicles	42,880	7,870	8,500
A21.1	Wages and salaries	11,700	14,500	14,500
21.2	Rent 800 ha @ £7.5	6,000	6,000	6,000
21.2	Seed	1,500	1,500	1,500
21.2	Fertilizer	11,300	11,300	11,300
21.2	Tractor work 15,000 hrs @ Sh.5.50/hr	4,125	4,125	4,125
21.1	Other overheads, spare parts, etc.	4,000	4,000	4,000
	Subtotal	105,095	49,295	49,925
Feeding ration 4				
	Maize grain 2,700 tons @ Sh.25/bag	–	37,500	37,500
	MUM 1086 tons	–	8,688	8,688
	CSC 195 tons	–	4,680	4,680
	Cattle purchases	22,600	118,780	240,125
	(number)	(1,000)	(4,600)	(9,300)
	Vet. and transport costs	1,000	4,600	9,300
	Cattle sales		207,568	433,795
	(number)		(4,450)	(9,300)
Net revenue		-128,695	-15,975	83,577
	Internal rate of return 33%			
	Present discounted value @ 10%	£521,430		
Feeding ration 5				
	Maize grain 5,934 tons	–	82,417	82,417
	MUM 1,669 tons	–	13,352	13,352
	CSC 294 tons	–	7,047	7,047
	Cattle purchases	22,600	158,200	349,170
	(numbers)	(1,000)	(6,000)	(13,160)
	Vet. and transport costs	1,000	6,000	13,160
	Cattle sales		270,127	646,341
	(number)	–	(5,500	(13,160)
Net revenue		-128,695	-46,184	131,270
	Internal rate of return 41%			
	Present discounted value @ 10%	£870,662		

Notes:

1. All projections are in real terms. Any rise in real wages is assumed to be offset by an upward trend in the beef/maize price ratio, or downward trend in fertilizer costs.

2. Cattle are NEP Borans, all purchased at the medium run price of Sh.2.26/kg live. Cattle for grazing purchased at 200 kg, others at 250 kg. Throughput of pastures = 4,000 head p.a. Growth rates on ration 4 are 1 kg/day, on ration 5 1.2 kg/day, for 90 days.

3. It might be argued that the increased throughput with ration 5 might increase feedlot costs. If feedlot capital were increased pro rata, and wages/salaries were also increased (less than pro rata) extra costs would amount to £5,400 p.a. or about 3 per cent reduction in the IRR.

4. The PDV is calculated assuming that incomes and expenditure occurs on average at mid year.

large amount of working capital (and its very specific form), whilst it is also difficult to conceive of many of the mechanized operations being replaced by more labour intensive alternatives. One example will suffice—the early feeding trials used rations which had been fork mixed rather than machine mixed in the expensive mixer feeders. This permitted the cattle to feed selectively on the low energy silage and led to very low weight gains: later trials with more homogeneous rations gave significantly better rates of growth and conversion ratios.

Another appropriate comparison is with a breeding herd, which under reasonably good conditions will permit an offtake of 25 per cent of the live weight of the herd per annum. In the feedlot itself the figure of live weight produced to average live weight present would be 142 per cent on ration 5; crudely compared, the feedlot has a capital-output ratio at accounting prices of 2.6, and the breeding herd would have a ratio approaching 4, possibly higher.

Of course, the notion of capital-intensity must be interpreted rather loosely here, as must such measures as 'capital employed' or the capital-output ratio. The second method of computing the rate of return avoids such concepts and the unnecessary conundrums involved in reducing a dated stream of inputs to a single value; though for shorthand summary descriptions the concept of capital is useful and not too misleading. Of course, the whole object of a good method of cost-benefit analysis is to go behind such potentially misleading summary statistics as the capital-output ratio, and to take account of *all* scarce factors.

If the project is not very capital-intensive, it is more difficult to say that it is labour-intensive. The cost-benefit analysis has taken the benefits of extra employment into account, but, again, crude summary statistics are useful to give a feel for the project. Labour employed per hectare is probably double that for a commercially run maize or wheat farm at 12.3 ha/man, though it is difficult to compare it with employment on smallholding schemes using similar land. G. Gwyer[1] reports labour inputs for growing maize at anything between 75 man days/ha to 400 man days, equivalent to between 1.7 and 3 ha/man if all the farm is sown to maize; a practice which is doubtful for rotational reasons. Thus compared with commercial agriculture or cattle herding the project is more labour intensive, whilst compared with smallholding it is substantially less labour intensive. Again one must be wary of placing too much emphasis on one summary statistic.

The last point to make is that the project is sensitive to the quality of management; small variations in the fattening efficiency of the cattle will have a large effect on the rate of profit. Machinery breaking down at vital moments, poor discipline of the workforce in feeding the cattle on time, failure to measure rations accurately and several other factors could easily turn the large profit into a loss. On the other hand, it is difficult to describe the project as management-intensive when salaries are only 7 per cent of costs, or 7 per cent of profits.

24.3 THE MOST PROFITABLE PROJECT UNDER ALTERNATIVE ASSUMPTIONS

The previous section analysed the best project at 1972 maize export-parity prices and specific assumptions about supply prices, and discussed some of the general features of the project. Here we perform a similar exercise (much condensed) for alternative assumptions to test the sensitivity of the previous result to uncertainties in some of the parameters and prices, and to explore the changing supply situation in the very short and long run. Table 24.3 gives the best estimates for the same size farm-feedlot, relating total profit (including the 10 per cent

[1] In *Employment in Kenyan Agriculture*, IDS Nairobi, March, 1972.

Table 24.3

Social Profit Under Various Assumptions

Assumption	Supernormal profit per head incl. grazing profits Sh. (1)	Normal profit per head Sh. (2)	Total profit per head Sh. (3)	Standard deviation Sh. (4)	Rate of return per cent p.a. (5)
Short run					
NEP Borans ex LMD at slaughter value, fed ration 5					
at 1972 accounting prices	224	50	274	67	54% ± 13%
at 1972 market prices	154	41	195		47%
Medium run					
NEP Borans from graziers, fed ration 5					
at 1972 APs	147	52	199	67	38% ± 13%
at 1972 MPs	99	43	142		33%
at 1970 APs	64	43	109	67	25% ± 16%
at 1970 APs exporting to Europe	230	45	275	67	60% ± 15%
at 1972 APs maize import parity prices	83	59	142	67	24% ± 11%
NEP Borans from graziers, on ration 4					
at 1972 APs	130	60	190	67	31% ± 11%
Long run					
Crosses etc. on ration 5	91	60	151	77	25% ± 13%
Variations in profit in NEP Borans due to uncertainties in					
Conversion ratio			20		4%
Supply price of immatures			37		7%
Allocation of costs at KMC			30		6%
15% variation in shadow wage rate and associated APs			20		4%

Notes:

(1) Col. (1) Grazing profits can be calculated from Table 21.8 in conjunction with the appropriate supply prices in Table 20.2.

(2) Col. (2) Normal profit per head is 10 per cent of the total capital allocated per head (using the same scheme as in Table 24.1.) Total capital per head is then 10 times this column.

(3) Maize germ meal is assumed to be available at export parity prices to substitute for maize grain when that is imported.

(4) In the very long run, of course, supernormal profits will drop to zero as rents to ranches producing crossbreds rise.

(5) Variations in profit are derived from Table 23.2. Rates of return assume a medium run capital value per head at 1972 APs.

return implicitly included in earlier calculations) under different assumptions.

Whilst the uncertainty surrounding the best estimate is quite large, and whilst different assumptions about the opportunity cost of immatures make a considerable difference to the rate of profit, it would be very surprising if the project were not profitable, assuming it to be managed efficiently.

It is worth noting that errors in calculating the basic accounting prices (particularly the shadow wage rate and the standard conversion factor) have a negligible effect on the estimated profitabilities. This is not surprising since the rate of return at market prices is not very different from that at accounting prices, and it is a reflection of the offsetting effects of cattle being underpriced in the market whilst most other inputs are overpriced.

24.4. POLICY IMPLICATIONS

In Chapter 18 it was pointed out that a feasibility study ought to produce the information needed to design the best investment project. At the same time it is likely to lead to wider policy recommendations, as the way in which the benefits of the project are to be dispersed and the costs met will not have been well defined in advance. The Government has very extensive control over the allocation of the income generated within the beef industry, because it sets the producer prices for different grades of beef, arranges the marketing of a large proportion of NEP Borans through the Livestock Marketing

Division and at present operates the only exporting slaughterhouse. It therefore seems reasonable to assume, as has been done so far, that the profits generated by intensive beef fattening are as valuable as if they accrued to the Government—since the Government could arrange for this in fact to happen. Whether this is desirable obviously depends on the other alternatives available and the objectives of the Government, so the next section discusses the effect of different possible policies on the distribution of the gains.

24.4.1 *Alternative Policies and the Distribution of the Social Profits*

If the Government wanted to capture the profits of beef fattening for its own use, several possible alternatives suggest themselves. The most straightforward would involve Government ownership of the feedlot industry (indirectly through a parastatal subsidiary free to hire good management and devise its own condition of employment). The price of feeder steers from the LMD would be raised to the point that would make it just sufficiently attractive for ranchers to background them for sale to the feedlots. The producer price of high grade beef would be reduced to make the return to intensive feeding just unattractive to the private sector, whilst the price of locally sold high grade beef would be related to its export parity. (The exact relationship would depend essentially on the extent to which the Government thought high grade beef a luxury item worthy of a high rate of indirect tax.) The profits would be mainly generated in the LMD and KMC, and would be transferred direct to the Government or via a tax on throughput. Alternatively the feedlot industry would be left in the private sector with prices again set to reduce profits to the lowest level consistent with the continued operation of the feedlots. Again the LMD would set prices of NEP Borans competitive with crossbreds from the breeding herds. The main difficulty with this approach is that until the feedlot industry expanded to a size capable of handling all crossbred and NEP cattle, each feedlot would earn supernormal profits. In the very long run competition between them (assuming the industry were kept competitive) would raise the price of crossbreds (or allow the producer price of all grades to be lowered).

The other difficulty is that the large margin between the producer and consumer price would provide an incentive for illegal slaughtering. This is unlikely to be serious as high grade beef cattle movements are already carefully controlled, and the consumers of high quality beef will be anxious that it has been properly inspected, and prepared to pay for this service.

Parenthetically we note that whilst it is reasonable to suppose that the Government has extensive control over the producer and consumer price of high grade beef the same is not true for low grade beef, which is readily diverted to local butchers if the margin between the two is wide enough. If we suppose the margin between producer and consumer prices cannot therefore exceed a certain amount, the Government is faced with only one price to choose for low grade beef. A high producer price will generate higher incomes for beef producers (some of whom are already quite wealthy) and probably elicit a larger marketed surplus (though this will depend on other factors, such as the availability of stock routes, watering facilities, etc.) High beef prices would also tend to reduce urban beef consumption (perhaps encouraging the consumption of other meats), and urban real incomes. Conversely low producer prices involve income transfers from producers to the (comparatively) wealthy urban consumers, with a possible decline in marketed surplus and exports.

Another possibility is that the Government sets the producer price schedule at the accounting prices determined here (or at export parity, which is very similar). If the feedlot industry were controlled by a privately owned monopoly the substantial profits would then accrue to that monopoly, and if they also controlled the marketing of the exported beef these profits might be generated abroad and avoid Kenya profits taxation. Even without a monopoly the beneficiaries in the early stages of development would be the large farmers with the resources and organized ability to operate the feedlots, until competition for immatures riased their price and reduced feedlot profits. At this stage the profits would accrue to the suppliers of immatures raised their price and reduced feedlot profits. At this ranchers in the Disease Free Area.

Finally, it should be emphasized that the price policy for beef cannot be considered independently of the price policy towards other agricultural products, particularly milk and grains. It should also be obvious from the previous discussion that an agricultural price policy necessarily involves a policy for the distribution of income, so that the simple and appealing rule of bringing market prices into line with accounting prices no longer holds. Market prices must also reflect judgements about distributional equity.

24.5 THE TREATMENT OF UNCERTAINTY

We can distinguish two types of uncertainty—that resulting from our ignorance of the exact values taken by some of the parameters (the conversion ratio, the supply price of immatures, etc.) and 'environmental uncertainty' due to weather, disease, fluctuations in world prices, etc., which will always remain. What will be the probable effect of the latter on social profitability? It can be plausibly argued that a feedlot industry will *reduce* uncertainty for the economy as a whole, though the magnitude of the effect is likely to be rather small (certainly smaller than Stern found for tea, and even this was not significant—see Stern, 1972). It is logical for the feedlots to carry substantial stocks of feed, particularly grain, thus possibly reducing the fluctuations in exports of grain, and stabilizing farm incomes from maize. These stocks will reduce uncertainty to the feedlot industry, and also to the backgrounders and other cattle breeders—if the pastures fail the immatures can be shipped to the feedlot and fed there. The flow of cattle through KMC will be less variable—this reduces their costs and has already been allowed for. In addition, the credit-worthiness of cattle ranchers and backgrounders will be increased by the existence of a well-defined purchase price and sales prospects for their immature cattle.

Apart from the weather and price fluctuations, the other main source of uncertainty is disease, particularly foot-and-mouth. It is difficult to quantify the consequences of an outbreak, and more difficult to gauge the differences in costs of an outbreak with and without a feedlot industry. At the least, an outbreak outside the Disease Free Area might impede the supply of immatures for a period, though the cattle already on pastures within the DFA provide a stock to insulate supplies to the feedlot from short interruptions. More serious would be an outbreak within the DFA, which, under OIE/WHO regulations would require the suspension of exports to Europe until six months after the last sign of the disease within the DFA. The cost of this would depend on the price differential between European and other markets, which in 1972 seemed negligible, and/or the decrease in profit from holding cattle for longer periods—in other words during the period of prohibited exports the cattle can be further fattened, at least for a while. The extra cost of doing this will be the rising feed costs per kg of weight gain, which might be as high as 15-20 per cent. The worst possibility would be an outbreak of the disease within a feedlot, requiring a prolonged suspension of activity on the feedlot. The losses would be the interest foregone on the capital, the avoidable overheads, and the costs of feeding the diseased cattle, who would be unlikely to gain weight and would probably lose condition, incurring the double cost of the feed and the reduced value of the animal. The costs of an outbreak on a feedlot would therefore be higher than on a ranch; on the other hand, an outbreak ought to be less likely as feedlots will impose better quarantine control over the cattle with their system of game-proof fences than the more open ranches can manage. It is difficult, therefore, to come to any simple conclusion, except to note that it may well *seem* more hazardous to the individual feedlot, which faces considerable costs (and financial or liquidity problems) than it is to the country as a whole. On balance it is not clear that the *extra* costs are significant (and we have already allowed for a 2 per cent mortality risk well above the actual average experienced to date of more like ½ per cent).

Finally, the increased share of beef in the export 'portfolio' can be expected to reduce fluctuations in unit value and total export revenue.

24.6 OTHER CONSEQUENCES OF THE PROJECT

The main difficulty in valuing the more indirect consequences of the establishment of a sizeable feedlot industry lies in predicting what these consequences will be. At the feasibility study stage it seems sensible to try to indicate what these might be, so that if they are likely to be significant they can be determined with greater precision as the industry gradually expands. The following consequences are thus mentioned only briefly and would not appear likely to reduce the already attractive return to the project.

The North-East will be monetized, the extent of over-stocking *may* be reduced,[1] and its integration into the economy accelerated. The ecological consequences would be beneficial if the threat of soil erosion were reduced—though the social consequences of monetization can neither be predicted nor readily evaluated.

Competition between abattoirs may reduce costly inefficiency. The knowledge gained in feeding beef may lead to the development of other feedstuffs, the breeding of more suitable forage crops and the profitable feeding of other animals, particularly dairy cattle. The use of other by-products will tend to raise their value, and, in the case of molasses, reduce a present pollution threat (to several lakes). All these are beneficial, and strengthen an already attractive case. On the other hand, if the feedlot industry were left for private exploitation without careful price policies the gap between the smallholder and the larger farmer would be widened, and at least initially it is likely that the main beneficiaries would be the high-income landowners, managers and investors. The demand for skilled workers (mechanics, tractor drivers, etc.) will increase, and the spur to organizational efficiency will be unavoidable, because the profits of the feedlot depend on organizing high throughputs on a quite narrow margin.

24.7 THE RETURNS TO RESEARCH AT THE BEEF RESEARCH STATION

At first sight the Beef Industry Development Project appears to be quite expensive—the estimated budget for the period 1948-72 implies a UN contribution of US $1,175,100 or £420,000, whilst the Kenyan government contributes

[1] Though the main inpact will probably be on the herd *structure* (higher proportion of young cattle) than on total numbers. Monetization might tend to *increase* numbers.

£410,000. During this period 288 'expert man-months' were budgeted, and the experimental farm is comparable in size to the optimum commercial farm described in this study. Is such an expenditure justified by the likely maximum size of a feedlot industry in Kenya of 100,000 head per annum (in the medium term at least)?

It would require another, more difficult, project appraisal to answer this question, but the following features ought to be mentioned. First, the research project was unusual in that it generated a significant income which offset at least part of the research costs—it is estimated that during the period in question it produced value added at market prices of £250,000 (at a rough estimate about £320,000 at accounting prices) and this directly offsets the Kenyan contribution. In 1971 and 1972 the station produced about 12 per cent of all high grade cattle slaughtered at KMC, and a much higher proportion still of choice and prime grades.

At the level of straightforward scientific research it has established that Kenyan cattle perform as predicted, with certain provisos (that NEP Boran tend to experience 'compensatory' growth and to finish earlier or with a higher fat proportion on medium and high energy rations), and that maize plants form a satisfactory roughage source. It has shown the importance of adequate ration mixing to prevent selective grazing of the low energy ration constituents. Furthermore, it has established its findings for a very large number of animals—the trial lots were typically 50 head compared with the usual research station's more modest experiments involving single animals or very small groups. On the other hand it could be argued that a small research station could have been set up specifically to test the hypothesis that existing theory provided a good predictor for designing a feedlot industry. If such a research station had been based on an economic evaluation, such as the present study, it could have directed its experiments to measuring the most economically decisive parameters—such as the daily weight gain and the conversion ratio, and the ability of cattle to respond to high energy rations, as well as to measuring the energy value of a wide range of different possible feedstuffs. To some extent research over the past decade at the East Africa Veterinary Research Organization at Muguga near

Nairobi had been directed at these questions, though these had been proceeding at the leisurely pace of routine scientific research. To date there have been few such research projects in which experimental design was based on economic sensitivity analysis, but the returns to such projects must be significantly higher than to ordinary research.

However, it would be a mistake to confine the evaluation of the research station to its purely scientific findings. Its main impact has been to demonstrate in a short period of time that large scale commercial cattle fattening is not only feasible but commercially attractive, and it has done this not only by making observations of cattle performance but also by exerting pressure on the marketing agency (pressure increased by collecting obviously relevant information on costs and market prospects), on the Government (particularly in setting the producer price schedule) and on the Maize and Produce Board (to supply feed maize at export parity prices). It has created the market that now exists in immatures, and must have had some effect in orienting the LMD towards a commercial/economic approach to the marketing of cattle from the NEP. It has field-tested important new pieces of equipment, in particular the forage harvester and the mixer feeder, and demonstrated their importance. It has devised commercial farm plans which have formed the basis of submissions by commercial ranchers to the Agriculture Finance Corporation for credit to establish feedlots, and by the latter part of 1972 a significant number of feedlots were already being established. Finally, it has enabled the Kenyans to excercise pressure to market beef in Europe, and with the recent granting of conditions under which this is possible, it has probably increased Kenya's marketing strength not only in the new market but also in existing markets (at least once prices have risen in these markets to European levels). Moreover, in the next phase of the research it was planned to reduce the scale of operations considerably but to widen their scope to evaluate other crops and ration combinations in other parts of the country. Now that it has become clear what particular factors are important, the research can be more finely focused (and therefore conducted on a more modest scale). For example, now that it has proved economically interesting to feed NEP Boran on quite high energy rations, attention can be directed to finding the best supplements to add to try to prevent or minimize the veterinary problems that Borans have on high energy rations; early experience showed a tendency for these animals to founder.

To summarize, the approach represented by social cost-benefit analysis has wider implications than may be apparent at first glance. In particular any research projects designed to explore the economic feasibility of some proposal can almost certainly be made more cost effective by a preliminary cost-benefit analysis designed to identify the crucial parameters to measure, and by continuing the dialogue between the research project and the project evaluators.

24.8 APPLICABILITY OF THE FINDINGS FOR OTHER COUNTRIES

If Kenyan cattle behave as theoretically predicted, the natural question to ask is whether cattle in neighbouring countries (or even distant countries) would not do the same. It ought to be possible to do a rough feasibility study for cattle feeding in such countries using the methodology of the present study to derive a quick estimate of profitability.

24.9 THE APPLICABILITY OF THE LITTLE-MIRRLEES METHOD

The particular project considered in this study certainly lent itself to the application of the Little-Mirrlees method. Working *consistently* in terms of world prices was both feasible and obviously sensible in this context, and it was seen to be so both by the staff of the Beef Research Station and the Ministry of Agriculture. On the other hand it could be argued that the project was atypical of agriculture in that it was not very labour-intensive and was comparatively insensitive to the shadow wage rate—in great contrast to the settlement schemes reported in Part II. Moreover, it was argued that the Government has potentially a great deal of control over income distribution generated by the project, partly because it already owns the mains marketing channel, but also because as a quite capital-intensive operation the feedlot industry would comprise a small number of large producers, who could be Government owned, or could be subject to reasonably effective income taxes.

Whilst the project may be atypical of much of agriculture, it does highlight the importance and attractiveness of some agricultural projects in development. The product offers a highly profitable outlet for considerable public and private investment, and has the additional attraction of going counter to the evident 'urban-bias' of much industrial and infrastructural investment.

Not only was it reasonably straightforward to calculate the appropriate accounting prices but there were good reasons for thinking that to do so would make a significant difference to the attractiveness of the project. The prices of the main inputs and outputs are not freely determined market prices reflecting relative scarcities, but prices fixed by the Government or its statutory Boards and intended to reflect a complex range of policy decisions. If the Government is to be well informed in drawing up its agricultural pricing policy it obviously needs to go behind the existing prices (which are its own creation) and find the underlying scarcity prices. In this particular case the market prices turned out to be quite a good guide to social profitability, though to some extent this was the result of a series of offsetting factors. In 1970 the situation looked rather different, and it is clear that the market prices could easily get out of line with accounting prices, unless the Government were adjusting the agricultural prices appropriately.

GLOSSARY TO PART III

Backgrounders	Ranchers who buy immatures and graze them up to a suitable weight for feedlots (i.e. they background the cattle).
Boma	The pen used to hold cattle prior to slaughter.
Boran	A type of zebu, the breed of cattle native to Kenya and Ethiopia.
Carton of canned beef	1 carton = 24 cans of 12 oz or 0.34 kg.
Condemned (meat)	Unsuitable for human consumption, used for by-products.
Dressing out percentage	The percentage of cold dressed weight to liveweight.
Extract	Concentrated beef essence obtained as a by-product in canning.
Feedlot	A small pen in which animals can be fed a controlled diet.
Feeder stock	Immature beef cattle suitable for intensive feeding in a feedlot.
Finished (animal)	Ready for slaughter.
Foot-and-mouth	A disease affecting cattle.
Forage	Greenchop (q.v.) fresh or ex-silo.
Full weight	See shrunk weight.
Gilson Cuts	Type of primal cut (q.v.)
Green chop	The whole maize plant (stalk, leaves and cob) chopped while still green into small pieces; a basic constituent of low energy cattle feed.
Measles	Measle cysts (*cysticercus Bovis*) which give rise to tapeworm in humans unless treated.
Pistolas	Type of primal cut (q.v.)
Primal cuts	High grade cuts of beef such as fillets which can be marketed as specific cuts. Bone has been removed and they have a high value/weight ratio.
Reject	See condemned.
Shrinkage	The loss of weight of an animal incurred (usually in transit) as a result of a period of inadequate feeding; about 8-10 per cent.
Shrunk weight	The weight after shrinkage from the full weight.
Silage	Greenchop (q.v.) ex-silo.
Zebu	See Boran.

LIST OF REFERENCES

Agricultural Research Council, *The Nutrient Requirements of Farm Livestock, No. 2, Ruminants,* London, 1965.

Aldington, T.J. and Wilson, F.A., *The Marketing of Beef in Kenya,* Institute of Development Studies, University of Nairobi, 1968.

Allan, A.Y., 'Is it still profitable to grow maize?', *Trans Nzoia Show Supplement,* October 1969, reprinted by Kenya Seed Company, Kitale.

Allen, R.G.D., *Mathematical Economics,* Macmillan, London, 1956 (2nd edn. 1965).

Alvis, V.Q. and Temu, P.E., *Marketing Selected Staple Foodstuffs in Kenya,* West Virginia University, March 1968.

Balassa, B. and associates, *The Structure of Protection in Developing Countries,* Johns Hopkins Press, Baltimore, 1971.

Beddoes, G., *Meat Processing Costs in the Kenya Meat Commission,* AGA: SF/KEN 20 Technical Paper No. 1, UNDP/FAO, Rome, 1971.

Beef Research Station, *Studies in Forage Production,* Draft Technical Report, No. 1 (mimeo), Lanet, December 1970.

——— *Enterprise Costings for Commercial Feedlot Companies,* ad hoc *Report, Part II* (mimeo) Lanet, October 1971.

——— *Trials using Maize Grain, Nov. 1970–Aug. 1971,* ad hoc *Report, Part III,* (mimeo), Lanet, October 1971.

Bhagwati, J. and Desae, P., *India: Planning for Industrialization,* Oxford University Press, London, 1970.

Carey-Jones, N.S., 'The Decolonisation of the White Highlands of Kenya', *Geographical Journal,* Vol. 131, 1965.

Clough, R.H., *Some Economic Aspects of Land Settlement in Kenya,* Egerton College, Kenya, June 1965.

Crampton, E.W. and Harris, L.E., *Applied Animal Nutrition* (2nd edn.), E.H. Freeman & Co., San Francisco, 1969.

Dahl, H.E., *Household Demand for Consumer Goods in Kenya 1963-65,* Parts I, II and III (mimeo, draft report), Chr. Michelsen Institute, Bergen, February 1969 and December 1968.

Denison, E.F., *Why Growth Rates Differ,* Brookings Institution, Washington, 1967.

Desai, M. and Mazumdar, D., 'A Test of the Hypothesis of Disguised Unemployment', *Economica,* February 1970.

Diamond, P.A. and Mirrlees, J.A., 'Optimal Taxation and Public Production', *American Economic Review,* March and June 1972.

Dorner, P., *Land Reform and Economic Development,* Penguin, 1972.

East African Community, East African Income Tax Department, *Report for the Period 1st July 1970 to 30th June 1971,* Nairobi (undated).

——— East African Customs and Excise, *Annual Trade Reports of Tanzania, Uganda and Kenya.*

——— *East African Customs and Excise Tariffs,* Nairobi, October 1968.

East African Railways, *Tariff Book No. 5,* Nairobi, 1968.

East African Statistical Department, Kenya Unit, *Reported Employment and Earnings in Kenya, 1959,* Nairobi, June 1960.
Economist Intelligence Unit, *Study of Transport in East Africa,* (unpublished), October 1969.
Etherington, D.M., 'Land Settlement in Kenya: Policy and Practice', *East African Economic Review,* Vol. 10, No. 1, 1963.
FAO., *Production Yearbook,* 1955, 1970.
——— *Trade Yearbooks,* various years from 1959 to 1969.
——— *Pre-investment Survey, Report of Ranching Potential, Kaputiei Section, Kajiado District, Kenya,* Nairobi, 1969.
——— *Report of the joint FAO/OIE Working Group to review the criteria governing the importation of beef from countries not entirely free from virus disease exotic for Europe* (mimeo), Rome, 1971.
Fellner, W., *Ten Essays in the Tradition of Irving Fisher,* John Wiley, New York, 1967.
Gwyer, G.D., *The Agricultural Labour Markets for Two Smallholder Areas of Kenya,* Report prepared for I.L.O. (mimeo), October 1971.
Gwyer, G.D., *Employment in Kenyan Agriculture,* Institute of Development Studies, University of Nairobi, March 1972.
Hall, M., Knapp, J. and Winston, C., *Distribution in Great Britain and North America: a Study in Structure and Productivity,* Oxford University Press, London, 1961.
Harberger, A.C., 'On Measuring the Social Opportunity Cost of Labour', *International Labour Review,* June 1971.
Harris, J.R. and Todaro, M.P., 'Migration, Unemployment and Development: a Two-Sector Analysis', *American Economic Review,* March 1970.
Hirschman, A.O., *The Strategy of Economic Development,* Yale University Press, New Haven, 1958.
International Bank for Reconstruction and Development (World Bank), *Study of the Availability of Fattening Beef Breeding and Dairy Breeding Stock in East Africa, 1970-75,* IBRD/PMEA, January 1972.
International Labour Office, *Employment, Incomes and Equality—a Strategy for Increasing Productive Employment in Kenya,* Geneva, 1972.
Jefferys, J.B. and Knee, D., *Retailing in Europe, Present Structure and Future Trends,* Macmillan, London, 1962.
Jepsen, O.S., *Intensive Backgrounding of Beef Cattle on Pasture* (mimeo), Beef Research Station, Lanet, 1973.
Johnson, G.E., *The Determination of Individual Hourly Earnings in Urban Kenya* (mimeo), Institute for Development Studies, University of Nairobi, Discussion Paper No. 115, September 1971.
Kenya, Colony and Protectorate of, *Kenya European and Asian Agricultural Census 1958: an Economic Analysis,* 1960.
——— *Agricultural Census 1959,* 1961.
(Also other census reports, variously titled).
Kenya Government, *Economic Survey* (Annual).
——— *Kenya Statistical Digest* (Quarterly).

Kenya Government, Statistical Abstract (Annual).
——— Department of Settlement, *Annual Reports.*
——— Settlement Fund Trustees, *Annual Reports* (unpublished).
——— *Survey of Distribution, 1960,* 1963.
——— *African Socialism and its Application to Planning in Kenya,* Sessional Paper No. 10, 1965.
——— 'An Economic Survey of Settlement Schemes 1964-65—Some Preliminary Results', *Kenya Statistical Digest,* Vol. IV, No. 2, 1966.
——— *Mission on Land Settlement in Kenya (Van Arkadie Mission) Report,* 1966 (unpublished).
——— *Development Plan 1966-70,* 1966.
——— *Development Plan 1970-74,* 1969.
——— *Report of the Maize Commission of Inquiry,* June 1966.
——— ('Central Province Survey'), *Economic Survey of Central Province 1963/4,* 1968.
——— *Report of Working Party on Storage and Handling of Wheat and Maize,* 1969.
——— *Census of Population 1969,* Vols. I, II and III, April 1971.
——— ('Ndegwa Report'), *Report of the Commission of Inquiry (Public Service Structure and Remuneration Commission), 1970-71,* May 1971.
——— ('Settlement Appraisal'), *An Economic Appraisal of the Settlement Schemes 1964/5-1967/8,* November 1971.
——— *New Lower and Middle Income Cost of Living Indices, 1971,* January 1972.
——— *Urban Household Budget Survey 1968/9* (unpublished) (for reference, see ILO as above, Technical Paper No. 4).
——— Central Land Board, *Review of the Activities of the Land Development and Settlement Board, January 1961-July 1962.*
——— Central Land Board, *Annual Report 1963/4, Final Report 1964/5.*
——— Farm Economics Survey Unit Report No. 2, *Farm Profits and Costs, Trans Nzoia Area 1958/9,* April 1960.
——— Farm Economics Survey Unit Report No. 6, *Report on Economic Survey of Farming in the Njoro Area, 1959/60,* June, 1961.
——— Farm Economics Survey Unit Report No. 16, *Farm Production Costs in the Uasin Gishu Area, 1959/62,* December 1963.
——— Farm Economics Survey Unit Report No. 19, *Farm Production Costs in the Molo and Mau Narok Areas 1959/62,* May 1964.
——— Farm Economics Survey Unit Report No. 22, *Farm Production Costs in The Trans Nzoia Area, 1958/61,* March 1965.
——— Farm Economics Survey Unit Report No. 25 ('Nyeri District Survey'), *Some Aspects of Agricultural Development in Nyeri District 1964,* 1968.

Kenya Government, Farm Economics Survey Unit Report No. 28, *An Economic Survey of African-Owned Large Farms in the Trans Nzoia 1967/8-1970/1,* 1972.

——— Nottidge, C.P.R. and Goldsack, J.R., *The Million-Acre Settlement Scheme, 1962/66,* Department of Settlement, Nairobi, 1966.

Kenya Maize and Produce Board, *Annual Reports.*

Kenya Meat Commission, *Annual Reports.*

Kenya Tea Development Authority, *Annual Reports.*

Kenya Wheat Board, *Annual Reports.*

Knight, J.B., 'Wages and Employment in Developed and Underdeveloped Economies', *Oxford Economic Papers,* March 1971.

Lal, D., *Wells and Welfare,* OECD Development Centre, Paris, 1972.

Lewis, S.R., *Pakistan: Industrialization and Trade Policies,* Oxford University Press, London, 1970.

Little, I.M.D., 'Nuffield College Research on Project Analysis in Agriculture' in 'Symposium on Project Appraisal on Less Developed Countries', *Journal of Agricultural Economics,* Vol. XXII, No. 3, September 1971.

Little, I.M.D. and Mirrlees, J.A., *Manual of Industrial Project Analysis for Developing Countries; Vol. II, Social Cost-Benefit Analysis,* OECD Development Centre, Paris, 1968.

——— 'Reply to Some Criticisms of the OECD Manual', *Bulletin of the Oxford University Institute of Economics & Statistics,* February 1972.

——— *Project Appraisal and Planning for Developing Countries,* Heinemann, London, 1974.

Little, I.M.D., Scitovsky, T. and Scott, M. FG., *Industry and Trade in Some Developing Countries,* Oxford University Press, London, 1970.

Little, I.M.D. and Tipping, D.G., *A Social Cost-Benefit Analysis of the Kulai Oil Palm Estate,* OECD Development Centre, Paris, 1972.

MacArthur, J.D., 'The Economic Study of African Small Farms: Some Kenya Experiences', *Journal of Agricultural Economics,* Vol. XIX, No. 2, 1968.

——— 'Agricultural Settlement in Kenya', in *Agricultural Planning in East Africa,* ed. G.K. Helleiner, East African Publishing House, Nairobi, 1968.

——— 'The Application of the OECD Method of Social Cost-Benefit Analysis to Agricultural Projects', in *Project Appraisal and Evaluation in Agriculture,* ed. R. Raikes and C.F. Åmann, Makerere Univ., Kampala, 1974.

McClelland, W.G., *Costs and Competition in Retailing,* Macmillan, London, 1966.

Maina, J.W. and MacArthur, J.D., 'Land Settlement in Kenya', in *Change in Agriculture,* ed. A.H. Bunting, Duckworth, 1970.

'Mathare Valley Survey': Etherton, D. and others, *Mathare Valley, a Case Study of Uncontrolled Settlement in Nairobi,* Housing Research and Development Unit, University of Nairobi, 1971.

Massell, B.F., 'Consistent estimation of expenditure elasticities from cross-section data on households producing partly for subsistence', *Review of Economics and Statistics*, Vol. 51, No. 2, May 1969.

Meyn, K., 'A Breeding Policy for Borans', *Kenya Farmer*, February 1969.

Miles, D.G., *Animal Production on Rhodes Grass Pastures* (mimeo), Beef Research Station, Lanet, 1973.

Mitchell, B.R. and Deane, P., *Abstract of British Historical Statistics*, Cambridge, 1962.

Newbery, D.M.G., *A Feasibility Study of Intensive Cattle Feeding* (mimeo), Churchill College, Cambridge, June 1972.

——— 'A method of estimating the underlying input-output relations for beef cattle from large-scale experimental trials', *Journal of Agricultural Science*, 1974.

Nottidge, C.P.R. and Goldsack, J.R. *The Million-Acre Settlement Scheme, 1962/6*, Department of Settlement, Nairobi, 1966.

Odingo, R.S., 'Land Settlement in the Kenya Highlands', in *Education, Employment and Rural Development*, ed. J.R. Sheffield, East African Publishing House, Nairobi, 1967.

——— *The Kenya Highlands: Land Use and Agricultural Development*, East African Publishing House, Nairobi, 1971.

Phelps, M.G. and Wasow, B., *Measuring Protection and its Effects in Kenya*, Institute for Development Studies, University of Nairobi, Working Paper No. 37 (undated).

——— (*See also* I.D.S. Discussion Paper No. 147, 1972.)

Price, J.E., 'Productivity Changes in Kenyan Agriculture', in *South of the Sahara: Development in African Economies*, ed. S.P. Schatz, Macmillan, London, 1972.

Rempel, H., *Labour Migration into Urban Centres and Urban Unemployment in Kenya*, unpublished D. Phil. thesis submitted at the University of Wisconsin, 1970.

Schaefer-Kehnert, W., *Economic Aspects of Intensive Beef Cattle Feeding in Kenya* (mimeo), IBRD/PMEA, Nairobi, March 1971.

Scitovsky, T., *Welfare and Competition*, Allen & Unwin, London, 1952.

Scott, M. FG., 'Supply and Demand Refurbished', *Oxford Economic Papers*, July 1967.

——— *Note on the Estimation of Accounting Prices for Some Non-Tradeable and Tradeable Goods in Kenya* (mimeo), Nuffield College, Oxford, March 1970.

——— *Estimates of Accounting Prices for some Agricultural Products in Kenya* (mimeo), Nuffield College, Oxford, August 1970.

——— *Accounting Prices for Goods and Services in Kenya* (mimeo), Nuffield College, Oxford, March 1972.

——— *Estimates of Accounting Prices for Mauritius* (mimeo), Nuffield College, Oxford, April 1972.

——— *Estimates of Shadow Wages in Kenya* (mimeo), Nuffield College, Oxford, February 1973.

Sen, A.K., 'An Aspect of Indian Agriculture', *The Economic Weekly* (Annual Number), February 1962.

Seton, F., *Shadow Wages in the Chilean Economy,* OECD Development Centre, Paris, 1972.

Silberston, A., 'Economies of Scale in Theory and Practice', *Economic Journal* (Supplement), March 1972.

Simpson, M.C., *Alternative Strategies for Range Land Development in Kenya,* Department of Agricultural Economics, University of Leeds, March 1973.

Stern, N.H., *An Appraisal of Tea Production on Small-Holdings in Kenya,* OECD Development Centre, Paris, 1972.

——————— *Welfare Weights and the Elasticity of the Marginal Valuation of Income* (mimeo), St. Catherine's College, Oxford, August 1973.

Stewart, F. and Streeten, P., 'Little-Mirrlees Methods and Project Appraisal', *Bulletin of the Oxford University Institute of Economics and Statistics,* February 1972.

Stiglitz, J.E., *Alternative Theories of Wage Determination and Unemployment in LDCs: I: The Labour Turnover Model,* Cowles Foundation Discussion Paper No. 335, April 1972.

Storrar, A., 'A Guide to the Principles and Practices of Land Settlement in Kenya', *Journal of Local Administration Overseas,* Vol. III, No. 1, 1964.

Usher, D., *The Price Mechanism and the Meaning of National Income Statistics,* Oxford, 1968.

Von Haugwitz, H,W. and Thorwart, H., *Some Experiences with Small-Holder Settlement in Kenya, 1963/4 to 1966/7,* Weltforum Verlag, Munich, 1972.

Westlake, M.J., *Tax Evasion, Tax Incidence and the Distribution of Income in Kenya,* Institute for Development Studies, University of Nairobi, December 1971.

Whetham, E.H., 'Land Reform and Settlement in Kenya', *East African Journal of Rural Development,* Vol. 1, No. 1, 1968.

Wilson, F.A., *An Economic Assessment of the Structure and Organisation of Small-Scale Marketing Systems,* M. Phil. Thesis, University of Leeds, 1972.

United States Department of Agriculture, *Livestock and Meat Statistics,* SB 333, (various years).